CHEVROLET
CORVETTE

CLASSIC CORVETTE

THE FIRST THIRTY YEARS

MIKE MUELLER

MBI Publishing Company

This edition published in 2002 by MBI Publishing Company, Galtier Plaza, Suite 200, 380 Jackson Street, St. Paul, MN 55101-3885 USA

MBI Publishing Company books are also available at discounts in bulk quantity for industrial or sales-promotional use. For details write to Special Sales Manager at Motorbooks International Wholesalers & Distributors, Galtier Plaza, Suite 200, 380 Jackson Street, St. Paul, MN 55101-3885 USA.

Library of Congress Cataloging-in-Publication Data Available

ISBN 0-7603-1358-X

On the front cover, clockwise from upper left: Fuel filler door of the 1963 Sting Ray.

On the title page: 1971 LS-5.

On the back cover: 1963 Z06 and 1971 LS-6.

Printed in China

Contents

Corvette 1953–1962

Corvette Sting Ray 1963–1967

Corvette 1968–1982

CORVETTE
1953-1962

Acknowledgments

We could still see all the stars even though the Kentucky skies that Thursday night were grey and rainy. Country singer George Jones serenaded us before dinner. And the *Beach Boys* were waiting in the wings to welcome the estimated 100,000 visitors scheduled to start arriving full-force in and around Bowling Green the next day. As for that evening, all the great names were seated around us. Chevrolet general manager Jim Perkins. Chief Corvette engineers Zora Arkus-Duntov, Dave McLellan and Dave Hill. Designer Larry Shinoda. Et cetera, et cetera. For fiberglass fanatics, this was the VIP dinner to end all VIP dinners. After all, you only get one chance to celebrate the grand opening of anything. And "anything" in this case was the National Corvette Museum, the long-awaited Valhalla for Corvette lovers that officially opened on Friday, September 2, 1994.

The feeding frenzy began once the ceremonial ribbon was cut and the faithful started flooding in. By Monday the turnstiles had clicked over 118,047 times. It wasn't exactly a madhouse, but it was close. Luckily I was one of the fortunate folks invited to see the place for myself in less hectic fashion with all those VIPs the night before the grand opening. And it was there that I ran into a good friend, Ray Quinlan, who was beaming like a new father who'd just had triplets.

Ray got invited to that Thursday night VIP reception, too, but for a much different reason than me. I'm not very important at all. I'm a journalist. Ray, on the other hand, simply couldn't be overlooked when it came time to assemble all the people—big, little or otherwise—who helped make that night possible. He was among those who first started the NCM ball rolling long before ground was even broken on the site directly across from the Corvette assembly plant in Bowling Green. Ray was the first to donate a car—appropriately enough, a 1953 Corvette—to the museum collection. He obviously had confidence in the dream when others weren't so sure. In return, he now carries NCM founding membership card number 1, a lifetime honor.

I, too, owe a major debt of gratitude to Ray Quinlan, who was also among those who gave me a break when I was first trying to make it as an automotive writer/photographer. I first got to know Ray after graduating from the University of Illinois in 1983 when I joined his car club in Champaign, Illinois. His supercharged Studebaker Avanti was one of the first cars I photographed for a magazine feature in 1984. Ever since, Ray has been there each time I've looked for help or support, and he has always treated me like family, even going so far as to let me drive his A.C. Cobra two summers ago. I'm sitting at my Macintosh in sunny Florida right now hammering out this book instead of digging ditches somewhere in the frozen north due to people like Ray Quinlan. Thanks, however, is simply not a big enough word. I'll say it anyway, Ray, but not until I see you the next time I'm hunting down some rare car to photograph in the Midwest.

As for all the other very important people who helped make this book possible, where to start? Perhaps at the beginning, say, with my parents, Jim and Nancy Mueller, who also just happen to be my biggest fans—I think. The old Mueller homestead in Illinois outside Champaign has also come in handy many times during the various 5,000-mile photo junkets required to piece this and other epics of mine together. And those trips would've been far more work and much less fun if my various "assistants" hadn't come along now and again. First and foremost is my brother Dave Mueller, who now knows this work probably better than I. But I can't forget my other brothers, Jim Jr. and Ken, as well as my brother-in-law, Illinois State Police Trooper Frank Young, and his boy, Jason. All your overtime was greatly appreciated. The checks are in the mail, honest.

As usual, my former cohorts at the Dobbs Publishing Group here in Lakeland, Florida, were ready, willing and able to let me use and abuse them for my own personal gain. Thanks go to DPG's Donald Farr, who gave me my first full-time job in this field in 1987; *Corvette Fever* editor Greg Pernula, who again let me ransack his files; and former *CF* chief Paul Zazarine, who didn't really do anything for me this time, but I still owe him from many times before.

Rob Reaser, another DPG editor and the hardest working photo technician outside Hollywood, also once again came through when I needed mucho B&W processing and printing work done absolutely, positively overnight. Right up there with Rob is Lakeland's Ollie Young, who opened his darkroom for me on short notice in Reaser's absence.

Noted Corvette expert Noland Adams again saved the day for me on this project, just as he did concerning my 1963-67 Sting Ray book two years ago. Noland is a man of his word, which is probably more than can be said about me.

Historical photographic support came from automotive writer/historians Bob Ackerson and Mike Lamm, veteran West Coast racing photographer Bob Tronolone, and Jonathan Mauk at the Daytona International Speedway archives.

Support of another kind came from various Corvette crazies and collectors around the country who either helped me during photo shoots or pointed me in the right direction when I was looking for a specific car to photograph. Among these friends in Florida are Bill Locke, *Road & Track* photographer Bill Warner, Ed Kuziel, and Brent Ferguson, of the the Classic Corvettes of Orlando Club.

Elsewhere, this list also includes Elmer Lash in Champaign, Illinois; Robin Winnan at Harmony Corvette in Marengo, Illinois; Dick Hubbard, of the Hubbard GM Center in Monticello, Indiana; Ellen Kliene at the Indianapolis Motor Speedway Hall of Fame Museum, Indianapolis, Indiana; musclecar collector Milton Robson and his ace righthand man, Wayne Allen, in Gainesville, Georgia; Chip Miller and all the great folks at Carlisle Productions in Carlisle, Pennsylvania, home to the annual "Corvette at Carlisle" extravaganza; Chip's main man, Paul Cherchuck, also of Carlisle; Tom Biltcliff and Guy Landis, both of Kutztown, Pennsylvania; Terry Michaelis and his guys at Pro Team Corvette Sales in Napoleon, Ohio; and Dan Gale, Danny Gillock, Tim Reilly, and Patrick Hayes at the National Corvette Museum in Bowling Green.

Last, but certainly not least, I must mention another great friend, Bill Tower, in nearby Plant City, Florida. Not only has Bill repeatedly bent over backwards to allow me to photograph his fantastic fiberglass collection (you'll see inside), he has also been a great companion on more than one automotive adventure over the last few years. A former GM engineer and NASCAR race engine builder, he has always been more than willing to help open doors for me as well. Bill, I know a free lunch for as long as you live isn't quite enough in exchange, but you know me. Say hi to Betty for me, too.

I'm reasonably sure I've left out a name or two in here somewhere. Perhaps I can make it up in my next book, that is if my Motorbooks editors will ever forgive me for this one. Finally, let me not forget all the car owners who gave their time and energy so I could capture their great cars on film for these pages. In general order of appearance, they are:

1953 Muntz Jet, Fred and Lyn Hunter, Ft. Lauderdale, Florida; 1953 Nash-Healey, Paul Sable, Fleetwood, Pennsylvania; 1954 Kaiser-Darrin, Edwin Hobart, Naples, Florida; 1953 Corvette, Chip Miller, Carlisle, Pennsylvania; 1954 Corvette, Bill Warner,

AL's BARBER SHOP

A very proud Ray Quinlan with his 1953 Corvette at the National Corvette Museum in Bowling Green, Kentucky, on the night before the NCM's long-awaited grand opening, September 2, 1994. Ray donated his car to the NCM group long before there was a NCM, becoming one of the first Corvette fanatics to help transform the Bowling Green museum from dream into reality.

Jacksonville, Florida; 1955 Corvette, Elmer and Dean Puckett, Elgin, Illinois; 1956 Corvette, Frank Diefenderfer III, Orlando, Florida; 1956 Corvette SR-2 (Bill Mitchell's) and "Betty Skelton beach racer," Bill and Betty Tower, Plant City, Florida; 1956 Corvette SR-2 (Jerry Earl's), Rich Mason, Carson City, Nevada; 1956 Corvette SR-2 "low-fin" (Harlow Curtice's), Richard and Carolyn Fortier, Swartz Creek, Michigan; 1957 Corvette "Airbox" fuelie, Milton Robson, Gainesville, Georgia; 1957 Corvette 270hp, Bob and Diane Colfer, Macungie, Pennsylvania; 1957 Corvette 250hp fuelie, Brent and Janet Ferguson, Orlando, Florida; 1957 Corvette SS, Indianapolis Motor Speedway Hall of Fame Museum, Indianapolis, Indiana; 1958 Corvette 230hp, Ron Cenowa, Shelby Township, Michigan; 1958 Corvette 245hp, Gary Gudla, Norridge, Illinois; 1958 Corvette fuelie, Dick Hubbard, Monticello, Indiana; 1958 Corvette "retractable hardtop," Terry Michealis, Pro Team Corvette Sales, Napoleon, Ohio; 1959 Corvette, Bruce and Karen Slattery, Cincinnati, Ohio; 1960 Corvette 270hp, Kevin and Sally Waspi, Urbana, Illinois; 1960 Corvette 230hp, Bob and Shirley Stallings, Orlando, Florida; 1961 Corvette 230hp, Steve Weimer, Weston, Florida; 1961 Corvette "Big Tank" fuelie, Elmer and Sharon Lash, Champaign, Illinois; 1962 Corvette 250hp, Bob and Shirley Stallings, Orlando, Florida; 1962 Corvette 340hp, Doug and Lee Mann, Bourbannais, Illinois; 1962 Corvette SCCA racer, Tim and Carol Partridge, South Barrington, Illinois.

Thanks to all.

Illinois
Land of Lincoln
WHU 181

Chapter 1

Introduction
Speaking Of Sports

Calling Chevrolet's Corvette "America's only sports car" was for years a relatively quick way to start an argument, especially with those indefatigable souls who forever subscribe to the belief that a sports car is only a sports car if it both taxes and excites the senses. Wind-in-your hair thrills must also bring along rain-down-your-neck compromises. Up-close-and-personal two-seat grand touring should also mean knocking knees and elbows. Roll-up glass windows? Hell no; it has to be side curtains or nothing at all. And if you're not forced to carry a tool kit along on every ride, you're simply not driving a true sports car.

Of course, that rudimentary ideal, once prominent in the heyday of the fabled, finicky British sports car, has long since lost favor as technological advances and basic changes in taste have redefined the way the world looks at sporty automobiles—and automobiles in general, for that matter. Today, the top world sports cars offer the best of everything; few, if any, compromises here. That the certainly classy, relatively comfortable, reasonably-luxurious Corvette is a true sports car has been a foregone conclusion for quite a few years now; not so early on.

As for the "America's only" aspect, that too has required some liberal interpretation over the years. Many sports-minded devotees—from those

Before the sensational Sting Ray, there were the so-called "solid-axle" Corvettes, the first-generation models built between 1953 and 1962. This 1962 edition shows off the same quad-headlight nose that graced the solid-axle cars for the last five years of that production run.

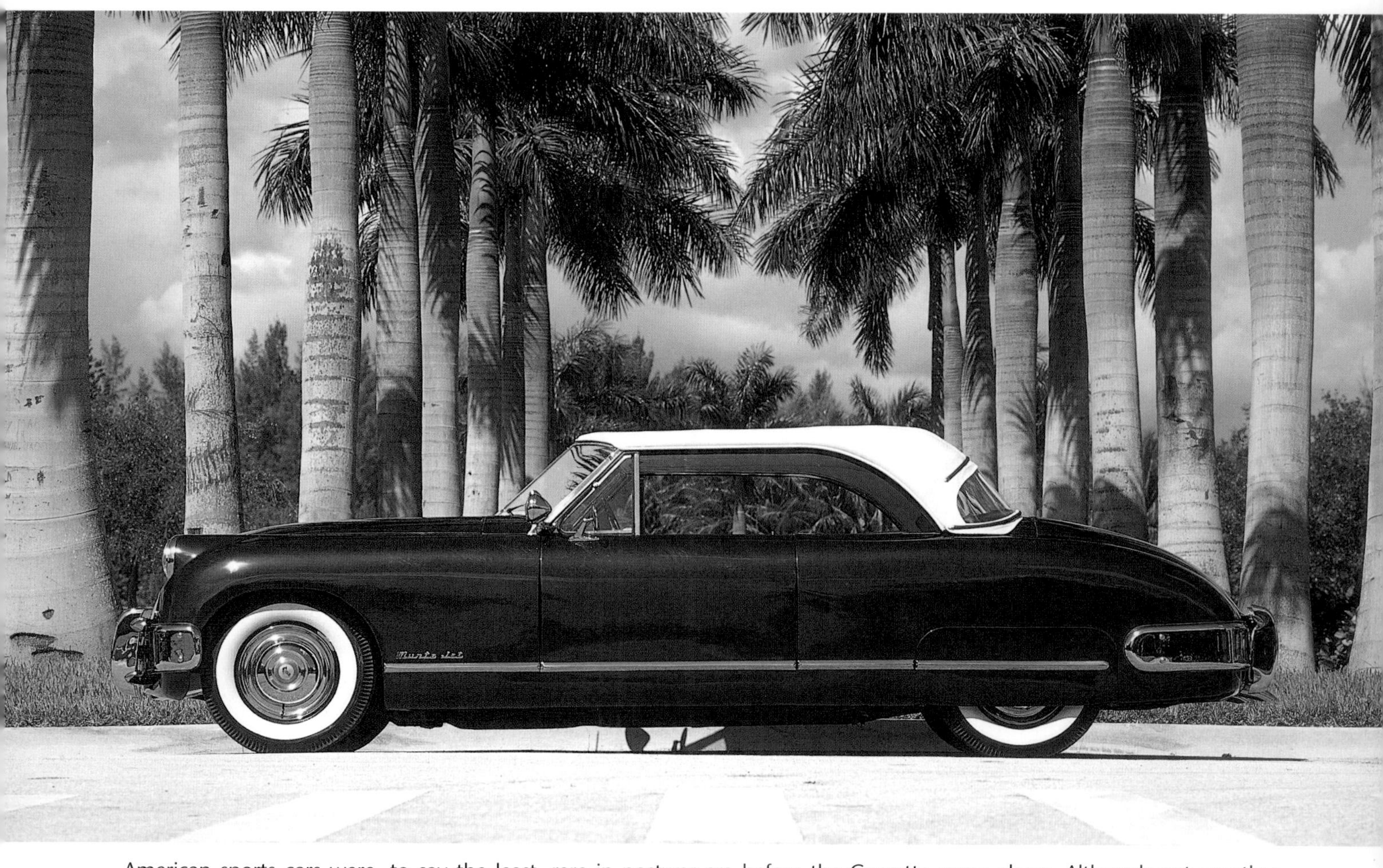

American sports cars were, to say the least, rare in postwar era before the Corvette came along. Although not exactly a sports car by the book—it was too large and had an equally large backseat—the Muntz Jet was a sporty machine born of a sports car. Before Earl "Madman" Muntz bought the rights to produce this car in 1949 it was a product of the Kurtis-Kraft company. Veteran racer Frank Kurtis originally created the vehicle in 1949. When first built by Kurtis, the car rolled on a shorter wheelbase and had only two seats

lucky enough to have experienced the rarely seen Nash-Healey Euro-Yankee hybrid in the early 1950s, to ponycar promoters hot on AMC's two-seat AMX in 1968, to today's victims of the Dodge Viper's venom—just might have a bone to pick with Chevy's hypemasters for making that bold claim. Yet when you consider no automaker in this country has ever done it any better, or for anywhere near as long as Chevrolet has now for more than four decades, it becomes easier to overlook the Bow-Tie boys' over-enthusiasm. Sure, a better description might be "America's only long successful sports car"—no, Viper fans, Dodge hasn't proven spit yet. But it's only right to continue bestowing upon the Corvette an honor it has for some time deserved simply for being out there and proving it all night. "America's only sports car" isn't a dictionary definition, it's a statement.

Earning that honor took more than a few years of hard work, both on the street and at the track. After struggling for its very life during its first three years, Chevrolet's fiberglass two-seater then took flight in a flurry in 1956, and continued gaining altitude each successive year as performance improved and a competition reputation grew—at least from a purely American perspective. Sport-minded chaps overseas, however, continued pooh-poohing the car, as did some Yankees here at home who still believed that only Brits, Germans and Italians could build real sports cars.

Those biases began to fall in a big way in 1963 with the arrival of the all-new Sting Ray, a stunning redesign that did its first-generation forerunners, built from 1953 to 1962, more than one better with its sleek, timeless lines and state-of-the-art (in American terms) independent rear suspension. Even long-time Corvette chief engineer Zora Arkus-Duntov was finally fully impressed. "For the first time," he commented to the press, "I now have a Corvette I can be proud to drive in Europe."

Racer Frank Kurtis with his Kurtis-Kraft sports car, built in California from late 1949 through 1950. Its body was mostly aluminum and power, in most cases, came from a "hopped-up" Ford flathead V-8. Only 36 were built before Earl Muntz bought Kurtis' factory and moved it to Evanston, Illinois.

A slap at the first-generation Corvette? Although it certainly did sound like one, what Duntov meant was that his baby had finally reached a goal he had been chasing seriously since 1957; the Corvette had become a world-class sports car, at least in the opinion of many more curbside critics than ever before. That achievement, however, did not diminish gains made previously. After all, progress can only be progress if the first step is taken.

Sure, the first-generation Corvettes had their glitches. Total weight was a bit much in comparison to foreign rivals. Brakes were never quite up to snuff. And the yeoman-like chassis was always limited considerably—even with top racing options—by that meat-and-potatoes live axle in back. Nonetheless, the so-called "solid-axle" Corvettes did represent more driving excitement than most Americans would ever experience—on U.S. roads and racetracks, they were all but unbeatable.

Most importantly, they were true pioneers on the Detroit scene. They represented a totally new kind of performance, a sensual brand of speed that bridged the gap between the existing foreign sports car ideal and the expectations, as well as demands,

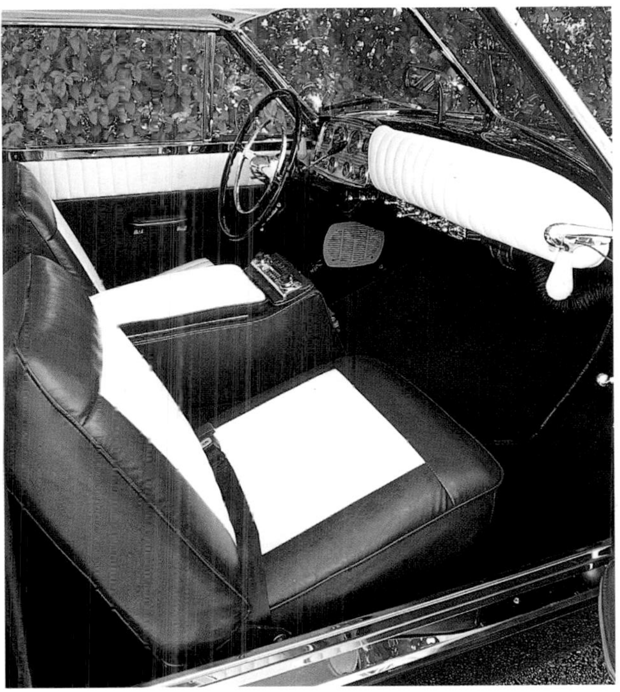

The Muntz Jet featured its radio mounted in a center console between two "bucket" seats, representing the first modern console/bucket arrangement in an American car. Also notice the seatbelts and padded dash, two more innovative features.

of this country's typical drivers. As it was, most Americans couldn't have cared less about whether or not the early Corvette qualified by accepted sporting standards since so few customers in those days had even seen an honest-to-goodness sports car, let alone driven one.

Sports cars in America were still a rare breed in the days just prior to the Corvette's birth in January 1953. U.S. registrations of sporty two-seaters amounted to only 11,199 in 1952, a nearly unnoticable figure that represented ever so slightly more than one-quarter of one percent of the total 4.16 million automobiles registered on these shores that year. Of that relatively meager sum, 7,449 were MG TDs, the latest lovely little roadster from Morris Garages, the British builder that had turned more than one Yankee serviceman's head with its carefree two-seaters in England during World War II. Second behind the TD at 3,349 registrations was Jaguar's classic XK120, a more expensive, much more powerful sporting machine compared to its fellow countryman from MG.

At a glance, these statistics didn't exactly support the notion that sports cars were turning many heads here in the States in those days. But, among others, Zora Duntov didn't believe that numbers told the whole story, which he tried to explain in a 1953 address before the Society of Automotive Engineers. "Considering the statistics," he said, "the American public does not want a sports car at all. But do the statistics give a true picture? As far as the American market is concerned, it is still an unknown quantity, since an American sports car catering to American tastes, roads, ways of living and national character has not yet been on the market."

Duntov wasn't the first in this country to speak out in defense of the sports car. Legendary automotive journalist Ken Purdy had, four years before, predicted that a sporty flair would soon be finding its way into Detroit's hum-drum, everyday automobiles. Again. In a 1949 *True* magazine feature entitled "The Two-Seater Comes Back," he told of how everything that goes around probably comes around:

"Before the Kaiser War, when Americans were serious about their motoring, the fast, high-performance two-seater automobile was as common as the 5-cent schooner of beer, and a lot more fun. But time passed, and inevitably the U.S. automobile began to change from an instrument of sport, like a pair of skis, into a device for economical mass transportation, and the two-seater was lost in the shuffle. Comes now a cloud on the horizon bigger than a man's hand which may portend a revival on this side of the water of the sports car—an automobile built for the sole purpose of going like a bat out of hell and never mind whether the girl friend likes it or not."

That Purdy found himself reaching back 35 years into the glory days of big, burly stripped-down machines like the Mercer Raceabout and Stutz Bearcat for a point of reference did not mean Americans were not treated to a little taste of speed in the years between the two World Wars. While sporty two-seat travel was indeed almost non-existent during those years, performance machines were available, although primarily only to the very rich. The Great Depression then changed all that, doing in, among others, the classic Auburn-Cord-Duesenberg triumvirate, which had been among the 1930s leaders in both power and price. And once World War II helped wipe the slate clean even further, the U.S. market was left open for whatever new form of travel buyers would accept. Sports cars perhaps?

Argosy's Ralph Stein thought so. "There is no good reason why America should not be able to produce a good sports car," he wrote in 1950. "We have engineers and designers with enough on the ball to create a crackerjack car, but, from observations, it looks very much as if they don't know what it takes. With a fast-growing band of sports-car fans, however, the demand will gradually make itself felt."

But that demand was at first considerably slow in coming as the 1950s dawned, for various reasons. Yes, some military men had brought back the sports car bug from Europe in 1945 and 1946. Most, however, remained immune as resuming (or starting) their family life was the main priority—a two-seater was definitely out of the question once kids came into the picture. On top of that, typical American car buyers with typical American car-buying budgets had yet to discover that there was nothing wrong with expecting a little pizzazz along with their practical transportation. And since they weren't exactly asking for such a combination, Detroit wasn't in any particular hurry to offer it.

Yet there were small pockets of sporty car interest present during the early postwar years. One of these was nurtured by U.S. Air Force General Curtis LeMay, who hoped to help boost military morale by arranging sports car races at various Strategic Air Command bases. A good friend of General Motors Styling head Harley Earl, it was LeMay who reportedly put a bug in Earl's ear concerning the prospects of GM building a true sports car. Also helping further the cause was the Sports Car Club of America (SCCA), which in its first years immediately following the end of World War II essentially only showcased foreign cars since domestic counterparts were essentially nowhere to be found.

Probably the first real American sports car of the postwar era was the Nash-Healey. Representing a meeting of the minds of Nash-Kelvinator's George Mason and British racer Donald Healey, the Nash-Healey featured a warmed-over Nash six-cylinder engine, a Healey-prepared chassis and Italian coachwork from Pinin Farina. Only 506 Nash-Healey sportsters, roadsters and coupes, were built from 1951 to 1954. Some leftover coupes were sold as 1955 models.

Commonly taking the credit for leading the foreign sports car wave (actually, it was more like a ripple) onto these shores was MG; again an arguable claim, but a presumption that does help explain the aforementioned relative popularity of the TD by 1952. Introduced to the U.S. market in 1950, the TD had picked up where the cute, little MG TC, born in 1945, had left off. Americans loved them, even with their cramped quarters, crude soft-tops and weak-kneed four-cylinder power. Of the 29,664 TDs built between late 1949 and 1953, 23,488 were imported to this country.

Jaguar's first XK120 reached the East Coast in August 1949. Priced at about $3,500, nearly twice as much as the MG TD, the long, low XK120 didn't draw nearly as much as attention, at least not at first. But what few early looks it garnered it did for good reason. With a 160- or 180-hp dual-overhead-cam six-cylinder be-tween those flowing fenders, a top end of 120mph was a distinct possibility—thus the car's name.

Power for the Nash-Healey sports car came from Nash's Dual Jetfire Le Mans six-cylinder, a 252ci engine that produced 135hp. The twin-carb Dual Jetfire Le Mans six was also an option for the Nash Ambassador in 1953 and 1954.

Yet another British manufacturer, Triumph, jumped into the game in 1953 with its familiar TR-2, a 90-mph sportster priced at around $2,300, a little more than the MG, a lot less than the Jag. An additional $600 or so that year bought a fourth two-seater from England, Austin Healey's new 100/4, a thoroughly modern-looking brute of a sports car that could really satisfy an American driver's need for speed.

German contributions to the sports car invasion in the early 1950s included Porsche's 356 and the Mercedes-Benz SL models. Even higher up on the rich boy's playtoy scale were the truly exotic, hand-built Italian specials from Maserati and Ferrari.

U.S. responses to the European offensive? While Duntov wasn't entirely correct in 1953 when he said an American sports car "has not yet been on the market," early postwar attempts in this country to build and market a successful sporty machine were certainly easy to overlook. Right out of the blocks, we can forget all about the host of small-time, privately built sportsters that came and went in the late 1940s and early 1950s like spent lottery tickets in a windswept convenience store parking lot.

Earliest of note from a "major" manufacturer was the Crosley Hot Shot, yet another tiny offering from National League baseball team (Cincinnati Reds) owner and refrigerator magnate Powel Crosley. Wearing no doors and an equally small price tag of about $860, the two-seat Hot Shot debuted in 1949, powered by a 26.5hp four-cylinder engine. Optional doors were added in 1950, creating the Super Sport. Neither versions were ever really given serious consideration, nor was the Crosley firm itself. It was history by the end of 1952.

Debuting as well in 1949 was an intriguing two-seat convertible conceived by veteran race car builder Frank Kurtis. His California-based company, Kurtis-Kraft, attempted to market his slab-sided creation, which was powered by a Ford flathead V-8 commonly spruced up with an aftermarket hot rod piece or two. On top was a low, clean body made of mostly aluminum. Kurtis' cars impressed many with their speed potential, including Ken Purdy, whose aforementioned *True* article featured one, along with a Crosley Hot Shot and a Jaguar XK120. Although Purdy was told that Kurtis-Kraft production would reach about 300 models a year, only 36 cars were built before Kurtis sold everything to renowned used car dealer Earl "Madman" Muntz. After briefly continuing production of his own modified version of the car in California, Muntz then moved production to Evanston, Illinois.

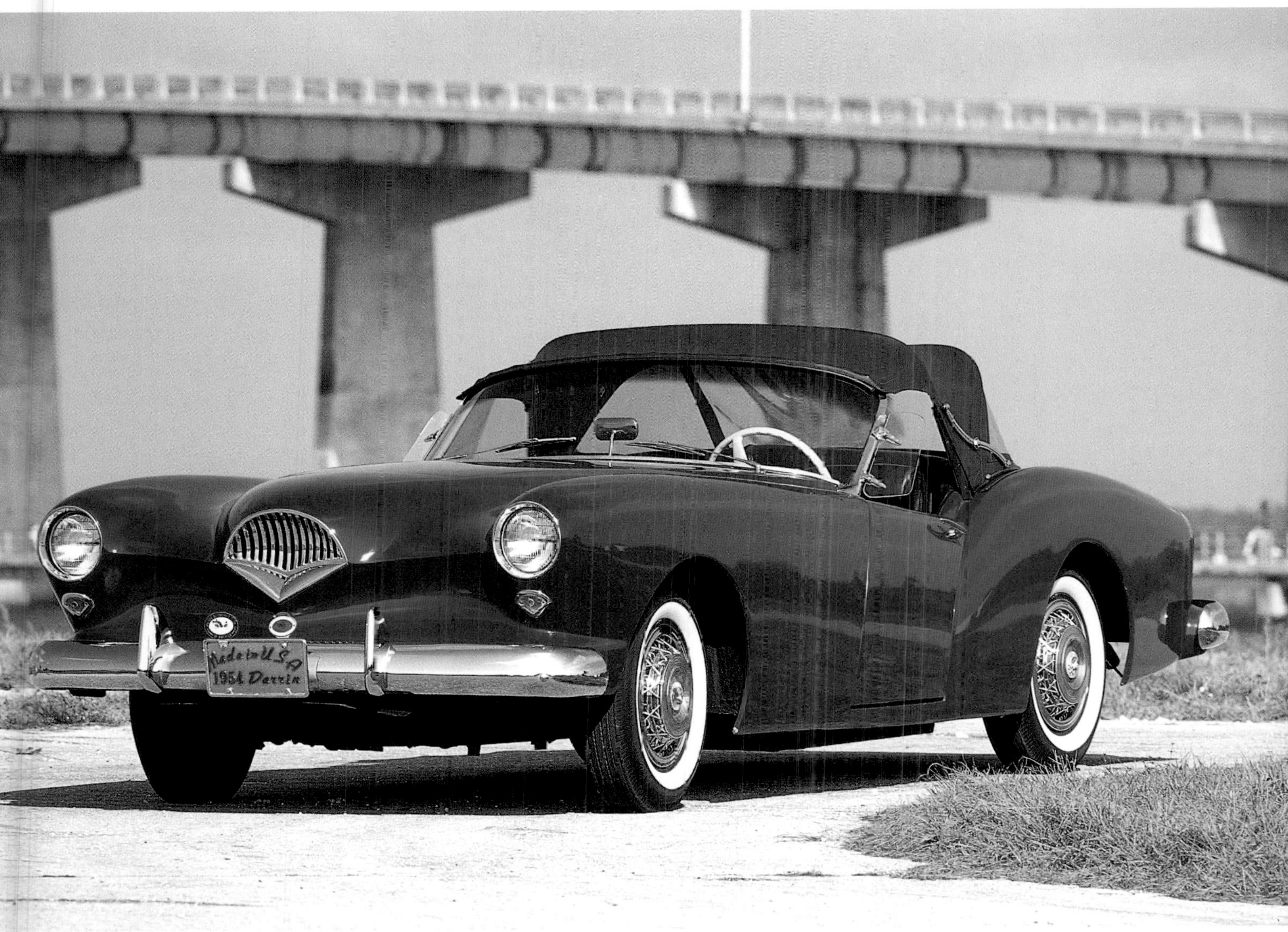

Originally conceived by legendary stylist Howard "Dutch" Darrin, the Kaiser-Darrin was built by independent automaker Henry J. Kaiser at the urging of his wife in 1954. Its fiberglass body wasn't its only innovative feature. The Darrin's soft top could fold halfway down in landau fashion and its doors disappeared forward into the front fenders.

In the hands of the Madman, the convertible's wheelbase was stretched by about a foot, aluminum was traded for steel, a custom Carson top replaced Kurtis' folding unit, a backseat was added, and horsepower was upped considerably—first by a 331ci Cadillac V-8, then eventually by Lincoln's excellent 317ci overhead-valve V-8 after it debuted in 1952. Completing the package was a new name—Muntz Jet. Even while falling a reported $1,000 behind on each car sold, Madman Muntz still managed to build roughly 500 of his speedy Jets before finally cutting his losses. The very last Muntz Jet was built in 1954.

While the 160hp Muntz Jet was definitely a hot performance car, was it a sports car? No, not considering its size, weight, corresponding big-car handling and the plain fact that it had more than two seats. It does, however, deserve credit for making a major contribution to sporty car design: the Muntz Jet apparently was the first American postwar car to show off a modern console/bucket seat combination. A padded dash and standard seat belts represented two other ground-breaking features.

If any one automobile did deserve credit as this country's first postwar sports car it was the Nash-Healey, a hybrid that at least was part American. A brilliant combination of British chassis, Yankee drivetrain and Italian bodywork, the Nash-Healey represented the meeting of minds between Nash-Kelvinator's George Mason and famed British sports car builder Donald Healey.

Certainly small, even by accepted sports car standards of the day, Powel Crosley's Hot Shot debuted in 1949 as a carefree, inexpensive sportabout. Doors were later added, creating the Super Sport. Crosley built these four-cylinder-powered roller skates up through 1952, the last year for his automaking venture. *courtesy Robert Ackerson*

If Crosley's Hot Shot or Super Sport didn't trick a budget-conscious buyer's trigger there was always the Skorpion fiberglass body kit, which first appeared in 1950. Ranging from about $450 to $600, the Skorpion kit could drop right onto a Crosley chassis.

The idea behind the Nash-Healey was launched in December 1949 aboard the *Queen Elizabeth*, then heading west across the Atlantic from England to America. Both Mason and Healey were aboard, the latter bound for the U.S. in search of a suitable American engine to power an export model he wanted to build. A chance meeting ensued, inspiring Mason to make a proposal: why not use Nash's overhead-valve six-cylinder as the base for this new sports car? Healey would get his horses—125 to be exact—while Mason would reap the rewards of a high-performance image, something Nash automobiles weren't exactly dripping with in the early 1950s. Healey agreed and the two company names then became joined at the hyphen.

A competition prototype using Nash's 234ci six and a 102-inch wheelbase Healey chassis was built in 1950 and raced at Le Mans that year, finishing fourth overall. More than 100 production versions with British-built bodies were then rolled out in 1951. Not fond of the body used that year, Mason then contracted Pinin Farina—the Italian coachworks that had created Nash's new regular-production body for 1952—to reshape the Nash-Healey sportster into a more distinctive machine. Although the results were certainly worthy of the Pinin Farina badge, the Nash-Healey convertible never really caught on with American buyers. Nor did the Nash-Healey coupe, which joined the lineup in 1953 and carried on alone into 1954. Production finally ended in August that year, with only 506 Nash-Healeys built over the four-year run. A handful of the 90 coupes built for 1954 ended up as "leftover" 1955 models.

About the time the Nash-Healey was rolling off into the sunset, another American sports car was just coming into being. And again the manufacturer was an independent, not one of Detroit's "Big Three."

Called "The Sports Car the World Has Been Awaiting," the Kaiser-Darrin was a distinct departure from the more practical product line Henry J. Kaiser had been offering since 1946. Actually, Henry J. reportedly wanted nothing to do with this idea when he first saw it in the California studio of Howard "Dutch" Darrin, he of prewar Packard fame. Darrin had been with Kaiser-Frazer off and on during the independent automakers early years, and was then "off" in 1952 when he borrowed a chassis from a Henry J—Kaiser's little compact car named after the boss—and used it as a base for the sports car Mr. Kaiser didn't like. Initially. Reportedly, Mrs. Kaiser, on the other hand, was thoroughly impressed. And it was she who, legend has it, whispered in hubbie's ear that he should build this car.

That he did, beginning in December 1953. Rolling on a 100-inch wheelbase, the long, low, rakish Kaiser-Darrin featured a three-position folding landau top, wire wheelcovers and curious doors that, instead of swinging open, disappeared forward into the front fenders, an idea Dutch Darrin had patented in 1946. Intriguing at a glance, the Darrin was, on the contrary, disappointingly powered by the mundane Willys F-head six-cylinder rated at 90 horsepower. Its obsolete power source alone might have been enough to keep the Kaiser-Darrin from going places had the reorganized Kaiser-Willys firm not left the U.S. market for South America in 1955. Only 435 Kaiser-Darrins were built in 1954 before that defection occurred.

Although shortlived and often overlooked, the Kaiser-Darrin did make one important automotive fashion statement before rolling into obscurity. The two-seater's distinctive body wasn't made from steel or aluminum, it was moulded from glass-reinforced plastic, or "GRP."

Discounting various synthetic body panel experiments in the 1930s, the wonders of modern GRP was basically first fully exploited during World War II as military manufacturers searched for a construction material to fill in for steel, aluminum and other metals then in very short supply. The solution was simple: mix together hardening polyester resins with a reinforcing woven mat made of fine glass fibers. Presto, "fiberglass," not to be confused with the trade name "Fiberglas" that Owens-Corning has long used for its glass-fiber insulation.

Once peace resumed, it was only a matter of time before the automaking industry discovered the merits of this then "high-tech" material. As early as 1944 Henry Kaiser was working with Owens-Corning on an experimental GRP car body. Mover-and-shaker William Stout also used Owens-Corning know-how that year to help fabricate a GRP prototype shell for his rear-engined Scarab.

Southern California then became the hub of the GRP universe as various small-time firms began trying their hand at marketing small, sporty fiberglass body kits, one of the most notable being the Skorpion, which for around $500 could transform a Crosley chassis into an open-air fun machine. When the Skorpion kit car appeared at the Los Angeles Motorama in November 1951, it shared the limelight with Bill Tritt's "Brooks Boxer," a custom-built, fiberglass-bodied Jeep. It was Tritt who undoubtedly deserves the most credit early on for helping advance the use of fiberglass in auto body construction.

Tritt's first experience with GRP fabrication came in 1949 when he was asked to build a fiberglass

THE WOODILL

A TRULY AMERICAN SPORTS CAR!

Assemble your own sports car for less than half the cost of a foreign sports car. The Woodill Wildfire is a complete kit. We furnish the materials and necessary detailed instructions —you furnish the labor.

Write for detailed drawing of the WILDFIRE body and frame—detailed instructions on "How to Build Your Own Sports Car"—see what you get before you buy—all for only $2 which will be returned on your first order.

See the Wildfire in "Knock On Wood," a Paramount picture starring Danny Kaye.

See the Wildfire in "Johnny Dark," a Universal picture starring Tony Curtis and Piper Laurie. See the Wildfire as the X150, watch it being built, watch it win the "border to border" race.

Build the Wildfire: See how easy it is to "do-it-yourself" and beat the high cost of sports cars.

THE WOODILL

"WILDFIRE"

Probably deserving credit as America's first "regular-production" fiberglass-bodied sports car was the Woodill Wildfire, which featured a body produced by Bill Tritt's Glasspar company atop a Willys chassis. The Wildfire was built in Downey, California, by local Willys dealer B.R. "Woody" Woodill. According to Woody, about 300 Wildfires were sold between 1952 and 1956, most of those in kit form.

FROM
0
TO
60
M.P.H.
IN 10.5 SECONDS
The Austin-Healey '100' offers you today's outstanding combination of performance and value. For less than $3,000 you get light, precise steering, pool-table flat cornering and stable four-footed roadability. These advantages plus an excellent weight-to-power ratio enable the Austin-Healey '100' to dominate Class D cars and many larger.
ONLY $298
FULLY EQUIPPE

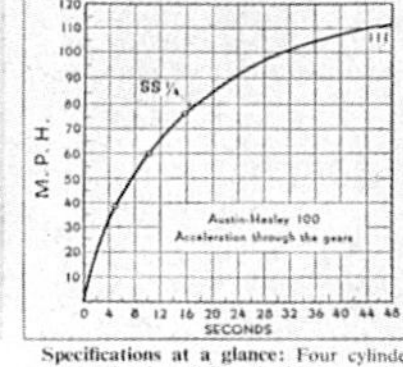

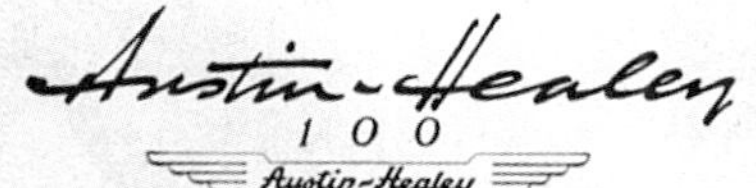

The British invasion of the 1950s brought many great sports cars to America, including the MG TD and Jaguar XK120. Probably representing the "best bang for the buck" was the Austin-Healey 100, which arrived in the U.S. in 1953.

boat for a friend. He then opened the Green Dolphin Boat Works in Montecito, California, a small outfit that quickly grew into the Glasspar Company in 1950. That year, Glasspar was contracted by Air Force Major Ken Brooks to fashion a fiberglass sports car shell for a military Jeep he had given his wife. Completed in the spring of 1951, the resulting Brooks Boxer then caught the eye of officials from the U.S. Rubber Company, one of Glasspar's suppliers.

It seemed U.S. Rubber's Earl Ebers was hot on the idea of promoting the use of GRP by convincing Detroit that fiberglass automobiles were indeed the wave of the future. When Detroit declined to be convinced, Ebers then teamed up with Tritt in February 1952 to try marketing yet another fiberglass body kit for a short-wheelbase chassis.

About the same time, Tritt was also contacted by Downey, California, Willys dealer B.R. "Woody" Woodill to help design a GRP body to sit atop a special chassis featuring a Willys drivetrain. Called the Wildfire, the final product basically became America's first "regular-production" fiberglass sports car since it was offered to the public in complete fashion, not as a kit, right off the showroom floor at the Woodill dealership. Most of the roughly 300 Woodill Wildfires sold from 1952 to 1956, however, were kits as Woody later explained only about 15 were actually built in-house at his small "factory."

As for Tritt and Ebers' plans, they were given a major boost off the ground when Life magazine detailed their efforts in a February 25, 1952, article entitled "Plastic Bodies for Autos." Once the public got wind of the apparent merits of GRP body construction, Glasspar was mobbed with inquiries and requests. One such contact later came from Henry Kaiser, who contracted Glasspar to mould the Kaiser-Darrin's GRP bodyshell.

But easily the most important inquiry came from a Chevrolet engineer, who in early 1952 invited U.S. Rubber officials in Mishawaka, Indiana, to come northeast to Detroit and show GM how this newfangled manufacturing process worked. They

If any one man can be called the father of the Corvette it's Harley Earl, famed styling chief at General Motors from 1927 to 1958. Having toyed with two-seat dream car designs from the late 1930s, it was Earl who transformed an experimental two-seater ideal into an American sports car reality.

Extremely hard to find in 1953, Chevrolet's earliest Corvettes started rolling out of the division's St. Louis assembly plant in force the following year—from auto show stage to the mainstream in less than two years. *courtesy Noland Adams*

immediately did, and the seed was planted.

Later in 1952, GM Styling began exploring the feasibility of GRP construction by fabricating a complete Chevrolet convertible body using fiberglass. Tests went exceptionally well. According to research and development chief Maurice Olley, who Ed Cole had brought aboard after he had been made Chevrolet chief engineer in April 1952, the GRP material differed little from the wood components that had made up most auto body reinforcements not all that long before.

As Olley reported, GRP construction produced "a very usable body, somewhat expensive, costing a little less than a dollar a pound, but of light weight, able to stand up to abuse, which will not rust, will not crumple in collision, will take a paint finish, and is relatively free from drumming noise. A fiberglass panel of body quality three times as thick as steel will weigh half as much and will have approximately equal stiffness." Additional testing then followed as fiberglass began showing up in the bodies (and elsewhere) of various experimental GM showcars.

Bystanders were also quick to jump on the GRP bandwagon. Writing in *Motor Trend's* December 1952 issue, Jim Potter called fiberglass's potential as an automotive body material "terrific." "Especially," he continued, "when the know-how in the use of the material is in the hands of individuals who are willing to share their experiences with others who want to help satisfy the growing demand for American-built sports cars."

Already having proven they were more than willing to share their experiences, U.S. Rubber officials again showed off what they had helped wrought in March 1952 when they put the Brooks Boxer—renamed the Alembic I—on display in Philadelphia at the National Plastics Exposition. Immediately following that appearance, the Alembic I was taken to Detroit where it was shown to the GM Styling staff. On hand, of course, was longtime Styling mogul Harley Earl. To say an impression was made was an understatement.

Not long after came a prediction from *Motor Trend's* Jim Potter. "Watch 1953," he concluded. "Plastic bodies are not only the coming thing—they have come, and they are too good not to stay."

Little did he know they'd still be staying around more than four decades later.

Chapter 2

1953-55

Born In A Rush

That America's only sports car has been running strong now through four generations for more than four decades stands as an impressive achievement on its own, given the constant tugs and shoves of an ever-changing market. Almost cut loose in its early years when demand failed to materialize as planned, Chevrolet's Corvette did manage to find its niche, and has with ease survived at least one major malaise, that coming in the second half of the 1970s. An all-new fifth-generation Corvette is being readied for release even as you gaze at the pictures on these pages, all this happening while rumors still persist concerning a final end of the road for Chevy's fiberglass two-seater. Or at least a trip down an off ramp as plans to merge the F-body Camaro and upscale Corvette have been discussed.

Long forgotten, yet far more amazing than the car's longevity record, was the short time Chevrolet originally required to create the Corvette some 40 years ago. In most cases, simply updating an existing model line in Detroit requires maybe three years or so. The typical time needed to kick off an entirely new breed is anyone's guess, but obviously you can start at "years," plural.

From initial sketches to the first Corvette off the production line in June 1953 incredibly amounted to less than 18 months—and this for an untried ideal (for a major postwar manufac-

All 300 1953 Corvettes were painted Polo White with red interiors. That "toothy" grille would remain a trademark up through 1960. Wearing 13 teeth from 1953 to 1955, it would loose four of those beginning in 1958.

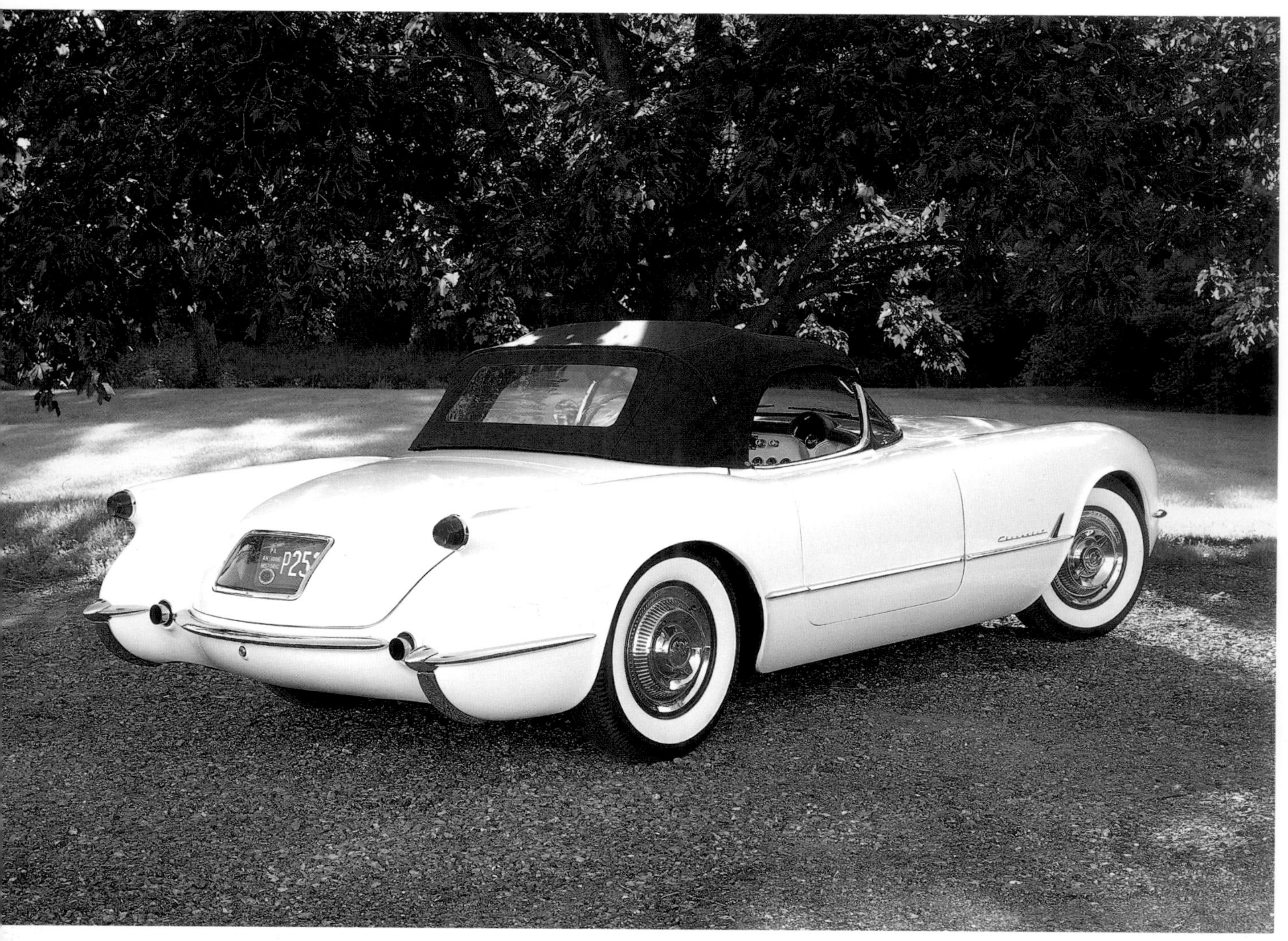

One way to identify a 1953 Corvette is by its black canvas top; the color was changed to beige in 1954. Also notice the short, stubby exhaust tips. These were lengthened on 1954 models, undoubtedly in an attempt cure an exhaust staining problem on the rear bodywork.

turer) that, at a glance, didn't stand much of a chance of gaining a foothold in the American consciousness of the time. This was a sports car, after all, a machine that served no purpose whatsoever other than making merry. Even more incredulous was the fact that this fun-mobile was a Chevrolet, long a low-priced sales leader. "Yeoman" was a fair description for most Chevrolet models in the early 1950s, although "dull" would've certainly worked in a pinch.

Yet there it was, Chevrolet's first Corvette, that somewhat unsure progenitor of more than 1 million more fiberglass two-seaters to follow over the succeeding 40-something years. If you were lucky enough to have bought one in 1953, you could've had a Corvette in any color you liked—as long as you liked Polo White. Same went for the Sportsman Red interior. Equipment choices were limited as well; the one-and-only power source was the "Blue Flame" six-cylinder backed by a Powerglide automatic transmission. A humble beginning, yes, but it was a beginning.

Responsibility for this hastily prepared product launch was typically shared by so many, from Chevrolet general manager Thomas Keating on down; the division's chief engineer Ed Cole, r&d's Maurice Olley, body engineer Ellis "Jim" Premo, and stylist Robert McLean to name just a few. As much as devoted fiberglass followers today like to respectfully refer to Zora Arkus-Duntov as the "father of the Corvette," he didn't arrive at General Motors until May 1953, four months after the car's public debut in prototype form.

But if any one man does deserve credit for single-handedly starting the Corvette ball rolling it has to be Harley Earl, longtime head of General Motors

Styling. A big man at GM, literally and figuratively, it was Earl who used his weight to push his dream for an American sports car into production.

Dream cars were nothing new for the six-foot-four Stanford graduate, who in the 1920s began his career in California designing custom bodies for some of Hollywood's flashiest characters while working for Los Angeles Cadillac dealer Don Lee. There, Earl was discovered by GM president Alfred Sloan, who brought him to Detroit to work for bodybuilder Lawrence Fisher. As a Fisher Body man, one of Earl's first responsibilities was to create a compelling look for the 1927 LaSalle, Cadillac's new, less-expensive running mate. The results were classic, and the LaSalle has since been called Detroit's first truly styled automobile.

Impressed by what a few well-planned good looks could do for his products' image, Sloan then founded GM's Art and Colour Section on June 23, 1927, and made Earl its head. Just like that, Sloan had taken automobile design responsibilities out of the hands of engineers and given them to Earl's 50-man staff, a move that both signaled an end to the era of independent coachworks and helped boost Earl to greatness. Once his greatness reached sufficient prominence, he took it on himself to paint over the Art and Colour sign, changing that "sissy name" to "Styling Section" in 1937. And with that stroke, he and his people then became "stylists."

The list of stylists who rose to greatness on their own after tutoring under Earl is long. Notables include Virgil Exner, he of Chrysler's "Forward Look;" Frank Hershey, responsible for Ford's Thunderbird and Crown Victoria in 1955; Buick's Ned Nickles; Clare MacKichan, credited with Chevy's legendary "Hot One" of 1955; and William Mitchell, who became Harley's "favored son" and eventually replaced Earl at the top of GM Styling in 1958.

Under Earl's directions, GM stylists put Detroit's first tailfins on the Cadillac in 1948, then started adding trendy wraparound windshields to various models five years later. Earl himself was also responsible for Detroit's first "dream car," the stunning Buick Y-Job. Built in 1938, the Y-Job not only featured futuristic hideaway headlights and an exceptionally clean body devoid of running boards, it also dramatically demonstrated Earl's faith in long, low lines. Later in a 1954 interview he touched on the logic behind this style:

"My primary purpose has been to lengthen and lower the American automobile, at times in reality and always at least in appearance. Why? Because my sense of proportion tells me that oblongs are more attractive than squares, just as a ranch house is more attractive than a square, three-story, flat-roofed house. Or a greyhound is more graceful than a bulldog."

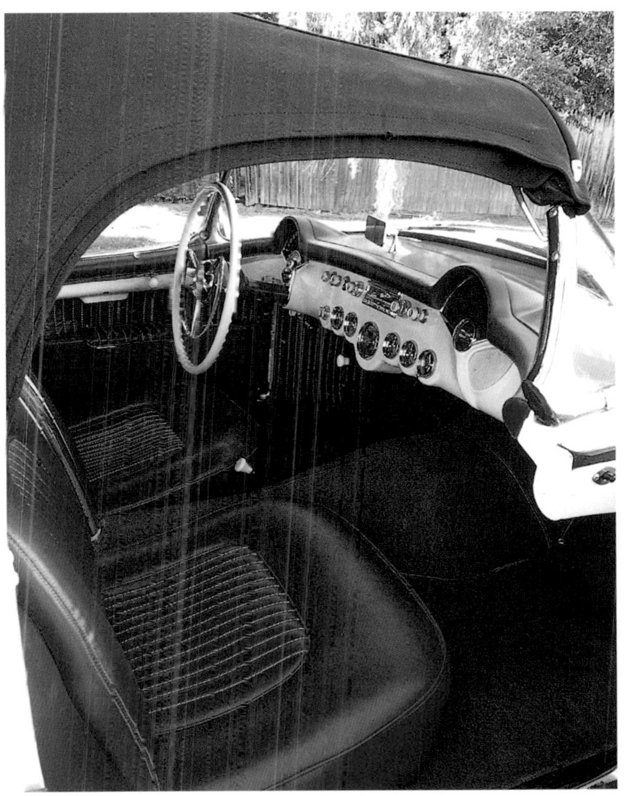

The early Corvette dash—which carried over in basically the same fashion up though 1957—may have appeared sporty looking, but was far from sports-car functional. Tach location was especially poor—it's the large round pod at the bottom of the instrument panel directly in the center.

The early Corvette's Blue Flame six breathed in its good air through three bullet-shaped inlets that were filters in name alone. Low hood clearance influenced various engine compartment installations, including, most prominently, the carburetors. Three side-draft Carters fit nicely on a special aluminum intake manifold.

Projects like the Y-Job then helped inspire yet another new practice for GM, this one involving the way the corporation introduced its products—and products-to-be. General Motors' first Motorama auto show was held in January 1949 in New York's Waldorf-Astoria hotel, kicking off a proud tradition that would serve its purpose well throughout the 1950s as a public proving grounds of sorts. Motorama stages quickly became the best places to see the latest automotive ideas from GM, some far-fetched, others ably predicting the future ahead.

Showcars then became a passion of Earl's, as were sports cars and racing. In 1950 and early 1951, he oversaw the production of two more experimental machines, Buick's LeSabre and XP-300, both sporty, albeit large, two-seaters.

A serious idea for a GM-built, regular-production, two-seater first came to Earl late in 1951. In this case, he envisioned more of a true sports car, a vehicle both relatively small in stature and price. While foreign sports cars, like Jaguar's XK120, did serve as inspiration, so too did the newly introduced Willys Jeepster, a perky, practical, open-air machine priced at less than $2,000. But Earl knew the only way to build a comparably priced GM sportster would be to keep production costs low by, say, using an existing chassis and/or other components right off the shelf. His idea initially went no further than a few private sketches and a bit of model building in hushed surroundings.

Earl's plan finally came into the light after he saw the fiberglass-bodied Alembic I during its showing on the 11th floor of GM's Styling's Milwaukee Avenue offices in the spring of 1952. Now ready for real action, he escalated his approach, bringing in Bob McLean and assigning him the task of establishing the basic parameters for the head stylist's latest dream machine.

McLean's drawings depicted a low, two-place sportster with a wide stance and a short 102-inch wheelbase. Engine location was key. Using Chevrolet's existing six-cylinder inline powerplant as a model, McLean placed it about three inches lower and seven inches closer to the dash than in typical Chevy installations. An externally mounted spare, reminiscent of the Jeepster's, was first considered, then dropped to help keep things clean in back. Earl's direct contributions to the initial layout included the trendy wraparound windshield and clear headlight cov-

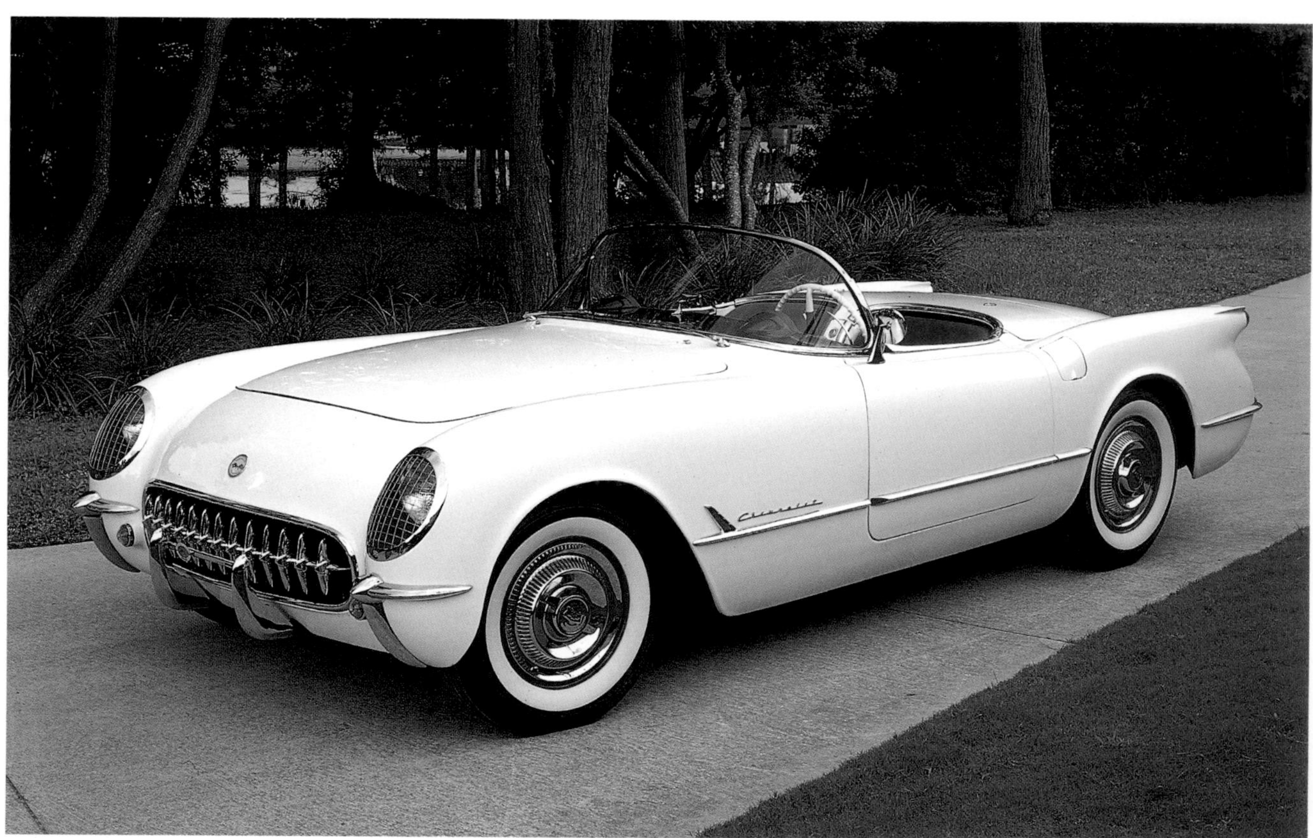

Most innocent bystanders never even noticed the arrival of the second-edition Corvette in 1954, basically since it appeared almost identical to its rarely seen 1953 forerunner. Chevrolet officials at the time didn't even bother to differentiate the two officially in writing.

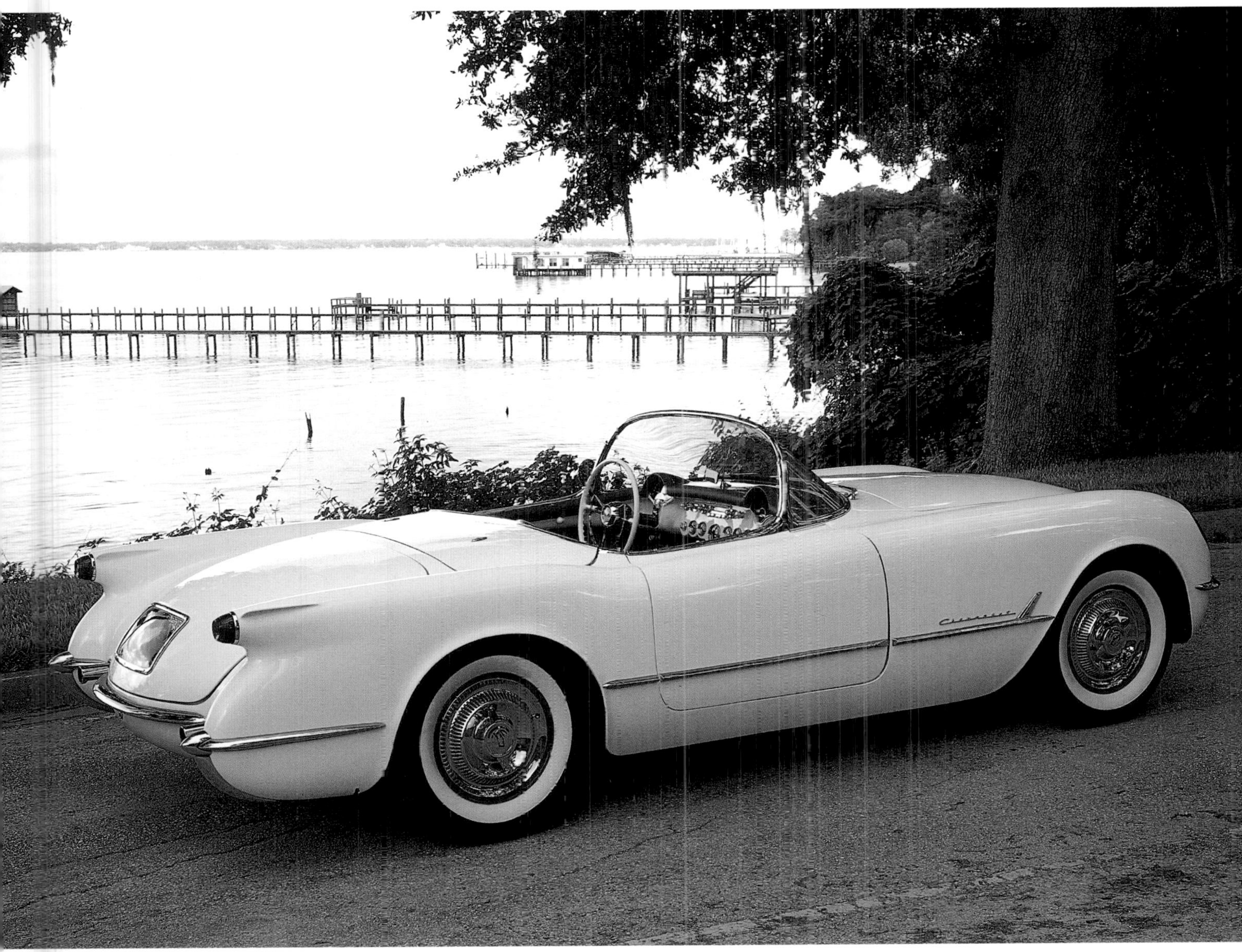

Various changes here and there help differentiate a 1954 Corvette from a 1953, but the easiest at a glance from the outside involves the lengthened exhaust tips used in 1954—compare these tips to the ones appearing on the 1953 model shown on page 24.

ers that fared the recessed headlamps into the rounded fenders.

Momentum quickly gathered from there. A lifesize clay mockup was hastily prepared in April 1952, followed equally as quick by a full-sized plaster model, which was then shown to Ed Cole. Cole was ecstatic and immediately promised his complete support for the project. Cole and Thomas Keating then showed the model to GM president Harlow Curtice with hopes of receiving Curtice's approval for plans to build an experimental version for the upcoming 1953 Motorama at New York's Waldorf-Astoria in January. He approved.

Next came the engineers. On June 2, Maurice Olley's research and development crew were shown the model and asked to create a suitable chassis. According to Olley, "the need was to produce a sports car, using components of known reliability, with adequate performance, a comfortable ride, and stable handling qualities, in something less than seven months before showing, and 12 months before production." No problem. A mere 10 days later, Olley had already sketched the basic chassis layout—codenamed "Opel"—a drawing that all but predicted the final product to the letter. Along the way, Chevrolet officially named the car "Corvette," a moniker borrowed from a lightly protected, lightly armed war-

The Corvette's 235ci Blue Flame six was rated at 150 horsepower in 1953 and through early 1954 production, as advertised on the valve cover of this 1954 model. A cam change then boosted output to 155hp for remaining 1954 Corvettes and the few six-cylinder models built for 1955.

ship class built both during World War II and long before in the days of wooden-hulled sailing vessels.

Olley's chassis design featured a very rigid, yet reasonably light X-member frame with fully boxed side rails. Weight was slightly more than 200 pounds. While front suspension featured many stock Chevy pieces, rear suspension was by leaf springs created specially to help locate the rear axle since modern Hotchkiss drive was used in place of the standard Chevrolet's torque tube. A short, 36-inch-long driveshaft delivered engine torque to a modified stock rearend that featured rebound straps to keep excess travel under control. Rear axle ratio was 3.55:1.

Per standard specs, front shock absorbers were mounted inside the coil springs squeezed between the typical A-arms. The front stabilizer bar, however, was larger than stock and mounted differently than in passenger car applications. Brakes were also off-the-shelf Chevy units, with 11-inch drums at all four corners. Steering was by a Saginaw worm-and-sector box featuring a mildly quick 16:1 ratio.

With Chevrolet's first modern V-8 still two years away, Cole's engineers were left with no choice but to rely on Chevy's yeoman-like "Stovebolt" six-cylinder engine, which by 1953 at least featured lightweight aluminum pistons and improved lubrication and more durable main bearings. Displacing 235 cubic inches, this tried-and-true, overhead-valve inline six produced 115 horsepower at 3600rpm in standard passenger car trim—just fine for everyday transportation, but not near enough to put the sports in sports car.

Again, no problem. Various modifications transformed Chevy's thrifty six-cylinder into the Blue Flame six, a Jekyll and Hyde transformation if there ever was one. Top Blue Flame horsepower was 150hp at 4200rpm, while maximum torque output went from the stock six's 204lb-ft at 2000rpm to 223 at 2400 revs. How'd they do it?

For starters, compression was raised from 7.5:1 to 8:1 and a more aggressive solid-lifter cam was stuffed inside with a .405-inch lift on the intake end, .414 on the exhaust. A metal cam gear replaced the stock fiber piece, all the better to let this powerplant rev beyond 5000rpm and survive to rev again. Valvetrain gear was also beefed with dual valve springs and stronger exhaust valves.

Three Carter one-barrel carburetors—mounted in horizontal sidedraft fashion in order to stay clear of the car's low hood—fed fuel/air to those six combustion chambers through a special aluminum intake manifold. Although three round air cleaners were originally used in the prototype application, they were replaced in production by a trio of small "air inlet extensions." Handling exhaust chores was a split manifold dumping into dual pipes and mufflers.

Additional special features included a "high-efficiency" water pump and shielding for the distributor and plug wires. The latter was added to prevent ignition voltage from wrecking havoc with radio reception since fiberglass panels don't suppress this interference the way typical steel bodies do. As for the high-volume water pump, it was relocated low on the front of the Corvette engine to again allow more hood clearance, this time for the four-bladed fan.

Also mounted low for obvious reasons, the Blue Flame six's radiator required a remote header tank, which on the Motorama prototype was located on the driver's side of the valve cover running parallel with the engine. In regular production, this tank was switched to the opposite side. Yet another change from showcar to streetcar involved the carbs; the Motorama prototype's automatic choke was exchanged for a cable-operated manual setup in production.

Behind the Blue Flame six went the un-sports-car-like two-speed Powerglide automatic transmission, a choice that may have made purists cringe but represented the simplest, least costly (from an engineering standpoint) way of putting the driveline together on such short notice. Powerglide modifications for the Corvette application included a revised tail housing (since a driveshaft was used in place of the standard torque tube) and some internal beefing (shift points came at higher rpm) to better handle the additional engine torque. If it was any consolation, at least the Corvette Powerglide was equipped with a floor-mounted shift lever.

On top of all this went a GRP bodyshell hand-laid in plaster moulds pulled from McLean's original clay model. But while fiberglass would, of course, end up the material of choice for regular-production bodies, it wasn't exactly the first choice. As Jim Premo later told the SAE, "the body on the show model was made of reinforced plastic purely as an expedient to get the job built quickly. At the time of the Waldorf Show, we were actually concentrating on a steel body utilizing Kirksite tooling." Kirksite dies were cheaper and could be fabricated quicker than typical steel dies, but, on the downside, had much shorter working lives. All that, however, was rendered moot once Chevrolet people gained confidence in both the new GRP material's merits and the construction techniques behind its successful use.

Once on its stage at the New York Motorama in January 1953, Chevrolet's GRP-bodied Corvette prototype was turning heads with ease, both with its intriguing fresh face and its apparent state-of-the-art makeup. "People seemed to be captivated by the idea of the fiberglass plastic body," explained Premo. "Furthermore, information being given to us by the reinforced plastic industry seemed to indicate the practicability of fabricating plastic body parts for automobiles on a large scale."

Beyond that, the public was simply in awe of the little Polo White sports car with its low, wide stance, "toothy" grille, wire-mesh stone guards over recessed headlights, wraparound windshield, gloriously red two-seat interior, and dual exhaust tips exiting through its rounded tail. Prospective buyers almost immediately began clamoring for Corvettes of their own right away. Reportedly, original Chevrolet plans called for a production run of 10,000 two-seaters in 1954. Customers wouldn't wait, however, convincing officials to kick off a limited run of 300 'glass-bodied 1953 models that June, meaning Premo and his men had less than six months to get their GRP act in gear.

GM then began accepting bids for the production of Corvette bodies. U.S Rubber, working through GM's Fisher Body Division, tried its hand with a bid, as did the Molded Fiber Glass Company, located in Ashtabula, Ohio. Although the Ohio firm won the contract, worth a reported $4 million, it wasn't exactly prepared for the job. The company's founder, Robert Morrison, first had to establish a second plant, the Molded Fiber Glass Body Company, itself founded in April 1953. He then had to scramble to assemble the various equipment needed to produce the requested GRP panels fast enough. For more than a year, the MFG Body Company relied on a subcontractor to help meet its contract as Morrison's own fiberglass body process wasn't fully up and running until July 1954.

All told, the Corvette's various GRP body parts weighed 340 pounds. Once fabricated in Ohio, they were shipped to GM's makeshift assembly line in Flint, Michigan, where they were glued together and finished by hand. The completed body weighed in at 411 pounds and was mated to the chassis at eleven mounting points.

Another mid-year production change for 1954 involved exchanging the three small air inlets atop the Carter carburetors for a more functional air cleaner arrangement featuring two round filter housings.

The first of 300 regular-production 1953 Corvettes rolled off the short, temporary Flint line on June 30, 1953, looking very much like the Motorama prototype save for various minor exceptions, some already detailed here. On the outside, the showcar had "Corvette" identification on its nose and tail and "Chevrolet" badges accompanied by a small trim piece on each front fender. Production cars did not have the nose and tail i.d., and their bodyside "Chevrolet" badges were joined by a long trim piece that ran from wheel opening to wheel opening. Headlamp bezels and wheelcovers were different on the showcar, which also featured exterior door pushbuttons and small "scoops" atop each fender—both these features were deleted in production.

Deleted as well were the Motorama model's various chrome touch-ups on the engine, the fan shroud under the hood, and the hydraulic assists for both the hood and doors. On the flipside, additions made to production models included windshield end seals and drip mouldings also with seals. Inside, the showcar's chrome door knobs and painted upper dash edge were exchanged for white knobs and a vinyl-trimmed dash.

As mentioned, all 300 Flint-built 1953 Corvettes were painted Polo White with contrasting red interiors. And all were identically equipped, again save for a few less-than-earth-shaking running changes here and there. The most notable—at

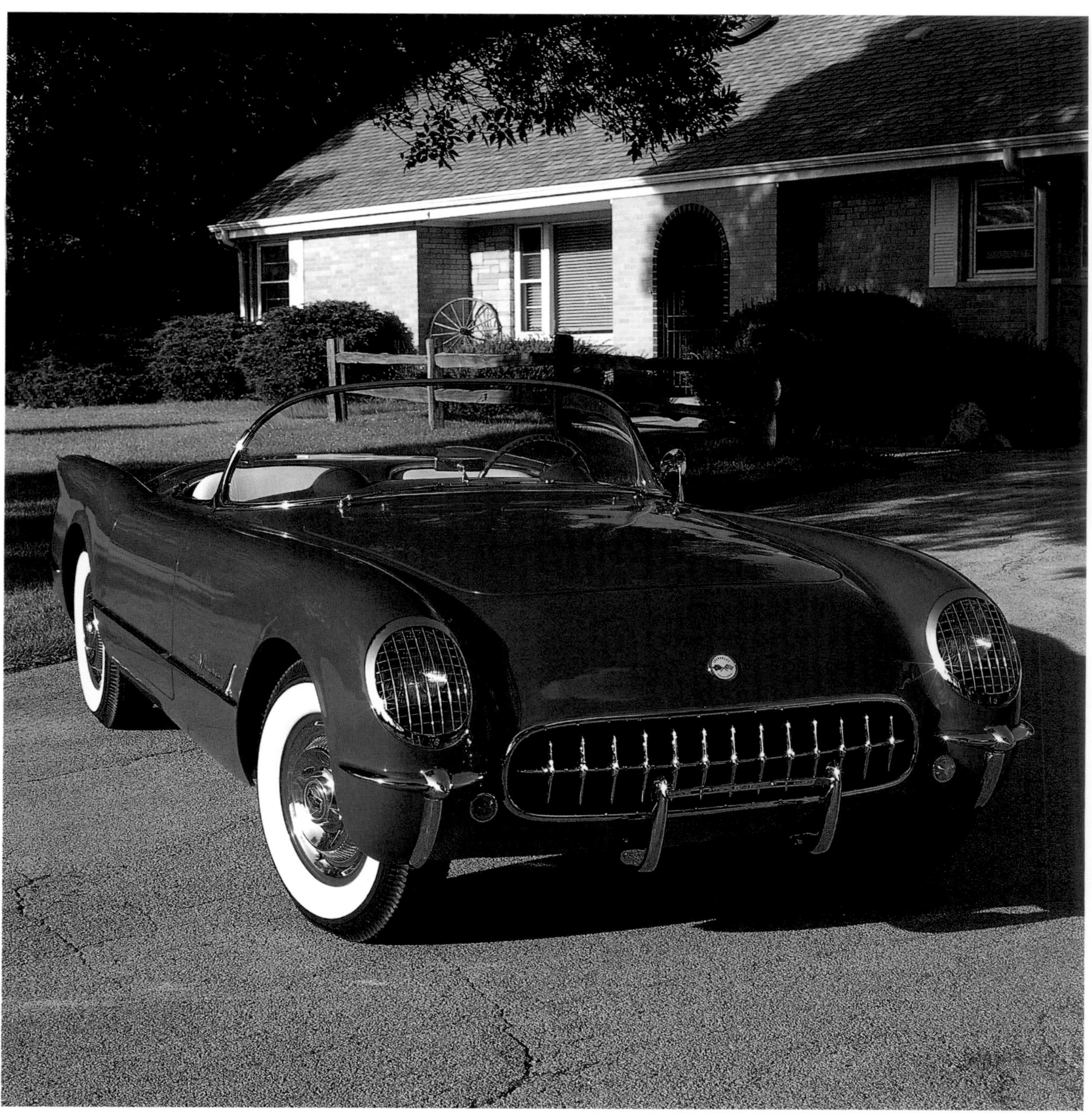

Gypsy Red was reportedly the second most popular Corvette color in 1955, a year when only 700 fiberglass two-seaters were built. Although paint choices had been introduced in 1954, the original Polo White finish dominated that year, and it remained the top choice in 1955.

least on the car itself—came at all four wheels. With tooling of the Corvette's "spinner" wheelcover then apparently not complete, the earliest cars off the line wore covers pirated from passenger-line Bel Airs. According to estimates, at least the first 25 Corvettes were so equipped.

The most prominent "running change" involved the Corvette's production site. From the beginning, the Flint assembly line had served only as a stop-gap measure while Chevrolet officials prepared a more suitable production area at GM's St. Louis assembly plant. St. Louis plant manager William Mosher had been informed in March 1953 that his facility would become home to Corvette production. And it was there that the first 1954 Corvette was completed on December 29,

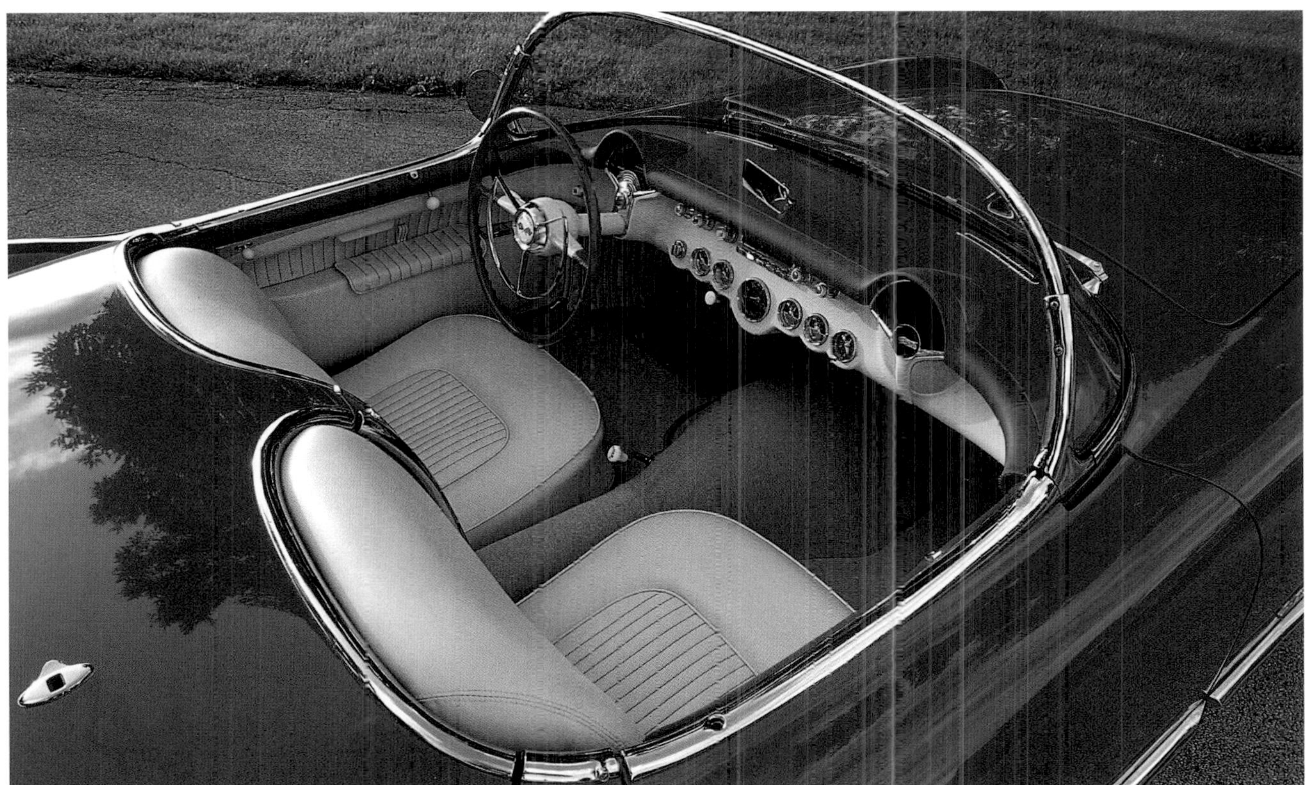

All Corvettes in 1953 and 1954 and most in 1955 featured two-speed Powerglide automatic transmissions—notice the small Powerglide shift lever on this 1955 model. A long-awaited manual transmission, a three-speed, was first offered in 1955, but only about 70 or 80 were installed.

1953. Reportedly, 15 1954 Corvettes were built that month in St. Louis before production really got rolling in January.

Distinguishing between those 300 1953 Corvettes and the following 1954 models wasn't all that easy at first glance, save for the addition of new exterior paint choices and interior trim shades. While nearly 85 percent of the 1954 Corvette population still featured the Polo White paint with red interior, Chevrolet also introduced Pennant Blue and Sportsman Red exterior finishes, along with Shoreline Beige and blue interior trim. Black paint was also apparently introduced, although in somewhat mysterious fashion. Non-documented estimates claim 1954 exterior color breakdown came to about 300 blue cars, roughly 100 red and perhaps less than 10 black. Factory paperwork in 1954 briefly mentioned Metallic Green and Metallic Bronze paint as well, but both are unknown. Chevrolet also changed the rubberized canvas convertible top color in 1954, replacing black with beige. Reportedly some early 1954 Corvettes may have come with the 1953 black top.

Discounting various hard-to-find technical changes, made both as St. Louis production began

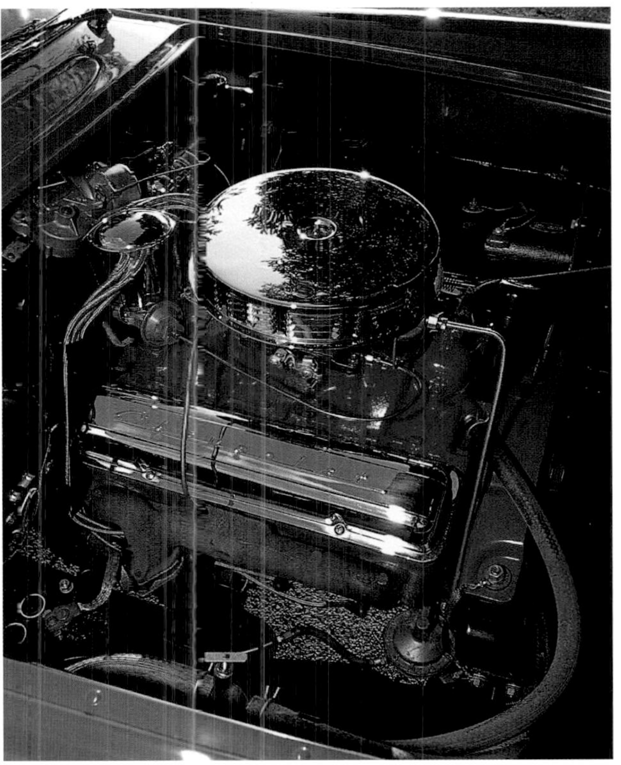

Big news in 1955 was the arrival of more Corvette power, courtesy of Chevrolet's all-new overhead-valve 265ci V-8. Output for the bechromed Corvette 265 was 195hp.

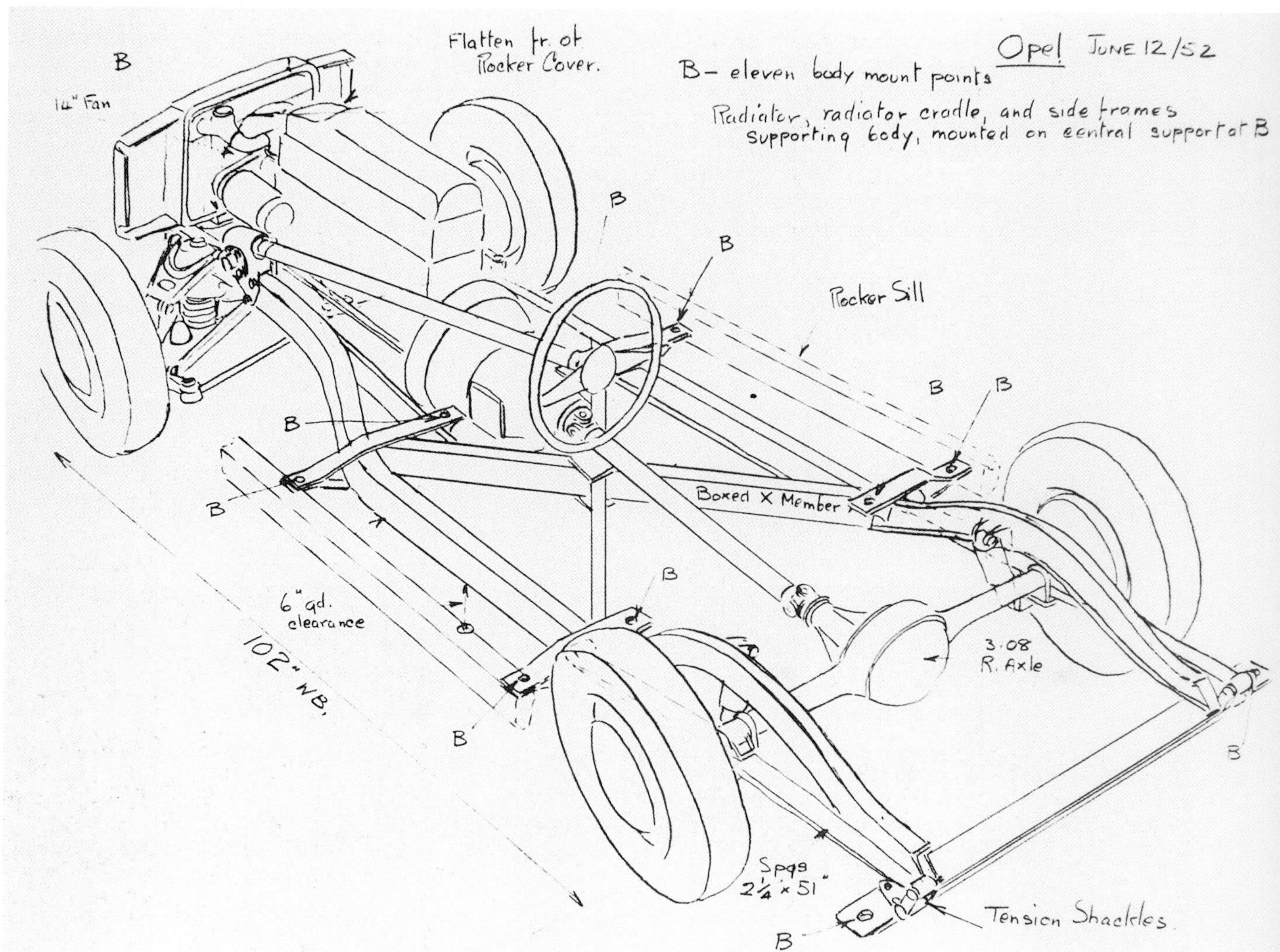

Research and development chief Maurice Olley penned the Corvette's chassis layout in June 1952. Early code name for Olley's engineering project was "Opel." Notice the driveshaft with U-joints instead of Chevrolet's standard torque-tube design. *courtesy Noland Adams*

and in "running" fashion throughout the year, the easiest way to readily identify most 1954 models comes in back. Early in 1954 production, the short exhaust extensions used on all 1953 Corvettes were exchanged for longer tips, undoubtedly to help cure an exhaust staining problem that continually plagued the first Corvettes.

Yet another running change for 1954 came under the hood, where a different cam upped advertised output for the Blue Flame Six to 155 horsepower. Both 150- and 155-hp 1954 Corvettes were built. At some point along the line, engineers also traded the triple carburetors' three bullet-shaped air inlets for a more functional setup made up of two round air cleaners perched in conventional upright fashion. Most 1954 Corvettes also used a hood latch mechanism with only one interior release, while some early cars and all 1953 models featured two hood releases, one for each latch. The Corvette frame differed slightly (concerning component mounting) in 1953 and 1954, as it also would in 1955.

That so little evidence was present to readily differentiate a 1953 Corvette from a 1954 was only right since Chevrolet officials themselves simply grouped them together under the same model year designation. And most witnesses at the time were none the wiser anyway since the 300 early cars were considerably slow in hitting the streets. On top of that, Chevrolet wasn't able to make an official press introduction until late September 1953 when journalists were invited to try out the new sports car at GM's Milford Proving Grounds in Michigan.

Chevrolet general manager Thomas Keating introduced the Corvette that day in an official press release: "In the Corvette we have built a sports car in the American tradition. It is not a racing car in the accepted sense that a European sports car is a race car. It is intended rather to satisfy the American public's conception of beauty, comfort and convenience, plus performance. Just as the American production sedan has become the criterion of luxury throughout the world, we have produced a superior sports car. We have not been forced to compromise with the driving and economic considerations that influence so broadly the European automotive design."

As a performance car, the new Corvette did well off the line by standards of the day. Top end was just short of 110mph and reported acceleration figures were 11 seconds from zero to 60, 18 seconds for the quarter-mile. In the words of *Motor Life's* Hank Gamble, "the Corvette is a beauty—and it *goes*!"

But was it really a sports car? *Road & Track's* staffers asked that very question in their June 1954 issue. Overall, they "liked the Corvette very much," calling straight-line performance its most "outstanding characteristic." And in their opinion, "the second most outstanding characteristic of the Corvette is its really good combination of riding and handling qualities." Concluded the *R&T* report, "the Corvette corners flat like a genuine sports car should."

In the words of *Motor Trend's* Don MacDonald, "Chevrolet has produced a bucket-seat roadster that will hold its own with Europe's best, short of actual competition and a few imports that cost three times as much."

Nonetheless, could a sports car be a sports car without a clutch and a stick? Many felt not. In defense of the Corvette's Powerglide-only status, Maurice Olley had earlier addressed the car's one apparently major disappointment.

A beautiful piece of art in itself, this mahogany body buck was used to make the first molds for the 1953 Corvette's fiberglass shell. *courtesy Noland Adams*

"The use of an automatic transmission has been criticized by those who believe that sports car enthusiasts want nothing but a four-speed crash shift," explained Olley. "The answer is that the typical sports car enthusiast, like the 'average man,' or the square root of minus one, is an imaginary quantity. Also, as the sports car appeals to a wider and wider section of the public, the center of gravity of this theoretical individual is shifting from the austerity of the pioneer towards the luxury of modern

Chevrolet chief engineer Ed Cole (left) and division general manager Tom Keating take a quick look at the Corvette prototype sitting on its Motorama stage at New York's Waldorf-Astoria hotel in January 1953. Notice the unique fender trim and small push-button door handles—regular-production Corvettes from 1953-55 had no exterior door handles.

ideas." Concluded Olley, "there is no need to apologize for the performance of this car with its automatic transmission."

"That statement," wrote *R&T's* John Bond, "should get a rise from 100,000 *Road & Track* readers!"

Even more defensive was an official Chevrolet statement explaining that the division's new two-seater was "not intended to be used as a racing car." More than one journalist was quick to respond to this disclaimer.

"Definitely being discouraged is [the] competition use of the Corvette though its name means 'sloop of war,'" wrote Floyd Lawrence in *Motor Trend*. "This stands in marked contrast to foreign sports car producers who try to get their first models into the hands of well known racing drivers to insure a racing reputation for the car. It is reported that Briggs Cunningham's order for two Corvettes for possible entry in the Le Mans race was quietly turned down at headquarters."

Chevrolet officials were no dummies. They knew the Corvette wasn't anywhere near ready to race in 1953. Hell, it hadn't even gotten out of the blocks yet.

While Olley saw no need to apologize for the Powerglide, Chevy sales executives quickly discovered that many prospective customers were unable to forgive various other apparent pitfalls of the two-seat roadster. It seemed American car buyers didn't much care for the Corvette's pesky, leaky plexiglass side curtains and folding top. In reference to the clumsy top, MacDonald's *MT* report explained that apparently Chevy's "conception of the Corvette market is that no owner will be caught in the rain without a spare Cadillac."

Less troublesome but still a negative was the prospect of fumbling around for the interior door panel knob to gain entrance—remember, no exterior door handles. Cockpit instrumentation was also questioned. While gauges and a tachometer were included, they were located low in the center of the dashboard. The passenger basically had a better view of the 5000rpm tach—situated dead center in the dash—than the driver. All this helped explain why early Corvette sales never even came close to projections.

Then again, perhaps Chevrolet officials shot themselves in their own feet. Hoping to promote an exclusive image for their new Corvette, they initially limited availability of the first production run to "V.I.P." customers only. Most of the eager show-goers who saw the Motorama Corvette in January 1953 never even had a chance to touch a regular-production version. "If you've got an itch to get behind the wheel of a Chevrolet Corvette," wrote *MT's* Lawrence, "you might as well scratch it. Better are your chances of winning the Mille Miglia on a kiddie car." After explaining that the very few cars then available in the late summer of 1953 were going to General Motors executives, Lawrence quipped, "if [the] present distribution pattern continues, the hoped-for output of 300 units this year will scarcely take care of the top GM brass."

By the end of the year, only about 180 of the 300 1953 Corvettes built were sold as Chevrolet's sales geniuses couldn't find enough very important people willing to come to their by-invitation-only party. Much momentum had already been lost by the time the V.I.P-only qualification was dropped in the summer of 1954. As Don MacDonald explained in *Motor Trend,* "the long gap between initial publicity and availability has cooled the desires of many buyers." Meanwhile, the stockpile of unwanted Corvettes continued to grow as the St. Louis plant was rolling out 50 a day.

Alarmed by this unexpected apathetic trend, Chevrolet officials in June cut back production and halted fiberglass body panel construction entirely in Ohio. The St. Louis plant ended up building only 3,640 of the 10,000 Corvettes planned for 1954, and nearly a third of those were still sitting unsold as of January 1, 1955. Future prospects for continued production of America's only sport car looked bleak, helping explain why a mere 700 1955 Corvettes were built. Many atop GM's executive pecking order wanted to see Chevrolet cut its losses and quit the sports car game right there. But Ed Cole, Harley Earl and the rest wouldn't have it—somehow they were going to save this unique automobile from early extinction.

The first step towards salvation came early in 1955.

By then, nothing could be done about the car's cruder characteristics since the same body was back for a third year. The only notable changes again involved color choices, although some additional mystery surrounds what was actually offered. On the outside, Polo White was once more the

Chevrolet's first production Corvette rolled off the very short makeshift assembly line in Flint, Michigan, on June 30, 1953. Early models used standard Bel Air passenger car wheelcovers because the planned "knock-off" style covers weren't ready in time

Chevrolet didn't offer the comfort and convenience of a removable hardtop for the early Corvettes, but that didn't mean a fiberglass two-seater customer couldn't come in out of the rain. Various aftermarket companies started offering removable tops of their own not long after the Corvette was introduced. Chevrolet then took it upon itself to offer an optional detachable hardtop beginning in 1956.

paint of choice (representing nearly half of the 700 cars built), with Gypsy Red and the newly offered Harvest Gold making up the bulk of the remaining orders. Pennant Blue was apparently briefly carried over from 1954 then dropped in April 1955. Some sources say that Pennant Blue was then replaced by "Corvette Copper," while others list a "Coppertone Bronze." By either name, this latter shade was all but unknown in 1955.

Interior colors included red, dark beige, light beige, green and yellow, the latter two appropriately reserved for the yellowish Harvest Gold exte-

Chevrolet returned to GM's annual Motorama show circuit in 1954 with a bevy of Corvette dream cars. Appearing at top with the standard 1954 model is the fastback Corvair coupe. Below it is the passenger-line-based Nomad wagon, which led to a regular-production follow-up in 1955. In front is a hardtop 1954 Corvette with roll-up windows and exterior door handles.

rior paint. Top shades were also expanded, as white and dark green (again, for the Harvest Gold cars) joined beige.

The real news, however, came under the hood where overall impressions were boosted considerably thanks to the addition of Chevrolet's overhead-valve V-8, introduced that year to the delight of speed-conscious buyers in the low-priced field. From a passenger-line perspective, the new OHV V-8 had overnight transformed the old, reliable Chevy into the "Hot One."

With development dating back to just before Ed Cole came on board from Cadillac in 1952, Chevrolet's first modern V-8 displaced 265 cubic inches and featured a lightweight valvetrain using individual stamped steel rocker arms. These ball-stud rockers—an idea borrowed from Pontiac engineers—helped the short-stroke 265 wind up like nobody's business. In "Power Pack" trim under a 1955 Bel Air's hood, it produced 180hp at 4600rpm. Its potential beneath the Corvette's forward-hinged fiberglass lid was obvious.

Injecting more power into the Corvette equation had been tried before almost as soon as the car had hit the streets. More than one private V-8 swap had been performed. But the quickest, easiest way to add more horsepower was by bolting on one of McCulloch's centrifugal superchargers. The Paxton division of the McCulloch Company in California sold supercharger kits for many cars in the 1950s, and even supplied forced-induction blowers as factory-offered options through Kaiser (standard with 1954 Manhattans), Studebaker-Packard and Ford. When force feeding the Blue Flame six's three Carter carbs, a Paxton blower reportedly increased the Corvette's rear wheel horsepower by 35 percent, translating into a 0-60 time of about nine seconds.

Although impressive, the supercharged six-cylinder was still just a six, and a six still couldn't produce the image Cole and crew really wanted for the Corvette, especially after Ford began showing models of its upcoming Thunderbird early in 1954. A winner on looks alone, the planned two-seat "T-bird" would also be powered by a V-8, nothing less. Chevrolet had no choice but to respond accordingly.

Before Zora Arkus-Duntov came along to oversee Corvette performance, the man in charge of such development was three-time Indy 500 winner Mauri Rose, at far right. Here, he shows off the new V-8-equipped Corvette. *courtesy Michael Lamm*

The third experimental Corvette produced (notice the Motorama-style fender trim was later rebuilt as the prototype for the V-8 installation planned for 1955. This airborne moment came during chassis testing at GM's Milford Proving Grounds in May 1954. *courtesy Michael Lamm*

A prototype V-8 Corvette was undergoing testing as early as May 1954 under the direction of performance consultant and three-time Indy 500 winner Mauri Rose. Cole had hired Rose in August 1952 to oversee the division's performance parts development projects, a position Vince Piggins filled later in the 1950s. Rose's earliest challenges included developing the triple-carb setup for the Blue Flame six. Far more prominent was his involvement with the V-8-powered Corvette, a creation requiring not all that much sweat. Maurice Olley's X-member frame needed only a minor modification to allow clearance for the 265's fuel pump, and a bigger radiator with a fan shroud was added.

With a lumpier cam and a Carter four-barrel carburetor topped by a low-restriction chrome air cleaner, the Corvette's 265 V-8 was bumped up to 195 horsepower. Compression remained 8:1. Additional chrome dress-up appeared on the valve covers and the distributor's suppressive shielding. And a new 12-volt electrical system and automatic choke came along as part of the deal. On the outside, the V-8 Corvette was identified by the large gold "V" added to the "Corvette" script on each fender.

While some (as few as 10 perhaps) very early 1955 Corvettes were equipped with the 155hp Blue Flame six, the vast majority featured the high-winding 265 V-8. In turn, most of these cars also were equipped with the Powerglide automatic. A second transmission choice, the long-awaited three-speed manual, was introduced sometime during the year, apparently available only behind the Corvette's V-8 (no six-cylinder/auto trans cars are known). Estimates put three-speed Corvette production that year at probably 75.

As for more important numbers, according to *Road & Track*, the muscled-up V-8 Corvette couldn't be denied as far as sheer brute force was concerned. Rest to 60mph required a reasonably scant 8.7 seconds, with the far end of the quarter-mile showing up only 7.8 ticks later. The car's real-world top end was a tad short of 120mph, definitely impressive. "Loaded for bear" was *R&T's* description. As *Motor Life's* Ken Fermoyle saw it, "the V-8 engine makes this a far more interesting automobile and has upped performance to a point at least as good as anything in its price class."

Yet in other areas the Corvette was still lacking, whether from the perspective of a typical American customer looking for typical American conveniences or from the angle of sports car buffs who hoped to finally see a Yankee machine capable of putting Europeans in their place. Help in both cases was on the way.

Enter Zora Duntov.

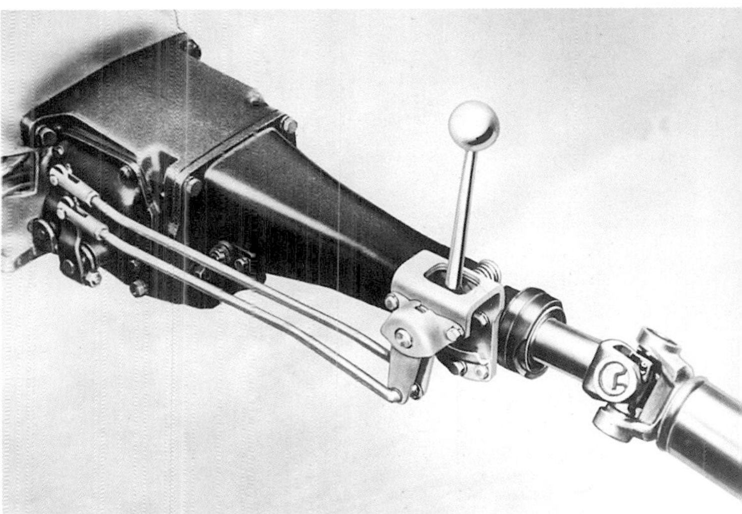

Easily the most common complaint concerning the early Corvettes involved its Powerglide-only status—an automatic transmission would never do if Chevrolet's two-seater was to ever take its place as a true sports car. That problem was solved late in 1955 production with the arrival of this three-speed manual transmission. *courtesy Noland Adams*

Chapter 3

1956-57

Off And Running

It easily ranks among the fastest stretches of sand in the world, an honor earned through both the various four-wheeled record runs once made there as well as the annual action still occurring today each spring when thousands of young, hormone-intensive collegiates hit these shores. For years, the Daytona area in Florida—roughly 25 miles of hard-packed, bullet-straight beaches—was home to high performance in America, beginning right after the turn of the century at Daytona's northern neighbor, Ormond Beach, the legendary "Birthplace of Speed."

There in April 1902, an Oldsmobile and a Winton both were clocked at a then-sizzling 57mph. Four years later, Fred Marriott's Stanley steamer hit 127mph, a world record, the first such international honor for the Ormond sands. Various other top end records followed, reaching 276mph in 1935 before speed freaks refocused their universe across the country to the Bonneville salt beds in Utah.

Florida's speed scene then shifted south to nearby Daytona Beach, where in March 1936, the area's first stock car race, sanctioned by the American Automobile Association (AAA), was run on a 3.2-mile course that led up the beach and down a closed-off section of the main coast road. In 1938, a young racer named Bill France took over promotion of the beach race, which that year became more than just an annual affair. Two races were run in 1938, three in 1939,

Exterior door handles, roll-up windows and optional two-tone paint schemes debuted along with a restyled fiberglass shell in 1956. Also notice the chromed headlight bezels—some early cars featured body-colored pieces.

and before France knew it he had a racing "season" in Florida. In December 1947, a France-led group voted to form the National Association of Stock Car Auto Racing. Nearly a half century later, NASCAR racing today is one of the sporting world's hottest tickets.

By 1956, Daytona Beach had again become the place to be in America for those with a need for speed. Along with the three annual beach races—Modified-Sportsman, Convertible class and Grand National—held in late February, the beach was also home to the various "Speed Weeks" performance trials for stock-class and modified-production factory cars, both foreign and domestic.

Domestic representatives that year included three specially prepared 1956 Corvettes. The trio arrived at Daytona Beach on a mission to prove that Chevrolet could indeed build a competitive sports car. Piloting the newly restyled two-seaters were two men and a woman, veteran racer John Fitch, aerobatic pilot Betty Skelton and a certain GM engineer named Zora Arkus-Duntov. For both Duntov and the car that had by then become "his baby," the 1956 Speed Weeks represented a "coming-out party" of sorts. By the time the sand settled, the man and his machine had grown forever entwined. And the Corvette's reputation as a real road rocket was born.

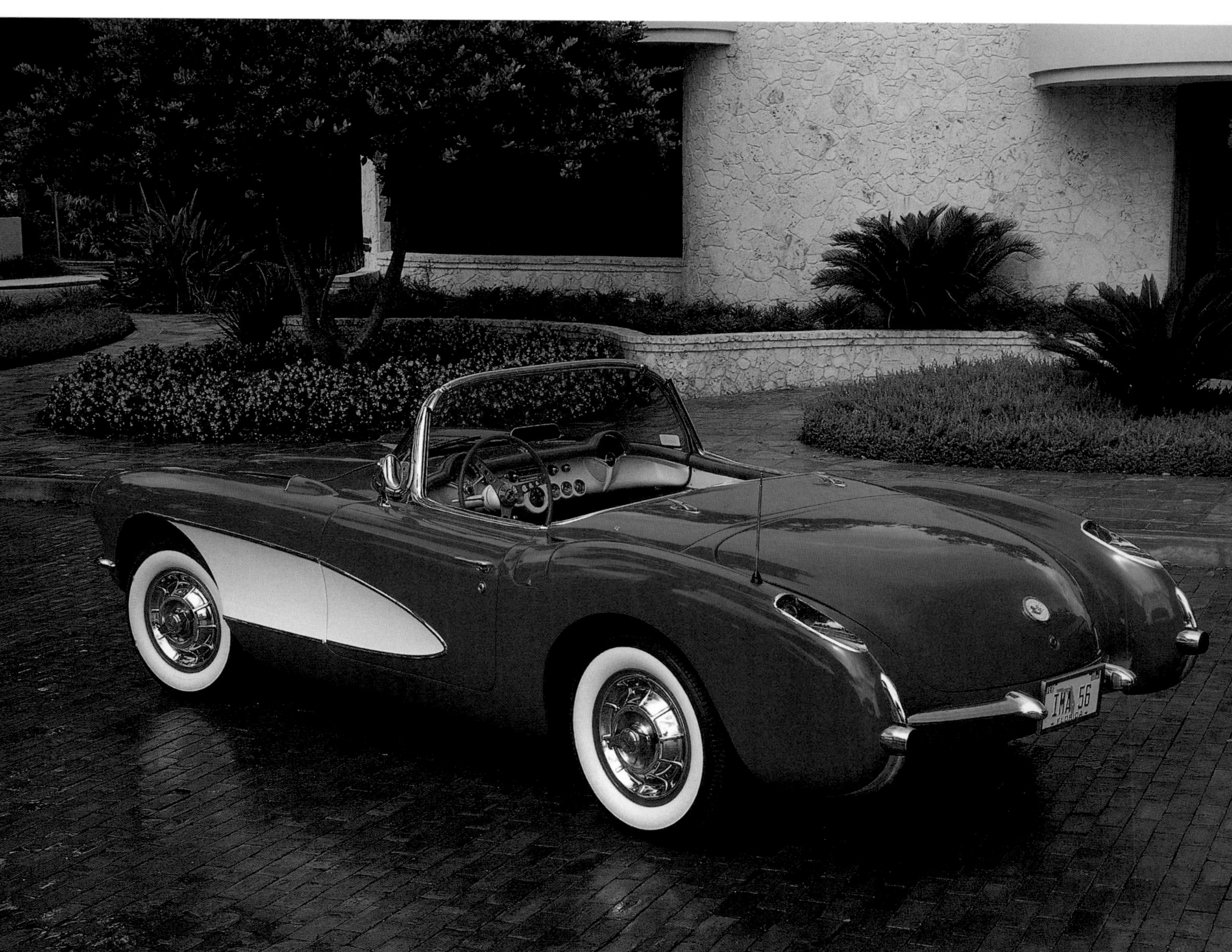

One of Zora Duntov's earliest jobs at GM engineering involved solving the exhaust staining problem on the tails of the early Corvettes. He proposed the twin exhaust tips be moved from the rear panel to the ends of the rear quarters for the 1955 model. The change, however, wasn't made until 1956.

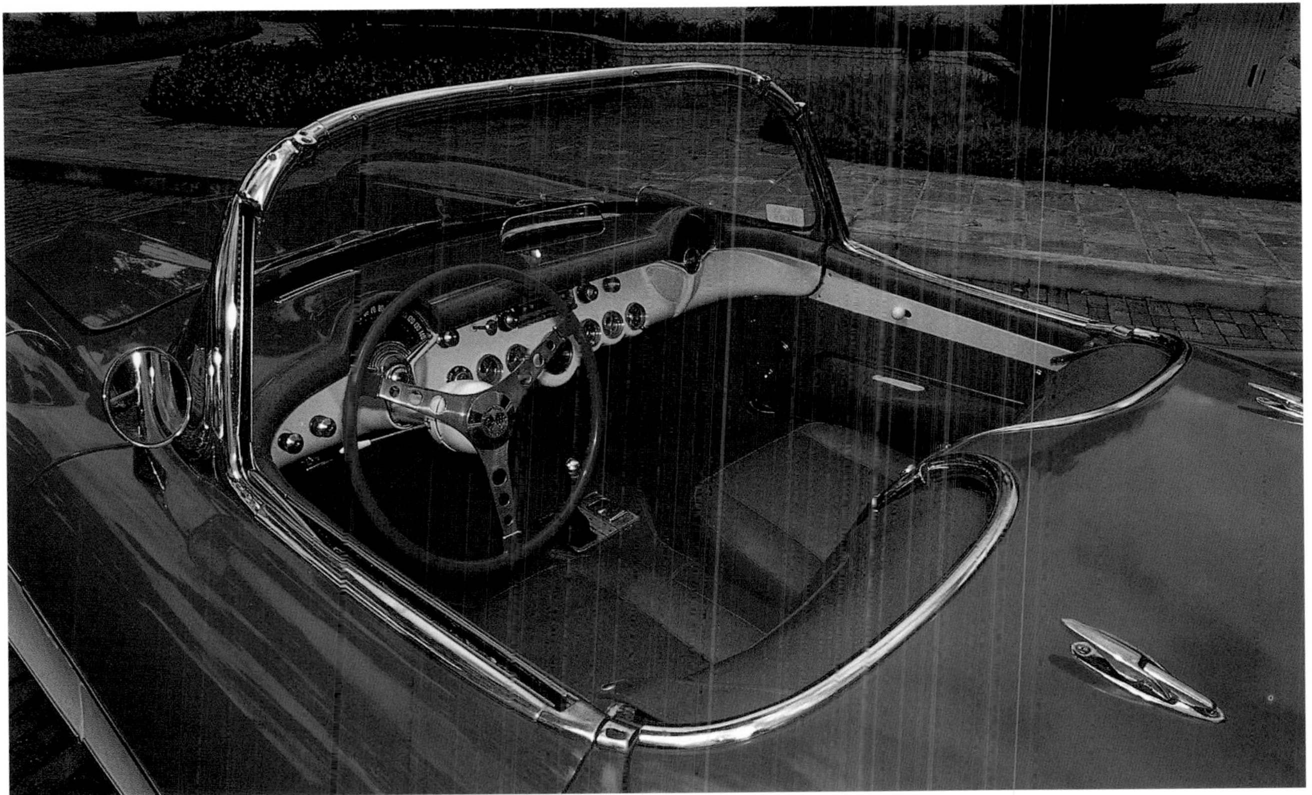

An attractive, truly sporty three-spoke steering wheel helped spruce up the 1956 Corvette's interior, which carried over in similar fashion from the style used previously. A three-speed manual transmission was also standard in 1956, with the Powerglide now an $188.50 option.

Serving as the Corvette's chief engineer until his retirement in 1975, Zora Duntov commonly receives the lion's share of the credit for nearly every one of the fiberglass two-seater's advancements made during the 1950s and 1960s. Of course, he didn't do it all singlehandedly. But it was his experience, both as an engineer and a race driver, that was mainly responsible for the Corvette's kick start after 1955.

Duntov was born to Russian parents in Belgium on Christmas Day, 1909. By the time he was a teenager, he was demonstrating an intense interest for internal combustion machines. After studying mechanical engineering at universities in Leningrad and Germany, his thesis paper on supercharging was published in Berlin in 1934. A job designing superchargers then followed, as did various other engineering positions in Belgium and Paris. It was about this time that he also began toying with sports cars and racing. But both his engineering and racing careers were temporarily stalled with the coming of war in Europe.

Duntov and his family left France in December 1940 for the U.S., where he first worked as a consulting engineer. In 1942, he teamed up with his brother Yuri to open a machine shop in New York. This business soon became the Ardun Mechanical Corporation, the company title coming from a shortening of the *Ar*kus-*Dun*tov name.

Six-cylinder power fell by the wayside after 1955. Top Corvette performance in 1956 came from a 265 V-8 with two Carter four-barrel carburetors. Advertised output was 225 horsepower. A single-carb 265, rated at 210hp, was also available, but few were installed. Various running changes made beneath the hood in 1956 included relocating the oil pan's dipstick to the driver's side of the engine. Early cars, like this one, had the dipstick on the passenger's side

One of three 1956 Corvettes specially prepared for the Daytona Beach Speed Weeks trials that year, this race-ready model was driven on the sands by aerobatic pilot Betty Skelton. Restored and owned today by noted Corvette collector Bill Tower, the Betty Skelton racer featured many speed-conscious modifications, including the addition of various aluminum trim pieces.

After the war, the Ardun company was contracted by Ford to help boost the power of Dearborn's old, reliable "flathead" V-8 for use in heavy-duty trucks. Zora then designed the legendary "Ardun head" overhead-valve conversion kit for Ford's valve-in-block flathead. These innovative aluminum cylinder heads featured hemispherical combustion chambers, centrally located spark plugs and inclined valves. But even though the Ardun heads did improve flathead performance considerably, Ford had already opted for the larger Lincoln V-8 for its trucks by the time Duntov's design was ready for market in 1949. Not all was lost, however, as Duntov heads then found their way into various Ford-powered race cars in the 1950s.

By far the biggest promoter of the Ardun-head V-8 was British sports car builder and racer Sydney Allard. He began offering the Ardun flathead engine in his J2 sports racer in 1949. Duntov himself went to work for Allard soon after, then returned to the States in late 1952 to work for Fairchild Aviation in Long Island, New York. Curiously, before he left England Duntov had contacted Chevrolet's Ed Cole about an engineering job, to no avail.

Then Zora saw the Corvette prototype at the Waldorf-Astoria in January 1953. "Now there's potential," he told *Hot Rod's* Jim McFarland in 1967. "I thought it wasn't a good car yet, but if you're going to do something, this looks good." Thus inspired, Duntov queried Cole's office a second time and was given a GM engineering position in May 1953. "Not for [the] Corvette or for anything of that sort," he told McFarland, "but for research and development and future stuff."

Nonetheless, it wasn't long before Duntov was tinkering with the Corvette chassis to improve overall handling. As he later explained, "this was not part of my normal assignment—just fiddling on the side." His first true Corvette assignment involved solving the exhaust staining problem in back, which he did by moving the twin tailpipe tips out to the farthest reach of each rear-quarter section. Considered then dropped for 1955, this design was incorporated the following year.

Duntov's involvement with the Corvette project then increased rapidly as first V-8 power was added and then additional chassis refinements were investigated. Finally in 1957, he was officially named Director of High Performance Vehicle Design and Development, with the Corvette, of course, being his top priority. America's only sports car would remain so for nearly two decades more.

As for the development of a better Corvette for 1956, it was Duntov's chassis experiments that paid off first. In his opinion, the early Corvette was a car with "two ends fighting each other" since considerable oversteer was designed in up front and almost as much roll understeer was inherent in back. All this was changed in 1956. As he wrote in *Auto Age*, "the target was to attain such handling characteristics that the driver of some ability could get really high performance safely. The main objects of suspension changes were: increase of high-speed stability, consistency in response to the steering wheel over a wide range of lateral accelerations and speeds, and improvement of power transmission on turns—that is, [the] reduction of unloading of [the] inside rear wheels."

These goals were accomplished by adjusting suspension geometry. Front suspension location was changed by adding shims where the front cross-member attached to the frame, a move that increased caster angle. Roll oversteer was also minimized by changing the steering's main idler arm angle, again by shims. In back, roll understeer was reduced by revamping the leaf spring hangers to lessen the slope of the springs.

Weight distribution was improved as well ever so slightly (by 1 percentage point) to 52 percent front, 48 percent rear, since the 265ci V-8, at 531 pounds, weighed 41 pounds less than the big Blue Flame six. And power was boosted considerably thanks to the addition of a second Carter four-barrel carburetor to the 265's induction setup.

Initially, two power choices were offered for 1956, the twin-carb 265, with 225 healthy horses, and a 210hp version with its single Carter four-barrel. Both engines featured a compression increase to 9.25:1. Some confusion still exists over which of these powerplants was actually standard, although the lower performance 210hp 265 has been logically listed as such over the years. The dual-four V-8, however, was apparently the first powerplant offered beneath a 1956 Corvette's hood. As for this engine's regular production option (RPO) number, 469, that came later in the run after the 210hp engine reportedly appeared on the scene to replace its twin-carb counterpart as base equipment.

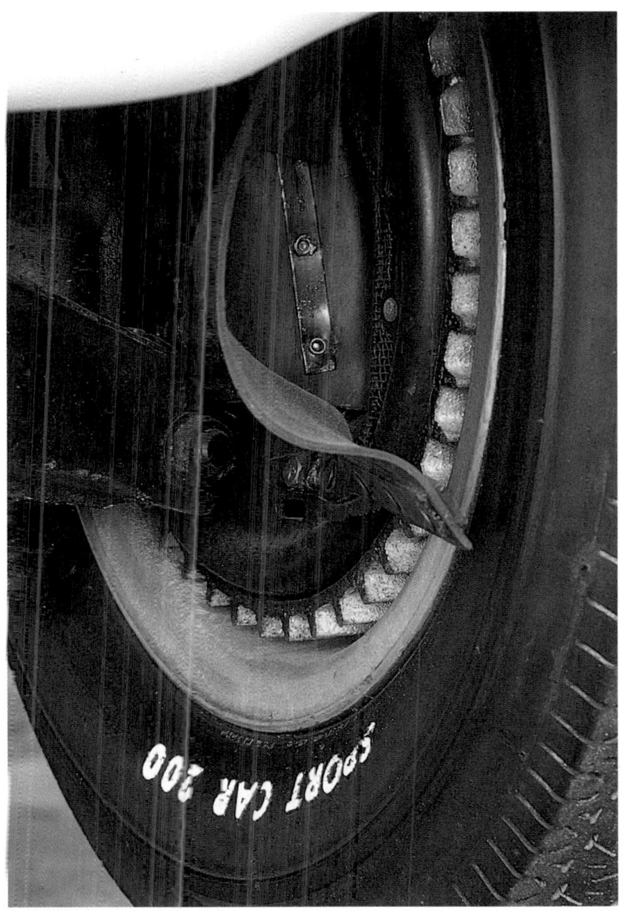

Beneath the Betty Skelton beach racer were special brakes fitted with finned drums, vented backing plates and special cooling ducts. Although not available for regular-production Corvettes in 1956, this type of equipment would become an official option the following year.

Some evidence to this move came early that summer via a *Road & Track* road test. In reference to the 225hp V-8's tendency for "'flatness' of carburetion on take-off," that report explained that "this appears to be a characteristic of the two four-barrel carburetors and possibly accounts for the change to a single four-barrel carburetor as standard equipment (210bhp)." According to official Chevrolet paperwork dated May 28, 1956, the 225hp 265 was about that time first listed as an option and

Famed Daytona Beach speed merchant Smokey Yunick did the prep work on the three 1956 Corvette beach racers. On Skelton's car, he reportedly installed a four-speed manual transmission, equipment that wouldn't be available to Corvette buyers until 1957. Yunick also added his trademark cool-air induction system, which drew in the denser, outside atmosphere from near the passenger's side headlight and delivered it via ductwork to the twin carbs. That setup has long since disappeared, although a small intake grille (not visible here) still exists at the right front corner of the engine compartment.

given the appropriate code, RPO 469. Oddly, this apparent switch is also marked by various trivial mechanical changes to the dual-carb V-8, including relocating the oil dipstick from the right side of the engine to the left. Coincidentally, the vast majority of the 3,467 1956 Corvettes built featured the 225hp 265. Very few 210-horse examples are known.

Whatever the engine choice, a base Corvette in 1956 did come equipped with an honest-to-goodness manual transmission, the same three-speed box briefly offered late in 1955. Gear ratios were 2.21:1, first, 1.31:1, second. Those who preferred shiftless driving could still have the two-speed Powerglide automatic, listed under RPO 313. Reportedly, installation totals of the two transmissions were split roughly right down the middle.

Again using 11-inch drums, the brake system basically carried over, save for new linings that were more fade resistant and wore longer. Standard axle ratio in 1956 was again 3.55:1, with a 3.27:1 differential listed as an option under RPO 471.

Truly new was the fresh, modern-looking body that went atop that revamped chassis in 1956. This restyle was quick to impress as both a marked improvement on what came before as well as a faithfully updated rendition of the original image. While the toothy grille up front helped remind onlookers that the 1956 model was indeed a Corvette, the more conventionally located headlights and recessed taillights gave the car more of an impression of forward motion.

Complementing those speedier-looking lines were twin "windsplits" on the hood and scalloped "cove" panels behind each front wheel opening. These coves could remain the same overall body color or could be painted a contrasting shade—the optional two-tone finish was a Corvette first. Solid color choices numbered six in 1956; Onyx Black, Aztec Copper, Cascade Green, Arctic Blue, Venetian Red, and Polo White. Priced at $19.40, the RPO 440 two-tone combination was also available in six forms. Interior trim shades were two, red and beige, while three folding top colors (depending on paint choice) were offered, black, white and beige.

Additional exterior firsts included the two simulated scoops added atop each front fender, items reminiscent of the 1953 Motorama prototype. Completing the exterior remake were new knock-off wheelcovers that amazingly carried over in nearly identical fashion up through 1962. In 1959, this design was modified with 10 rectangular slots added to help cool the brakes.

On the street, the restyled, muscled-up Corvette looked every bit as fast as it ran. According to *Road & Track*, that amounted to 0-60 in 7.3 seconds, 15.8 seconds for the quarter-mile, this in a three-speed model. Performance for its Powerglide-equipped counterpart was listed as 8.9 and 16.5 seconds, respectively. Nice numbers either way. *Sports Car Illustrated's* Roger Huntington thought so. He called the 1956 Corvette's 225hp V-8 "one of the hottest production engines in the world—regardless of piston displacement." And to think Duntov wasn't even done yet.

Both he and Cole, who would be promoted to Chevrolet general manager that July, wanted the world to know just how fast the revamped

Corvette had become by 1956. Zora was confident he could squeeze 150mph out of the car with some additional work. Cole quickly gave the go-ahead for that effort with the goal being a trip south to Florida to show off the results during the aforementioned Speed Weeks trials.

It was then that Zora developed the aptly named "Duntov cam," a potent solid-lifter bumpstick that really brought the little 265 V-8 to life. While lift was a bit less than Chevrolet's existing top performance V-8 cam, the Duntov cam's duration for both intake and exhaust was considerably longer. Found under RPO 448 or 449, depending on your source, the "Special High-Lift Camshaft" was only available for the 225hp RPO 469 V-8. Output for the Duntov-cam RPO 469 engine, although not officially listed, was commonly put at 240 horsepower. Chevrolet paperwork recommended that this combination only be used "for racing purposes only."

Duntov, Fitch and Skelton showed why on the sands of Daytona in late February 1956. For Skelton, an experienced pilot, test driver and corporate spokesperson who then worked for Campbell-Ewald, Chevrolet's ad agency, a day at the beach would never mean the same again. As she later told *Road & Track's* Andrew Bornhop, "it was very exciting because when the tide would go out it would leave these little puddles of water. And after the cars ran a few times through the measured mile, these pools would become deep ruts that would get you airborne. That was kind of fun. It was just a marvelous time, driving on the beach and being there in the early days of Corvettes with all those great people. It was such an honor to be part of the activity. And, of course, the Corvette was the star of the show."

Star, indeed. Duntov's prediction rang true as he drove one of the cars to a top two-way average speed of 150.533mph. Fitch's Corvette hit 145.543mph, while Skelton turned in a 137.773mph average. Without a doubt, the Corvette had arrived.

Then, just as quickly, it was off again, this time farther south to Sebring, Florida, home of the 12-hour endurance race that each spring brought the world's best sports-racing machines to America.

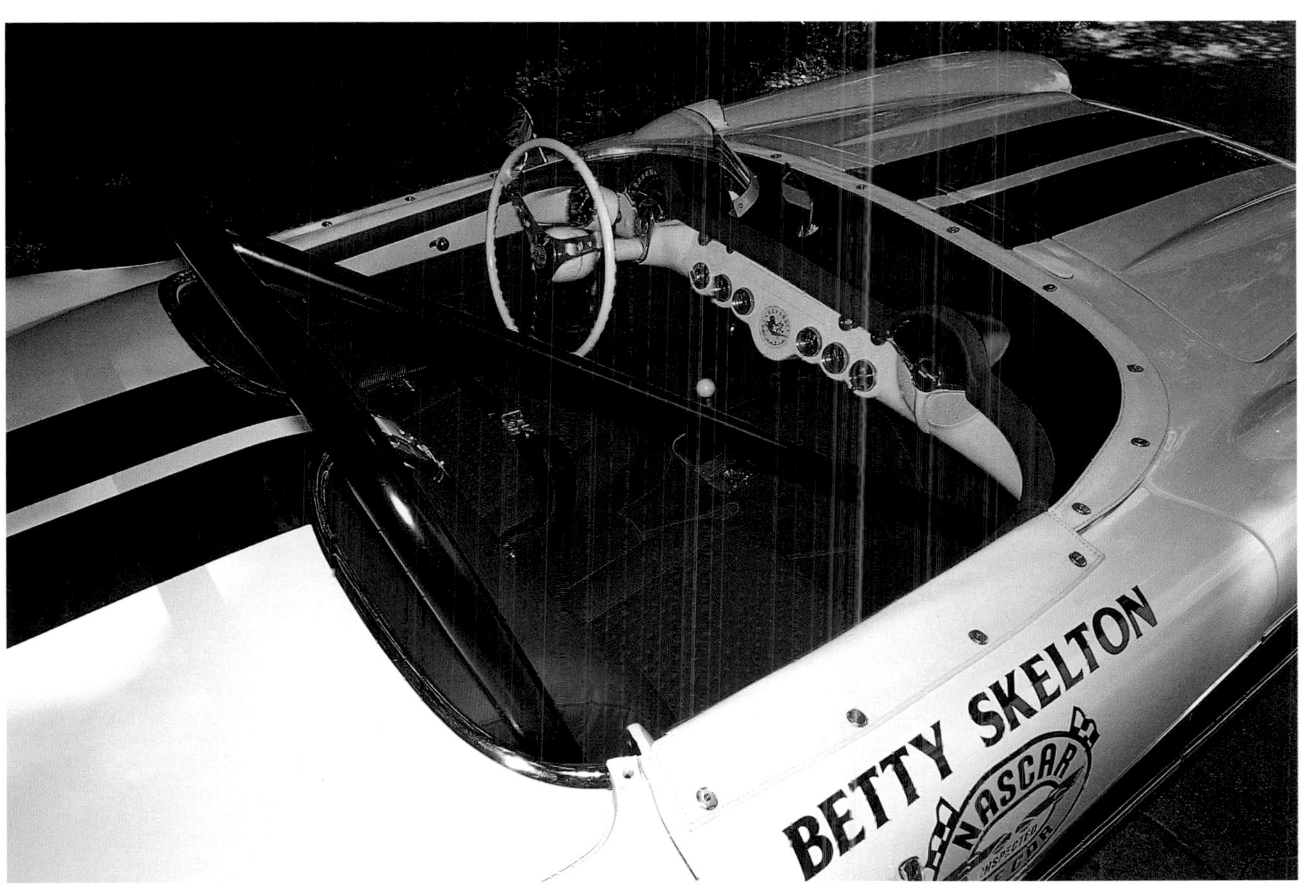

Raced at various venues in the years after its February 1956 appearance at Daytona Beach, Betty Skelton's Corvette was fitted with a rollbar somewhere along the line. The small windscreen was used at Daytona. Notice the tachometer, relocated on the steering column where it belonged. A plate covers the stock tach location in the center of the dash.

A bore job boosted displacement for Chevrolet's high-winding V-8 to 283 cubic inches in 1957. Two dual-carb 283s were offered that year, the hydraulic-cam 245hp version and this brute, the 270hp variety with its solid-lifter "Duntov cam."

After kicking up some sand on the beach, Chevrolet's Corvette showed up a month later in Sebring to hopefully show everyone it could do more than just go fast in a straight line. Duntov declined to take part this time, so it was up to John Fitch to lead the four-car Sebring team on March 24, 1956.

On the surface, Chevrolet officials did everything they could to distance themselves publicly from Fitch's four-car team, which was "fronted" through Dick Doane's Raceway Enterprises in Dundee, Illinois. All theatrics aside, the effort was definitely fully factory backed, right down to the engineering advancements hiding beneath the skins of each car. Springs and shocks were heavy-duty and

One more color choice, Inca Silver, was added for the 1957 Corvette, which basically carried over unchanged at a glance from the outside. This Cascade Green 1957, one of 550 Corvettes painted that color in 1957, is equipped with the 270hp 283cid V-8, RPO 469C. Price for RPO 469C was $182.95. Production was 1,621.

A four-speed stick was introduced as a Corvette option, RPO 685, in 1957. Priced at $188.30, this close-ratio gearbox was snapped up by 664 buyers that year.

brakes featured finned drums with wider shoes wearing sintered cerametallix linings. Three of the cars relied on the twin-carb 265 backed by the standard three-speed. The fourth featured an enlarged 307ci V-8 with 10.2:1 compression and headers. Behind this 275hp beast was a German-built ZF four-speed transmission. All four cars rolled on Halibrand knock-off magnesium wheels.

Painted white with blue stripes and coves, the team Corvettes were not easily missed at Sebring—for more than one reason. "The crowds watched half curiously, half mockingly as the Chevys lumbered around the tricky circuit turning practice laps," wrote Al Kidd, sports editor for *Motor Trend*. "The same Corvettes which had looked so low and racy to them around their home towns were hulking monsters compared to the nimble competition. Just about everyone wondered what in the world the Corvettes were doing there in such fast company, and some of the Chevrolet Division officials on hand weren't quite sure themselves."

Those officials had a fair idea after 12 hours of racing around the rough-and-tough 5.2-mile course. While two of the production cars fell out of the race—along with 35 rivals—the modified Corvette, driven by Fitch and Walt Hansgen, finished ninth overall and tops in its class with an average speed less than 8mph slower than the win-

Hands down, the most important addition to the Corvette package in 1957 was Ramjet fuel injection, an optional induction system that put America's only sports car into an entirely different league as far as performance was concerned. Fuel injection would remain the top Corvette performance option up through 1965.

ning Ferrari's 84mph clocking. The other "team" car finished 15th. Yet another Corvette, this one definitely a private entry, completed the race in 23rd, second from last.

Simply finishing at Sebring, however, represented a reasonably meritorious achievement, a fact not lost on Campbell-Ewald. Almost immediately, a magazine ad appeared featuring one of the Sebring Corvettes in the pits under the heading, "The Real McCoy." That ad described the 1956 Corvette as "a tough, road-gripping, torpedo-on-wheels with the stamina to last through the brutal 12 hours of Sebring." As for more innocent bystanders, most of them were also impressed, however humbly, by the Corvette's gutsy first-time effort in international competition. "The Corvette was once a joke at serious races," announced Kidd, "now it's a grudgingly respected underdog. What kind of a future can it have in such fast company?"

While that question remained then unanswered, the Corvette's future on the street appeared particularly bright once the new 1956 model appeared. Prospective customers who previously had been turned off the by the less amiable characteristics of the early Corvettes had next to nothing to complain about in 1956.

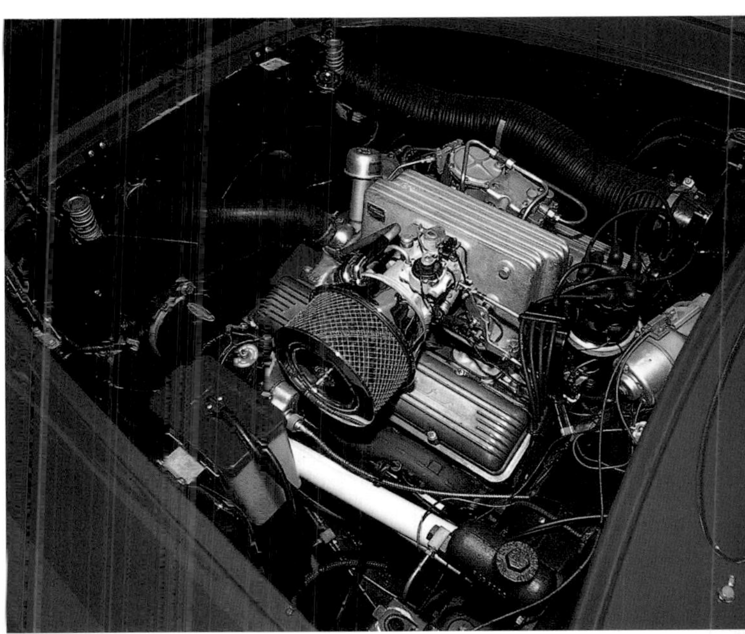

Supplied by Rochester, the Corvette's Ramjet "fuelie" setup went atop two very different 283 V-8s in 1957. The milder, hydraulic-cam version was rated at 250 horses. With the Duntov cam inside, the injected 283 was rated at 283hp, making it the second American car to offer one horsepower per cubic inch of displacement—Chrysler had been the first the previous year.

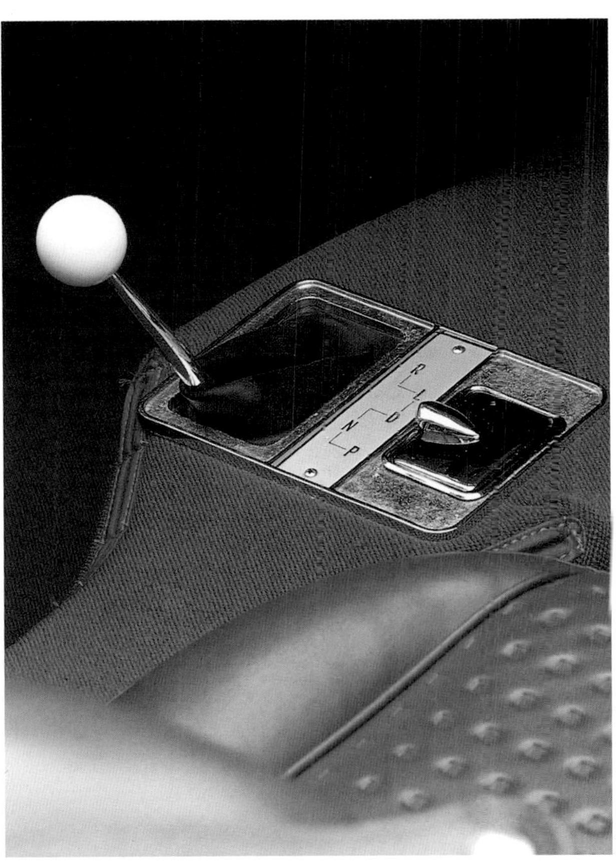

The topless 1957 fuel-injected Corvette shown here is equipped with the 250hp Ramjet-equipped 283 backed by a Powerglide automatic transmission, a package listed under RPO 579C that year. Only 102 RPO 579C 1957 Corvettes were built. Another 182 featured RPO 579A, which consisted of the 250hp fuelie V-8 and a manual transmission.

Fiberglass firsts from a convenience standpoint that year included real side windows that actually rolled up and down, exterior door handles, an adjustable seat for the passenger, and a fresh-air heater instead of the previously used recirculating unit. Additional newfangled features came on the options list, including power windows (RPO 426) and hydraulic operation for the folding convertible roof (RPO 473). Seat belts also appeared for the first time, albeit as dealer-installed equipment. But topping everything was the new removable hardtop, a stylish, fully functional option that added both class and convenience.

Removable hardtops had appeared for the Corvette in 1954 and 1955 thanks to various aftermarket companies. As a factory option (RPO 419) in 1956, Chevrolet's removable top could have been added at no cost in place of the standard folding soft top or as an accompaniment along with the nylon top for $188.30. The former installation was chosen by 629 buyers, the latter by 1,447 others. All were probably tickled pink about the way that top kept wetness away.

Was it any wonder Corvette sales jumped 400 percent in 1956?

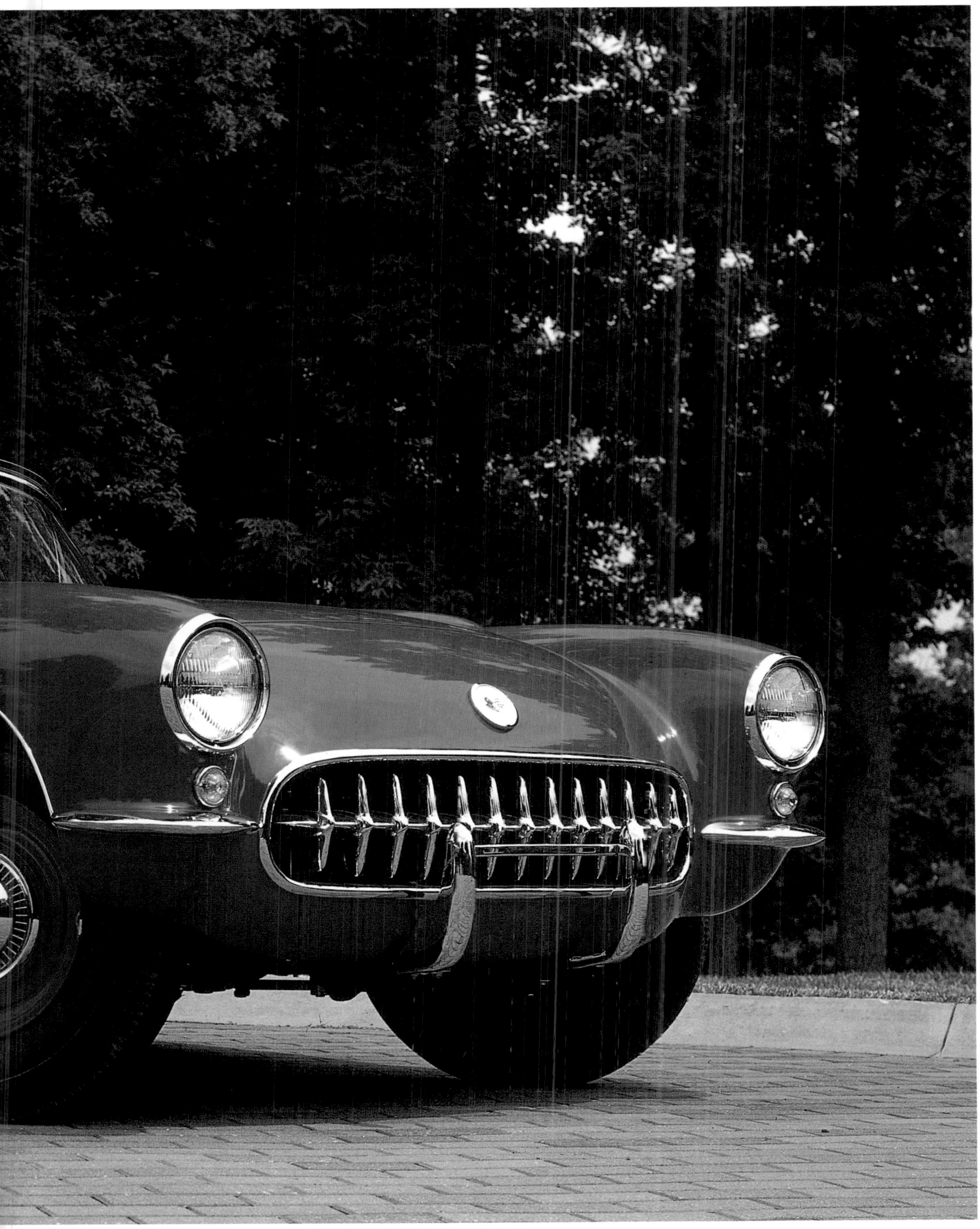

Previous page
At the top of the fuel-injection heap in 1957 was RPO 579E, the so-called "Airbox" fuelie. Priced at $726.30, RPO 579E added a special induction system much like the equipment previously used by Smokey Yunick at Daytona. Only 43 Airbox Corvettes were built in 1957. This model also has the optional 15x5.5 wheels (RPO 276 with their small hubcaps. Production of the removable hardtop, RPO 419, was 4,055 in 1957.

Yet another major leap came in 1957 when Chevrolet sold 6,339 Corvettes, nearly twice as many as in the previous year. Having redeemed itself, Chevrolet's fiberglass two-seater was finally off and running as public confidence in the concept took root. Not much more than a cute curiosity in 1953-55, the Corvette had overnight been transformed into a real sexpot. So much so, customers apparently couldn't care less that the 1957 model was essentially a carbon copy of the 1956. At a glance, that is.

The quickest way to identify a rare Airbox Corvette without opening the hood comes inside, where the tachometer was relocated from the dash to the steering column. A round plate then went in place of the opening left in the center of the dash.

Beneath the skin was another story.

First and foremost was the 1957 Corvette's "new" engine, a bored-out version of the proven 265 V-8. Now displacing 283 cubic inches with 9.5:1 compression, the 1957 V-8 was rated at 220 horsepower in standard form with a single Carter four-barrel. The dual-four option was again available in two forms, this time identified as RPOs 469A and 469C. RPO 469A added twin Carter carbs and a hydraulic cam, while 469C used the mechanical Duntov cam. Advertised output for RPO 469A was 245hp at 5000rpm, while its solid-lifter brother produced 270hp at 6000 revs. The standard transmission was again a three-speed manual, with the Powerglide automatic available optionally at the same price listed in 1956.

The performance boost supplied by the 270hp 283 was more than enough to bring 'em running into Chevrolet dealerships. A *Sport Car Illustrated* road test (using a three-speed model with 3.55:1 gears) produced a scintillating 0-60 pass of only 6.8 seconds. Quarter-mile performance was 15.0 seconds at 95mph, while top end reached 123mph. But wait, there was more.

A whole host of hot performance options were introduced for Corvette customers in 1957, a few of them coming along a bit after the new cars themselves debuted in the fall of 1956. Priced at $188.30, RPO 685, a four-speed manual transmission, was released on April 9, 1957. The Chevrolet-designed, Borg-Warner-built T-10 four-speed featured gear ratios of 2.20:1, first; 1.66:1, second; and 1.31:1, third. According to a Chevrolet press release, "the four forward speeds of the new transmission are synchronized to provide a swift and smooth response. The close-ratio gears also permit easy downshift to make maximum use of the engine for braking as an added safety factor."

"When you can whip the stick around from one gear to any other the way you'd stir a can of paint, that's a gearbox that's synchronized," responded Walt Woron in the September 1957 issue of *Motor Trend*. "And when you can downshift from second to first at 40mph without double clutching, that's slightly more than just an 'easy downshift.'" Corvette buyers snatched up 664 four-speeds that first year.

But easily the most impressive new option for 1957 was an innovative induction system for the 283 V-8. Wearing a definitely heavy price tag of $484.20, the legendary "Ramjet" fuel injection setup was offered for the first time that year to Corvette customers and passenger car buyers alike. Its roots went back to development work by engineer John Dolza. Early in 1955, Ed Cole also put Zora Duntov on the Dolza project, which quickly escalated. A prototype fuel injection installation was being tested on a Chevrolet V-8 by the end of the year. And not even a 1956 test track crash that put Duntov in a body cast could keep him from finalizing the de-

Feeding cooler, denser air to the 283hp 283 fuelie beneath an Airbox Corvette's hood was a special plenum box (at top just to right of master cylinder) mounted to the driver's side inner fender panel. Ductwork at the front of that box drew outside air from the left of the radiator; additional ductwork led from the filter inside the plenum box to the Rochester injection unit.

sign, which was being readied almost right up to the date the new 1957 Corvettes were introduced.

The Rochester Products-built "fuelie" system did typical carburetors one better by, among other things, eliminating flooding and fuel starvation caused when hard turns sent the gas supply in the carb bowl centrifuging off sideways away from the pickup. This latter problem in particular had worked against the dual-carb racing Corvettes at Sebring in March 1956.

In place of those carbs, the Ramjet system not only delivered fuel more evenly in a much more efficient manner, it did so instantly. Throttle response for the fuel-injected Corvette was superb. In *Road & Track's* words, "the fuel injection engine is an absolute jewel, quiet and remarkably docile when driven gently around town, yet instantly transformable into a roaring brute when pushed hard."

Various problems, however, plagued the early fuelie cars, the most prominent one involving hard starts. Uninformed owners didn't help matters during starting by typically pumping the accelerator, a definite no-no. Once hot, the fuelie engine simply refused completely. While these starting maladies were soon minimized, the Ramjet unit remained

Special brake and suspension features like those used at Daytona and Sebring in the spring of 1956 became Corvette options in 1957. This is the rear wheel assembly included in RPO 684, the heavy-duty racing suspension package. Finned drums and an intricate brake cooling duct setup (notice the air inlet scoop above the leaf spring at the front of the backing plate) were part of RPO 684, as were various beefed suspension components.

This styling studio clay model shows the 1956 Corvette shape to come, minus the scoops that returned atop each fender after first appearing on the Motorama prototype of January 1953. Notice the body-colored headlight bezels. *courtesy Noland Adams*

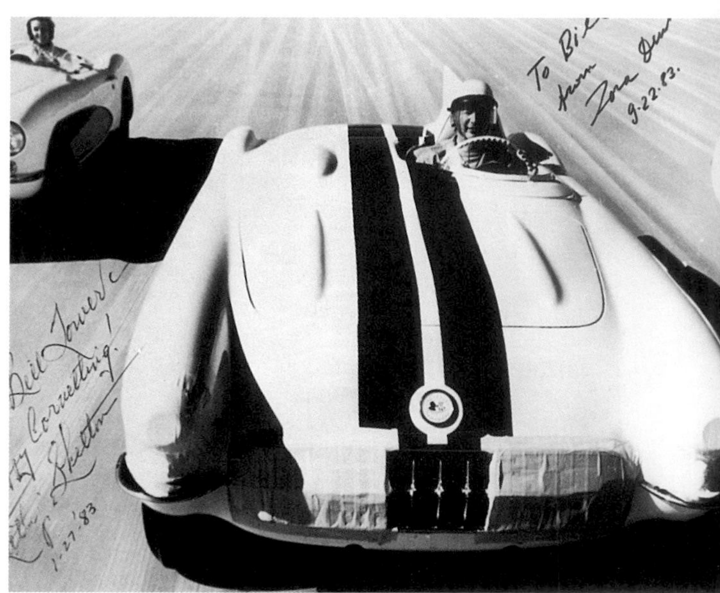

Zora Duntov at the wheel of the 1956 Corvette he took to Daytona Beach, Florida, in February 1956. There, he topped 150mph during speed tests. To the left is Betty Skelton; to the right is the rear wheel of John Fitch's Corvette. *courtesy Bill Tower*

Discounting a few minor changes, most made as part of the switch from six-cylinder power to V-8, the Corvette's chassis remained quite similar to its 1953-55 predecessor. The most apparent change here is the new dual-carb 265 V-8.

Veteran American race driver John Fitch went along with Duntov and Skelton to Daytona in 1956 to prove just how high the new Corvette could fly. After the 1956 Speed Weeks trials, he then took another Corvette team to Sebring to test the car up against live competition from Europe. *courtesy Bill Tower*

finicky when it came to keeping it in "proper tune." And compounding this situation over the years was the plain fact that so few typical garages were prepared to service this rarely seen equipment. More than one owner of an early fuelie Corvette gave up entirely and exchanged the Ramjet setup for the more conventional carburetor, even though in some cases the frustrations encountered were the result of unrelated problems mistakenly blamed on the fuel injection equipment.

In its first year, that equipment was available in various forms, all listed under RPO 579. RPOs 579A and 579C both featured the hydraulic-cam 250hp 283 fuelie, the former including a manual transmission, the latter the Powerglide automatic. RPO 579B was the fabled 283hp 283 F.I. V-8, a certified screamer with 10.5:1 compression, the solid-lifter Duntov cam and a manual trans only. Chevrolet promotional people have long loved to claim that this engine was Detroit's first to reach the magical one-horsepower-per-cubic-inch barrier. But they have also long overlooked Chrysler's 300B of 1956, which could've been equipped with an optional 355hp 354ci "hemi" V-8. Production of the 283hp fuelie in 1957 was 713. Another 284 250hp versions were built, 182 manual transmission cars, 102 automatics.

Performance for the top fuelie Corvette was simply stunning. *Road & Track's* testers managed 0-60 in just 5.7 seconds and the quarter-mile in 14.3; excellent results even for today, totally outrageous nearly 40 years ago. Published top end for the "283/283" Corvette was 132mph.

Yet another version of the 283/283 fuelie was offered in 1957, this one clearly built with competition in mind. One of the lessons learned during the high-speed runs at Daytona and Sebring in 1956 was the value of allowing cooler, denser outside air entry into an engine's induction system, as opposed to simply letting it breathe in the hot underhood atmosphere. Experimentation with "cold-air" induction setups led to the creation of the so-called "Airbox" Corvette.

The idea was simple. A plenum box was fabricated and mounted on the driver's side fenderwell panel. Up front, this box led to an opening in the support bulkhead beside the radiator where outside air could be "rammed" into it. Inside the box was an air filter; connected to the box's side was a rubberized duct sealing that filter to the Ramjet injection unit. All this added up to a few more ponies as the airbox Corvette's injected 283 breathed in its denser supply of precious oxygen. The Airbox option was listed as RPO 579E, priced at $726.30. Only 43 579E 1957 Corvettes were built, bringing total fuelie production that year to 1,040.

Additional Airbox modifications included moving the tachometer from its less-than-desirable stock spot in the center of the dash to atop the steering column where it could do its job like it should. The old tach location opening in the dash was then

Along with being a treat to the eyes, Betty Skelton was an accomplished pilot and record-setting driver. She also served as an advertising spokesperson for both Dodge and Chevrolet. *courtesy Bill Tower*

Campbell-Ewald, Chevrolet's advertising agency and Betty Skelton's employer, wasted little time after the record-setting runs at Daytona in February 1956. The Corvette had arrived as a true competitor, at least in Yankee terms.

covered by a round plate. And since Airbox Corvettes were meant for racing, both a radio and heater were not available. Coincidentally, with the a radio not present, ignition shielding wasn't required. This in turn meant plug wires could be run more directly from the distributor to the spark plugs over the valve covers as far away from the hot exhaust manifolds as possible. Plug wires on all other 1957 Corvettes were routed the long way down along the cylinder heads below the manifolds since this was the easiest place to mount the static-suppressive shielding.

The Airbox equipment wasn't the only new-for-1957 performance option inspired by earlier racing activities. A Positraction differential and wide 15x5.5 wheels were also introduced that year. Three different "Posi" rearends were available, RPO 677 with a 3.70:1 ratio, 678 with 4.11:1 gears, and the stump-pulling 679 with 4.56:1 cogs. The steel wheels, RPO 276, were a half-inch wider than stock rims and came only with a small, plain hubcap in place of the standard, ornate "knock-off" wheelcover.

A heavy-duty suspension option, listed under RPO 581, also entered the fray early on. Included were beefed springs front and rear; larger, stiffer shocks; a thicker front stabilizer bar; and a quick steering adapter. Sometime early in the 1957 model run, this option was repackaged under RPO 684 as a heavy-duty brake package was added along with the suspension components.

Sounding very much like the equipment list found on the four Sebring Corvettes of 1956, the RPO 684 brakes featured cerametallix linings, finned drums, and vented backing plates with scoops to catch cooling air. Helping deliver this air to the rear wheel scoops was a somewhat odd ductwork arrangement that began at each side of the radiator, ran back through the engine compartment, down around each front wheelwell to inside the lower rocker panels. At the trailing end of each rocker was was a short, fiberglass deflector duct that directed the airflow inboard towards the scoops on each vented backing plate.

Mounting this extensive ductwork meant a few additional changes were required. The horn relay had to be relocated beneath the hood and apparently modified mounting plates were needed in back for the heavy-duty shock absorbers.

A Positraction rearend was mandatory along with RPO 684, which itself was only available with the 270- and 283-horse engines. Its price was

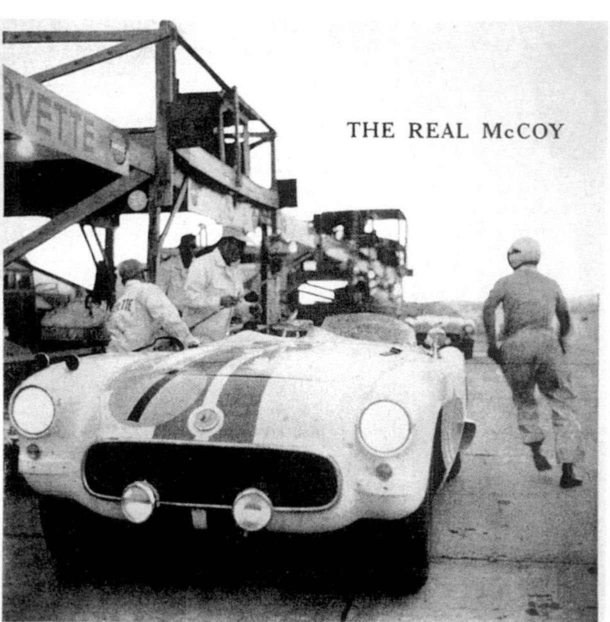

One month after Duntov's three-car team kicked up the sands at Daytona, a second group went farther south to Sebring, Florida, to compete in the annual 12-hour endurance race. And again, a popular ad campaign resulted.

In 1957, a Corvette team returned to Sebring, this time with a production-car effort (foreground) and the all-out SS (car number 1). Bill Mitchell's 1956 SR-2 also competed that year.

Along with fuel injection, Corvette buyers were also treated to an optional four-speed manual transmission in 1957.

$780.10. Only 51 1957 Corvettes were built with this Sebring-inspired performance package.

Apparently armed to the teeth, Chevrolet's Corvette returned to Daytona Beach in February 1957, this time taking top standing-start mile honors in the production class as Paul Goldsmith's fiberglass two-seater ran 91.301mph. And in March, two 1957 airbox Corvettes equipped with all the goodies—four-speed and RPO 684—took to the starting grid at Sebring, where they were joined for the annual 12-hour enduro by Bill Mitchell's SR-2 (see chapter four) and Duntov's SS (see chapter five). While the ill-fated SS dropped out early, the SR-2 soldiered on, and finished 16th. As for the production cars (which, by the way, ran with their airboxes removed), one finished one place ahead of the SR-2, the other managed to come in 12th and win its class—yet another public relations feather for caps of Ed Cole and crew.

By 1957, the Corvette had, at least from an American perspective, established itself as a top performing grand tourer. As *Road & Track* explained it, "Chevrolet said, back in 1954, that they were in the sports car business to stay, and their competition successes of the past two years certainly show that they mean it."

While those successes would continue, they were basically limited to SCCA competition on these shores. After driving a Corvette to an SCCA C/Production national title in 1956, Dr. Dick Thompson, the "Flying Dentist" from Washington D.C., won another SCCA title (B/Production) in a Corvette in 1957. That same year, J. E. Rose piloted his Corvette to the SCCA's B/Sports-Racing crown. This was just the beginning as Corvettes would go on to dominate SCCA competition throughout the 1950s.

But most hopes—primarily fostered by Duntov—to take the Corvette to international racing heights were all but dashed that summer when the Automobile Manufacturers Association stepped in. Alarmed by Detroit's escalating "horsepower race," the AMA board issued the following decree in June 1957:

"Whereas, the Automobile Manufacturers Association believes that automobile manufacturers should encourage owners and drivers to evaluate passenger cars in terms of useful power and ability to provide safe, reliable, and comfortable transportation, rather than in terms of capacity for speed. Now therefore, this board unanimously recommends to the member companies engaged in the manufacture and sale of passenger cars that they:

"Not participate or engage in any public contest, competitive event or test of passenger cars involving or suggesting racing or speed, including acceleration tests, or encourage or furnish financial, engineering, manufacturing, advertising, or public relations assistance, or supply 'pace cars' or 'official cars,' in connection with any such contest, event, or test, directly or indirectly.

"Nor participate or engage in, or encourage or assist employees, dealers, or others in the advertising or publicizing of (a) any race or speed contest, test, or competitive event involving or suggesting speed, whether public or private, involving passenger cars or the results thereof; or (b) the actual or comparative capabilities of passenger cars for speed, or the specific engine size, torque, horsepower or ability to accelerate or perform in any context that suggests speed."

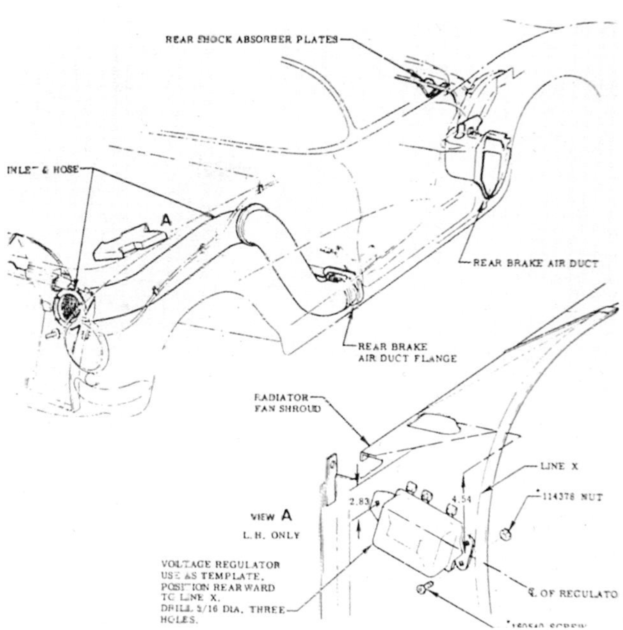

Long ducts ran down both sides of 1957 Corvettes equipped with RPO 684, the racing suspension package. These ducts took cooling air in from behind the headlights and directed it, via the rocker panels, into the scoop on each rear backing plate.

With the AMA "ban" in place, Chevrolet was forced by GM's upper office to cease and desist as far as shenanigans like the Corvette SS project and the Sebring racing efforts were concerned. While much clandestine factory support of competition Corvettes continued, and performance developments were by no means derailed, one can only wonder what might've resulted had Cole, Duntov and the rest been allowed to keep up the pace set in 1956 and early 1957.

They didn't do a bad job after 1957 as it was. Even with the AMA raining on Chevrolet's parade, the Corvette continued rolling on as America's only sports car.

CORVETTE
SR-2

Chapter 4

Executive Privileges

1956 Corvette SR-2

Chevrolet people had grown duly excited about their Corvette by the summer of 1956. Nearly put on ice a year or so before, Chevy's fiberglass two-seater had almost overnight been transformed from an average-performing curiosity into a sizzling sporting machine. First came V-8 power in 1955, followed by a totally fresh, certainly sexy body the following year. And if prospective Corvette customers still weren't sure about just how hot America's only sports car had become, they only needed to watch Zora Duntov, John Fitch and Betty Skelton during their high-flying record runs down Daytona Beach in February 1956. After Fitch's trip to Sebring that March, it was time to "bring on the hay bales"—the Corvette was now an honest-to-goodness race car.

These were high times indeed. As Bill Mitchell, then Harley Earl's righthand man at GM Styling, later wrote in 1984, "the 1954 Corvette looked great, but was a weak performer. Its six-cylinder engine was not exactly what you would expect in a sleek-looking sports car. Fortunately, along came the V-8 and Zora and we beat some Jags and Mercedes at Elkhart Lake and Watkins Glen, and when that happened, boy, the Corvette became something! We were really inspired then."

Mitchell was especially inspired when it came to the Corvette, which in his words would become "my baby" once he replaced Earl at the top of GM

Chevrolet built three SR-2 Corvettes in 1956, this one for styling executive Bill Mitchell. Mitchell's car, like the first SR-2 built for Harley Earl's son Jerry, were race cars. The third, built for GM president Harlow Curtice, was a street-going showboat.

Bill Mitchell's SR-2 was the first "high-fin" car; when originally built, Jerry Earl's SR-2 featured a much small, symmetrical "low fin" on its decklid, as would the SR-2 built for Harlow Curtice.

Styling following Harley's retirement in 1958. Mitchell also loved racing, as ably demonstrated by the 1959 Stingray, his so-called "private" race car that won a Sports Car Club of America (SCCA) championship in 1960 piloted by Dr. Dick Thompson. Based on the chassis of the 1957 SS "Mule," Mitchell's Stingray foretold much of the all-new classic Corvette look that would debut for 1963 wearing the same name, only spelled "Sting Ray."

Without a doubt, Mitchell's Stingray racer was a "privateer" in name alone, a ruse carried out to help innocent, hopefully naive bystanders believe Chevrolet was still adhering 100 percent to the Automobile Manufacturers Association's "ban" on factory racing involvement set down in 1957. Thompson, the legendary "Flying Dentist," was also commonly referred to as an independent racer, even though the backdoor to Chevrolet Engineering was always left wide open for him.

Such shenanigans had not been needed in 1956 when Mitchell asked Chevrolet designers to create his first personal Corvette racer, the SR-2. And he wasn't the only top GM officer to take advantage of executive privileges that year. Two other SR-2

Corvettes were built in 1956, one by request of Harley Earl, the other for GM president Harlow "Red" Curtice. Like Mitchell's, Earl's SR-2 was built for racing, while Curtice's was a street car. And like so many of the special Corvette racers and experimental machines created over the years, all three SR-2s are still around today to help demonstrate just how privileged GM execs were some four decades ago.

Clearly those were different times, a "more personal" era when a corporate heavy hitter could easily throw his weight around with his own interests in mind. This is exactly what GM vice president Harley Earl did when son Jerry decided to go racing in 1956. The younger Earl's first choice for track duty was a Ferrari, a decision that didn't exactly make father proud. It seemed Jerry Earl wasn't all that impressed with the restyled Corvette, even with its new dual-carb V-8 injecting more optional horsepower into the equation. Nonetheless, Harley Earl wasn't about to let his son campaign an Italian exotic instead of Detroit iron. Or Detroit fiberglass.

The elder Earl's solution to the problem was simple. "Jerry," he probably asked, "what if I had my people build you a custom-bodied Corvette race car using all those wonderful chassis modifications track tested at Sebring in March by John Fitch's competition Corvette team?" Maybe he didn't ask. After all, Mr. Earl was a very big man. Either way, Jerry Earl did agree to the deal. And just like that, the first SR-2 Corvette was born.

Explaining the car's name is simple enough. Inside Chevrolet Engineering, the special performance components created for the Corvettes that had scorched the sands at Daytona and competed valiantly at Sebring early in 1956 were known by an "SR" designation, a reference to either "Special Racer," "Sports Racing" or "Sebring Racer," depending on your source. Mixed messages aside, those early Corvette factory racers were the first SR models. Logically, any purpose-built racing machines to follow would wear the name "SR-2."

SR-2 production began with Jerry Earl purchasing a new 1956 Corvette, serial number E56F002522, off the showroom floor at Ray White Chevrolet in Grosse Point, Michigan. In early May, the car went into GM Styling, under shop order number 90090, where the body was hastily modified and the chassis beefed up. Amazingly, the completed SR-2 rolled out less than four weeks later, leading some to conclude that the reworked shell was simply dropped atop an existing race-ready chassis from one of Fitch's Sebring racers. Just like the Fitch cars, Earl's SR-2 featured quick steering, stiffer springs and shocks, a limited-slip differential, and bigger brakes with sintered cerametallix linings, finned drums and special cooling "scoops" mounted on vented backing plates. Halibrand knock-off wheels were also used. Dual exhaust pipes dumped out, in typical race car fashion, directly in front of each rear wheel.

The modified metallic blue fiberglass shell that went on top featured an extended nose and a somewhat peculiar—albeit small—tailfin protruding from the center of the decklid. The stock windshield was replaced by two small windscreens, while the interior was dressed up to a far greater degree than your average race car. Footwells remained carpeted with padded vinyl inserts on each side. Vinyl covered the transmission tunnel, which was topped with a chrome-plated fire extinguisher. Along with the original-equipment power window lifts, the car's stock seats were retained, but were re-upholstered in blue vinyl. Extra instrumentation included a tachometer on the steering column and gauges mounted in a stainless steel panel located in the center of the dash. Oddly, a radio was initially present, although no antenna was noticeable. Completing the interior makeover was a wood-rimmed steering wheel.

Back on the outside, large turn signal lamps were added beneath the headlights, and a series of louvers were formed into the hood to help keep engine compartment temperatures within reason. Cooling was the also the goal behind the rather ornate scoops incorporated into the bodyside cove panels on both doors. Although these bright baubles did look like nothing more than typical styling tricks, they were fully functional.

Each scoop directed air flow into internal ductwork that ran back out the door's trailing edge through a seal in the doorjam into another duct in the body. From there, flow was channeled into the rear wheelhouse where it was aimed at the cooling scoop attached to the leading edge of the brake drum's backing plate. Hopefully, the precious outside air then entered the backing plates through vents and made its way inside the drum to help bring down internal temperatures. Simple, right?

While the functional aspects of the SR-2 body modifications were top priority—remember, this was a race car—the aesthetic end results proved to be every bit as successful. Most critics of the day loved everything about the SR-2 look, including that little fin in back. As *Motor Life's* Art Dean saw it, "[this] custom Corvette from the factory could be the forecast of things to come from Chevrolet, and if it is, they've got a winner." The one forecast the SR-2 did make involved its louvered hood, which eventually resurfaced—in nonfunctional form—as a production Corvette feature for 1958 only.

Telling the 1956 SR-2 tale from a power perspective also involves a little forecasting. Today, all three cars feature fuel injection and four-speed manual transmissions, both Corvette options not made available officially until 1957. On top of that, Curtice's street-going SR-2 is powered by a 283ci V-8, which also first appeared for 1957, replacing the

All three Corvette SR-2s appeared together, for the first time since 1985, at the 13th annual "Corvettes at Carlisle" event in Carlisle, Pennsylvania, in August 1994. From left to right: Jerry Earl's car, now owned by Rich Mason of Carson City, Nevada; Harlow Curtice's "low-fin" SR-2, owned by Richard and Carolyn Fortier of Swartz Creek, Michigan; and Bill Mitchell's high-fin model, owned by Bill Tower of Plant City, Florida.

1956 Corvette's 265ci small-block. Both racing SR-2s now have bored and stroked small-blocks, Earl's car displacing 333 cubic inches, Mitchell's 336.

Were the three SR-2 Corvettes predicting the near future when built in 1956? Many have long believed the powertrain features were prototype installations. Apparently partly yes, partly no.

Still basically in original condition, Curtice's street SR-2 undoubtedly represents a yes. Since the last of the trio was built late in the 1956 model year, it's certainly easy enough to believe that the all-new production parts planned for 1957 were then available—however unofficially—to satisfy the whims of the division's top executive. Other than that, the only existing "hard and fast" documentation appears in a short September 1957 *Motor Trend* feature on Curtice's SR-2, which, considering deadline lead time, would have been prepared earlier that summer. *MT's* Walt Woron raved most about the car's four-speed trans—"whoever's responsible should take a deep bow," he wrote—representing the earliest known reference to that installation.

Hard and fast facts are not all that readily available concerning Earl's SR-2, although it is reasonably clear it was not originally equipped with fuel injection and a four-speed. Like most long-running race cars, various powertrain changes were made to the first SR-2 over the years, muddying the waters even further. But according to noted Corvette collector Bill Tower, who now owns Mitchell's SR-2, Earl's car was basically stock (without a doubt it was carbureted) under that louvered hood when first built. Having contacted various insiders (including Bill Mitchell) to help him during the restoration of the second SR-2, Tower was told by a GM design staffer that, in the haste to simply complete the job, the original drivetrain—a dual-carb 265 V-8 backed by a three-speed—was initially retained. That combo undoubtedly didn't last long in the racer, but when it was replaced by more muscular equipment is anyone's guess.

As for Mitchell's SR-2, Tower was told it was indeed fitted, in prototype fashion, with a fuel-injected 283 V-8 and a four-speed when built later that summer in 1956. And reportedly, the 283 was then bored and stroked to 336 cubic inches by Smokey Yunick early in 1957 as part of various modifications made for yet another Corvette speed run down Daytona Beach.

The high-speed debut for SR-2 number one came in June 1956 at Elkhart Lake in Wisconsin, where first Jerry Earl and then Dick Thompson race tested the car. Both, however, discovered the same thing—the machine was just too heavy, what with all that extra "plushness" and such. Problems with the trunk-mounted, oversized, unbaffled fuel tank were also encountered. The only choice was to head back to the GM studio drawing board.

There, junior stylist Robert Cumberford—today automotive design editor for *Automobile* magazine—removed all the excess baggage: stock seats, heater, radio, windows and lift hardware, etc. Cumberford even donated a set of Porsche speedster bucket seats to help finish the job.

By that time, work was also finishing up on the second SR-2, the red racer Bill Mitchell had requested almost immediately after he had first set eyes on the Earl car. Built under Mitchell's direct supervision, this model differed here and there compared to its predecessor, the most prominent change coming in back. Instead of the small symmetrical decklid fin, the Mitchell car was fitted with a large tailfin structure offset to the driver's side. The so-called "high fin" functioned as both a driver's headrest and rollbar, and also housed the filler cap (hidden behind a flip panel) to a baffled 45-gallon fuel tank.

Compared to the basically decorative "low fin" on Earl's car, SR-2 number two's high fin obviously served more than one real purpose. Its functional aspects weren't lost on Jerry Earl, who had his racer's tail rebuilt along the lines (the two high fins are not identical) of the Mitchell machine's about the time the original SR-2 was brought back into GM Styling to be lightened. At a glance, the two cars then appeared much like twins. Closer examination, however, told the true tale.

Unlike its blue predecessor, Mitchell's red SR-2 was apparently fabricated "from scratch," not simply created by cannibalizing a standard production Corvette. It does wear an official 1956 VIN (vehicle identification number) plate with serial number E56S002532. But, again according to Bill Tower's Chevrolet design sources, that tag was apparently added later to help hide its "non-production" status from racing rulesmakers.

Evidence to this fact can be found with a ruler. Although it does use the same Sebring-inspired chassis features found on Earl's car, the highly modified frame under Mitchell's SR-2 has a three-inch wider track. A special cowl was required since the engine was mounted father back and offset to the passenger's side. Additionally, the fiberglass shell is considerably lighter throughout, meaning it was probably specially laid up by hand. Mitchell's design team also left off the twin simulated scoops found atop each fender of all 1956-57 Corvettes—including the two other SR-2s. This absence represents the easiest way to differentiate the second SR-2 from the first—after Earl's was converted from low fin to high, that is—in the various 30-something-year-old photos of the two siblings. This task was made more difficult during the time both were painted red—each has been resprayed more than once over the years.

Many other differences between the two racers came inside. Mitchell's men installed racing bucket seats right off the bat to help shave off pounds. The lightly skinned doors were also gutted, but were nicely trimmed instead of simply being left bare. Rudimentary pull-cords were used in place of the stock door handles.

Instrumentation again included a column-mounted tachometer, only this tach differed in design compared to its counterpart in the Earl car. Differing as well was the gauge layout in the stainless steel panel located in the center of the dashboard. Mitchell's car also received a special shifter plate identifying it as a "Chevrolet SR-2 Corvette." A wood-rimmed steering wheel and full carpeting completed the cockpit package.

The third SR-2 differed even more in comparison to its two track-ready forerunners. Watching as Jerry Earl's low-fin racer was going together in May 1956, Harlow Curtice decided he wanted a daily driver just like it. "How soon would you like that, Mr. President," probably came the reply from the Chevy design people who by then undoubtedly had the whole SR-2 trick down pat.

Curtice's SR-2 was completed in either June or July using a production-line Corvette, serial number E56S002636. Built only with street driving in mind, it was basically stock underneath, save for the aforementioned 1957 drivetrain installation. Outside, the third SR-2 received the typical extended snout and symmetrical low fin, only this ap-

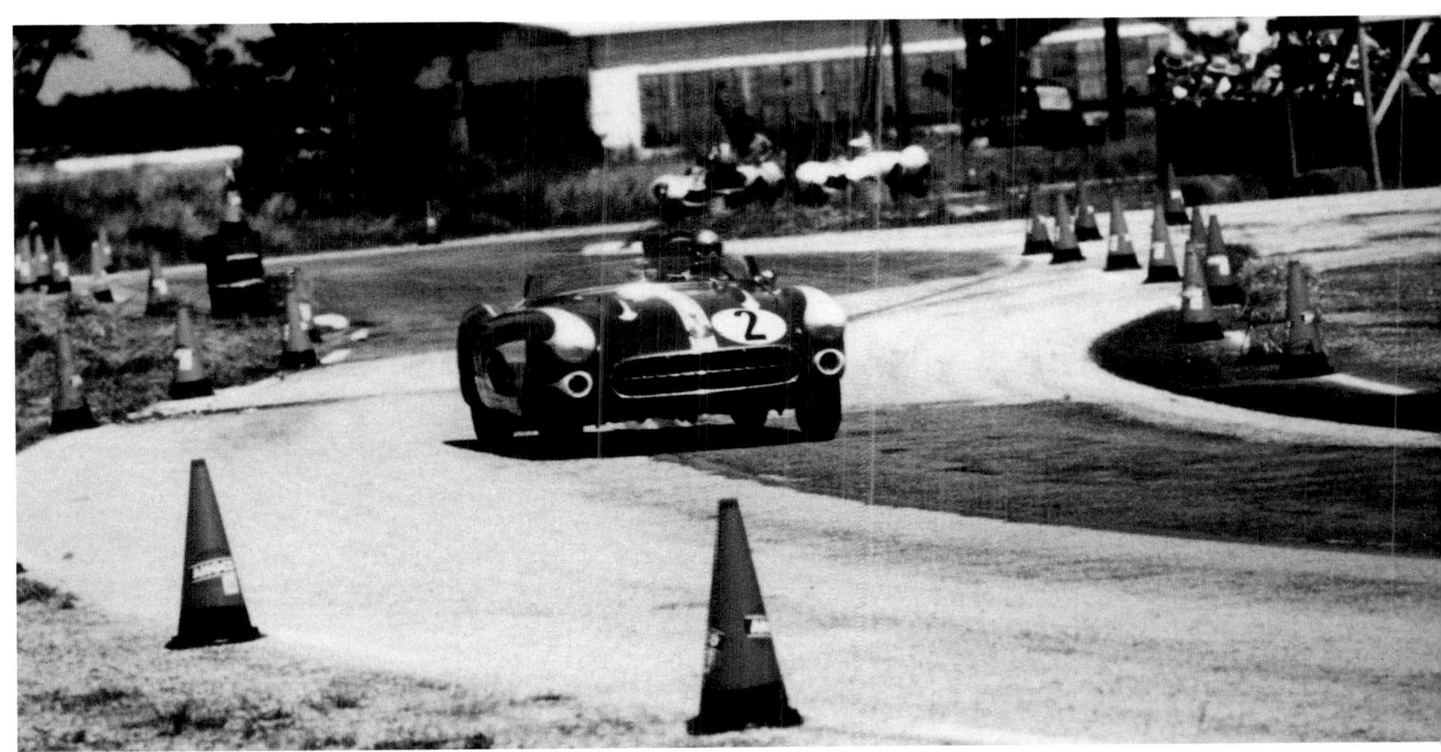

Jerry Earl's SR-2 eventually became an SCCA racing champion, but not until Earl sold it to Nickey Chevrolet's Jim Jeffords late in 1957. Among track honors for Bill Mitchell's SR-2 was a 16-place finish at Sebring in March 1957. Here, the Mitchell SR-2 weaves its way around the airport course in Florida with two D-Type Jaguars off in the distance behind. *courtesy Bill Tower*

Interior treatments for the second SR-2, although stripped down, were still quite plush for a racer. Notice the non-essential trim pieces found at the shifter's base, on the dash and inside the door panels. Racing buckets, full instrumentation, a column-mounted tachometer, and a wood-rimmed steering wheel were included.

Although much mystery still exists concerning the three SR-2's powertrains, apparently the Mitchell SR-2 was equipped with a fuel-injected 283 V-8 backed by a four-speed, both prototype installations. Reportedly, Smokey Yunick bored this 283 out to 336 cubic inches early in 1957 in preparation for some high-speed runs down Daytona Beach.

The scoops at the back of the SR-2's cove panel on each door were functional on the two race cars (not so on the Curtice SR-2). They fed cooling air to the rear brakes through ductwork that ran through the door into this opening in the doorjam. From here, the air was directed into the vented backing plates at the rear wheels.

pendage was slightly larger and more rounded. A louvered hood and annodized aluminum side cove scoops were again used, only in this case they were non-functional. Unlike the non-functional hood added on production Corvettes in 1958, the simulated louvers on Curtice's car were recessed, a trick that required much reinforcement, which in turn added considerable weight. Reportedly, that hood weighed about 100 pounds.

Interior appointments included blue leather seats and door panels. Curtice's own "personal shade" of metallic blue paint was applied outside, complemented by whitewall tires on dazzling Dayton wire wheels. Topping it all off was a stainless steel removable hardtop.

A certified showboat that reportedly cost some $50,000 to build in the summer of 1956, Curtice's SR-2 did indeed make more than one appearance on a Motorama stage as a GM showcar before the president began driving it on the street. About a year later, he sold it to a neighbor, who later passed it over to another buyer, and so on. Remaining in Michigan throughout its life, the third SR-2 managed to survive in decent original condition (discounting a 1960 minor accident repair repaint resulting in a slightly different shade of blue) over its life and has been in the hands of Swartz Creek's Richard Fortier for some 25 years now.

The two racing SR-2 Corvettes didn't have it quite so easy, the demands of racing being not nearly as forgiving as those of a quiet Sunday drive. Both were typically thrashed and went through various identities as their competition careers progressed.

Earl's SR-2 was the most successful of the two, although not while in the hands of Harley Earl's son. In November 1957, Jerry Earl and NASCAR founder Bill France took the first SR-2 to the Bahamas to race with longtime NASCAR ace

The trailing edge of the SR-2's door shows the opening (with seal) through which cooling air flowed from the bodyside scoops into the rear wheelhouse area.

This June 1956 photo shows the first SR-2's chassis, which probably came directly from one of the John Fitch's Sebring team cars. Notice the cerametallix brake linings and the special scoops mounted to each backing plate. While Jerry Earl's SR-2 was undoubtedly built with the twin-carb 265 shown here, it was soon retrofitted with a fuel-injected 331ci V-8, which it has today.

Curtis Turner doing the driving and Smokey Yunick typically behind the scenes with a wrench. After winning an early heat at the Nassau event, the Turner-piloted SR-2 lost its lunch on the main course, running off the road unable to return.

Earl then sold his racer to Jim Jeffords, who drove for Nickey Chevrolet in Chicago. Wearing Nickey's distinctive—if not slightly disturbing—"Purple People Eater" paint scheme, Jefford's SR-2 managed to roar off with an SCCA B/Production national title in 1958. Bud Gates Chevrolet in Indianapolis then raced the car in 1959 and 1960. From there, a couple more owners followed before the once-proud machine somehow ended up in a junkyard in Terre Haute, Indiana, in the early 1960s. It was later restored and today is owned by Corvette collector Rich Mason of Carson City, Nevada.

Bill Mitchell's SR-2 first showed up before the public eye when it arrived in Daytona on February 7, 1957, to once more kick up some sand like the first SR Corvettes had done the year before. As mentioned, Smokey Yunick was again present to help make the Mitchell car everything it could be mechanically. To help cheat the wind, the car was also adorned with a plexiglass canopy for the driver, a hard tonneau cover for the passenger side of the cockpit, full wheel discs and rear fender skirts. Up front, the headlights and large turn signal lamps were covered with conical farings.

With stock car veteran Buck Baker doing the driving, the odd-looking Corvette took top standing-mile honors in its modified class, turning an average speed of 93.047mph. Its flying mile speed was 152.866mph, second to a Jaguar D-Type.

Jerry Earl's SR-2 in its early "low-fin" days. Its racing debut came at Elkhart Lake, Wisconsin, in June 1956. Not long afterward, the car was returned to Chevrolet Engineering where it was lightened and modified with a "high fin" similar to the one used on Bill Mitchell's SR-2.

When first built, the Earl SR-2 featured an interior that resembled a showcar more than a race car. All this extra plushness meant a lot of extra weight. Accordingly, the car did not do well when first raced in this trim.

The Earl SR-2 after its conversion to "high fin" in the summer of 1956. Notice the stock Corvette scoops atop each fender; these features represent the easiest way to tell the first and second SR-2s apart—Bill Mitchell's car didn't have these.

Following in the early SR's tire treads, Mitchell's SR-2 then went south to Sebring in March as part of Chevrolet's competition Corvette team effort, highlighted by the Corvette SS's debut (see chapter five), however ill-fated. At the end of the 12-hour endurance run, one regular-production-based Corvette ended up first in its GT class and 12th overall. Another production car finished 15th overall. While the Mitchell SR-2, piloted by Pete Lovely and Paul O'Shea, was right behind in 16th, a victim of too many pit stops. All told, the befinned racer did 166 laps totalling 863.2 miles at an average speed of 71.93mph. A decent effort, but as Bill Tower points out today, once a new, rebodied Corvette came along for 1958, the SR-2—with its obsolete image—became old news basically overnight.

Mitchell's SR-2 went into storage in a GM basement sometime in 1958. Chevrolet racer Don Yenko bought the car and campaigned it in the early 1960s, then sold it in November 1965 to Charles Knuth, who began restoring the well-worn racer. Tower took over ownership in 1979 and completed the job. Today, Chevy's second SR-2 resides proudly in Florida as part of Tower's impressive Corvette collection, which includes one of the five 1963 Grand Sports, Betty Skelton's 1956 beach racer and a 1967 L88.

Looking much like they did nearly 40 years ago, all three SR-2 Corvettes converged on the fairgrounds in Carlisle, Pennsylvania, in August 1994 for the 13th annual "Corvettes at Carlisle" event. It was the first time since 1985 that the trio was reunited; one can only wonder when they will come together again. One thing is for sure: those who were lucky enough to be on hand for the historic reunion this time were the privileged ones.

Too many pit stops plagued the Mitchell SR-2 during its run at Sebring in 1957. Here it speeds through a turn hot on the heels of a Maserati, the marque that won the 12 Hours that year.

Chapter 5

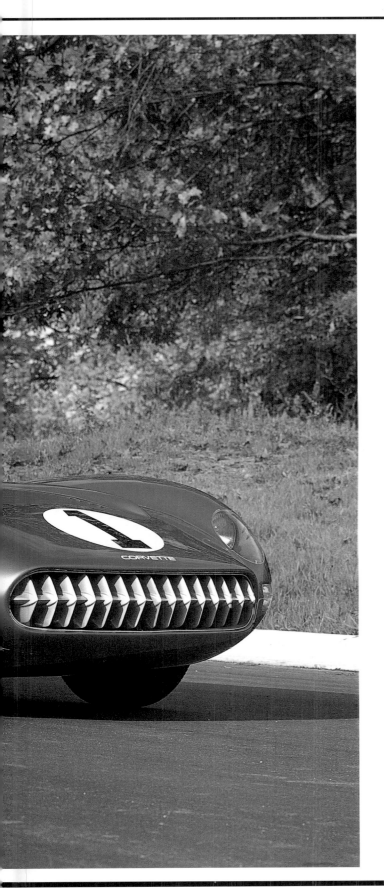

Stillborn At Sebring

Duntov's Corvette SS

That this ill-fated racer today resides among the many four-wheeled legends at the Indianapolis Motor Speedway Hall of Fame Museum is only right, regardless of its meager track record. Twenty-three problem-plagued tours around Sebring's rough-and-tumble endurance course in Florida in March 1957. A few serious hot laps at General Motors' Arizona proving grounds in December 1958. A sizzling 155-mph sprint through the high banks to help celebrate the opening of NASCAR founder Bill France's Daytona International Speedway in February 1959. Not much more, certainly nothing less; that basically portrays the high-speed history of the Corvette SS in a steel-blue nutshell.

Yet there is much more to the SS tale, perhaps one of the greatest "what-if" stories in American sports-racing history. What if Chevrolet's movers and shakers had approached the SS project, designated XP-64, with all the fervor and financial backing then commonly displayed by their sports-car-building rivals in Europe? What if Zora Duntov and his engineering team had been allowed more time to design, test and sort things out? What if GM hadn't put the clamps on in-house competition development and support in the summer of

While John Fitch was leading a team of production-based Corvettes to Sebring in March 1956, Zora Duntov was busy with his own idea of how Chevrolet's two-seater should be raced. Later that year, he began planning for an all-out racing version of the Corvette to better compete with Europe's finest sports-racers. The result was the Corvette SS.

Chevrolet designated the SS Corvette project XP-64. The XP-64's cove panel shape represented the only real tie to the production Corvette from a tail view. Wheels are racing Halibrand knock-offs.

1957 following the AMA's ban on factory racing involvement? Then again, what if Duntov, Ed Cole, Harley Earl and the rest hadn't even tried?

Apart from everything the ill-fated SS didn't do, it did represent Chevrolet's first serious, all-out attempt to put the Corvette name on the international racing map, something that many at GM recognized could only help enhance the regular-production two-seater's image back on Mainstreet U.S.A. Although worn out today, a certain now-familiar gearhead adage definitely rang true in the Corvette's early days. Racing did, and still does, indeed improve the breed, if not through mechanical enhancements alone, then by direct association with a competition-winning, record-setting reputation. Although the SS never won a race—or finished one for that matter—it did serve notice in high-profile fashion that Corvettes and competition would always be companions.

Long recognized, but only then gaining real momentum in the 1950s as a major promotional tool was the relationship between racing victories at the track and popularity (translated: sales) on the street. Duntov himself had described this very relationship in September 1953 during an address before a meeting of the Society of Automotive Engineers in Lansing, Michigan. "All commercially successful sports cars were promoted by participation in racing with specialized or modified cars," he explained.

Continued Duntov, "even if the vast majority of sports car buyers do not intend to race them, and most likely will never drive flat out, the potential performance of the car, or the recognized and publicized performance of its sister—the racing sports car—is of primordial value to its owner. The owner of such a car can peacefully let everybody pass him, still feeling like the proud king of the road, his ego and pride of ownership being inflated by racing glory."

Improving both streetside performance and competition potential by adding V-8 power in 1955 had already helped boost Corvette popularity, saving the car from certain extinction. Further evolution clearly hinged on how well the Corvette would continue to compete, thus the reasoning behind the Daytona Beach speed runs and John Fitch's four-car assault on Sebring early in 1956.

But while Duntov had been there at Daytona to help establish the Corvette as a record-setting speedster, he kept his distance when it came time to go racing at Sebring with modified stockers up against Europe's best thoroughbred sports-racers, then led by Jaguar and Ferrari. He knew only a specialized racing machine bearing the Corvette nameplate would ever do if Chevrolet seriously wanted to compete on an international level. Nonetheless, it was a top class finish at the fifth running of Sebring's annual 12-hour endurance event that served as inspiration for Campbell-Ewald to proclaim in print in 1956 that America's only sports car truly was "the real McCoy."

Those popular ads aside, claiming title as this country's one true sports car was one thing. Qualifying the Corvette as a world-class sporting machine represented a whole 'nother hurdle entirely. Overemphasized (and soon to be overlooked) minor production class wins at Sebring didn't quite cut it. Nor would various Sports Car Club of America production-class victories to come, not as long as true international racing glory remained an unfulfilled goal.

Winning top honors at Sebring against the world's best specially prepared sports-racers, however improbable, of course would've been a step in the right direction in 1956. But in the opinion of Duntov and others, the only real glory awaited American challengers in France. The legendary Le Mans 24-hour torture test had long served as a launchpad to greatness for the sporting crowd, most recently for Jaguar's chaps who watched as their dominating D-Types took "Las Vingt-quatre Heures du Mans" laurels in both 1955 and 1956. And again for a third time the following year.

Introduced in 1954, the D-Type Jaguar relied on its purpose-built, slippery shell and state-of-the-art disc brakes (first used by Jaguar on its racing C-Types in 1953) to overcome its main rivals from Ferrari. A Briggs Cunningham-backed D-Type won at Sebring in 1955, and another finished third in the 12 Hours the next year. Interestingly, it was this particular Jaguar that helped directly inspire the creation of the Corvette SS.

Duntov wasn't the only one at GM to recognize the realities of international sports car competition. At Sebring in March 1956 it had become clear from chief engineer Ed Cole on down that Chevrolet would never match up against the likes of Porsche, Ferrari, Jaguar, Mercedes, Maserati and so on with merely a modified production Corvette. Yet for an American manufacturer to become involved in an expensive, time-consuming, all-out race car development project was almost unthinkable. No U.S. automaker had tried such a thing since Studebaker had sent a five-car racing team to Indianapolis in 1932. And as spring was blossoming in Detroit in 1956 it appeared that streak would remain alive.

Leave it to GM Styling mogul Harley Earl. Again. Whether he meant it seriously or not, it was Earl who brought a yellow D-Type Jaguar—the aforementioned third-place finisher at Sebring—into his Styling studio in the early summer of 1956 with hopes of rebuilding it with a Chevy engine and racing it as an experimental Corvette. Some body modifications here and there, a switch to lefthand drive, and no one would've been the wiser.

No one, that is, save for Zora Duntov. Once he got wind of Earl's plan he quickly determined that such a hybrid would never fly. Besides, it would still be a Jaguar in disguise. Inspired into action, Duntov then immediately began work on a proposal for a purpose-built race car that would wear the Corvette name with pride. Amazingly, the proposal was quickly approved.

In July 1956, Chevrolet styling studio head Clare MacKichan began work on a clay model depicting a state-of-the-art race car with a low, rounded, bulging body looking a bit like the Jaguar Harley Earl had apparently used to wake up his cohorts. Had Earl's plan to modify that D-Type into a Corvette racer been a mere ploy to bluff Cole, Duntov and the rest into taking the situation into their own hands? Only his hairdresser knew for sure.

Not long after he had risen to Chevrolet's general manager position, Ed Cole, along with other division executives, were given their first look at MacKichan's clay near the end of July. All were impressed with the sleek, aerodynamic-looking shell, which resembled its regular-production Corvette counterpart only through its toothy grille and bodyside cove areas. From there, the XP-64 effort quickly escalated.

Official paperwork detailing the project was sent down from the top in September. According to those orders, XP-64 was to "be a competition racing car with special frame, suspension, engine, drivetrain, and body." Right out of the blocks, however, production plans were assigned very tight, incredibly short deadlines. Initial specifications mentioned building four XP-64 race cars, one intended for show duty in New York in December 1957, the other three to be completed in time to test and compete at Sebring—the stepping stone to Le Mans—the following March.

Cobbling together a show car for static display in less than three months may have been a possibility. Carefully crafting three additional

1

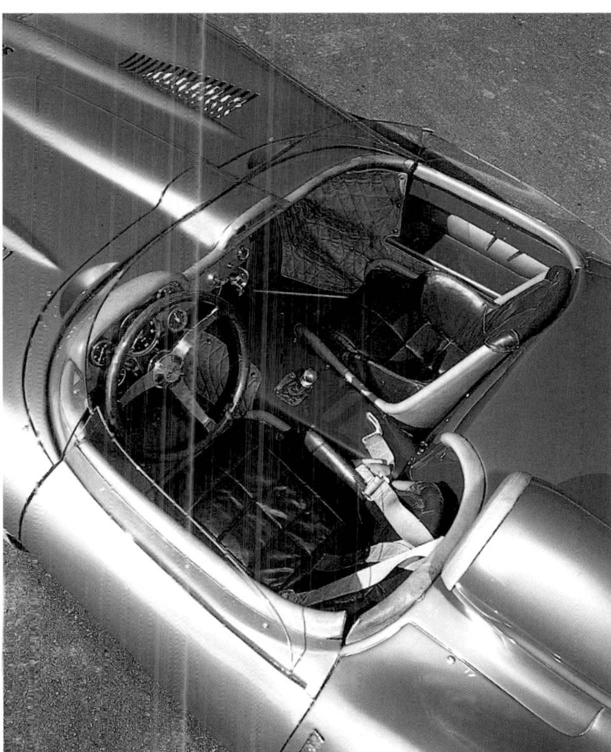

No nonsense here, save for perhaps the wood-rimmed steering wheel. The SS interior was certainly competition-ready, although it gave all new meaning to the term "hot seat" on race day at Sebring in 1957.

world-class racing machines from scratch at the same time, to be ready for action in only three months more, was completely out of the question given the money and manpower available. Final approval for the XP-64 project realistically involved only one race car, dubbed the Corvette SS.

Duntov's hand-picked crew immediately began assembling the Corvette SS's chassis and driveline, working night and day in a partitioned corner in Chevrolet Engineering. By October, MacKichan's styling crew had finalized the body design, which was then hand formed in magnesium, not fiberglass, to help keep overall weight as low as possible. Distinct exterior features included flush-fit headlamps and driving lights, tilt-up nose and tail sections, side-exiting exhausts, cooling louvers on the hood and rocker panels, semi-enclosed rear wheelhouses, and a somewhat futuristic headrest "pod" that doubled as a rollbar.

Duntov's engineers didn't even use fiberglass for the SS, opting for lightweight magnesium instead. This decision ended up helping assist in the SS racer's downfall at Sebring in March 1957 as the magnesium shell didn't dissipate heat well at all—both man and machinery were basically baked.

Power for the SS came from an injected 283 with aluminum heads and long, tuned headers. Additional weight-saving features included a special magnesium oil pan with baffles and fins to help cool the oil supply.

The original body design also featured a large, recessed inlet in the center of the hood area meant to feed denser air directly into the engine below. But wind tunnel tests in December showed that the inlet negatively disrupted air flow over the nose. Unable to find time to correct the design, Duntov had no choice but to delete the opening. Wind tunnel testing did, however, prove that the SS body exhibited minor lift characteristics and was comparable to the D-Type Jaguar as far as overall aerodynamic drag was concerned. The sexy shell was as superbly functional as it was good looking.

Deadline pressures also influenced chassis construction. To save time by keeping things as simple as possible, a tubular space frame design was chosen over the more desirable, and more complex, monocoque body/frame layout used by Jaguar. And to help beat the clock even further, Duntov's crew simply brought in a Mercedes-Benz 300SL tube frame to serve as a model. In the end, the cage-like SS chassis showed only a few minor similarities to the 300SL layout. One-inch-diameter chrome-moly steel tubing was used throughout, with the majority being round. Square tubing was used where some components were mounted to the frame. Weight for the tubular frame was a mere 180 pounds, a typical figure for race cars of the day. At 92 inches the SS chassis' wheelbase was a half foot less than the production Corvette.

Suspension was by variable-rate coilover shocks in back, typical coils (with shocks inside them) at the nose. Up front, the hand-fabricated sheet steel A-arms, ball joints and forged-steel steering knuckles looked very much like a regular-production arrangement. Two short links connected each end of an anti-sway bar to the underside of the lower A-arms. And steering equipment consisted of a specially built Saginaw recirculating-ball unit and a three-piece track rod. Steering ratio was a race-car-quick 12.0:1.

A tried-and-true de Dion axle was used in back instead of a fully independent arrangement, again to help save extra developmental time the engineering team simply didn't have to spare. Located by four lightweight (together they only weighed roughly six pounds) tubular trailing links, the curved de Dion steel tube axle wound its way from wheel hub carrier to wheel hub carrier behind a frame-mounted Halibrand quick-change rearend. Each trailing link used rubber bushings where they pivoted at their frame mounting points, while ball joints connected them to the de Dion axle.

The Halibrand unit was picked to once more help save production time, although Duntov's engineers only kept the existing housing, filling it instead with their own ring and pinion gears and quick-change cogs, all being specially machined and shot peened to resist fatigue. Interestingly, the differential inside that Halibrand housing was not a limited-slip unit. A limited-slip differential was prepared for the SS, but the appropriately beefed-up half shafts needed to couple it to the wheel hubs were not ready in time. The various quick-change gears available made for final drive ratios ranging from 2.63:1 to 4.80:1.

As for brakes, up-to-date discs would've certainly been nice, but such pieces were still in the developmental stage as far as GM was concerned. In their place, Duntov's men used the brawniest drum brakes they could fashion, combining Chevrolet's existing sintered cerametallix linings with big 2.5-inch wide shoes in equally big 12-inch drums—finned for cooling—at all four wheels. Ductwork at each wheel delivered the air for cooling those drums. And while the front drums were typically found nestled within XP-64's Halibrand aluminum knock-off wheels, the two rear units were mounted inboard on the Halibrand quick-change housing, a relatively simple trick that helped reduce unsprung weight in back.

Completing the Corvette SS's beefy brake system was an advanced vacuum-servo-controlled power booster setup designed to distribute stopping power proportionately from back to front to hopefully help avert rear wheel lock-up during hard stops. While front braking force was always relative to pedal pressure, a cockpit-mounted mercury switch controlled a valve that limited the power boost to the rear brakes. When the mercury in the switch responded to the negative g-forces created by deceleration, it electrically shut down that valve, meaning rear braking force would not increase beyond whatever level it was at that moment regardless of how hard the brake pedal was depressed. Front brakes would continue to work harder at

Both the nose and tail of the SS flipped up, in this case to allow access to the spare tire and rear coilover suspension.

stopping the car as the pedal went farther down, while the rears would not work too hard and lock the wheels once the tires began losing their grip as the tail started lifting. The idea sounded good. And it looked good on paper. Real world tests, however, proved otherwise.

Supplying the impetus to test those brakes was a race-prepped V-8 based on the Corvette's newly enlarged 283ci small-block. Inside, compression was kept at a definitely docile 9:1 to help ensure this powerplant would stick around for 12 hours at Sebring. Atop the iron block went specially prepared, lightweight aluminum heads featuring reworked ports and stock-size valves treated to some minor recontouring. Inserts were added to the exhaust valve seats to protect the relatively soft aluminum from the vicious pounding experienced at, say, 6500rpm. Intake valve seats, however, received no inserts.

Feeding this hungry V-8 was Chevrolet's new Rochester fuel injection setup, which itself sucked in the atmosphere through a duct running from the grille opening to the fuel/air metering unit. Reportedly, this ram-air setup translated into an extra 10 horsepower at 150mph. Also of great help were the tubular steel headers, hot hardware that not only shaved off unwanted pounds but also boosted output by another 20 horses. All told, XP-64's 283 produced 307hp at 6400rpm on the dynamometer. Redline was

The Corvette SS's tubular space frame was based, however minimally, on the design used beneath the Mercedes-Benz 300SL. Weight for this frame was only 180 pounds. Wheelbase was 92 inches, six less than the standard Corvette.

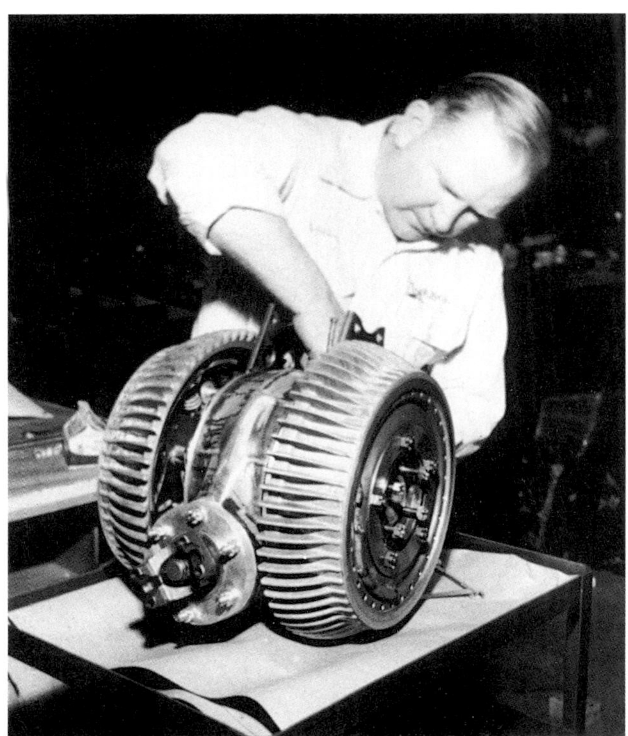

A Halibrand quick-change rearend, with Chevrolet-prepared internals, was chosen for the SS. And inboard mounted drum brakes were also typically added to reduce unsprung weight. The downside of this design was that the drums transferred unwanted heat to the differential housing and vice versa.

put at 6800 revs, 200 below the accepted safe limit for Chevy's little "hot one" in top performance trim.

Additional weight was trimmed by using an aluminum water pump and a special magnesium oil pan featuring a finned bottom panel and baffled internal passages to help keep the lubricant supply cool. On the scales, the entire SS power package weighed 450 pounds, about 80 less than a typical Corvette 283. Weight-saving aluminum was also used in manufacturing the bell housing, transmission case and radiator core. Overall, the completed SS weighed 1,850 pounds; Jaguar's D-Type carried roughly 100 more. A production Corvette was about a half-ton heavier.

A typical single-disc hydraulic clutch, beefed up with heavy-duty facings and stouter springs, delivered those 300+ horses to XP-64's aluminum-case four-speed transmission. Specially chosen for Sebring, first gear was 1.87:1, followed by 1.54:1 for second, 1.22:1 for third.

All in all, the finished product—painted a beautiful metallic blue—looked like a formidable warrior. Proving that fact was another matter. Needing basically every minute from the start of production in October 1956 almost up to race day at Sebring on March 23, 1957, to create his SS racer, Duntov knew he'd never have the time to properly test the car and iron out all bugs prior to going into action. Luckily, he managed to squirrel away enough extra parts to assemble an unauthorized second SS, the so-called test "Mule." Almost enough. When the Mule arrived at Sebring for testing, it did so minus a few body panels and headlights. Its interior was incomplete and its crudely formed, white fiberglass shell helped bring total weight up 150 pounds compared to the magnesium-bodied SS. Available power was also down slightly.

All that aside, the SS Mule did its job well while running about 2000 test miles at Sebring. Various problems surfaced in time to make some changes on the blue SS. And as crude as the Mule looked, it proved itself to be quite formidable in action. During test sessions just prior to race day, legendary driver Juan Fangio took a seat behind the Mule's wheel and proceeded to rip off a lap time of three minutes, 27 seconds—about two seconds faster than the best lap run in 1956. Stirling Moss then took a turn and recorded a 3:28 lap. If the slapped-together Mule could run like that, what could its refined sibling achieve?

Then again, the blue SS was not as refined as it looked. Hampered from the start by the tight deadline, Duntov's men were still working on the SS

XP-64's four-speed transmission featured an aluminum case, a weight-saving idea that would become standard for four-speed production Corvettes in 1961.

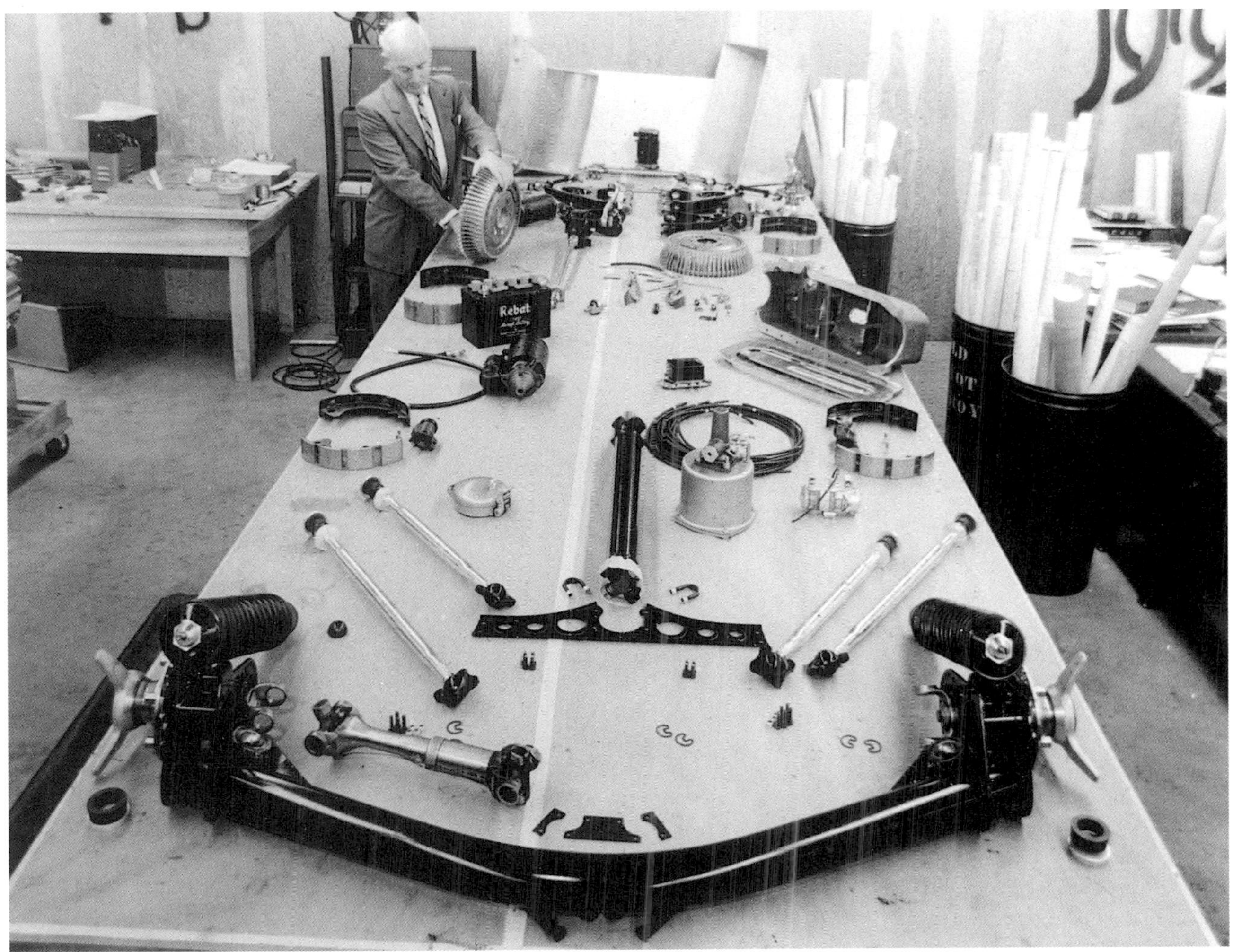

Zora Duntov admires the SS racer's basic layout, with the many innovative features including finned brake drums, large ceramet-allix brake linings, and a baffled magnesium oil panel (at middle right on its side hanging over edge of table). In the foreground is the tubular de Dion axle.

even as it arrived in Florida via transport van at the proverbial last minute. Not only was the car not entirely ready to race, it was also without a driver. Fangio had been the original choice, with Moss considered as a co-driver. Moss, however, was already committed, while Fangio was released from a signed agreement with Chevrolet once it became clear the SS would never arrive at Sebring in time for proper testing and appraisal.

John Fitch was then asked to step in. Having led Chevrolet's production-based Corvette racing team to Sebring the previous year, he was again placed in charge of the stock-class competition effort in 1957. While his experience did indeed qualify him as a top candidate for the SS job, it was the time element that mattered most. Fitch wasn't just a good choice to pilot the SS at Sebring. On short notice, he was basically the only choice. And on even shorter notice, Chevrolet contacted 50-year-old Piero Taruffi—by Fitch's request—in Italy early in the morning on Tuesday, March 19, asking him to co-drive the car. He agreed and was flown in just in time to take a few practice laps.

What Taruffi and Fitch discovered during the SS racer's all-too-short practice time was that the car was definitely a different animal compared to the Mule. First, the magnesium body helped keep interior heat levels almost unbearable, a problem that hadn't surfaced in the better ventilated (remember the missing panels) Mule. The Mule's fiberglass shell helped insulate the driver from heat, while the magnesium SS body served as a heat conductor. To compensate, various sections of the doors and rocker panels were cut away as part of an effort to let cooling air in and exhaust heat out. Extra cockpit insulation was also added, all to no avail.

Making matters worse were problems with the complicated brake system, which had worked fine for the Mule. Fitch and Duntov were still trying to repair those brakes 15 minutes before race time,

Racing rules required a top be at least available for a competition legal sports-racer in 1957, thus the reasoning behind this bubble, which was never used. That's Duntov doing the modeling.

again to no avail. Fitch even went so far as to warn fellow drivers of his stopping woes while lining up for the Le Mans-style running start that Saturday morning on the grid at Sebring.

Once underway, Fitch did manage to give it a valiant try, bad brakes and all. The SS ran with the best of them, turning one lap at 3:29, but soon fell behind as glitches took over. First came an unplanned pit stop to change front tires after only two laps—the right front had been badly flat-spotted when it locked up during Fitch's last-minute brake testing prior to the race's start. A few times around the 5.2-mile course and Fitch was back in with a dead engine, the result of a faulty coil connection that required some 15 minutes to identify and repair. The SS died again back out on the course, forcing Fitch to replace the coil entirely. Meanwhile, heat in the cockpit continued to be a major problem. Finally, a failed rubber bushing on one of the de Dion

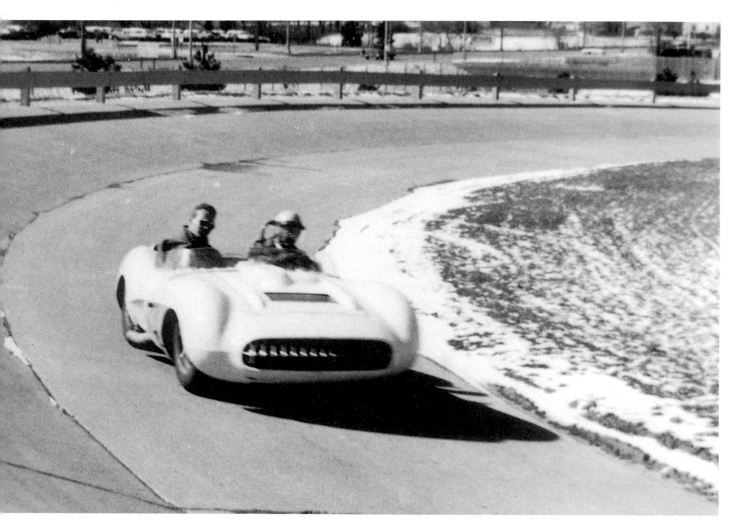

Despite no authorization for a second SS, Duntov's crew did manage to cobble together a fiberglass-bodied test "Mule," which here undergoes testing in Michigan late in the winter of 1956-57. Although considerably crude compared to its magnesium-bodied cousin, the Mule wowed many during practice at Sebring with its speed potential. And it didn't fry its driver like the SS ended up doing to John Fitch.

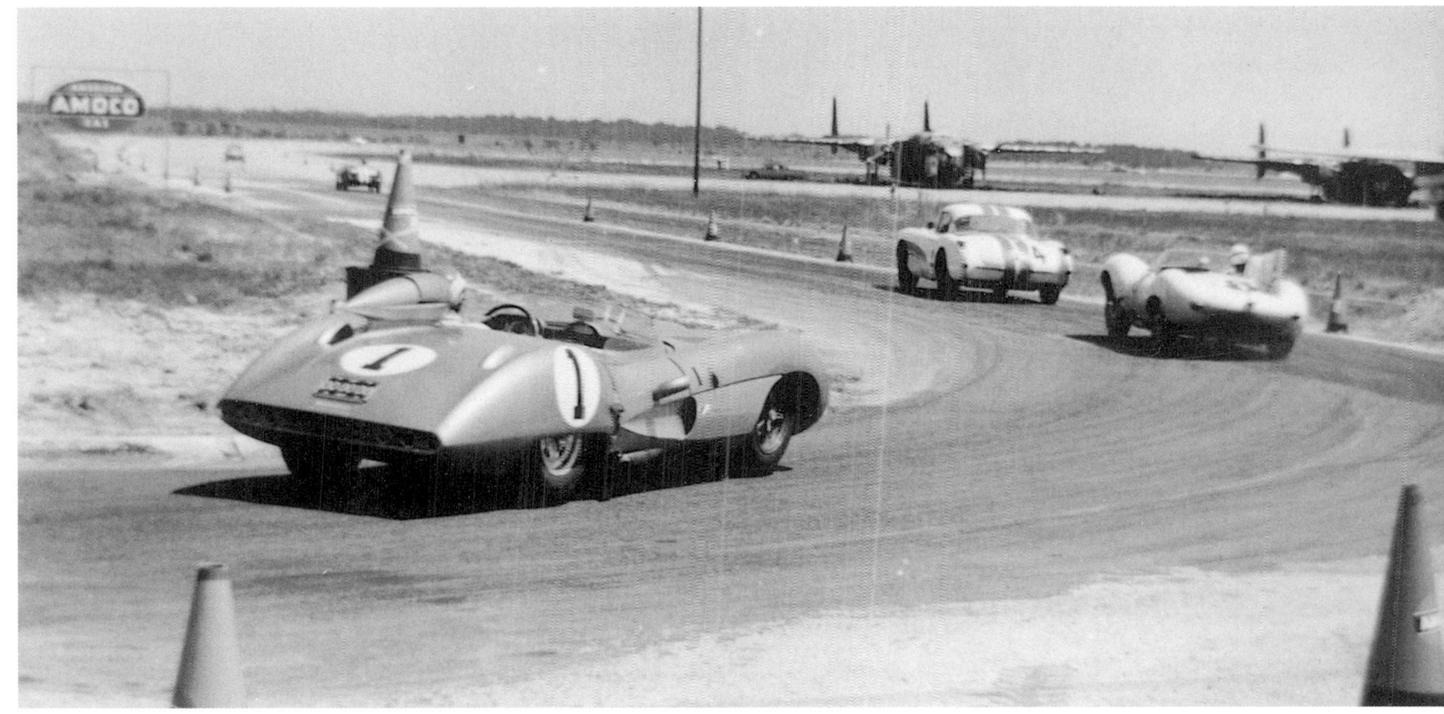

The racing career of the SS lasted only 23 laps at Sebring in March 1957. Brakes problems, a coil failure, a broken rear suspension, and continual over-heating difficulties caused the car's demise. Here, U.S. Air Force "Flying Boxcars" stand by as the SS chases a D-Type Jaguar and one of the production-based 1957 Corvette racers.

axle's trailing links in back made the SS all but unmanageable. After only 23 laps—22 by Fitch, one by Taruffi—the SS was forced to retire from the race.

The Corvette SS clearly had shown some powerful potential, and even in failure did represent a remarkable achievement considering how little time was allowed for its creation. As John Fitch later wrote, "I felt that we had somehow been cheated, that if we had only been allowed another month, the wrinkles would have been ironed out." Others were also quick to note what the car could be given time to flush out the gremlins. "Without a doubt," wrote *Autocar's* Jesse Alexander, "Chevrolet [has] a car that could win Le Mans in the hands of the right driver... given a proper share of luck."

Ed Cole was also confident of the SS's potential despite the Sebring debacle in March, so much so he immediately approved a proposal for putting together a three-car SS team for Le Mans later that summer. Continued Alexander, "under proper guidance, a team of three or four of these machines with top drivers could put the United States on the sports-racing car map." But a Chevrolet-backed Corvette team did not make it to France in 1957.

Even as plans were being considered for an improved Corvette SS, word began to spread concerning impending action by the Automobile Manufacturers Association to squelch factory-supported racing activities. While the AMA "ban" on factory racing didn't arrive until June, GM officials had already announced in early May that they would be dropping any and all competition connections. Although clandestine underground support for certain racers did continue from both Chevrolet and Pontiac, high-profile projects like the Corvette SS were obviously doomed. The quick retirement at Sebring had been the end of the road.

The book on the Corvette SS, however, didn't exactly close there. Both the blue SS and the white Mule survived the GM axe, with the Mule's chassis resurfacing in 1959 as the base for Bill Mitchell's Stingray racer, a machine driven to competition glory by Dr. Dick Thompson. As for the unfortunate SS, it made it back to the track, too. In December 1958, Duntov's blue baby ran an incredible 183mph during testing at GM's proving grounds in Phoenix. Then in February 1959, Zora himself drove the SS around the new Daytona International Speedway's 2.5-mile highbank, hitting 155mph along the way.

Eventually, the Corvette SS was donated to the Indy 500 museum, where it was refurbished in 1987. And when the National Corvette Museum opened its doors in Bowling Green, Kentucky, on Labor Day weekend in 1994, there stood the still-proud SS to help greet visitors in the main lobby, up front where it belonged.

Chapter 6

1958-60

Onward And Upward

While the AMA factory racing ban of June 1957 did cut short the SS racer's career and put the clamps on Zora Duntov's plans to expand the Corvette image onto the international stage, it did little to inhibit the continuance of that image here at home. Fuel injection, the Duntov cam, competition brakes—these and other hot performance parts remained on the Corvette options list in 1958 for anyone to add to their fiberglass two-seater. Whether or not these private owners then took their Corvettes racing was purely up to them. Many did, some with more than a little unauthorized "back-door" support from Chevrolet Engineering. Most prominent among these alleged "privateers" was Dr. Dick Thompson, who commonly led the way as Corvettes went on to dominate SCCA racing in this country during the late 1950s and early 1960s.

As for action off the track, Chevrolet's Corvette began, in 1958, a perceived progression even further away from the European sports car ideal as size and weight grew and styling started falling more in line with typically trendy Yankee tastes. Sports car purists may have cringed, but they couldn't deny the Corvette's increasing popularity among the American jet set. Sales continually jumped up after 1956; 3,467 that year, 6,339 in 1957, 9,168 in 1958, and 9,670 in 1959, the last year production failed to surpass the 10,000-unit prediction first made for 1954. That barrier was finally broken in 1960 when 10,261 Corvettes were built.

Corvette updates for 1958 included quad headlights, simulated louvers on the hood and equally non-functional "vents" at the leading edges of the cove panels. The paint appearing here, Charcoal, was a one-year offering for 1958 alone.

A totally restyled interior was finally added in 1958. Dash modifications included putting the gauges and tach in front of the driver where they belonged, but they still remained tough to read.

Distinguishing between those last three model years wasn't all that easy at a glance since the 29,099 Corvettes built between 1958 and 1960 were all based on the same restyled body that had replaced the clean, classic look of 1956-57. Simple, even elegant, the 1957 Corvette has long been considered by many bystanders, innocent or otherwise, as the best of the first-generation, "solid-axle" breed, thanks both to its ground-breaking fuel-injected performance and uncluttered, crisp lines. This car was, at the same time, wholly American and like nothing else then seen out of Detroit. All arguments temporarily shoved aside, it represented the epitome of the American sports car ideal. Or at least it did until the stunning Sting Ray came along for 1963.

Nonetheless, lasting impressions left behind by the 1957 Corvette shouldn't be allowed to overshadow what followed. Just because so many fiberglass fans loved, and still love the 1957 model in no way means the restyled 1958 went unloved. A few slings and arrows were thrown, yes, but overall responses commonly involved patting Duntov's engineering crew on the back as performance carried on every bit as strong.

Now with 290 horses, the top 283 fuelie V-8 (with improved fuel metering and warm-up mixture control) was again capable of powering the 1958 Corvette through the quarter-mile in a shade more than 14 seconds. From there down you still had the 250hp injected V-8, as well as the 245- and 270hp dual-quad 283s. Outputs for all four optional

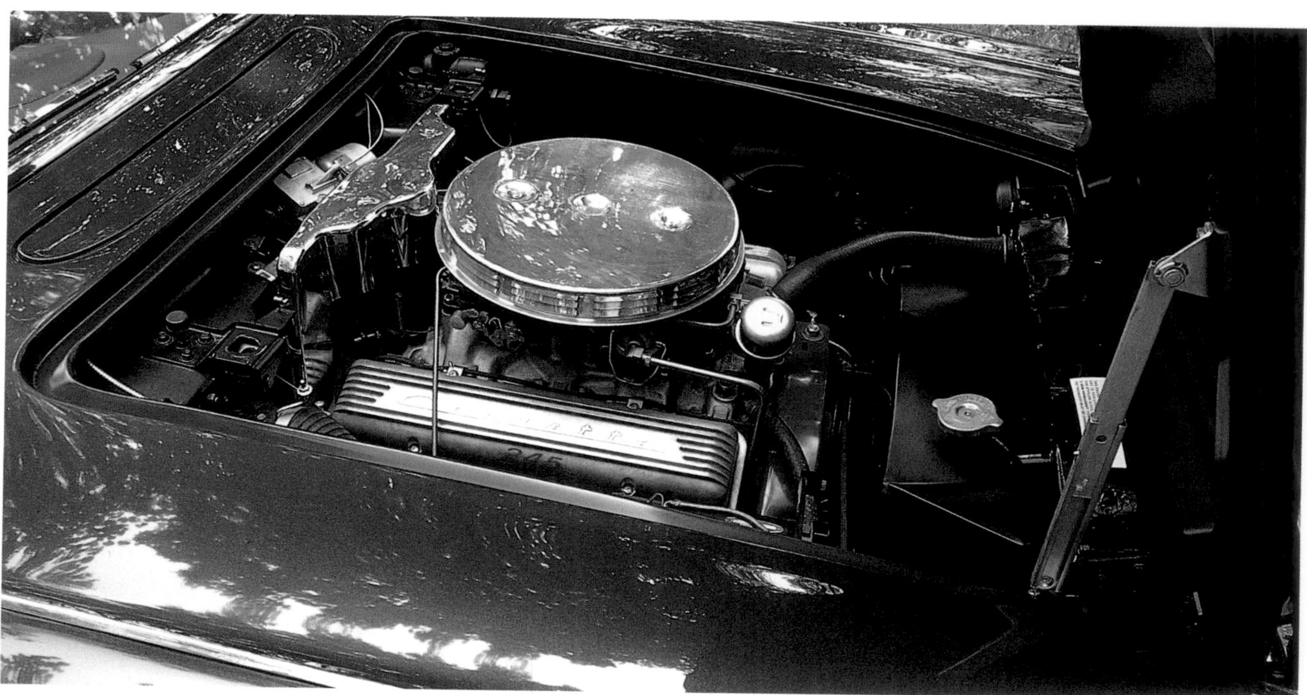

As in 1957, the optional dual-carb 283 with the hydraulic cam (RPO 469) was rated at 245 horsepower. At 2,436 sold, RPO 469 was second only to the base single-car 283 in popularity in 1958.

Twin chrome bands running down the decklid serve as a quick reminder as to what year Corvette you're looking at—the were only applied in 1958.

Corvette engines would remain unchanged up through 1960, as would the base 283 four-barrel, which beginning in 1958 was uprated 10 additional horses to 230. New for 1958 was the position of the 283 V-8's generator, relocated from the driver's side to the passenger's in order to improve fan belt "geometry," in turn increasing that belt's "grip" around the water pump pulley.

Transmission choices carried over unchanged from 1957, and would remain so for 1959 and 1960. Standard fare was again the three-speed manual, with the four-speed and Powerglide automatic coming at additional cost.

Styling was where the 1958 Corvette tended to take it on the chin. Its very prominent chin. In keeping with a corporate-wide trend, Chevrolet's latest 'glass body sprouted an extra pair of headlights up front, helping inspire *Road & Track* to call the new model "too fussy." In *R&T's* opinion, "that supposedly hard-to-sell commodity, elegant simplicity, is gone."

Painted valve covers always signified the presence of a base Corvette V-8; optional engines received various style finned aluminum valve covers. From 1958 to 1961, that base engine was the 230hp 283 backed by a three-speed manual.

America's only sports car in all its glory in 1958—top performance that year again came from a fuel-injected 283. This Snowcrest White fuelie is one of 1,511 built in 1958; 504 250hp versions, and 1,007 more with the upgraded 290hp 283.

Along with those quad headlights, new frontal treatment included two large simulated air ducts (which became functional with the optional racing brakes) and enlarged bumpers that were now mounted directly to the frame instead of the body as in previous years. Long, chrome accents went atop each fender, where they would stay up through 1962. Rear bumpers were also restyled in a much more prominent fashion, and two unexplained chrome bands were stretched up and over the decklid. These bands helped set a 1958 Corvette apart from the similar 1959 and 1960 models to follow—that parallel chrome trim treatment got the boot after appearing for one year only.

Additional "fussiness" came behind the front wheels where simulated vents were added to the previously uncluttered cove panel's leading edges. This design would stick around, too, in this case up through 1961. One feature that didn't stick around was the readily identifiable new hood with its 18 fake louvers, an arrangement that at least reminded some witnesses of the SR-2's fully functional louvered lid. Like the trunk chrome, the 1958 Corvette's simulated louvered hood did not make a return appearance.

Overall, the restyled shell, at 177.2 inches, measured more than nine inches longer than its 1957 predecessor, most of that increase coming up front. Total width grew as well, from 70.5 inches to 72.8. Weight accordingly also went up, by 200 pounds to 3,080, making for the first time a Corvette tipped the scales at more than a ton and a half. It was this newfound heft, along with all those extra styling baubles, that had some Chevrolet insiders in 1958 joking about how much "Cadillac-like" the new Corvette had become.

The car was, of course, very much "unCadillac-like" from behind the wheel, where performance belied the 1958 Corvette's somewhat bulked-up image and an updated cockpit surrounded the driver with fresh flair. Gone was the same basic dashboard used since 1953 as designers finally responded to complaints concerning gauge location. All instruments were in 1958 moved to directly in front of the driver in a modern-looking, recessed pod arrangement. A larger speedometer, calibrated to 160mph instead of 140, was added, as was a new 6000-rpm standard tachometer (a 7000-rpm unit had been used in 1957) located in a relatively prominent pod directly atop the steering column. Choosing either one of the two solid-lifter engines (270- and 290hp) meant that standard tach was exchanged for an 8000-rpm unit.

Additional updates included all-new inner door panels, a center "console" below the dash where the standard clock and optional heater and radio went, and a stylish "grab bar" across the concave area incorporated on the dashboard's passenger side. The steering wheel, however, was still basically the same sporty three-spoke unit introduced in 1956. And although upholstery was new, the seat design continued to leave many drivers sore and unsure of their placement in hard turns, problems inherent with the Corvette interior from the beginning.

Even Duntov admitted the new 1958 interior wasn't perfect by any means, the seats in particular. Instrument legibility was still on the tough side, but he preferred to point out that they did represent a marked improvement over what came before. That they did, although some weren't so easy to accept that rationalization. Nor was everyone particularly kind when it came time to acknowledge the deficiencies.

As in 1957, the lower performance fuelie V8 in 1958 featured a hydraulic cam and was rated at 250 horsepower. Minor modifications meant the top fuelie V-8, with its solid-lifter cam, was bumped up from 283 hp to 290. Price for the RPO 579 fuel injection setup was still $484.20.

Previous page
Chevrolet stripped off the bright trunk bands in 1959, but little else was changed in that year from a tail point of view.

Up front, the louvered hood used in 1958 disappeared once the 1959 Corvette debuted.

As veteran race driver Ken Miles wrote in *Sports Car Journal*, "in only two respects does the car fall short, and whilst the styling department is undoubtedly responsible for the miserably illegible instruments, I feel the engineering department is probably to blame for the totally inadequate seats. [These] are neither comfortable to ride in nor give any lateral support at all so that there is a constant temptation to drive round corners hanging on to the door with one hand in order to stay behind the wheel."

Miles did speak highly of the Corvette's maximum performance potential. As mentioned, all those hot pieces available in 1957 were still around in 1958. A Positraction differential with 3.70:1, 4.11:1 or 4.56:1 gears. Wide 15x5.5 wheels with their small hubcaps. And the race-ready RPO 684 package. Still priced at $780.10, RPO 684 again added quicker steering, stiffer suspension, finned brake drums with cooling scoops and cerametallix linings, and that somewhat complicated brake-cool-

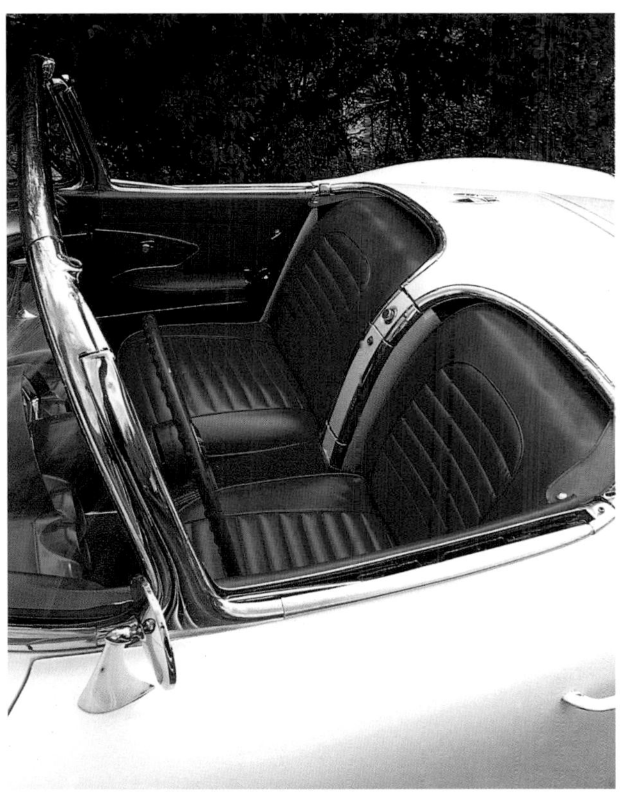

Interior updates for 1959 included different style seat upholstery and the addition of a storage bin to the passenger's side of the dash.

ing ductwork that this time took in air through the two normally fake vents (functionally opened up, of course) added beneath the 1958 Corvette's quad headlights. How convenient.

As before, it was highly recommended not to rely on those heavy-duty brakes for everyday use, as Miles was quick to explain. "When cold, the cerametallic lining is ferociously unpredictable," he wrote. "For low speeds the slightest touch on the brake pedal almost pitches both drive and passenger through the windshield. At normal freeway speeds incautious application of the brakes results in a hasty and unexpected change of lane." That was the downside. "But at high speeds," continued Miles, "the brakes really come into their own and haul this great big automobile down from maximum speed with no sign of fade whatsoever, time and time again."

Few drivers, however, found the chance to discover firsthand the realities of Chevrolet's cerametallix brakes since only 144 Corvettes were equipped with RPO 684 in 1958.

The same could've been said in 1959 when another 142 buyers checked off RPO 684, this time priced at only $425.05. Cost was slashed by deleting all that extra ductwork used in 1957 and 1958, leaving the vented backing plates to do the brake cooling on their own. On the other side of the coin, RPO 684 springs were stiffened further in 1959, which was probably only right considering the extra weight the Corvette had been saddled with the previous year. Spring rates went from 340lb/in to 550 in front, 125 to 145 in back.

New options for 1959 included stronger, high-speed 6.70x15 nylon blackwall tires—limited-production option (LPO) number 1408—and yet another brake package. This one simply featured special sintered metallic linings supplied by GM's Delco Moraine division. These metallic shoes didn't "eat up" the drums' inner surfaces as bad as their gnarly, ceramic-based counterparts did, nor did they work as poorly when cold. Metallic brakes were listed under RPO 686 at a cost of $26.90; 333 sets were sold in 1959, followed by another 920 in 1960.

Also introduced in 1959, on March 12, was LPO 1625, an oversized gas tank that upped the available fuel load from the stock 16.4 gallons to 24. This option's competition implications were obvious. Reportedly, Chevrolet had installed as many as seven enlarged 21-gallon fiberglass fuel tanks in 1957 Corvettes, but these cars were meant only for the track. LPO 1625 represented the first time John Q. Public could enhance his Corvette's range. Again, whether or not John Q. then used that increased range to run longer between pit stops on a race course of his choice was strictly his prerogative. Remember, Chevrolet wasn't involved in racing. No sir.

Logically filling up more space than usual behind the Corvette's bucket seats, the so-called "big tank" required the additional inclusion of RPO 419—the $236.75 removable hardtop—thanks to the fact there was not enough room left to mount the standard folding roof in its typical location. Yet another mandated modification involved the standard Corvette gas cap with its protruding tab or "handle," which wouldn't allow the filler door to close due to the 24-gallon tank's relocated filler neck. Assembly manual instructions offered a simple solution: "Rework cap by removing handle or bending it over to make it flat with surface of cap."

No production figures are available for the LPO 1625 option, but estimates claim less than 200 big tanks were installed between 1959 and 1962. Beginning in 1961, the cap clearance problem was dealt with differently as a lengthened neck was simply extended through a holed filler door, itself sealed to the body. A bright, smooth-faced cap with serrated grip edges topped off that neck, representing the easiest way to pick out a rare big-tank Corvette built in 1961 and 1962. But only if the original owner didn't cut down the neck and re-install the typical working filler door, something most apparently did due to the perceived unsightly appearance of the exposed cap. Very few exposed-cap big-tank Corvettes are known. In 1962, LPO 1625 was redesignated RPO 488, for which a production number is known—65.

Corvette production in 1960 surpassed the 10,000 level for the first time—that figure had been the original projection for 1954. Exact production was 10,261. By 1960, color combinations were almost endless, as the light blue convertible top on this Ermine White/Sateen Silver Corvette attests.

Among modifications made to the standard Corvette package for 1959 was the aforementioned deletion of the louvered hood and chrome decklid trim and the addition of 10 rectangular slots to the wheelcovers to help cool the brakes. Underneath in back, a pair of radius rods were added to tie each end of the rear axle more solidly to the frame. These trailing links helped at least partially cure the inherent shuddering and "wheel hop" problems common to solid-axle designs during hard acceleration. Early Corvettes were especially susceptible to these maladies.

Shock absorber mounting points were also moved to improve their damping effect. And the new 1959 shocks incorporated a nitrogen-filled bag inside to help prevent fluid foaming during hard use.

Inside, a convenient storage bin was added to the dash beneath the passenger-side grab bar, and the door knob was moved farther forward with added convenience in mind. Seats were slightly reshaped to hopefully keep the driver's butt more firmly planted, incremental calibration of the instruments were better defined, gauges received concave lens to assist legibility, and the four-speed stick was equipped with an innovative, safety-conscious reverse-lockout mechanism. Shifts into reverse could only be made by squeezing a T-handle added to the four-speed lever. Twin sun visors were also introduced as an option, RPO 261, for the 1959 interior.

All these improvements and additions of course meant a corresponding cost increase. Priced at around $3500 with essentially no individual options offered (they were listed, but apparently were all included on every car built) to hike that price during its first three years, the Corvette was by 1959

Base price for a 1960 Corvette was $3,872, a relatively minor increase over the $3,500 asking price listed during the car's first few years on the road. Options, however, were plentiful, making the possibility of seeing a bottom line soar beyond $5,000 quite common.

being offered at $3,875 in base form. Options had begun growing in number after 1956. Two years later, putting a Corvette bottom line well beyond the $5000 level was no problem at all.

Few onlookers, apparently, were discouraged by this fact. "For all around performance per dollar, the Corvette is hard to beat," wrote Stephen F. Wilder in a *Sports Car Illustrated* review of Chevrolet's 1959 fiberglass sports car.

Motor Trend's Wayne Thoms came to a similar conclusion after comparing the 1959 Corvette with Porsche's latest open-air two-seater. "Which one is the best buy?" asked his article. "Depends on what you want in a sportscar," came his reply. "If getting a lot of performance from a precision-built, small-

Early Corvette seats represented another area of complaint for customers who wanted to drive a sports car like a sports car. Improvements were made, but the 1960 rendition still apparently left much to be desired. According to *Sports Car Illustrated* they looked "more buckety than they are, offering little side support."

Introduced in 1959, Roman Red was again the hot color of choice for Corvette buyers in 1960, with 1,529 cars of this shade sold, second only to Ermine White at 3,717. Priced at $16.15, the optional two-tone paint scheme was still around as well, listed under RPO 440. Production of Roman Red/white 1960 Corvettes was 779.

Production of the solid-lifter 270hp 283 Corvettes in 1960 was 2,364, making it the second most popular power choice behind the base 230hp V-8. Price for this twin-carb engine, RPO 469C, was $182.95.

displacement engine is intriguing, then the Porsche is the answer. If you like the idea of having one of the world's fastest accelerating sports cars, then pick the Corvette. Truth is, both are excellent buys. They're sturdy, reliable, comfortable and above all, fun to drive. What more can you ask of a sportscar?"

Apparently not much, considering Chevrolet simply rolled out an essentially identical model for 1960—and this after so many Corvette watchers had earlier concluded that much greater things were planned.

"The changes to the car in the last six model years are not so great as we think will come about in 1960," claimed a report in the January 1959 edition of *Road & Track*. "We predict that this will be the year of the big changes for the Corvette."

Prime inspiration for this prediction came from two main sources, the XP-700 Corvette built for GM Styling chief William Mitchell early in 1959 and the "Q-Corvette" project, kicked off in the fall of 1957. Basically a typical personally customized flight of fancy intended for executive use, the XP-700 showed off what many in the press though was the upcoming new Corvette look for 1960. As it was, Mitchell's dream machine did predict a styling change, that being the "boat-tail" design that debuted in 1961.

The highly advanced Q-Corvette, on the other hand, was apparently initially considered for production beginning in 1960. Early design

William L. Mitchell took over as chief of GM Styling in December 1958. Future feathers in his cap would include the 1963 Sting Ray and Buick's Riviera.

models featured a startling coupe shell and an innovative driveline incorporating an aluminum V-8 sending torque to a transaxle located at the rear wheels. By trading a transmission typically located behind the engine for a rear-mounted transaxle, Duntov's engineers gave the Q-Corvette a more balanced stance as weight distribution moved away from the normally nose-heavy production Corvette standard.

But in the end, the costly Q-Corvette project was shelved. Temporarily. While the transaxle idea never resurfaced as a Corvette feature, that low, sleek shell ended up leading to the creation of the stunning 1963 Sting Ray coupe. With nothing else left in the oven for 1960, Duntov was left no choice but to keep the existing Corvette cooking as best he could for however long it took to develop a real all-new model.

"1960 will go down as the Year of Speculation for Corvette, *SCI* not being the only magazine that was caught well off base on predictions of radically changed styling and construction," wrote Karl Ludvigsen of *Sports Car Illustrated*. "New-type Corvettes along the lines theorized had actually been proposed, but the terrific engineering concentration on the Corvair project literally left no time for other developments. From the exterior

One of Bill Mitchell's many Corvette playtoys was this styling fling, XP-700, which appeared in the spring of 1959. While it was a bit futuristic up front, it did foretell the design change to come for 1961 in back.

Now You See It, Now You Don't
GM Designer Francis Scott's Retractable Hardtop Corvette

In the beginning Chevrolet's Corvette was a true roadster. No exterior door handles. No side windows. A nearly fully functional folding soft top that was best left stowed behind the seat. When it came time to drive your 1953, 1954 or 1955 Corvette top-up in bad weather, everything was just peachy as long as you didn't mind a little typical dampness and a lot of wind noise.

British sports car buffs never seemed particularly bothered by such annoyances—but then they didn't mind being left in the dark by their Lucas electrics, either. American sportsters, on the other hand, have always differed considerably from their European counterparts. Call us spoiled, think us blouse-wearing poodle-walkers, we Yankees have long tended to expect as many comforts of home as possible in our automobiles, sporting or not. No compromises. No trade-offs. Clumsy, less-than-transparent side curtains and leaking, booming canvas tops may have once represented an acceptable price the sporting crowd paid for their driving excitement, at least in foreign car terms. But it became clear not long after the Corvette was born that if an American sports car was going to thrive in sufficient numbers on these shores it would have to better appeal to American sensibilities.

So it was the Corvette was equipped with door handles and crank-up windows in 1956. New as well on the options list that year was an attractive, definitely functional—if not somewhat difficult to mount gracefully—removable hardtop. So what if a co-pilot was required to make the transition from open-air tourer to weather-proof status-mobile? There was no better way to have the best of both worlds in a sports car, right?

Wrong. Or at least according to GM designer Francis "Scotty" Scott. Inspired by a desire to both have his cake in hand and mouth, Scott contacted the U.S. patent office in September 1962 armed with his idea for a retractable hardtop design based on the Corvette. His design featured a full roof that simply retracted back and down into an oversized Corvette trunk, to be hidden away beneath a modified, forward-opening decklid. One minute a full-fledged hardtop. An honest-to-goodness convertible a flick of a switch later. Who'd a-thunk it?

The guys at Peugot for one. In 1936, they introduced what was probably the world's first regular-production, "split-personality," retractable hardtop model. Four years later, Chrysler's stunning LeBaron-built Thunderbolt show car also appeared with a retractable "hideaway" hardtop. Other Detroit show cars later featured similar retractable designs, and Scott himself contributed to one such GM Motorama machine very early in his career, which began in 1951. In his words, that Motorama project "was like fertilizer, it promoted the idea in my mind."

Additional promotion came in 1957 when Ford introduced this country's most successful attempt to combine wind-in-the-hair excitement with fixed-roof comfort. Built up through 1959, Ford's Skyliner featured a complex retractable roof arrangement incorporating three drive motors, four lock motors, eight circuit breakers, 10 limit switches, 10 power re-

Created by GM designer Francis Scott, this 1958 Corvette features a retractable hardtop that can be raised or lowered—here it is stowed away beneath the rear deck.

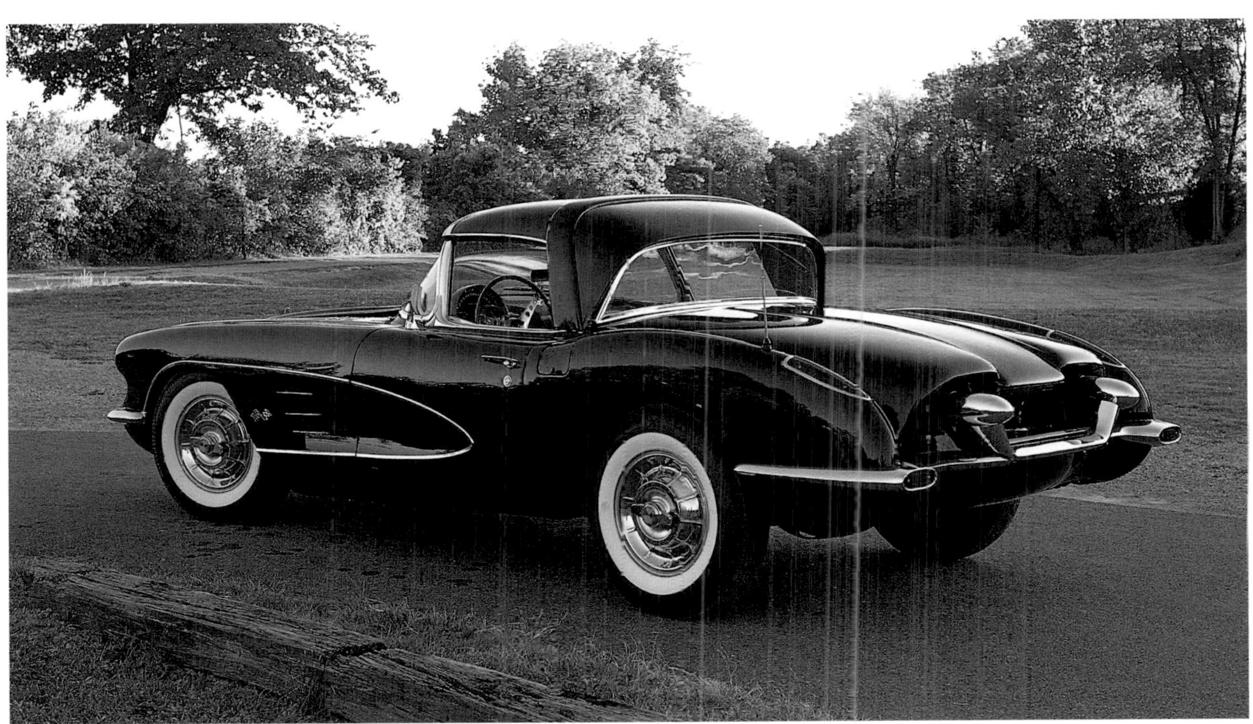

A push of a button and little help with the hands later and Scott's Corvette is a full-fledged hardtop. Scott borrowed various parts for this design from Ford, which marketed retractable hardtop models from 1957 to 1959.

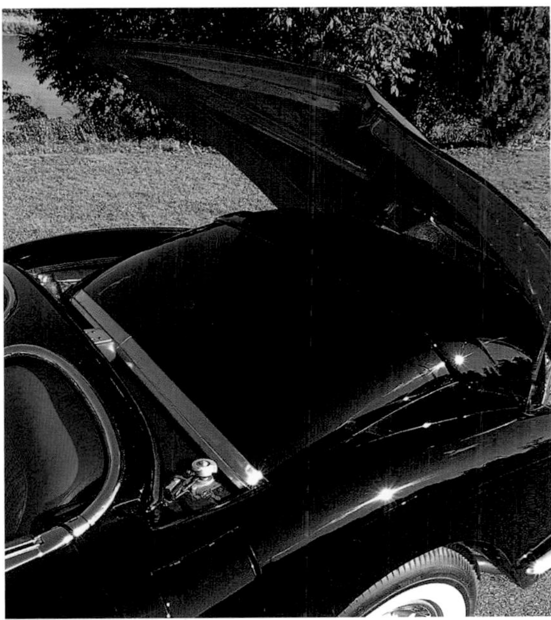

The fiberglass top simply rolls down channels into the trunk area where it is housed by a rear-hinged decklid restyled to add more space in back.

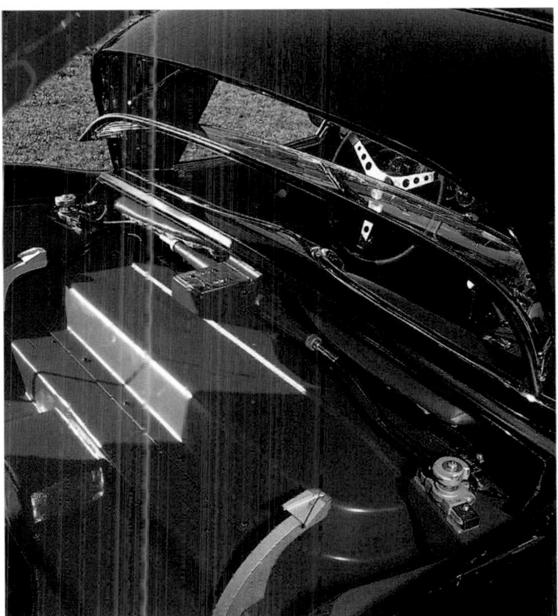

One of the keys to Scott's design was this hinged rear glass, which was first rotated before the top moved to add additional clearance for storage beneath the rear deck.

"Scotty" demonstrating its lift-up rear deck in front of Francis Scott's Michigan home in 1961. *Francis Scott photo*

lays and 610 feet of wire. Dearborn rolled out 48,394 of these mechanical marvels during the retractable Skyliner's relatively successful, certainly short, three-year production run.

Francis Scott, however, couldn't have cared less about a Ford product. Corvettes were naturally his favorites, although he couldn't quite afford one. A new one, that is. A few years after advancing up the ladder into GM Styling in 1953, he bought a rolled-over 1954 Corvette and rebuilt it as his daily driver.

Then in October 1958 he paid $900 for another trashed two-seater, "a jumbled up ball of wrecked Corvette hanging on a tow hook." What was left of that white 1958 model was delivered to his home in Warren, Michigan, where Scott's second restoration project began. Only this time the job would entail something completely different.

"I thought up the idea as I was putting the car back together," remembered Scott. "The back end was so badly damaged—there wasn't a back end there. And I saw that a retractable hardtop would fit down into the trunk and it all started going back together that way. I had to do some head-scratching in the beginning, but generally speaking it just fell together."

Scott used no drawings or models while building his retractable Corvette. Only three or four templates were needed. He also borrowed a lock motor, two flex cables and a pair of roof latches from a Ford parts shelf, all Skyliner components. One other electric motor was used to drive the decklid hydraulics, but that was basically it as far as heavy hardware was concerned. Far less complicated than Ford's better idea, Scott's retractable hardtop simple rolled on rails down into the trunk. Clever layout of the roller channels and use of a "fold-down" rear window made the design a veritable breeze. "Crude but effective" was Scott's description. "Why complicate the design?" he continued. "It was difficult enough to achieve as it was."

Unlatching the top from the windshield header and rotating the rear glass horizontally started the simple process. A switch on the console beside the driver's right knee opened the hydraulically controlled, rear-hinged decklid, which in turn moved the top up and backwards. From there, the top moved manually on rollers back and down into the trunk. As the decklid lowered, its knee-action hinges—pieces that also anchored the roller channels in back—dropped the top even deeper into the trunk, supplying ample clearance for the lid when closed. Did wrenches ever appear in the works? "I don't remember it ever not working," Scott said.

Kicked off in late 1958 in, of all places, the front room of his Warren home, Scott's retractable 1958 Corvette was completed by October 1961. Bodywork included fashioning a restyled top and a modified tail to house that top when retracted. Extra personal touches included adding two large bumper bullets and relocating the exhaust outlets from the bumper ends to the lower quarterpanels directly behind the rear wheels. A fresh 1958 Corvette nose was grafted on in place of the original shattered 'glass and a gleaming black finish completed the job. Scott estimated he invested 3,200 man hours and about $2,600 in the "strictly shoestring operation."

Budget constraints help explain why Scott's retractable Corvette ended up looking so different in

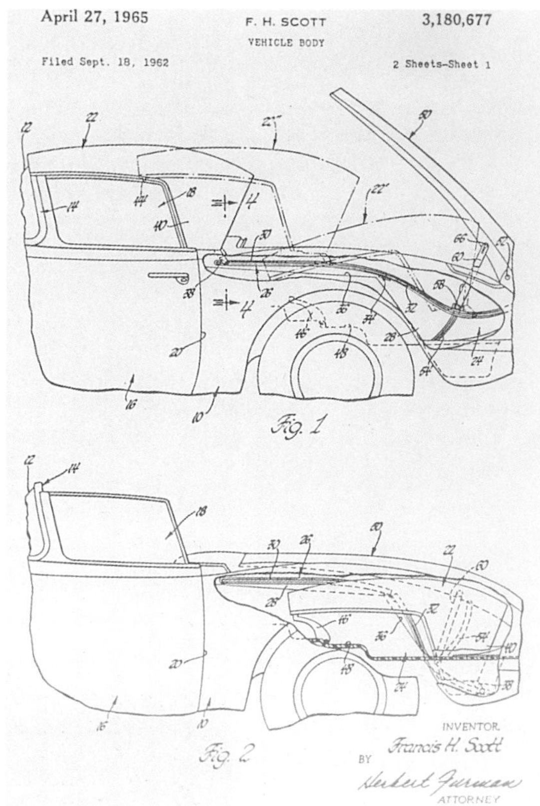

General Motors paid Scott one silver dollar for the rights to this patent. As for the idea of a retractable hardtop Corvette, little, if any thought was given to the idea.

Taken August 22, 1963, in front of GM Styling headquarters, this photo features more than 60 Corvette enthusiasts, all corporate employees. In front is Bill Mitchell with his Stingray racer; to his back is the XP-755 "Shark." Francis Scott is hidden in the left column with his retractable hardtop Corvette. His is the only quad-headlight car in that column, located sixth from the bottom. *Courtesy Francis Scott*

back. "Styling at the rear didn't quite satisfy me," he said, "but I didn't know what else to do to make it work. After I saw the car out on the street, it did look a little strange—I wished I had tried something else, but I'd already invested enough time in the project, I wasn't about to spend any more."

A little strange or not, Scott's creation did take a third-place trophy after its first big public appearance, a hot rod show in Detroit's Cobo Hall in December 1961. Soon afterward, Scott gave GM officials their own show in an executive garage. Present were Design Staff Engineering's Bob Lauer and Bill Mitchell himself. Recalled Scott, "Mitchell walked around the car once, completely ignoring me, said 'I'll be damned,' then just walked away. He was like that sometimes."

Lauer then suggested Scott contact the patent office. Patent number 3,180,677, detailing "a cover arrangement for convertible vehicle bodies," was issued to Francis H. Scott, assignor to General Motors, on April 27, 1965. GM traded Scott one silver dollar for the rights to the design, which were then filed away into obscurity.

As for the car, Scott drove it for about five years, then traded it for a used 1963 Chevy coupe. Details are sketchy until 1971, when Phil Wells, of Tallahassee, Florida, purchased the one-off retractable and began racing it. A pair of four-barrels had replaced the original-equipment single carb and white paint (with red coves) had superseded Scott's black exterior somewhere along the line. Wells sold the car to Miami's William Bruce in 1981. In March 1989, Terry Michaelis, of Pro Team Corvette Sales in Napoleon, Ohio, bought the unique Corvette from Bruce after seeing it featured in a national magazine.

Michaelis had seen the car once before in the early-1970s. "I knew [then this Corvette] was much more than someone's customizing project," he claimed, "as the cloth/resin layup was consistent with other GM concepts we've all seen before and since." Once in Michaelis' hands, the one-of-a-kind two-seater was quickly restored to "original" condition thanks to all-out efforts by Pro Team co-owner Fred Michaelis, body shop manager Dan Young, trim man Bob Hugo and ace assembly mechanic Billy Rodenhauser. "Scotty"—named by Terry Michaelis in honor of its designer/builder—was completed just in time for a special press introduction at a luncheon held August 27, 1994, during Carlisle Productions' 13th annual Corvettes at Carlisle extravaganza in Pennsylvania.

Although Francis Scott couldn't be there for the unveiling, he did supply much help to the Pro Team crew during the car's restoration. Having moved from the Detroit area to Oregon one month after his retirement from GM in October 1983, the 67-year-old forward-thinker still dabbles in out-of-the-ordinary design work, including a racing bicycle built for the Walt Disney movie "Ask Max." Scotty the man was, of course, happy to see Scotty the car come back to life. But he basically looked at it as old news. "I can't quite understand all this interest in the vehicle," joked Scott. "It was so completely ignored back then."

The car, maybe. But not the idea, as evidenced by Mitsubishi's recent release of its 3000 GT Spyder, the automotive world's latest attempt to marry carefree topless touring with fully functional, weatherproof practicality.

Another of Mitchell's personal rides was his Stingray racer, built late in 1958 using the chassis from the Corvette SS Mule of 1957. Many of the Stingray's lines would later reappear on the regular-production Sting Ray of 1963.

The Sting Ray's SS ancestry can be seen beneath its flip-up nose; compare this view with a shot of the SS's injected 283 V-8 in chapter five. *Bob Tronolone photo*

With veteran Corvette racer Dick Thompson at the wheel, Mitchell's Stingray became an SCCA champion in 1960. Here, Thompson works his magic at Riverside during the Times Grand Prix in October 1960. *Bob Tronolone photo*

After it was retired from racing, the Stingray was refurbished and put on the auto show circuit. Its debut on the stage was at Chicago's McCormick Place on February 18, 1961.

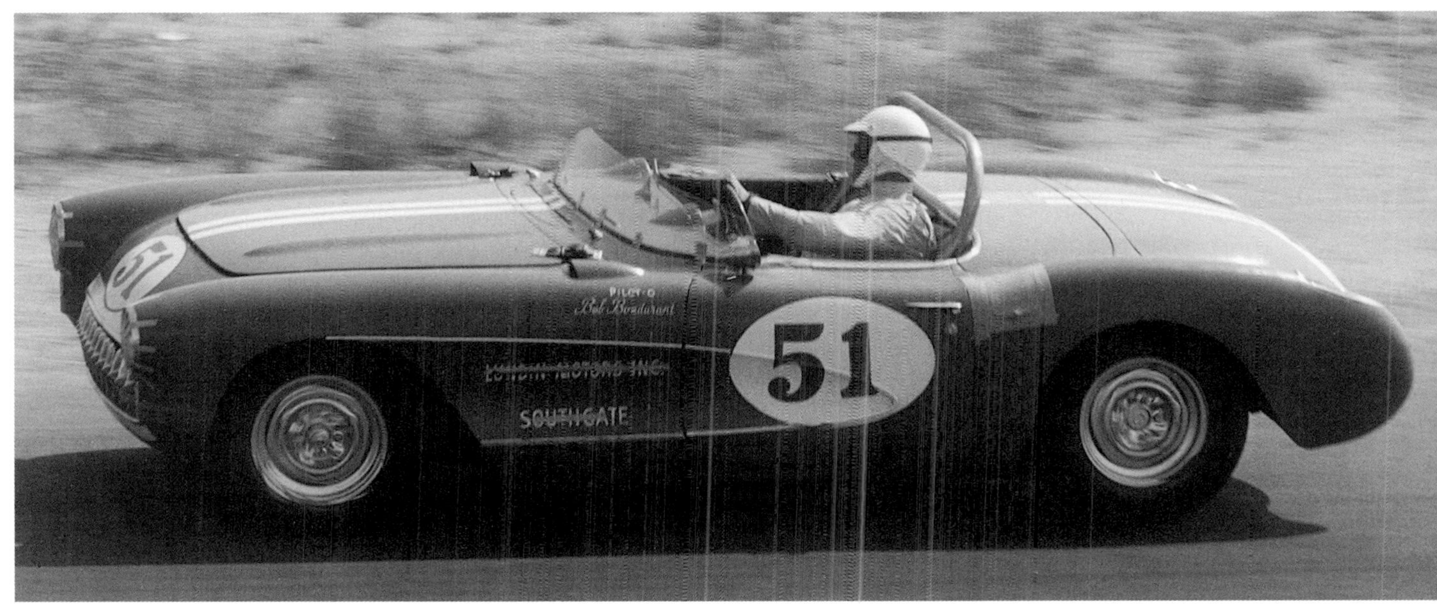

Along with Dick Thompson, other great Corvette racing names of the solid-axle era included Dave MacDonald, Don Yenko and Bob Bondurant, shown here at Riverside during the Kiwanis Grand Prix in July 1959. *Bob Tronolone photo*

and in all important respects, then, the 1960 Corvette is identical to last year's."

That's not to say the 1960 Corvette was devoid of improvements. Especially innovative was a standard rear stabilizer bar. Working in concert with a thicker (.70-inch) front stabilizer, this suspension upgrade meant stiffer springs weren't needed. Thus, higher-rate coils and leaves were dropped from the competition brake/suspension package formerly listed under RPO 684 in 1959.

In 1960, the corresponding option was RPO 687, which similarly included stiffer shocks, a quick-steering adapter, and finned brake drums with vented backing plates and cooling scoops. But this year, the brutish cerametallix linings were exchanged for the more civilized sintered metallic shoes previously listed on their own as RPO 686 in 1959. Also new was a clever 24-blade cooling "fan" mounted inside each brake drum. Price for the RPO 687 package in 1960 was $333.60. Production was only 119.

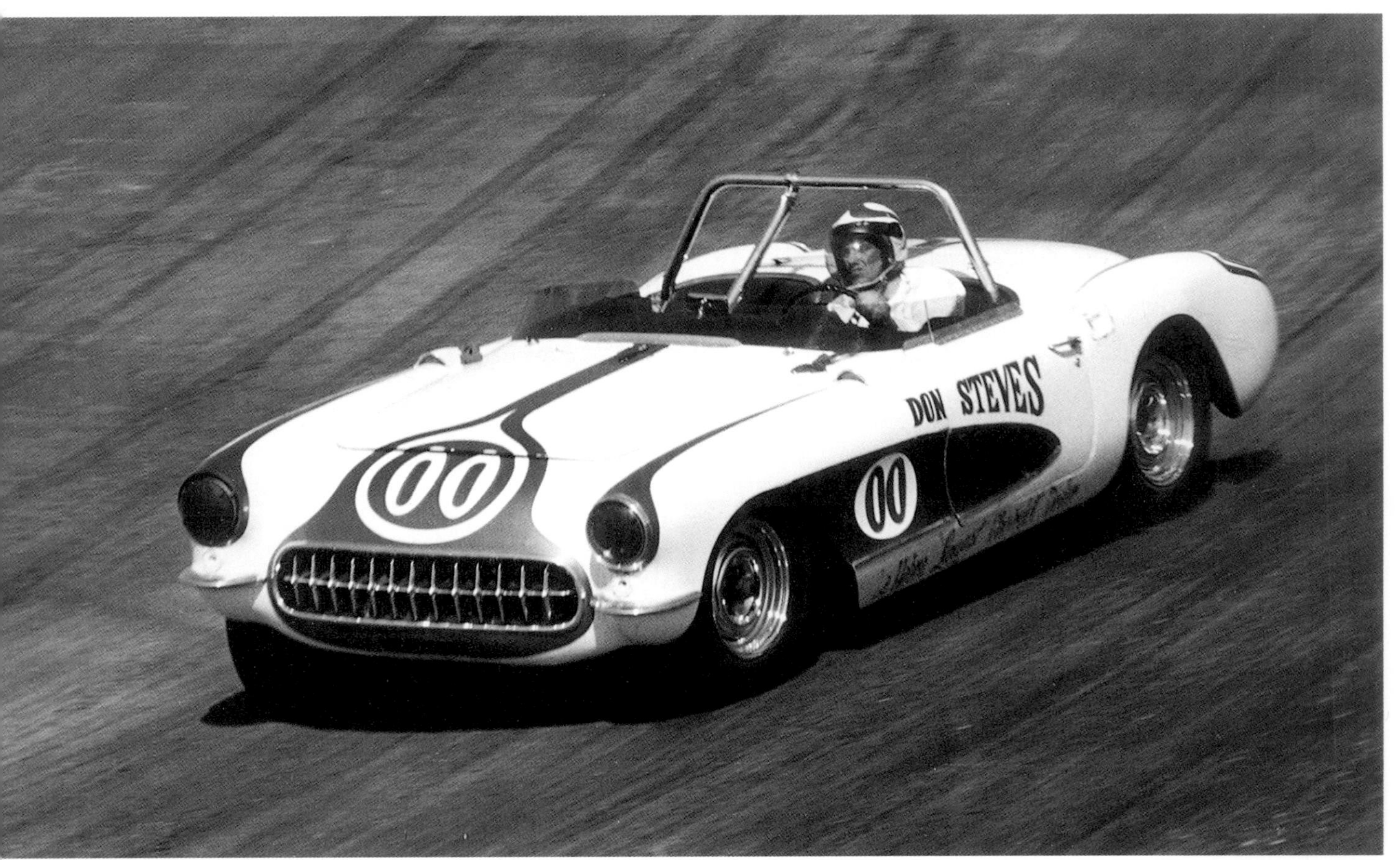

Dave MacDonald wheels his Corvette around the Marchbanks Speedway at Hanford, California, in September 1960. MacDonald would later die in a fiery crash at Indianapolis. *Bob Tronolone photo*

Easily the most important improvement came by way of the Q-Corvette's powertrain experiments, as well as the engine advancements used on the Corvette SS in 1957. Initially both the fuel-injected 283s offered for 1960, RPOs 579 and 579D, featured weight-saving heads with revised combustion chambers and larger intake valves. Cast out of aluminum, they helped shave off 53 precious pounds from the fuelie V-8. And, along with an enlarged injection plenum and an increase from 10.5:1 to 11:1 compression, these lightweight heads boosted fuel injection output from 250 to 275hp for the hydraulic-cammed RPO 579 V-8, and from 290hp to 315 horses for the solid-lifter 579D.

All this advancement, however, came basically only on paper, where advertisements touted this "major breakthrough in design and metallurgy" while announcing the arrival of the new 315hp Corvette for 1960. Casting difficulties quickly surfaced, as did problems with damage caused should the aluminum-head engine overheat. The "major breakthrough" was cancelled after only a few sets of these aluminum fuelie heads had become reality. Most were rejected due to casting irregularities. Left back at the drawing board, engineers then rolled out the 250- and 290-horse injected 283s for one more appearance. Production in 1960 was 759 for the latter, 100 for the former.

Despite the cylinder head setback, aluminum did find its way elsewhere on the 1960 Corvette. A new aluminum bell housing cut off 18 pounds, while a few pounds more disappeared from 270- and 290hp solid-lifter powertrains thanks to the addition of a Harrison radiator also made of aluminum. All other hydraulic-cam Corvette V-8s in 1960 used copper-core radiators. And all cars, regardless of which radiator was present, also received a spacer that moved the fan nearly two inches closer to that radiator for better cooling.

Additional changes for 1960 were quite minor. Inside, seat upholstery was changed from a horizontal pleat to a vertical (as it had been in 1958). The door panel design was revised ever so slightly. And the 7000-rpm tachometer appeared without a total rev counter, a feature previously found on all Corvettes since 1953.

But even though news concerning the 1960 Corvette was limited on Mainstreet U.S.A., there

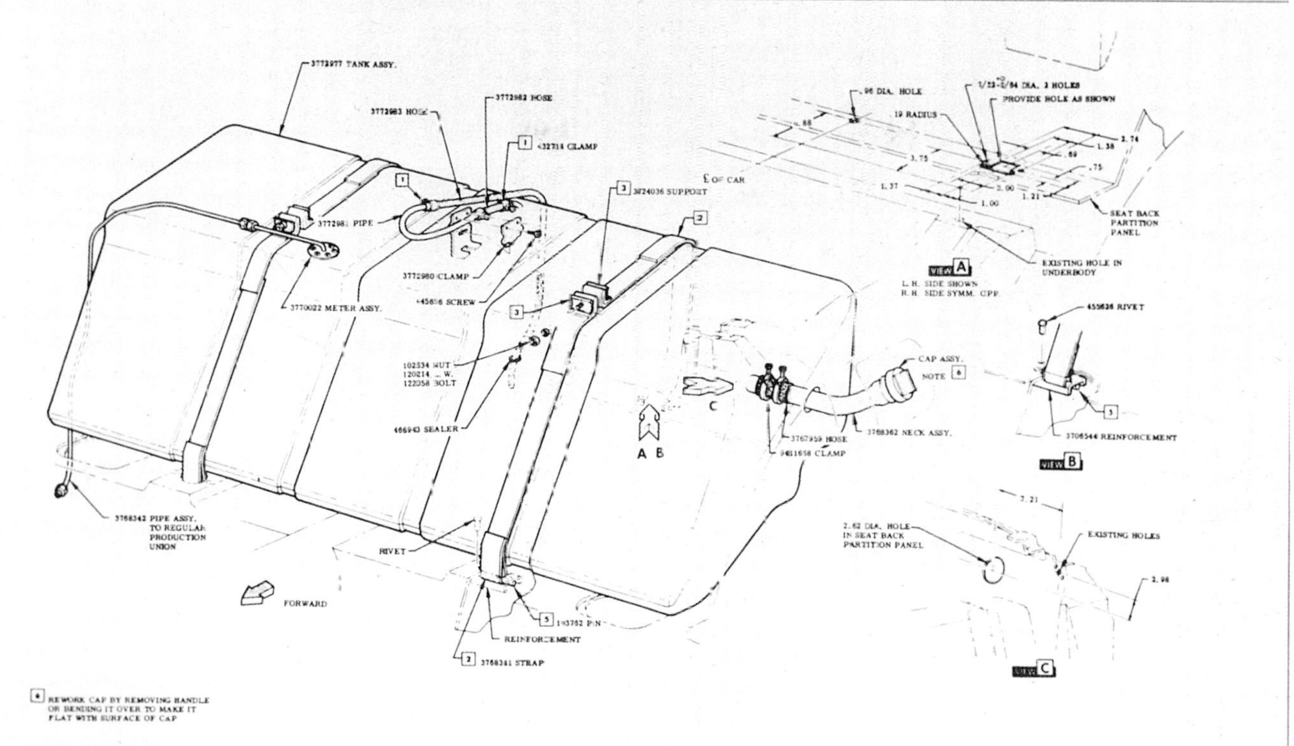

An oversized 24-gallon fuel tank became a Corvette option in 1959, listed under Limited Production Option (LPO) number 1625. In 1962, this option was redesignated RPO 488.

were big things happening overseas, where famed rich man racer Briggs Cunningham took a three-car Corvette team to France that year. A fourth competition Corvette also showed up for the prestigious 24-hour Le Mans event in June. Two of the three Cunningham cars failed to finish, although one of those did hit 151mph on the Mulsanne straight before melting its engine down after 207 laps. The third survived to finish eighth after turning 280 laps at an average speed of 97.92mph.

Without a doubt, eighth at Le Mans sure as hell beat tops in class at Sebring. And, in some respects, perhaps even an SCCA national championship. Even though it once more didn't represent a real victory, Cunningham's valiant effort at Le Mans in 1960 did impress more than one European as to the Corvette's status as a true sports car. Americans at the time were already sure.

Duntov had hoped to add aluminum heads to the two solid-lifter 283 V-8s (dual-carb and fuel-injected) in 1960, but production difficulties shelved the effort. This same design was then re-issued in 1961, this time in cast-iron. *courtesy Noland Adams*

Illinois

1961-62

Last Of The Solid Axles

The Corvette's true "father," Harley Earl, retired in December 1958 after directing General Motors' styling affairs for three decades. During that time, GM had become a leader in looks among this country's automakers. Whether it involved innovations, trends, or fads, Earl's cars from Cadillac on down were always at the forefront as far as exterior design was concerned. As for Chevrolet's Corvette, it never once failed to turn heads during the 1950s.

Keeping Earl's legacy alive would be no easy task, something Harley himself recognized fully. By 1958, he had already groomed his successor, a Pennsylvania man Earl had discovered in 1935 doing automotive sketches while working for the Barron Collier advertising agency in New York. Six months after they met, William L. Mitchell had joined Harley Earl's Art and Colour studio. After another six months, he had soared to the chief designer's position at Cadillac. His first notable contribution to GM's rich styling tradition was the 1938 Cadillac Sixty Special, recognized as one of the best design efforts from the prewar years. By the time he had returned to the corporation after serving in the Navy during World War II, Bill Mitchell had essentially become Earl's righthand man.

New emblems and a modern grille sans teeth represented new Corvette styling features for 1961. Also new that year was the optional oversized fuel tank's (LPO 1625) exposed filler cap which protruded through the sealed filler door. When introduced in 1959, this option simply included a gas cap with its grip tab bent over or removed to allow clearance for the stock filler door.

"Boat-tail" styling at the rear of the 1961 Corvette represented the greatest exterior change since quad-headlights were added in 1958.

That Mitchell's future at GM later became entwined with the Corvette's was only natural considering his taste for racing. Already informed by Earl of his eventual ascension to GM Styling's top position, Mitchell in 1956 put a design crew to work building his own personal competition Corvette, the second of the three SR-2 models (see chapter four). Later, he managed to buy the chassis out from under the Corvette SS Mule (see chapter five), using it as a base for his second "private racer," the Stingray. Work on the Stingray began in Mitchell's secret "Studio X" in the winter of 1958. About the same time, on December 1, 46-year-old William L. Mitchell was officially named to replace the retiring Earl as the prime mover and shaker at GM Styling.

Even as powerful was he had become, Bill Mitchell still had to fight off considerable flak from above concerning the Stingray. Chevrolet wasn't involved in racing, he was sternly reminded by various top level GM executives. But Mitchell was. So too was his Stingray, with more than a little support from Engineering insiders. GM Styling people, including a young designer named Larry Shinoda, had been of considerable help as well.

Debuting on the track at Maryland's Marlboro Raceway in April 1959, Mitchell's rebodied racer wore a bodyshell that borrowed most of its lines—courtesy of Shinoda's pen—from the sleek Q-Corvette project of 1957. Accordingly, the Stingray ended up predicting, quite accurately, the all-new Corvette look to come in 1963.

The musclebound machine also demonstrated a bit of what the ill-fated Corvette SS might've achieved had Zora Duntov and his men been given a second chance to iron out the bugs. With Dr. Dick Thompson at the wheel, Mitchell's Stingray roared to an SCCA national championship in the C/Modified class in 1960. Then, once retired from competi-

In 1961, racing brakes came under RPO 687, which also added a quick-steering adapter. Included in the deal, priced at $333.60, were metallic linings, vented backing plates with air scoops, finned brake drums and internal cooling "fans." Heavy-duty shocks were also thrown in as part of the package. In this case, standard linings are in place on this 1961 Corvette to prevent unwanted wear to such highly valued equipment. The correct sintered metallic shoes are shown on the pavement.

Convenience items like sun visors, windshield washers, a courtesy light and parking brake alarm were made standard equipment for the 1961 Corvette. Leg room was also increased that year thanks to a revised underbody panel that narrowed the transmission tunnel.

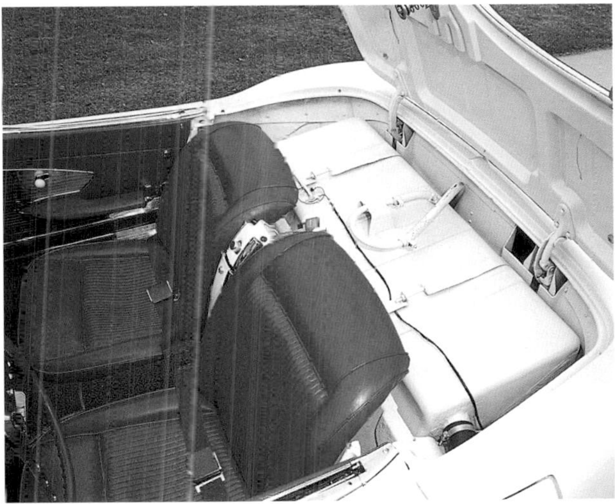

Adding LPO 1625 in 1961 also meant a customer had to order the optional removable hardtop, RPO 419, since the convertible soft top could not be installed in its typical location behind the seats.

Chevrolet had originally planned to up performance in 1960 by adding aluminum heads to the two solid-lifter 283 V-8s. Early advertisements even listed the two engines at 275hp (dual carbs) and 315 (fuel injection). But when the heads failed to make production, the standard power line-up for 1959 carried over. Not so in 1961. By recasting the same head design in iron, Duntov's engineers were able to make those power upgrades one year later. This is the 315hp solid-lifter 283 fuelie for 1961. Notice the missing ignition shielding—this particular fuelie came without a radio.

tion, the car was spruced up and in 1961 put on the auto show circuit, where it was a big winner as well.

Yet another eye-catching Corvette custom built for Bill Mitchell had appeared on the scene along with the Stingray in April 1959. Based on a stock 1958 Corvette, the XP-700 had been built that summer for Mitchell's personal use. It was a bit far-fetched up front with its extended snout and opened-up wheelhouses. In back, however, the XP-700 was quite pleasing, with inspiration for that look again coming from the Q-Corvette. Lines were more crisp, less rounded than the regular-production shape used in essentially identical fashion from 1956 to 1960. And four recessed taillights were mounted horizontally across the lower panel of the sharply creased tail. All in all it was certainly a fresh, modern-looking design.

And it was also the look Mitchell's stylists used to update the regular-production Corvette for 1961.

The new-for-1961 Corvette appeared quite similar up front in comparison to its quad-headlight forerunners of 1958-60. Changes included trading the chrome headlight bezels used previously for body-colored versions. And that bright, bullish grille with its nine "teeth" was finally retired after three years of service, replaced by a cleaner annodized rectangular mesh layout. "Corvette" block letters were also added across the nose above the grille.

From the rear, the 1961 Corvette was all new thanks to the addition of the XP-700's "boat-tail" design, which slightly expanded trunk space without increasing total length. And that boat-tail body not only totally transformed rearward impressions, but also changed the way the car expelled its bad

This somewhat soft shade, Jewel Blue, was another one-hit wonder as far as Corvette colors were concerned—it was only offered in 1961.

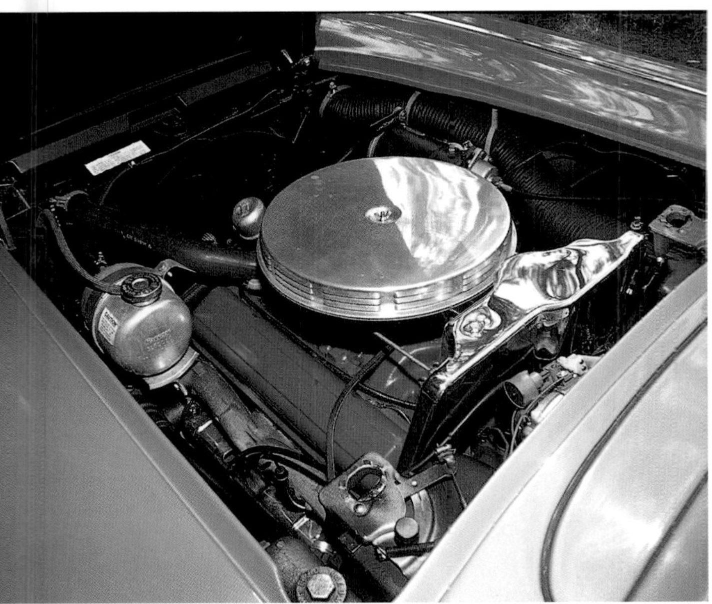

The old, reliable 230hp 283 was the standard 1961 Corvette powerplant, again backed by a three-speed manual transmission. Notice the barrel-shaped surge tank for the aluminum radiator—a new feature for all Corvettes in 1961.

air. For the first time, the Corvette's twin exhaust tips were not incorporated within its rear bodywork. Instead of exiting through the bumpers, as they had since 1956, the 1961 tailpipes turned down and dumped out directly behind each rear wheel, where, according to *Sports Car Illustrated*, "they rumble with a truly musical motorboat tone and beat a tattoo on the sides of the car you (frequently) pass."

Also included along with all that restyled fiberglass in back was a revised underbody panel featuring a narrowed (by about 20 percent) transmission tunnel. This, of course, meant an increase in interior room. Cockpit changes beyond that were minor—typically updated seat upholstery and door panel trim. Chevrolet did see fit to make the courtesy light, parking brake alarm, windshield washer and sun visors standard equipment for 1961. The first three of these features had been extra cost options since 1956, the last since 1959.

More optional power was a new 1961 feature as well. While the base V-8 was still the 230hp 283, and the 245- and 270hp dual-carb engines remained available at extra cost, the two fuel-injected powerplants were now rated at 275 and 315 horses. If these numbers sound familiar, they should, having been mentioned early in 1960 when Zora Duntov tried to add aluminum heads to the Corvette's fuelie V-8s. For 1961, these big-valve heads were simply recast in iron and mated to the injected 283s along with the other modifications previously planned—11:1 compression and an enlarged injection plenum.

Along with this power boost came new RPO codes. Since its introduction in 1957, the fuel injection equipment had been listed under RPO 579 with various alphabetic suffixes determining the various performance levels and transmission applications. In 1961, the 275hp hydraulic-cam 283 fuelie became RPO 353, while the solid-lifter 315hp variety was assigned RPO 354. Price for either fuelie V-8 remained at $484.20. Production in 1961 was 118 for the 275hp engine, 1,462 for the 315hp 283.

As for the carbureted 283s, the 245hp (hydraulic cam) version retained the RPO 469 code used previously. The mechanical-cammed 270hp 283, however, was redesignated RPO 468. Prices for these two optional powerplants also carried over, $182.95 for RPO 468, $150.65 for RPO 469. Chevrolet in 1961 sold 1,175 of the latter, 2,827 of the former.

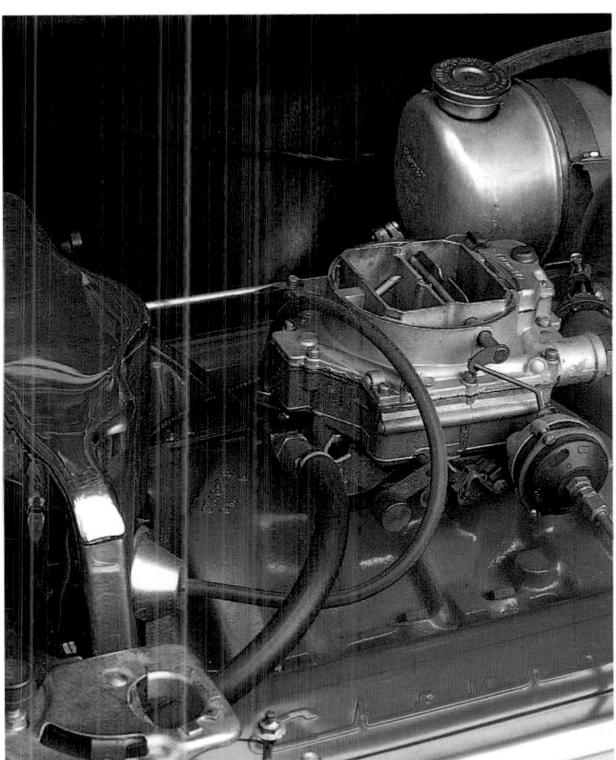

Another new feature for 1961 was RPO 242, a mandatory item for all Corvettes delivered in California. The large black hose in the center is part of a positive crankcase ventilation system, which superseded the existing practice of simply venting crankcase vapors into the atmosphere via a road-draft tube or such.

Another new grille, this one blacked out, helped set apart a 1962 Corvette from a 1961. Rocker panel moulding were also new for 1962, as was the cove panel "vent" treatment.

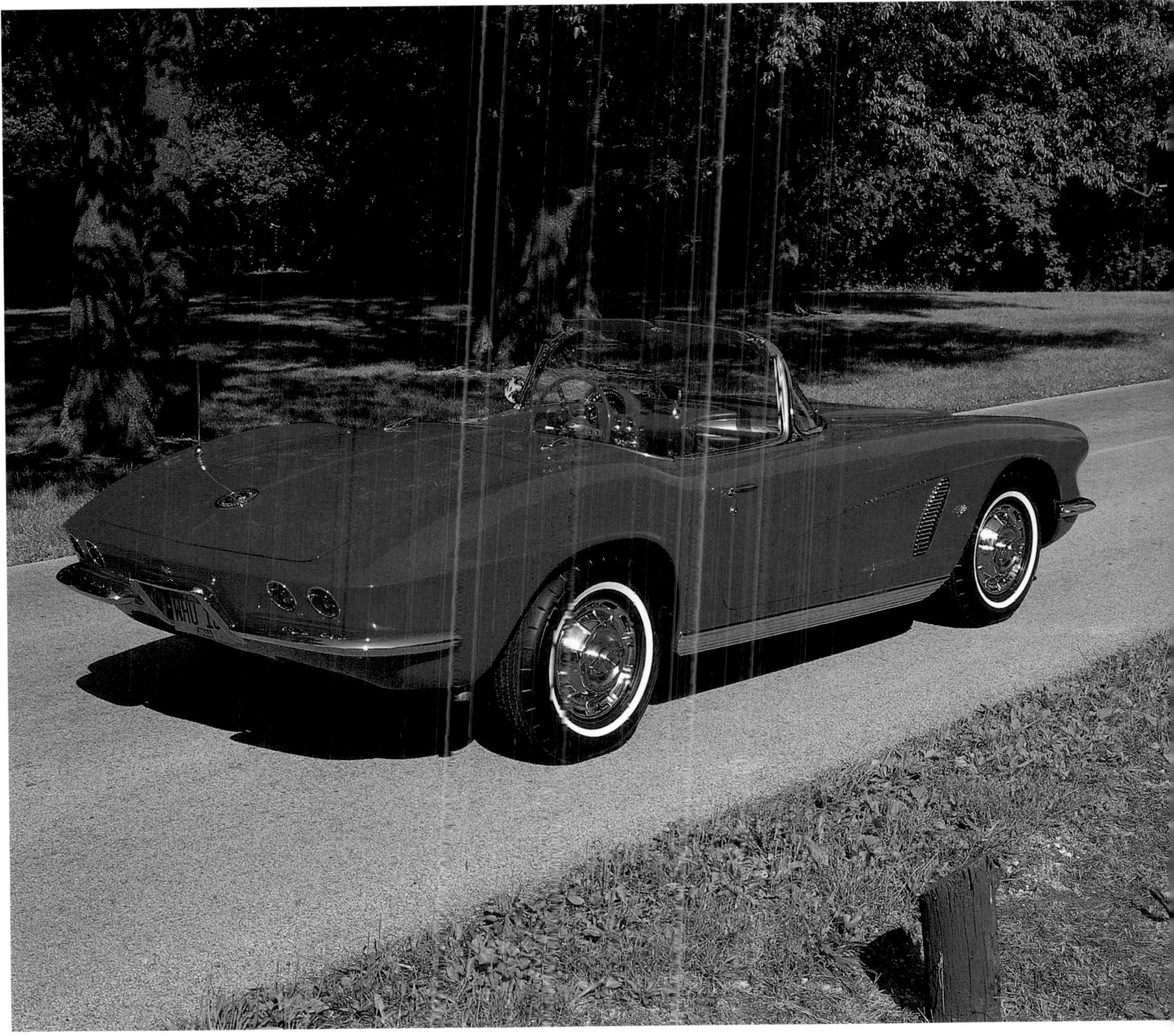

The Corvette base price went over four grand for the first time in 1962, reaching $4,038. Production jumped considerably, from 10,939 in 1961 to 14,531 the following year.

More fuel-injected horsepower wasn't the only thing new beneath the hood of the 1961 Corvette. Less weight also made big news as an aluminum radiator became standard and the RPO 685 four-speed's cast-iron case was traded for an aluminum one early in production. The lightweight transmission case saved 15 pounds.

First included along with the high-lift cam 283s in 1960, the aluminum radiator idea was revised for 1961 as a remote surge tank was used in place of an integral header tank. Looking much like a mini beer keg, this aluminum surge tank was mounted near the front of the driver's side valve cover. But not all 1961 Corvettes had this type radiator as Chevrolet first had to deal with leftover supplies of the previous year's header-tank units. This situation was explained in a factory bulletin:

"Approximately 1,700 early production 1961 Corvettes will be built with 1960 type radiators. One hundred ninety-two 1960 copper ra-

Chevrolet increased displacement for its V8 again in 1962, pumping the 283 up to 327ci. The base Corvette 327 that year was a 250hp version. Three optional 327s were offered two carbureted, one fuel injected.

diators will be used on Corvettes with standard equipment engines. One thousand five hundred 1960 type aluminum crossflow radiators, part number 3147516, will be used on all 1961 Corvettes after the copper radiator supply is exhausted. When the 1960 type aluminum radiator supply is exhausted, Corvette production will use aluminum radiator part number 3151116 on High Performance Engines and aluminum radiator part number 3150916 on all other type engines."

Completing the standard cooling system in 1961 was a temperature-modulated, clutch-controlled fan, a former Corvette option first offered in 1959.

Even with the various new standard features and its rear end makeover, the 1961 Corvette didn't go up in price all that much, its $3,934 base figure representing only a 1.6 percent increase over 1960's figure. Typically, all the same basic options available previously—bigger wheels, high-speed nylon tires, Positraction, metallic brakes, the RPO 687 big-brake/quick-steering package, oversized fuel tank, etc.—again made it easily possible to drive a $5,000 Corvette off the lot in 1961. And this prospect once more apparently failed to discourage the Corvette faithful as another 10,939 of them doled out about four or five grand for a fiberglass two-seater that year.

What they got for the money represented the most complete, most refined, best balanced Corvette package to date. And the 1961 model wasn't bad looking to boot. Even *Road & Track's* Euro-conscious critics were finally impressed.

"Once upon a time, just a few years ago," began *R&T's* review, "owners of America's only sports car were on the receiving end of constant gibes from the 'sporty car set,' which held that the only thing the beast had to offer was drag strip performance. It would go like the wind (in a straight line, they said), but it wouldn't corner, it wouldn't stop, it had a boulevard ride, and a glass body. And it took 265ci (4.5 liters) to get that performance. Well, these derogatory remarks probably were true at one time. At least, some of them were. But Chevrolet

The same basic interior offered since 1958 made one last appearance in 1962 before the totally redesigned Sting Ray came along to wipe the slate clean. Once again, a different door panel design and an upholstery remake made up the noticeable changes inside a 1962 Corvette.

engineers have now achieved an excellent package, combining acceleration, stopping power, a good ride and handling characteristics whose adequacy is indicated by the car's race-winning ways."

Zora Duntov explained this achievement to the editors of *Sports Car Illustrated* in 1961. "Originally, our plan was to develop the car along separate touring and racing lines, as Jaguar did with the XK series on one hand and the C-Type and D-Type on the other," he said. "With this in mind we first introduced racing options, then the SR2, and finally the SS, which was intended to be our 'prototype' competition car. When this project was cut off, we realized we had to approach the Corvette in some other way. Since we could no longer build two kinds of Corvettes with different characteristics, we

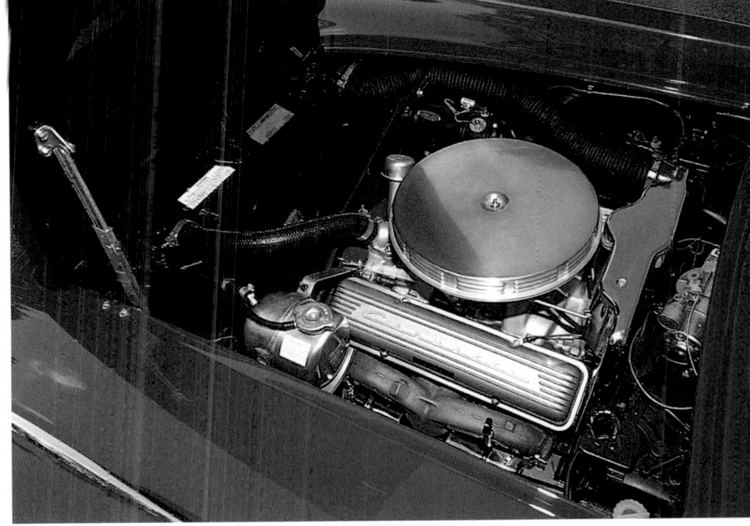

Chevrolet offered its last dual-carb V-8 for the Corvette in 1961. In 1962, the two performance options this side of the top-dog fuelie featured large Carter four-barrels in place of the twin-Carter arrangement offered since 1956. This is the top carbureted 1962 327, rated at 340 horses.

Gettin' Their Kicks In A Corvette
CBS Television's Route 66

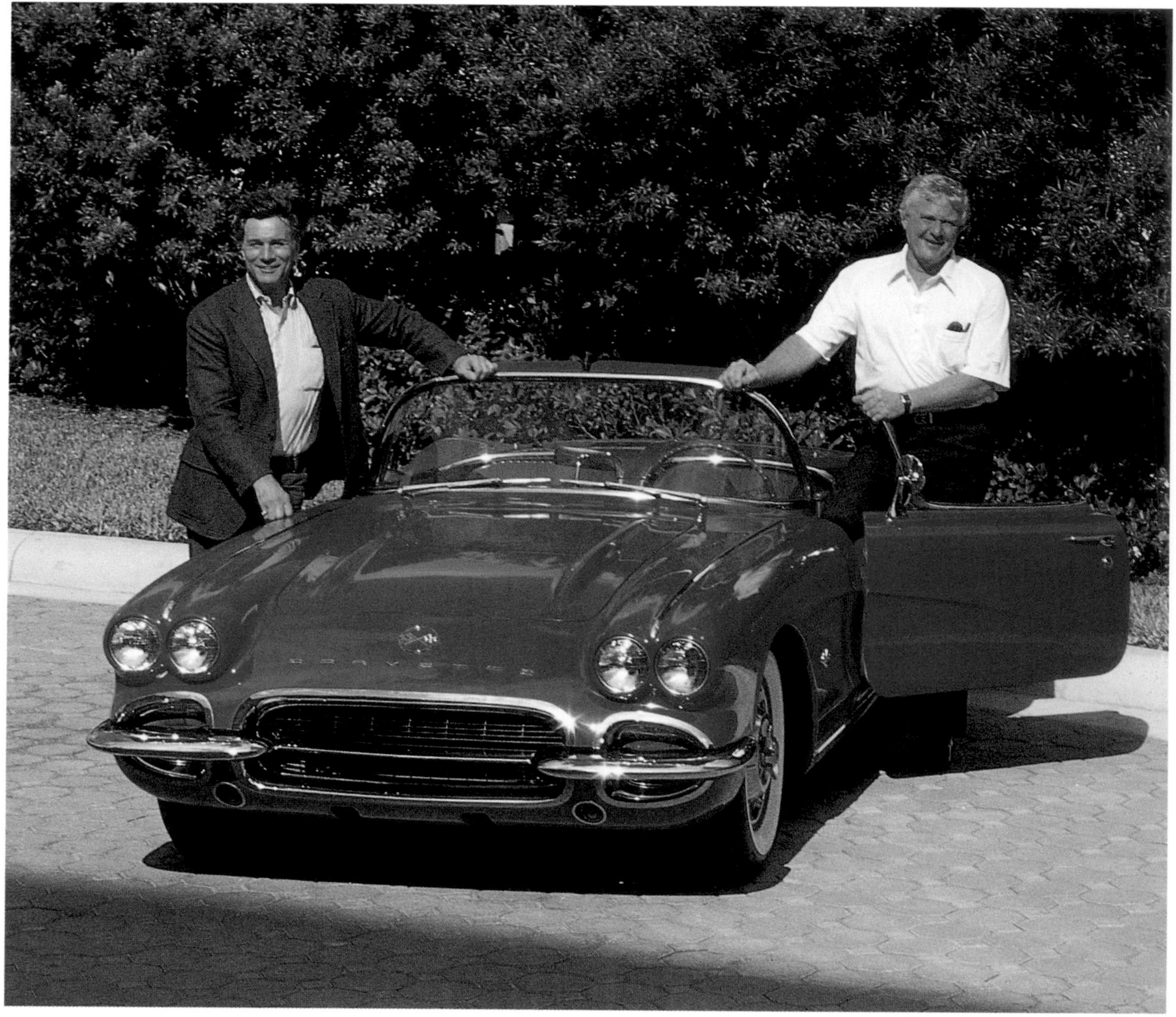

George Maharis (left) and Martin Milner of *Route 66* fame were together again during the "Route 66 Reunion" Corvette show, held November 6-8, 1987, at the Rocky Point Days Inn in Tampa, Florida. The Rocky Point Days Inn was once the Causeway Inn, which was where the final episode of the *Route 66* television show was filmed.

Nelson Riddle's jazzy hit theme was just fading out as Tod Stiles and a dozing Linc Case wheeled their way into Tampa's Causeway Inn in Stiles' 1964 Corvette. For Tod and Linc—alias Martin Milner and Glen Corbett—the Causeway Inn represented the end of the road. It was unique CBS television program Route 66 played out its final episode in two parts, with the second half of "Where There's A Will, There's A Way" airing on the evening of March 13, 1964.

For four seasons, beginning in late 1960, Route 66 had carried American television audi-

The National Corvette Museum honors both the *Route 66* show and the famed highway of the same name. Statues of George Maharis and Martin Milner are part of the display.

ences on a journey over the length and breadth of this country. What made the show unique was that nearly all episodes were filmed on location. The adventures of Tod Stiles and Buz Murdock, later replaced by Linc Case, were not staged on back lots or in studios. Everyone—actors, the director, the crew, their families—all travelled from site to site, setting up to film in the towns the scripts were written for.

"We trucked everything from place to place," remembered production manager Sam Manners, "and when Route 66 visited a city it was a big event—like the circus coming to town. In four years on the road we never paid for a hotel and rarely paid for meals." During those four years, the Route 66 troupe filmed 116 episodes, sometimes working 16 hours a day, six days a week, travelling from Savannah, Georgia, to Cascade, Oregon; from Grand Isle, Louisiana, to Cleveland, Ohio; from Butte, Montana, to Tampa, Florida. All but one episode appeared on CBS network television. Number 101, "I'm Here To Kill A King," about a political assassin, ironically was scheduled to appear the night of November 22, 1963. Network officials respectfully cancelled that episode following John F. Kennedy's assassination in Dallas earlier that day.

Producer Herb Leonard and writer Stirling Silliphant, who were responsible for Naked City, created Route 66 in the spring of 1959. The two came up with an idea to pair a poor kid from the streets with a wealthy preppie and then worked that storyline into a Naked City plot. Playing the part of the street kid was a young actor Leonard remembered from an earlier Naked City episode —George Maharis.

Once the "mini-plot" was aired, work began immediately on "Black November," Route 66's pilot episode. Although the show's "on-location" status, an industry first, was important to Silliphant, "Black November," meant to happen in the fictitious town of Garth, Alabama, was actually filmed in Concord, Kentucky, because a suitable site in Alabama could not be found. This was one

Buz Murdock (Maharis), at left, and Tod Stiles (Milner atop Tod's Corvette on the way to Garth, Alabama, during the *Route 66* pilot episode, which aired on October 7, 1960.

of the few instances Route 66 was not shot at the advertised location, fictional or otherwise. Completed in February 1960, the Route 66 pilot was then purchased by CBS.

"Black November" established the premise for the Route 66 adventures, briefly explaining how George Maharis' character, Buz Murdock, "the poor street-wise kid from New York," teamed up with the son of his boss, Tod Stiles, who worked with Buz at the Stiles family shipping business during summer vacations away from prep school. Tod's dad then dies, the business fails and the two, both with no family left, then set out to see the U.S.A. in a Chevrolet, this one being the 1960 Corvette Tod inherited from his father.

Leonard originally envisioned the two travelling in a Ferrari, but decided a domestic car better fit the show's theme. Chevrolet was more than happy to supply a brand new example. Each year. While accepting how young Tod ended up with his father's Corvette following his death was easy enough, no explanation was ever given as to how he continued to find a new model every 12 months. Ah, the wonders of television.

As for the role of Tod Stiles, Leonard initially pared candidates down to two—Martin Milner and "a good-looking kid with some stage experience." While Milner already had television experience, his rival had very little. "We liked him," Leonard later recalled, "but he had a tendency to scream every time he got emotional." Milner was then chosen over the "good-looking kid," Robert Redford to you.

Redford later made various guest appearances on the show, as did many other well-recognized stars: Gene Hackman, George Kennedy, Robert Duvall, Alan Alda, Rod Steiger, Suzanne Pleshette, Joey Heatherton, Martin Sheen, James Brown, Lon Chaney Jr., Soupy Sales, and Rin Tin Tin to name just a few. Many made encore appearances, some more than once.

Starring as well with Tod and Buz were those new Corvettes, beginning with a Horizon Blue 1960 model, followed by a Fawn Beige example in 1961. Each succeeding Corvette used on the show was brown. Maharis himself also drove a black Corvette away from work, courtesy of the show's main sponsor. He first opted for a fuel-injected model, but the sometimes harsh realities of life on backroad America quickly helped change his mind. Local small-town garages more often than not were unable to service the fuelie, convincing him to switch to a carbureted Corvette in 1961. A family man with his wife and

Stars and stars-to-be were plentiful during *Route 66's* four-year run. Here, Julie Newmar appears with Maharis in episode number 48, "How Much a Pound Is Albatross?"

kids along during location shoots, Milner passed on Corvettes, each year opting instead for a new Chevy station wagon.

On television, however, Milner was right there behind a Corvette's wheel every week delivering into our living rooms pieces of backroad America that have since all but disappeared. In Maharis' words, back then "the country had flavor." "You could drive 60 or 70 miles and find small towns with individual characteristics. Today, everything looks the same." Route 66 made a sincere effort to capture that flavor and feed it to viewers, many of whom would never taste it for themselves. So what if reality was stretched a bit. As Milner put it, "I think we inspired a lot of people, but it was a fantasy. You couldn't just drive into a town and get a good job the way we did." Maybe so, but what was wrong with a little fantasy once a week?

Apparently American television watchers didn't mind. By its third season, Route 66 had become a true ratings winner. The show "could have run for years," according to Leonard. "The people at Chevrolet and I had been discussing taking Tod and Buz to Europe after the fourth season. Route 66 could have been the first American series shot abroad." Instead, I Spy captured that honor as Route 66 fell by the wayside.

Problems began when Maharis contracted hepatitis early during third season filming. Then word got out he was squabbling over his contract. Milner was forced to appear alone as a recovering Maharis and network officials battled. Meanwhile, Buz Murdock's absence was not explained over the air as hopes for Maharis' return continued. Silliphant never did write in an end to Buz, "because we all felt [Maharis] might come to his senses and return to the show." He never did.

In his place, Silliphant eventually introduced Linc Case, fresh from a military stint, as Tod's new companion. Initially, Leonard had just the man for the job—Burt Reynolds. "But he didn't want to be any actor's replacement," said Leonard, who then chose Glen Corbett.

"Glen was a great guy," remembered Sam Manners, "and he tried very hard, but he just didn't have it."

Linc Case, played by Glen Corbett, was introduced in episode number 84, which aired March 22, 1963. Corbett replaced Maharis after a contract squabble took Buz out of the picture.

"We knew when George left the show it was over," added Leonard, "but we had our audience and the sponsor renewed us for the next season. Eventually, though, the audience got bored. It's really sad, when you think about the show's potential."

"It would be very hard today to duplicate what we did on Route 66," said Silliphant. "We were able to show the American character. The fact we were all over the map, with all kinds of people in every kind of situation, gave us a special richness. That would be difficult to show today since the country has become so homogenized. Places all look alike now—it's all Holiday Inns and freeways. Tod and Buz might not find the road so exciting anymore."

They'd also have a tough time finding what's left of the real Route 66, still the epitome of American backroads.

7
SVRA
BIGBK

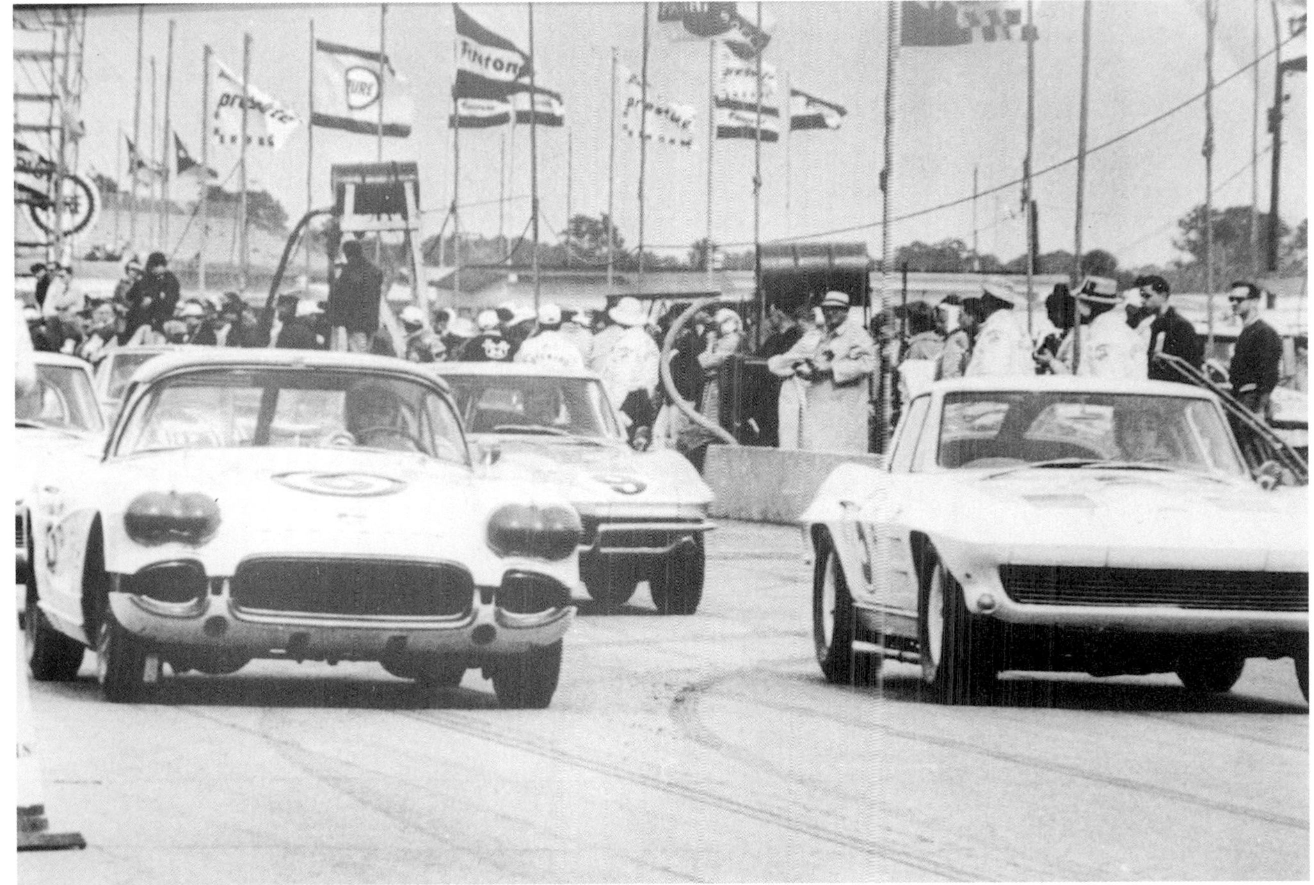
This is the #7 1962 Corvette as it looked when raced with great success by the late George Robertson. Robertson's fuelie even held its own up against Chevrolet's all-new Sting Ray at Daytona in 1963.

decided to give the Corvette buyer as much of both worlds as we could—to use our racing experience to combine in one automobile the comfort of a tourer and the ability of a racer. A big order, yes, but an interesting and worthwhile one. The 1960 Corvette was the first to reflect this thinking; the 1961 car is very similar."

SCI's review then went to call the 1961 Corvette "one of the most remarkable marriages of touring comfort and violent performance we have ever enjoyed, especially at the price."

Top reported 315hp Corvette performance for 1961 was a mere 5.5 seconds for the typically timed 0-60 acceleration run. The quarter-mile went by in 14.2 seconds at 99mph, and terminal velocity was listed at right around 130mph. Clearly, when you spent your hard-earned cash on an injected Corvette in 1961, you got what you paid for.

A Corvette customer received even more in return in 1962, the year the car's base price, at $4,038, went beyond the four-grand level for the first time. At a glance, not much changed as the same body used in 1961 carried over with only a few alterations. Mitchell's styling crew simply re-did the simulated vents at the front of each bodyside cove area and deleted the optional two-tone paint schemes and bright trim that had previously set off those coves. Minor additions included revised emblems, aluminum rocker panel mouldings and a black-out treatment for the grille.

Interior appointments were also all but identical, with restyled door panels and slightly revised seat upholstery representing the most notable updates. Heaters became standard in 1962, but could be deleted by checking off RPO 610.

Corvettes were kings of SCCA racing in the late 1950s and early 1960s, and would remain so until the arrival of Carroll Shelby's little Ford-powered Cobras in 1962. Some of those old warriors are still around, too—although it looks not at all like it did 30-something years ago, this Honduras Maroon 1962 fuelie was a very competitive production-class racer when new.

Yet another of Bill Mitchell's flights of fancy, the XP-700 "Shark," was built in 1961 based on then-developing styling exercises for the upcoming 1963 Sting Ray. The name later became Mako Shark, then Mako Shark I once the aptly named Mako Shark II appeared in 1965.

Really big changes did, however, come under the hood, where the five-year-old 283 V-8 was bored and stroked up to 327 cubic inches. Four different 327s were available, one fuel-injected version followed by three others fed by single Carter four-barrels. The costly, somewhat complex dual four-barrel option was dropped after 1961, and it would be another five years before the Corvette would again be fitted with a multi-carb setup, that being the triple Holley two-barrels found atop the 435hp 427 big-block V-8 in 1967.

With a more potent hydraulic cam, 10.5:1 compression and small-valve (1.72-inch intakes) cylinder heads, the base 327 V-8 was rated at 250 horsepower, 20 more than in previous quad-headlight Corvettes. Adding a larger Carter four-barrel and big-valve (1.94-inch intakes) heads produced the 300hp 327, RPO 583, priced at $53.80. The two top performance 327s both relied on the solid-lifter Duntov cam, big-valve heads and 11.25:1 compression. The Carter-fed version, RPO 396, was rated at 340 horsepower, while its injected counterpart, RPO 582, produced a healthy 360 horses. RPO 396 was priced at $107.60. RPO 582 typically cost $484.20. Production was 1,918 for RPO 582, 4,412 for RPO 396, and 3,294 for RPO 583.

Additional underhood modifications in 1962 included stronger pistons for the solid-lifter engines and distributor-driven tachometers on all four 327s. Previously, only the fuel-injected V-8s used distributor-driven tachs, with the carbureted cars featuring generator-driven rev counters.

Also, the Powerglide automatic was fitted with an aluminum case as weight consciousness continued. Still listed under RPO 313, the Powerglide was a $199.10 (itself, the same figure listed since 1959) option for the two lower performance, hydraulic-cam 327s only. The Corvette's fuel-injected V-8s had been limited to manual transmission installations since 1959. In 1962, a three-speed manual was once more a standard feature.

But few customers settled for that standard box. From its introduction in 1957, the Borg-Warner-built four-speed had grown in popularity each year. After only 664 were sold that first year, four-speed production made up 41 percent of the total run in 1958. That figure rose to 43 percent in 1959, 52 in 1960, and 64 in 1961. By the time the tire smoke had cleared in 1962, sales of four-speed Corvettes had soared to 11,318, representing 78 percent of total production.

For the first time, two different T-10 four-speed transmissions were available at extra cost that year, both listed under RPO 685. The existing close-ratio four-speed, with its 2.20:1 low gear, was intended for use behind the 340- and 360-horse solid-lifter 327s. A second four-speed, this one identical save for its 2.54:1 low, was offered for the two hydraulic-cam V-8s. This wide-ratio box also could've been accompanied by a new 3.08:1 "highway" axle, a no-cost option listed under RPO 203

Additional new options in 1962 included off-road straight-through mufflers (RPO 441), positive crankcase ventilation (RPO 242, mandatory on 1962 Corvettes delivered in California), and narrow

Extra body reinforcement represented one of the refinements made beneath the restyled (at least in back) Corvette body for 1961. *Courtesy Noland Adams*

whitewall tires (RPO 1832), which replaced the antiquated "wide whites" used up through 1961. And all the great go-fast options previously offered were 1962 carryovers, meaning top performance potential remained every bit as "violent" as it had been the previous year. "As always," claimed a *Car and Driver* review, "the fuel-injected Corvette engine is a sweetheart to drive."

More fiberglass fans than ever before found out just how sweet it was in 1962. With a second shift added at Chevrolet's St. Louis plant, Corvette production jumped up by 33 percent that year, reaching a new record of 14,531.

Credit for much of this increase could've easily belonged to Semon "Bunkie" Knudsen, who had came over from Pontiac to become Chevrolet general manager in November 1961 after Ed Cole had moved up to GM's ivory tower. Knudsen was no stranger to performance and racing, having resurrected Pontiac's image almost overnight after becoming PMD's general manager in 1956. Despite the AMA racing ban of 1957, Bunkie kept Pontiac heavily involved in competition-conscious performance developments. That he would continue such supposedly taboo tactics at Chevrolet was a foregone conclusion. And it was Corvette buyers/racers who would quickly benefit from his arrival.

Corvettes—most of them again "private racers" in name alone—continued to thrash their SCCA rivals on the track in 1962, as they had done in 1961. Dr. Dick Thompson's Corvettes won production-class national championships both years,

Duntov's CERV I at Riverside in November 1960. Although it probably could've raced, if GM sticks-in-the-mud would've allowed it, the CERV I vehicle served as an experimental test bed for various features, most notably the basic independent suspension layout applied in less complicated form to the 1963 Sting Ray.

This aluminum radiator became standard equipment for all Corvettes in 1961 once the supply of existing copper-core radiators was exhausted early in the year. In 1960, an aluminum radiator had been optional along with the two high-performance 283s.

while Don Yenko copped another in 1962. What better way to send off the last of the first-generation solid-axle Corvettes, easily the most successful of the fiberglass breed when it came to backing up its sexy image on the street with victorious results at the track.

By the time Knudsen had arrived, an all-new Corvette was already waiting in the wings. It would debut in the fall of 1962 with fully independent rear suspension and a sensational coupe bodyshell wearing low, flowing lines and hideaway headlights. Simply put, the stunning 1963 Sting Ray totally rede-

The top performance option in 1962 was once more a fuel-injected V-8, this time found under RPO 582. Atop the new 327 V-8, the Rochester injection equipment boosted output to a record high of 360 horsepower. Only one fuelie V-8 was available in 1962. Notice the plain plenum chamber, which first appeared in 1961. Previous fuel injection plenums had ribbed tops. *courtesy Noland Adams*

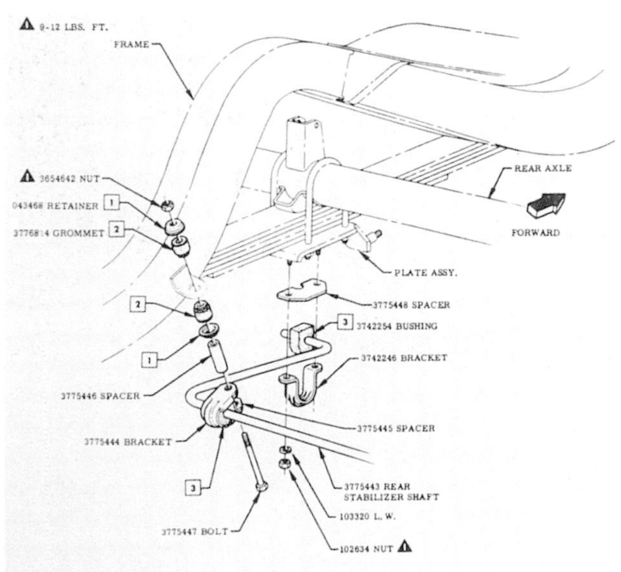

As in 1960, all Corvettes built for 1961 and 1962 came standard with a rear anti-roll bar.

fined the American sports car ideal, leaving the first-generation Corvettes to take their places as museum pieces. Then again, that Chevrolet had to produce such a superb automobile as the Sting Ray in order to supersede its existing sports car image surely represented an honorable testament to just how exceptional the solid-axle Corvettes were in their day.

Progress was the only challenger to ever leave these cars behind. Nothing on four wheels built in this country ever did. Nothing.

The solid-axle Corvette era came to an end in the fall of 1962 when Chevrolet introduced its sensational Sting Ray—for the first time a Corvette could be a coupe. Notice the attractive knock-off wheels. They were initially offered in 1963 then recalled due to production difficulties; they would finally debut in 1964.

67 "SUNSHINE STATE" 68
7W-54105
FLORIDA

CORVETTE STING RAY

1963-1967

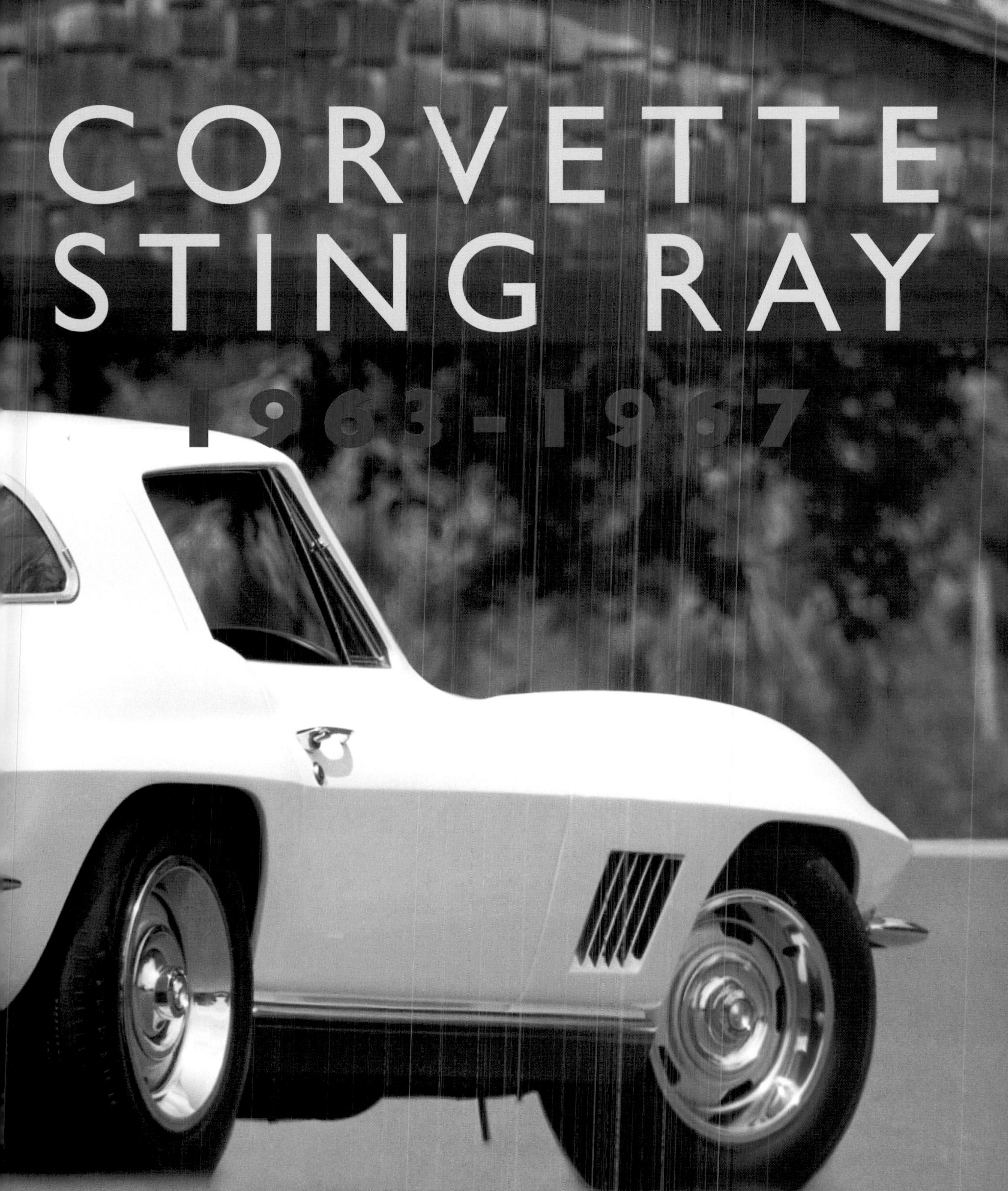

Corvette
Sting Ray

Acknowledgments

I've been a sucker for Sting Rays for as long as I can remember, even before the days when I first started making high-performance noises with my lips. Funny thing, I can't recall much of anything before the first grade, but I can still see that new 1963 Corvette like it was yesterday—and I was barely four years old when Larry Shinoda's stunning split-window coupe first hit the streets. Even then I must've had my priorities in order.

In any case, some 30 years and many, many pounds later I now find myself writing all about the cars I've loved—albeit from afar—for so long. Or not so long, considering your perspective. Not only that, but I've also been allowed to burn a few rolls of film on these lovely creations, a task that hands down represented much more pleasure than work. From any angle, these fiberglass two-seaters can be almost hypnotizing, a fact I'd filed away into the back of my Pabst-clouded brain only to rediscover it with only one look through my Hasselblad's viewfinder. Timeless? Classic? Sex on wheels? Decide for yourself—I've obviously already made up my mind.

If anything, the first-generation Sting Ray's ability to continue turning heads for five years with that same curvaceous body ought to be proof enough of this machine's claim to the gearhead's hall of fame. Most mere mortal automobiles become old news almost as soon as they hit the street, and the average American car buyer is certainly no stranger to the "what-have-you-done-for-me-lately" attitude. What did Zora Duntov and Bill Mitchell do for Corvette buyers in 1963?

First and foremost, they gave them a ride to the top of the world. Chevrolet's cute little two-seater had already salted away undeniable honors as this country's only sports car in the late 1950s—"only" was easy enough, it was the "sports car" part that the Corvette

had to earn. As for "this country's," with the Sting Ray in 1963 came the chance to extend those boundaries. Sure, Jaguars, Ferraris, and Aston-Martins were superior sports cars, but they were also priced much higher and weren't inhibited by the ebb and flow of Detroit's mass-market agenda.

That Duntov managed to slip independent rear suspension under his baby was achievement enough considering the dreaded retooling-cost hurdle ever present at every turn in Detroit. Pushing the envelope out even further by adding standard four-wheel discs in 1965 only helped reaffirm the legend of both man and machine. In its supreme form, the so-called "midyear" Corvette was a sports car that could go, stop, turn, and travel. And it could also haul, survive everyday traffic, and live long enough to see most of its foreign rivals become museum pieces—and all this for only a couple hundred bucks, plus four grand.

Of course, Zora Duntov was always looking well ahead of what reality could stand, and that's the only reason you can possibly mention "disappointed" and "Duntov" in the same sentence when talking about the

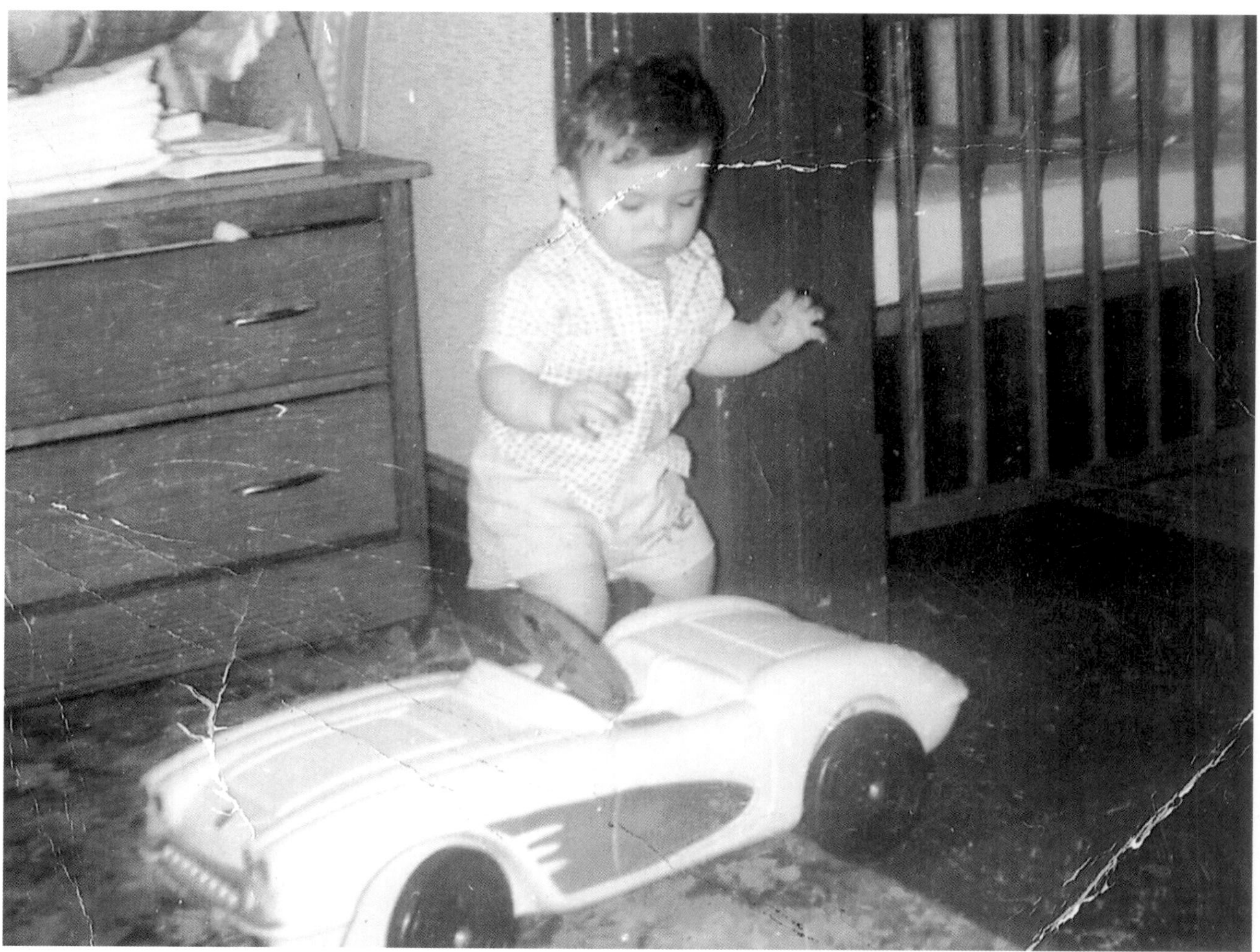

The author with his first Corvette, circa 1961. He's still looking for his second. *Nancy Mueller photo*

Sting Ray. Zora always wanted a supreme mid-engine sports car, a perfectly balanced world-beater that General Motors would never build in a million years. Looking at the car GM could build, Duntov wasn't quite happy with its weight, and there was very little he could do about its nasty habit to lift at high speeds. And adding a heavy big-block V-8 in 1965 wasn't exactly the direction he wanted to go, but it was the way peer pressure was directing the Corvette.

So what if Duntov's ideals were a bit high-minded? As so often is the case, shooting for the sky only helps raise the sights of those around you, while asking for far too much many times leaves you with more than you deserved. All this analogous mumbo-jumbo aside, the distance between Duntov's ideals and GM's production realities wasn't that much greater than the gap between the common Corvette's ultimate abilities and the expectations of most average buyers. Translation: Duntov may have wanted more than he ended up with, but what he ended up with was more than enough to thrill the typical Yankee. And it still is, or at least it is from this typical Yankee's point of view.

The first-generation Sting Rays were finally winding down their five-year run when *Car Life* magazine paid tribute to Chevrolet's fiberglass legacy late in 1967. As *Car Life*'s John Tomerlin saw it, the Sting Ray had emerged to fill needs that were uniquely American. "What was needed was an agile, responsive car, yet one that would be comfortable on long trips," he wrote. "What was needed was a high-performance, safe cornering, safe stopping car, yet one that any garage mechanic could service. What was needed was a car small enough to be road sensitive, powerful enough to blow off the (rolling living room) yet one that could be equipped with air conditioning, stereo tape deck and automatic transmission." No finicky E-type Jaguar with its cramped quarters, limited conveniences, and temperamental mechanicals would do, no sir. "What was needed," Tomerlin concluded, "was the Corvette."

As usual, putting together my tribute to the midyear Corvettes required much help from many people, all of whom deserve far more than the humble thanks I'm preparing to dish out here. First, I must take time to thank Donald Farr, editorial director at Dobbs Publishing Group in Lakeland, Florida. Donald somehow saw fit to give me my start in this business, and has continued to bend over backward to offer assistance whenever I've asked. Allowing me to use Dobbs' library for my initial research was instrumental to kicking this project off the ground. A tip of the hat also goes to DPG's Paul Zazarine and Greg Pernula, editor and managing editor, respectively, of *Corvette Fever*. Both never failed to pick up the other end of the phone line when I had a question and graciously allowed me to ransack *Corvette Fever*'s files.

Noted author and Corvette restoration expert Noland Adams also went well beyond the call of duty once I came pleading. National Corvette Restorers Society official Bill Locke down in West Palm Beach, Florida, was a great help as well. Spending a few hours with former Chevrolet engineer and fellow Floridian Bob Clift was both educational and entertaining, as has been my time with racing engine builder and Corvette collector Bill Tower of Plant City, Florida. Well-traveled Corvette enthusiast Ray Quinlan, of Champaign, Illinois, chipped in with his usual enthusiasm and helped locate various photogenic feature subjects.

Photographic support was also supplied by Melissa Garman at Chevrolet Public Relations, and I can't forget Lynn Cordaro, of Chevrolet's press fleet in Atlanta, who actually gave me the keys to a 1993 40th anniversary convertible, which I then promptly photographed with a 1963 split-window coupe owned by Ed and Diann Kuziel of Tampa. Roger and Dave Judski, of Roger's Corvette Center in Maitland, Florida, along with Roger's right-hand man, Jeff Harris, have been incredibly cooperative as well. Way to use your head, Dave.

Valuable historical photos also came from diehard Chevy fan Pat Chappell, Jonathan Mauk at the Daytona International Speedway archives, veteran racing photographer Dave Friedman, and Joy Laschober of Bob Bondurant's School of High Performance Driving in Chandler, Arizona. At the bottom of the pile was my good friend and ever-present photographic technician, Rob Reaser, who will never cease to amaze me with his all-American work ethic.

As for obligatory credits, there's my brother Dave Mueller, of Flatville, Illinois. It was Dave's able-bodied support during countless photo shoots in the Midwest heat last summer that undoubtedly allowed me to make it home alive. And speaking of those trips, they would've never been possible if my parents, Jim and Nancy Mueller, hadn't allowed me back into the old homestead in Champaign, Illinois, for a week here and a month there while I burned up the interstates in search of midyear Corvettes. Finally, there's my brother-in-law, Illinois State Trooper Frank Young, who kept my nights jumping during those trips with more Yahtzee than one human being could possibly stand. Frank, may the dice be with you.

Most important, a laurel and a hardy handshake are extended to all the Corvette owners who allowed their two-seaters to be photographed for this book. In general order of appearance, they are:

1961 Corvette, Elmer and Sharon Lash, Champaign, Illinois; 1962 Corvette, Ed and Diann Kuziel, Tampa, Florida; 1963 coupe, Ed and Diann Kuziel, Tampa, Florida; 1963 convertible, Roger and Dave Judski, Roger's Corvette Center, Maitland, Florida; 1963 Z06 coupe (silver), Bob Lojewski, Cook County, Illinois; 1963 vintage racing coupe,Ron Lowenthal, Davie, Florida; 1963 Grand Sport coupe #005, Bill Tower, Plant City, Florida; 1964 coupe (Saddle Tan), Howard and Ginny Coombs, Sanford, Florida; 1964 fuel-injected convertible, Al and Sharon Koeberlein, White Heath, Illinois; 1964 XP-819 rear-engined prototype, Marvin Friedman, Hallandale, Florida; 1965 396 convertible, Lukason and Son Collection, Florida; 1965 L79 coupe (maroon), Al and Sharon Koeberlein, White Heath, Illinois; 1965 fuel-injected coupe (maroon), Gary and Carol Licko, Miami, Florida; 1966 convertible (red), Ed and Diann Kuziel,Tampa, Florida; 1966 coupe, Bob and Linda Ogle, Champaign, Illinois; 1966 427 convertible, Sam Pierce, Anderson, Indiana; 1967 427 convertible (yellow), Bernie Siegel, Lakeland, Florida; 1967 L71 427 convertible, Chet and Deb Miltenberger, Winter Park, Florida; 1967 coupe, Ed Augustine, Clermont, Florida; 1967 L88 coupe, Roger and Dave Judski, Roger's Corvette Center, Maitland, Florida.

Thanks so much, everyone.

SUNSHINE STATE
3 - 41570
FLORIDA

Chapter 1

1953–1962

Sting Ray Roots

Forty years old and still running strong. Proving that "middle-aged" doesn't always mean on the downhill slide, Chevrolet's Corvette still stands tall today—four decades after its humble birth—as America's preeminent sports car. Rivals, copies, impostors, they've all come and gone, from Kaiser-Darrin, to Cobra, to Viper. While Detroit's latest attempt to unseat the King of the Hill does have an advantage as far as sheer brute force is concerned, Dodge's Viper roadster can't match General Motors' fantastic plastic two-seater in class, comfort, and convenience, not to mention tradition. Regardless of Chrysler Corporation's claims, a rich reputation of performance and prestige like this doesn't come about overnight.

And to think Chevrolet's top brass nearly gave up on their fiberglass roadster after only about 18 months on the road. Offered solely in Polo White with a red interior and six-cylinder power, the first Corvette rolled off a makeshift production line in Flint, Michigan, on June 30, 1953. A tad more than 40 years to the day later, car number one million—appropriately painted Arctic White with red upholstery—emerged from the Corvette plant in Bowling Green, Kentucky, on July 2, 1992, proving that at least someone at GM believed in the idea. Zora Arkus-Duntov, perhaps?

Despite the Corvette faithfuls' reverent references to Duntov as the father of their fiberglass fantasies, he wasn't even a member of the family at the Corvette's time of birth. When Duntov joined Chevrolet Motor Division's research and development team in May 1953, the original Corvette form was already cast and would roll on basically unchanged—save for the addition of V-8 power in 1955—through three model runs. Duntov's contributions didn't really kick in until the redesigned Corvette debuted in 1956.

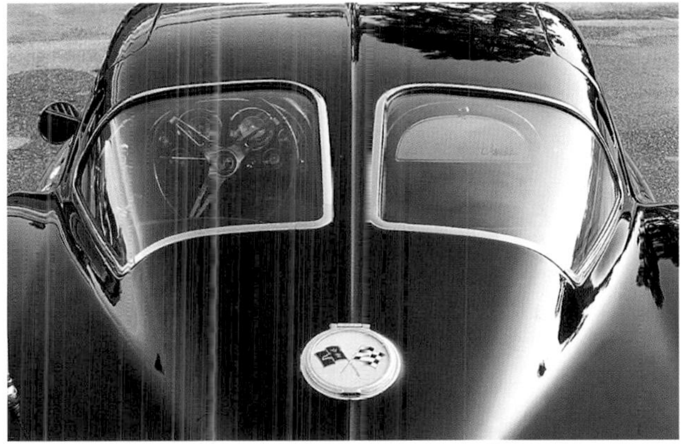

Then and now. Ten years made an incredible difference as far as the development of America's only sports car—comparing Chevrolet's first Corvette in 1953 with the stunning 1963 Sting Ray was simply no contest. Thirty years later the Corvette tradition is still running strong, a fact commemorated by Chevrolet in the form of a special 40th anniversary model offered as both a convertible and coupe in 1993.

An intriguing, innovative attraction, Chevrolet's initial Corvette turned quite a few heads early on, then quickly fell from grace. After 300 Polo White roadsters were built from June to December 1953, planners boldly projected sales of 10,000 second-year models. Actual production for 1954 reached only 3,640, however, with about one-third of the total sitting unsold at year's end, seemingly proving to many at GM that it was time to carefully consider the Corvette's fate. Although sales sunk to a mere 700 in 1955, not everyone was ready to give up and go home. It was Duntov's determined direction that helped turn things around, as Corvette production increased every year through 1966. Most notable among the many feathers placed in Duntov's engineering cap during the Corvette's early development were the fabled "Duntov cam" and Ramjet fuel injection, unveiled in 1956 and 1957, respectively.

Duntov's Roots

Born in Belgium to Russian parents on Christmas Day, 1909, Zora Arkus-Duntov took an interest in mechanics while a teenager living in Russia. By age 13 he was fascinated by motorcycles; at 14, he was at work designing a motor-driven "ice sled." After entering the university at Leningrad in 1924, Duntov followed his parents three years later to Germany where he studied at Darmstadt and Berlin. His graduation thesis paper on supercharging was published in Berlin in 1934, leading to a job designing supercharger compressors soon used on various European sports cars. From there, Duntov took a position with Mondiale in Belgium, where he penned a machine-tool lathe design. Next came work designing diesel engines for a locomotive manufacturer in Paris, during which time he continued toying with sports cars and took up race driving, a growing passion that was temporarily shelved with the coming of World War II.

Duntov joined a French bomber crew in 1939, but was grounded once Vichy France allied with its German occupiers. Then, as part of a U.S. plan to rob the Axis powers of as many valuable professional minds as possible, Duntov, along with about 5,000 other Europeans, was given an American visa and an invitation to leave France for the United States, which he and his family did in December 1940. After working a short time as a consulting engineer, Zora joined forces with brother Yuri in 1942 and opened a small machine shop in New York, an outfit that eventually became the Ardun Mechanical Corporation, Ardun being short for Arkus-Duntov. Wartime projects included various aviation components, but more to Zora's liking was a post-war contract with Ford Motor Company.

In 1947, Dearborn designers turned to the Ardun company looking for help in making Ford's venerable, somewhat underpowered "flathead" V-8 more suitable for heavy-duty truck applications. Duntov's solution was an overhead-valve conversion kit featuring aluminum cylinder heads with hemispherical combustion chambers, centrally located spark plugs, and inclined valves. Although the legendary Ardun heads did boost the flathead V-8's power, by the time they were ready for market in 1949 Ford had decided to use its own enlarged Lincoln V-8 for its truck fleet. Duntov's innovative OHV conversion kits were left to find homes in various race cars, some of which were still tearing up American drag strips into the early 1960s.

Chevrolet chief engineer Ed Cole (left) and division chief Tom Keating examine Harley Earl's Corvette show car at GM's Motorama auto show, held in January 1953 at New York's Waldorf-Astoria Hotel. It was Cole's enthusiastic support of Earl's sporting ideal that helped transform the Corvette from dream car to production reality. Having joined Chevrolet as its top engineer in April 1952, Cole later rose to the division's general manager chair in July 1956.

The first regular-production Corvette is shown here rolling off the makeshift assembly line in Flint, Michigan, on June 30, 1953. Note the plain Bel Air wheel covers. Exclusive Corvette covers were not ready in time for production, leaving Chevrolet no choice but to equip the early models with passenger-car wheel covers. Although it is not known exactly how many 1953 Corvettes left the line with Bel Air wheel covers, best guesses put the number at around 25. Total 1953 Corvette production was 300.

Although Zora Arkus-Duntov has long been hailed as the "father of the Corvette," it was Harley Earl who actually deserves the credit for the Corvette's creation. Earl, whose tenure as head GM stylist began in 1927, started toying with the idea of a small, sporty two-seater in 1951. A plaster model was constructed in 1952, followed by a Motorama show car in 1953. Corvette production commenced at the end of 1953 on a makeshift assembly line in Flint, Michigan. Earl retired as GM Styling's top man in December 1958, passing the baton to his hand-picked successor, Bill Mitchell.

Perhaps most prominent among Ardun head fans was Britain's Sydney Allard, who, in 1949, began offering Duntov's OHV Ford flathead conversion in his J2 Anglo-American sports racer hybrids. Soon afterward, Duntov sold his New York firm and went to work in England for Allard, both as an engineer and a race driver. Two years later, despite a campaign among the British automotive press to "keep Duntov," he returned to the United States, taking a job with Fairchild Aviation in Long Island, New York, in the fall of 1952. Before leaving England he had written Chevrolet chief engineer Ed Cole, hinting at his interest in a job, but received only a lukewarm response.

Duntov tried Chevrolet again after seeing the prototype Corvette at GM's Motorama auto show in January 1953. Duntov told *Hot Rod* magazine's Jim McFarland during a 1967 conversation that he remembered thinking, "Now there's potential. I thought it wasn't a good car yet, but if you're going to do something, this looks good." A subsequent interview finally landed Duntov an engineering position at Chevrolet in May. "Not for [the] Corvette or for anything of that sort," Duntov told McFarland, "but for research and development and future stuff." Once on Chevy's payroll, Duntov wrote another letter, this one detailing his feelings about the Corvette's future. This time Cole's response to Zora's words was quick and decisive—Duntov was made a member of the Corvette engineering team, where he would stay until his retirement in 1975.

Kicking Things Off

Of course, the list of prominent players in the Corvette game's early stages did not begin nor end with Duntov. Without a doubt, Ed Cole's support for the project, first as Chevrolet's chief engineer beginning in May 1952, then as the division's general manager and GM vice president in July 1956, was every bit as important to the Corvette's survival during those early years as Duntov's performance developments.

Suspension expert Maurice Olley, then head of Chevrolet's research and development department, designed the first Corvette's chassis in 1952. Body engineer Ellis Premo oversaw the initial GRP (glass-reinforced plastic) panel designs, which were then contracted out to the Molded Fiberglass Body Company in Ashtabula, Ohio. It was Harry Barr, along with Cole, who helped breathe life into Chevrolet's aging Stovebolt six-cylinder, transforming it into the

General Motors styling head William L. Mitchell (left) with legendary Can-Am race driver Denny Hulme. No stranger to the track, Mitchell had first gone to work in the late 1930s as one of Harley Earl's favored stylists in Earl's Art and Colour studio. Following Earl's retirement in December 1958, Mitchell became GM's top man in design and remained so for another 20 years. Along with overseeing development of Chevrolet's sensational 1963 Sting Ray, he is also credited with Buick's equally impressive 1963 Riviera.

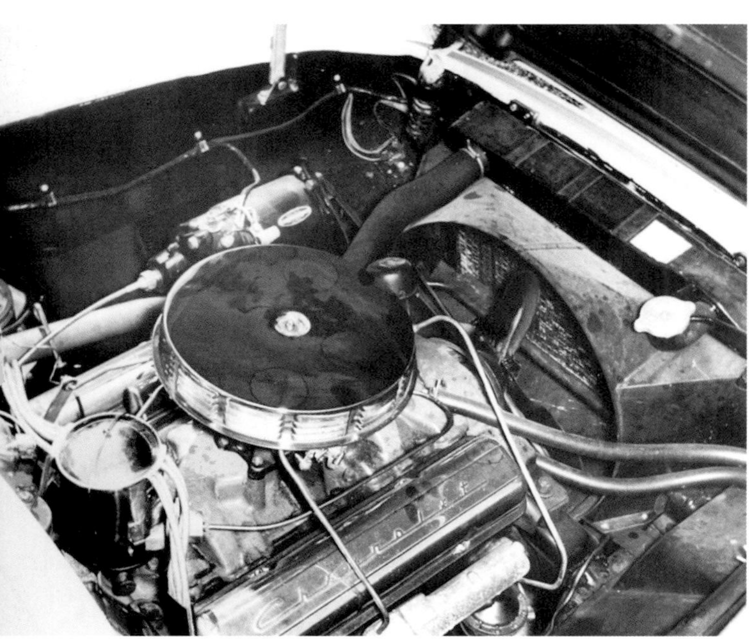

Although the first Corvettes were certainly sporty from an American perspective, many critics were not particularly fond of the car's "Blue Flame" six-cylinder engine and wimpy two-speed Powerglide automatic transmission, the only powertrain combo available in 1953 and 1954. Helping boost Corvette prestige considerably was this 195-horsepower 265-ci overhead-valve V-8, introduced in 1955. A rare three-speed manual transmission was also offered for the first time that year.

Although Chevrolet's styling crew had originally hoped to unveil an all-new Corvette shape for 1960, their plan was delayed three years while only the car's rear end was revised for 1961. Clearly hinting of what buyers would see in 1963, the 1961 Corvette's new "boat-tail" rear was basically lifted off Bill Mitchell's 1958 XP-700. Notice the exposed gas cap protruding through this fuel-injected 1961 Corvette's fuel filler door—this car is equipped with the rare 24-gallon fiberglass fuel tank, limited-production option (LPO) 1625.

Corvette's 150-horsepower Blue Flame six. And three-time Indianapolis 500 winner Mauri Rose was put in charge of early performance development.

But if any one man deserves the lion's share of the credit for the Corvette's conception, it was long-time GM styling mogul Harley Earl. As big a man as they came—both literally and figuratively—among GM's elite in the 1930s, 1940s, and 1950s, at 6 feet, 4 inches, Earl certainly carried considerable weight around the corporation's front office. Pushing cutting-edge projects through corporate red tape had never been a problem for him, almost from his first day on the job as a Fisher Body man in 1927.

After setting the American automotive world on its ear with his lovely, ground-breaking 1927 LaSalle—Detroit's first truly styled car—Earl was chosen by GM president Alfred Sloan to head the newly created Art and Colour Section in June of that year (Art and Colour later became the Styling Section in 1937). Almost overnight, Earl and his 50-man staff catapulted GM into Detroit's styling forefront, both on the auto show circuit and down Mainstreet, U.S.A. Under his direction, Cadillacs sprouted Detroit's first tailfins in 1948, and wraparound windshields became all the rage five years later. He also created Detroit's first "dream car," the sensational Buick Y-Job, in 1938, and helped inspire the lavish Motorama auto shows, which first showcased GM's dream car lineup at New York's Waldorf-Astoria Hotel in January 1949 under the "Transportation Unlimited" banner.

In the fall of 1951, Earl began thinking about producing a low-priced, sporty two-seater after toying with a pair of extravagant two-seat Buick dream cars, the LeSabre and XP-300, in 1950 and early 1951. Surrounding himself with his best people, including stylist Robert F. McLean, he somewhat secretly set out on what was perhaps his boldest venture. By April 1952, a plaster model was ready, and one look from Ed Cole a month later was enough to inspire his enthusiastic vote

A product of a very different time, the distinctive SR-2 Corvette was built by Chevrolet Engineering in 1956 at the request of Harley Earl. As the story goes, Earl's son Jerry wanted to race Corvettes and dad wasn't about to let him down. In all, three SR-2s were built: two racers and one street car. Originally criticized for being too heavy, Jerry Earl's SR-2 later proved itself after the younger Earl passed the car into the hands of Jim Jeffords, who won an SCCA B/Modified Production title in 1958. Here, Bud Gates pilots an SR-2 Corvette at Nassau, Bahamas, in December 1959. *Dave Friedman photo*

Considered to be America's best race driver at the time, Indianapolis-born John Fitch was the man Chevrolet turned to in 1956 to lead its Corvette racing effort. After teaming up in February with Zora Duntov and Betty Skelton to kick up some sand at Daytona in their record-setting Corvettes, Fitch led a four-car team to Sebring in March with meager, yet admirable, results. While Duntov was busy working on his purpose-built Super Sport racer, it was Fitch who toiled over the regular-production Corvettes, making them competitive on the world sports car scene.

for continued development. Chevrolet engineers got their look at the model in June, and from there it was a mad dash to prepare the working prototype that would inspire Zora Duntov at the Waldorf-Astoria in January 1953. As intriguing as Earl's baby appeared, his Corvette show car was almost overshadowed at the 1953 Motorama by a trio of luxurious GM dreamboats: Cadillac's Eldorado, Buick's Skylark, and Oldsmobile's Fiesta. Contrary to typical Motorama show cars, all four 1953 GM droptop prototypes ended up in regular, if limited, production by the end of the year.

Left
A standard three-speed manual transmission, more power, an optional removable hardtop, roll-up windows, and a snazzy new shell represented big news for the fiberglass faithful in 1956. With twin four-barrel carburetors, the 1956 Corvette's 265 V-8 was rated at 210 horsepower; adding the famed "Duntov cam," an option recommended for competition purposes only, bumped output to an unofficial 240 horses. Here, 24 of the 3,467 Corvettes built for 1956 pose in San Francisco.

Improving the Breed

Corvette production began in the summer of 1953 in cramped quarters in Flint, while Chevrolet officials prepared a proper assembly line in St. Louis. Missouri manufacturing started up in December 1953, kicking off a tradition that endured until August 1981, when the revered St. Louis plant produced its last Corvette.

CORVETTE

Zora Duntov poses proudly in his SS racer, XP-64, at Sebring in March 1957. Eschewing a role in Chevrolet's 1956 attempt at racing glory in Florida, Duntov saw no reason to waste his efforts on the stock Corvette with its excessive weight and substandard brakes. In his mind, the only way to beat the Europeans at Sebring—or, he hoped, Le Mans—was to specially build a racing Corvette from the ground up. With a tube frame, four-wheel independent suspension, finned drum brakes (mounted inboard on the differential housing), and a lightweight magnesium body, the 1957 SS was certainly a purpose-built racer. Overheating problems, however, doomed the car to failure at Sebring in March 1957, then the infamous AMA factory racing "ban" killed the project entirely later that spring.

Left
After receiving quad headlights in 1958, Corvettes were basically unchanged up front through 1962 when the last of the solid-rear-axle, convertible-only models were built. In 1962, one year before the totally new Sting Ray coupe made the scene, Corvette sales had jumped nearly 40 percent to an all-time high of 14,531 units. Wide whitewalls and red-painted wheels on this 1962 Corvette are incorrect.

Not long after the St. Louis assembly line started rolling, engineers began toying with a V-8 Corvette prototype in the spring of 1954. A regular-production V-8 Corvette debuted for 1955, as did an optional three-speed manual transmission, both features helping to at least minimize complaints concerning the car's original six-cylinder power and disappointing two-speed Powerglide automatic.

In 1956, Corvette news included an attractive restyle, roll-up windows, and an optional removable hardtop. A three-speed manual transmission was standard equipment behind the base 21 210-horsepower 265-ci V-8, which could be pumped up to 225 horses by adding the optional twin four-barrel carburetors. Although recommended "for racing purposes only," Duntov's special high-lift camshaft was available under regular-production option (RPO) number 448 (or 449, depending on your source). With the famed Duntov cam, the dual-carb 265 managed an unofficial 240 horsepower, enough to power a 1956 Corvette to 163 miles per hour during testing in Phoenix, Arizona. Impressive, but it was only the beginning.

Duntov knew the quickest way to the top of the sports car scene was through sanctioned competition and by 1956 Chevrolet had given him leeway to promote Corvette performance as far as it would go. In February he took a three-car team to Florida for the National Association for Stock Car Automobile Racings (NASCAR) annual Speed Week trials held on the beach at Daytona. Joining Duntov behind the wheels of the other two 1956 Corvettes were champion aerobatic pilot Betty Skelton and veteran race driver John Fitch. When the sand finally settled, Duntov had set a new sports car flying-mile record of 150.533 miles per hour, while Fitch had established a two-way average standard at 145.543 miles per hour. Skelton wasn't far behind, with a 137.773 two-way clocking.

A Fitch-led trip south for Sebring's 12 Hour competition in March wasn't as rewarding, however, a result Duntov predicted. Recognizing that straight-line speed tests and twisting, turning endurance racing represented two vastly different worlds, he wouldn't have any part of an assault on Sebring—at least not until he had a purpose-built, world-class Corvette race car capable of running long, hard, and fast with the best that Mercedes, Porsche, and Jaguar could offer.

While Duntov was at work planning just such a car, Dr. Dick Thompson, the celebrated "Flying Dentist" from Washington, D.C., was busy building a Corvette racing reputation of his own, copping the first of four Sports Car Club of America (SCCA) championships in 1956. With considerable factory support from Chevrolet, Thompson's SCCA Corvettes would repeat as production-class champions in 1957, 1962, and 1963 (he garnered SCCA C-Modified honors in 1960 as well). In June 1956, he also took a turn behind the wheel of Harley Earl's finned SR-2 racer, a

Washington, D.C.'s famed "Flying Dentist," Dr. Dick Thompson, was easily the most successful Corvette race driver in the 1950s and early 1960s. Even after the AMA ban supposedly had closed the door between Detroit and the track in 1957, Thompson continued receiving considerable support from Chevrolet, with the result being a steady string of victories in Sports Car Club of America competition. Thompson took turns behind the wheels of, among others, Harley Earl's SR-2, Bill Mitchell's Stingray and Zora Duntov's Grand Sport. He won SCCA titles in various classes in 1956, 1957, and 1960–1962.

modified 1956 Corvette built for Earl's son Jerry. One of three SR-2s produced (two competition versions, one street model), Jerry Earl's racer ended up taking the SCCA B-Modified Production title in 1958 with Jim Jeffords driving for Chicago's Nickey Chevrolet.

As for street-going Corvettes, buyers in 1957 were treated to various exciting new options, including a four-speed manual transmission and Ramjet fuel injection. Designed by Duntov at Ed Cole's request and supplied by Rochester, the Ramjet unit helped the Corvette's newly enlarged 283-ci V-8 reach the magical one-horse-power-per-cubic-inch level in top-performance trim. Along with the exceptional 283-horsepower 283 "fuelie," Corvette customers in 1957 could also add wider wheels, heavy-duty suspension, and beefy brakes featuring finned drums, ceramic-metallic linings, and special cooling ducts. A very rare oversized fuel tank was produced as well, although the few released undoubtedly went right into racers' hands.

Back on the track, 1957 also marked the debut of the first of Duntov's "dream" Corvettes, the Super Sport racer. First fashioned in clay in July 1956, the SS was intended to take Sebring by storm, and might have done just that had more time been invested in the project. Exceptionally innovative features included a fuel-injected 283 V-8 with aluminum heads, a tubular space frame, a lightweight magnesium body, coilover shock suspension, and a servo-controlled brake booster system designed to prevent the rear drums from locking up during hard stops.

Two Super Sports were built—a white fiberglass test "mule" and the beautiful blue, magnesium-bodied Sebring challenger—and both were hastily rushed to Florida before the bugs could be ironed out. SS power was certainly up to speed, as the mule proved during practice laps. Brakes, however, were far from adequate. And as John Fitch discovered during his short time in the blue SS, the magnesium shell couldn't dissipate heat like its fiberglass counterpart. All that fuel-injected might was wasted as Duntov's hopes for success at Sebring literally melted away after only 22 laps. Although Duntov regrouped with his sights set on Le Mans, the rug was pulled out from under him before the Super Sport team could take another shot at international racing glory.

By 1957, many among Detroit's auto-making elite had seen enough of the so-called horsepower race. Some believed performance had been promoted to unsafe levels, while underlying feelings questioned the logic of factory racing teams competing against their own customers running privately. Finally fed up, the Automobile Manufacturers Association (AMA) in June agreed to stop such shenanigans. The AMA statement read as follows:

"Whereas, the Automobile Manufacturers Association believes that the automobile manufacturers should encourage owners and drivers to evaluate passenger cars in terms of useful power and ability to provide safe, reliable, and comfortable transportation, rather than in terms of capacity for speed. Now, therefore, this board unanimously recommends to the member companies engaged in the manufacture and sale of passenger cars and station wagons that they:

"Not participate or engage in any public contest, competitive event or test of passenger cars involving or suggesting racing or speed, including acceleration tests, or encourage or furnish financial, engineering, manufacturing, advertising, or public relations assistance, or supply 'pace cars' or 'official cars' in connection with any such contest, event, or test, directly or indirectly.

"Not participate or engage in, or encourage or assist employees, dealers, or others in the advertising or publicizing of (a) any race or speed contest, test or competitive event involving or suggesting speed, whether public or private, involving passenger cars or the results thereof; or (b) the actual or comparative capabilities of passenger cars for speed, or the specific engine size, torque, horsepower or ability to accelerate or perform in any context that suggests speed."

Well aware of what was coming. Chevrolet's braintrust torpedoed the Super Sport project a few

Veteran *Mechanix Illustrated* writer Tom McCahill (left) checks out the new fuel-injected Corvette with Zora Duntov. Introduced for 1957, the Rochester-built Ramjet injection unit helped put the Corvette into another league of performance, though early bugs often left many "fuelie" owners on the bench. In top form, a 1957 fuel-injected 283 V-8 was rated at 283 horsepower. Chevrolet bragged of having the first engine to produce 1 horsepower per cubic inch, but Chrysler had actually been the first the year before with its 355 horsepower 354 hemi, a brute of an engine offered as an option for the equally brutish 300B luxury performance bomb.

months before the AMA verdict came down. While the so-called "ban" on factory racing and performance did cool things off considerably, GM's back door remained open to certain prominent racers. Winners such as Dick Thompson continued receiving covert factory support, and much of the race-bred equipment—heavy-duty suspension pieces, metallic brakes, fuel injection, oversized fuel tanks, and so on—stayed on the Corvette options list through the 1950s.

Duntov's Super Sport carried on, too, though in another form. Late in 1958, GM styling chief William Mitchell—who had just replaced Harley Earl at the top following Earl's retirement—obtained the SS mule's chassis, then used it as a base for a private race car. In keeping with the AMA ban, at least as far as the public was concerned, Chevrolet made it clear to any and all innocent bystanders that Mitchell was to use his own resources to campaign the ensuing "Stingray" racer, a machine he reportedly owned, not Chevrolet. As Allan Girdler later wrote in *Road & Track*, "Mitchell somehow managed to get title to [the SS] chassis signed over to him. Heck, yes, it was a political thing, and it probably didn't fool anybody but the point was Mitchell was allowed to have the best guys in the shop work on his racing car, all for experimental purposes and/or as a hobby, ho ho."

Rebodied with a sleek, sexy fiberglass shell, Mitchell's "hobby racer" more than hinted at things to come in 1963, and not in name alone. As for its abilities at the track, the first Stingray was an easy SCCA C-Modified class champion in 1960 with the ever-present Dr. Dick Thompson at the wheel.

Compared to Earl's SR-2, Duntov's SS, and Mitchell's Stingray, regular-production Corvette advances during the late 1950s were relatively ho-hum. Top engine output did increase over that span, but the same small-block V-8 (283-ci from 1957 to 1961; 327-ci in 1962) tied to a solid rear axle prevailed in typical Yankee meat-and-potatoes fashion. Major styling changes were limited to the addition of quad headlights (1958) and Bill Mitchell's ducktail rear (1961), the latter inspired by Mitchell's XP-700 prototype of 1958.

That the Corvette carried on in such similar fashion from 1958 to 1962 was grounds enough to help inspire alarm among the fiberglass faithful upon witnessing the transformation made in 1963. That that transformation still stands today as one of the most stunning automotive renditions in this or any other country's history only helps make the legend loom larger. With breathtaking styling and an excellent chassis featuring innovative independent rear suspension, the 1963 Sting Ray emerged as the greatest Corvette to that point. Looking back at the original 1953 Corvette, it was hard to believe only 10 years separated the two. And from today's perspective, it's nearly as tough to accept that the Sting Ray is now 30 years old. A timeless classic? You decide.

Although Chevrolet's movers and shakers probably relied on that same beautiful body one year too long, it wasn't like they were beating a dead horse. Even though the nameplate was used through 1976 (as one word after 1969), whether someone says "Stingray" or "Sting Ray," most red-blooded Americans automatically think of the Corvettes built between 1963 and 1967.

Z06

1963

The Sting Ray Makes Its Splash

Although it looked as though Chevrolet's Corvette was all but dead after 1954, Ed Cole and crew were, in fact, regrouping for a second shot at breaking into the sports car game. While purists scoffed at the Powerglide automatic, Europeans laughed at the somewhat thinly disguised Stovebolt six, and pampered Americans questioned the crude soft top and side curtains, Cole was busy paying close attention to what was going on in Dearborn. If any one thing saved the first Corvette from a quick death, it was the appearance in 1954 of a prototype Thunderbird, a wonderfully sporty luxury toy loaded with amenities, as well as V-8 power. Although Ford's two-seater was a different breed, Chevrolet wasn't about to be one-upped, and from there the sky became the limit. Introducing Chevy's new overhead-valve V-8 between fiberglass fenders in 1955 was only the beginning.

Corvette popularity began to soar once the Duntov factor entered the equation and a fresh fiberglass form made the scene in 1956. With that new body, a better chassis, some serious V-8 power, and a few added "luxuries" such as roll-up windows and an optional removable hardtop, almost overnight the 1956 Corvette silenced critics and brought raves from buyers. Production of America's only sports car jumped to 3,467 in 1956, nearly doubled to 6,339 in 1957, surpassed the 10,000 unit level in 1960, and reached 14,531 in 1962. GM's front office seemed satisfied with such success, especially considering the Corvette's relatively tight market niche. Duntov, however, was never quite happy, at least not as far as his goal of building a supreme sports car was concerned.

By 1960, kibitzers in this country were no longer questioning the Corvette's status as a sports car, thanks in part to several victorious SCCA racing campaigns, most notably Dr. Dick Thompson's. Nonetheless, Duntov's high-flying ideals still dominated his thinking. Winning races at Riverside in California or Elkhart Lake in Wisconsin certainly did a lot for the Corvette image, but in Duntov's mind the only avenue to real glory was the Mulsanne Straight in France, the famed high-speed stretch at Le Mans. America's sports car? Zora wanted a *world* sports car, an agile, high-powered performance machine capable of beating Europe's best on their own turf.

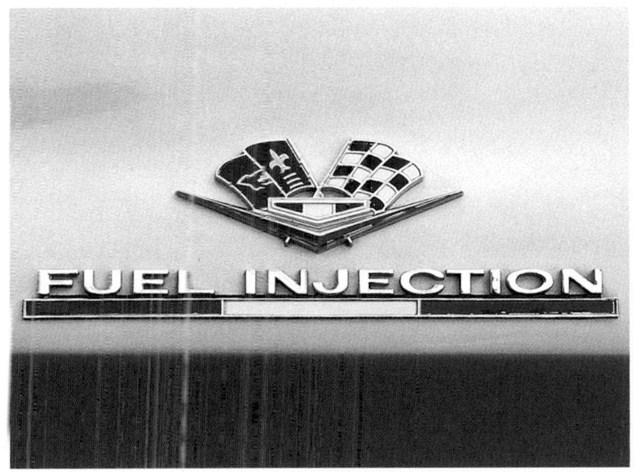

When first listed, RPO Z06 was priced at roughly $1,800. Once the oversized fuel tank and stillborn knock-off wheels were dropped from the package, the price was lowered to a tad less than $1,300. Production of 1963 Z06 coupes was only 199. The Sebring Silver paint on this Z06 Sting Ray was an extra-cost option priced at $80.70. Listed under RPO 941, Sebring Silver paint was chosen by 3,516 Corvette buyers in 1963.

Even with the performance advancements made beginning in 1956, Duntov and his engineering crew knew they could never reach such a lofty goal with the existing Corvette design. Power was plentiful, but a proliferation of mundane passenger-car suspension components hindered ride and handling, especially in back where a solid rear axle limited performance developments. Brakes never had been up to snuff, and

Corvettes had been nearly unbeatable in SCCA production-class competition in 1960, 1961, and most of 1962. But just when it looked as if the new 1963 Z06 Sting Ray would help continue the clean sweep, a little Anglo-American hybrid racer—built by Carroll Shelby—using Ford's Windsor small-block V-8 entered the picture. Both Chevrolet's Z06 and Shelby's 260 Cobra debuted at Riverside, California, in October 1962. Although Chevrolet won the first battle, Shelby quickly dominated the war. Here Shelby-American pilot Ken Miles' Cobra leads longtime Corvette racer Bob Bondurant's 1963 Z06 Sting Ray at Dodger Stadium in February 1963. This was a view that would become all too common for Chevrolet competitors as the Cobra supplanted the Corvette as America's top sports racer. *Dave Friedman photo*

weight posed an ever-present problem; not only were early Corvettes too heavy relative to international rivals, but they also were balanced improperly, in Zora's opinion, with about 53 percent of total weight resting on their front wheels. As Duntov had learned from Germany's dominating mid-engined Auto Union race cars of the 1930s, a rearward weight bias greatly assisted traction and lightened steering effort. By his estimates, a 40/60 (percentage, front and rear) weight distribution was preferred, though attaining such a ratio was next to impossible with a heavy V-8 sitting between a car's front wheels.

Although Duntov's first attempt at building the supreme Corvette, his SS racer of 1957, saw the engine mounted up front in typical fashion, its super lightweight body and tubular frame suspended independently at all four corners did represent state-of-the-art design. After the infamous AMA ban of June 1957 snuffed out the SS project before it could prove itself at Le Mans, Duntov began rethinking his approach. In 1958, his thoughts turned seriously to a mid-engined layout, an idea he would campaign right up to his retirement in 1975. (Chevrolet officials finally squelched his mid-engined Corvette proposals in 1974.)

Early inspiration for Duntov's dreams of a mid-engined Corvette came in the form of the stillborn Q-Corvette. Initially involving a Chevrolet passenger-car proposal made in 1957, the Q-code project featured an innovative rear-transaxle layout with independent suspension and inboard drum brakes. By moving the transmission to the rear while the engine stayed up front, designers at least gained ground, however minimal, toward a preferred weight distribution. Independent rear suspension and inboard brakes also

Although it was a little overdone up front and a lot gaudy overall, Bill Mitchell's 1958 XP-700 did lay the groundwork for the 1961 Corvette's restyled rear end, which in turn carried over basically intact into the Sting Ray era.

Below
Bill Mitchell's private race car, the XP87 Stingray, was built in the winter of 1958–1959 using the 1957 SS mule's chassis. Both a familiar styling exercise and a successful racer, Mitchell's Stingray was driven by Dr. Dick Thompson to an SCCA C/Modified Production title in 1960. Following its retirement from the track, the Stingray took to the showcar circuit, debuting at Chicago's McCormick Place on February 18, 1961.

greatly reduced unsprung weight, the prime negative aspect of the age-old solid rear axle setup.

Too much unsprung weight (the mass not supported by the springs, such as tires, wheels, brake components, differential, axle housing, and so on) relative to the amount of sprung weight (body, frame, engine and transmission, passengers, fuel, luggage) translates into severe vertical wheel motion under harsh driving conditions (road bumps, hard acceleration, radical direction changes). Simply put, the mass of sprung weight must be substantial enough to dampen the unsprung mass' natural tendency to react proportionally to uneven road surfaces, changing loads during cornering, and inadequate traction. Reducing unsprung weight not only helps handling, but it also greatly improves general ride quality.

Such was the aim of the Q-code project, originally slated as the new Chevrolet for 1960. Of course, the project's performance potential couldn't be overlooked, and it almost immediately became the platform for an all-new Corvette also proposed for 1960. Duntov penned the Q-Corvette's unit-body chassis on an extremely short 94-inch wheelbase, down 8 inches from the standard model, while stylist Bob McLean fashioned a sleek, low coupe body standing only 46 inches tall. Planned for production in steel, McLean's startling shell debuted full-scale in clay in November 1957. Slim, flowing, and compact with "pop-up" headlights, a pointed fastback roofline, and stylish bulges atop each wheel opening, it was a look that would survive even though the Q-Corvette wouldn't. Although the front-engined, rear-transaxle arrangement would appear beneath the skin of Pontiac's new Tempest in 1961, Chevrolet quickly gave up on the Q concept once retooling costs were determined to be too great.

Hopes for an all-new, world-class Corvette were temporarily derailed, therefore, leaving Duntov to his drawing board. He admitted that the proposed rear-transaxle layout still hadn't done enough, in his mind, toward a better-balanced Corvette. Yet at the same time, he also recognized the budgetary realities—made even more crucial by the impending national recession of 1958—common to all of Detroit's auto makers. Concerning future Corvettes, Duntov wrote the following memo to engineer Harry Barr in December 1957:

Larry Shinoda's touch was clearly present from any angle on the all-new 1963 Corvette Sting Ray. As Hot Rod's Ray Brock wrote, "those who may have seen the experimental Stingray in action the past couple of years will immediately note a strong resemblance." Shinoda had designed Bill Mitchell's Stingray in 1958, and much of that look carried over five years later. Base price for a 1963 Sting Ray coupe was $4,257. Production was 10,594.

> We can attempt to arrive at the general concept of the car on the basis of our experience, and in relationship to the present Corvette. We would like to have better driver and passenger accommodation, better luggage space, better ride, better handling, and higher performance. Superficially, it would seem that the comfort requirements indicate a larger car than the present Corvette. However, this is not so. With a new chassis concept and thoughtful body engineering and styling, the car may be bigger internally and somewhat smaller [externally] than the present Corvette. Consideration of cost spells the use of a large number of passenger car components which indicates that the chassis cannot become so small that [those components] cannot be used.

Larry Shinoda, shown here in January 1993 at the annual Corvette extravaganza held at Cypress Gardens, Florida, penned the 1963 Sting Ray's stunning lines, as he had Bill Mitchell's Stingray racer, built during the winter of 1958–1959. During his stay at GM Styling from 1956 to 1968, Shinoda also had a hand in the design of both the CERV I and CERV II, Mitchell's Shark (later renamed Mako Shark I) and Mako Shark II, the rear-engined XP-819, and various mid-engined Corvette prototypes. In 1968, he defected from GM to Ford, following his boss, Bunkie Knudsen. In a somewhat odd twist of fate, Shinoda found himself designing the image for Ford's famed Boss 302 Mustang not long after he had helped create Chevrolet's Z/28 Camaro, both cars ending up as heated rivals on the SCCA Trans-Am circuit.

Cost-consciousness notwithstanding, Duntov's next major engineering experiment ran about as far from regular-production realities as it could possibly get. With the Q-Corvette gone, he refocused his efforts in 1959 on mid-engined designs, resulting in his first Chevrolet Experimental Research Vehicle. Appropriately named CERV I (CERV II would appear in 1963, CERV III in 1990), Duntov's open-wheel follow-up to his ill-fated Super Sport made its public debut at Riverside, California, in November 1960 looking every bit like an Indy-style race car even though Chevrolet was notably not in the business of building race cars. Accordingly, official press releases diplomatically described the machine as "a research" tool for Chevrolet's continuous investigations into automotive ride and handling phenomena under the most realistic conditions."

Along with its aluminum V-8 mounted directly behind the driver, innovative CERV I features included a tubular space frame, a specially constructed lightweight fiberglass body, and independent rear suspension (IRS) with inboard aluminum drum brakes. Similar to the design proposed for the Q-Corvette, the CERV I's IRS setup—the work of Duntov and his senior engineers, Harold Krieger and Walt Zetye—was of a relatively simple three-link arrangement using the U-jointed half-shafts as the upper locating link. Typical chrome-moly tubes took care of lower linking chores, while a boxed-steel combination hub-carrier, radius-arm on each side made up the all-important horizontal third link, the point where forward thrust was transmitted to the frame.

Whether or not the mid-engined CERV I could have proven its merits at the track is anyone's guess. Despite hints at a possible Indy 500 entry, GM officials never would have allowed such behavior, leaving the vehicle to do its "research tool" thing in private. As a consolation of sorts, at least it did do that job well. Like McLean's Q-Corvette body, the CERV I's IRS pieces would come in handy soon enough.

By 1960, work on an honest-to-goodness all-new regular-production Corvette was indeed under way. While Duntov had been busy toying with his mid-engined ideals, Bill Mitchell's stylists had been hard at work envisioning a more readily acceptable future for Chevrolet's fiberglass two-seater. Mitchell, a Harley Earl protégé who went to work for the famed finman at his Art and Colour Studio in the late 1930s, had been picked by the retiring Earl as his successor atop GM Styling in December 1958. Almost immediately, Mitchell made his first contribution to the next-generation Corvette, "borrowing" much of the Q-Corvette's shape for his Stingray race car built that winter.

Young Larry Shinoda, at work at GM Styling for barely a year, was most responsible for the Stingray's stunning lines, a thoroughly modern look that Mitchell and his crew knew would become the new Corvette's image. Their first attempt to transform that look into a production reality as a facelift for 1962 failed miserably during the winter of 1958–1959. More successful, however was Mitchell's XP-700 prototype,

This April 1960 Larry Shinoda sketch depicts the CERV I racer, which debuted at Riverside in November 1960. Its mid-engine design was just the layout Zora Duntov had in mind for the future Corvette of his dreams. As it was, that idea was a dead end, but the CERV I's innovative three-link IRS setup would find its way beneath the regular-production 1963 Sting Ray.

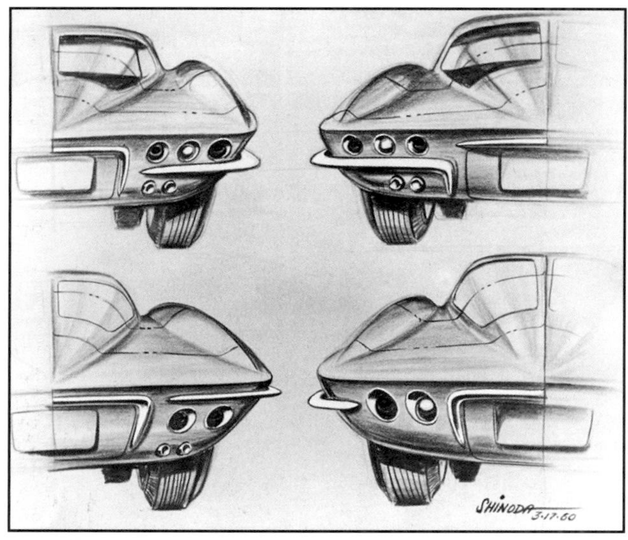

Left
These Shinoda sketches, dated March 17, 1960, show differing approaches to taillight and bumper layouts. Interestingly, the triple-taillight arrangements appearing in the top two drawings became a popular customizer's trick not long after the 1963 Sting Ray hit the streets.

built that previous summer. A bit far-fetched up front, the 1958 XP-700 featured a much more pleasant duck-tail rear end, a shape that was accepted as a standard Corvette styling revision for 1961.

That year, Mitchell also had Shinoda design yet another Corvette show car, the XP-755, called the Shark. Although many felt the Shark—later renamed the Mako Shark I—was a precursor to the all-new Corvette to come, it was actually a copy, its lines being drawn directly from the regular-production prototype already well under way at the time. XP-755 was a personal flight of fancy for Bill Mitchell; the true working model for future development was the XP-720, born earlier in the fall of 1959 in a cramped basement area known as Studio X.

Shinoda, again, did the sketchwork for the XP-720 project. And after watching his proposal for a mid-engined Q-Corvette follow-up fall by the wayside the previous year, Duntov then supplied a suitably advanced front-engined chassis to match the XP-720's wonderfully modern coupe body. Once refined, the XP-720 prototype did indeed became a production reality, with Chevrolet's long-awaited redesigned Corvette hitting showrooms in both traditional convertible and welcomed coupe forms in the fall of 1962.

"For the last five years, we've been bombarded with rumors of an 'all-new' Corvette that was supposed to be just around the corner," wrote Roger Huntington in *Motor Trend*'s January 1963 issue. "It was going to feature just about everything that was new and exciting in modern sports car design. We waited anxiously." From an automotive journalist's perspective, the waiting ended in June 1962, when Chevrolet unveiled its startling Sting Ray coupe for the press at GM's Milford Proving Grounds. Rave reviews quickly followed.

"This is the one we've been waiting for," gushed Huntington. "And it's all the rumors promised—and more. This is a modern sports car. In most ways it's as advanced as the latest dual-purpose sports/luxury cars from Europe—and this includes the new Jaguar XK-E, Ferrari GT, Mercedes 300-SL, and all the rest. The new Corvette doesn't have to take a back seat to any of them, in looks, performance, handling, or ride." Although considerable ink would flow in praise of the 1963 Sting Ray, perhaps its arrival was best summed up by Zora Duntov himself after the car's introduction to the press: "For the first time I now have a Corvette I can be proud to drive in Europe."

No stone was left unturned during the Corvette's total transformation from uniquely American sportster to world-class legend, beginning with Shinoda's sexy Sting Ray shell. Revered for its low, lovely lines, as well as its ground-breaking status as Chevrolet's first closed Corvette, the 1963 Sting Ray coupe was exceptionally modern looking, sleek, and compact, measuring nearly three 3 lower, 3.5 inches thinner side-to-side, and 2 inches shorter than its 1958–1962 forerunners. Wheelbase was also down, from the traditional 102 inches to 98 inches, and both front and rear tracks were narrowed slightly.

Even with these reductions, interior room and comfort were improved, thanks to, among other things, a lower floor and repositioned bucket seats. Although forward and aft travel of the buckets was a meager four inches, legroom was relatively substantial, more so for the driver since the engine and transmission were located 1 inch to the right. And as the 1963 owner's manual explained, "additional adjustments to tailor the seat location to your personal requirements can be performed by your Chevrolet Dealer." Backrest angle could be changed mechanically as well, as could seat height, through a maximum range of about 1.25 inches. Impressed by these surroundings, *Hot Rod*'s Ray Brock wrote: "The first thing we noticed about the 1963 Corvette was that you feel at home the minute you slip behind the wheel. Our former Corvette tests always required a 'break-in' period to get accustomed to the seating and steering. Not so this one—you feel at ease immediately. A few sharp turns later and you know you've found a friend."

Back on the outside, muscular wheel bulges at all four corners and the prominent break line running completely around the body were, by no coincidence,

Ed Cole briefly pushed for this four-place Sting Ray, a model that fortunately never survived past the prototype stage. Looking definitely ungainly on a stretched wheelbase, this enlarged Corvette earned a thumbs-down from Bill Mitchell and Zora Duntov.

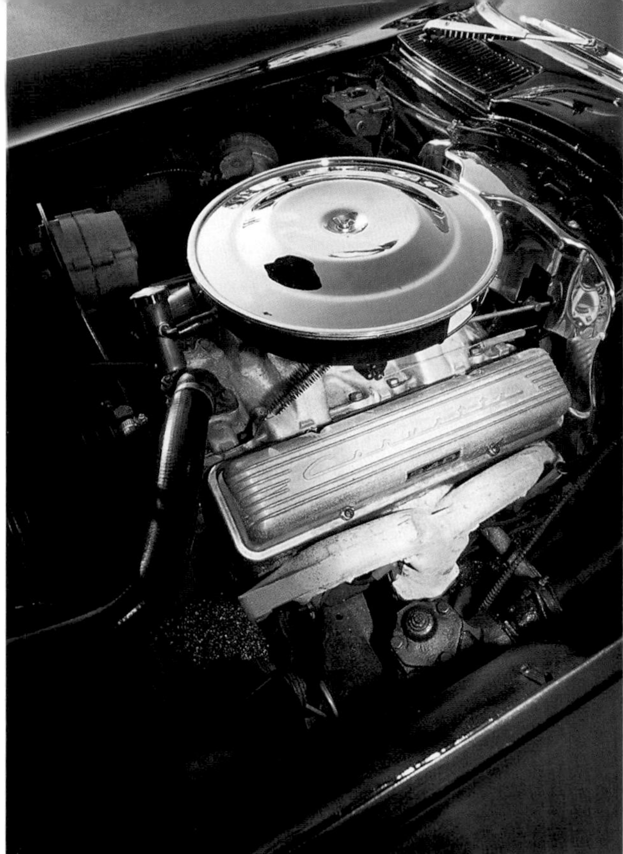

Four 327-ci V-8s were available for the 1963 Sting Ray. The top carbureted Corvette engine option in 1963 was RPO L76, the 340-horsepower 327. Sharing a Carter AFB four-barrel carburetor with the L75 300-horsepower 327 (the base 250-horsepower 327 was equipped with a smaller Carter four-barrel), the L76 had solid lifters and 11.25:1 compression. The L75 had hydraulic lifters and 10.5:1 compression. Unique to the L76 was the louvered, round air cleaner, while the finned valve covers were also used on the L84 fuel-injected 327. Price for this L76 327 was $107.60; the milder L75 cost $53.80.

particularly reminiscent of Mitchell's Stingray racer, as were the twin dummy hood vents. Original plans to make the 1963 Sting Ray's vents functional, like the Stingray's, were reportedly dropped to prevent hot underhood air from flowing directly into the passenger compartment's cowl intakes.

Q-Corvette ties were also prominent in the form of the tapered fastback roof and hideaway headlights up front. Representing Detroit's first use of hidden headlights since Chrysler Corporation's 1942 DeSoto, the Sting Ray's "flip-up" design required more than its fair share of midnight oil, with five different systems tried before a suitable electrical mechanism was perfected.

As for the tapered roof, it was an extension of Mitchell's "stinger" concept, a Sting Ray styling queue that began as a blade-shape bulge (Mitchell's "phallic symbol," in Shinoda's words) running from nose to cowl, then carried over the roof down to the tail in the form of a raised ridge. Along the way, that ridge parted the rear glass area into two sections, resulting in the renowned "split-window" theme. An obvious case of function falling victim to form, Mitchell's split-window idea didn't work at all for Duntov, who questioned its negative impact on rearward visibility. GM's styling guru, however, was adamant. "If you take that off," said Mitchell, "you might as well forget the whole thing." The stinger stayed, but Duntov didn't forget.

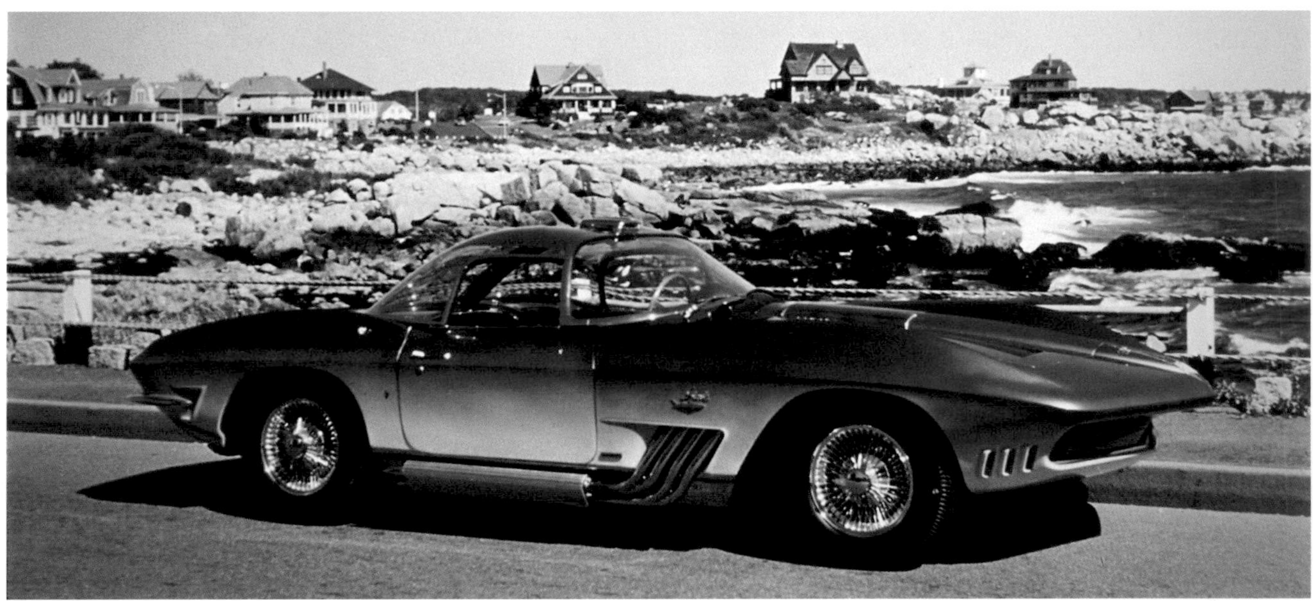

Bill Mitchell turned to stylist Larry Shinoda once more in 1961, directing him to copy the basic lines of the XP-720 Sting Ray prototype and create a personal car for Mitchell himself. Completed in a few months, XP-755, the so-called "Shark," was painted at Mitchell's request to match the ocean predator for which it was named. When Mitchell again asked Shinoda to apply a similar finish to another Corvette prototype in 1965, XP-755 was renamed the Mako Shark I as that new car became the Mako Shark II—an experimental model that led the way for the coming of the redesigned 1968 Corvette.

Standard power in 1963 came from this 250-horsepower 327 backed by a Saginaw three-speed manual transmission. Like the optional L75 327, the base small-block featured 10.5:1 compression and hydraulic lifters. Also common to both the 250- and 300-horse 327s were painted valve covers and a dual-snorkel air cleaner. Only 18 percent of Sting Ray buyers stayed with the base 327 in 1963, while a mere 919 buyers—4 percent—chose the standard three-speed manual transmission. The most popular power option was the L75 327, with 8,033 sold. Favorite optional drivetrain features included the M20 four-speed and G81 Positraction differential—84 percent of 1963 Corvette customers opted for RPO M20 and 82 percent chose RPO G81.

Shinoda's attractive new body also featured aircraft-style doors cut into the roofline to aid entry and exit. Yet another aircraft-inspired design trick helped freshen up the basic form that Shinoda had first penned five years before. Aeronautical engineers had discovered in the 1950s that adding a "pinched waistline" to a fighter jet's fuselage was a key to maximizing supersonic flight envelopes; by doing the same thing to the 1963 Sting Ray shell—letting the front and rear quarters bulge outward slightly in relation to the doors—Shinoda updated the image he had originally helped create for the Stingray racer.

From a wind-cheating perspective, however, the all-new Corvette looked more supersonic that it actually was. Wind-tunnel testing under the direction of Dr. Peter Kyropoulos at the California Institute of Technology demonstrated that, like the SS and Stingray racers, the 1963 Sting Ray was a real "lifter," as Duntov called it. Aerodynamically, the new Corvette did offer considerably less frontal area (meaning less drag) compared to its predecessors, but that age-old problem of high-speed lift caused by air pressure buildup beneath the car wasn't solved.

Nonetheless, the 1963 Sting Ray coupe body was light-years ahead of previous Corvette designs, thanks in part to assistant staff engineer Walter Horner. Stouter, yet lighter, the all-new shell featured Horner's reinforced steel "birdcage" beneath all that fiberglass, a development that helped guarantee a sure, solid feel. The Sting Ray's welded "birdcage" weighed 82 pounds, compared to the 1962 Corvette, which had 48 pounds of steel reinforcement. But its added strength meant less fiberglass was required—with a convertible version of the birdcage reinforcement, a 1963 droptop weighed 397 pounds, down 8 pounds from 1962.

On the other hand, overall weight wasn't much less than in 1962, despite a reduction in every exterior dimension, a fact that greatly disappointed Duntov. Helping make the 1963 Sting Ray heavier than planned was, among other things, the hideaway headlight system, beefier exhaust pipes with thickened walls for increased durability, a 20-gallon gas tank in

The Sting Ray frame's widely spaced perimeter rails meant the car's passenger compartment could lie down between those rails, which in turn translated into a truly low roofline (49.6 inches) without sacrificing headroom. Also notice the exhaust pipes running through the transmission cross-member (just below the steering column in this view)—a necessity to ensure ample ground clearance. Another innovation was the adjustable steering column, which could be relocated mechanically (from under the hood) in or out up to 3 inches.

place of the previous 16-gallon unit, and bigger brakes. Duntov's totally redesigned chassis may have appeared heavier, but like the reinforced body atop it, his new frame greatly improved the Corvette's rigidity without a typical corresponding increase in weight.

The Sting Ray's ladder-type frame design differed greatly from the antiquated X-member frame used under all previous Corvettes, offering 50 percent more torsional stiffness while weighing in at 260 pounds, the same as the discarded 1962 design. Five cross-members tied together the two boxed perimeter rails, which were widely spaced to allow the interior floor pan to drop between them, meaning the design crew could lower the 1963 Corvette's roofline dramatically without reducing headroom. The second cross-member from the front incorporated a pair of tubular inserts that made room for the exhaust pipes to run up close to the floor pan, a necessity as far as suitable ground clearance was concerned. Cross-member number three included a slight recess on top where the driveshaft ran above it. Member number three also worked in concert with number four atop the frame's kicked-up tail section as mounting points for the Sting Ray's innovative independent rear suspension (IRS).

IRS advantages include the obvious ability of both wheels to respond independently to changing road conditions. Depending on the design, an IRS setup also can be adjusted for negative camber, meaning the tires lean in slightly on top. Negative camber translates into better adhesion for the outside tire during hard cornering since more of the tread remains planted as the car rolls away from the turn. Standard solid axle suspensions tend to lift the tread's "footprint" off the road during hard turns as the outside rear tire is forced to lean out; needless to say, the first and foremost requirement for good handling is to keep as much tread as possible on the road at all times. IRS designs also considerably reduce unsprung weight when compared to solid rear axles, since only the tires, wheels, and brakes are suspended by the springs.

Duntov had been well aware of the advantages of IRS, having first tried the idea on his Super Sport race car in 1957. But the SS used a somewhat antiquated,

Although some may have initially scoffed at the Sting Ray's transverse "buggy spring," there was nothing funny about the way this IRS layout performed. With the center section bolted to the frame through rubber bushings, total unsprung weight was down considerably compared to the conventional solid rear axle used in 1962. A simple three-link design, the Corvette's IRS setup used each half-shaft as an upper locating link. Typical control rods made up the lower links, while the horizontal trailing arm hub carriers completed the triangle.

European-style DeDion rear axle. A more advanced, relatively simple three-link IRS arrangement was Duntov's choice for the CERV I, and it was that experimental arrangement that laid the groundwork for the Sting Ray's design.

Similar in form to the CERV I setup save for springing, the 1963 Sting Ray's IRS relied on each U-jointed halfshaft as upper locating links from the differential to the hubs. Typical control rods made up the lateral lower links from differential to hub carriers, which came at the end of a pair of boxed-steel trailing arms that supplied the longitudinal third link to the frame on each side. Space constraints ruled out the CERV I's coilover shocks, forcing the engineering team to use what Duntov called an "anachronistic feature"—a transverse multi-leaf spring mounted below and behind the differential. Undoubtedly representing the only feature a Model T and a Corvette ever shared, that nine-leaf transverse spring may have appeared out of place, but it did the job it had to do in lieu of the more expensive coilovers.

Typical full-sized Chevrolet suspension components (unequal-length A-arms with coil springs) were used up front, as they had been since 1953, to help keep a lid on production costs. But as part of the Corvette package, the standard A-arms were located differently to raise the Sting Ray's front roll center, which translated into less tire lean in relation to body roll during hard turns, which in turn meant more tread on the road. Other modifications included moving the steering linkage from ahead of the suspension arms, where it resided in passenger-car applications, to behind. Steering itself was greatly improved as the worm-and-sector steering box used in 1962 was replaced by a new recirculating-ball setup.

Sting Ray owners could also choose between two steering ratios: the standard 20.2:1 or a faster 17.6:1. Previous Corvette quick-steering options relied on a bolt-on adapter that adjusted the steering gear geometry at a point where the tie-rods joined in the middle. All 1963 Sting Rays were delivered with two holes drilled in each spindle's steering arm. Turning to the faster ratio was as easy as unbolting the tie-rod ends from the standard "setting" and moving them to the holes closer to the spindle. Steering wheel turns lock-to-lock were 3.4 for the standard ratio, 2.92 for the quicker setting. Yet another mechanical adjustment, this one found under the hood, could telescope the steering column, moving the steering wheel in or out up to 3 inches to suit the driver.

Standard Sting Ray interior features included a color-keyed, plastic-rimmed steering wheel; a 160-mile-per-hour speedometer; and a 7,000-rpm tachometer. Tachs differed depending on engine choice. The two hydraulic-lifter 327s, the base 250-horsepower version and the optional 300-horsepower L75, came with tach faces showing an orange band from 5,000 to 5,300 rpm and a red band from 5,300 to 5,500 rpm. The mechanical-cam engines, the 340-horsepower L76 and 360-horsepower L84 fuelie, were equipped with a tach showing an orange band from 6,300 to 6,500 rpm and a redline beginning at 6,500 rpm. Interior trim colors of black, red, saddle, or blue were offered. The leather seats shown here were an $80.70 option chosen by 1,334 buyers in 1963.

The star of the Z06 show was the special heavy-duty brake package included as part of the deal. Linings were sintered "cerametalix" while the enlarged drums were finned for cooling. Also helping keep things cool were internal "fans," screened backing plates with "elephant ear" air scoops, and special openings in the drums' faces.

Sting Ray brakes were improved 18 percent by adding wider drums all around. In front, the 11x2-inch drums used in 1962 were replaced by 11x2.75-inch units, while the rears went from 11x1.75 inches to 11 x2 inches, translating to an increase in total swept area from 259 square inches to 328. New brake equipment also included a self-adjusting feature (engaged in reverse) and optional power assist, RPO J50, priced at $43.05. Optional power steering, RPO N40, was offered to Corvette buyers for the first time in 1963. The N40 price tag was $75.35.

A Z06 Corvette was equipped with the top performance powerplant available in 1963, the L84 fuel-injected 327, rated at 360hp. Only one transmission, the close-ratio Muncie four-speed, was bolted up to the L84 when RPO Z06 was selected. The base three-speed was available behind the 360hp 327 in non-Z06 cars, as it was with the L76 small-block, though only fifty-nine such combinations (both L76 and L84) were sold. Notice the power brake booster and dual-circuit master cylinder at the top of the photo; it's a combination unique to the Z06 options group. Priced at a healthy $430.40, RPO L84 was checked off by 2,610 Corvette buyers in 1963.

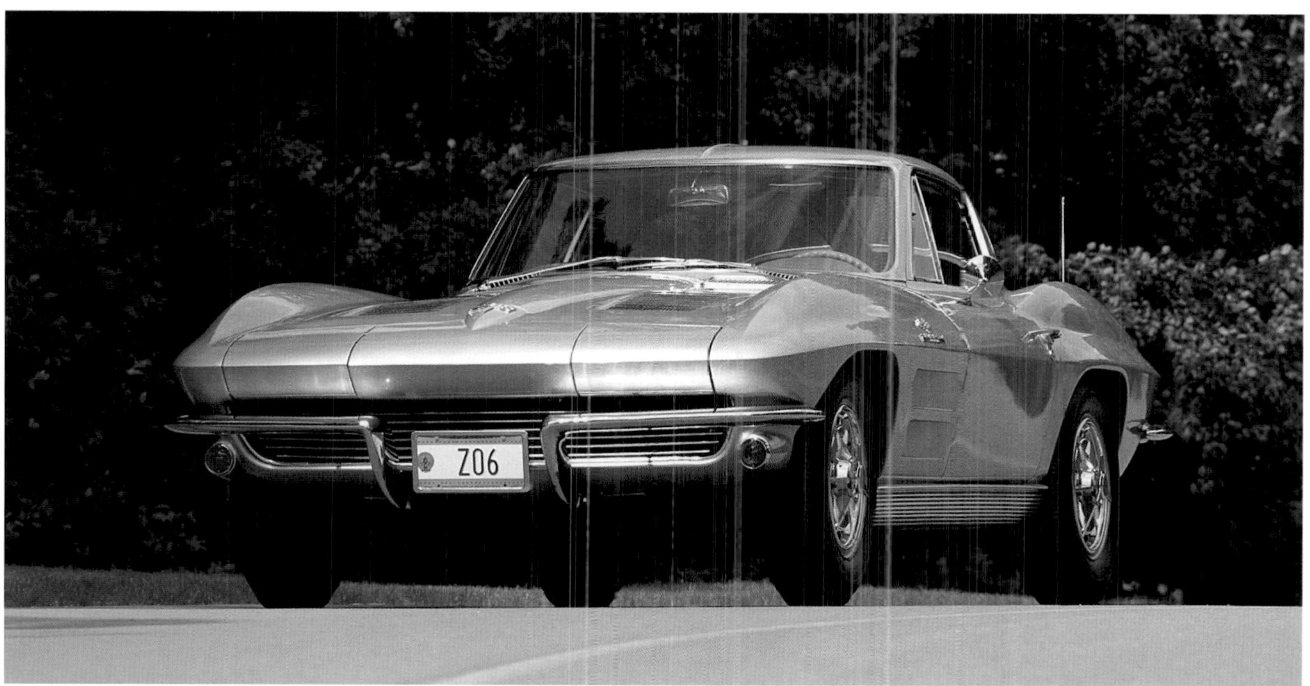

Obviously intended to go directly to the track, the Z06 Sting Ray represented the top of the heap in Corvette performance for 1963. Available only for coupes, RPO Z06 included the 360-horsepower fuel-injected 327, special heavy-duty brakes and suspension, and a Positraction differential. Early paperwork also listed the large 36.5-gallon fuel tank and cast-aluminum knock-off wheels, but both were quickly dropped from the package. While the big tank remained as a separate option, RPO N03, the wheels never made production due to casting defects that led to air leaks.

Overall, the 1963 Sting Ray chassis represented a marked improvement in every respect. Although they still left ample room for improvement, the bigger brakes were welcomed. Steering was more precise and ride was softer, thanks mostly to the reduction in unsprung weight in back—roughly 300 pounds for the 1962 Corvette's solid rear axle setup compared to only 200 pounds for the Sting Ray's IRS. The total ratio of sprung to unsprung weight increased considerably from 5.27:1 in 1962 to 7.98:1. Referring to that improvement, *Motor Trend*'s Roger Huntington pointed out that "many Corvette owners use the car as they would a Thunderbird—as a two-seater personal car. These people want a plush ride. The early Corvette wasn't bad in this department, but this new one is unbelievable for a car of its weight and wheelbase."

Even though Duntov's dream of a mid-engined Corvette had remained just that, he did manage to favorably redistribute the car's weight by shifting the powertrain and passenger compartment rearward on the Sting Ray's shortened wheelbase. A more acceptable 48/52 weight bias, combined with less unsprung mass, improved both handling and off-the-line capabilities. Not only could the new Sting Ray go around corners better than any Corvette yet, it also could launch out of the hole unlike any of its forerunners.

Contrary to all the changes made, 1963 horsepower numbers carried over unchanged from 1962. Standard Sting Ray power came from a 250-horsepower 327-ci V-8 fed by a single Carter WCFB four-barrel carburetor and backed by a Saginaw three-speed manual transmission sending torque to 3.36:1 gears in back. A Positraction differential (RPO G81) was available at extra cost ($43.05), as were various gear ratios running from a 3.08:1 Special Highway Axle to a 4.56:1 stump puller. Optional engines included three more 327 small-blocks: 300- and 340-horsepower versions, both with Carter AFB four-barrels, and the top-dog 360-horsepower variety, RPO L84, with the potent yet fussy Rochester fuel injection. Hydraulic cams and 10.5:1 compression were features of the standard 327- and 300-horsepower L75 V-8, while the higher-performance 340-horsepower L76 and 360-horsepower L84 fuelie got solid-lifter cams and 11.25:1 compression.

The aging two-speed Powerglide automatic transmission (M35) was an option behind the 250- and 300-horsepower 327s. Two optional Borg-Warner T-10

It was called "the birdcage," and its welded steel structure is what held the Sting Ray's fiberglass shell together firmly. Weighing nearly twice as much as the steel reinforcement found beneath a 1962 Corvette convertible's skin, the birdcage meant less fiberglass could be used—the pounds gained by the steel frame were more than offset by a much lighter body, which was also stronger thanks to its additional reinforcement.

four-speed manuals were also available, both listed under RPO M20. A wide-ratio M20 with a 2.54:1 first gear was offered only for the-two lower-powered 327s, while a close-ratio version with a 2.20:1 low could be mated to the higher-output L76 and L84 small-blocks. Later in the year, the Borg-Warner box was traded for a Muncie four-speed, itself also built in close- and wide-ratio forms, with the Muncie wide-ratio having a 2.56:1 first gear. Price for RPO M20, Borg-Warner or Muncie, close ratio or wide, was $188.30.

Additional performance options included an off-road exhaust system (N11)—which was officially offered but probably didn't appear until 1964—and sintered-metallic brakes (J65), priced at $37.70. Along with the metallic linings, RPO J65 also added finned drums, both features going a long way toward reducing brake fade, a constant complaint lodged against Corvette binders. Comfort and convenience features on the options list included power windows (A31), Soft Ray tinted glass (A02, windshield; A01, all glass), the $236.75 removable hardtop for convertibles (C07), a woodgrain plastic steering wheel (N34, introduced midyear), leather seats (priced at $80.70), and air conditioning (C60).

For Sting Ray buyers who couldn't care less about comfort and convenience, there was RPO Z06, the Special Performance Equipment group. A somewhat mysterious options package that went through various changes during its short, one-year run, RPO Z06 was clearly intended for one thing—and cruising the club wasn't it. Even if the first six 1963 Z06 Sting Ray coupes hadn't gone directly to top race drivers in October 1962, it wouldn't have taken a rocket scientist to figure things out.

Obviously aimed at competition venues, RPO Z06 included an impressive lineup of heavy-duty speed parts. First and foremost was the 360-horsepower fuel-injected 327 mated to a four-speed, the only powertrain combination available as part of the Special Performance package. A Positraction differential, special heavy-duty power brakes, heavy-duty suspension, an oversized 36.5-gallon fiberglass fuel tank, and five cast-aluminum knock-off wheels completed the deal, at least at first.

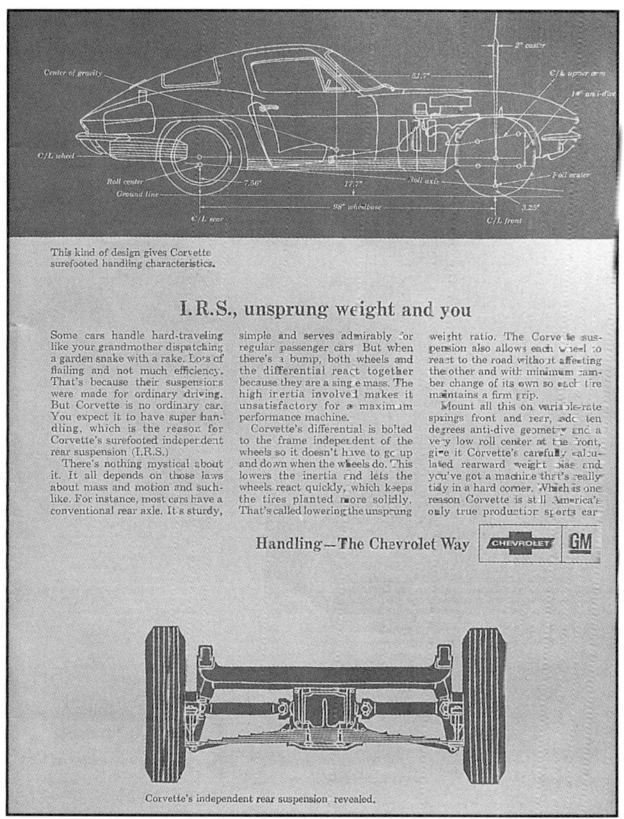

C/L wheel
Roll center
Ground line
7.56"
17.7"
Roll axis
98" wheelbase
3.25"
C/L rear
C/L front
This kind of design gives Corvette surefooted handling characteristics.
I.R.S., unsprung weight and you
Some cars handle hard-traveling like your grandmother dispatching a garden snake with a rake. Lots of flailing and not much efficiency. That's because their suspensions were made for ordinary driving. But Corvette is no ordinary car. You expect it to have super handling, which is the reason for Corvette's surefooted independent rear suspension (I.R.S.)
There's nothing mystical about it. It all depends on those laws about mass and motion and suchlike. For instance, most cars have a conventional rear axle. It's sturdy, simple and serves admirably for regular passenger cars But when there's a bump, both wheels and the differential react together because they are a single mass. The high inertia involved makes it unsatisfactory for a maximum performance machine.
Corvette's differential is bolted to the frame independent of the wheels so it doesn't have to go up and down when the wheels do. This lowers the inertia and lets the wheels react quickly, which keeps the tires planted more solidly. That's called lowering the unsprung weight ratio. The Corvette suspension also allows each wheel to react to the road without affecting the other and with minimum camber change of its own so each tire maintains a firm grip.
Mount all this on variable-rate springs front and rear, add ten degrees anti-dive geometry and a very low roll center at the front, give it Corvette's carefully calculated rearward weight bias and you've got a machine that's really tidy in a hard corner. Which is one reason Corvette is still America's only true production sports car
Handling—The Chevrolet Way
CHEVROLET
GM
Corvette's independent rear suspension revealed.

No, not that IRS; this acronym referred to the Sting Ray's innovative independent rear suspension, a design that helped cut unsprung weight in back by 33 percent. Save for springing, the Corvette's IRS setup was basically a copy of the design used three years before on Duntov's CERV I experimental open-wheeled racer.

Most notable among that group was the brake system, beginning with the vacuum-assisted, dual-circuit master cylinder, a unit unique to the Z06 application, It was not the standard J50 power brake setup, as some have mistakenly concluded. Also contrary to common claims, the brakes themselves were not the J65 sintered-metallic pieces either. Z06 brake linings were sintered "cerametalix" and the shoes measured 11.75 inches long, compared to the J65's 11-inch shoes. And since engineers logically concluded that Z06 Sting Rays would spend most of their time on a track, where most drivers, it is hoped, never used reverse, the automatic adjusting feature new to Corvette brakes for 1963 was modified to work with the car in forward motion, as opposed to the standard setup that was activated while backing up.

Like the J65 equipment, the Z06 cast-iron drums were finned for cooling, but efforts were made to help dissipate heat even further. Z06 backing plates were vented with screened openings allowing cooling air to enter the drum, where a fan mounted on the wheel hub helped keep the flow going. Rubber scoops, affectionately known as "elephant's ears," were attached to the backing plates to direct cool breezes into the fire. A Corvette performance option that dated back to 1957, elephant ears were delivered in a box inside a new 1963 Z06 Sting Ray, along with instructions on how to make the installation.

Heavy-duty Z06 suspension components included stiffer shocks, beefier springs, and a thick 0.94-inch front stabilizer bar. The attractive, aluminum knock-off rims—reportedly the result of Corvette racer and Gulf Oil executive Grady Davis' request for a quick-change road-racing wheel—measured 15x6 inches and included a special hub adapter that allowed attachment by a single three-pronged, threaded spinner (early prototypes used a two-eared spinner) in place of the typical five lugs.

Soon to be all the rage among the Corvette elite, the distinctive knock-offs (RPO P48) proved troublesome to produce early on and couldn't hold a tire seal. Dealers were forced to turn down requests for the $322.80 option and controversy still exists concerning how many 1963 Corvettes rolled off the lot with factory-installed P48 wheels. It is known that roughly a dozen pilot installations were attempted in St. Louis, but a regular-production example sold to the public has yet to be documented.

As it was, both the P48 wheels and oversized fuel tank were dropped from the Z06 lineup in December 1962 in a move to bring the option's initial hefty asking price of $1,818.14—almost half of the 1963 Corvette's base sticker—down to a more palatable $1,295. Adjusting the lineup also served to make the Z06 Sting Ray more attractive to brave nonracers who wanted to drive it on the street, as they then weren't forced to trade luggage space for the big fiberglass tank that had previously intruded into the cockpit area. Although no longer included as part of the Special Performance package, Z06 customers and standard Sting Ray fans could still order the 36.5-gallon tank since it remained available (for coupes only) as RPO N03, priced at a somewhat hefty $202.30. Incomplete factory records (actual production undoubtedly was higher) show sales of 63 N03 big tanks, both for competition purposes and some obvious nonracing applications where owners simply wanted extended range for long trips.

Not all successful Corvette racers built in 1963 were high-profile Z06 models. This coupe was originally equipped with a 340-horsepower 327 and saw regular street service until its original owner decided to put it to work on autocross circuits and in hillclimbs in Washington and Oregon beginning in 1965. Five years later, he went one step further, entering the car in SCCA B/Production competition. Today, this independent competition veteran is still proving itself in vintage racing events.

Right
Even though Chevrolet prognosticators had predicted the new Sting Ray coupe would dominate 1963 production, convertible sales picked up considerably late in the year, and the topless cars eventually overtook their closed counterparts. Total convertible production for 1963 was 10,919. Base price was $4,037. An optional removable hardtop, RPO C07, was also available and could be ordered at no extra cost if the folding-top mechanism was deleted. Ordering RPO C07 with the folding top meant a buyer had to fork over an additional $236.75. In all, 5,739 Corvette convertible customers checked off RPO C07, including 1,099 who simply traded the soft top for the clamp-down roof. Original rubber in this case has long since been replaced by modern radials. Standard tires for 1963 were 6.70x15-inch four-ply rayon blackwalls. Two 6.70x15-inch tires were available at extra cost: the $15.70 P91 four-ply nylon blackwall and the $31.85 P92 four-ply rayon whitewall. P92 production dominated at 19,877 sets sold.

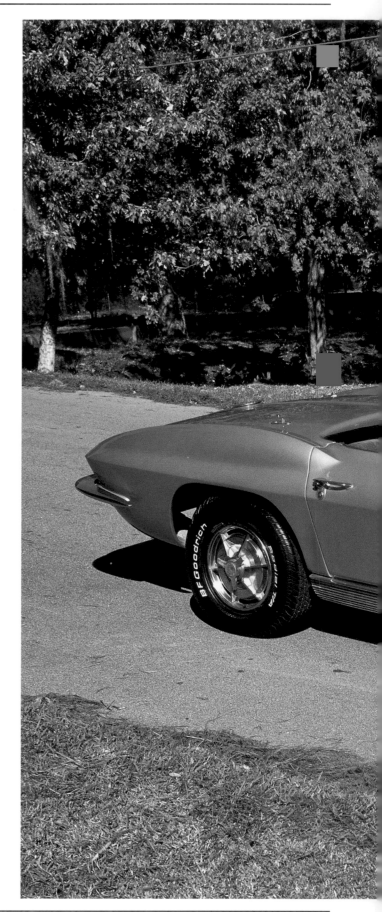

Another December 1962 change in the Z06 package involved model availability. Originally offered only with Model 837 coupes, RPO Z06 was also officially listed as an option for Model 867 convertibles for the first time in a distribution bulletin dated December 14. Although rumors of one Z06 convertible have floated about for years, no record of such a mating exists. Total Z06 coupe production was 199, with probably less than half of those surviving today as highly valued examples of just how hot a Corvette could get in 1963.

Even in standard trim, the 1963 Sting Ray was no slouch when it came to turning heads, either in motion or while standing still. Requests for the all-new models, *any* model, quickly swamped dealers in the fall of 1962 as soon as word got around.

"For the first time in its 10-year history," wrote *Motor Trend's* Jim Wright, "the Corvette is in such demand that the factory has had to put on a second shift and still can't begin to supply cars fast enough. The waiting period is at least 60 days, and dealers won't 'deal' a bit on either coupes or roadsters. Both are going for the full sticker price, with absolutely no discount and very little (if any) over-allowance on trade-ins." Total Corvette production

BFGoodrich
Radial T/A

Offered only for the base 250-horsepower 327 and the 300-horsepower L75, the M35 Powerglide automatic transmission is shown here in a 1963 prototype installation. Missing in this photo are the two oil cooler lines that normally ran from the Powerglide case's right side near where the dipstick tube appears from behind the transmission's ribbed center section.

Below
This prototype photo shows the 1963 Corvette's base Saginaw three-speed manual transmission. Among other things, the shift rod layout differed in regular production. Although originally listed behind all Sting Ray powerplants for 1963, the undesirable three-speed box was later dropped from the availability list for the top-two performance powerplants early in 1964 production.

for 1963 topped 20,000 for the first time, with a near equal balance between the two bodystyles. After coupes started off the year as the hot ticket, convertible sales later caught up and passed them. In the end, coupes numbered 10,594, convertibles 10,919.

Driving a coupe or convertible, *Car Life*'s staff was so impressed with the Sting Ray, they awarded it their Award for Engineering Excellence based on the fact that the Corvette had finally "achieved the refinement needed to match its great brute strength." Continued *Car Life*'s report, "the Sting Ray represents leadership in automotive design. It is tomorrow's car, on the street today."

Road & Track's curbside critics were especially fond of the Sting Ray's IRS advantage, especially compared to what came before. "The tendency for the [earlier Corvette's] rear wheels to spin freely on acceleration and for the rear end to come sliding around rather quickly during hard cornering was always there. Chevrolet engineers had done a good job with what they had at hand, but there just wasn't enough with which to work. That production-component live rear axle could hop and dance like an Apache with a hot foot." Three years after they had last tested a Corvette, *Road & Track*'s staff couldn't say enough about the way the redesigned 1963 model handled the road. "In a word, the new Sting Ray sticks! Whether you slam the car through an S-bend at 85 or pop the clutch at 5000 rpm at the drag strip, the result is the same—great gripping gobs of traction."

Car Life's editors couldn't agree more. "Tricky, twisting roads are this Corvette's meat," read their December 1962 report. "With its new suspension it seems to lock onto them, going precisely where directed and sticking to the tightest corners without the shadow of a doubt. Where the old Corvette had an annoying penchant for swapping ends when cornered vigorously, the new one just sticks and storms. This suspension is the best thing since gumdrops!"

Jim Wright liked the way the Sting Ray stopped, once the sintered-metallic linings were in place and working. Explaining that "the car really deserves" discs, Wright at first pointed out that the standard drums were a bit lacking. "Sintered iron brake linings are optional and will certainly be found necessary for anyone planning to race, as fade is easily provoked with the standard linings, although the cooling-off period required to restore full efficiency is very short." As for the J65 brakes, "it's true that they require more pedal pressure to operate and are a trifle noisy on cold mornings," continued Wright, "but once they get warmed up they're excellent. The brakes in our test car pulled the Sting Ray down to quick straight-line stops time and again without any sudden locking of the wheels and without apparent fade. Several stretches of mountain roads showed that they could stand up to prolonged hard use without failure."

Hot Rod's Ray Brock was impressed by the 1963 Corvette's polite side. In his opinion, the newly offered optional "power steering should help immeasurably in increasing sales (as if they need it this year) because we've often heard ladies of all ages express a liking for Corvette styling and size but a dislike for the steering effort required to drive one daily." Proving that political correctness is a relatively recent phenomenon, Brock then concluded that "gals of all ages can also enjoy a Corvette thanks to power steering, power brakes and other accessories."

Drivers overseas could enjoy the car as well. Both *Autosports* and *The Motor* were treated to England's first encounters with the greatest American sports car yet to come down the pike. According to *Autosport's* Patrick McNally in an early 1964 review, the 1963 Sting Ray coupe was a bloody winner: "Performance in a straight line is tremendous, the appearance not displeasing and the effect on the fair sex rewarding." "In most respects," reported *The Motor* in December 1963, "the Chevrolet Corvette Sting Ray is the equal of any G.T. car to be found on either side of the Atlantic." These comments seemed to prove *Car and Driver's* claim that "at long last America has a formidable weapon to challenge Europe's fastest grand touring cars on their home ground."

Complaints, although minor relative to all the raves, were present and accounted for. *Car Life's* crew didn't exactly like the prospect of wrestling heavy luggage into the "adequate-sized" storage area by way of the passenger compartment (since there was no rear deck lid, as there had been in 1962), nor were they thrilled by the hideaway headlights, calling them "a little too fussy for such an elegantly functional car." Fussy or not, those headlights didn't stop *Car Life* from enthusiastically labeling the 1963 Sting Ray "the best Corvette yet!"

Pointing to the typically imperfect fiberglass finish, Wright felt that "for a car that sells in the $4500-6000 range, [the Sting Ray] doesn't reflect the degree of quality control we feel it should." Continued his May 1963 *Motor Trend* report, "there still seems to be some difficulty in manufacturing a really smooth fiberglass body. While this isn't too apparent in a light-colored car, it becomes all too noticeable in some of the darker ones. When the light hits these from almost any angle, there's a definite rippled effect."

Such disappointments paled, however, in comparison to the runaway number one negative response, a complaint made by practically every automotive journalist who dared tried to look over his shoulder while at the 1963 Sting Ray's wheel. As much as he undoubtedly hated to admit it, Bill Mitchell was wrong; Duntov was right: the rear window "stinger" had to go. Although all magazines wholeheartedly agreed with Duntov, it was perhaps *Hop-Up's* Ed Phillips who put the split-window situation in its proper perspective. "Visibility from the rearview mirror isn't too good," he wrote in a September 1963 review. "Chances are you'd probably *hear a* motorcycle cop on your tail before you could see him.'

Why would a motorcycle cop be on a Sting Ray's tail? While *Car Life's* test of a 300-horsepower L75 Corvette coupe equipped with the optional Powerglide automatic produced an average quarter-mile time of 15.5 seconds at 86 miles per hour, Motor *Trend* demonstrated what the top-of-the-heap 360-horsepower fuelie could do for straight-line performance. With a close-ratio four-speed and a 3.70:1 Positraction rear end, *Motor Trend's* L84 Sting Ray coupe tripped the lights in 14.5 seconds, topping out at 102 miles per hour. Sixty miles per hour from rest took but 5.8 seconds, while top speed was listed as 130 miles per hour. With that kind of power, who needed to look behind anyway?

As for Z06 performance, that was proven on the track at Riverside on October 13, 1962, when Doug Hooper's Sting Ray bested a Porsche to win the *Los Angeles Times* Three-Hour Invitational. It was a win, sure, but Duntov didn't exactly feel like celebrating after watching another production racer launch its career that day. After Carroll Shelby's 1962 proposal to build a few rebodied, lightweight Corvettes had been rejected by Chevrolet, he turned to Dearborn as a power source for an exciting Anglo-American hybrid machine. With a warmed-over Ford Windsor V-8 beneath its British-built aluminum skin, Shelby's AC Cobra was easily the Z06's match, and perhaps only a Cobra breakdown saved the four-car Corvette team from a discouraging defeat during both sports cars' Riverside debut. That debut was only the beginning for the Cobra-Corvette wars.

Long a dominant force in SCCA competition, Chevrolet's Sting Ray would end up being bumped out of the 1964 A-Production championship by Shelby-American's Ford-based Cobra, and it would be five years before another Corvette would make its way back to the top. But Duntov had been considering a more competitive Corvette even before the Cobra had entered the scene. Based on the all-new 1963 Sting Ray, Zora's lightweight racer would be everything his 1957 Super Sport had been and much more. The car would be a "Grand Sport."

MECHANIC
Bill Scott
TRACO
Jim Hall
Roger Penske
2
5
2

Heirs to the Throne

Duntov's Ill-Fated Grand Sports

All five of them still exist, to the dismay of General Motors' officials who 30 years ago had demanded they be done away with. Corvette Grand Sports—three coupes and two roadsters—were first conceived in the summer of 1962. These burly, lightweight, all-out racing machines represented the best Zora Duntov could offer as far as world-class, *Federation Internationale de l'Automobile* (FIA)-sanctioned Grand Touring competition was concerned. Problem was, Chevrolet—like all of Detroit—wasn't supposed to be involved in racing, on this country's tracks or any other's; the Automobile Manufacturers Association's so-called ban on factory-supported competition had seen to that in June 1957. But ban be damned, Duntov powered up his Grand Sport project five years later, with enthusiastic backing from Chevrolet general manager Semon "Bunkie" Knudsen, only to have the plug pulled once GM's top brass decided enough was enough. In January 1963 the order came down from the 14th floor to end such politically incorrect shenanigans, effectively concluding the Grand Sport story before it could be written.

Nonetheless, various chapters did follow as the five Grand Sports built before GM's ax fell rolled out Chevrolet Engineering's back door into a succession of racers' hands, some supposedly independent, others definitely so. After that came an even longer line of collectors bent on preserving these high-priced pieces of Corvette racing history.

Through it all, the awesome Grand Sports have persevered, although all five have taken on differing identities over the years. Paint schemes varied with each succeeding racing team, bodywork was modified as scoops and flares were experimented with, and both small-block and big-block power was used. Once in the collector realm, a Grand Sport posed an interesting problem for restorers as "originality" in this case could be translated so many different ways. Unmistakable, however, is what the Grand Sports could have meant to Duntov's dreams of racing glory had the project been allowed to fully develop. Sure, the Grand Sports did race, but not while proudly waving the Chevrolet banner as Knudsen and Duntov had intended, nor in the optimum form originally planned.

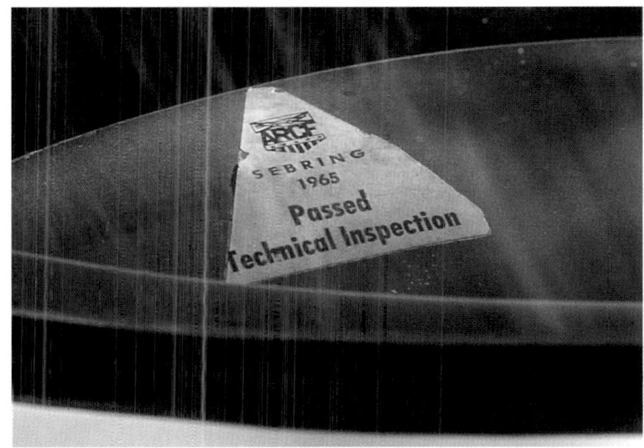

Various modifications were made to the Grand Sports almost immediately after they hit the track in 1963 as demands of competition were met. Among these modifications was the addition of a huge hood scoop to aid engine cooling (as well as to clear the four sidedraft Weber carburetors underneath) and equally large fender flares, which were required to house wider wheels (8.5-inch fronts, 9.5-inch rears) and Firestone tires. A series of openings was also added across the tail to improve both brake and differential cooling.

In the end, the disappointing display was reminiscent of the Corvette Super Sport debacle in 1957. After heat dissipation difficulties abruptly ended the car's competition debut at Sebring, the ensuing AMA anti-racing decree brought the entire project to a screaming halt. From there, any and all racing involvement by the Corvette engineering crew was completely covert, with much unauthorized, underground support going to Dr.

Early Grand Sport plans called for an unconventional 377-ci alloy small-block with special heads featuring two spark plugs per cylinder, but that powerplant never saw an engine bay. This more conventional 377-ci aluminum small-block, with its four Weber two-barrel carburetors, did make it under the Grand Sport's hood. In 1963, this engine was reported to produce 485-horsepower at 6,000 rpm, more than ample power as ably demonstrated during Nassau Speed Week that year. *Dave Friedman photo*

Dick Thompson's supposedly independent efforts on the SCCA circuit.

Duntov tried again in 1959, creating the enigmatic CERV I. Although early discussions did mention possible appearances at Pikes Peak and Indianapolis, GM management, still sticking tight to the AMA ban, wouldn't have anything to do with it, instead making it quite clear the CERV I was intended for nothing more than tire and suspension testing. But Duntov wanted a full-blooded racing Corvette, not a test track queen, and he wouldn't be denied.

The arrival of both Bunkie Knudsen in November 1967 and the all-new regular-production Sting Ray in late 1962 represented major stepping-stones toward Duntov's next attempt to put his Corvette on the international racing map. With its improved chassis, the 1963 Sting Ray obviously offered distinct advantages for building a production-based racing version. Weight remained a problem, however, even though Duntov had hoped the all-new Corvette coupe would end up considerably lighter than its forerunners.

As for Knudsen, his reputation as an avid performance promoter was well established before he slipped into Chevrolet's general manager shoes. As Pontiac's chief from 1956 to 1961, Knudsen had been the driving force behind the once-stagnant division's newfound youthful image, an image that wasn't hurt in the least by Pontiac Motor Division's growing dominance

Shown here is the Grand Sport's rigid tube frame and large 36.5-gallon gas tank. Notice the conventional 360-horsepower fuel-injected 327 originally installed in lieu of the larger, more exotic small-block initially planned for the Grand Sport. Grand Sports also initially rolled on relatively skinny Halibrand knock-off wheels wearing equally skinny rubber—all of which changed once the cars got a taste of the track. Unlike a standard 1963 Sting Ray, a Grand Sport featured a rear deck lid to supply access to that spare tire.

Top right
Semon E. "Bunkie" Knudsen had joined Pontiac in 1956 as GM's youngest ever divisional general manager and then successfully turned Pontiac's image around, thanks to a heavy dose of performance and youthful design pizzazz. Always a big fan of high performance, Knudsen was just the man Duntov needed at the top when Bunkie moved over to Chevrolet in November 1961. It was Knudsen's enthusiastic support that helped Zora Duntov kick off his Grand Sport project. But Knudsen didn't make all the decisions, and GM's anti-racing edict of January 1963 brought an abrupt end to Duntov's project. Knudsen later jumped GM's ship in 1968 and tried the same high-powered practices at Ford before he was abruptly fired by Henry Ford II some 18 months later.

of the early 1960s NASCAR stock car scene. Clearly, Bunkie and Zora thought a lot alike, especially concerning the value of victories at the track relating to future developments. Wrote *Car and Driver*'s Jan Norbye, "with a genuine sports car on his hands, and an attitude several degrees off perfect alignment with the AMA resolution, [Knudsen] may find the means of letting Duntov take up where he left off in 1957. Surely this would be the logical thing, for nobody at Chevrolet Engineering, least of all Zora Arkus-Duntov, allows himself to forget that they have to have a still better Corvette 10 years from now."

But what of the infamous AMA anti-racing resolution? Obviously Pontiac's performance developments under Knudsen's directions were contrary to the 1957 edict, and Ford and Chrysler had already begun showing little regard for the ban a few years before Bunkie joined Chevrolet. Then, in June 1962, Henry Ford II issued a press release announcing his company's plans to ignore the AMA directive and actively pursue racing successes. The 300-word release mentioned how Dearborn initially adhered "to the spirit and letter of the recommendations." However, the release continued, "as time passed, some car divisions [Pontiac, perhaps?] interpreted the resolution more and more freely, with the result that increasing emphasis was placed on speed, horsepower, and racing. As a result, Ford Motor Company feels that the resolution has come to have neither purpose nor effect. Accordingly, we have notified [the AMA] that we feel we can better establish our own standards of conduct with respect to the manner in which the performance of our vehicles is to be promoted and advertised."

Chrysler issued a similar statement soon after, helping kick off a fierce four-year battle between two of Detroit's Big Three on NASCAR's superspeedways.

At the same time, Dearborn's Total Performance campaign was marching toward glorious victory at Le Mans, where on June 19, 1966, Ford Motor Company became the first American auto maker to win France's legendary 24 Hours classic as three Ford-powered GT-40s convincingly crossed the finish in succession. It was the glory Duntov had long sought, and it was the satisfaction he would be continually denied.

In 1960, Duntov and a few of his men had assisted racing tycoon Briggs Cunningham in his attempt to field a three-Corvette team for Le Mans. Along with another 1960 Corvette, Cunningham's three cars impressed the Europeans with their power and appearance, but various mishaps limited their performance. Bad breaks aside, one of the Cunningham Corvettes, driven by John Fitch and Bob Grossman, did manage a respectable eighth-place overall finish, high enough to rank as one of the greatest track achievements to date for Chevrolet's fiberglass two-seater. Zora, however, still wanted more. Much more.

After briefly toying with the possibilities of taking the CERV I ideal to the track, Duntov began considering plan B. Greatly influencing his next competition approach was a 1962 FIA announcement detailing a restructuring of its World Manufacturers Championship rules. In 1963, Grand Touring cars would be eligible for that championship as long as a manufacturer "homologated" (legalized) its GT entry by building at least 100 "regular-production" examples in a given 12-month period. Also announced was the intriguing fact that no upper displacement limit would be put on these GT competitors, a point not lost on either Duntov or Carroll Shelby. Both were immediately at work on rival GT projects; Duntov, of course, for Chevrolet, Shelby for Ford.

With Chevrolet's performance-minded Knudsen now at the top running interference for him, Zora felt confident enough in 1962 to attempt an all-out GT racing project, with or without upper office approval. He would use the new Sting Ray as a base, although a lot of unnecessary, speed-robbing weight would have

Although Zora Duntov initially planned to build 125 Corvette Grand Sport racers, only 5 were unleashed late in 1962 before GM officials squelched the project. Featuring a tube frame and an especially lightweight, one-piece fiberglass shell, a Grand Sport coupe weighed in at roughly 1,000 pounds less than its regular-production Sting Ray counterpart. This is Grand Sport number 005, owned by NASCAR engine builder and Corvette collector Bill Tower of Plant City, Florida. Grand Sport coupe numbers 001 and 002 were converted into roadsters in 1964 in an attempt to improve aerodynamics.

to be trimmed before a suitable racing version could emerge at a competitive level. Simply referred to as the "lightweight Corvette" early on, that racing Sting Ray would become the Grand Sport.

Duntov's engineers kicked off the Grand Sport project in the summer of 1962 with a tubular-steel frame modeled after the standard Sting Ray's ladder-type design on an identical wheelbase (98 inches) with narrowed, parallel tubes instead of wide perimeter rails. Both lighter and stronger, the Grand Sport's purpose-built frame reportedly weighed 94 pounds less than its regular-production counterpart, and it also incorporated mounting points for a full roll cage. Equally light was the aluminum alloy differential housing used in back. With its transverse leaf spring and three-link arrangement, the Grand Sport's IRS design was certainly familiar, but differences between these pieces and stock parts were like night and day. Beefed throughout, the Grand Sport IRS layout also helped trim the fat with modified sheet-steel trailing-arm hub carriers drilled for reduced weight.

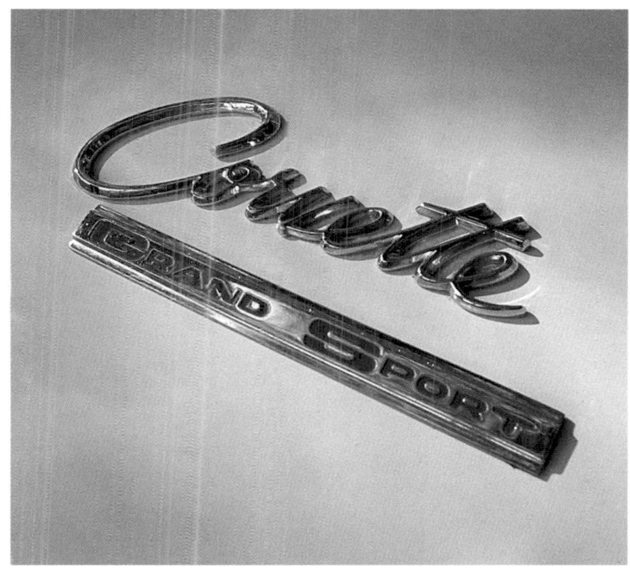

In 1957, Duntov's first attempt at international racing glory failed somewhat miserably as his purpose-built Super Sport succumbed early to overheating problems at Sebring. Five years later he was ready to try again with another purpose-built Corvette, a car that looked like its regular-production counterparts but was considerably modified beneath the skin.

Specially hand-laid to paper-thin specifications (0.040 inch) with an eye toward keeping weight down, the Grand Sport's fiberglass body was also "trimmed down" here and there to improve aerodynamics. Among other things, the roof is narrower and the windshield raked back farther compared to a standard 1963 Corvette. Owner Bill Tower calls the Grand Sport "a 7/8ths model of the stock Sting Ray." Notice the exposed fitting on the front fender (directly behind Bill Scott's name); it's tied to a hydraulic jacking system installed to expedite pit stops.

The Grand Sport's greatest days in the sun came in the Bahamas in December 1963 during Nassau Speed Week. Three Cadillac Blue Grand Sports, chassis numbers 003, 004, and 005, showed up under the Mecom Racing Team banner to put Carroll Shelby and his Cobras in their place. Along with the Grand Sports, wealthy Texan John Mecom also brought along a Lola-Chevrolet, a Cooper-Chevrolet, a Scarab, and the Zerex-Cooper Special. Mecom drivers included Roger Penske, A. J. Foyt, Jim Hall, Dr. Dick Thompson, and Augie Pabst. Shown here is Penske in Grand Sport 004 (car number 50 at lower left) leading the pack at Nassau during practice laps. Pabst's Chevy-Lola, car number 00, is directly behind Penske, followed by Thompson in GS 005 (car number 80) and Hall driving Grand Sport 003. Although none of the Grand Sports finished first in the three races held that week, they did beat the Ford-powered Cobras at every turn, which in itself was enough of a victory in Duntov's eyes. *Dave Friedman photo*

Contributing as well to the Grand Sport's diet was an aluminum steering box, special front suspension A-arms welded up from sheet steel, and a set of 15x6-inch Halibrand magnesium knock-off wheels. Each wheel tipped the scales at only 16.5 pounds. Solid 11.75-inch Girling discs with three-piston calipers were mounted at all four corners, while heavy-duty front coil springs, various hardened, reinforced steering pieces, and stiff Delco shocks completed the chassis.

Atop that chassis went a special one-piece fiberglass shell laid up by hand with superthin panels for additional lightness. Certain measurements here and there—such as slightly more windshield slope and a lower, narrowed roofline—differed from stock standards as Duntov's designers attempted to improve, however minimally, on the new Sting Ray's less-than-desirable high-speed aerodynamics. Relative to entrenched European rivals, Chevrolet's 1963 Corvette was still a veritable brick in the wind even though it looked so sleek and slippery. Although measurably smaller than typical American designs, Sting Ray frontal area remained considerable, from a competition perspective, and also contributed to the body's tendency to lift as speeds increased. It was this unwanted lift that plagued Grand Sports, as well as all racing Corvettes built from 1963 to 1967, throughout their abbreviated competition careers.

Additional differences between the stock Sting Ray shell and its flimsy Grand Sport copy included enlarged wheelhouses to allow the use of bigger tires, a rear deck lid for spare tire access, and fixed headlights mounted behind clear plexiglass in place of the heavy hideaway units. Even more weight was trimmed by using plexiglass windows (the windshield remained glass) with hand lifts instead of regulators, while aluminum underbody reinforcement did the job normally performed by the Sting Ray's steel birdcage. In back, Mitchell's pesky stinger window partition was not included for obvious reasons, and a fuel filler for the 36.5-gallon fiberglass gas tank protruded from the roof behind the passenger door.

Inside, a standard Sting Ray dash housed a typical collection of gauges, but most notable was the stock-looking speedometer that, on closer inspection, registered 200 miles per hour. Although the steering wheel appeared stock, it was actually modeled after the standard Sting Ray unit using a stainless-steel three-spoke rim wrapped in teakwood. Certainly not stock was the exceptionally quick steering ratio requiring only two turns lock-to-lock. Untypically plush (for a race car) full carpeting and fiberglass bucket seats completed the package.

As for power, Duntov's initial plans called for an exotic all-aluminum small-block displacing 377 ci. With four Weber 58-millimeter IDA two-barrel carburetors, twin spark plugs in each combustion chamber, and headers, the 377-ci Grand Sport V-8 reportedly made 550 horsepower on the dyno, more than enough muscle, it was hoped, to overwhelm the car's disappointing aerodynamics. While awaiting its engine, Grand Sport number 001 was fitted with an aluminum version of the Sting Ray's fuel-injected 327 and readied for testing at Sebring in December 1962. It was the first of 125 lightweight Corvettes Duntov intended to build for GT competition, with homologation papers being filed with the FIA that same month. In those papers, the Grand Sport's weight was listed as 1,908 pounds, more than a half-ton less than the standard 1963 Sting Ray.

As Duntov stood poised to unleash his Grand Sports on the world, fate once again stepped in to cut him off at the knees. On January 21, 1963, GM chairman Frederick Donner and president John Gordon dropped their ax in the form of a memo informing all division heads to cancel certain performance projects then under way. Victims of Donner's ax included Pontiac's NASCAR-dominating Super Duty program and Chevrolet's Mark II Mystery Motor, itself a promising NASCAR weapon of the future. The Grand Sport, of course, was canceled as well.

One month later, Donner explained GM's apparent change of heart at a February 16 press conference. "Ever since the AMA adopted—I think you can term it

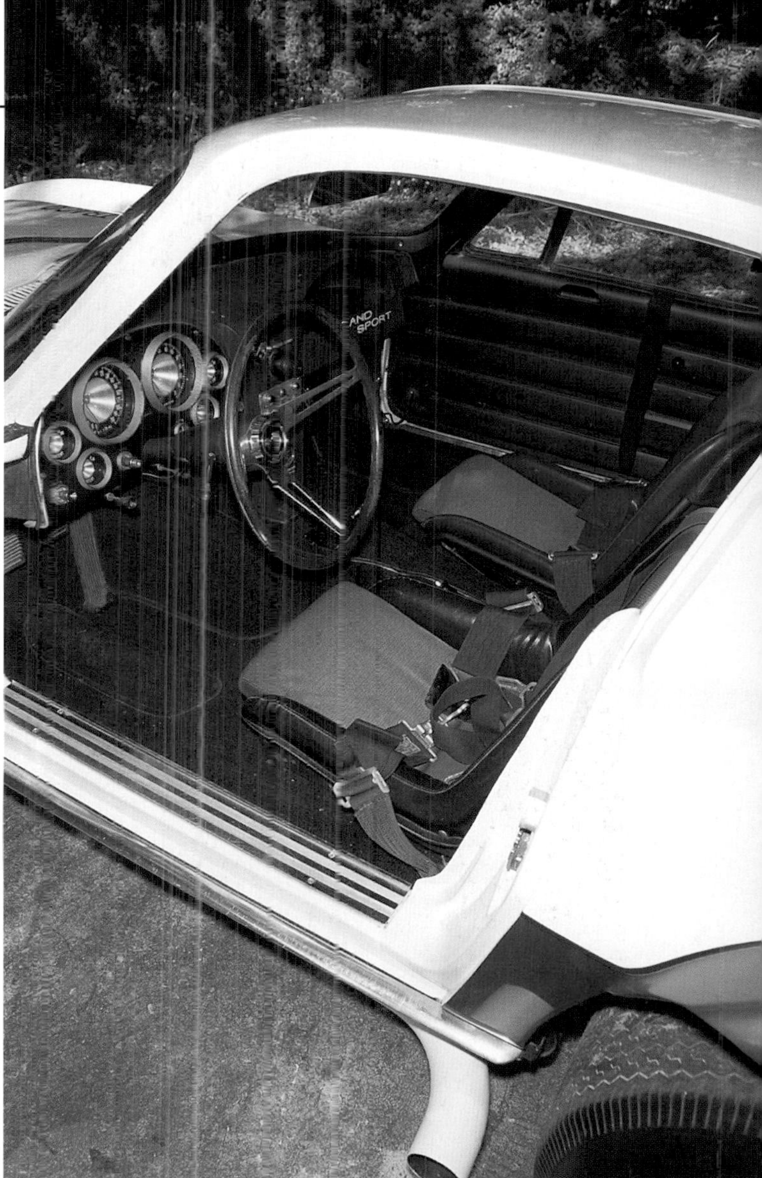

With somewhat plush full carpeting, a stock-looking dash, and a teakwood-rimmed steering wheel, the Grand Sport's interior appeared almost civilized, even though the car itself was a real beast. Notice the bulge in the driver's footwell where the tube frame member runs under the compartment floor. While a Grand Sport's main perimeter tubes ran parallel from front to back, a standard Sting Ray frame featured widely spaced perimeter rails that kicked out under the door sills to maximize passenger compartment floor space.

Following pages
In an attempt to improve the Grand Sport's wind-cheating abilities, the first two Grand Sport Coupes were transformed into roadsters in 1964. But before the idea could be proven on the track at Daytona, GM officials again ordered an end to the racing involvement they had supposedly canceled in January 1963. After sitting in storage for nearly two years, the two roadsters went to Roger Penske early in 1966. Penske let Grand Sport 002 go to George Wintersteen, who, like Penske, dropped in a 427 big-block and went racing. Penske's 427-powered 001 roadster debuted at Sebring in March 1966 but broke down after only three hours. *Dave Friedman photo*

GOODYEAR

This movie camera was installed by Chevrolet to investigate the Grand Sport's performance on the track, both visually and through audio pickup. The film not only allowed engineers to see how the car made it through the turns, it also let them listen to engine sounds that indicated the driver's choice of shift points, both up and down.

Hiding beneath those exotic 58-millimeter Weber side-draft carburetors is an aluminum 377-ci small-block, an all-out racing version of the 327 found under a standard 1963 Sting Ray's hood. The special intake was of cross-ram design, meaning the Webers on the right fed the heads on the left, while the Webers on the left fed the heads on the right.

Right
The Grand Sport's dash does appear stock at first glance, but closer inspection reveals that the standard 160-mile-per-hour Sting Ray speedometer has been replaced by this more suitable 200-mile-per-hour unit.

a recommendation—back in 1957," he said, "we have had a policy on our books, and we haven't had any change in it." But how could Duntov have built the Grand Sport if GM truly had been adhering to the AMA recommendation? "Very often you run into interpretations of policies that to an outsider might look like violations—that distance between interpretation and violation is a very delicate one."

What these words smelled like wasn't delicate at all. Donner and Gordon's people obviously had looked the other way until outside pressures forced them to rein in what were perceived to be runaway performance practices. General Motors might have liked everyone to think it was responding to growing government concerns over automotive safety, but perhaps closer to the truth was GM's concern over impending federal antitrust action. By putting a stop to Chevrolet and Pontiac's racing activities, GM officials succeeded in diverting any additional unwanted federal attention,

90
100
110
120
130
140
150
160
170
180
190
200
+40
WIPER

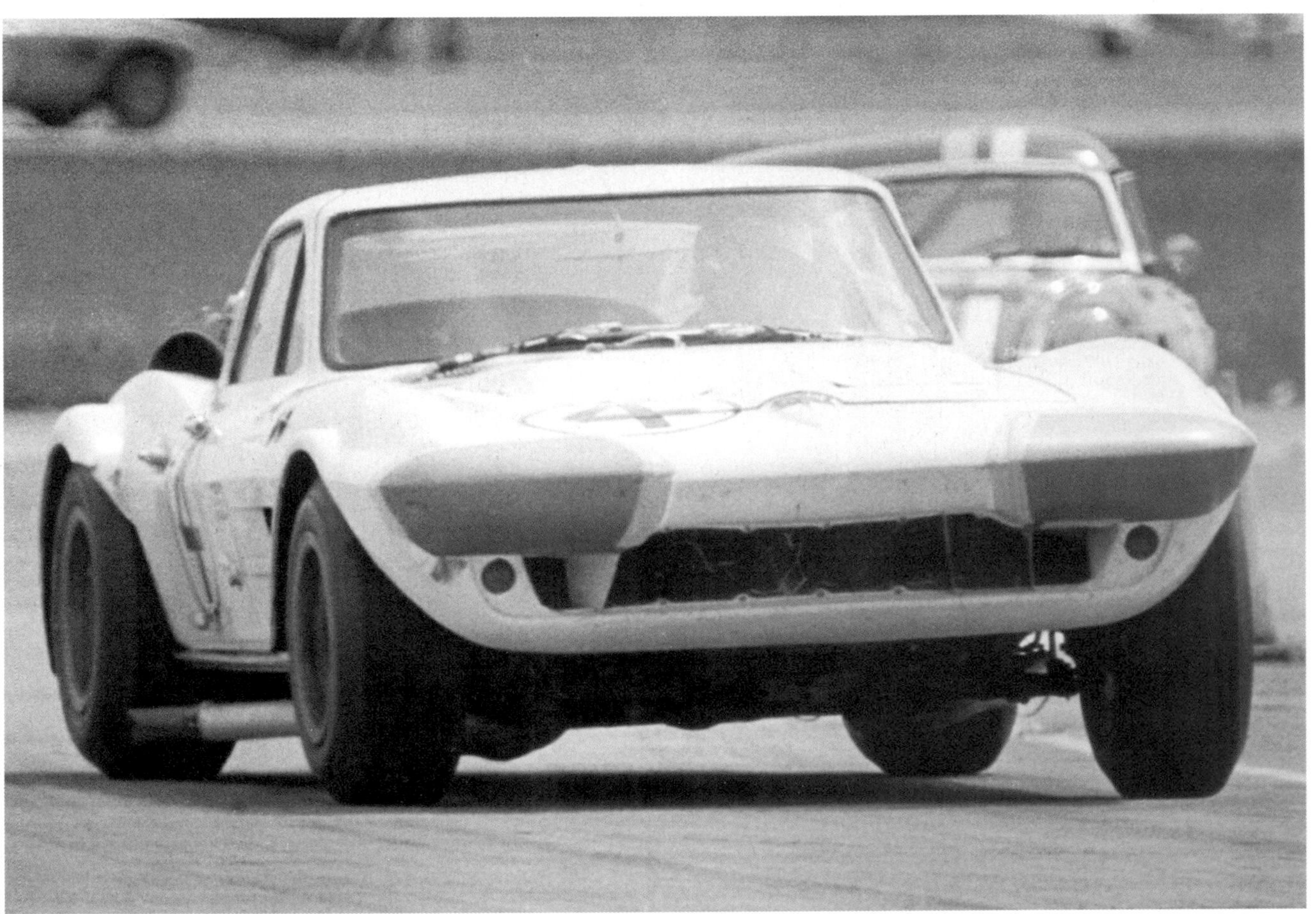

Co-driven by Roger Penske and Jim Hall, Grand Sport 005 demonstrates the breed's propensity toward excessive nose lift at high speeds during the 12 Hours of Sebring in March 1964. On the way to finishing 18th overall, Penske nearly broke the Sebring lap record in GS 005, touring the 5.2-mile course in 3 minutes, 12.2 seconds, just short of John Surtees' 3 minute, 11.4 second lap turned in a Ferrari two years before. *Dave Friedman photo*

in essence keeping their nose clean while they continued to tiptoe around what some legislators viewed as monopolistic business practices.

No matter how you sliced it, though, the end result remained a stillborn birth for Duntov's Grand Sport. The 377 aluminum engine never reached "regular" production, and only five GS chassis had been completed before the project was canceled.

Case closed?

Not at all. From there, the five Grand Sports managed to sneak out Chevrolet Engineering's still-open "back door" and enter the racing world with much unauthorized support from Duntov and his engineers. Two of the cars were equipped with 360-horsepower fuel-injected 327s and "loaned" to Chevrolet's racer "friends" Dick Doane and Gulf Oil executive Grady Davis. Since they failed to meet standard production class requirements, the Grand Sports were considered prototypes, and thus ended up in SCCA's C-Modified class, where they ran—with little success—against such unlimited racing machines as the Scarab and Chaparral, both also powered by Chevrolet V-8s.

Once the Grand Sport coupes were in the wild, they began sprouting various louvers, holes, and vents for added cooling, as well as spoilers and fender flares, while the transparent headlight shields were later replaced with covers. Early in 1964, a pneumatic jacking system was included to make pit stops easier and quicker. An imposing scoop was added to the hood, wheels and tires grew massive, and different engines were tried, including the 427 Mark IV big-block in 1966. But most prominent among the long list of Grand Sport modifications made over the years was the conversion of chassis numbers 001 and 002 from coupes into roadsters.

By removing the roof and cutting down the windscreen, Duntov had hoped to cure the Grand Sport's

George Wintersteen at the wheel of Grand Sport 002 at Ontario's Mosport track in June 1966, the last major competition appearance for the GS roadsters. Wintersteen reportedly sold his Grand Sport soon afterward for $6,700. *Dave Friedman photo*

aerodynamic difficulties, with the specific goal being to better the cars' chances during the Daytona Continental, to be held February 16, 1964. Along with the short windscreen, the Grand Sport roadsters also got a fiberglass-encased roll bar. Determining whether the roadster conversion improved the Grand Sport's ability to cut the wind was delayed, however, as the two cars didn't make it to Florida, at least not in 1964.

GM killjoys stepped in once again, this time after reading the papers, where headlines, including the New York *Herald Tribune*'s "Don't Look Now but That's a Chevy Tooling Up in the Pits," had them hopping mad. For a car that was supposed to be scrapped, the Grand Sport had been mysteriously active in 1963, including a wild foray to the Bahamas by an all-star racing team fielded by Texan John Mecom. Arriving November 30 on the docks for the Nassau Speed Weeks, the Mecom Racing Team showed up with a lot of factory support, three Grand Sports, and legendary drivers Roger Penske, Augie Pabst, Jim Hall, and A. J. Foyt. When the dust had cleared by week's end, the Grand Sports had thoroughly embarrassed Carroll Shelby's Cobras—and they had also drawn the ire of GM chiefs who thought they had put an end to such extracurricular affairs.

They then stepped in again, this time hitting Bunkie Knudsen where it hurt, threatening him with his annual bonus unless he put a stop to the Grand Sport project once and for all. That he did; the three coupes were eventually sold off, as were the two freshly converted roadsters. From there, the three Grand Sport coupes went through various racers' hands, including those of John Mecom, Jim Hall, and Roger Penske. Penske also bought the two roadsters, dropping a 427 into one of them and taking it to Sebring in March 1966. All five cars continued to compete at various levels, with the last major appearance for a Grand Sport roadster (number 002) coming in June 1966 at Mosport in Ontario. A Grand Sport coupe (number 004) toured a big-time track (Daytona) for the last time in February 1967.

Although there were racing successes, the Grand Sport legacy certainly didn't develop the way Duntov had intended when he first envisioned his lightweight Corvette in 1962. But interference from the front office alone couldn't be blamed. At best, the Grand Sports were brutal beasts, both advanced and crude at the same time. Even if Chevrolet had been allowed to produce all 125 cars, and fit them with that hot 377-ci aluminum V-8, the lightweight Corvettes still would have represented old news almost overnight. By the mid-1960s, the world racing scene was changing rapidly, and as we all know today, technology waits for no one. As Dick Guldstrand later told *Automobile Quarterly*'s John Heilig, "the mid-engined trick cars started to show up around mid-1965, making the Grand Sports little more than plastic pachyderms."

Grand Sport performance, however, was by no means peanuts. Those lucky enough to have seen one of Duntov's lightweight Corvettes in action will never forget.

1964

Split Decision

Sure, the 1963 Sting Ray was a great car, a veritable landmark in American automobile production history. Styling was sensational, mechanicals were state of the art (at least from a Yankee perspective), and all-around performance was as good as it got within these shores 30 years ago. But being a man-made machine, there were glitches, however minor. For the most part, complaints could be written off, considering that this was a sports car, and sports cars do have certain inherent deficiencies. Physical laws being the same in most states, there was only so much room to work with considering the Corvette's tight parameters, both literally and figuratively.

Typically, more room for legs would have meant less room for the engine. More room for hats would have meant disruption of the classic lines Shinoda had pained over for so long. More room for seats would have upset the balance Duntov desired. OK, there wasn't a trunk lid and stowing heavy bags was a little tough through the passenger compartment, but at least there was ample storage. Just think, you could have had an MG!

Base price for a Corvette convertible was $4,037 in 1964. As in 1963, the standard convertible-top color was black, with either beige or white available at no extra cost. Installed on 7,843 1964 convertibles, the white top was most popular that year, followed by black (4,721), and beige (591). Another 1,220 1964 Corvette convertibles were not equipped with soft tops as customers chose to opt for the C07 removable hardtop as a no-cost option. Again, when RPO C07 was ordered along with the folding top, the removable hardtop became a $236.75 option.

Maybe the ride was a bit harsh for some—again, remember, this was a sports car; a big, brawny American sports car. Enough said. As for brakes, well, there was no excuse here except for the plain fact that American auto makers had yet to get serious about stopping power. In Corvette terms, a proper response was a year away. There was, however, one problem area that wouldn't wait another year for a solution. You had to be blind to miss it, for even if you had never seen a 1963 Sting Ray, you could have read all about it in any popular magazine.

"Our only complaint about the interior was in the coupe," explained *Road & Track*, "where all we could see in the rearview mirror was that silly bar splitting the rear window down the middle." According to *Car Life*, "the bar down the center of the rear window makes it all but impossible to see out via the rearview mirror." As *Motor Trend*'s Jim Wright saw it, "the rear window on the coupe is designed more for looks than practicality, and any decent view to the rear will have to be through an exterior side mirror." *Car and Driver* concluded that "luggage space is surprisingly roomy but [the] central window partition ruins rear view." Slings and arrows even came from overseas, with England's *Autosport* reporting that "nothing can be seen of the tail through the divided rear window, which makes reversing in confined quarters rather precarious."

Even Bill Mitchell was quick to admit that the original Sting Ray's split-window layout, the pet theme he had battled Duntov for, was indeed a hazard.

Nonfunctional in 1963, the small roof vents behind the Sting Ray coupe's door were brought to life in 1964, at least on the driver's side. Used in both 1964 and 1965, this standard electric ventilation system used those vents to exhaust interior air. The idea worked much better on paper than in real life.

Not long after the all-new 1963 Corvette coupe had hit the streets, buyers were already cutting out Mitchell's stinger, replacing the two curved glass panes with one solid piece of plexiglass. Of course, that was a trend later reversed once the split-window Sting Rays started gaining considerable value as collectible classics. But who could have known 30 years ago?

On the other hand, predicting in 1963 what would happen to the Corvette body one year down the road was a stone-cold cinch in everyone's eyes. Rolling out in basically identical form, Chevrolet's second-edition Sting Ray debuted sans stinger in the fall of 1963, much to the delight of drivers who preferred seeing what they were about to back over. Describing the next great Corvette as "docile but no fossil, and agile but not fragile," *Road & Track*'s reviewers pointed out the obvious in their March 1964 report. "The body design of the 1964 Sting Ray remains little changed from 1963," they wrote, "although we were pleased to note that the central division in the rear window has been eliminated, with a consequent improvement in vision."

Other exterior changes were minor, with typically restyled wheel covers representing the most noticeable new feature. Harder to spot were the revamped rocker moldings with only three black-painted horizontal indentations instead of eight. Responding to barbs aimed at various unnecessary, nonfunctional trim tricks, Mitchell's crew removed the two dummy grilles in the hood; however, cost-awareness resulted in a return of the two hood depressions where the grilles had resided in 1963. Equally purposeless the year before, the 1963 coupe's so-called air outlets behind the doors were restyled and made functional, at least on the driver's side, where an electric ventilation motor, located in cramped quarters behind the left rear wheelwell, tried somewhat vainly to push out the 1964 Sting Ray's bad air. A nice idea, but it was severely limited by the small, three-speed motor's weak lungs. The equipment was deleted after 1965.

Remaining welcomed advancements came beneath the skin and addressed certain customer complaints concerning a gremlin Detroit's acronym artists like to call "NVH"—noise, vibration, and harshness. After determining that the 1963 frame had transmitted too much road noise inside the body, Duntov's engineers upgraded the body mounts (modifications varied from coupe to convertible) for 1964 using "rubber biscuit" insulators. New cotton-fiber insulation was added below the carpet and a foil-backed "insulation blanket" went on the firewall in the engine compartment. Stiffened fiberglass bodywork in back also helped reduce resonation, a common problem with GRP (glass-reinforced plastic) construction.

Other NVH attacks were turned back inside, where the shifter's annoying buzzing was cured with a new rubber boot and rubber linkage bushings. Underneath, noise and vibration were minimized by revising muffler internals and adding a more flexible tailpipe hanger also made of rubber. Additionally, front exhaust system mounts were moved from the frame cross-member to the transmission mounting hardware, further cutting pesky vibrations.

As for harshness, an already relatively "soft" ride (from a performance perspective) was softened even more by adding variable-rate springs and recalibrated shocks. Wound tighter at the top than bottom, the front coil springs "relaxed" during normal operation, yet firmed up when compressed. A similar variable-rate effect was created in back by forming the downward-curved transverse spring's shorter leaves with less curvature, meaning they would only add more stiffness to the spring as a whole under heavy compression. Overall, the 1964 Corvette's standard suspension easily represented America's best compromise between all-out road-hugging performance and pleasant boulevard-bound comfort.

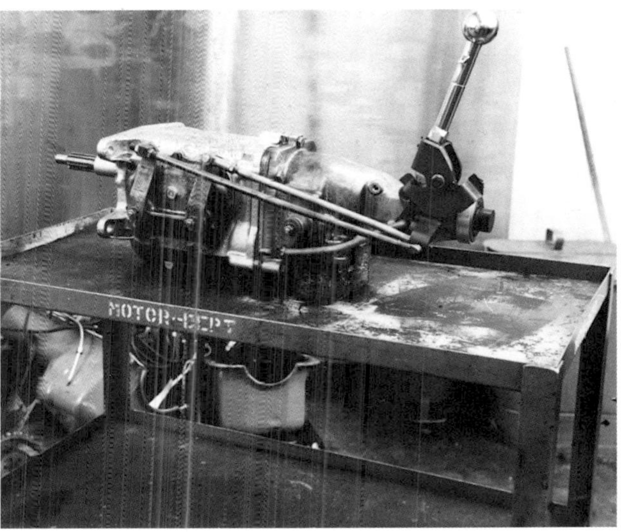

Chevrolet's excellent aluminum-case Muncie four-speed, RPO M20, was nearly identical to the Muncie gearbox that had debuted midyear in 1963 save for the shift rods, which were beefier in 1964. Price for the 1964 M20 box, wide- or close-ratio, was $188.30.

"By using relatively soft (for sports cars) springing and firm damping," reported *Car Life*, "the Sting Ray avoids the choppiness expected from such a short wheelbase." *Road & Track*'s test drivers agreed, claiming "the suspension is stiffer than we expected but not uncomfortable and does a good job on very bad road surfaces. It is helped considerably by a weight distribution [with] a slight rearward bias and this distribution has also done a lot for steering to the extent that we feel it makes power steering unnecessary under most circumstances."

Car Life's lead-foot journalists also liked how Duntov's soft-spoken suspension let its presence be known when angered. "Full-throttle acceleration from rest caused the car to hunker down and leap off, with only minimum wheelspin." Again, *Road & Track* was right there to back up *Car Life*'s bragging: "The Sting Ray tended to squat down on its rear suspension when leaving the line, with never so much as a chirp from its tires, and then gobble up the strip." It certainly appeared as if the 1964 Corvette had all bases pretty well covered.

Along with reducing NVH, Mitchell, Duntov, and the boys also paid closer attention to quality control during body construction, which, beginning late in 1963, was split between the St. Louis assembly plant and Dow Smith, a division of the A. O. Smith Company

continued on page 195

ONE STEP BACKWARD

XP-819—Chevrolet's Rear-Engined Corvette Prototype

General Motors' long, seemingly endless line of Corvette prototypes, competition machines, and show cars has featured more than its fair share of legendary vehicles, some more notable than others.

Having essentially rolled right off a GM Motorama stage itself in January 1953, Chevrolet's first-edition Corvette served as the base in 1954 for three more Motorama dream cars: a hardtop version, the fastback Corvair, and the Nomad sport wagon, the last model serving as inspiration for the regular-production passenger-line Nomads of 1955–1957. Three innovative racing Corvettes, the production-based SR-2, the tube-frame Super Sport, and the sleek Stingray, hit the track in 1956, 1957, and 1959, respectively. One year later, Bill Mitchell's futuristic, duck-tailed XP-700 appeared, tipping off the 1961 Corvette's rear-end restyle.

More renowned are GM's two engineering experiments—CERV (Chevrolet Experimental Research Vehicle) I and II—and the intimidating Grand Sport racers. CERV I was built in 1959 and helped lay the groundwork for the 1963 Sting Ray's standard independent rear suspension, while the 427-powered, all-wheel-drive CERV II emerged in 1963. Duntov's brutal Grand Sports were initially conceived in late 1962 as all-out responses to Carroll Shelby's Ford-powered Cobras, with only five produced before corporate anti-racing pressures nipped the project in the bud.

Recognizable Corvette styling studies included Larry Shinoda's XP-755 Shark (later the Mako Shark 1) of 1961 and the Mako Shark II of 1965, originally a nonfunctional mock-up that later reappeared in running form as the Manta Ray in 1969. Between the Mako Shark II and Manta Ray came the unconventional Astro I with its mid-engined layout, an idea introduced earlier by the CERV vehicles and probably best demonstrated in the form of the aluminum-bodied XP-895 (a steel-shell version was also built) in 1972. Even more unconventional were two mid-engined prototypes unveiled in 1973 using Wankel rotary power.

But as intriguing as the various experimental, or "XP," Corvettes have

Credited to Chevrolet engineer Frank Winchell, the rear-engined XP-819 was built in 1964 and foretold much of the new Corvette look that would debut for 1968—which was no coincidence since the body was designed by Larry Shinoda, the same man who created both the 1963 Sting Ray and 1968 Corvette restyle. XP-819's body-colored urethane front bumper and lift-off one-piece top (removed in this photo) were also signs of things to come. Overall height was only 44 inches.

The XP-819's Kamm-backed tail hinged upward, exposing a small-block V-8 perched backward off a Pontiac automatic transaxle, while the nose section tilted up as well—in a fashion similar to today's Corvettes—to allow access to the battery and radiator. A small storage compartment—accessed through an exterior deck lid—was incorporated behind the seats.

been over the years, not all made it into the show circuit limelight. Perhaps most prominent among the forgotten prototypes was XP-819, a radical rear-engined Corvette that came and went in 1964 before anyone outside GM's inner circle had a chance to even raise an eyebrow, let alone debate its merits, or lack thereof. Thirteen years later, XP-819 mysteriously returned from apparent oblivion to take its place in the show field at the annual Bloomington Gold Corvette event in Illinois, to the amazement of Duntov and Shinoda, who were both sure the car had met its end a decade or so before.

Even more amazing is the fact that Duntov had next to nothing to do with the XP-819 project. Credit for the idea belonged to Frank Winchell, then chief of the Corvair engineering program. At the time Ralph Nader's Corvair-damning book, *Unsafe At Any Speed,* was still a year away and Winchell's enthusiasm concerning the performance potential of Chevrolet's little rear-engined compact was running

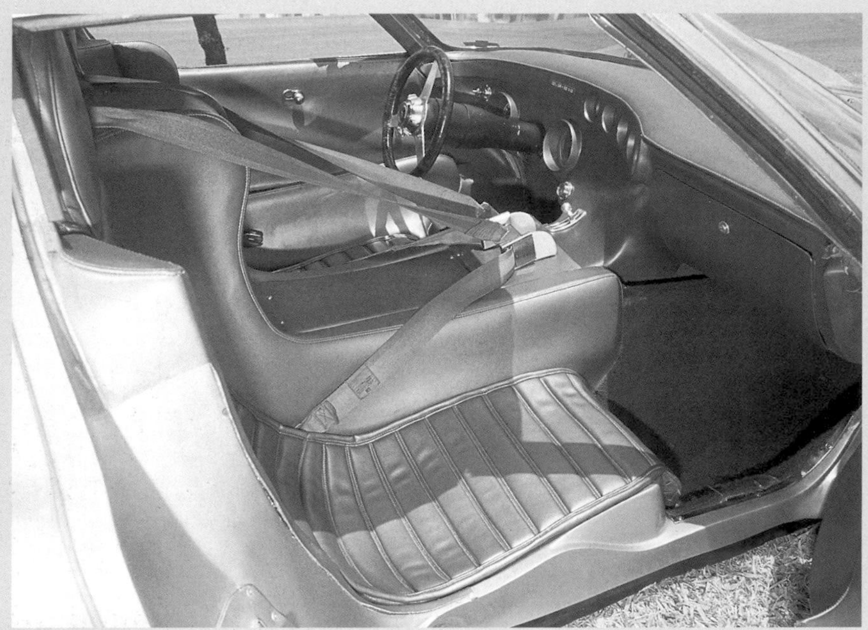

Some parts, such as the inner doorknobs, were right off the standard Sting Ray parts shelf, but nearly everything else seen here was custom fabricated for the XP-819, including the shoulder harnesses and exotic bucket seats. Seats were fixed, meaning the foot pedals had to be adjustable—in this case electrically—to meet varying driver reaches. The small lever just ahead of the seatbelt perched on the front of the console is the automatic transaxle shifter, while the electric pedal adjustment switches are between those perches. A particularly unique feature of the XP-819 prototype was its form-fitting inner door panels, which when closed made up the outside bolsters for the deeply recessed, somewhat cramped bucket seats. Notice the small black stick-on label just to the left of the gauges at the top of the dash. It reads "DEV. CAR—SEE NIES," a reference to engineer Larry Nies, who designed the backbone-type chassis for this odd developmental machine.

high. Among his pet projects was a V-8–powered Corvair, a proposal he hoped might also help vault him and his design team into the Corvette game. In Winchell's opinion, if a rear-mounted V-8 could work for a sporty Corvair application, why couldn't the same tactic succeed under Corvette guise?

Duntov didn't like the Corvair guy's idea, nor did stylist Bob McLean, especially since Winchell's initial drawings—based on a standard Sting Ray body—were downright ugly. Undeterred after a disappointing morning meeting with Duntov and McLean, Winchell then turned to his "styling expert," Larry Shinoda, who claimed he could make the design appealing. With the help of Allen Young and John Schinella, Shinoda did just that, returning right after lunch with a drawing that changed Duntov's and McLean's minds. "Where did you cheat?" Duntov reportedly asked.

With the go-ahead given, Winchell, Shinoda, and crew wasted little time; two months and a reported $500,000 later, XP-819 was a rolling reality demonstrating both an innovative rear-engined chassis and prophetic styling. Although various small details were right off the Corvette parts shelf, Shinoda's fiberglass shell was something totally new, its soon-to-be familiar "Coke-bottle" figure, Kamm-back tail, and wedge-shaped, pointed nose predicting styling queues later used on the restyled 1968 Corvette. Signs of things to come also included the XP-819's lift-off top, side-guard door beams, and body-colored urethane front bumper, which would appear as a standard Corvette feature in 1973. Interior innovations included foot pedals that adjusted electrically to meet the driver's reach, and molded door panels that became part of the seats when closed.

Beneath Shinoda's attractive fiberglass skin was a steel "backbone" frame built by a team of fabricators under the direction of engineer Larry Nies. Disc brakes and coil springs were used at all four corners, but the real news was the 287-ci alloy V-8 suspended rearward in back from a modified Pontiac Tempest two-speed automatic transaxle. Although relatively lightweight compared to the typical cast-iron V-8s of its day, the XP-819's experimental small-block still represented more than enough mass to tip the scales in favor of a distinct tail-end weight bias—reportedly, 70 percent of the car's 2,700 pounds rested on the rear wheels.

Duntov had been skeptical from the beginning, figuring the tail-heavy XP-819 would be a bear to handle in the turns. Shinoda begged to differ, claiming the car's specially mismatched tires would compensate, within reason, for the extreme weight imbalance. Two-piece alloy wheels, the same used on Jim Hall's Chaparral racers, mounted special-order Firestone rubber that was the same diameter front and rear, but considerably wider in back. As Shinoda later told *Road & Track*'s Ray Thursby, "like a mid-engined Can-Am car, when you overcook it, it's damn hard to catch. But driving it normally, the XP-819 worked pretty well."

Normal driving, however, never has been a Corvette selling point, and it's doubtful the average driver would have been able to adjust to the XP-819 prototype's unique control characteristics. According to former

Longtime race car builder Smokey Yunick is shown here on Florida's Daytona Beach in 1956. Notice the pre-1955-style wheel covers on this 1956 Corvette speedster. Yunick's Daytona Beach shop, home to many of Chevrolet's high-performance development projects, including the legendary "Mystery Motor" Mk II big-block V-8s that turned all heads during the 1963 Daytona 500. Yunick's garage also became the apparent final resting place for the XP-819 prototype when Chevrolet officials allowed Smokey to take possession only after he agreed to cut the rear-engined experiment into pieces. A collector later found those pieces in 1976, salvaged the mess, and restored the unique piece of Corvette history. Daytona International Speedway photo

Chevrolet engineer Paul Van Valkenburg, "the car could be set up to handle properly on a skid pad in steady-state cornering, but transient or dynamic response was nearly uncontrollable at the limit." Proof of Van Valkenburg's claim was apparently supplied when a driver plowed the XP-819 into a test-track guard rail in 1965, although Shinoda was quick to point out that the accident occurred because the car was rolling on standard narrow street tires at the time. Regardless, Chevrolet gave up on Winchell's rear-engined Corvette idea almost overnight following the crash—as if it really had been seriously considered at all. From there, the plot truly thickened.

With even less fanfare than it received during its short, somewhat

Total weight for XP-819 was roughly 2,700 pounds, with 70 percent of those pounds perched on the car's fat rear tires. Hard acceleration was not advised since that extreme rearward weight bias could quickly translate into a serious wheelstand that would make a veteran rail dragster pilot proud.

mysterious testing career, what was left of Winchell's XP-819 was quietly rolled out Chevrolet Engineering's back door, like many other GM performance experiments, to legendary race car builder Smokey Yunick's shop in Daytona Beach, Florida. Chevrolet general manager Bunkie Knudsen agreed to Yunick's request for the prototype with the understanding Smokey would salvage certain XP-819 parts for a Chevy-powered Indy car project he was working on, then trash the rest. By no means did Chevrolet brass intend for the rear-engined Corvette to survive, at least not in one piece.

Yunick, however, had other plans, and hitting the Brickyard with

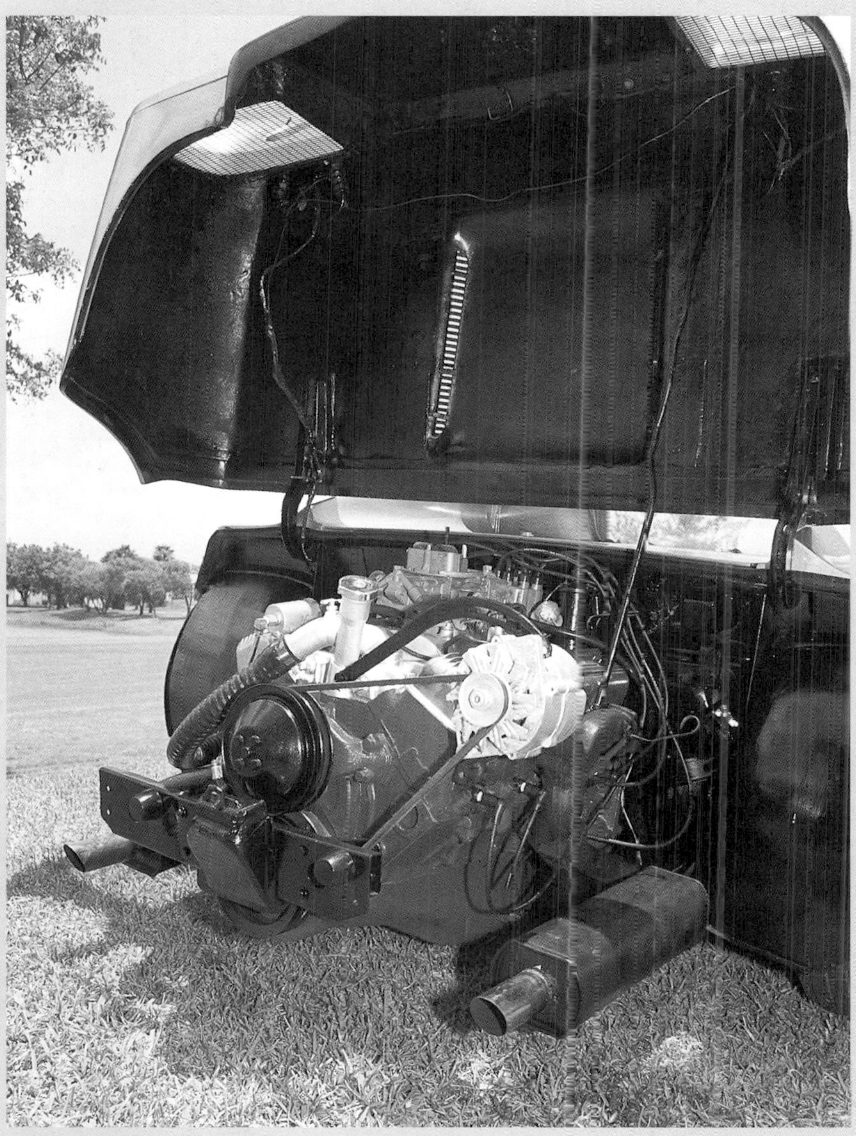

Originally, the XP-819 was powered by an aluminum 287-ci V-8, but that engine disappeared after the car went from Chevrolet Engineering into the hands of famed Daytona Beach race car builder Smokey Yunick. When XP-819 was restored in the late 1970s, a conventional iron-block 350-horsepower V-8 was used in place of the missing alloy small-block.

XP-819 remnants was not one of them. Some 25 years later, he confessed to *Corvette Fever* contributor Terry Jackson, explaining that his request for parts was only a ruse of sorts. "It didn't make sense to me that the car should be destroyed when Duntov was saving those CERV cars," he said. "I was building an Indy car and I concocted a story that I needed parts off the [XP-819] Corvette. They went for that."

Almost. Yunick's hope for preserving a piece of Corvette history was quickly squelched by a GM legal department order directing him to cut XP-819 into four pieces and document the dissection with a notarized photo. Captured on film as directed, the operation finally occurred in January 1973. From there, the pieces were stashed away to collect dust in a paint booth, where they were discovered by Missouri Corvette enthusiast Steve Tate in 1976 during one of Yunick's renowned "garage sales."

Tate bought the mess, which included nearly all the original components save for the 284-ci alloy small-block V-8. Working almost blind, since GM people weren't interested in supplying any support—remember, as far as they knew, XP-819 had been "shredded" as ordered—he restored XP-819 as best he could, substituting a 350-horsepower 327 for the missing original engine. All other details were put back as correctly as could be surmised under the circumstances, right down to the nonfunctional hideaway headlights, which were nonessential (from a prototype perspective); motor drives were never installed in 1964. Overall, the restoration wasn't exactly perfect, but then again, neither was the original. Tate's project was completed in time for the 1978 Bloomington Gold show, where the majority of Corvette followers simply walked right by without so much as a nod in recognition, an understandable situation considering the event represented the odd prototype's first public appearance.

Tate sold his rear-engined Corvette to Terry Dahmer in the late 1980s, who a few years later passed it on to well-known Duesenberg collector Rick Carroll in southern Florida. Following Carroll's death in a 1989 auto accident, the prototype was bought at auction in May 1990 by Hallandale, Florida, exotic car dealer Marvin Friedman, who went out of business in 1991. Legal entanglements have since driven the unique rear-engined Corvette underground once more—a somewhat fitting fate for the mystery machine known as XP-819.

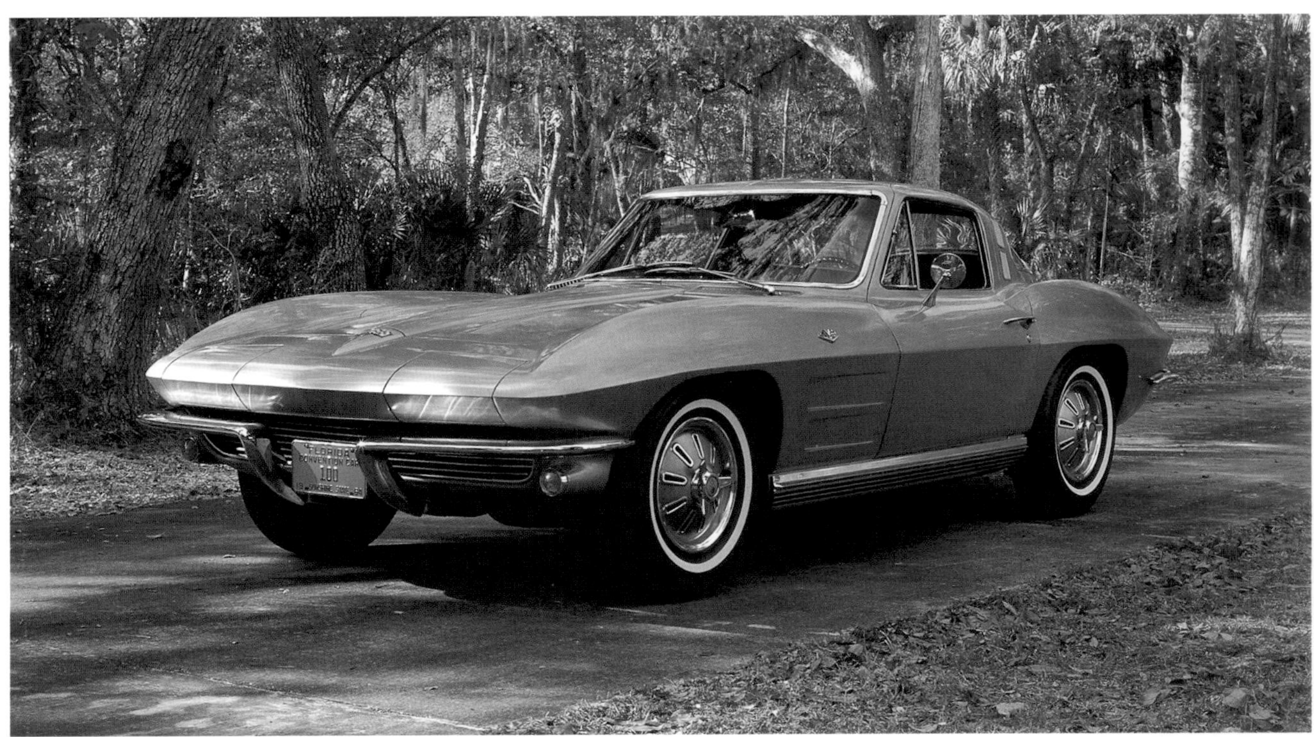

Chevrolet's Sting Ray had been in the works well before Jaguar's E-type debuted in 1961, but many among the press couldn't help circulating rumors claiming Bill Mitchell's men had copied the British sports car's lines. The rumors were false, but that didn't stop the inevitable comparisons, some of which were not so flattering. According to *Car Life's* August 1964 issue, "the Sting Ray's appearance is certainly striking, though it has been said to resemble a Jaguar XK-E with hiccups."

Corvette customers began to favor the convertible Sting Ray in 1964, with sales of coupes topping out at 8,304 models, compared to the 13,925 convertibles built. Base price for a 1964 coupe was $4,252. Saddle Tan, RPO 932, was one of seven exterioror colors offered in 1964. The others were Tuxedo Black (900), Silver Blue (912), Daytona Blue (916), Riverside Red (923), Ermine White (936), and Satin Silver (940). This paint lineup was a carryover from 1963 save for the last color, which replaced the extra-cost Sebring Silver, RPO 941. Notice the optional backup lights, RPO T86, which carried a $10.80 price tag in 1964.

continued from page 187

in Livonia, Michigan. Although paint and fiberglass panel quality would remain inconsistent through the years, many noticed a higher-grade look in 1964.

"There was some criticism of the quality of the fiberglass body when the Sting Ray first appeared," read *Road & Track*'s report, "but we were unable to find any ripples or other faults on our test car. Furthermore, the other characteristics normally associated with fiberglass, such as a tendency toward drumming and magnification of noise, were not present at all." Concerning that tendency, *Motor Trend's* Bob McVay was suitably impressed by the improved Sting Ray shell. "Although previous Corvettes had some noise problems with their fiberglass bodies," he wrote, "we're happy to report that ours was as quiet as a sedan—no squeaks, no rattles, no resonance."

Like its body, the 1964 Corvette's interior showed few changes. As *Car Life* described it, "a pair of giant 6-in. dials, styled to look for all the world like the snuggly side of Jayne Mansfield's Maidenform, dominates the instrument cluster and registers (quite accurately, too) speed and rpm. Other instruments, scattered about like a meteorite-pocked moonscape, continue this inverted cone motif." Once more responding to customer complaints, designers did trade the instrument's reflective silver center sections for glare-resistant flat-black pieces. Minor modifications were also made to the bucket seat upholstery, and a simulated woodgrain-rim steering wheel became standard.

Beneath the hood, Corvette buyers had a choice of four 327 small-blocks, only this time the output ante was upped for the top two engines. The yeoman 250-horsepower 327 remained the standard powerplant, as did a three-speed manual transmission. The optional L75 300-horsepower 327 and Powerglide automatic carried over from 1963 as well. From there, however, the 1964 power lineup was upgraded significantly.

At the top was the L84 327 topped by its Rochester fuel-injection setup. Producing 15 more horses than its 360-horsepower predecessor, the 1964 L84 featured revised heads with bigger valves (2.02-inch intakes, 1.60-inch exhausts) and a new mechanical camshaft with longer duration and more lift, 0.485 inch, compared to the previous Duntov cam's 0.394/0.399-inch intake/exhaust specs. Since the

While the 1964 Corvette's two lower-powered 327s remained as carryovers from 1963, the L84 fuelie received 15 more horsepower, and the 340-horsepower L76 was replaced by a much more aggressive 365-horsepower version. Shown here is the 300-horsepower L75 327, which again was priced at $53.80 and also repeated as the most popular power choice—10,471 were sold. Note the incorrect, owner-installed finned valve covers; as in 1963, both the base 250-horsepower 327 and the 300-horsepower L75 wore painted valve covers in 1964, while the 365-horsepower L76 and 375-horsepower L84 received the flashier finned pieces.

added lift meant the valves were intruding farther into the combustion chamber, machined reliefs were required for the piston tops, which in turn meant a slight reduction in compression to 11:1. As in 1963, L84 exhaust manifolds were larger and more efficient than those used on the 250- and 300-horsepower 327s.

L84 performance for 1964 easily convinced the small dogs to stay on the porch. A heavily optioned Sting Ray fuelie with 4.11:1 gears tested by *Motor Trend* went 0–60 miles per hour in 5.6 ticks of the clock, then stormed through the quarter-mile in 14.2 seconds at 100 miles per hour. After producing similar results at the strip, *Car Life*'s editors came away with nothing but praise for the fuel-injected 327: "Once underway, the engine exhibits a smoothness that was akin to turbines, with a fantastically sensitive throttle response that is unmatched by anything else produced in this country. Moreover, throttle response is instantaneous; there are no ragged spots while the rev counter swings hurriedly around the dial as the accelerator pedal is mashed to the floorboard."

Basically the same engine as the 375-horsepower L84, with a big Holley four-barrel in place of fuel

The simulated woodgrain steering wheel, a Corvette option in 1963, became standard in 1964. Among other things, minor interior modifications also included exchanging the black plastic doorknob used in 1963 with a chrome-plated piece for 1964. Ample storage space behind those buckets remained an attractive Sting Ray feature, although not all were enthused about the route required for baggage to enter that compartment. "Access to this space is through the doors alone," reported *Road & Track*, "which is extremely awkward when bulky items are concerned, and if the rear window could be hinged in Aston Martin style it would be a great improvement." Options appearing here include the M20 four-speed, priced at $188.30, and the $176.50 AM/FM radio, RPO U69.

injection, the 1964 Corvette's second-strongest 327, RPO L76, was advertised at 365-horsepower, the highest output Chevrolet would record for its carbureted 327 small-block. In 1964, 7,171 buyers chose the $107.60 L76 option, while the L84's healthy $538 asking price helped keep total fuel-injection numbers down to 1,325. Production of 300-horsepower L75 327s, priced at $53.80, was 10,471, and 3,262 customers stayed with the standard 250-horsepower V-8.

As in 1963, the wimpy Powerglide automatic transmission couldn't be mated to the L76 or L84 327s. Although the standard three-speed manual was apparently listed early on as being available behind the two solid-lifter small-blocks, records show no such combinations, and the three-speed reportedly became "N.A." (not available) for the 365- and 375-horsepower engines after January 1, 1964. L76 and L84 327s did get the M20 Muncie close-ratio four-speed, while the L75 and the 250-horsepower standard 327 could have been bolted up to the optional wide-ratio M20.

Once more, 3.36:1 gears were standard for the two calmer, hydraulic-lifter small-blocks, with a shorter 3.70:1 ratio specified along with the L76 and L84 options. Bonneville-bound L76 or L84 buyers could have picked the optional 3.08:1 highway flyers (in a Positraction differential), while gears of choice for solid-lifter street warriors were the ever-popular 4.11:1 cogs. Serious Saturday night soldiers could have chosen the gut-wrenching 4.56:1 ratio.

The M20 four-speed was built in Muncie, Indiana, and featured an aluminum case, wider-faced gears, and larger synchronizers, and was both beefier and smoother than the old Borg-Warner four-speed it had replaced midyear in 1963. *Car Life* called it "a faultless gearbox." Bob McVay was convinced Chevrolet's new four-speed was "one of the best we've tested." Continued McVay in his September 1964 *Motor Trend* review, "it gives lightning-fast shifts, up or down, without ever hanging up, [and] it has short, positive throws between gears."

Additional performance options included the $43.05 G81 Positraction differential—ordered again, as in 1963, by 82 percent of Corvette buyers—and the rare $202.30 N03 36.5-gallon gas tank, installed in 38 1964 Sting Ray coupes. Two extra-cost features promised in 1963, off-road exhausts and the five cast-aluminum 15x6-inch knock-off wheels found under RPO P48, actually did appear in 1964, the Kelsey-Hayes knock-offs adding a tidy $322.80 to the Corvette sticker. That high price, combined with continued tire sealing problems, helps explain why only 806 P48 sets were sold.

Priced at $37.70, off-road exhausts, RPO N11, consisted of a low-restriction muffler with its own tailpipe in place of the standard muffler-tailpipe

This shot of a prototype 1964 Corvette wheel cover demonstrates the difference between the chrome-plated and frosted wheel covers.

combo. Other than welded front joints (stock mufflers used clamps), the N11 system was externally identical to the standard pieces. The difference came inside the N11 muffler, where only three baffles were present, compared to the five found in the regular-issue mufflers. Fewer baffles meant lower back pressure, as well as a much more prominent exhaust note, both results representing music to performance buyers' ears.

Although N11 could be ordered along with the 375-horsepower L84, 365-horsepower L76, and 300-horsepower L75/M20 powertrains, it wasn't available for the standard 250-horsepower 327, nor the L75/M35 combination since these engines used 2-inch exhaust pipes. Off-road mufflers fit larger 2.5-inch pipes, which the manual-transmission 300-horsepower 327s and the two solid-lifter small-blocks used. Another hot exhaust option, this one featuring sexy side-mount pipes, was planned for 1964 production, but didn't arrive until 1965.

New options on the 1964 list included the $75.35 K66 ignition and $86.10 F40 suspension. Installed only on the high-performance L76 and L84 327s, RPO K66 replaced the ignition's conventional points and condenser with a solid-state, transistorized system. Only 552 buyers checked off the K66 option during its first year. Much more rare, the F40 heavy-duty suspension became available in late January 1964 and was officially offered only with the 375-horsepower 327, although F40-equipped L76 Corvettes are known. Among F40 heavy-duty components were beefier springs, stiffer shocks, and a thicker front stabilizer measuring 0.94 inch, as opposed to the standard 0.75-inch sway bar. F40 production was a mere 82 units.

Returning for an encore in 1964 were the J65 metallic brakes, a welcomed option that this time also included the J50 power brake booster. In 1963, an average customer could have ordered J50 and J65 separately for a Sting Ray at a total cost of $80.75. The following year Joe Average could have had the same power-assisted metallic brakes by simply checking off RPO J65 alone—and spent only $53.80 while doing it. It was a great deal, one that 4,780 1964 Corvette buyers couldn't pass up. And anyone who doubted J65's value needed only pick up a car magazine, *any* car magazine, for further convincing.

"Though production drum brakes (with organic linings) have been as prone to fade as any other on Detroit cars," read an August 1964 *Car Life* report, "opting for the metallic linings will let Sting Ray buyers avoid this problem." In *Road & Track*'s opinion, "to match performance, the [stock] brakes are adequate for normal fast driving but they will definitely fade and become uneven when used to the limit. When one considers both the weight and speed of the Sting Ray, it would appear to be an excellent car for a disc brake system, and it is surprising that General Motors has not yet adopted discs for this model."

While discs were still a year away, there was one more high-performance Corvette brake option in 1964, but it didn't come cheap. Carrying a formidable $629.50 asking price RPO J56 picked up where RPO Z06 left off in 1963. J56 equipment included the Z06's special sintered cerametalix brake linings, finned drums, internal drum-cooling fans, elephant-ear backing plate scoops, and unique dual-circuit master cylinder with power assist. Even though dealers had taken orders for Z06 Corvettes in the fall of 1963, the option wasn't carried over for 1964, but in fact was broken up into individual components. Having established that heavy-duty suspension was available as RPO F40 and that the special brakes were then listed under RPO J56, a dealer bulletin dated December 26,1963, detailed the new arrangement:

More than one wheel-cover finish was used in 1964. Apparently, early 1964 Corvettes were equipped with wheel covers featuring a chromed center section and a "frosted" gray-painted rim. This Silver Blue fuel-injected Corvette convertible wears the reversed "frosted" wheel covers used later. Notice the center is painted while the rim is chromed.

Above
Bigger valves and internal improvements to the Rochester fuel-injection unit helped boost the L84 327's output to 375-horsepower in 1964. As the price for RPO L84 jumped to $538, demand fell considerably, with production dropping to 1,325. Notice the J50 power brake booster, a $43.05 option. RPO J50 production for 1964 was 2,270.

Right
In response to customer complaints about reflective glare, black instrument centers replaced the silver centers used in 1963. Also notice the 6,500-rpm tach redline, a standard feature when either the 365-horsepower L76 or 375-horsepower L84 327s were ordered. The four-speed stick shown here is tied to a close-ratio M20 transmission. Production of the close-ratio M20 four-speed, used behind the L76 and L84 only, was 8,496 in 1964. Another 10,538 wide-ratio M20s were installed behind the base 327 and the 300-horsepower L75.

"In connection with the release of the above options [F40 and J56], your attention is directed to the special performance package (RPO Z06) initially released for the 1964 model Corvette. The contemplated design modifications and refinements did not materialize. However, in line with customers and dealer requests, the basic performance suspension and brake components have been separated and re-released as indicated above. Thus, the customer can now select the option that meets his particular requirements or order both of them depending on the intended usage of his Corvette.

"Some zones have orders in their Special Z06 Suspense File that they were instructed to hold by dealers. It is requested that zones immediately contact

WE MAKE VERY FEW CORVETTES LIKE THIS

Look closely. Those are cast aluminum wheels. They're one of several optional-at-extra-cost performance items Corvette supplies to the handful of enthusiasts who demand them.

If you want a 36.5-gallon gas tank, we have it. There are special performance equipment packages too. They include heavy-duty brake and suspension parts, and they're available only with the 375-hp Ramjet fuel-injected V8, 4-speed shift and Positraction equipment.

Why all these extra-cost options for a handful of enthusiasts? Well, we built the Corvette Sting Ray when we found that not everybody wants the same kind of car. And the options came in when we found that not everybody wants the same kind of Corvette. Options let you get just the Corvette you want. To the exact degree.

You can't fit people to the car. So we fit the car to the people....Chevrolet Division of General Motors, Detroit, Michigan. **'64 CORVETTE STING RAY**

Originally offered in 1963, these Kelsey-Hayes cast-aluminum knock-off wheels did not make regular production until 1964 thanks to various casting defects that resulted in poor tire sealing. Price for a set of five knock-offs, listed under RPO P48, was $322.80. Only 806 sets were sold in 1964. Notice the reference to the $202.30 N03 36.5-gallon fuel tank, itself a rare option. RPO N03 production was a mere 38.

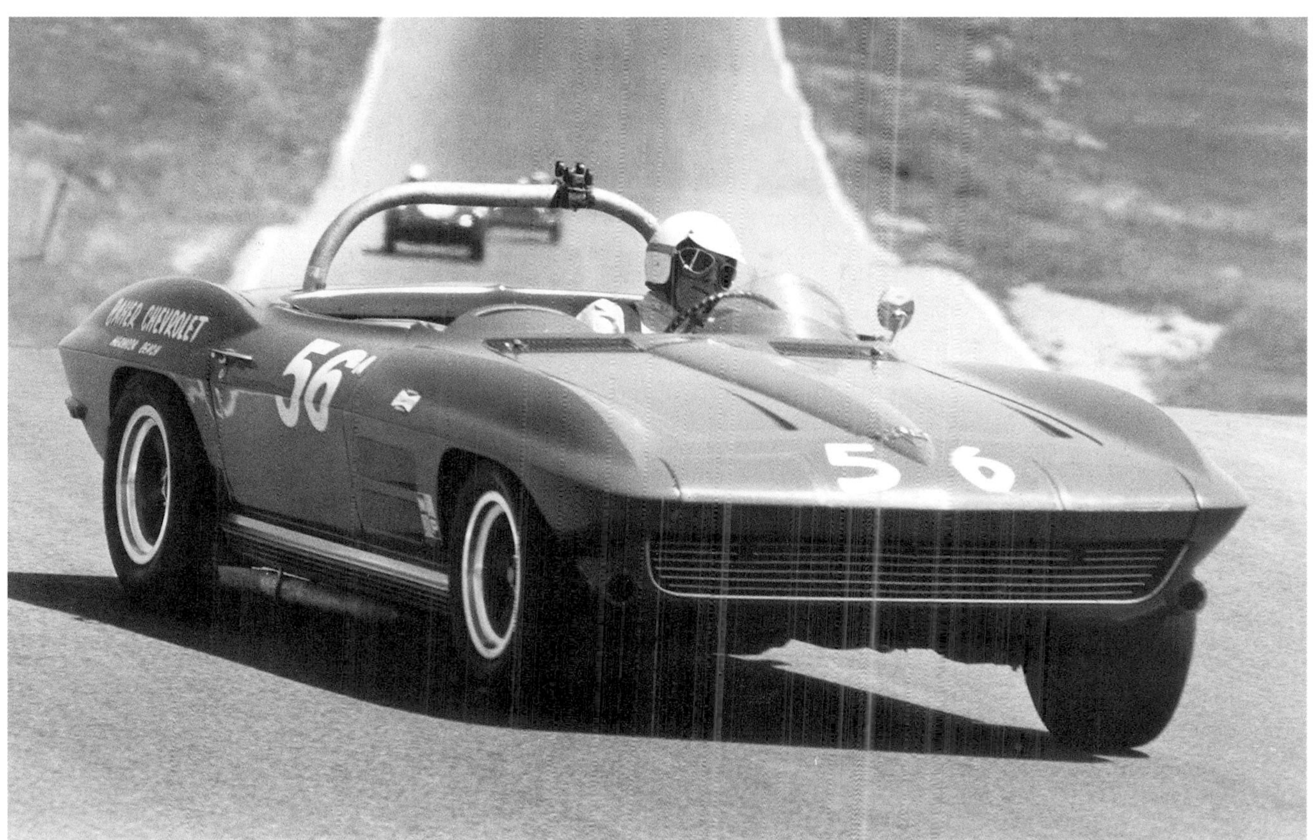

Along with Dr. Dick Thompson and Bob Bondurant, Dick Guldstrand stood out as one of the most prominent Sting Ray race pilots in the early 1960s. Here, Guldstrand does his thing at Riverside, California, in April 1964. After a wheel failure resulted in a serious end-over-end wreck at Riverside in 1963, a roller skate was attached to Guldstrand's roll bar as a joke. It would become his trademark. *Dave Friedman photo*

each dealer regarding such orders to determine exactly what type of performance equipment the customer wants. The zone should then delete Z06 as originally specified on the dealer's order and use the blank space(s) on the order form to indicate the performance option(s) the customer desires."

Officially, the J56 heavy-duty brake option was listed only for L84 Corvette customers in 1964, but like the F40 suspension equipment, it too has been found on L76 Sting Rays. Total production of J56-equipped 1964 Corvettes was a mere 29, including the fuel-injected coupe wearing knock-offs that floored Bob McVay of *Motor Trend*.

"Stopping power was amazing and adequate for the car's red-hot performance," he wrote. "We put it through stop after grueling stop from speeds of 100 mph up to 134 mph, and the brakes never faded completely. They smelled terrible and they'd pull slightly when hot, but they cooled down quickly and kept working no matter how much we asked of them."

"Oh, joy! What brakes!" screamed *Car Life*, calling all other binders "puny" in comparison. Nonetheless, *Car Life*'s report still questioned whether or not J56 advantages were worth $629. "Dissipation of the rapidly built-up heat in these brakes is, of course, hastened by the special drums," it explained, "but there is no reason to suspect that the stock drums with metallic linings wouldn't do substantially as well in less severe service." McVay questioned the cost, too, but for a different reason. "Somehow, we can't help feeling that four-wheel discs would be more practical, and we hear they're slated for 1965." He heard right.

Yet another new-and-improved fiberglass two-seater for 1965 would both stop and go better than any of its forerunners. But until it arrived on the scene, the 1964 Sting Ray was the best Corvette yet. As *Car Life* concluded in the summer of 1964, "there is no more go-able, roadable, steerable, adjustable, comfortable, respondable, or stoppable car mass-produced in this country today." Period.

1965

Easy Come, Easy Go

At first glance, it appeared that nothing all that different awaited Corvette customers at new-model introduction time in the fall of 1964. Slight exterior variations on the Sting Ray theme included a revised, blacked-out grille; a reformed, totally flat hood devoid of those disliked indentations present in 1963 and 1964; rearranged fender "gills" with three functional vertical louvers; restamped mag-type wheel covers; and restyled rocker trim with only one black line running end to end. Inside, plusher, reupholstered vinyl buckets offered a little more support, while a switch from conical instrument faces to a fully flat style helped drivers view the dashboard in a better light. Seatbelt retractors, molded door panels with integral armrests, a few reshaped baubles here and there, and that was basically it—Chevrolet's new Corvette for 1965. If prospective buyers never turned beyond page one, that's all they saw.

But the 1965 Sting Ray's storybook couldn't be judged solely by its dust jacket. Introduction of Chevrolet's third-edition Sting Ray marked the debut for a long-awaited standard feature, while the end of the model run spelled farewell for a long-revered performance option. Disc brakes—true state-of-the-art, world-class, bolted-to-the-ground binders—were finally added to the Corvette's arsenal in 1965, and not only up front, but at all four corners. Meanwhile, Rochester fuel injection, the famed fuelie equipment, was dropped from the Corvette's list of extra-cost power sources after 1965.

And if all that wasn't enough front-page news for Sting Ray followers, 1965 also brought the Corvette's first big-block V-8, the brutish 396 Turbo-Jet—425 horses' worth of tire-melting muscle more than capable of helping lead-footed, hell-bent drivers forget all about the fuelie's eminent demise. An obvious response

Corvette colors numbered eight in 1965: Tuxedo Black, Ermine White, Nassau Blue, Glen Green, Milano Maroon, Rally Red, Goldwood Yellow, and Silver Pearl. This maroon coupe is one of 771 1965 Sting Rays equipped with the 375-horsepower L84 fuel-injected 327, the last of the famed fuelie Corvettes.

to escalating enemy activity in Detroit's heated battle for cubic-inch supremacy, the 396-ci Mark IV V-8 debuted as a Sting Ray option in February and quickly left larger big-block rivals in the dust thanks in part to its innovative "porcupine" cylinder heads. Not since 1963 had there been so many high-powered headlines on the fiberglass front.

No slouches when it came to burning rubber, Duntov's fuel-injected small-block V-8s had been the Corvette's crown jewels since 1957. Manufactured by Rochester Products, a GM division in Rochester, New York, the Ramjet continuous-flow fuel-injection system was originally the work of engineer John Dolza, who first developed a working unit in 1955, hot on the heels of Mercedes' announcement of standard fuel injection for its classic gull-wing 300SL in 1954. Driven to make the Corvette a world-class competitor, chief engineer Ed Cole then put Duntov on the project in 1956, reportedly telling him that if he weren't so

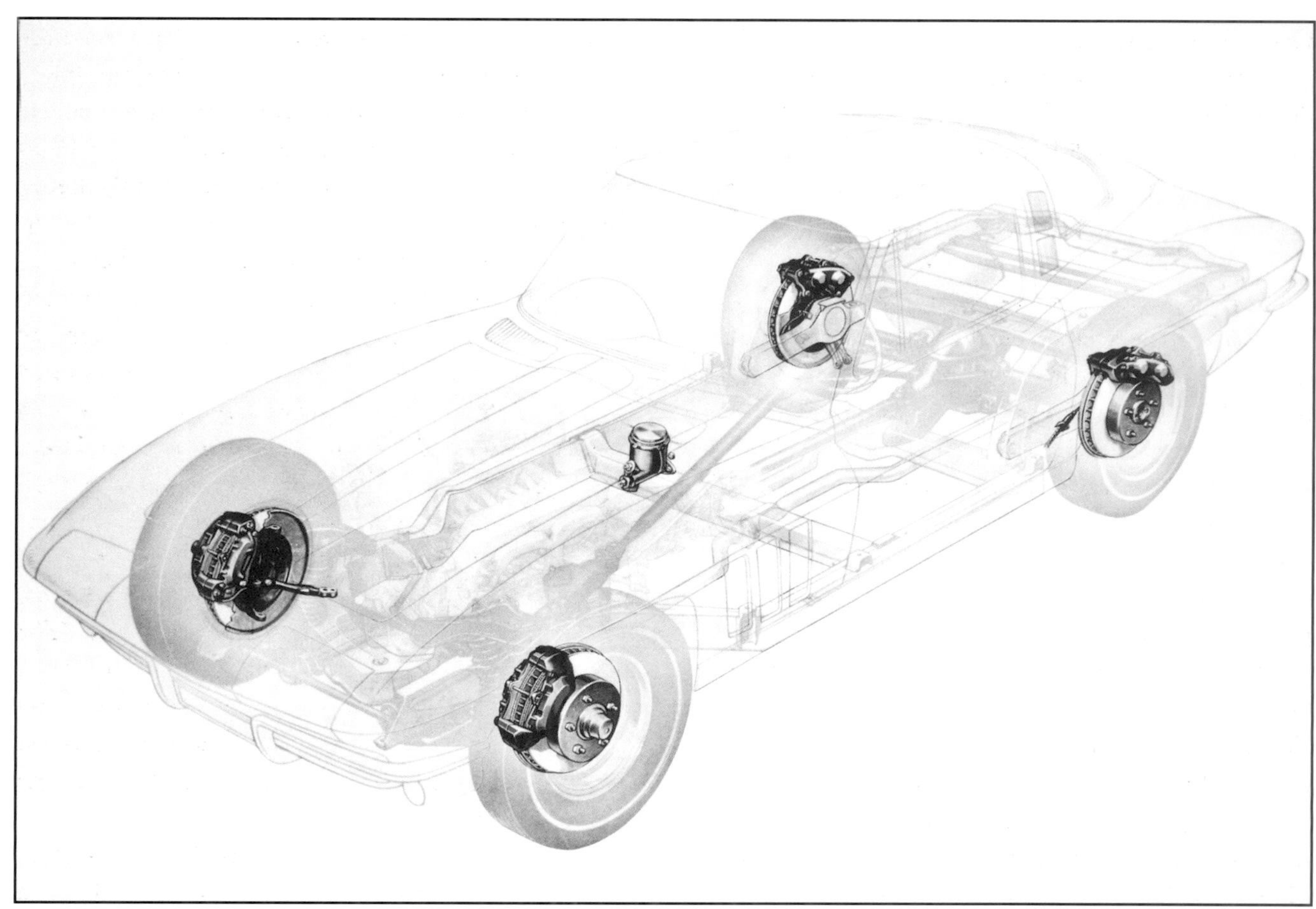

Although they were developed by the Kelsey-Hayes Company, the 1965 Corvette's standard four-wheel disc brakes were manufactured by Delco. Representing state-of-the-art stopping power, at least from an American perspective, these standard brakes could still be deleted by Corvette buyers who preferred to live in the past. RPO J61 both replaced those discs with drums and put $64.50 back into a customer's pocket as a credit. Notice the short section of emergency brake cable appearing just in front of the rear disc at right. The Corvette design cleverly incorporated the center of that rotor assembly as a drum for a conventional parking brake.

busy running things, he'd be right there in the shop working with Dolza on fuel-injection development. Not long afterward, Cole was promoted to general manager of Chevrolet and GM vice president; six months later, the regular-production Ramjet fuel-injected unit was introduced.

Early Ramjet fuel injection certainly had its share of bugs, but performance was exceptional with the temperamental unit in top tune. Two varieties were offered, 250- and the 283-horsepower, atop the newly enlarged 283-ci V-8 for 1957. Of the 283-horsepower Corvette, *Road & Track* reported that "the fuel-injection engine is an absolute jewel, quiet and remarkably docile when driven gently around town, yet instantly transformable into a roaring brute when pushed hard. Its best feature is its "instantaneous throttle response, completely free of any stutter or stumble under any situation." Zero to 60 for the 283-horsepower fuelie came in a mere 5.7 seconds—fast even by today's standards, downright frightening relative to what Detroit was building some 35 years ago.

Continued development helped iron out bugs and boost performance as fuel-injection reliability improved and maximum fuel-injection horsepower grew: 290-horsepower in 1958, 315 in 1961, 360 in 1962, and 375 in 1964. At the same time, fuelie production varied, from 1,040 units in 1957, up to 1,511 in 1958, down to 859 in 1960, followed by a steady upward trend reaching a peak of 2,610 for the 1963 Sting Ray. That trend turned back down the following year, with fuelie sales dropping to 1,325, then 771 for 1965.

Helping bring about the demise of fuel injection was the development of bigger, better four-barrel carburetors and improved intake manifolds, which made

Chevrolet's conventionally aspirated, yeoman-like V-8s nearly as powerful as their more expensive, finicky fuelie brethren. The appearance in 1964 of the truly formidable 365-horsepower L76 327 perhaps represented, the straw that broke fuel injection's back. Handwriting on the wall quickly followed.

"If you have fuel injection on your Corvette," scrawled Ed Janicki in *Car Life*'s November 1964 issue. "you have some sort of distinction. Few late model Corvette owners have it, even though it's been available from Chevrolet for about eight years now." Janicki's explanation for the decline? "If you bought a fuel-injection system this year you know that it cost you as much as a vacation to the World's Fair," he claimed. "Fuel injection is becoming less appealing for just that reason—price. Sports car enthusiasts don't feel they're getting their money's worth. As an example, the highest rated Chevrolet engine (365bhp) costs only $107 extra. Put fuel injection on that engine and it goes to 375bhp. That's only 10bhp more and you have to pay $538 to get it ... $53 for each additional horsepower."

Fuel injection had never come cheap, but at least the price had remained the same, at $484.20, from 1957 to 1962. RPO L84's cost was even cut to $430.40 in 1963. However, the L84 option's limited-production status forced Chevrolet to tack on that $107.60 price increase in 1964, and as a result the percentage of fuel-injection installations dropped by half, from 12 percent in 1963 to 6 percent the following year. By late 1964 it was clear the fuelie days were numbered. As *Motor Trend*'s clairvoyants predicted in their December 1964 issue, "Chevrolet will probably drop fuel injection on [its] 1966 Corvettes. Fewer and fewer buyers are ordering it. Chevy's officials feel [$538 is] too much to pay for an extra 10hp and slightly better throttle response. Looks like [fuel injection] could go the way of air suspension and swivel seats." That it did.

Before it left, however, Corvette fuel injection did have one last dance in 1965, and its partners were, as usual, quite impressed especially after the standard four-wheel discs joined the party. "Ten years ago, who could have guessed that the 1965 Corvette would have fuel injection, 4-speed manual transmission, limited slip differential, all independent suspension and, wonder of wonder, disc brakes?" read *Road & Track*'s report on a 1965 375-horsepower L84 coupe with F40 suspension and the 3.70:1 Positraction differential. "The Corvette has become a car any manufacturer would be proud to produce, and a far, far cry from the 6-cyl phut-phut with [a] 2-speed automatic transmission that was standard in the first model to bear the Corvette name."

Proving the Rochester unit hadn't lost a step, *Road & Track*'s testers managed 0–60 miles per hour in 6.3 seconds, with the end of the quarter-mile coming up 8.1 seeconds later. Trap speed was 99 miles per hour. As usual, a confident launch contributed greatly to the 1965 L84's 14.4-second elapsed time (ET). Reported *Road & Track*, "making a fast start, thanks to good weight distribution, independent

Basically an L84 327 with a big Holley four-barrel carburetor in place of the Rochester fuel-injection unit, the 365-horsepower L76 was introduced in 1964 and carried over unchanged into 1965. This airbrushed piece of factory artwork simply added the L76 features to an earlier image of a 1963 small-block. In 1965, 5,011 Corvette customers shelled out an extra $129.15 for RPO L76, which could only be ordered with the close-ratio Muncie four-speed.

A blacked-out grille, revised rocker moldings, and restyled fender louvers set the 1963 Corvette apart from its predecessors. As in 1964, coupes again represented a distinct minority in 1965, with production reaching 8,186. Base price for a 1965 coupe was $4,321. Options shown here include the $134.50 sidemount exhausts (RPO N14), $322.80 knock-off wheels (P48), and $50.05 "goldwall" nylon-cord tires (T01). RPO P48 sales for 1965 totaled 1,116, with 130 of these knock-off sets wearing the 7.75x15-inch goldwall tires. Another 859 sets of the T01 tires were also sold on standard steel wheels.

As in 1964, those vents in the roof pillar behind the door were functiona for 1965, serving as exhausts for the electric system. Notice the backup lights: in 1965 they became a part of the Comfort and Convenience Group, RPO Z01. Priced at $16.16, RPO Z01 also included a day/night rearview mirror.

rear suspension and Positraction, the big machine simply squats and squirts."

Leaving their mess behind, *Road & Track*'s fuelie fans walked away all smiles. "Summing up, the car does a masterful job of hitting the market bulls-eye. [It's] keyed to the boulevardier sports/racey types who account for the great majority of its sales. It has enough pizzazz for a movie set, or crumpet collecting, or nymphet nabbing, or for the types who get their jollies from looking at all that glitter. It encourages the Walter Mittys to become Fangios or Foyts. Yet it also goes well enough to suit the driver who is sincere about going fast, and can handle that much performance with skill."

Ten years later, *Road & Track*'s nostalgic staff remained impressed enough to take another look at Chevrolet's last fuel-injected Corvette. Though obviously enhanced in relation to a perspective based on experiences with the ho-hum collection of so-called performance machines being built in 1975, *Road & Track*'s retroactive response was still well worth reading:

Once the revs begin to build up, hang on! By the time the big tach needle reaches 3000rpm, things are beginning to happen so fast it's dizzying. The fuel-injection cars always had the close-ratio 4-speed gearbox; this car had the numerically high 4.11:1 final drive ratio, which makes the most of the close ratios. Even with the 4.11 it takes a good bit of clutch slipping to get the car off the line and it's a nice long climb to the redline at 54mph. But after that the driver works hard just to keep up with the engine, so fast does the redline come up in second and third, and it takes very little time to redline the engine in fourth gear either for that matter. The pull begins to fall off above 5500rpm, but it is a brilliant show up to that point."

After its retro road test, *Road & Track* couldn't help but ask the question how Chevrolet engineers could let mid-1960s peer pressures promoting more cubic inches over balanced performance convince them to let the polite yet potent fuelie Corvette die in favor of a less flexible, muscle-bound, big-block bully? "It seems funny, doesn't it, in the context of 1975 to remember that a leading manufacturer had airflow-controlled, continuous-flow fuel injection and dropped it? The Rochester system was just that, and though it was quite different in detail and designed for a lot of power rather than low emissions, it answers the same basic description as the system now used on Volvos and Porsches, for instance, to meet 1975 emission regulations. How times change." Seven years later, fuel-injection performance returned to the Corvette lineup, this time as standard equipment in the form of the 1982 200-horsepower 350-ci small-block with Cross-Fire Injection.

Of course, most Corvette buyers in 1965 probably would have agreed that the arrival of disc brakes was ample consolation for the eventual loss of fuel injection at year's end. Car owners and critics alike had long been begging for better brakes, even more so after Studebaker made front discs standard in 1963 on its equally timeless fiberglass sportster, the Avanti. Duntov's crew weren't blind, nor deaf, it was just that

If you'd just spent fifty miles twisting down a mountainside in this '65 CORVETTE, you'd be taking the words right out of our mouth about its new 4-wheel disc brakes.

Praise comes easily to Corvette's big caliper-type disc brakes. They're fade-resistant, heat-resistant, water-resistant and fuss-resistant.

Adjustment and maintenance? What adjustment and maintenance? These discs can get along swell without much help.

All this peace of mind is standard equipment on all '65 Corvettes. But even this doesn't complete the improvements.

We've added a new 327-cubic-inch V8. This new one is the best behaved 350-hp V8 you ever met. Loaded with all kinds of good things a high-performance engine ought to have. But tamed to a civilized purr. You can order it or a 300-, 365- or Ramjet fuel-injected 375-hp V8 on any Corvette.

As for appearance, it's brushed up. Smooth new hood, magnesium-style wheel covers, new grille design and functional front fender louvers. And a revised interior that treats you even more elaborately than before.

We didn't change all those lovely items you can specify, like 4-Speed fully synchronized transmission, cast aluminum wheels, Positraction—the lot.

All in all, Corvette for '65 adds up to a lot more car in every way. Which we think is the best possible reason for changing it.

Chevrolet Division of General Motors, Detroit, Michigan

Chevrolet ads in the fall of 1964 couldn't say enough about the Sting Ray's standard disc brakes, news that would soon be overshadowed by the debut of the Corvette's first big-block V-8 in the spring of 1965. Notice the reference to the equally new 350-horsepower L79 small-block. In *Car and Driver's* opinion, dropping the wonderfully docile, wildly energetic L79 beneath the fiberglass hood of a $4,500 car with four-wheel discs and independent rear suspension represented one of the best buys on the sports car market, Europe included.

development of suitably superior disc brakes for the Corvette required some suitably intensive, time-consuming testing.

Automotive disc brake designs date back almost as far as automotive history itself, with England's Frederick William Lanchester taking out the first patent for such a setup in 1902. Various approaches to the idea followed over the years, but disc brake development truly got rolling once WWII military men began looking for suitable ways to haul down heavy, high-powered aircraft during landing. Both Lockheed, a renowned U.S. aircfaft manufacturer, and England's Girling firm had entered the game in the 1930s, while another British outfit, the Dunlop Rubber Company, stopped everyone in their tracks after the war with its own ground-breaking disc brake design that established standards still used today.

In 1951, Girling bought a license to produce the Dunlop design for passenger-car applications. Equipped with Girling brakes, a team of C-type Jaguar roadsters brought worldwide acclaim for the innovative binders by winning the 24 Hours of Le Mans in 1953, embarrassing Enzo Ferrari's much faster V-12 coupes in the process. Two years later, all British racing machines featured disc brakes as did Ferrari by 1958. Across the Atlantic, Chrysler and Crosley each offered a somewhat crude disc brake system in 1949.

General Motors' experiments with disc brakes began in 1937, although Detroit's advancement in the field lagged far behind what European engineers were doing to surely, safely, stop their cars. After both Chrysler's and Crosley's designs failed to impress anyone, GM's Delco-Moraine Division did manage to produce an experimental disc brake system—featuring "ventilated" rotors for increased cooling capacity—in 1954, with working examples ending up on Pontiac's Firebird II gas turbine show car in 1956.

Halibrand discs were tested briefly on the Corvettes John Fitch took to Sebring in 1965, and Duntov chose Girling disc brakes for his lightweight racing Sting Rays late in 1962. Although Girling's competition-proven design couldn't handle the standard Corvette's weight, it was able to haul in the much lighter Grand Sport racers. Earlier that same year, Delco's four-wheel discs had been tested on a prototype Sting Ray at Sebring, and finally arrived as Corvette standard equipment in 1965.

Once development of Corvette discs got serious after 1962, it was primarily longtime test driver and engineer Bob Clift who helped make them a production reality. The Kelsey-Hayes Company actually received the contract for developing the Corvette's four-wheel disc design, and it was the K-H people with whom Clift worked closely for three years. But when it came time to manufacture the resulting four-wheel disc brake equipment, Delco outbid Kelsey-Hayes.

Advantages of the Corvette's Delco discs were various, not the least of which was their fade resistance. Brake fade is a product of high heat, itself an inherent reality where friction is involved. Conventional drum

Continuing a Corvette tradition, the 1965 Sting Ray's standard wheel cover featured a simulated knock-off spinner. Though certainly distinctive, the 1965 covers were not exactly loved by all. According to *Car Life's* curbside critics, they were "less happy, for now they imitate not only knock-off hubs, but mag wheels as well.

brakes are especially sensitive to fade because they do not dissipate heat well, and thermal expansion tends to increase the clearance between the drum wall and brake lining. Discs naturally develop less heat since they work "out in the open," with their caliper-activated friction pads and rotor faces fully exposed (discounting the presence of thin splash shields) to ambient air temperatures.

Heat buildup inside an internal-acting drum brake has no place to go unless such clever optional tricks as the Z06's finned drums, cerametalix linings, internal cooling fans, and vented-backing plates with air scoops were used. Adding the Z06 brakes in 1963, followed by their J56 counterparts in 1964, did greatly reduce operating temperatures, and thus fade, but the merits of all that extra baggage—and its accompanying huge price tags—was rendered a moot point once four-wheel disc brakes made the scene.

Introduced for 1965 as a milder version of the 365-horsepower solid-lifter L76 327, this L79 small-block had civilized hydraulic lifters and 11:1 compression. Fed by a Holley four-barrel carburetor, the L79 327 produced 350 horsepower at 5,800 rpm. Production of RPO L79 was 4,716, making the 350-horsepower 327 the third most popular Corvette power choice in 1965 behind the 300-horsepower L75 327, which found 8,356 buyers that year, and the 365-horsepower L76. The L79's price was $107.60. Adding even more to this L79 coupe's original asking price was the optional air conditioning, RPO C60, which cost $421.80 in 1965. Air conditioning sales hit 2,423 that year, up nearly 25 percent from 1964.

You might have missed the fender badge, but you couldn't have overlooked the 1965 396 Sting Ray's bulging hood. Listed under RPO L78, the Corvette's first big-block V-8 produced 425 real horsepower. Checking off the L78 option meant adding $292.70 to a 1965 convertible's $4,106 base price. Total convertible production that year was 15,376, with 1,409 of those powered by the L78 396. Another 748 1965 coupes were built with the 425-horsepower big-block V-8.

Described by *Motor Trend's* Jim Wright as "fade-proof," the 1965 Corvette's discs were kept even cooler thanks to their aforementioned ventilated design. As opposed to some early disc brake arrangements that featured solid rotors, Delco rotors essentially were two separate discs joined together by webbing. Compared to racing discs, which are commonly drilled full of holes, Corvette discs were "hollow," meaning cooling air was able to flow through them with the same effect created by the racing-style holes. Standard American brakes in 1965 simply didn't come any cooler.

Another disc brake advantage involved the relationship between the driver's right and the road, a concept known as "pedal modulation." Conventional drum brakes are self-energizing, meaning that the energy used to stop a wheel from turning when the shoe comes in contact with the drum also helps squeeze the shoe against the drum. Although this effect translates into "free" stopping pressure, it also hinders pedal feel, as driver effort and actual braking power are not proportional. Among other things, a drum brake system's inherently weak pedal modulation relationship contributes to wheel lockup during hard stops. As Duntov told *Corvette News* in 1964, with the new disc brakes a Corvette's "retardation is directly proportional to pedal pressure so that the driver can modulate his retardation very precisely. So the degree of braking control is much greater with discs than with self-energizing drum brakes."

Underlying all this was the plain fact that the Corvette disc brakes simply offered more pure stopping power, measured in part by total swept area, which is the amount of rotor face (multiplied by four) covered by the friction pads through one revolution. Like the drums they replaced, the Sting Ray's durable, cast-iron discs were big, measuring 11.75 inches in diameter and 1.25 inches in thickness. Effective lining area for each brake pad was about 20 square inches, translating into a total swept area of 461.2 square inches, up considerably from the 1964 drum brake system's 328 square inches. Mashing those pads against the rotors were four-piston calipers with 1.857-inch pistons in front, 1.375 inches out back. Stopping power was split 65/35, front to rear.

As much as everyone in 1965 rushed to praise the Corvette's four-wheel discs, one thing did need to be said:

New bucket-seat upholstery, inner door panels with integral armrests, and flat-faced gauges were among interior revamps for 1965. This 1965 fuelie coupe also features the $48.45 teakwood steering wheel and M20 close-ratio four-speed transmission, the only tranny offered behind the L84 327 in 1965. One popular option this coupe doesn't have is the $203.40 AM/FM radio, RPO U69. Ninety-four percent of Corvette buyers checked off RPO U69 in 1965.

the big Corvette drum brakes left behind weren't entirely bad. As *Car Life* explained in its August 1965 issue, "though the old standard drums were liberal in size and adequate for everyday stopping, they weren't always even in their action and could be made to fade fairly easily; still, relative to the contemporary domestic production, they were among the better standard brakes available."

Even better were the optional J56 heavy-duty drum brakes. In their heyday, these beefy brakes easily represented state-of-the-art pieces, at least as far as American performance cars—as well as average American drivers—were concerned. As Duntov later told Karl Ludvigsen, author of *Corvette: America's Star-Spangled Sports Car*, "although brutal, [the J56 drums] had the highest energy-dissipating ability and durability of all brakes we could visualize on our Corvette." All that was forgotten, however, in 1965 as the Sting Ray's discs simply embarrassed everything else on U.S. roads.

In Bob McVay's opinion, "the 1965 Corvette has the finest, smoothest-acting, and strongest set of stoppers available on any American automobile." "Disc brakes are big news on the automotive scene this year," he wrote in *Motor Trend*'s April 1965 issue, "but Corvette builders don't believe in doing things halfway."

Stated a *Road & Track* report, "long ago we gave up (read chickened out) on doing stomp-down, all-out panic stops in American cars, but the Corvette restored our faith to such an extent that we did 0-80-0-80-0 time after time and grew bored, almost, with the ease and lack of fuss with which the car stopped straight and true. No lock up, no fade, no muscle-straining increases in pedal pressure. Just good dependable stops. Wonderful."

Even though those wonderful disc brakes were indeed included as standard equipment in 1965, the Sting Ray options list still carried the old drums as a $64.50 credit under RPO J61, basically so that Chevrolet could dispose of leftover supplies. Only 316 customers helped cut down the pile, however, leaving Chevy's idea guys poised to try again with their J61 "inventory clearance" in 1966; but the credit option did not return.

Options that did return for 1965 included the aluminum knock-off wheels; power brakes, steering, and windows; leather seats; air conditioning; F40 heavy-duty suspension; K66 transistorized ignition; NOB 36.5-gallon fuel tank; and N11 off-road exhausts. Again offered as a coupe option only, RPO N03 was chosen by a mere 41 Corvette customers in 1965. Newly offered extra-cost items that year included a cockpit-controlled telescopic steering wheel (N36), an honest-to-goodness teakwood steering wheel (N32), and another off-road exhaust system, the $134.50 N14 pipes. Priced at $48.45, the classy teakwood wheel was yet another Corvette option hinted at one year, then introduced the next.

Mentioned as well in 1964 paperwork, RPO N14 featured a pair of sexy, side-mount exhausts with crimped restrictor pipes (mufflers in name only) hidden behind bright aluminum heat shields. Installing the N14 system meant completely deleting the standard dual exhausts and replacing the rear body panel, its two lower openings no longer needed. Fiberglass modification was also required along the body's lower edge to make room for the installation, which when completed was not easily missed, either by eyes or ears. As much an appearance option as a performance feature, the N14 system was labeled "off-road" by Chevrolet in order to shirk liability for any noise ordinance violations. Whether included with a tried-and-true 327 small-block or the newly offered L78 396 Turbo-Jet, those side-mount exhausts didn't keep a secret very well at all. Neither could Chevrolet, in 1964, concerning the impending arrival of its new big-block V-8.

That summer the rumor mill was overloaded with speculation surrounding the return of Chevrolet's appropriately named Mystery Motor, an all-out racing big-block V-8 created by engineer Dick Keinath in July 1962. Keinath's Mystery Motor, officially known as the Mark II, was similar on the bottom end to Chevrolet's other clandestine racing big-block, the super-stock Z11 powerplant, also developed midyear 1962. Both powerplants featured identical displacements, 427-ci, but that's where comparisons ended. While the Z11 drag-racing V-8 was old news—it was simply a highly modified, stroked 409—the Mark II big-block was like nothing else seen before, especially up top where a pair of exceptional, free-breathing cylinder heads featured innovative staggered valves laid out in a seemingly haphazard fashion reminiscent of a porcupine's quills. Dyno-measured output for the Mark II easily topped 500 horsepower.

Literally laughing in the face of the AMA factory-racing ban, Chevrolet Engineering, in cahoots with veteran Daytona Beach speed merchant Smokey Yunick, prepared a Mark II stock car (one of five built) for the February 1963 running of NASCAR's Daytona 500. General Motors' top brass, however, got the last laugh when they sent down their infamous cease and desist memo in January. Having seen enough of Duntov's semisecret Grand Sport shenanigans, as well as what was going on in Yunick's shop, GM chairman Frederick Donner brought both projects to a halt, but not before the Mark II made its record-shattering debut in Florida. As impressive as they had been during the two 100-mile Daytona 500 qualifiers on February 22 (a Mark II Chevy stocker won both, averaging in excess of 160 miles per hour), mechanical mishaps left the five Mystery Motor Chevrolets back in the pack while five Fords took top honors at Daytona's big show February 24. With all of GM's divisions then officially out of racing, Chevrolet's Mark II 427 was apparently headed for the scrap heap following its Daytona 500 failure.

Such was not the case. Regardless of GM's new-found anti-racing stance, the Mark II V-8's potential as a street performer wasn't overlooked. Equally hard to miss were the two 427-powered Corvette competition specials built late in 1962 at Mickey Thompson's shop in Long Beach, California. Driven by Bill Krause, one of these beasties took third in the Daytona Challenge Cup in January 1963, setting the stage for a possible production follow-up. But Duntov was not exactly thrilled about the prospect of a big-block Corvette, preferring instead to concentrate on much lighter powerplants with high horsepower-per-cubic-inch ratios; smaller, stronger engines better suited for his ideal of a tail-heavy Sting Ray. Nonetheless, he was overruled, and about a year after the Mystery Motor's Daytona debut, Zora found himself forming a special design team of engineers including Fred Frincke, Cal Wade, and Denny Davis. The team's goal? To build a street-going counterpart of the Mark II big-block, a major chunk of cast-iron guaranteed to tip the scales toward a Corvette's nose.

As it was, a Ford man may well have had more to do with the initial development of a big-block Corvette than Duntov. Carroll Shelby, former Le Mans winner and builder of the fastest "production" machine ever to hit the American road, quite simply forced Chevrolet's hand. In 1963, Shelby's Ford-powered AC

Cobras eclipsed Duntov's Sting Rays on the American sports car racing front, although it wasn't exactly a fair fight. Shelby's Cobra was nearly a half-ton lighter and wasn't even close to being a true production automobile, with only 1,003 built mostly by hand during the entire five-year model run—at its peak, the Corvette plant in St. Louis rolled that many Sting Rays off the line in two weeks. Regardless of this "apple-orange" situation, comparisons between America's only two-seat sportsters were continually made, and the Corvette continually got the short end.

Initially armed with a 260-ci Ford Windsor small-block, followed by a 289-ci Windsor, the lithe, beastly Cobra always held a distinct power-to-weight ratio advantage over the larger, heavier, much more civilized Corvette. That advantage grew by leaps and bounds late in 1964 when Shelby-American started stuffing Ford's NASCAR-proven 427-ci Le Mans big-block V-8 beneath that little aluminum bonnet, instantly injecting 425 horses' worth of venom into the Cobra's bite. In or out of racing, Chevrolet had little choice but to retaliate.

Duntov's engineers were, of course, already working on a big-block Corvette when Shelby's outrageous 427 Cobra hit the streets. Grist for that ever-present rumor mill had been piling up all through 1964, then spilled out that fall. As *Motor Trend* claimed in its September issue, "Chevrolet may revive the Mark II Daytona engine for passenger car use. This is the engine that shook the troops at Daytona in 1963, developing about 550hp from 427 inches, giving lap speeds up to 166mph. It disappeared when GM dropped out of racing. But recent reports mention prototypes under test powered by this basic engine reduced to 396ci." *Motor Trend* readers were instructed to keep an eye out for this new big-block come spring.

As a Corvette ad announced just months into 1965, "You heard the rumors. Now hear this ... There *is* a Turbo Jet 396 from Chevrolet." *Sports Car Graphic*'s Jerry Titus almost couldn't believe it, writing that "while General Motors continues to pursue its non-racing policy and promote the theme of Proving Grounds Development as the ONLY answer, it is about to put an engine in production that was developed specifically for racing." Production of 396 Turbo-Jet big-blocks began in January 1965, with the first Mark IV–equipped Chevrolets hitting the streets in April.

Like the L84 fuelie small-block, the 425-horsepower L78 big-block could only be ordered with the close-ratio M20 Muncie four-speed. Mandatory options also included the K66 transistorized ignition and the G81 Positraction differential. This L78 convertible also has the optional J50 power brakes—notice the vacuum booster and dual-circuit master cylinder.

Chevrolet general manager Bunkie Knudsen made it all official in February during a press gathering at GM's Mesa, Arizona, proving grounds. Introduced to reporters was the Mark IV V-8, the downsized 396-ci Mark II derivative mentioned by *Motor Trend*. Knudsen proudly pointed to three new big-blocks: a hydraulically timed 325-horsepower Turbo-Jet for the topline Caprice; a 375-horsepower 396 (also with hydraulic lifters) for the equally new Z16 Malibu, Chevrolet's first SS 396 Chevelle; and a solid-lifter, 425-horsepower maximum Mark IV for the Corvette, which Titus then described as a "fiberglass porcupine," a reference to those wonderful, wild Mark IV cylinder heads.

The Mark IV head's staggered-valve porcupine arrangement was made possible by Chevrolet's trademark individually mounted ball-stud rocker arm design, a trick that had helped make Chevy's first overhead-valve V-8—the high-winding "Hot One"—so hot in 1955. Not only did those ball-stud rockers greatly reduce valvetrain weight, they also allowed engineers to put the valves where they would work best. Instead of designing the all-important combustion chamber around a limited valve position, the ball-stud rockers' flexibility gave Duntov's crew a clean slate.

Mark IV intake valves were located up high near their ports and inclined slightly, making for a straighter flow from intake manifold to combustion chamber. An opposite inclination was applied (to a slightly lesser

Since this fuel-injected 1965 coupe was ordered without an optional radio, there was no need for the ever-present ignition shielding required on a Corvette. As in 1964, the 1965 L84 327 produced 375 horsepower at 6,200 rpm. Notice the dual-circuit master cylinder (bottom right) included as part of the J50 power brake package. This L84 small-block also has the optional K66 electronic ignition. Carrying a $75.35 price tag, RPO K66 found 3,686 buyers in 1965. Only 304 K66/L84 combos were sold, with 17 of those cars built without the U69 radio.

Engineer and Corvette test driver Bob Clift poses with a Canadian-built 1974 Bricklin SV-1—a gullwing creation he helped design—at a November 1993 Bricklin club meet in Orlando, Florida. The man behind the development of the Corvette's four-wheel disc brake system, Clift joined innovative independent automaker Malcolm Bricklin in Fredricton, New Brunswick, in 1973 after retiring from Chevrolet Engineering.

degree) on the exhaust end to the same effect. In between, those inclined valves opened into a "modified wedge" (some classified it as semi-hemispherical, semi-hemi for short) combustion chamber that featured improved flame propagation and superb volumetric efficiency. Along with exceptional breathing characteristics, the inclined valve setup also offered slightly more room for the Mark IV's truly big valves, 2.19-inch intake and 1.72-inch exhaust.

Activating those valves was a serious solid-lifter cam, a lumpy loper with a 0.497-inch lift on the intake side, 0.503-inch on exhaust. Duration was 348 degrees with a 127 degree overlap. Feeding coal to the Mark IV's fire was a job handled by a big Holley four-barrel carb atop an aluminum intake, while the K66 transistorized ignition—mandatory with the L78 option—supplied the spark to start that fire. Inside the bores, impact-extruded aluminum pistons squeezed the fuel-air mixture to an octane-intensive 11:1 ratio. Free-flowing, header-type cast-iron exhaust manifolds directed spent gases down the pipes in short order.

Everything else about the 396 Turbo-Jet was beefier or better than your average big-block. The Mark IV's forged-steel crank (with cross-drilled journals for added lubrication) and rods were about as tough as they came, as was the block itself. Pumped up where it counted, on the bottom end, the L78 cylinder block featured huge bulkheads, massive bearing surfaces, and four-bolt main bearing caps. All this extra rigidity, combined with an

Corvette buyers who opted for the optional removable hardtop in 1965 numbered 7,787. Of that RPO C07 total, 1,277 were added at no cost in place of a folding top. Although the $236.75 hardtop was certainly attractive, it wasn't easy to handle. "Definitely not a one-man job," wrote *Motor Trend's* Bob McVay. "Taking off [the] top can be a chore. Once in place, it rattled and required lots of muscle to lift up in order to get into [the] luggage compartment." Ten years later, Road & Track remained displeased in a retro-review of a 1965 fuelie, claiming the removable hardtop required "a lot of bolting and unbolting to install or remove, and one assumes the body designers saw it as an all-winter proposition."

exceptional lubrication system, relatively lightweight valvetrain, and excellent breathing characteristics translated into sky-high rev limits for the L78. Maximum output of 425 horsepwer came on at 6,400 rpm, higher even than the 375-horsepower L84 fuelie, which developed its top power at 200 rpm less. Torque output for the L78 was 415 foot-pounds at 4,000 rpm.

Even with a slight displacement disadvantage, the 396 Turbo-Jet was an able opponent for anything Detroit could offer in 1965. As *Motor Trend*'s Roger Huntington wrote, the L78 "can't quite match the cubes of the '427' Ford or the '426-S' Dodge/Plymouth option, but breathing may be enough to more than make up the difference." *Motorcade*'s Jim Wright agreed, claiming Chevrolet's new big-block wasn't "as spectacular as the all-out racing engines from Ford and Chrysler, but as a high performance street engine it's going to be hard to beat."

Dropping the optional L78 big-block between fiberglass fenders for 1965 required various revamps, not the least of which was an impressive, bulging hood with functional louvers. Cooling the beast beneath that bulge meant adding a larger fan and a wider radiator with an appropriately large shroud. And like the K66 ignition, Chevrolet's close-ratio M20 four-speed and G81 Positraction differential were mandatory with RPO L78.

As for chassis and drivetrain modifications, a revised-frame cross-member was needed to mount the big-block in place of the more comfortable 327 small-blocks, as were stiffer front springs. Clutch diameter, at 10.4 inches, remained the same, but plate pressure was increased to handle all that Turbo-Jet torque. Beefed up as well were the rear halfshafts and U-joints, each being made of high-strength 4240 alloy steel and shot-peened to fight fatigue. Also added was a thicker 0.875-inch stabilizer bar (compared to the standard 0.750-inch bar) up front, while a new 0.562-inch sway bar was bolted on in back to help counteract the new-found understeer effects created by all that extra weight planted on the front wheels.

All told, the 396 big-block weighed about 680 pounds, easily 100 pounds more than its 327-ci little brother. To Duntov's dismay, substituting Turbo-Jet power into the Sting Ray equation equaled an inherent forward weight bias. Wearing about 150 additional pounds—most coming at the nose—compared to its small-block brethren, a 1965 396 Corvette's front-to-rear weight distribution was 51/49; nothing frightening, mind you, but a marked departure from the direction Duntov had long envisioned for America's only sports car.

In all, six V-8s were available to Sting Ray buyers that year, with the standard 250-horsepower 327 and optional 300-horsepower L75 small-block carrying over from 1964. Although initial reports had the solid-lifter 365-horsepower L76—also a 1964 carryover—being replaced midyear by the L78 396, such was not the case. A 1965 *Interim Shop Manual* did mention that planned small-block/big-block trade, but an announcement in the March edition of the *Chevrolet Service News* cleared up the confusion. "The important midyear change in engine lineup for Corvette is the addition of the extra-cost 425hp Turbo-jet 396 V-8," it read. "Limited availability of the 365hp 327 V-8 is expected for the balance of the model year." L76 Turbo-Fire production did drop considerably following the L78 Turbo-Jet's release that spring, then picked up again during the last month of the 1965 run, ending in a final sales tally of 5,011.

Chevrolet's other new Corvette engine for 1965 offered much of the L76's might without the fuss and muss of solid lifters. Featuring a slightly milder hydraulic cam, the 350-horsepower L79 327 produced its maximum power at a more usable 5,800 rpm as compared to the L76's 365 horsepower at 6,200 rpm. The L79 was identical to the L76 on the outside with its chromed, round air cleaner and cast-aluminum, finned valve covers. Holley four-barrels and 11:1 compression were also shared by the two optional small-blocks. The most noticeable differences were on the sticker, where the $107.60 L79 was $21.55 cheaper, and on the street, where the 350-horsepower 327 was much more civilized while still possessing more than enough brute force to keep sports car rivals at bay.

Like Jerry Titus in reference to the 396, *Car and Driver's* crew could barely believe their eyes. "A new engine for the Corvette? With hydraulic lifters? Three hundred-and-fifty horsepower at 5800rpm? Silky-smooth? No rough idle? No pushrod clatter? One hundred more horsepower than the [Ferrari] 250/GT? Sixty-eight more than the Aston-Martin [DB-5]?" After turning in an impressive 6.2-second 0–60 run and a 14.9-second 94-mile-per-hour quarter-mile pass for an L79 Sting Ray—a car they also lauded for its "outstanding" four-wheel discs, "stable" four-wheel independent suspension, and "silent" sophistication—*Car and Driver's* testers were still scratching their heads. "You aren't suggesting that it's one of the best GT cars in the world, or are you?" Only L79 Corvette owners knew for sure.

Most major questions concerning the L78 big-block Corvette's place on this planet were answered almost immediately. According to Titus, "it goes like the proverbial scalded cat, will be cheaper than an injected 327 model, and has all the attributes of the normal Sting Ray to boot: quietness, weather-proofing, and comfort." Compared to the L84 fuelie's intimidating $538 asking price, the $292.70 L78 power option certainly appeared cheap. And when you consider what that option did for Sting Ray straight-line performance, the deal couldn't be beat.

Road & Track's stopwatch punchers had seen few cars like it. "Easing off the line with a chirp and then being careful to keep the tires just this side of broken loose gave us a 14.1 [quarter-mile time in seconds]," read *R&T's* August 1965 review. "This is quick. Quicker than any other standard production car we've ever tested except the AC Cobra. Quick enough that nobody is likely to give you much trouble getting away from a stoplight. Except the law, maybe." But as impressed as they were over its newfound muscle, *Road & Track's* editors couldn't help but question the Corvette's redirected approach to performance.

"It is difficult to describe precisely the 425bhp Corvette's place in the automotive scheme of things," continued *Road & Track*. "It's an interesting technical exercise, building a nice big engine like the 396 and putting it in a good chassis like the Corvette, but it honestly isn't a very satisfactory car for driving in everyday traffic. It's too much of a brute for that. And with all that power, any manner in which it is driven on anything except dead dry paving, the car is going to be a very large handful. It is not a car for the inexpert or the inattentive—two blinks of the eye and a careless poke of the toe and you could be in serious trouble." Contrary to other press claims that ride and handling weren't harmed to any substantial degree by the presence of all that cast-iron up front, Corvette engineer and racer Jerry Thompson minced few words when he later referred to the first big-block Sting Rays as "real cows."

Earlier, before RPO L78 was introduced, *Road & Track* had openly questioned the need for Chevrolet's Corvette to chase Shelby's Cobra in a cubic-inch battle it could never win. In their December 1964 edition, *R&T's* reporters claimed that "though 400-425bhp is certainly going to propel the [Sting Ray] along at even higher rates of speed than the present 375, we're not at all certain that more horsepower is the answer so far as competition is concerned. The Corvette is simply too far overweight when it comes to competition like factory Cobras." Nonetheless, *Sports Car Graphic's* Jerry Titus was still rooting on the Corvette-Cobra war in the March

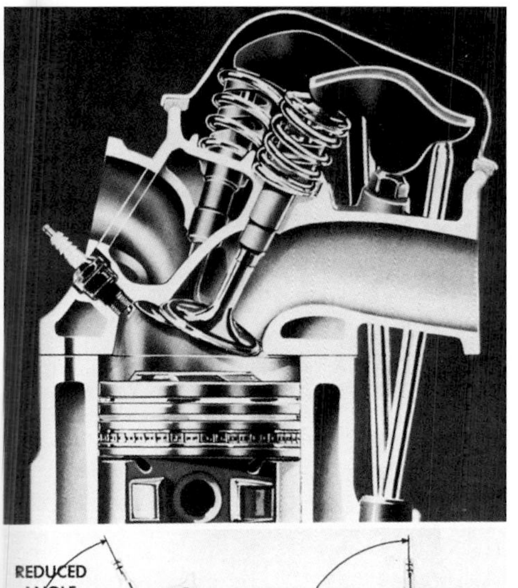

The 396-ci Mk IV big-block V-8 featured innovative "porcupine" cylinder heads, a design that drew its name from the way the staggered, canted valves protruded up from the combustion chambers in varying angles akin to a porcupine's quills. Individual stamped-steel rocker arms allowed engineers to angle the valves towards their respective ports to minimize flow restriction caused by sharp bends in the intake and exhaust passages.

1965 issue: 'The big question, 'Will [the 396 Corvette] beat the 427 Cobra?' is a long way from answered yet.'"

Setting Titus' big question aside for the moment, *Road & Track* followed up with a plea of sorts for a return to sanity. "The proper approach, we think, is to make the most efficient use of a good design—which is what the fuel-injected 327 did—not simply to stuff in a bigger, stronger engine. There are many sports cars that honestly need more power. But the Corvette isn't one of them." Regardless of what *R&T* editors thought, or Duntov for that matter, more power would be on the way in the form of an even bigger Sting Ray big-block in 1966.

Small-block/big-block arguments notwithstanding, *Road & Track* did have a long list of good words for the 1965 Corvette. *R&T* especially liked the car's heater, which was "almost alone among sports cars in that it really works—even in cold weather." And in the magazine's words, the Muncie four-speed was "about as near faultless as any we've ever encountered."

As in previous years, 3.36:1 gears and a three-speed manual were standard for 1965, behind the equally rare base 250 and predominant L75 300-horsepower 327s. And again, the optional Powerglide was available for these two small-blocks only, as was the wide-ratio M20 four-speed. Like the L78 big-block, the 365-horsepower L76, 350-horsepower L79, and 375-horsepower L84 small-blocks were delivered with the close-ratio Muncie gearbox and 3.70:1 rear gears. Optional axle ratios once more included 3.08:1 highway cogs, 4.11:1 street-racers, and 4.56:1 drag-strip specials. A super-heavy-duty Muncie four-speed, the soon-to-be-legendary M22 Rock Crusher, was also planned for 1965 production but didn't make the lineup.

Appearing prominently, on the other hand, was a finer fiberglass form, at least according to *Car Life*, which concluded that the 1965 Corvette "has improved somewhat in the quality of its finish. It seems that each year the characteristic ripples of the panels get a little less noticeable." Noted Corvette restoration expert Noland Adams agrees, explaining in his excellent *Corvette Restoration & Technical Guide, Volume 2* that "competition between [A. O. Smith and the St. Louis assembly plant] resulted in continuous improvements in Corvette body fit and finish. Although 1963-67 Corvette body quality was probably at its highest in 1966, 1965 was certainly a good year."

Hands down, it was a great year as far as the fiberglass-wrapped package as a whole was concerned. As in 1963 and 1964, Sting Ray production for 1965 set another record, this time reaching 23,562: 15,376 convertibles and 8,186 coupes. The 1965 Corvette remained simply irresistible. Continued *Car Life*, its "combination of ride and handling is unchallenged among American cars and right up with the best production sports cars made anywhere. It goes, it stops, it handles, and it does all in comfort, silence and reliability. And, above all else, it's great fun to drive. There's just nothing quite like it at within $1,000 of its price."

Motor Trend's Bob McVay couldn't have agreed more. "Unique on the Detroit scene," he wrote in the April 1965 issue, "that's still Chevrolet's Corvette Sting Ray. It's as yet the only true American sports car. It makes no concessions for carrying more than two people and a reasonable amount of luggage, and it doesn't claim to be anything except what it is. What is the Corvette? It's one of the hottest performing, best handling, most comfortable sports cars on the market, and some think it's one of the best looking as well. Each year since its 1953 introduction, the 'Vette has been getting more refined, faster, better handling, and gentler riding. In standard form, Corvette's 1965 offerings are smooth, quiet, comfortable sports cars, capable of staggering performance depending on what engine you order. A better all-around sports car would be hard to find at any price. We loved it."

No kidding.

FLORIDA

1966

Building a Bigger, Better Big-Block

When the so-called Mystery Motor first appeared at Daytona in February 1963 its displacement measured 427-ci, thanks to a 4.25-inch bore and 3.76-inch stroke. Two years later, when Chevrolet engineers finally decided to reintroduce their porcupine powerplant for street duty, the resulting Mark IV big-block displaced 396 ci due to a slight bore reduction made to allow the new Turbo-Jet V-8 authorized entry into Chevy's second-edition mid-sized Chevelle. Late in 1964, the killjoys at General Motors had established a 400-ci maximum displacement limit for its divisions' intermediates in an attempt to keep a lid on performance passions, which at the time were just starting to boil again after GM officials had supposedly cooled things off with their infamous anti-racing edict of January 1963.

There were, however, no such limits at the top of Chevrolet's performance ladder, where the 1965 Sting Ray had made do with the 396-ci version of the Mark IV V-8. No one complained, though, since the 396 Turbo-Jet's 425 horses stood ready, willing, and able to make Chevy's first big-block Corvette the meanest, nastiest American performance machine this side of Shelby-American's uncivilized 427 Cobra. But if curbside critics thought the 1965 396 Corvette was wild, they had another thing coming—and it arrived in 1966, when Zora Duntov's Sting Ray joined Carroll Shelby's Cobra atop the sports car realm's cubic-inch leader board.

The transition from 396 Turbo-Jet to 427 Turbo-Jet was as simple as boring the Mark IV cylinder block to match to its Mark II roots. As Duntov told *Car and Driver* in the fall of 1965, "this was done primarily to save weight. You must remember that cast iron is very heavy, and by removing 30 cubic inches of it we have made a significant reduction in weight." Of course Zora was kidding, but there was nothing funny about the

Base price for a 1966 Corvette convertible was $4,084. Production was 17,762. Sales of the options appearing here were 3,617 for the $131.65 N14 sidemount exhausts, 1,194 for the $316 P48 Kelsey-Hayes knock-off wheels, and 5,557 for the $46.55 T01 goldwall tires. Notice the incorrect bright center cones (behind the knock-off spinners) on these P48 wheels. Corvette's knock-offs in 1964 and 1965 had chrome-plated cones, while 1966 P48 wheels used brushed-finish cones (see the Sunfire Yellow 1966 coupe shown in this chapter).

Corvette's 427, a brutal big-block that owed nothing to any other regular-production powerplant on the planet.

"Unless you're wheelin' a 'street hemi' or a 427 Cobra," warned *Cars* magazine's Martyn Schorr, "steer clear of Chevy's hottest street stinger." The 427 Corvette can "literally walk away and hide from any domestic production car, except for the Shelby 427

A 1966 small-block Corvette rolls down the St. Louis assembly line, followed by two big-blocks and another small-block in the distance.

Cobra and MoPar street hemi. Even though Chevrolet insists on being divorced from anything that even hints of racing the 1966 Sting Ray can be ordered with a fantastic amount of genuine racing equipment."

Available in two forms, the optional 427 Turbo-Jet V-8 topped off that equipment list in high-powered fashion. Buyers who wanted a big, bad Turbo-Jet that didn't have a big, bad attitude could check off RPO L36, priced at $181.20. Based on a Mark IV cylinder block with two-bolt main bearing caps, the L36 427 featured domesticated hydraulic lifters, reasonably mild 10.25:1 compression, cast-aluminum pistons, and a hefty Holley four-barrel on a cast-iron intake manifold. Intake valves, at 2.06 inches, were smaller than those used in the 1965 L78 396, and valve lift (0.461-inch intake, 0.480-inch exhaust) was down as well. Maximum output for the L36 big-block was originally listed as 400 horsepower at 5,400 rpm, and then was almost immediately lowered to 390 horsepower at 5,200 rpm. Maximum torque was a whopping 460 foot-pounds at 3,600 rpm.

Chevrolet's other 427 Turbo-Jet cost quite a bit more, and for good reason. Priced at $312.85, RPO L72 started with a cylinder block held together on the bottom end by four-bolt main bearing caps. Like its smaller L78 predecessor, the L72 427 was stuffed full of 11:1 impact-extruded aluminum pistons and a lumpy solid-lifter cam. The L78's mechanical cam certainly had been no wimp in 1965, but the L72's 0.519-inch lift unit made it look weak in comparison. Mandatory K66 transistorized ignition, a 780-cfm Holley four-barrel on an aluminum intake, and free-flowing exhaust manifolds completed the L72 package, a burly power source that was even more mighty than its 396-ci Mark IV forerunner. Just as the L36 was originally listed as 400 horsepower, L72 output was originally listed as 450 horsepower at 6,400 rpm, and then was quickly adjusted down, in the case to 425 horsepower at 5,600 rpm. Top torque was identical to the L36's rating, but came on 400 rpm higher.

No specific explanation for those horsepower adjustments exists, though it's not difficult to guess why they happened considering the long-running battle between Chevrolet's performance planners and GM's anti-racing faction, the latter group especially conscious of the federal government's growing concern over automotive safety. Someone high up surely must have stepped in, once Duntov's engineers started playing with more than 400 horses. At the time, GM was preparing to institute yet another power-restricting rule of thumb, this one limiting passenger cars to no less than 10 pounds of curb weight per 1 advertised horsepower, although again, this limit didn't apply to America's only sports car. Nonetheless, 450-horsepower in an automobile that weighed only 3,300 pounds was asking for a bit too much leeway from the brass on the 14th floor. Lowering that red flag, on the other hand, was as easy as pulling out an eraser and writing in a less threatening advertised figure. A new decal on the L72's chrome air cleaner and it was back to business as usual. Few, however, were fooled.

Among others, *Motor Trend* noted the change, and then took a shot at answering why. "One explanation for this curious state of affairs making the rounds is that, since the congressional safety inquisition, there has been a gentlemen's agreement among parties concerned not to advertise more than 425hp. No official explanations have been offered [for the L72's drop from 450hp], and Chevrolet's sticking to the 425hp figure in its latest literature. A similar situation is said to exist at Ford and Chrysler, too, whose high-performance engines are believed capable of gross power ratings far in excess of the 425hp they each claim."

Anyone who believed Chevy's 425-horsepower claim needed only to drop the hammer once on an L72 Corvette. As *Car and Driver*'s road testers reported, "Chevrolet insists that there are only 425 horses in there, and we'll just have to take their word for it. Though we feel compelled to point out that these are 425 horses of a size and strength never before seen by

Corvettes received yet another distinctive, restyled, standard simulated knock-off wheel cover for 1966.

man—horses as tall as houses, with hooves as big as bushel baskets. When you have *this* many of *those* horses exerting their full force against the small of your back, you are profoundly impressed, and you will most likely lose all interest in counting anyway."

Motor Trend's Bob McVay was equally skeptical. Chevrolet "coyly rates [the L72] at 425hp," he wrote in the March 1966 issue, "but we think an extra two teams of Borax mules lie hidden behind the barn door. Engineers call it 'porcupine,' but that refers to the valve layout and not its agility." McVay's test of a 425-horsepower 1966 Corvette convertible with optional 4.11:1 rear gears produced some sizzling results: 0–60 miles per hour in 5.6 ticks, and the quarter-mile in 13.4 seconds at 105 miles per hour. Top speed at the 6,500 rpm redline was listed as 135 miles per hour.

All numbers—advertised or whatever—aside, McVay simply couldn't say enough about the L72's raw-boned muscle. In his words, "the 427 has the kind of torque that made World War II fighter planes try to wrap themselves around their propeller on take-off. In the relatively light, front-end-heavy Corvette this verve tends to pave the highway with your rear-tire treads." Echoed *Car and Driver*, "there's power literally everywhere, great gobs of steam-locomotive, earth-moving torque."

Doing McVay one better, *Sports Car Graphic*'s Jerry Titus reported an even more impressive 0–60-mile-per-hour time of 4.8 seconds for an L72 coupe also fitted

A new egg-crate grille and "Corvette Sting Ray" script added to the hood represented the quickest way to identify the mildly revamped 1966 model. New exterior colors for 1966 included Laguna Blue, Trophy Blue, Mosport Green, and Sunfire Yellow, joining Tuxedo Black, Ermine White, Rally Red, Nassau Blue, Silver Pearl, and Milano Maroon.

with a 4.11:1 differential. "The porcupine engine—which first saw the light of day as a 427, not a 396—is a beaut," wrote Titus. "There's gobs of low end torque and a willingness to grab revs that belies its size. It'll turn seven grand, so the 6500 redline is conservative. Tell us you'd like a hotter performing road machine than this and we'll call you some kinda nut!"

Perhaps most amazing was *Car and Driver*'s test of an L72 convertible sporting somewhat mild 3.36:1 cogs. "With the normal 3.36 rear axle ratio it'll turn a quarter mile that'll give a GTO morning sickness, and still run a top speed of around 150mph," claimed a report in the magazine's November 1965 issue. Rest to 60 miles perhour took only 5.4 seconds, according to that report, while the quarter-mile's far end arrived in a sensational 12.8 seconds, with trap speeds hitting 112 miles per hour. The 425-horsepower Sting Ray "accelerates from zero to 100 in less than eleven seconds," continued *Car and Driver*, "and is so smooth and controllable in the three-figure speed ranges that it all becomes sort of unreal."

In that same issue, *Car and Driver* also thrashed one of Shelby-American's Ford-powered 427 Cobras, proving that physical laws simply can never be broken. Weighing a mere 2,890pounds—a quarter-ton less than the L72 Sting Ray convertible—the 425-horsepower Cobra seared the track to the tune of 12.2 seconds at 118 miles per hour in the quarter-mile, and 4.3 seconds for the time-honored 0–60-mile-per-hour run. Most alarming was the Cobra's ability to hit 100 miles per hour *and* return to rest in a scant 14.5 seconds. Clearly Duntov's engineering crew could have done themselves a favor by setting their sights lower, perhaps in the direction of Shelby-American's other Ford-powered sportster, the GT-350 Mustang. As it was, Shelby's superquick snake would become extinct within a year anyway, leaving the GT-350, and its soon-to-be-announced GT-500 big-block brother, to carry on the battle with Chevrolet's fiberglass two-seater. It came by default, but the tables finally would be turned on Shelby in 1967, at least on the street.

In 1965, there had been five 327 small-block V-8s available to Corvette buyers. In 1966, there were only two, as the yeoman 250hp 327 and solid-lifter 365hp L76 were dropped, leaving the 300hp 327 as the base Sting Ray powerplant, while this 350hp L79 (missing its air cleaner decal) remained as the one optional small-block. Air conditioning, RPO C60, was priced at $412.90 in 1966. RPO C60 production was 3,520.

Left
Options appearing here on this 1966 convertible include air conditioning (C60), AM/FM radio (U69), the tweaked steering wheel (N32), Powerglide (M35), leather seats, and the telescopic steering wheel (N36). The telescopic wheel ($42.15) was adjusted through a three-inch range by the finned-locking nut located between the horn button and steering wheel center. Leather seats cost $79, the teakwood wheel $47.40, $199.10 bought the U69 radio, and Powerglide was a $194.85 option.

As for the 1966 427 Corvette, like the 396 Sting Ray the previous year, it featured a strong supporting cast including that same bulging hood. Suspension was beefed and a 0.562-inch rear anti-sway bar was incorporated. Standard transmission fare was the wide-ratio M20 four-speed (2.56:1 low) for the 390-horsepower L36, while the 425-horsepower L72 was mated to the close-ratio Muncie (2.20:1 low), which became an option in itself, RPO M21, for 1966. The milder L36 could also be backed by the M35 Powerglide automatic, although only 20 buyers made that choice. Equally rare was the new M22 heavy-duty Muncie four-speed, available for the L72 only.

Rumors of a special, bulletproof gearbox had been floating around since early 1965. More than one press report at the time hinted at a wide array of purpose-built, SCCA-legal racing components to come, including such prominent pieces as aluminum heads and a stout four-speed capable of handling more than 500 horsepower. But none of these parts appeared for 1965, though RPO M22 was planned for production

THE DOOR TO RECOGNITION

Although the same basic Sting Ray shell carried over from 1963 to 1967, differentiating one model from the next is not particularly difficult, as long as you know where to look. Rocker moldings and wheel covers changed every year, various grilles and fender louvers were used, and of course you couldn't miss a 1963 coupe with its twin hood grilles and that trademark rear "stinger." Another identifying feature was the fuel filler door, which received a distinctive treatment each model year. Study these photos carefully; you will be tested.

1964

1965

1963

1966

1967

that year. When it did appear in 1966, the M22 four-speed was aptly named Rock Crusher due to its noisy operation. Inside, an M22 differed from its M20 and M21 brethren by using beefier gears with heavier teeth cut at a lesser angle—it was the gnashing of these teeth that inspired the Rocker Crusher's name. Externally, all three Muncie boxes were quite similar. Compared to the 13,903 M21s and 10,837 M20s sold, both costing $184.35, only 15 L72 buyers spent another $237 for RPO M22.

Chevrolet also introduced a new, stronger, fully synchronized Saginaw three-speed manual transmission as standard equipment for the base 300hp 327 small-block (the 250hp 327 was dropped after 1965) in 1966. Both the M20 four-speed and Powerglide automatic were available behind the base 327. Backing up the

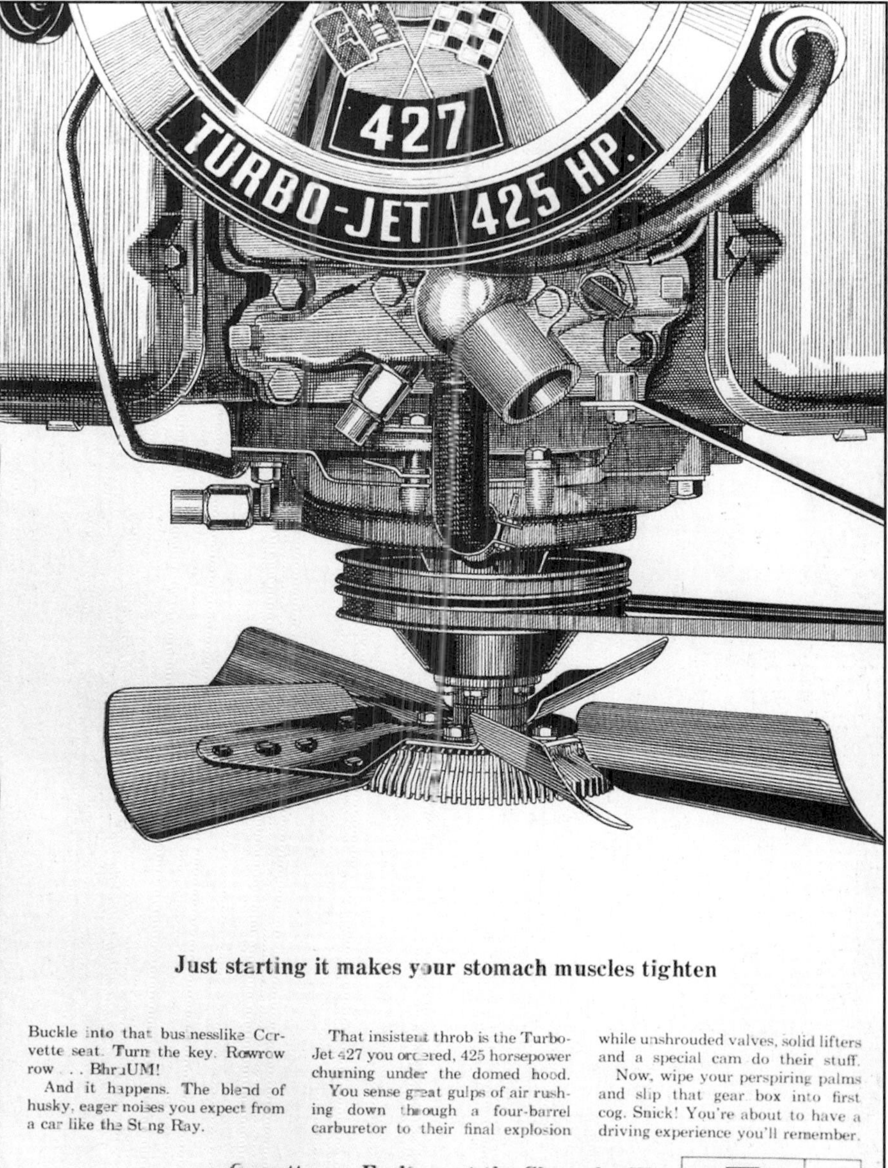

427
TURBO-JET 425 HP.
Just starting it makes your stomach muscles tighten
Buckle into that businesslike Corvette seat. Turn the key. Rowrow row . . . BhrrUM!
And it happens. The blend of husky, eager noises you expect from a car like the Sting Ray.
That insistent throb is the Turbo-Jet 427 you ordered, 425 horsepower churning under the domed hood.
You sense great gulps of air rushing down through a four-barrel carburetor to their final explosion while unshrouded valves, solid lifters and a special cam do their stuff.
Now, wipe your perspiring palms and slip that gear box into first cog. Snick! You're about to have a driving experience you'll remember.
Corvette . . . Excitement the Chevrolet Way

Rest to 60 miles per hour in less than 5 seconds. Seeing the far end of a quarter-mile in about 12.8 ticks of the clock. This type of performance would've tightened more than your stomach muscles.

fourth engine in the 1966 Corvette lineup—the 350hp L79 327—was either the M20 or M21 Muncie four-speed. Neither the standard three-speed nor the optional Powerglide could be ordered with RPO L79.

Standard gear ratio for the L72 427 was 3.55:1, with additional choices including the aforementioned 3.36:1 and 4.11:1 axles, joined by a 3.70:1 unit. M20-equipped L36 427s came with 3.08 gears, while an M21 or M35 Powerglide behind a 390-horsepower big-block meant a 3.36:1 differential was in back.

Among returning popular performance pieces were both the $36.90 N11 off-road exhausts and the more noticeable N14 side-mounts, the latter option dropping in price to $131.65 as demand naturally picked up. Offered alongside all four engines, the loud, sexy sidepipes were selected by 3,617 Corvette customers in 1966. Less common, undoubtedly due to their still heavy $316 asking price, the P48 Kelsey-Hayes aluminum knock-off wheels remained suitable complements for the N14 exhausts. RPO P48 sales totaled 1,194.

Coupe buyers could still opt for the big 36.5-gallon tank (66 did), while all customers choosing the three optional powerplants were also able to add the K66 transistorized ignition. Leather seats; tinted glass power brakes, steering, and windows; telescopic steering column; teakwood steering wheel; air conditioning; removable hardtop—all the familiar comfort and convenience pieces were present and accounted for. New attractions included bucket seat headrests (RPO A82), shoulder harnesses (A85), and four-way hazard warning lights (V74), the last feature coming in response to the growing number of states requiring cars to have some form of onboard traffic warning system. A sign of things to come also appeared in the form of an air-injection reactor made mandatory for the first time in 1966 on all Corvettes (except L72 models) delivered in California and listed as RPO K19 for Sting Rays sold elsewhere. Last, but certainly not least, among the group of new options for 1966 were two packages bound to put a twinkle in the

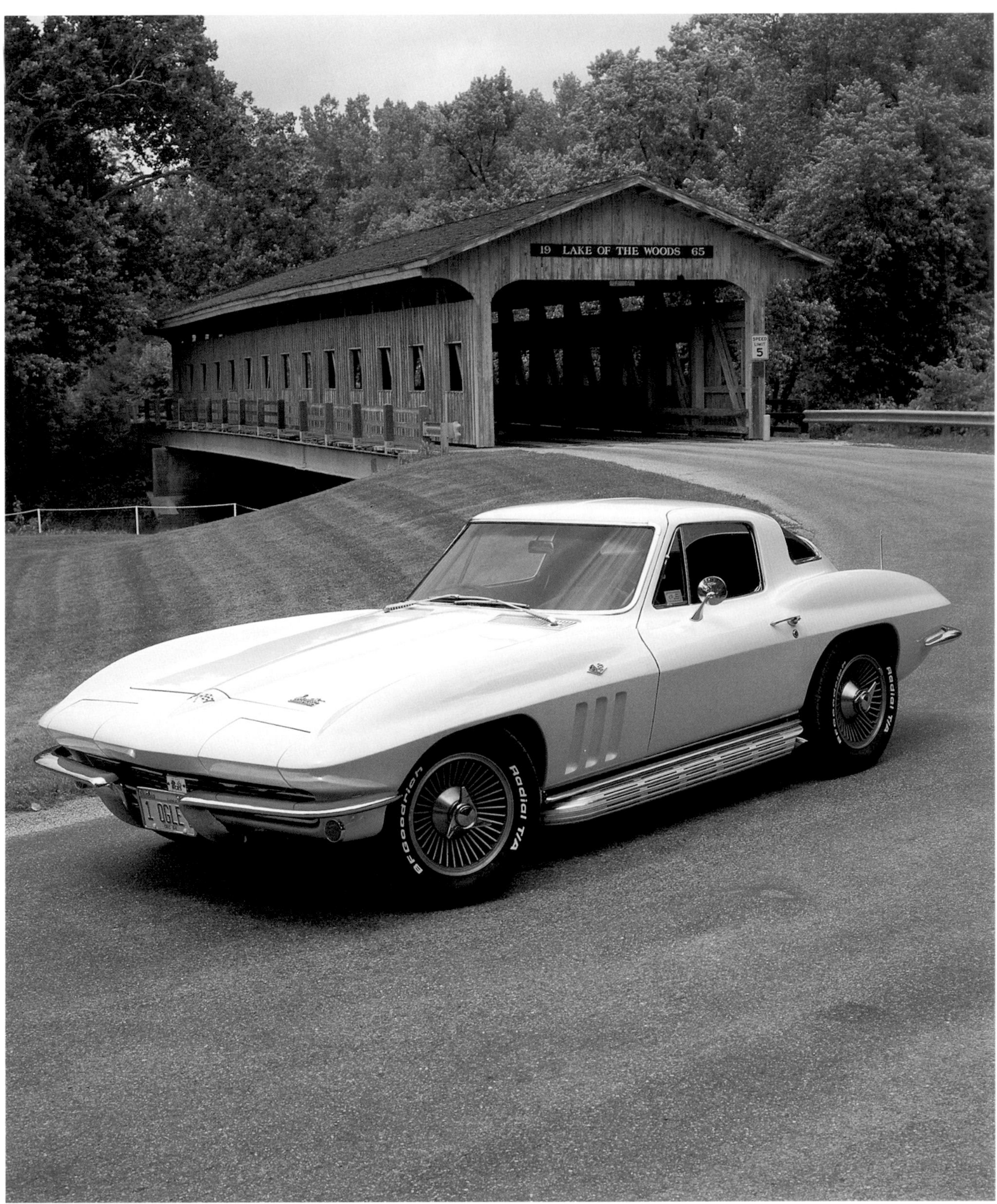

The crossflags on the fender meant that one of the two small-block V-8s was beneath the hood; in this case it's the standard 300-horsepower 327. Notice that the familiar red, white, and blue markings on these P48 knock-off spinners have long since faded from this basically original, one-owner 1966 coupe, a car that has seen its fair share of both daily driving and long-distance touring. Gone as well is the original rubber, replaced by modern radials. Standard equipment included either Goodyear or Firestone two-ply nylon cord tires. Available at extra cost were the P92 rayon whitewalls and T01 goldwall nylon tires.

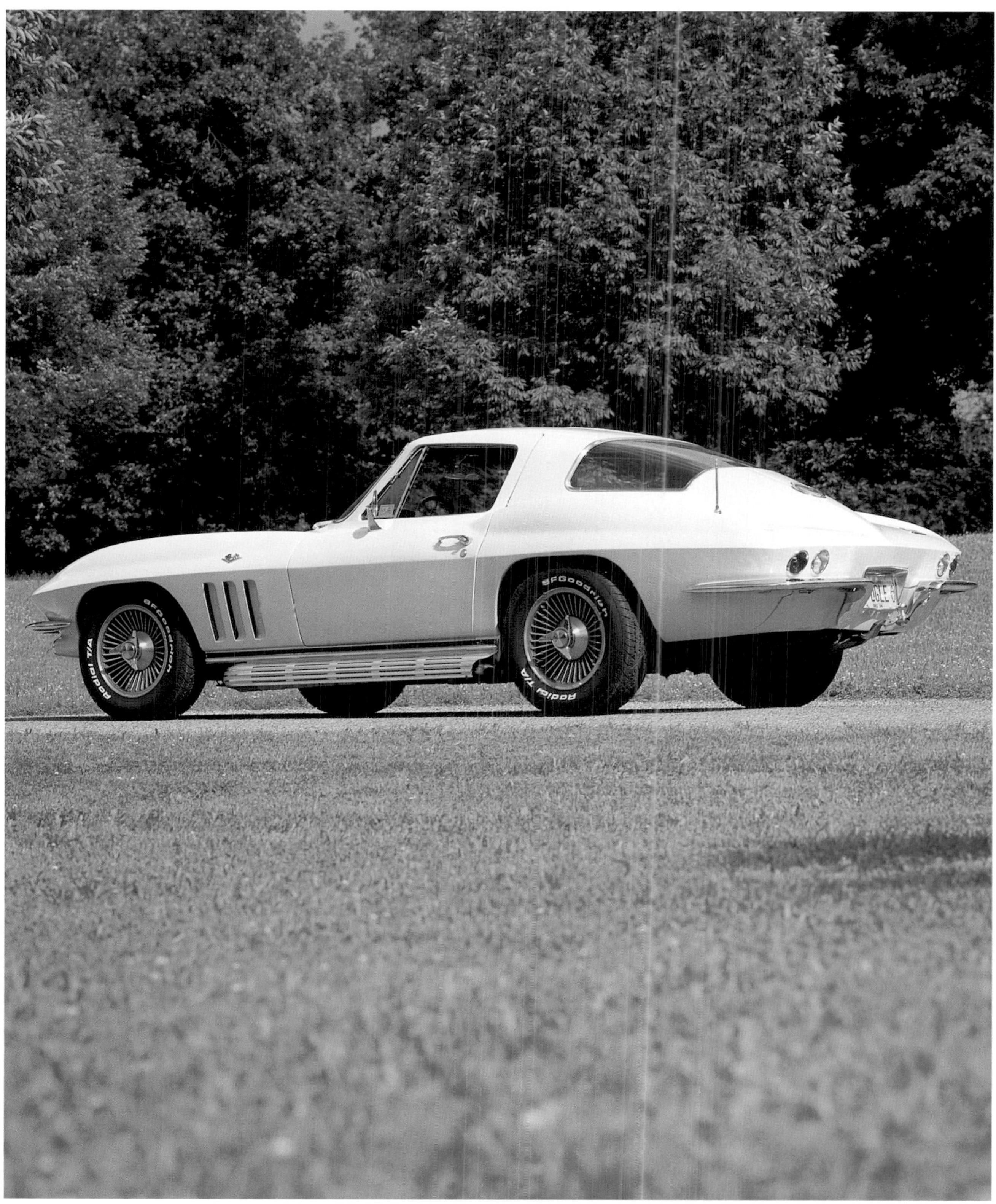

Base priced at $4,295, the 1966 Corvette coupe again was outsold by its topless counterpart by a wide margin: 17,762 to 9,958. Notice the backup lights; both this feature and the day/night rearview mirror, items offered in 1965 as part of the optional Comfort and Convenience Group (RPO Z01), became standard equipment in 1966. Alert readers may have already noticed the Rally Red 1966 convertible shown in this chapter does not have the correct backup lenses. The trailer hitch appearing here is an owner-installed item.

RPO N32 featured a classy teakwood rim glued and fitted to the typical steel three-spoke wheel. Also notice the tachometer with its "mild" redline, meaning this small-block coupe has the base 300-horsepower 327. Adding the optional 350-horsepower L76 in 1966 automatically included a tach with a 6,000-rpm redline.

eye of those continually winking at the commonly held notion that "Chevrolet wasn't in racing." The first, RPO J56, was a familiar code, having been present in 1964 for buyers who had wanted the best brakes possible. The second, RPO F41, would kick off a Chevrolet tradition of exceptional sport suspension setups that still survives today. Together, the two were unbeatable.

Of course, standard brakes were still the excellent Delco four-wheel 11.75-inch discs, equipment that inspired *Cars'* Martyn Schorr to call the 1966 427 Sting Ray the "quickest, fastest, stoppingest 'Vette yet!" Even during the roughest street play these super binders were up to the task, but inhumanly harsh use could bring out their mortal side, however briefly. As *Car Life* explained, "only when we made a series of consecutive stops from 120mph did demon fade rear his smelly head." Everything, even Corvette's excellent four-wheel disc setup, has its limits.

Big-block Corvette customers who wanted to push those limits in 1966 could have shelled out an extra $342.30 for the new J56 disc brakes. Like its 1964 drum-brake predecessor, the 1966 J56 heavy-duty disc option included metallic linings. Compared to standard discs (with organic linings), these semimetallic pads were larger and were bonded, not riveted, to beefier nickel-alloy backing plates held in place by two retaining pins instead of one. Each front caliper was also reinforced by an iron brace, and a proportioning valve was included to help balance braking pressure between front and rear wheels. Completing the J56 package was the J50 power booster and dual-circuit master cylinder—standard brakes were energized by a single-chamber master cylinder. Perhaps because of its price, perhaps because it represented more brakes than the average Corvette driver would ever use, sales of the J56 option totaled only 382 units.

Another 427-exclusive option, RPO F41, replaced the 1965 F40 option and apparently was offered only with the 425hp L72 big-block (once again, 327- and

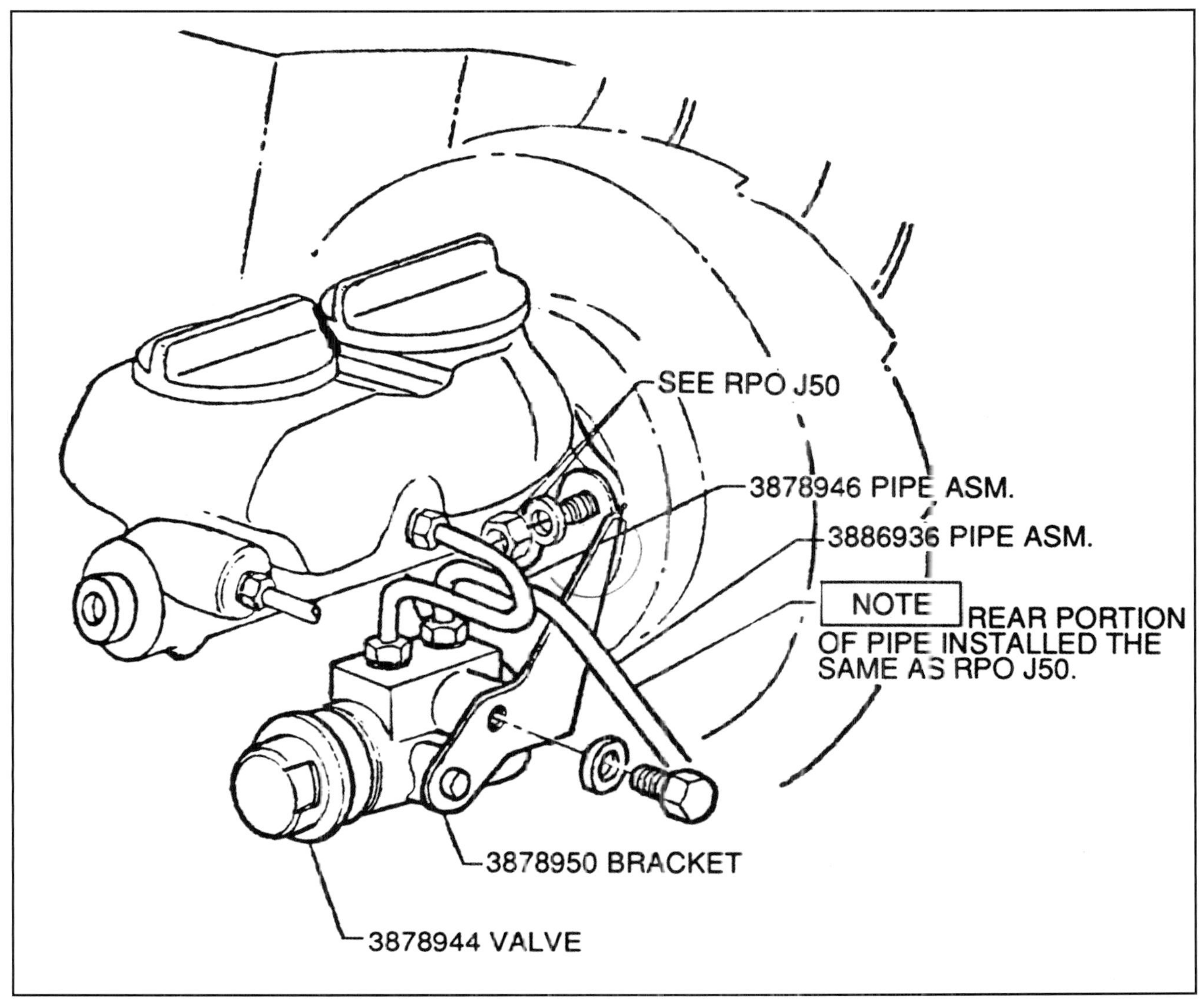

The heavy-duty J56 brake option reappeared for 1966, adding power assist, metallic linings, and special beefed-up brake pad retainers up front. Also included was a proportioning valve (at bottom) that allowed the driver to adjust the balance between front and rear braking power.

L36-equipped 1966 Corvettes with F41 are known) at a humble price of $36.90. F41 features included heavier, nonvariable-rate springs front and rear, stiffer shocks, and a 0.94-inch front sway bar. F41 production was 2,705.

Already appropriately beefed up, an L72 Corvette's standard suspension worked well enough on its own in many critics' eyes, although anyone who had come to appreciate the truly agile 327 Sting Ray in top trim knew that most compliments aimed at the big-block Corvette's ride and handling were made with many obvious qualifications left unsaid. Simply put, heavy and nimble rarely go hand in hand. But regardless of physical laws, most reviews of the big-block chassis were on the positive side. According to *Car and Driver,* "the extra weight of this big engine doesn't really seem to affect the car's handling at all. There's a general feeling of ponderousness that one associates with any of the bigger sports machines at low speeds, but when you're going fast it's quick and responsive."

Describing the F41 ride was a slightly different call, as Jerry Titus discovered during his test of an L72 coupe. "With the optional suspension," he began in *Sports Car Graphics* December 1965 issue, "the ride is very firm, pleasant enough for smooth roads, but almost uncomfortable on bumpy, wavy surfaces." Bumpy or not, Titus' ride still left him impressed with the compromise made between pleasure and performance. "We logged almost 350 miles in

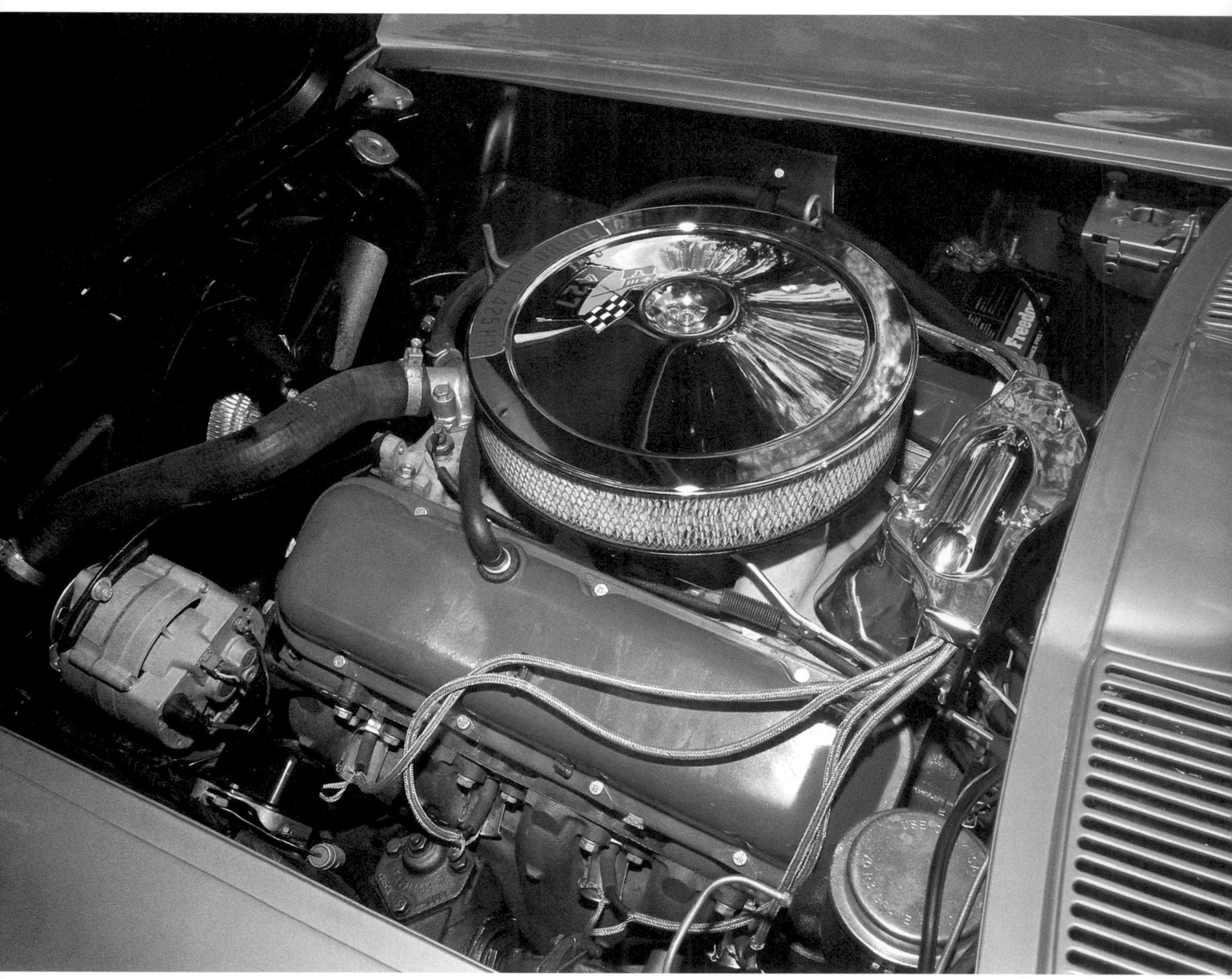

Previous pages
Two 427-ci big-blocks replaced the 425-horsepower 396 Turbo-Jet as the top Corvette power option for 1966. RPO L36, the 390-horsepower 427, was priced at $181.20, while the meaner 425-horsepower L72 427 cost a healthy $312.85. This Mosport Green L72 Sting Ray is one of 5,258—coupe and convertible—built in 1966. Another 5,116 L36 big-block 1966 Corvettes were also produced. Like the Rally Red convertible appearing in this chapter, this 1966 427 Corvette also has the bright knock-off wheel center cones instead of the proper brushed-finish pieces.

Above
Anyone who drove a 1966 L72 Corvette questioned that 425-horsepower rating, and Chevrolet didn't help matters by initially advertising this big-block at 450 horses. As *Motor Trend's* Bob McVay wrote, "for drivers who have the guts and skill to master it—and the maturity to recognize it for what it is and handle it accordingly—the 427 Turbo-Jet Corvette is a road king. The other 99 percent of the population is likely to be much happier and safer in either of the two 327 models. In conclusion, McVay reiterated his position, explaining that "for those rare individuals who want and can handle its potential, the 427 Turbo-Jet is a red-hot machine, but if it gets away from you, don't say we didn't warn you."

To be specific, the price for a 425-horsepower coupe in 1966 was more than $4,500, and could crowd $5,000 in a hurry if a buyer found himself unable to resist the wide array of optional teasers.

one day covering all kinds of roads," continued Titus, "and neither driver nor passenger felt any overall discomfort. As a matter of fact, the firmness represented security as the right foot kept getting heavier and heavier.'

With all the attention given such prominent new features as the F41 suspension, J56 brakes, and the big, beautiful 427s, basic model upgrades were lost in the shuffle, a result by no means undeserved. Basic exterior changes for 1966 again were limited to different rocker moldings, restyled wheel covers, and a redesigned grille, this one an attractive egg-crate design. Less noticeable trim adjustments included adding the familiar "Corvette Sting Ray" script to the hood's leading corner on the driver's side. And Chevrolet finally gave up entirely on the roof vents behind the doors, deleting them along with the electric interior ventilation system used, albeit weakly, in 1964 and 1965. Another resewn bucket seat style with additional horizontal pleats, a vinyl-covered foam headliner in place of the previously used fiberboard, chrome door-pull handles, and standard backup lights were also new for 1966.

Overall, Chevrolet offered Corvette buyers in 1966 the best of both worlds with two polite small-block models and two big-block bullies. Among the former, the 350-horsepower L79 Sting Ray was still the same car that had *Car and Driver* comparing it in 1965 to some of Europe's best. In the upper ranks, the 390-horsepower L36 427 Corvette was a relatively affordable way for a driver to enter Chevrolet's super-car fraternity without all the fuss and muss commonly associated with the all-out Mark IV motors. The two bookends, the 300-horsepower standard Sting Ray and the outrageous 425-horsepower L72 screamer, were as different as night and day. But all were Corvettes, and Corvettes still stood at the top of Detroit's ever-changing pecking order as far as class, luxury, pizzazz, and performance were concerned.

It just didn't get any better.

1967

Unintended Encore

Once the all-new Sting Ray hit the streets in the fall of 1962 Chevrolet couldn't build them fast enough, not even after putting on an extra shift at the St. Louis assembly plant. Corvette model-year sales jumped by 50 percent in 1963, reaching an all-time high of 21,513 cars. Convertible sales alone that year missed topping the entire 1961 total by only 20 units. And if that wasn't good news enough for Chevrolet's bean counters, Sting Ray sales continued upward each year: 22,229 in 1964; 23,562 in 1965; and a healthy 27,720 in 1966. As a sidelight, after predicting in 1963 that the new coupe would end up dominating future sales, those same product planners watched as topless Corvettes slowly gained momentum, then completely overwhelmed their fastback running mates. Following a near even split in 1963, the coupe's share of the market dropped to 37.3 percent in 1964 and stayed near that level until 1969.

This 1967 roadster is equipped with the L71 435-horsepower 427. It also sports the N14 sidemount exhausts, priced at $131.65, and the redesigned bolt-on cast-aluminum wheels, RPO N89. Only 720 buyers shelled out $263.30 in 1967 for the N89 wheels. Production of L71 Corvettes, coupes and convertibles, was 3,754.

Clearly, William Mitchell and Zora Arkus-Duntov knew a little about what they were doing while overseeing the creation of the all-new Corvette. The sporty, sexy 1963 Sting Ray certainly was deserving of every rave and more. But resting on laurels represents the easiest way to miss the bus in Detroit, where today's news ends up old news almost as soon as it's fit to print. Working three to four, sometimes five years in advance has long been the norm when it comes to building new cars; by the time that new machine is turning heads on Mainstreet U.S.A., the next edition is already well under way.

Timeless classic or not, the Sting Ray was no exception. Even as thrilled buyers were flocking by the proverbial droves to their nearest Corvette dealer in late 1962, Bill Mitchell was busy dreaming up another exciting, all-new look for America's only true sports car, an image all at Chevrolet hoped would wow the masses again in 1967. By the spring of 1965, Mitchell had his next new look in the form of Larry Shinoda's Mako Shark show car, a long, low, sleek concoction with bulging wheelhouses at all four corners. Initially a nonrunning mockup, Shinoda's Mako Shark soon became the Mako Shark II once it was decided to rename the XP-755 Shark of 1961 the Mako Shark I. Later in the year, work began on a fully functional Mako Shark II using the new Mark IV big-block V-8.

At the same time, Duntov was back working on his mid-engined dream Corvette, an effort that once again would prove fruitless. Much closer to reality was the project then under way in stylist Henry Haga's studio under the direction of Chevrolet chief stylist David Holls. Using Shinoda's Mako Shark II image as a base, Haga's studio had created the next new Corvette's shell midway through 1965, with a working prototype running under test at the Milford Proving Grounds that fall.

Larry Shinoda's Mako Shark II was designed in 1965 as the inspiration for the next new Corvette, which was initially planned for 1967. Developmental difficulties eventually delayed that debut until 1968, meaning the so-called "midyear" Sting Ray body had to run one extra year.

Track tests, however, showed the new model suffered from high-speed lift characteristics, and Duntov didn't like the way those bulging corners inhibited visibility. Both these negatives could be fixed, but not within what little time was left between that point and the planned 1967 new-model introduction. So it was back to the drawing board for Haga and Shinoda's 1967 Corvette, a more-than-modern-looking machine that then became Chevrolet's 1968 Corvette.

Stylists were left with no choice but to dress up the old familiar Sting Ray for one more encore, after they thought they'd already done that job in 1966. While it very well could have ended up a rubber-stamp effort, the resulting 1967 makeover emerged as perhaps the best of the breed in the opinion of many fiberglass fans, both then and now.

Car and Driver subscribers liked the 1967 Corvette so much they voted it the Best All-Around Car for 1967, a first for Chevrolet's performance machine, which also copped Best GT and Best Sports Car over 3,000 cc that year in *Car and Driver*'s annual readers' poll. "As it sits, the Sting Ray is the most sophisticated passenger car made in America—in terms of engine, drivetrain, suspension and brakes—and among the best engineered sports cars made anywhere," claimed the May 1967 report. "If that isn't good enough to make it the Best All-Around Car of 1967, we'd like to know what is."

Road & Track's staff was also impressed: "The Sting Ray is in its fifth and probably last year with that name and body style, and it finally looks the way we thought it should have in the first place. All the funny business—the fake vents, extraneous emblems and simulated-something-or-other wheel covers—is gone, and though some consider the basic shape overstyled, it looks more like a finished product now."

All typically minor exterior changes were performed in the best interests of letting the pure Sting Ray form shine through. Engine identification, small-block or big-block, was stripped from the fenders,

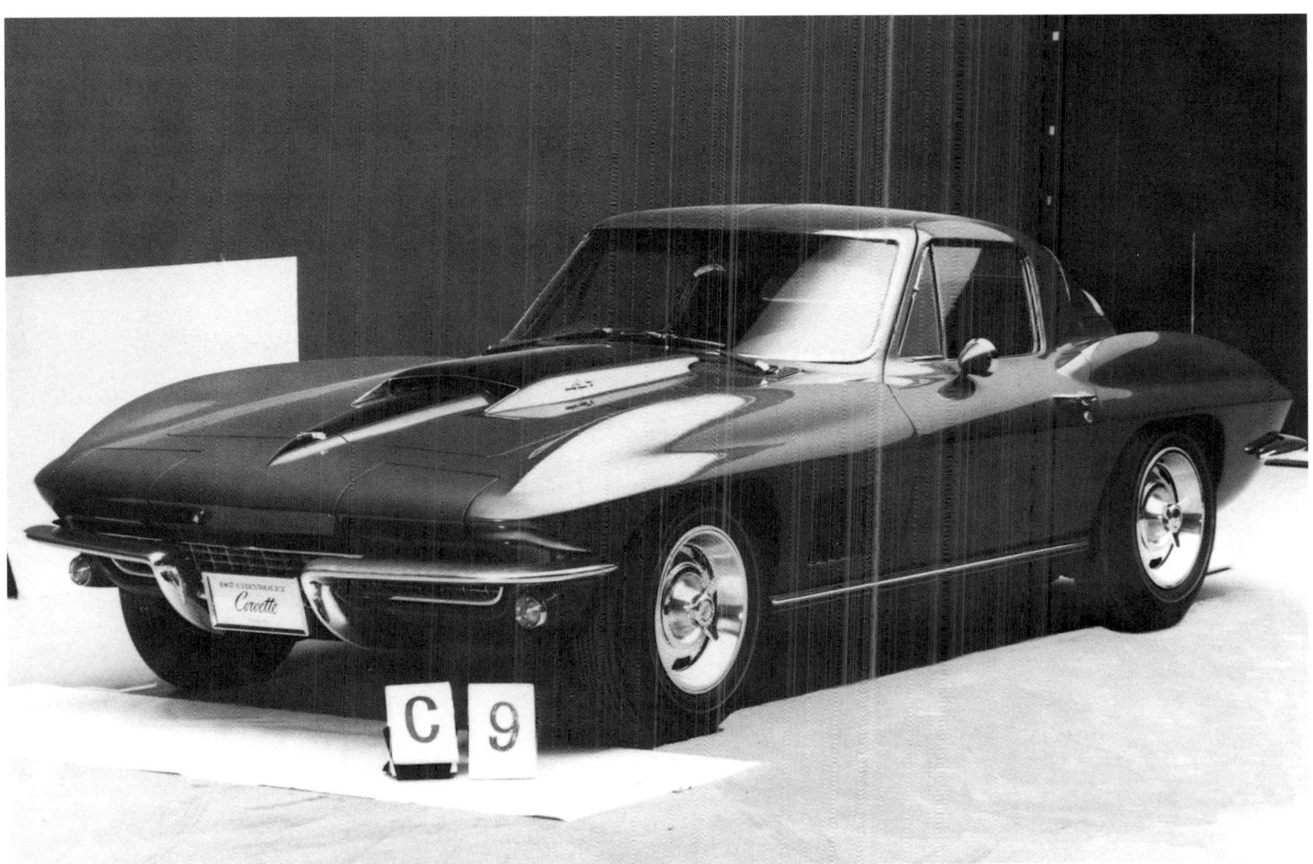

Shown here is a prototype 1967 427 Corvette coupe. Notice the proposed three-bladed spinners on the wheels' hubcaps, items that clashed somewhat with the "cleaned up" image applied to the last of the first-generation Sting Rays.

which became even cleaner with the addition of a smaller, more modern louver arrangement that featured a slight forward rake. Accentuating those clean bodysides were new rocker moldings that were nearly completely blacked-out. Up front, the traditional crossflag emblem was smaller and the "Corvette" script used on the hood in 1966 was deleted.

If anything bordered on "funny business" it was the 1967 Sting Ray's bold big-block hood, although nearly all critics agreed the new "stinger"-style non-functional scoop was both extremely attractive and a marked improvement over the somewhat crude big-block bulge used in 1965 and 1966. Not all big-block hoods hid big-block 427s in 1967, however, since a mishap involving molds for the flat small-block hood left St. Louis plant officials no choice but to assemble 327 Sting Rays with 427 hoods for a few days in late February or early March 1967. Dealers undoubtedly made the same swap themselves in response to customer requests for that sexy scoop atop a small-block, a combination the St. Louis plant wouldn't perform under normal circumstances.

Along with that scoop, the 1967 big-block hood also received a set of paint stripes that either contrasted or complemented the exterior finish, depending on the interior trim. For example, a black Sting Ray with a black or red interior received red striping, while a black car with saddle or green appointments inside were adorned with a white scoop. In addition to the red and white stripes, hood scoops were also painted black, dark teal blue, or medium bright blue. Thanks to problems perfecting the painting process, some early 1967 427 Corvettes were delivered with no stripes at all.

Overall, paint and body quality earned high marks in 1967. Calling the 1967 Corvette's paint its "most arresting aspect," *Hot Rod*'s Eric Dahlquist claimed the finish "does a pretty good job at being smooth and free of orange peel." According to *Road & Track*, the 1967 Sting Ray's paint "was better than on any Corvette we've tested." *Motor Trend* writer Steve Kelly liked the

Many critics lauded the 1967 Corvette for its clean appearance as the so-called excess clutter, including the 1966 model's fender emblems and hood script, were deleted. The restyled functional fender louvers were also less obtrusive. Completing the package was a set of standard Rally wheels that were both attractive and helped cool the four-wheel disc brakes through the slots in the rims' center sections. Chevrolet built 8,504 coupes in 1967, offering them at a base price of $4,388.75.

general finish, explaining that "Chevrolet has had over 15 years to learn about working with fiberglass, and it shows in the almost flawless workmanship of the body." Dahlquist, however, disagreed, pointing out that "early Sting Rays endured a session of poor-fitting fiberglass components, a situation we thought had been put behind years ago but appears to crop up in places, like the way our doors failed to match the rear quarters by almost a half inch."

On the other hand, you had to go a long way to find a bad word about the new standard Corvette wheel introduced in 1967. Curbside hacks had continually taken pot shots at the somewhat overdone simulated mag-style wheel covers used in 1965 and 1966. The spinners previously mounted on all Sting Ray wheel covers since 1963 were also considered to be a little too much by many. In contrast, the 1967 Rally wheel was simple and stunning at the same time, its painted steel center section set off by chrome trim rings and an equally bright understated hubcap. Functional as well as attractive, the 15-inch Rally wheel featured brake-cooling slots and was a half-inch wider than the previous 15x5.5-inch standard steel rim.

Designers modified the optional cast-aluminum wheel as well, basically because they had to. Ever-growing federally mandated automotive safety standards in 1967 precluded the use of the Corvette's racing-inspired knock-off wheel, its adapter arrangement

Standard Sting Ray power for 1967 again came from the 300-horsepower 327, which 6,858 buyers opted for that year. Another 6,375 customers chose the other available small-block, the optional 350-horsepower L79, priced at $105.35. Air conditioning, RPO C60, cost $412.90 and was installed on 3,788 1967 Sting Rays. Notice the dual-circuit master cylinder (directly above the chrome ignition shielding), a new standard brake feature in 1967.

and three-pronged spinner deemed by government agencies as being not fit for human consumption. Behind the 1967 N89 aluminum wheel's simple Bow-Tie center cap were the typical five lugs found on conventional wheels. Even though the "romance" of the knock-offs was lost, the new wheel finally did its weight-saving thing like an aluminum wheel should—in previous years, any pounds trimmed by the addition of RPO P48 were offset by the adapter equipment required to convert from the standard five-lug mounting setup to the quick-change knock-off design.

Safety concerns also helped inspire a long list of additional new standard Corvette features for 1967. Under the hood, a dual-circuit master cylinder—optional with J50 power assist and the J56 heavy-duty brake package in 1966—replaced the previously used single-chamber brake cylinder. Included as well was a malfunction warning system that informed the driver of his potential demise by flashing a red light on the instrument panel.

This Sunfire Yellow 1967 convertible is equipped with the 390-horsepower L36 427—total 1967 L36 production, both coupes and convertibles, was 3,832. Price for RPO L36 was $200.15.

Inside, both that panel and the steering column were redesigned with energy-absorbing characteristics. A thicker lip was added to the foam dash pad, and the shatter-resistant day/night mirror got a vinyl-padded frame and breakaway support. Dashboard

Zora Duntov grins as engineer Denny Davis dyno tests an L88 prototype (notice road draft tube on the right valve cover) in May 1966. This particular version has iron cylinder heads; regular-production L88s used the aluminum heads also offered as RPO L89 for the street-legal L71 427.

knobs were mushroom-faced, and window regulator knobs were plastic, while the door handles themselves free wheeled, meaning they were rendered inoperative once the locks were set. Seatbelts got push-button releases and the buckets' backrests got positive latches. Four-way flashers, another 1966 option, became standard in 1967 and the turn signal system was revised with a "freeway lane change" feature—a little pressure in the desired direction activated the signal, allowing the busy driver to forgo clicking the lever fully in and out of place.

Also among interior revamps was an easier-to-use parking brake handle, relocated from beneath the dash to between the seats. Although it was practical and possessed a certain sporty flair, the new handbrake made it all but impossible to carry an extra stowaway passenger, an undesirable, yet sometimes performed practice of previous years. 'This is good from an insurance company's point of view," wrote *Cars* magazine's Martyn Schorr, "but it further limits the already limited passenger space. Third passengers, especially females, will have to think a few times before accepting a ride in a 1967 Ray!"

Safety-conscious options again included shoulder harnesses, headrests, and tinted glass, items joined in 1967 by RPO U15, a speed-warning indicator incorporated, somewhat paradoxically, into the 160-mile-per-hour speedometer. By turning a small knob in the speedo's center, the driver could preset a maximum mile-per-hour limit; once he surpassed that limit on his way around the dial a buzzer would remind him of his transgression, it was hoped, before a state trooper stepped in to do the honors himself. And for drivers conscious of the safety of their removable hardtop's finish, a new vinyl covering, RPO COS, was available for an extra $52.70, on top of the C07 roof's $231.75 asking price.

Positraction continued as the overwhelming choice on the options list (89 percent of the buyers forked up $42.15 for RPO G81 in 1967), and the attractive side-mount exhausts remained popular as well. Still present among the RPO codes were the N11 off-road exhausts, K19 air injection reactor, J50 power brakes, J56 heavy-duty brakes, K66 transistorized ignition, F41 special suspension, and N03 oversized fuel tank, offered for the last time, and for good reason—only two NOB tanks were sold in 1967. Except for the discontinued teakwood steering wheel, all extra-cost comfort and convenience features were carryovers from 1966.

Quite different, though, was the 1967 powertrain lineup. Things remained unchanged at the bottom of the list, where the base 300-horsepower 327 and optional 350-horsepower L79 small-block soldiered on. Familiar as well was the L36 427 big-block with its hydraulic lifters, single Holley four-barrel, and 390 horses at the ready. Again, the Saginaw three-speed manual transmission was standard behind the 300hp small-block, with the M20 wide-ratio Muncie four-speed and M35 Powerglide still around on the options list. L79 327 buyers could choose between the M20 and M21 close-ratio four-speed, as could L36 customers, who could also select the Powerglide automatic if shiftless big-block performance was desired. Once more, Powerglide was not available behind the 350-horsepower small-block.

From there, the powertrain pecking order was revamped considerably thanks to the appearance of three little Holley two-barrel carburetors. Triple carburetion—an idea first introduced to GM's lineup in

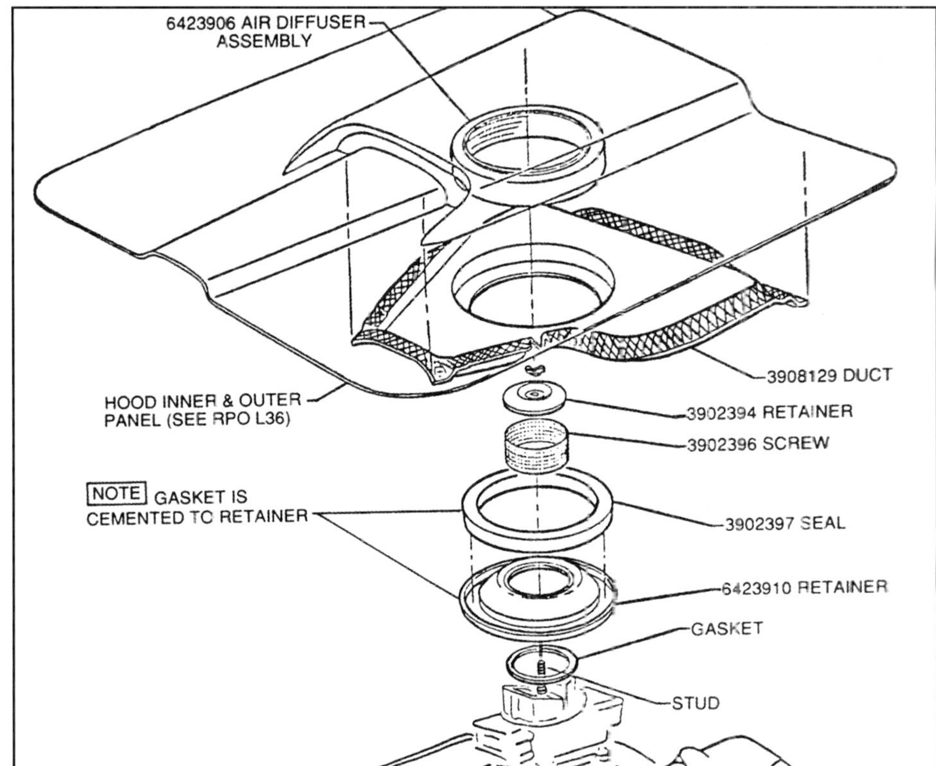

The familiar 1967 big-block hood was for looks only on all models except the L88. The small, open-top air cleaner sealed to the hood's underside and drew air through a duct running to the back of the scoop where denser air gathered at the windshield's base at high speeds.

1957 both as Oldsmobile's legendary J2 option and under the hoods of Bunkie Knudsen's Pontiacs—was finally made available atop Chevrolet big-blocks in 1967, but only for Corvette customers. Pontiac had been using its famed Tri-Power equipment as the top GTO power option since 1964, then was forced to discontinue the setup (as was Oldsmobile) after 1966 following yet another anti-performance decree from GM's front office, this one banning the use of all multicarburetor (dual-four and 3x2) induction systems on its divisions' passenger-car engines. The Sting Ray's status as America's only sports car excluded it from this ban, leading to a new big-block Corvette for 1967 that was even more brutal than the previous year's 425-horsepower model.

Chevrolet's 3x2 induction design began with an aluminum intake manifold. Mounted atop that manifold were those three Holleys, with the center two-barrel being the primary fuel-feeder for normal operation. Throttle plates in the two secondary Holley venturis remained closed until revs reached roughly 2,000 rpm, when a mass-air vacuum signal sent directly from the primary carb's venturi (as opposed to a typical central vacuum source) brought the front and rear two-barrels into the fray in a progression relative to the weight of the driver's foot. By the time engine speeds hit 4,000 rpm, all three throats were wide open and wailing. Releasing the accelerator activated a mechanical link, which positively closed the two secondary throats to avoid instantly overfeeding the engine when it no longer wanted to be fed. Topping everything off was a chrome, triangular, open-element air cleaner.

Benefits of the 3x2 setup involved the best of both worlds. Excellent fuel economy resulted during normal operation as only the humble middle two-barrel was shoveling coal into the fire. But when it came time to fan those flames, the other two Holleys quickly entered the fray, almost instantly increasing the system's total flow from roughly 300 cfm to a whopping 1,000 cfm, making even the biggest four-barrel look like a choker in comparison. Of course, Chevrolet's innovative mass-air 3x2 operation didn't hurt things, either. As Martyn Schorr wrote, "performance characteristics of [this] three-two setup are unlike those usually associated with a tri-power vehicle. [The] newly developed secondary carburetor control system eliminates the abrupt throttle opening characteristics usually found in most [tri-carb] setups."

After experiencing Chevrolet's tri-carb big-block, *Car and Driver*'s thoroughly impressed writers couldn't resist making comparisons to an earlier innovative Corvette fuel delivery system. 'The new system . . . results in an astoundingly tractable engine and uncannily smooth engine response," claimed the magazine's review. "With a venturi area about the size of a barn door, it's possible to drive off in high gear with very little slipping of the clutch or feathering of the throttle. As soon as it's rolling, say at 500rpm, you can push the throttle to the floor and the car just picks up with a turbine-like swelling surge of power

Another marked improvement over previous styling tricks, the distinctive 1967 Corvette's big-block hood may not have been functional, but it could certainly turn heads.

that never misses a beat all the way up to its top speed of over 140mph. On the whole, the Corvette's three deuces are as smooth and responsive as fuel injection."

Chevrolet's "three deuces" were offered in two forms for 1967 Corvettes. RPO L68 replaced the L36 427's four-barrel with those three Holleys, resulting in a power increase from 390 to 400 horsepower. While most powertrain RPO numbers referred to an engine as a whole, L68 represented the tri-carb setup alone, which was only natural since everything else about the 390- and 400-horsepower 427s was pretty much identical. Window stickers on a 400-horsepower 1967 Corvette showed both RPOs: L36, priced at $200.15, combined with L68, which tacked on another $105.35, for a total of $305.50. And like the "standard" L36, the 400-horsepower 427 could be backed by the $194.35 Powerglide automatic.

One step beyond was RPO L71, a potent package that almost overnight made the fiberglass faithful forget all about the formidable 425-horsepwer L72 of 1966. Everything that had made the L72 so tough—four-bolt mains, a lumpy solid-lifter cam, 11:1 compression big-valve heads, K66 electronic ignition—was in that package, save, of course, for the big 780cfm Holley four-barrel. With the triple Holleys taking care of fuel-air mixing, the L71 427 produced 435 horsepower at 5,800 rpm, more than enough muscle to keep Chevrolet's big-block Corvette at the top of Detroit's super-car ranks.

Calling the L71 Sting Ray the "hottest 'Vette yet," Eric Dahlquist explained that it didn't take a powertrain engineer to figure out how the new big-block Corvette stacked up to the competition. Wrote Dahlquist in *Hot Rod*'s May 1967 issue, "ask any kid you meet what the hottest thing going off the showroom floor is and you get one answer: a 435 'Vette." Driving an L71 convertible with the mandatory M21 close-ratio four-speed and standard 3.55:1 Positraction gears, Dahlquist recorded quarter-mile numbers of 13.80 seconds at 108 miles per hour. "GM may not

Above
A whole host of safety-conscious features were added inside a Corvette in 1967. Among these were free-wheeling door handles (they were rendered inoperative when the locks were set), four-way flashers, a shatter-resistant day/night mirror, and a "freeway lane change" turn signal system that activated the signal at a touch of the stalk. Also notice the optional headrests, RPO A82, which debuted in 1966.

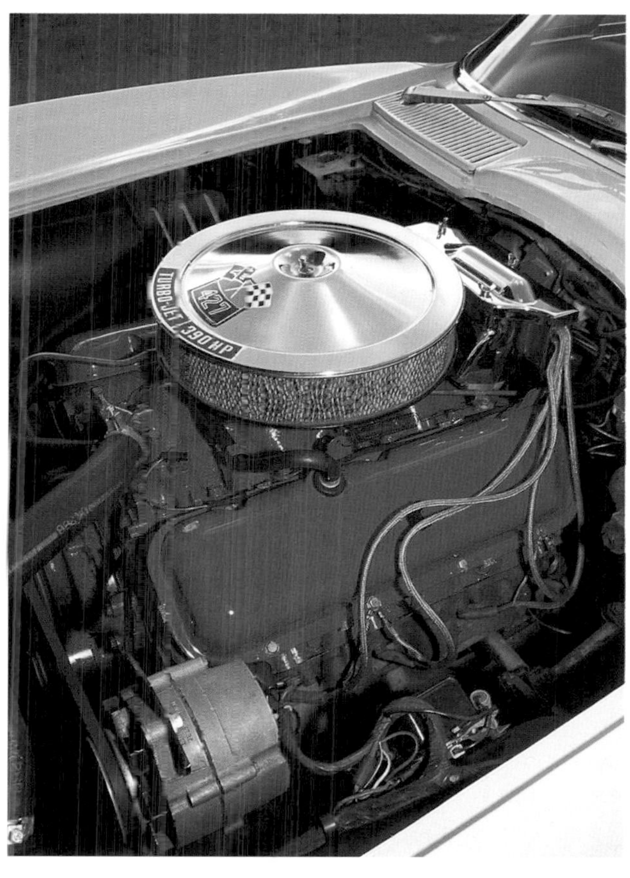

Right
Three street-legal 427 big-blocks were offered in 1967: this 390-horsepower L36, the 400-horsepower L68, and the 435-horsepower top-dog L71. The L36 used a single four-barrel carburetor, while the L68 and L71 were fed by three Holley two-barrels. Basically identical to the L36 save for the triple carbs in place of the single four-barrel, the L68 was priced at $305.50. L68 production was 2,101.

be in racing," he continued, "but its divisions build the best darned line of production competition cars in the world. The 435 Sting Ray is kind of king of these kings."

Thrashing an identically equipped 1967 convertible, Martyn Schorr bettered Dahlquist's results to the tune of a 12.90-second, 111-mile-per-hour time slip and 0–60 miles per hour in 5 seconds flat. In his words, driving an L71 Sting Ray was "sort of like guiding a

Deuces wild!

Talk about a winning hand! Three deuces to a full-house 427, the Turbo-Jet V8's got it, cold. And that's precisely what Corvette offers, among other things, in the new '67 Sting Ray. In fact, you can order it two ways: 400 horsepower with hydraulic lifters or 435 horses with solid lifters and a real special performance camshaft.

On the other hand, you traditionalists can still get the 427 V8 with a big four-barrel on top, putting out 390 horses. The whole works comes with that well-known Corvette independent rear suspension, 11¾-inch disc brakes all around, new 1967 styling touches and comforts galore. And it has safety features like the GM-developed energy-absorbing steering column and seat belts with pushbutton buckles, standard.

Take the base 300-horsepower Turbo-Fire 327 V8 or order any of the other four engines available. Decide on the extras, like AM-FM radio, you can add. Choose the standard three-speed or Powerglide or the four-speed gearbox you can order. Shuffle up the equipment the way you want it, and deal yourself a Sting Ray.

'67 Corvette

Corvette Sting Ray Sport Coupe with passenger-guard door locks standard for added safety

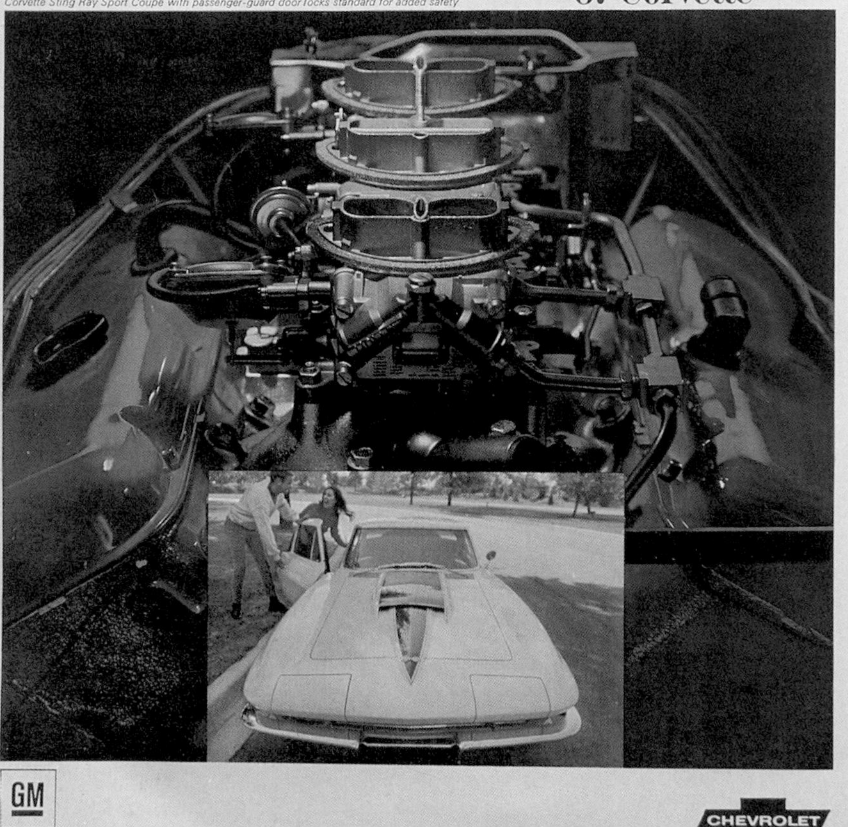

Chevrolet's triple-carb setup was a mass-air system, meaning it drew vacuum activation for the front and rear Holleys directly from the middle two-barrel's venturi, as opposed to the intake manifold. The effect was a smooth flow of power as all three carburetors began to feed the beast as rpm rose.

four-wheeled, two-passenger rocket sled with license plates, an AM-FM radio and stereo tape system!" Concluded Schorr, "the 435-hp Corvette is super-boss, super-quick, super-expensive, [and] super-impossible to insure."

It was also a bit on the super rough side when it came to ride, thanks again to all the weight up front combined with the stiffer springs required to handle that weight. "As such, the 427 model is strictly a smooth-road machine at the posted speed limits," commented Dahlquist. "Granted, once you get wailing, the suspension evens out and sticks to the ground doing it, but there are few places left to run a hundred-twenty for sustained periods." Continued Dahlquist, "the ride is just too severe for any kind of protracted driving, which is a real shame because the Sting Ray's other attributes—steering, balance, adequate leg room, good seat-to-steering-wheel relation, disc brakes that are far superior to anything else we've tried and, of course, the spine-snapping response—are just the right ingredients for a Grand Touring car in anybody's language."

Although only 16 pairs of L89 cylinder heads were sold in 1967, *Car and Driver* did manage to test a coupe with an aluminum-head L71 427. Explaining that the L89/L71 big-block weighed only 40 pounds more than the 327 small-block, *Car and Driver*'s editors recorded a front-to-rear weight distribution of 46/54 for their test Corvette, while a typical 327 Sting Ray's distribution was 47/53. Quarter-mile results were listed as 13.6 seconds at 105 miles per hour. By the magazine's account, the L89 option did go a long way toward making a big-block Corvette ride and handle like its small-block brother, basically because those aluminum heads helped put weight distribution back where Duntov knew it belonged.

Of course, overall weight was critical as well, and the Sting Ray had never been as light on its feet as Zora originally had envisioned. After 1963's Grand Sport debacle, it was clear that another lightweight, purpose-built, no-nonsense, high-profile racer would never fly in the face of GM's anti-racing policy.

To end-run the anti-performance types, Duntov's engineers kicked off another lightweight Corvette development project in 1965, but this one was based on regular-production options. By essentially "hiding" a collection of race-ready components in Chevrolet parts books, Duntov figured he'd skirt the anti-racing issue. He was right.

Fred Frincke, Cal Wade, and Denny Davis had barely begun work on that parts project when rumors started flying. Writing in *Sports Car Graphic's* March 1965 issue, Jerry Titus mentioned various performance parts then being planned for the Corvette. "Among the options that will make the car competitive is a new four-speed gearbox designed to handle a 'prodified' [homologated] version of the [Mark IV] engine," claimed Titus. "An estimated 470 horsepower is expected with application of allowable SCCA modifications. We didn't have a chance to test the box. We understand it is quite a bit noisier than the standard Muncie." The "box" Titus referred to was, of course, the M22 Rock Crusher four-speed, officially introduced for 1966. As for the "prodified" engine, that was the fabled L88 427 big-block, easily the greatest Corvette powerplant yet to come down the road. Or racetrack.

From top to bottom, the L88 427 was as "purpose-built" as it got. Although its cylinder block was identical to a typical street-going Mark IV, that certainly was not a detriment considering the standard high-performance block's four-bolt mains, and terrifically stout lower end. Equally stout was the L88's crankshaft, which was specially forged out of 5140 alloy steel, then cross-drilled for sure lubrication and tuftrided for hardness. Attached to that crank by shot-peened, magnafluxed connecting rods (with heavier 7/16-inch bolts) were eight forged-aluminum pop-up pistons that squeezed the fuel-air mixture at a molecule-mashing 12.5:1 ratio. Topping things off were the same weight-saving aluminum heads—with their big 2.19-inch intake and 1.84-inch exhaust valves—that eventually would be listed under RPO L89.

Feeding the beast was a huge 850-cfm Holley four-barrel on a special aluminum intake manifold with its internal partition removed to create an open plenum. Designed by engineer Denny Davis, the L88's solid-lifter cam was radical, to say the least, with 337 degrees duration on the intake side, 340 degrees on exhaust, and

Bob Bondurant and Dick Guldstrand's L88 Corvette leaves the famous starting line at Le Mans in June 1967. Performance early on during the 24 Hours was impressive, with top speeds topping 170 miles per hour on the Mulsanne Straight, but a blown engine during the night torpedoed the effort. *Dave Friedman photo*

lift of 0.5365 inch for the intake valve and 0.5560 inch for the exhaust. Pushrods were thick 7/16-inch pieces with hardened ends. On top, special "long-slot" stamped-steel rockers rocked on heat-treated, hardened ball-studs, while heavy-duty valve springs were held in place by beefed-up retainers and locks. Spark was supplied by the K66 transistorized ignition equipment.

Although a token advertised output of 430 horsepower was bestowed upon the L88 427, to avert any unwanted attention—both from within the corporation and without—actual horsepower was much more than 500. According to engineer Fred Frincke, dyno tests of an L88 with headers produced figures of between 550 and 570 horsepower. Any way you looked at it, the L88 427 was far and away the strongest Corvette powerplant ever produced.

Initial plans called for the L88's release as a 1966 Corvette option. Duntov's engineers had a working example running on a dyno in October 1965, and official 1966 factory paperwork was full of L88 availability references. Chomping at the bit, Jerry Titus couldn't wait to get his hands on an L88 Corvette, and was set to test one late in 1965. The car did not arrive, however, leaving Titus to explain a performance offering he was hoping he wouldn't have to wait much longer to see.

"What was supposed to fill these pages was a track test of an optioned 427, a hundred of which are supposed to be built by January 1 and homologated with

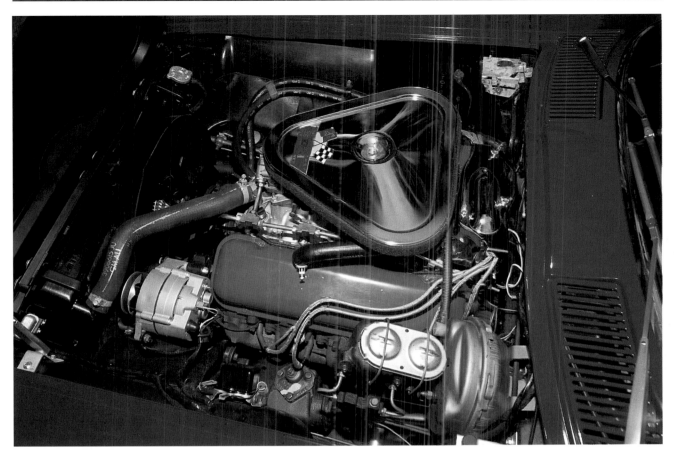

Beneath that distinctive triangular air cleaner are three Holley two-barrels feeding about 1,000 cfm into the L71 427. The L71 made 435 horsepower at 5,800 rpm. Compression was 11:1.

both FIA and SCCA," began Titus in December's *Sports Car Graphic*. "Since their retirement from active competition, Chevrolet has been besieged by customers and dealers to at least make hardware available so they could go racing on their own. This program was strictly that, to give the customer something to work with. The package is still in the mill at this writing and may see a production line. If rumors are correct, it's nothing too wild; several alloy options—including cylinder

Right
The $42.15 telescopic steering wheel. RPO N36 returned for 1967 with a restyled locking nut/horn button combination. N36 buyers numbered 2,415.

Left
Redline 7.75x15-inch four-ply nylon tires, RPO QB1, were introduced for 1967 carrying a $46.65 price tag. Sales of RPO QB1 reached 4,230. Total 1967 convertible production, with all engines, was 14,436. New colors included Marina Blue, Lynndale Blue, Elkhart Blue, Goodwood Green, and Marlboro Maroon.

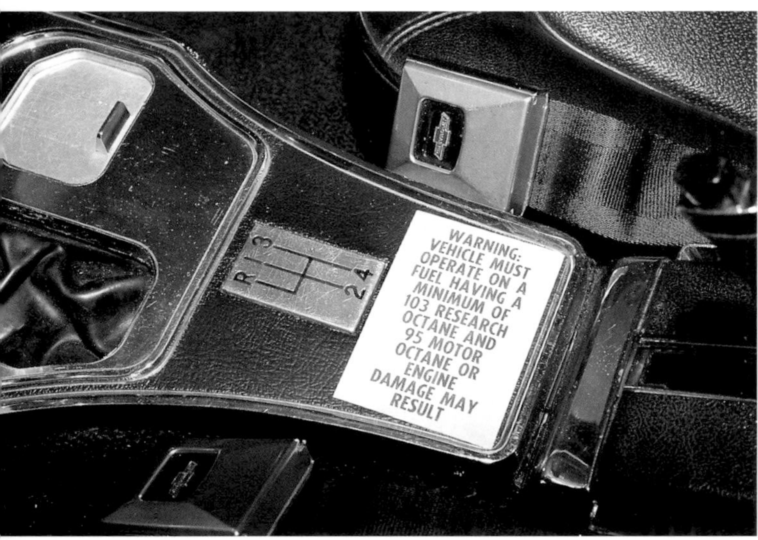

There was little doubt that the L88 was intended only for the track. But those who thought otherwise might have been reminded what they were facing on the street by this warning label on the car's console. Chevrolet press releases made the situation perfectly clear, explaining that "because the L88 is an off-road engine, no provision has been made for anti-pollution control. For those states that require smog-control devices, it cannot be registered for street use in a passenger-carrying vehicle."

heads—that enable you to reduce the curb weight to around 2600 pounds, and mild engine rework that puts output above 500 horsepower."

Later, in the spring of 1966, *Cars'* Martyn Schorr also made mention of the mysterious new big-block. "Although not listed in the official Chevrolet AMA Sting Ray specifications book," wrote Schorr, "there is another optional 427 which is even more suited for competition. All we know at this time is that this engine does exist. Before ordering a Sting Ray for all-out competition it would be wise to check with . . . any dealer who engages in sports or drag competition on the availability of this 'not listed' option."

Duntov had filed L88 homologation papers with both the Sports Car Club of America (SCCA) and the French-run FIA, the governing body for worldwide racing, late in 1965, then quickly delivered a red 1966 427 Corvette coupe, equipped with the L88's big Holley four-barrel and intake, to Roger Penske, who was planning to enter the car in the Daytona 24 Hours race in February 1966. Not even a wreck or a punctured radiator could stop Penske's coupe from finishing 1st in its class and 12th overall at Daytona. The car was then repaired, repainted Sunoco Blue, and sent to Sebring, where it was also joined by Penske's Grand Sport roadster, itself now armed with a 427 big-block. Although the Grand Sport would drop out with a blown engine, the coupe ended up 9th overall for the 12 Hours. It hadn't exactly beaten the world, but Penske's Corvette had proven to Duntov that he definitely needed to get the rest of the L88 parts into production.

Actual release of RPO L88 as an official Corvette option available to the public came in the spring of 1967. Priced at $947.90, the L88 427 was complemented by an impressive list of mandatory heavy-duty pieces. K66 ignition, J56 power-assisted metallic brakes, F41 suspension (which was offered only as an option with the 1967 L71 427), G81 Positraction, and the M22 Rocker Crusher four-speed were all standard equipment along with the L88 427. RPO C48, the heater-defroster delete option offered for Sting Ray buyers since 1963, was included as part of the L88 deal as well since it was relatively easy to assume these cars wouldn't be seeing very much duty away from a racetrack. Deleting the heater/defroster also helped cut loose a few additional pounds.

Another standard feature that helped discourage a driver from taking a 1967 L88 Corvette to the streets (as if the high-strung aluminum-head 427 and brutal Rocker Crusher gearbox weren't convincing enough) was its heavy-duty Harrison aluminum cross-flow radiator, which was installed without a fan shroud—an item race cars rarely need anyway since they almost never end up stuck in traffic. California customers had no choice concerning the car's off-road status since all L88s were delivered with a road draft tube that vented the crankcase directly into the atmosphere, meaning the engines would never meet even the most forgiving emissions standards, let alone the toughest in the country.

As it was, even if a Californian could have driven an L88 legally on the street he would have thought twice about it as soon as he turned the key. The emissions-illegal (in some states, including California) L88's 850-cfm Holley four-barrel wasn't equipped with a choke—although a retrofit kit was offered by Chevrolet—so starting that hungry, cranky animal was no easy task. Then once running, an L88 427 didn't like to sit calmly as its open-plenum intake, long-duration high-lift cam, and large-port heads completely sacrificed low-speed cooperation for all-out high-rpm performance. Idle speed was a cupboard-rattling 1,000 rpm. And thanks to that head-cracking 12.5:1 compression, only the next best thing to jet fuel could keep this bomb from predetonating. According to delivery paperwork included with an L88, "this unit operates only on

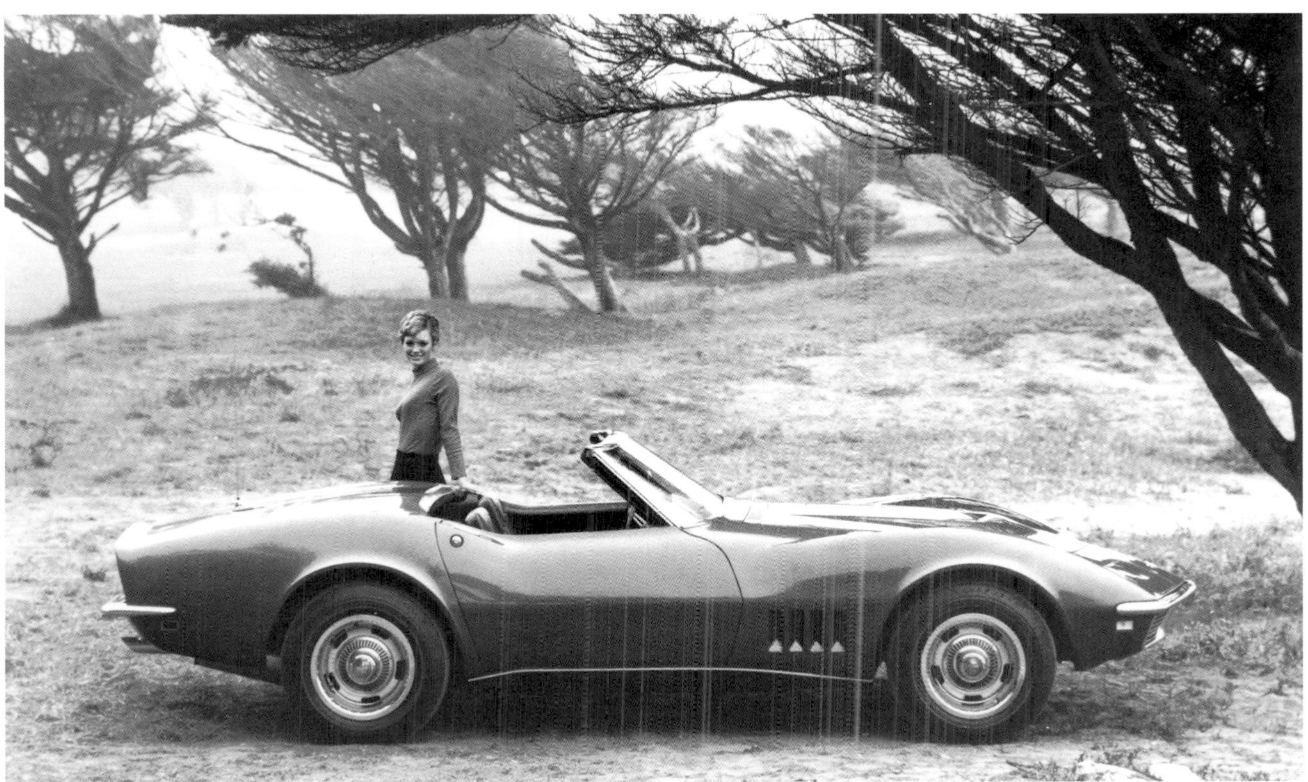

With its "Coke-bottle" body, bulging wheelhouses, and pointed nose, the all-new 1968 Corvette followed the first-edition Sting Ray as a proud representative of Chevrolet's long-running legacy of sporty performance and sexy pizzazz.

Sunoco 260 or equivalent gas of very high octane. Under no circumstances should regular gasoline be used." Those instructions were repeated inside on a label near the shifter: "Warning: vehicle must operate on a fuel having a minimum of 103 research octane and 95 motor octane or engine damage may result." If all that wasn't enough to make everyday operation a drag, L88 Corvettes also couldn't be equipped—no way, no how—with radios. Or power windows. What a bummer.

Completing the L88 lineup was a smaller flywheel, a heavy-duty clutch, and a unique air cleaner. Looking much like no air cleaner at all, the L88 unit featured an open "pan" mounted atop the big Holley carb. In the center of the pan was a small filter; around its edge was a foam gasket. With the hood closed, the gasket sealed the air cleaner to the hood's underside, where ductwork ran back to the rear edge of the Corvette's normally nonfunctional big-block hood scoop. By making this scoop functional, engineers allowed the L88 to take its breaths from the denser air mass that typically gathers at the base of a car's windshield at speed—a clever idea, one that had proven itself under Chevrolet hoods during the Daytona 500 in 1963.

How did the L88 Corvette do on the track? Four aluminum-head 427 Sting Rays went to Sebring in 1967, with the Don Yenko–Dave Morgan car finishing 10th overall and first in class. The 24 Hours of Le Mans in France was the true test, however, and that's where a 1967 L88 coupe showed up that summer with sponsorship from California dealer Dana Chevrolet. With Dick Guldstrand and Bob Bondurant driving, the Dana L88 ran strong in the early going, hitting 171 miles per hour on the Mulsanne Straight. But hopes for glory were dashed during the night when a connecting rod exited the side of the block.

Though disappointing, the 1967 Le Mans effort was only the beginning as the L88 kicked off a Corvette racing revival. A second-edition L88 would appear in 1968, followed by a third in 1969. In the hands of Jerry Thompson and Tony DeLorenzo, the famed Owens-Corning Fiberglass L88 roadsters went on to win 8 of 11 SCCA A-Production races in 1968, reviving memories of the glory days before Shelby's Cobras made the scene late in 1962. Production of L88 Corvettes was only 20 in 1967, 80 in 1968, and 116 in 1969.

Chevrolet gave the L88 a token 430-horsepower rating, which was a joke in light of this powerplant's muscular abilities. With a big 850-cfm Holley four-barrel, 12.5:1 compression, and aluminum heads, the L88 427 easily produced more than 500 horsepower. The K66 transistorized ignition was another mandatory option. Notice the road draft tube equipment exiting the left valve cover. This antiquated setup simply evacuated the crankcase directly into the atmosphere, which is the main reason the L88 was labeled an "off-road" engine.

While Shelby-American's 427 Cobra was still around to taunt Corvette racers on the track in 1967, production of those gnarly monsters had all but ceased that year, leaving Sting Ray drivers on American streets unlimited bragging rights as the baddest boys in the valley. With the big-block Cobra gone, the automotive press turned to Shelby's Mustangs as new measuring sticks for this country's only true sports car, and of course the conclusions this time finally favored the Sting Ray hands down. *Motor Trend* squared off a base 300-horsepower 1967 Corvette with a small-block Shelby GT-350 in its April 1967 issue, then followed that with a 435-horsepower Sting Ray big-block versus GT-500 shootout in the May edition. In both cases it was no contest on the road, although *Motor Trend*'s Steve Kelly did point out that insuring the Shelby Mustangs would be considerably less traumatic than getting coverage for Chevrolet's fiberglass slingshots.

Overall conclusions concerning the last of Chevrolet's first-generation Sting Rays were typically glowing. "The Sting Ray's four-wheel disc brakes are in a class of their own among American cars, and up to the highest standards set abroad," commented *Car and Driver*. They continued, "We have just about exhausted our cherished supply of superlatives for these brakes, so suffice it to say that they're the best." According to *Road & Track*, it was "hard to find fault with the Corvette's handling; it's as near neutral as any car we know and of course there's always enough torque available to steer with the throttle." "All things considered," continued the magazine, "the Sting Ray is a big value for the money. It matches any of its European competition for useful performance and walks away from most of them; it's quiet, luxurious and comfortable under ordinary conditions; easy to tune and maintain; and even easy on fuel if its performance isn't indulged too often. It remains unique among American cars—and among sports cars."

Chevrolet's 1967 Sting Ray may have been an unintended encore, but what a performance. Five years after the breed first appeared in stunning fashion in the fall of 1962, the last of the so-called midyear Corvettes exited stage right to a standing ovation. Although faster, more modern, better-selling models would follow, they haven't dimmed the first-generation Sting Ray's image in the least. All remain unforgettable.

No readily available external evidence gave away the awesome L88's identity, at least while one was standing still. But with roughly 500 horses beneath that functional hood scoop, there was little doubt that this animal was the wildest Corvette yet. Not street legal in many states in 1967 thanks to its nonexistent emissions equipment, this L88 Corvette is 1 of only 20 built.

Appendix

Corvette Sting Ray Production Figures

1963

coupes	10,594
convertibles	10,919
Total	21,513

Other totals:

Standard 250hp 327 V-8	3,892
L75 300hp 327 V-8	8,033
L76 340hp 327 V-8	6,978
L84 360hp 327 F.I. V-8	2,610
Standard three-speed manual transmission	919
M20 Four-speed manual transmission	17,973
M35 Powerglide automatic transmission	2,621
C07 Auxiliary hardtop for convertibles	5,739
C60 Air conditioning	278
G81 Positraction rear axle	17,554
J50 Power brakes	3,336
J65 Sintered-metallic brakes	5,310
N03 36.5gal fuel tank (coupes only)	63
N40 Power steering	3,063
Z06 Special Performance Equipment (coupes only)	199

New Sting Rays roll down the St. Louis assembly line in 1963. Notice that the hood vents have been inexplicably airbrushed out on the lead car.

1964

coupes	8,304
convertibles	13,925
Total	22,229

Other totals:

Standard 250hp 327 V-8	3,262
L75 300hp 327 V-8	10,471
L76 365hp 327 V-8	7,171
L84 375hp 327 F.I.V-8	1,325
Standard three-speed manual transmission	715
M20 Four-speed manual transmission	19,034
M35 Powerglide automatic transmission	2,480
C07 Auxiliary hardtop for convertibles	7,023
C60 Air conditioning	1,988
F40 Special suspension	82
G81 Positraction rear axle	18,279
J50 Power brakes	2,270
J56 Special sintered-metallic brakes	29
J65 Sintered-metallic brakes, power-assisted	4,780
K66 Transistorized ignition	552
N03 36.5gal fuel tank (coupes only)	38
N11 Off-road exhaust system	1,953
N40 Power steering	3,126
P48 Cast-aluminum knock-off wheels	806

1965

coupes	8,186
convertibles	15,376
Total	23,562

Other totals:

Standard 250hp 327 V-8	2,549
L75 300hp 327 V-8	8,358
L76 365hp 327 V-8	5,011
L78 425hp 396 V-8	2,157
L79 350hp 327 V-8	4,716
L84 375hp 327 F.I. V-8	771
Standard three-speed manual transmission	434
M20 Four-speed manual transmission	21,107
M35 Powerglide automatic transmission	2,021

C07 Auxiliary hardtop for convertibles	7,787
C60 Air conditioning	2,423
F40 Special suspension	975
G81 Positraction rear axle	19,965
J50 Power brakes	4,044
J61 Drum brake substitution credit	316
K66 Transistorized ignition	3,686
N03 36.5-gallon fuel tank (coupes only)	41
N11 Off-road exhaust system	2,468
N14 Sidemount exhausts	759
N32 Teakwood steering wheel	2,259
N36 Telescopic steering column	3,917
N40 Power steering	3,236
P48 Cast-aluminum knock-off wheels	1,116

1966

coupes	9,958
convertibles	17,762
Total	27,720

Other totals:

Standard 300hp 327 V-8	9,755
L36 390hp 427 V-8	5,116
L72 425hp 427 V-8	5,258
L79 350hp 327 V-8	7,591
Standard three-speed manual transmission	564
M20 Four-speed manual transmission (wide-ratio)	10,837
M21 Four-speed manual transmission (close-ratio)	13,903
M22 Heavy-duty four-speed manual trans. (close-ratio)	15
M35 Powerglide automatic transmission	2,401
C07 Auxiliary hardtop for convertibles	8,463
C60 Air conditioning	3,520
F41 Special suspension	2,705
G81 Positraction rear axle	24,056
J50 Power brakes	5,464
J56 Special heavy-duty brakes	382
K66 Transistorized ignition	7,146
N03 36.5gal fuel tank (coupes only)	66
N11 Off-road exhaust system	2,795
N14 Sidemount exhausts	3,617
N32 Teakwood steering wheel	3,941
N36 Telescopic steering column	3,670
N40 Power steering	5,611
P48 Cast-aluminum knock-off wheels	1,194

1967

coupes	8,504
convertibles	14,436
Total	22,940

Other totals:

Standard 300hp 327 V-8	6,858
L36 390hp 427 V-8	3,832
L68 400hp 427 V-8	2,101
L71 435hp 427 V-8	3,754
L79 350hp 327 V-8	6,375
L88 430hp 427 V-8 (with aluminum cylinder heads)	20
L89 Aluminum cylinder heads for L71 427	16
Standard three-speed manual transmission	424
M20 Four-speed manual transmission (wide-ratio)	9,157
M21 Four-speed manual transmission (close-ratio)	11,015
M22 Heavy-duty four-speed manual trans. (close-ratio)	20
M35 Powerglide automatic transmission	2,324
C07 Auxiliary hardtop for convertibles	6,880
C60 Air conditioning	3,788
F41 Special suspension	2,198
G81 Positraction rear axle	20,308
J50 Power brakes	4,766
J56 Special heavy-duty brakes	267
K19 Air injection reactor	2,573
K66 Transistorized ignition	5,759
N03 36.5-gallon fuel tank (coupes only)	2
N14 Sidemount exhausts	4,209
N36 Telescopic steering column	2,415
N40 Power steering	5,747
N89 Cast-aluminum wheels	720

Shown here is Chevrolet's 1965 Corvette convertible with small-block power.

Corvette Engine Specifications

RPO	CID	Horsepower	Torque	Induction	Comp.
1963					
Std.	327	250 @ 4400rpm	350 @ 2800rpm	Carter 4-bbl.	10.5:1
L75	327	300 @ 5000rpm	360 @ 3200rpm	Carter AFB 4-bbl.	10.5:1
L76	327	340 @ 6000rpm	344 @ 4000rpm	Carter AFB 4-bbl.	11.25:1
L84	327	360 @ 6000rpm	352 @ 4000rpm	Rochester fuel-inj.	11.25:1

Note: Base engine and L75 327 had hydraulic lifters; L76 and L84 high-performance 327s had solid lifters.

RPO	CID	Horsepower	Torque	Induction	Comp.
1964					
Std.	327	250 @ 4400rpm	350 @ 2800rpm	Carter 4-bbl.	10.5:1
L75	327	300 @ 5000rpm	360 @ 3200rpm	Carter AFB 4-bbl.	10.5:1
L76	327	365 @ 6200rpm	350 @ 4000rpm	Holley 4-bbl.	11:1
L84	327	375 @ 6200rpm	350 @ 4400rpm	Rochester fuel-inj.	11:1

Note: Base engine and L75 327 had hydraulic lifters; L76 and L84 high-performance 327s had solid lifters.

RPO	CID	Horsepower	Torque	Induction	Comp.
1965					
Std.	327	250 @ 4400rpm	350 @ 2800rpm	Carter 4-bbl.	10.5:1
L75	327	300 @ 5000rpm	360 @ 3200rpm	Carter AFB 4-bbl.	10.5:1
L76	327	365 @ 6200rpm	350 @ 4000rpm	Holley 4-bbl.	11:1
L78	396	425 @ 6400rpm	415 @ 4000rpm	Holley 4-bbl.	11:1
L79	327	350 @ 5800rpm	360 @ 3600rpm	Holley 4-bbl.	11:1
L84	327	375 @ 6200rpm	350 @ 4400rpm	Rochester fuel-inj.	11:1

Note: Base engine, L75 and L79 327s had hydraulic lifters; L76 and L84 327s had solid lifters, as did the 425 hp 396 big-block V-8.

RPO	CID	Horsepower	Torque	Induction	Comp.
1966					
Std.	327	300 @ 5000rpm	360 @ 3400rpm	Holley 4-bbl.	10.25:1
L36	427	390 @ 5200rpm[1]	460 @ 3600rpm	Holley 4-bbl.	10.25:1
L72	427	425 @ 5600rpm[2]	460 @ 4000rpm	Holley 4-bbl.	11:1
L79	327	350 @ 5800rpm	360 @ 3600rpm	Holley 4-bbl.	11:1

[1]L36 was briefly advertised at 400 hp early in production [2]L72 was briefly advertised at 450 hp early in production

Note: Base engine, L79 327 and L36 427 all had hydraulic lifters; the 425hp L72 427 had solid lifters. The L36 390hp 427 also had two-bolt mainbearing caps, while the L72 big-block had four-bolt mains.

RPO	CID	Horsepower	Torque	Induction	Comp.
1967					
Std.	327	300 @ 5000rpm	360 @ 3400rpm	Holley 4-bbl.	10.25:1
L36	427	390 @ 5400rpm	460 @ 3600rpm	Holley 4-bbl.	10.25:1
L68[1]	427	400 @ 5400rpm	460 @ 3600rpm	3 Holley 2-bbls.	10.25:1
L71	427	435 @ 5800rpm	460 @ 4000rpm	3 Holley 2-bbls.	11:1
L79	327	350 @ 5800rpm	360 @ 3600rpm	Holley 4-bbl.	11:1
L88[2]	427	430 @ 5200rpm	450 @ 4400rpm	Holley 4-bbl.	12.5:1
L89[3]	427	435 @ 5800rpm	460 @ 4000rpm	3 Holley 2-bbls.	11:1

[1]L68 option added the 3x2 Holley carburetor setup atop the L36 427 in place of the 390hp 427's single Holley four-barrel, upping the advertised output to 400 hp.

[2] L88 option featured special race-only 427 with aluminum heads and no provisions for street-legal emissions controls. Advertised horsepower and torque figures shown here were token numbers—actual output was much higher, easily surpassing 500 horsepower.

[3] L89 option simply added aluminum heads to the L71 435hp 427 resulting in no changes for advertised output.

Note: Base engine, L79 327, L36 427, and L68 427 all had hydraulic lifters; the 425hp L71 427 and L88 special-performance 427 had solid lifters. The L36 390hp and L68 400hp 427s also had two-bolt main bearing caps, while the L71 and L88 big-blocks had four-bolt mains.

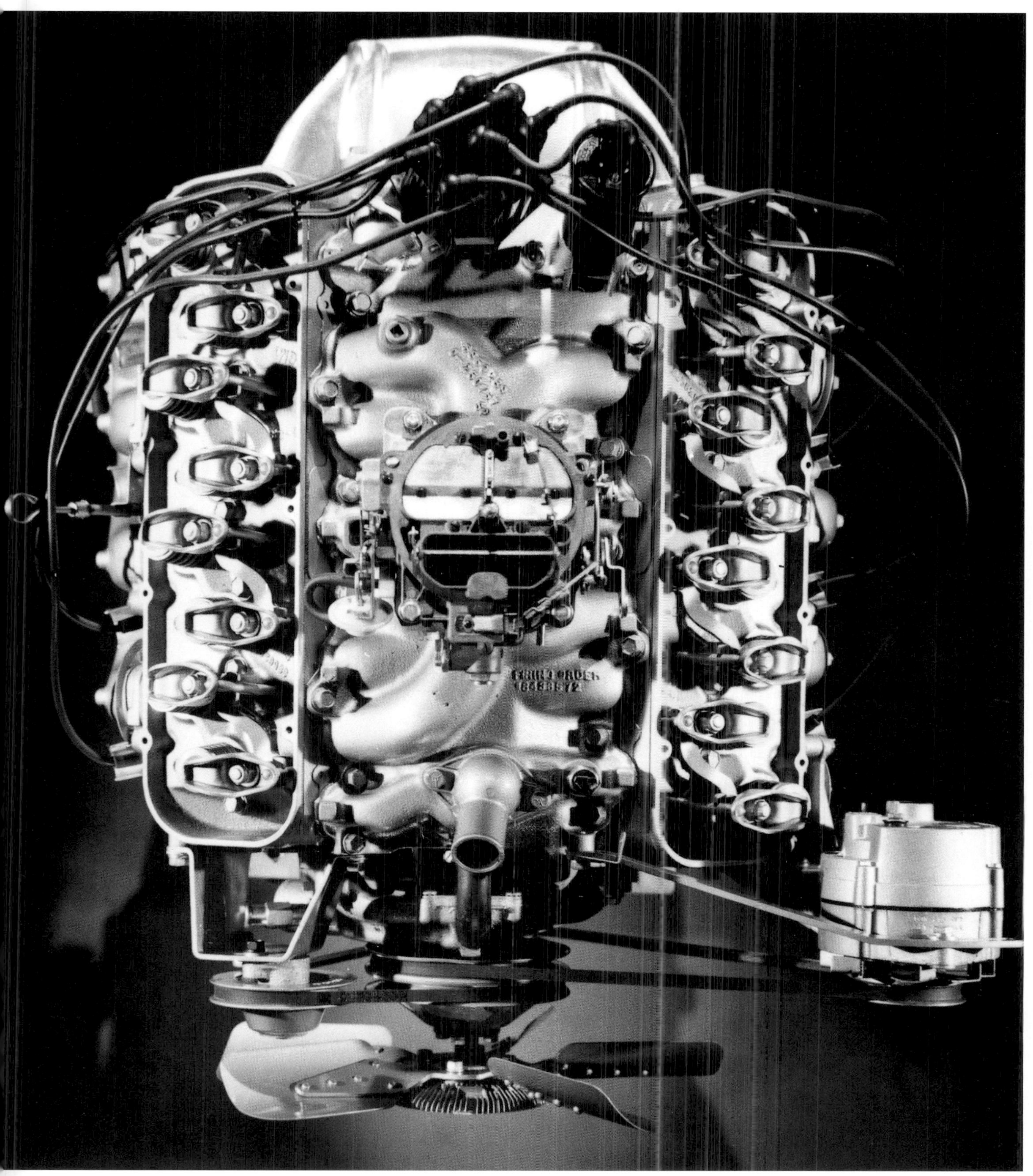

Chevrolet's Mk IV big-block shows off its "porcupine" canted-valve heads.

EAGLE ST
GOODYEAR

CORVETTE

1968-1982

Acknowledgments

I can't let any of you read any further into this epic without introducing you to the many people who went above and beyond the call of duty to help me miss yet another deadline. First, I have to do the obligatory family kudo thing, beginning with my sister, Kathy Young, and her husband, Master Sergeant Frank Young of the Illinois State Police. Kathy and Frank once made the mistake of insinuating that their fabulous home in Savoy, Illinois, was mine too. Can't take it back now. Same goes for Ma and Pa—Jim Sr. and Nancy Mueller—in Champaign, Illinois. Don't know what I would do without a free place to stay during my many photo junkets through the Midwest.

My brother-in-law, Officer Frank, has also proven especially helpful during photo shoots, as have my brothers Dave Mueller of Thomasboro, Illinois, and Jim Mueller Jr. of Champaign. Don't worry, guys, the check's in the mail, as always.

Worth more than all of that free labor combined is my wife, Joyce, who truly does know how to put the mule in Mueller. Her contributions to my projects can't be listed here, nor would she want some of them to be. Suffice it to say that I am one of the luckiest men on the face of the earth, if not the luckiest.

And speaking of incredibly good-looking young women, I would like to offer thanks to the "Comets," my 10-and-under Sandy Plains League girls softball team. While they didn't help me meet this deadline, they did make the struggle much more enjoyable. Chelsea Tucker, Michelle Gergel, Wesleigh Coskey, Savannah and Sierra McGrath, Carly Migdall, Courtney Nicklas, Kendall Reed, Kristi Lemieux, Caitie Cirou, Bridget Monroe, Colleen Evans, Lauren Smith, Casey Baker—you go, girls!

Back to business . . .

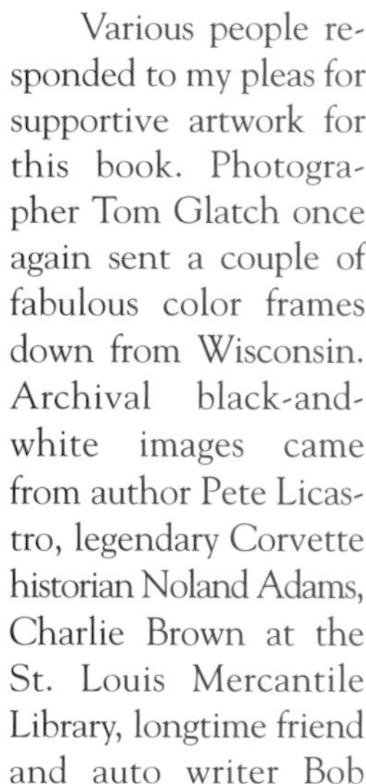

Various people responded to my pleas for supportive artwork for this book. Photographer Tom Glatch once again sent a couple of fabulous color frames down from Wisconsin. Archival black-and-white images came from author Pete Licastro, legendary Corvette historian Noland Adams, Charlie Brown at the St. Louis Mercantile Library, longtime friend and auto writer Bob Ackerson, and automotive literature collector/dealer Walter Miller. Two former bosses of mine, Donald Farr at Petersen Publishing in Florida and *Automobile Quarterly* editor Jonathan Stein, graciously helped me locate literally tons of valuable historical photography—too bad I couldn't use it all here. And I'll never be able to repay Chuck Schifsky, senior editor at *Motor Trend*, for coming to my aid as if I was an old friend in need. Such kindness must be catchy out west. *Motor Trend*'s editor-in-chief, C. Van Tune, has also never failed to pick up the phone with a friendly hello whenever I've called for help or advice. Former *Motor Trend* (and *Hot Rod*) editor Eric Dahlquist's patience and kind cooperation over the last few years ranks as priceless as well.

Gary and Eric Mortimer of the National Corvette Restorers Society saved my bacon more than once too. Any Corvette fan couldn't lose by joining the NCRS—call them in Cincinnati at (513) 385-8526. NCRS judge and 1970–72 Corvette expert Terry MacManmon in Berwyn, Illinois, was especially helpful when it came time to write about the stillborn LS-7 454 V-8. Like all NCRS guys, Terry knows his stuff.

So do Bill Tower (Plant City, Florida) and Ray Quinlan (Champaign, Illinois), two veteran Corvette enthusiasts who have always been there to help keep me from stumbling too much. GM Powertrain man Jack Underwood too has often made it his job to take me in and raise. Thanks to Jack, I was able to spend more than one moment on the phone with veteran GM engineering legends Tom Langdon and Gib Hufstader, who both were there in 1969 when Duntov was promoting Corvette horsepower like it was going out of style. Too bad it was.

Finally, I have to make mention of Mike Yager and Steve Wiedman at Mid America Designs, Inc. Not only have Mike and Steve always welcomed me into their fabulous shop and museum, located among the cornfields outside Effingham, Illinois, they also invited me to serve as a VIP (their designation, not mine) judge for their 25th anniversary Corvette Funfest, held September 18–19, 1999. There, I had the pleasure of spending about three hours listening to former chief engineer Dave McLellan spin a yarn or two. Like Zora always did, Dave seems to have cornered the market in patience. What a gentleman and scholar.

Last, but certainly not least, I can't close without offering my gratitude to all the men and women who took the time to roll out their Corvettes for my Hasselblad. In general order of appearance, they are 1972 LT-1 coupe (blue), Larry Tritt, Woodstock, Georgia; 1977 coupe (red), Bill Nollenberger, Alpharetta, Georgia; 1967 Sting Ray, Bob Wolter, Champaign, Illinois; 1982 Collectors Edition, Dan Holton, Gainesville, Florida; 1996 Collectors Edition, Jim Morris, Winter Haven, Florida; 1969 ZL-1, Roger and Dave Judski, Roger's Corvette Center, Maitland, Florida; 1968 L-89 427 coupe (blue), Elmer and Dean Puckett, Elgin, Illinois; 1968 427 coupe (silver), Guy Landis, Kutztown, Pennsylvania; 1970 coupe (yellow), Phil Vitale, Port St. Lucie, Florida; 1971 454 convertible (blue), Tom Biltcliff, Topton, Pennsylvania; 1972 coupe (dark red), Dennis Hold, Punta Gorda, Florida; 1967 L-88, Bill Tower, Plant City, Florida; 1968 L-88 coupe, Lou Groebner, Corvette City, Highland Park, Illinois; 1971 LS-6 coupe, Jim MacDougald, Port Richey, Florida; 1970 LS-6 Chevelle SS 454, Dr. Sam TreBeck, Knoxville, Illinois; 1970 LT-1 convertible, Phil Vitale, Port St. Lucie, Florida; 1972 LT-1 coupe, Steve and Nora Gussack, Winter Springs, Florida; 1970–1/2 Camaro Z/28, Kevin Emberton, Edmonton, Kentucky; 1975 convertible (yellow), Bill Tower, Plant City, Florida; 1973 coupe (yellow) and 1974 454 coupe (blue), Robert Boynton Jr., Palm Harbor, Florida; 1975 convertible (silver), Bob Bateman, Port Charlotte, Florida; 1976 coupe (orange), Paul and Nancy Pearson, Lakeland, Florida; 1978 Indy Pace Car replica, Bill Tower, Plant City, Florida; 1979 L-82 coupe (black), Jerry Miller, Zephyrhills, Florida; 1981 two-tone coupe, Mike and Sharon Kelly, Portage, Indiana; and 1984 coupe serial number 00001 Dick Gonyer, Bowling Green, Ohio.

A hearty thanks and best wishes go to you all.

—*Mike Mueller*

Introduction

America's Sports Car Pursues Perfection

Preparations for one of the biggest birthday parties Detroit has ever seen are underway even as you read this, and the anniversary date itself is still some three years away. Forget all that ridiculous Y2K paranoia. The real headlines will be made in 2003 when Chevrolet's fantastic plastic two-seater will mark its 50th year on the automotive scene.

A half-century old? The Corvette? A half-century young would be more like it. All those years, all the trials and tribulations, and the Corvette looks none the worse for wear. That no other American car (Ford's F-series pickup truck celebrated its 50th in 1998, Cadillac's DeVille doesn't really count and Eldorado's many different faces rules it out on a technicality) can claim anything close to this longevity record is one thing. Zora Arkus-Duntov's dream machine is not only an unprecedented survivor, it also stands out as one of the few pleasures of life that actually has gotten better with age. Make that much better.

If only Corvette drivers could say the same. But then they wouldn't need cars like this to lead them to the nearest fountain of youth. From its humble beginnings in 1953, the Corvette has never failed in its role as a time machine capable of restoring its middle-aged owner's slackening sex appeal, at least in his mind. To hell with reality. Once behind a Corvette's wheel, any man becomes irresistible to women of all ages, preferably half his. That's a supernatural fact.

Back in the real world, the plain truth is that the Corvette also has never failed to excite all kinds of drivers, male or female, young or old, as this country's supreme performance machine. They don't call it 'America's only sports car" for nothing. With absolutely no apologies whatsoever to the Dodge boys, the Corvette deserves this exclusive honor for various reasons, not the least of which is its established track record. Come back in 50 years, Viper fans, and we'll see what you've got.

Fifty years and five generations of Corvettes—one can only wonder if Harley Earl himself could have envisioned such a lengthy legacy when he first began the push for his little six-cylinder showcar in the early 1950s. While no one today dares doubt the Corvette's reason to be, there are, however, some who do feel the numbers don't quite add up. One, two, three, four, five—five generations? In many opinions, the figure should read six: 1953–55, 1956–62, 1963–67, 1968–82, 1984–96, and 1997–present. According to these kibitzers, even though the 1953–62 group all rolled on the same basic solid-axle chassis, the many upgrades made in 1956 should have established a break between the Corvette's first three pioneering models and the much improved solid-axles that followed. *Road & Track* apparently agreed in its March 1983 issue, which trumpeted the arrival of the "new 5th-generation Corvette."

According to General Motors' finger- and toe-counters, the fifth-generation Corvette arrived in January 1997. It was Chevrolet officials who cast the Corvette bloodline in stone by letting it slip a few years back that the next great model would be coded "C5"—the 5, of course, for five generations. Clearly Chevy people didn't

The third-generation Corvette began life with chrome bumpers at both ends and ended it with plastic-covered bump-resistant structures front and rear. The Stingray in the foreground is one of the rare air-conditioned LT-1 cars built late in 1972. The Corvette in the background is a 1977 model.

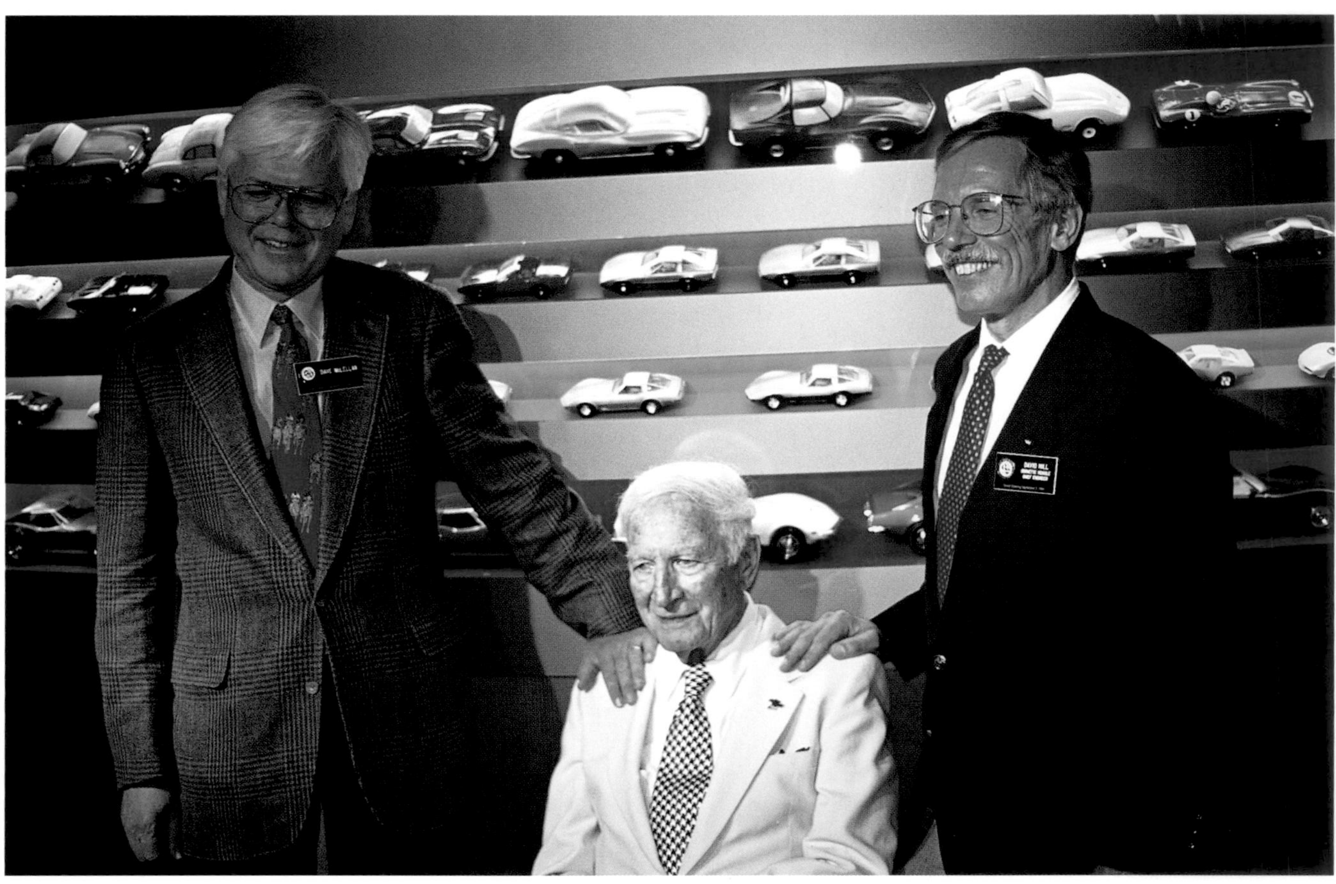

All three Corvette chief engineers were on hand for the National Corvette Museum's grand opening in Bowling Green, Kentucky, on Labor Day weekend 1994. Dave McLellan (left) joined the late Zora Arkus-Duntov and David Hill in front of a promotional model display. *John Heilig*

see any need to break up the solid-axle years. Once the C5 code became popularized, it was then only natural to retroactively rename the four forerunners: 1953–62 became C1; the Sting Rays of 1963–67, C2; the 1968–82 run, C3; and the 1984–96 cars, C4.

Whatever your count, one thing can't be argued: year in, year out, the Corvette has proved it all night unlike any other car ever sold in any numbers in this country. Its sex appeal has never been questioned, nor imagined. The same goes for its reputation as one of the world's best handling, hottest running fun machines for the money. There have been and still are many world-class sports cars, including Viper, that offer more power and speed. But they also cost many thousands more than Chevrolet's 'glass-bodied babies. Many, many thousands more.

No matter how you slice it, no rival at any price can match the Corvette as far as relative comfort and driver friendliness are concerned. Again, they don't call it "America's only sports car" for nothing. In the beginning, the British sports car ideal encompassed quite a few pains along with its pleasures. Cramped quarters. Sadly lacking weatherproofing. Untrustworthy mechanicals. Nonexistent creature comforts. Chevrolet's movers and shakers, on the other hand, recognized early on that Yankee car buyers would never put up with such inconveniences. Thus the reasoning behind the addition of conventional exterior door handles, roll-up windows, and an optional removable hardtop to the updated Corvette equation in 1956. Yet another concession to American sensibilities came seven years later in the form of a truly closed coupe body.

The pursuit of perfection has been a major component of the American sports car ideal ever since. But a qualification of terms, however paradoxical at a glance, is required. Perfection in the Corvette's case has always involved a supreme compromise; a balance of things often considered polar opposites. At one end of the scales are all the track-ready features that heat up the blood of a driver familiar with the fast lane. At the other are as many of the commonly taken for granted sedan-like comforts and conveniences that can fit within the two-seater's tight parameters. Of course that balance has always leaned toward the former. But lessons learned and radically improved technologies have since evened out things by bringing the two poles, performance and practicality, much closer together.

Chief engineer David Hill wasn't just bragging in 1997 when he described the C5 as "the best Vette yet." Today's Corvettes are both the hottest to drive at the limit and the coolest to live with in everyday operation. But the same could be said for similar claims made a few decades earlier by Zora Duntov and Dave McLellan. The stunning Sting Ray was indeed the greatest Corvette yet to set tread on American roads in 1963. Some even felt it was more than that. "For the first time I now have a Corvette I can be proud to drive in Europe," said Duntov. McLellan's pride and joy was the redesigned C4 Corvette, *Motor Trend*'s "Car of the Year" for 1984.

In between these two milestone moments in Corvette history came the only model years anyone would dare label as anything less than legendary. Some modern-day critics might even use the word *lackluster*. The longest span of the five generations at 15 years, the C3 run of 1968–82 encompassed both some of the hottest, wildest Corvettes ever built and easily the weakest of the breed. Buyers in 1968 and 1969 could choose between seven different power sources, including the aluminum-head L-89 option for the L-71 427-ci tri-carb big-block. The count in 1969 technically was eight if you added the all-but-unique aluminum ZL-1 427. Outputs in those two years ranged from the standard 300 horses all the way up to the L-71's 435 rompin', stompin' ponies. By 1974, however, only two optional engines were being offered, and the top advertised output had fallen to 270 net-rated horses. Seven years later, all Corvettes sold outside of California were fitted with one engine only, the 190-horse L-81 350 small-block.

Although Corvettes did remain this country's most powerful cars after 1973, that they paled in comparison to their outrageous forerunners left them easy targets for retrospective naysayers. Horsepower-challenged Corvettes of the late 1970s and early 1980s today remain the most overlooked members of Chevrolet's historic, half-century-old performance legacy, especially so from a value-driven collector's standpoint. At best, vintage Corvette dealers

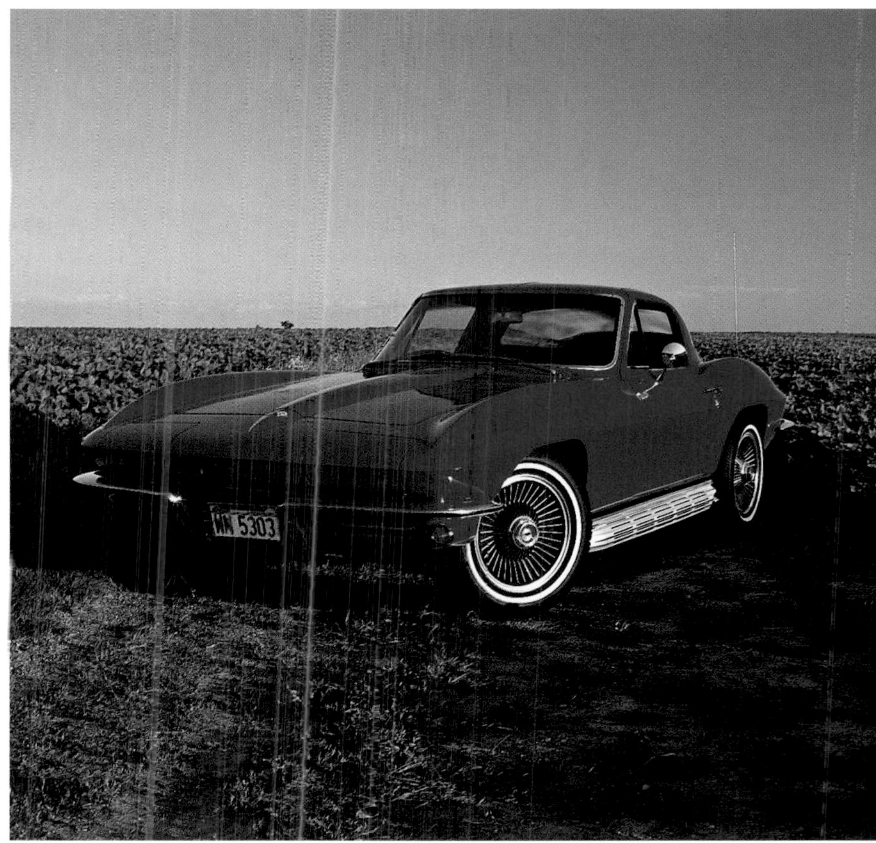

The second-generation "midyear" Corvette run lasted only five years, one more than intended. The first C3 was planned for 1967, but various snafus delayed it a year. In its place came one of the most popular Corvettes of all time, the 1967 Sting Ray.

Like Zora Duntov, GM styling guru Bill Mitchell was among the last of the all-powerful "car guys" to help shape things around General Motors. Mitchell took over from Harley Earl, GM's first great designer, in 1958, then went on to greatness himself. Feathers in his cap included the 1963 Sting Ray, 1968 Corvette, and 1963 Buick Riviera. *Chevrolet Public Relations*

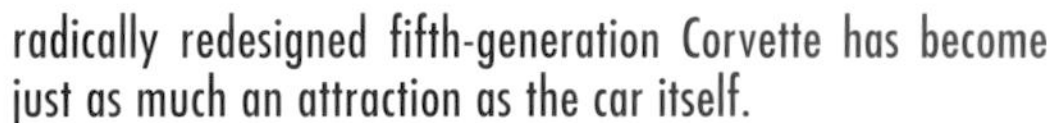

Where Legends Go to Live

The National Corvette Museum opened across the street from the Corvette assembly plant in Bowling Green, Kentucky, during a massive gala held Labor Day weekend 1994.

The Blue Grass State has been the mecca for the fiberglass faithful since 1981, the year, of course, when Corvette production was transferred east from General Motors' venerable St. Louis facility. The not-so-old Kentucky home to Corvette assembly today is found right off I-65 at exit number 28 on Bowling Green's northeast side. Yankees heading south for the winter can't miss it. Many don't. Nearly 50,000 visitors tour the facility each year. While the plant tour has always drawn a strong and steady stream of Corvette lovers, its popularity has increased noticeably since the C5 was introduced in 1997. It seems that assembling the radically redesigned fifth-generation Corvette has become just as much an attraction as the car itself.

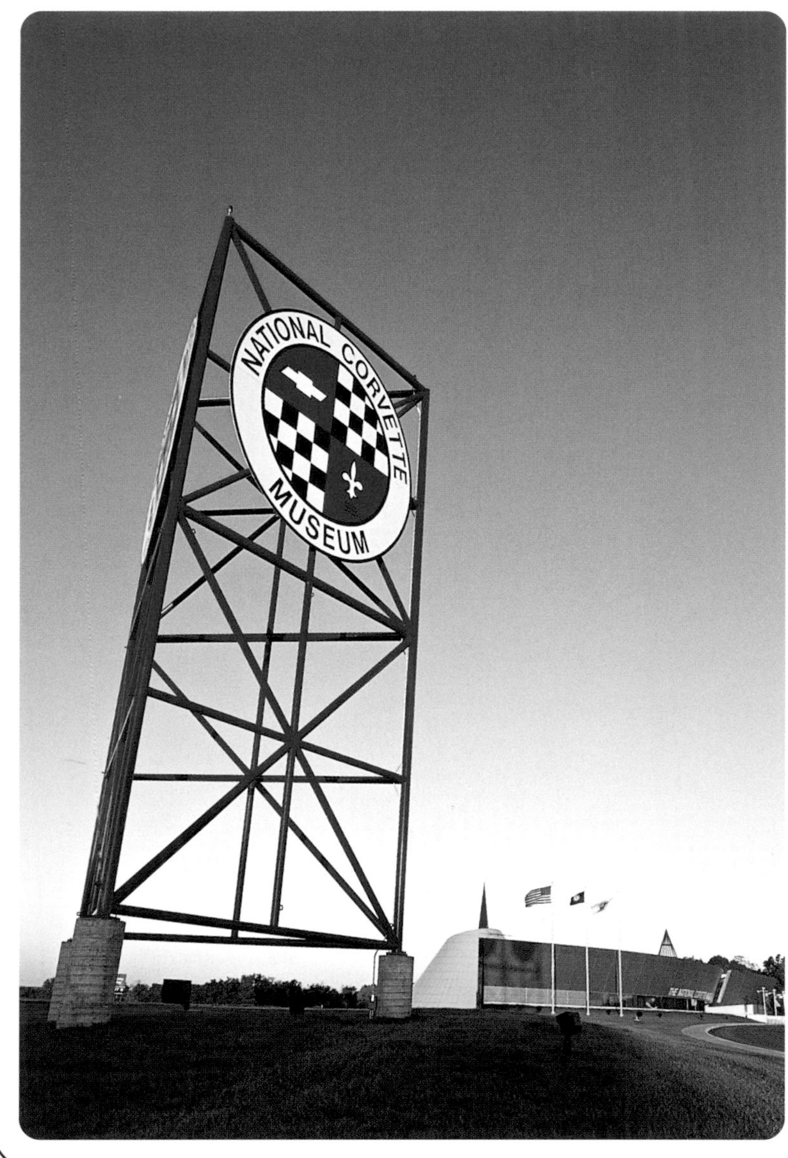

Enhancing exit number 28's attraction even further is the National Corvette Museum, found just as easily across the street from the Bowling Green assembly plant. Passersby truly can't miss this edifice; its bright yellow rotunda topped by the red Mobil 1 Signature Spire, at 11-stories tall, stands as the tallest structure between Louisville and Nashville. The entire complex itself takes up nearly 70,000 square feet on 33 acres, and hopes are to build onto this palace of the past in the near future.

"We will need more room soon, especially for the library," explained Wendell Strode, the NCM's executive director since December 1996. "Within three to five years we'll be running out of space there." That's the good news for Corvette historians and researchers hungry to learn as much as they can about the car of their dreams.

The not-so-good news is that the NCM's prosperity has not matched initial predictions made during the museum's grand opening in September 1994. Strode himself is not shy about admitting the obvious. Public support has not materialized as strongly as the museum's founding fathers envisioned so optimistically earlier in the decade. As the next millennium nears, bringing with it the Corvette's 50th birthday in 2003, NCM people find themselves hustling to find new ways to bolster the NCM's somewhat lukewarm fortunes. According to Strode, about 156,000 people a year have spun the turnstiles over the last 3 years. Nearly 10 years ago, members of the Kentucky Tourism Cabinet claimed that as many as 500,000 Corvette fans would make the trek to Bowling Green each year to visit an automotive valhalla that simply begged to become a reality.

Pioneers including Terry McManmon, Jon Brookmyer, and Ray Battaglini of the National Corvette Restorers Society first began dreaming the dream back in the 1980s. Many others, like former Bowling Green assembly plant human resources manager Darryl Bowlin, quickly joined in, leading to the founding of the National Corvette Museum Foundation in 1988. A temporary home to nearly a half century of Corvette history, the Corvette Museum Annex, opened in downtown Bowling Green in November 1990. In attendance at that opening was the "father of the Corvette" himself, Zora Arkus-Duntov. "Please build this museum and save the things that I've built," was Duntov's plea during his speech.

Two years later, on June 5, 1992, Duntov was at the controls of a one-of-a-kind "Corvette bulldozer" for the National Corvette Museum's ceremonial ground-breaking. Donations of cash, archival materials, even the cars themselves had been arriving in Bowling Green long before that date. Big-time backing for the project came from, among others, General Motors, Chevrolet, Mobil, Goodyear, and the American Sunroof Corporation. About $4 million in private support was supplied by various loyal Corvette owners, parts suppliers, and dealers worldwide. United Auto Workers members at the Bowling Green plant chipped in $270,000 as well.

The culmination of all that generosity came on Labor Day weekend 1994 in one of the grandest grand openings ever witnessed. Among the 120,000 people who flocked to Bowling Green that weekend were Duntov, Larry Shinoda, Dave McLellan, David Hill, and Jim Perkins, to name just a few of the men behind the machine. Country singer George Jones serenaded luminaries and humble journalists alike during the VIP dinner the night before the ribbon cutting. The Beach Boys were also on hand to do a little harmonizing.

More than 4,000 Corvette owners clicked off about 250,000 miles traveling from points all across the country in 10 Corvette caravans to make it to this big show. Motorists in mere mortal automobiles on I-65 on Saturday morning, September 2, found themselves spit out of luck as police closed down the interstate to through traffic while these caravans wound their way onto the NCM grounds. It was an unforgettable weekend, so much so that museum officials mark it with an annual birthday party every September.

But some onlookers were soon left wondering just how many birthdays lay ahead not long after the Beach Boys packed up their surfboards and went home. Financial difficulties quickly arose, due partly to the museum board's inexperience in such matters as fund-raising, banking, and corporate relations. The founding fathers themselves were the first to admit that they were basically "just a bunch of Corvette guys." That those guys managed to transform their dream into a reality is a testament to their steadfast dedication. Keeping that dream alive, however, has proven to be a much higher hurdle, a task requiring sure-handed management. Even Dan Gale, the driving force behind the museum's opening, admitted that "we made a bunch of mistakes."

A solution to the problem involved turning to professional help. When Wendell Strode arrived in late 1996, he brought along 25 years of banking experience—that, and he's a died-in-the-wool Corvette guy, too.

Among Strode's first goals was to restore credibility with everyone: GM, bankers, sponsors, and Corvette lovers themselves. He was amazed to find a chasm growing between the museum and the Corvette guys and gals who should be, in his mind, the NCM's main source of support. Foundation membership was shrinking, and it was this trend that Strode felt he had to reverse first in order to get things back on track. The museum would never survive without growth. And according to Strode, "the key to such growth is the membership. Corvette people have to love this place." Since Strode arrived the foundation roll call has increased from 1,600 to 4,000. "Membership is on the rise," he said, "but of course I would like to see more."

One of the two 1969 ZL-1 Corvettes built (this one owned by Roger Judski) is shown here while on display in December 1997. Next to the car is an all-aluminum ZL-1 427 V-8.

Strode's plans for future growth also involve adding "second-season exhibits," displays created with "more casual visitors" in mind. Meant to entice non-Corvette people through the turnstiles during slower times, these exhibits feature fun topics like dinosaurs and NASA-related activities. General car shows are also planned for a summertime schedule already full of Corvette-related gatherings. To that end, 25 additional acres adjacent to NCM property were purchased in November 1998 to make room for more parking.

Among Strode's top goals today is the library, which remained incomplete five years after the museum's grand opening due to Chevrolet officials' hesitancy to donate records, build sheets, and such. It was left up to the NCM team to prove that their facility could indeed adequately house and securely preserve the material. That proof can now be found in the present growth nurtured by Strode and his staff.

As Wendell Strode says, the rest is up to you. The future of one of the finest automotive museums in the country depends on your support. If you would like to make a difference—simply a visit would be a start—call the National Corvette Museum at (502) 781-7973 for information. Web surfers should check in at *www.corvettemuseum.com* for all the latest news.

Sculptor Karen Atta cast more than 20 statues of some of the great men who made Corvette history. You decide which is the real Dave McLellan. Dave and his likeness were on hand for the VIP party the night before the NCM's ribbon-cutting ceremony.

The Corvette's status as a true sports car grew more controversial in 1956 when Chevrolet civilized its little fiberglass two-seater even further by adding roll-up windows, exterior door handles, and an optional lift-off hardtop. *Chevrolet Public Relations*

consider these underpriced relics as little more than affordable, entry-level opportunities for less wealthy Corvette crazies to join the fiberglass fraternity.

Clearly, as far as investment opportunity is concerned, the bulk of the C3 generation rank among the least desired Corvettes of all-time. At the same time, casual history too seemingly ignores this group. Enthusiast clubs across the country that use the label "Classic Corvette" always cut memberships off at the knees at 1967, almost as if Chevrolet stopped building fiberglass two-seaters then. Granted, the so-called "midyear" models of 1963–67 deserve their status as the easiest recognized, most popular vintage Corvettes out there. But is it fair that the C3s, affectionately known as "Sharks" by Corvette followers who refuse to turn a blind eye, be forever lost in the giant shadow cast by the original Sting Ray?

It remains difficult, of course, to completely overlook the C3 cars, what with such luminaries as the L-88s of 1968–69, the 1969 ZL-1, the LS-6 454 big-block of 1971, and the LT-1 small-blocks of 1970–72 present and well accounted for. On the flipside, however, other historic milestones posted during the third-generation run tended to signal that what once was, might never be again. The last big-block Corvette was built in 1974. The last convertible (for the moment) came a year later. The fabled "Stingray" badge (made one word after its return to Corvette flanks in 1969 following a one-year hiatus) was last used in 1976. On a lesser note, conventional chromed bumpers began to disappear in 1973 as the car's nose went the monochromatic, 5-mile-per-hour crash resistant route. The tail then followed suit in 1974.

A changing of the guard also occurred in 1975 as Zora Duntov retired in January. Dave McLellan then became the Corvette's second chief engineer. Another legendary figure, William Mitchell, traded his powerful perch atop GM Styling for the golf course in 1977 after 19 years of essentially single-handedly deciding the future face of the next year's Corvette. The fate of America's only sports car would never again hinge on the will of any one man, however strong, after Mitchell's departure. McLellan, Hill, Chuck Jordan, Jerry Palmer—although Jordan might disagree, none of these top players in the C4/C5 game came close to matching the individual impacts

made by Mitchell and certainly Duntov in their heydays.

Revisionist historians and exploitative entrepreneurs might look disparagingly at the C3 editions today, but in their own heydays the cars themselves did quite well for themselves, thank you. Sales were by no means lackluster. The first Shark in 1968 established a new production high of 28,566 coupes and convertibles, breaking the previous record of 27,720 set in 1966. The 1969 Corvette then became the first to surpass 30,000 in annual sales on the way to a new all-time high of 38,762 cars. Of course it should be mentioned that newly appointed Chevrolet chief John DeLorean allowed the 1969 model run to work overtime into December after a strike delayed production for two months early in the year. This in turn restricted 1970's effort, resulting in a drop to 17,316 Corvettes.

From there, sales increased each year up through 1977. Total production for 1973 again reached the 30,000 plateau, a first as far as a regulation 12-month model run was concerned. As it was, 1969's "asterisk" was finally rendered moot in 1976 when the 40,000 barrier was breached. Now made up of coupes only, 1976's new sales standard totaled out at 46,558. Yet another record, one that still stands, was established in 1979 as sales surpassed 50,000 for the first time. The final tally for 1979 was 53,807.

So what's up with that? How could these cars be so popular then, yet so easily overlooked today? One answer involves the basic law of supply and demand. All that supply may have made Chevrolet beancounters happy a quarter-century ago, but it also naturally hindered nostalgic demand later on. Why would anyone have worried about preserving one of these babies for the ages when there were so damned many of them around?

Resale values in turn suffered from the outset. C3 models stuck around on used car lots, wearing unaccustomed used car price tags, far longer than any other Corvette breed. Some occasionally can still be found there with soaped-up windshields even today. Why even consider restoring a later C3 when you'd spend far more green than anyone would ever pay for the final product?

Many critics, cruel or otherwise, also feel that the C3's apparent popularity in the 1970s didn't exactly reflect reality. Forget for the moment that the third-generation Corvette ran up against certainly the heaviest odds ever faced by its creators: stumbling blocks included

Dave McLellan's team bid a fond farewell to the C3 in 1982 by putting together the classy Collectors Edition package. David Hill's crew pulled off a similar trick with a Collectors Edition model of their own (background) to mark the last C4 Corvette in 1996.

The C3 was basically a rebodied midyear Corvette. Initially, the third-generation chassis with its independent rear suspension carried over unchanged from the 1963 Sting Ray, shown here. Standard four-wheel disc brakes were added in 1965. *Chevrolet Motor Division*

AC
Shark by Chevrolet—ACtion sparked by AC
The same AC Spark Plugs that add power to this car of tomorrow are available for your car today! Engineers specify ACs for experimental cars like the Corvette Shark because of AC's self-cleaning Hot Tip. It heats faster to burn away fouling carbon deposits—delivers longer peak power—greater economy for every car! Don't experiment with your spark plugs, ask for ACtion . . . ask for AC.
AC
FIRE-RING
SPARK PLUGS

C3 Corvettes are lovingly known as "Sharks." That nickname dates back to the Shark showcar of 1961, which was later renamed Mako Shark I after the Mako Shark II appeared in 1965. The Mako Shark II body showcased the shape that would become the production Corvette in 1968.

the emergence of ever-tightening government-mandated emissions standards and safety regulations in 1968; soaring insurance rates for performance cars during the period of 1969–72; skyrocketing gasoline prices resulting from the 1973 energy crisis; another federal mandate, this one specifying new fuel economy standards in 1978; even higher gas prices; and a national economic disaster in 1979. All that aside, more than one armchair historian has concluded that the C3 breed deserves little relative respect today because much of the attention it received 25 years ago came by way of mirrors. Sure, those record production figures seemingly said that Americans then couldn't get enough of Chevrolet's fiberglass two-seater. Those numbers, however, were apparently part of a mirage. Perhaps Chevy wouldn't have sold nearly as many Corvettes in the decade's latter half had not nearly all the competition retired from the race.

All-American horsepower was all but dead by 1973, a victim of changing times. Hemi Mopars, Super Cobra Jet Fords, and all the other ultra-high-performance big-block machines saw their last days in 1971, the year

Dave McLellan (at left) took over control of the Corvette's future after Zora Duntov retired in January 1975. His impact was first felt in 1978 when a new "fastback" rear-end treatment debuted. With a 1978 Indy Pace Car replica and the Corvette's second chief engineer here are Chevrolet general manager Robert Lund (far right) and GM exec Robert Stempel (second from right). *Chevrolet Motor Division*

when automakers radically slashed engine compression as part of a federally mandated detuning plan aimed at cleaning up Detroit's internal combustion act. Although a few steadfast survivors, mostly from Pontiac, held out to the very last breath in 1972, 1973, and 1974, the breed known as America's musclecar died a quick death as the environmentally conscious 1970s dawned.

While major price differentials set Corvettes and musclecars well apart as far as direct competition was concerned, the two forms of fast transportation still shared the same segment of the car-buying market. And that piece of the pie was soon sliced down to almost nothing in the 1970s. By 1973, performance-minded buyers could pick from two plums: Pontiac's Trans Am and Chevrolet's Corvette. Like the Corvette, the more affordable Trans Am also experienced a sales spike in the 1970s, this one even more dramatic. Production soared from 4,800 in 1973 to more than 117,000 six years later. Clearly both cars benefited greatly from the "captive audience" left searching for ways to satisfy their need for speed after the musclecar's demise.

In the Corvette's case, that 1970s sales spike also featured a downside that helped trigger additional slings and arrows. Setting and re-setting sales records increased both revenues and quality control maladies. Chevrolet had had a hard enough time consistently molding and painting the midyear Sting Rays to high enough standards, and this was at an average production rate of about 20,000 cars a year. Raising that rate by half, then doubling it only helped make matters worse. Complaints about poor fitting, wavy panels and "orange-peel" paint surfaced immediately in 1968 and could be heard throughout the C3 run.

But also heard were comments most bystanders today seem to have forgotten. When *Car and Driver* tested the new "soft-nosed" 1973 Corvette, not one whine about diminishing horsepower was printed. "Zora Arkus-Duntov reckons the new Corvette to be the best ever," read *Car and Driver*'s December 1972 report. "And after exhaustive testing of four different models, we're inclined to agree."

Sound familiar? Even with less-than-perfect bodywork and ever-weakening engines, the C3 models were still Corvettes. And Corvettes have never been anything less than kings of the hill—for nearly 50 years now.

Long live the king.

Chevrolet's St. Louis assembly plant was home to Corvette production from December 1953 to July 1981. The Fisher Mill Building, located in the far upper left corner of the complex (behind the white water tower to the left of the smokestack), housed the Corvette assembly line. *St. Louis Mercantile Library*

Various strikes hindered GM production efforts in the late 1960s and 1970s. The three picketeers shown here were among 8,100 employees idled by a strike at the St. Louis plant that began April 10, 1969. Corvette production that year ran into overtime (it ended in December) due to such delays. *St. Louis Mercantile Library*

SHARK SIGHTINGS

Development of the Third-Generation Corvette

The Corvette, like your best girlfriend in high school, has never been able to make it downstairs on time for the big date. Consider the C5. Early hopes around Chevrolet in the late 1980s had an all-new fifth-generation Corvette debuting in time for the car's 40th birthday bash. That meant 1993. Then along came various trials and tribulations, not the least of which was General Motors' red ink bath in the early 1990s. The proposed delivery date slipped to 1994. Then 1995. Then 1996. Before we knew it the project was all but dead. Fortunately a rebirth followed, resulting in the long-awaited C5's introduction in January 1997. All was forgiven.

Similar tales, with far fewer chapters, were written earlier each time the best Vette yet stood poised to make its anticipated appearance. Who can forget 1983? Chevrolet did, this after ever-present gremlins helped push the C4's planned debut back more than six months. The C3's record run finally ended in 1982. The comparably lengthy C4 stretch began with the 1984 model. How time flies when you're having fun following fiberglass futures.

Twenty-five years before, the rumor mill had the public anxiously awaiting a radically redesigned Corvette for 1960. In this case a perceived tease was probably more the result of premature press predictions than any real stumbling or bumbling on GM's part. Chevrolet simply would sell no Sting Ray before its time. That moment arrived in 1963, and anyone with eyes agreed the results were well worth the wait. No question about it, this was the best 'Vette yet.

But then Duntov and crew found themselves seemingly painted into a corner. How do you top a classic? And how much time should you take trying? The solid-axle Corvette had carried on for 10 years, much longer, in many critics' minds, than it should have—thus the 1960 prophecies. Chevrolet's braintrust apparently agreed, or at least they recognized that Sting Ray customers were bound to begin wondering, "What have you done for me lately?"

The second-generation Corvette's days became numbered almost as quickly as they began. Duntov and Bill Mitchell began independently brainstorming new ideas concerning the Corvette's next move even before the original Sting Ray's well-earned raves died out. A legend in its own time or not, the midyear models would be history by the fall of 1966. Four years and out was the plan, as was topping a classic—literally. The original Sting Ray had already pushed retooling costs to the limit with its independently suspended chassis and reinforced, restyled bodyshell. Busting the bank again only a few years down the road was out of the question. The bulk of the job of building the third-generation Corvette was then left to Mitchell as a new body atop the existing platform was planned. For 1967.

Luckily for midyear worshippers, that plan typically did not end up in the best-laid category.

As always, improving performance was Duntov's prime goal. And this time he desperately

Designer Larry Shinoda's touch is clearly evident in the lines of the rear-engined XP-819, which was first conceived by R&D man Frank Winchell in 1964.

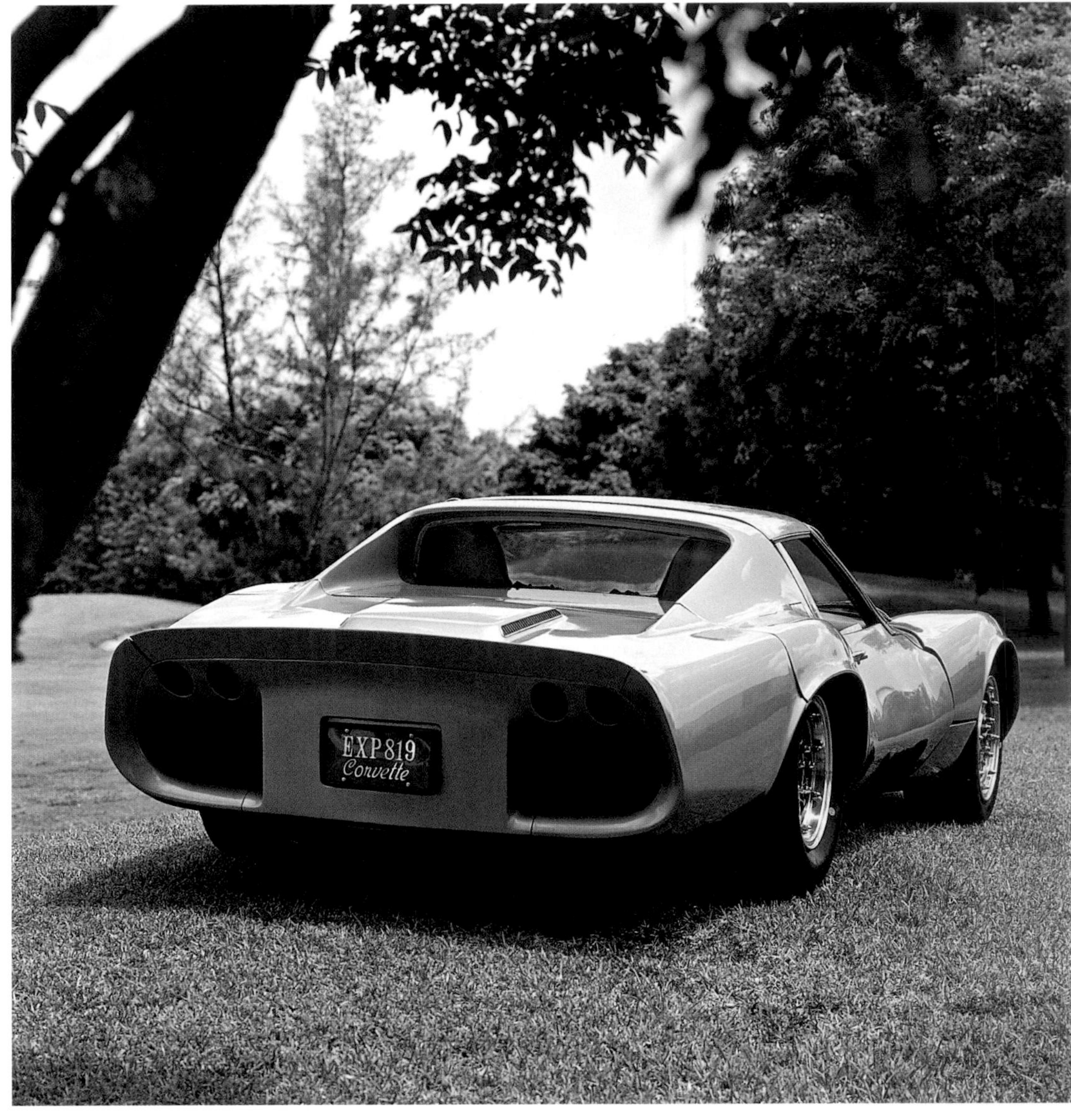

Various XP-819 features, such as the one-piece lift-off roof and inner-door steel guard beams, foretold later Corvette developments. That fat tail hinged upward to reveal a small-block V-8 perched backward, Corvair-style, behind the rear wheels.

wanted to concentrate on one particularly disappointing aspect of the second-generation Corvette's go-fast personality. A *Car and Driver* report later in 1971 described "the contempt Duntov feels for the body shape of the 1963–1967 Sting Ray." In Zora's own words, that body possessed "just enough lift to be a bad airplane." Duntov's Grand Sport racers of 1963 never had a chance of keeping pace with the world's best sports cars due to, among other things, their inherent preference to take flight instead of sticking to the track. That his Grand Sport project was abruptly cancelled by GM executive office decree only spared Zora and the Corvette additional embarrassment on the international stage.

Designer Larry Shinoda, Mitchell's right-hand man, described the situation to *Corvette Fever* contributor Don Sherman in 1989. "GM wind-tunnel engineers attempting to justify their theories spent untold sums studying the 1963 Corvette," said Shinoda. "What they found was a drag coefficient of 0.53. In essence, it was a flying machine."

Of course aerodynamic automotive design was still not exactly a science in the 1960s, certainly not to the degree it is today. John Cafaro's C5 design team three decades later was totally dedicated to transforming the latest, greatest Corvette into the slickest shape ever to slip out of not only Bowling Green, but Detroit too. Cafaro achieved the 1997 Corvette's unprecedented

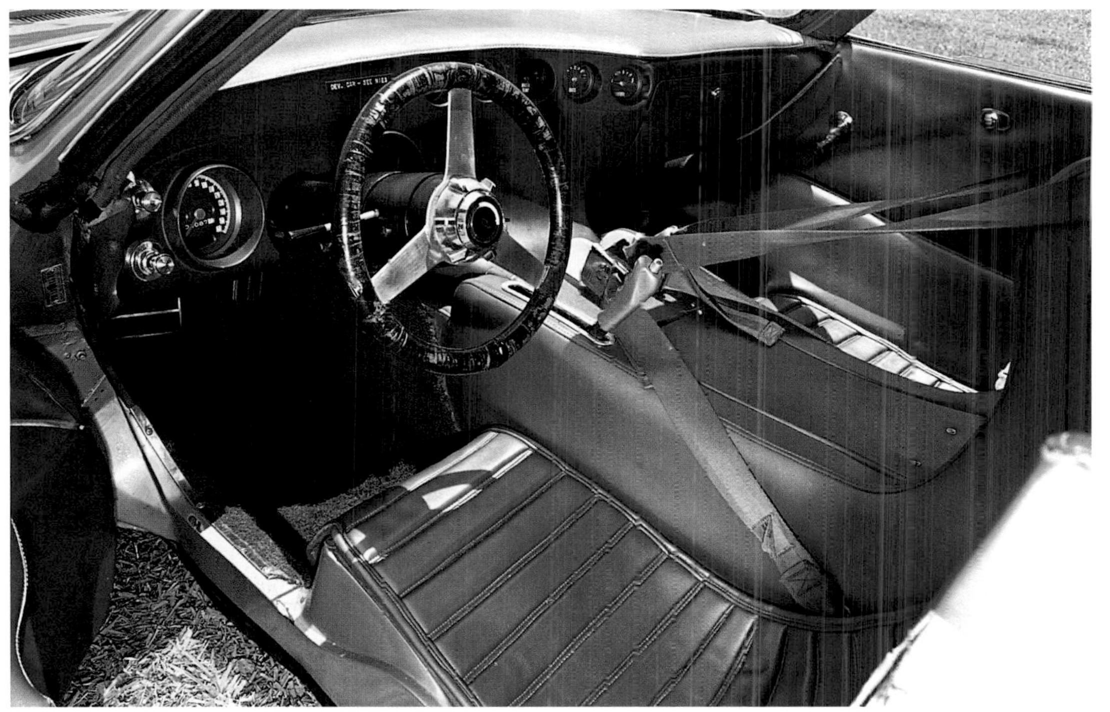

XP-819's inner door panels serve double duty (when closed) as a side bolster for the tight-fitting bucket seats. The label on the dash reads "Dev. Car See Nies." Larry Nies was the engineer responsible for the car's unique rear-engine design.

0.29 drag coefficent by doing what the wind tunnel told him to do, and this meant sticking with an aspect of the tunnel-tested shape that drew the most negative comments at unveiling time—the car's sharp-edged, flat-backed tail.

"That is there specifically for aerodynamics," said Kurt Romberg, the engineer responsible for the C5's abrupt ending. "We spent a lot of time locating that hard edge, and what it does is it separates the air cleanly off the car." The newest Corvette couldn't top out at a definitely world-class 180 miles per hour without that clean cut. Style-conscious critics may have cringed, but clearly the days of form following function have been replaced with function dictating form.

It was thoughts to the opposite that primarily dictated styling decisions in Bill Mitchell's day. In the 1960s, looking like the wind was a friend remained a much more important priority than actually cutting through the air with precision. Mitchell had already proven himself more than willing to place form well ahead of function before work on the C3 began—witness the visibility-inhibiting "stinger" that split the 1963 Sting Ray coupe's rear window in two. Duntov knew that one would never fly for long and tried to remove it, but Mitchell was adamant. "If you take that off, you might as well forget the whole thing," he snorted.

That's not to say that Mitchell was totally blind to the importance of a fully functional Corvette form. He was no fu-fu designer walled up in an ivory tower studio far from the realities experienced by his designs. He was a certified car nut, with one of his many favorite sayings (borrowed in part from his mentor, Harley Earl) being "you've gotta have gasoline in your veins to be a real car designer." He was also a speed freak who loved his Corvettes to be of the balls-out, full-race variety—witness his 1956 SR-2 and 1959 Stingray.

"From the time that Bill started driving sports cars, he has never taken his foot off the gas," wrote fellow designer Strother MacMinn in *Automobile Quarterly* in 1988. Said Mitchell in 1984, "As long as there's a Corvette on four wheels, a hot bike on two, that I can do something with, I'll stay young." Yes, Bill Mitchell was a lead-footed gearhead, one of the last truly great "car guys" to rule with heart and soul in Detroit. Yet he was a style-conscious designer first, and it was fashion that governed his hand.

"When they were doing the [C3]," he told *Automobile Quarterly*, "I went down there, and it was all square-cornered, and I put on an act and said, 'We're never going to do a box around my place.' I wanted it to look like it was born in a wind tunnel." Even though he actually used the term *wind tunnel*, he was basically only

The first Mako Shark II showcar was a nonrunning mockup featuring dummy side exhausts. The "Mark IV 396" badges on the hood scoop were also dummies—there was no engine, big- or small-block, beneath the hood. *Chevrolet Motor Division*

concerned with creating an analogy. The key words here were *look like*. Appearances and impressions were always his top priorities.

A boxy, brick-shaped Corvette was not his bag primarily because it didn't look good, and in Mitchell's own words, "If it doesn't look good, why bother getting in?" Many of his famous one-liners resulted from his apparent belief that it was better to look good than to feel good: "Barrymore's nose is better looking than Churchill's." "A collie is better looking than a bulldog." "A shark looks better than a grouper."

That latter profundity also related to another of Mitchell's pet preferences. He was especially fond of aggressive sea creatures—stingrays, for example. He kept a stuffed mako shark on his studio wall, and its graduated toning intrigued him, so much so that he demanded that the XP-755 showcar be finished to match. Created in 1961, XP-755 showcased much of the upcoming 1963 Sting Ray's look. But it didn't start showing off that look until it was finally painted, and that took some doing. As the oft-told legend has it, Mitchell continually rejected the paint crew's futile efforts to match the shark's natural shadings. The O.K. was finally given only after painters sneaked into Mitchell's office one night and colored the fish to match the car. Believe it or not.

XP-755, of course, then became the Shark, and therein lies the origins of the third-generation Corvette's pet name. A second showcar, the Mako Shark, appeared in 1965. Not long after its birth, the Mako Shark was rechristened Mako Shark II as XP-755 was retroactively renamed Mako Shark I. And just as XP-755 foretold the Sting Ray's arrival, so too did the Mako Shark II allow show-goers at least a partial look at the C3 Corvette—which, remember, was promised for 1967.

Transforming the Mako Shark II image into reality, however, proved more difficult than expected. Function truly suffered with this form as driver visibility, engine ventilation and, yes, aerodynamics fell well below acceptable standards. Per Mitchell's prerogative, the prototype Shark shape looked great. But it functioned more like a flying fish as unwanted lift again proved to be a troublesome hitch. Duntov found himself forced to push the C3's introduction back a year while these problems were ironed out. In the meantime, one more midyear Sting Ray was rolled back out for 1967—an unintended encore, if you will. That car, as fate would have it, has since attained its own legendary status. Sometimes the worst-laid plans end up the best.

Delaying the C3's introduction by a year not only allowed the 1967 Sting Ray a chance at immortality, it also gave Duntov the time to deal with bugs as best he could, which he found himself doing right up to the 1968 Corvette's press introduction. But that's not to say that Zora played the hero to Mitchell's goat. Not at all. Mitchell simply did his job, Duntov did his. New model development back then wasn't anywhere near as integrated as it is today. As Larry Shinoda wrote in *Shark Quarterly* in 1997, "Bill and Zora didn't agree on the design at first. But this was in the era when design came first and engineering then got to work within the major parameters we set."

People may have listened when Duntov spoke, but Mitchell clearly was no stranger to having the last word concerning the Corvette. And as much as it appeared that some of his demands and directions proved to be more trouble than they were worth, his contributions to the Corvette legacy remain every bit as legendary as Zora's.

According to Henry Haga, who headed the Chevrolet 2 studio where the final C3 form was fashioned, Mitchell was "the Corvette's most important ally at GM." "In Bill's influence, those of us in the design studios had something to guide us: his feeling of what the Corvette should be," continued Haga in *Corvette: The Legend Lives On*. "He had a facility for setting a trend that you could put into production. That's what was so great about Bill, he had the foresight to leap out and do show cars and production cars that needed doing. In a world where there was no Mako Shark and no Sting Ray, he suddenly made them."

Of course he didn't make them without help. Overseeing Henry Haga and his Chevy 2 gang during Shark development was Chevrolet chief stylist David Holls. Larry Shinoda was head of the mysterious Chevrolet 3 studio in 1965 and 1966. Chevy 3 became known as "the warehouse" because it was hidden away in a GM Styling storage building on the Tech Center's south side. Among the stylists who worked there with Shinoda was John Schinella, who later went on to head GM's Advanced Concepts Center in Southern California. In 1990, Schinella's Advanced Concepts team created the sensational Sting Ray III showcar, a stepping stone of sorts to the C5. In 1965, Schinella assisted Shinoda with the C3's stepping stone, the Mako Shark II. Chevrolet 3 was also the home to the earliest C3 prototype theme, which Shinoda then passed on to Haga at Chevrolet 2 for final refinements on the way to production.

Watching over it all—design and engineering—was Elliott "Pete" Estes, who had filled the vacated general manager's seat at Chevrolet in 1965 after Semon "Bunkie" Knudsen left to climb the GM corporate ladder. Like Knudsen prior to 1961, Estes had previously held the reins at Pontiac. Also like Bunkie, Pete was no stranger to the fast lane, he being the mover and shaker who had had the foresight to shepherd the supposedly taboo GTO through GM red tape into production in 1964. As was often the case when a new face arrived atop a GM division, Estes' move to Chevrolet helped open the door to fresh ideas, as well as the possible rethinking of earlier proposals shot down by the previous regime. The time was ripe to create the next new Corvette.

One of the earliest steps toward this creation actually came before Estes' arrival by way of a long-forgotten engineering presentation made by Duntov to Bunkie Knudsen in April 1964. Zora's initial premise in this presentation involved the obvious fact that the 1965 Corvette would be wearing the identical body seen in 1963 and 1964. This, in his learned opinion, could not continue if Knudsen expected America's only sports car to stay out in front ahead of the times. At the least, Duntov wanted a rebody for 1966. At most, he asked for a totally re-engineered Corvette for 1967.

Included in his proposal was a relatively mild facelift for 1966, an estimated $5 million upgrade that didn't differ all that much from the

The second Mako Shark II built was a fully functional model without sidepipes. This time beneath the hood was the 427 big-block, which was just then being readied for use in production Corvettes for 1966. *Chevrolet Motor Division*

existing Sting Ray. He also pitched another radical race car, the GS 3, with the two letters being short for "Grand Sport." Duntov wanted to build 10 Grand Sport 3 racers in 1966 at a cost of $1.125 million. These machines would closely resemble the mid-engined, all-wheel-drive CERV II and would be used to promote Chevrolet engineering advances at the track.

More radical were the two production alternatives he proposed for 1967. Both offered significant weight cuts by way of a stronger, yet lighter frame featuring a central tunnel "backbone." And each wore completely modernized bodies. But while one of these 1967 proposals was of conventional design with the engine in front, the other, like the CERV II, would mount its engine amidships between the driver and rear wheels. Rough cost estimates were $20 million for the former, $38.5 million for the latter. Projected curb weights for the two were 2,200 pounds for the front-engined proposal, 2,475 for the midshipman.

While keeping the Corvette's weight in line was always one of Duntov's top priorites, so too was balancing that weight. He was well aware of the importance of weight bias long before he joined Chevrolet's engineering team in May 1953. Getting the bulk of a car's poundage off the front wheels has always been one of the main keys to maximizing road-handling capabilities. Doing so, however, has never been an easy task with a big V-8 mounted up front in typical American style.

Moving the transmission to the rear—like engineers in the 1990s did for the C5—to reduce the forward weight bias was considered as early as 1957 for the "Q-Corvette" project, which foretold the 1963 Sting Ray. It was considered, but never put into development. However, the mid-engined CERV I engineering practice was. It appeared in 1960, and then was followed by the CERV II four years later. Although Duntov's April 1964 midengined proposal never made it beyond the drawing board stage (nor did his 1966 makeover), various other engine relocation plans did. And not all stopped at the midengine ideal.

Frank Winchell's research and development team hastily put together the XP-819 Corvette in 1964. At the time, many minds around GM had high hopes for a high-performance variation on the rear-engined Corvair platform. Winchell had even gone so far as to build a V-8-powered Corvair prototype, a layout he felt might also work well beneath the Corvette's skin.

Duntov, however, never did like Winchell's rear-engined Corvette idea, especially so after initial drawings appeared downright ugly. Enter the ever-present Larry Shinoda. Shinoda had already drawn up the XP-755 Shark, Mitchell's Stingray, the production Sting Ray, and CERVs I and II, to name a few. Now he was promising he could make Winchell's idea work in pleasing fashion. "Where did you cheat?" asked a surprised Duntov upon seeing Shinoda's sketches.

Taking XP-819 from paper to fiberglass amazingly required only a few months. Engineer Larry Nies' team built a backbone chassis with independent coils at the corners. Wheelbase was a stubby 90 inches. In back, Nies suspended an alloy 287-ci V-8 rearward off a modified Pontiac Tempest automatic transaxle. Seventy percent of XP-819's 2,700 pounds rested on the rear tires, which were super-wide Firestones.

Despite Shinoda's claim that all that rubber helped compensate for XP-819's radical rearward weight bias, other witnesses weren't so sure. According to automotive journalist and former Chevrolet engineer Paul Van Valkenburgh, "The car could be set up to handle properly on a skid pad in steady-state cornering, but transient or dynamic response was nearly uncontrollable at the limit." Rolling proof of Van Valkenburgh's conclusion came when XP-819 careened into a guard rail during testing. So much for the rear-engine idea.

Much more significant to the continuing Corvette legacy was the XP-819's shell. Shaped by Shinoda and Schinella, its "Coke-bottle" body introduced many elements that would later show up in the third-generation Corvette via the Mako Shark II. The low, pointed nose. Those high wheel bulges. That ducktailed rear. Guard beams inside XP-819's doors also predicted a Shark feature, as did the tunneled rear window. The urethane body-colored front bumper foretold a Corvette upgrade to come in 1973. The one-piece lift-off roof did the same for a comparable top design unveiled along with the new C4 for 1984.

Few witnesses noticed XP-819's prophecies however, as it was shuffled off into history as quickly as it had arrived on the scene. And soon after it was gone, Shinoda and Schinella turned their attentions toward the car that nearly everyone predicted would become the next new Corvette.

Bill Mitchell first laid down the law concerning this machine to Shinoda's team midway in 1964. Mitchell's specifications included a coupe body with a "pinched" center section ala that "Coke-bottle" trend. The wheels would be prominently displayed with fender areas that appeared well-defined yet fully integrated into the body. The low, low roof too would be melded into that slim center section so it wouldn't look like a separate top tacked onto a convertible. A tapered tail in the best tradition of the original Sting Ray coupe would end things. Per Mitchell's mandate, all this futuristic fashion would have to fit on the existing Corvette chassis—with its engine up front. And the whole works would have to be fully fashioned in time

The Mako Shark II's 427 V-8 was fitted with an air-conditioning compressor and the newly introduced Turbo Hydra-Matic automatic transmission. Turbo Hydra-Matic didn't become a Corvette option until 1968. *Chevrolet Motor Division*

Drawing On Experience

Zora Arkus-Duntov was, of course, "the father of the Corvette." It didn't matter that he wasn't even around when conception occurred. Nor does saying this represent a slight to the many other proud father figures. Duntov deserves such an honor because it was he above any other who helped steer the car away from an early demise in 1955 into the history books. "The greatest of the Corvette prophets," as *Corvette Fever* called him in 1999, was being revered as highly as his beloved two-seat babies even before his retirement in 1975. "Zora Arkus-Duntov is so firmly identified with Corvettes they could bear his name," wrote *Car and Driver*'s Jan Norbye in 1962. Most of history's prime movers and shakers have to wait until after their deaths to attain mythical stature. Duntov's legend, on the other hand, was looming larger than life long before his mortal presence left this world for the next on April 21, 1996.

That Zora still casts a giant shadow goes without saying. It is so large it all but obscures many of the other great names associated with the half-century-old Corvette legacy. One of the more prominent entries on that list, at least from a Shark fan's perspective, reads "Shinoda."

A legend in his own right, veteran designer Lawrence Kiyoshi Shinoda knew more than a little about the short end of the stick. He was an 11-year-old Nisei child growing up in southern California when Pearl Harbor was attacked on December 7, 1941, meaning he and his Japanese-American family were then locked up in the Manzanar interment camp. Ironically, he later served with the Air National Guard in Korea.

Shinoda had the unfortunate honor of working under another of GM's large-than-life giants, Bill Mitchell. What Duntov was to Corvette engineering, Mitchell was to Sting Ray styling. Same for the Shark. Although Zora had a lot to say about what did or didn't fly, Mitchell was certainly no slouch when it came to throwing his weight around. And he was also more than willing to accept all the kudos for the new Corvette bodies unveiled in 1963 and 1968. Sure, it was Mitchell who rode herd over Corvette styling in the 1960s. It was he who supplied the direction and decision-making. But it was Larry Shinoda who first put it on paper.

A few decades passed and Shinoda found himself pushed aside by history again as the fiberglass faithful flocked to praise the almighty father in his waning years. Being overshadowed, however, was something an aging Shinoda never did accept. His dissenting opinions concerning Duntov's dominance of the nostalgic limelight were openly expressed more than once during the 1990s.

"He was the Don Rickles of the design world, a colorful individual who spoke his mind and occasionally ruffled the wrong feathers," wrote good friend and *Sports Car International* editor

Larry Shinoda worked for both Ford and Chevrolet in his younger years, and he had the unique honor of creating images for two arch-rivals, Ford's Boss 302 Mustang and Chevy's Z/28 Camaro. Shinoda was caught on film here during the VIP dinner held the night before the National Corvette Museum's grand opening in September 1994.

D. Randy Riggs following Shinoda's death on November 13, 1997. "But that was why I admired him—there wasn't a phony bone in his body. He was our kind of car guy."

Shinoda never liked taking a backseat to anyone, which explains why he was such a demon behind the wheel. A red-blooded American hot-rodder from the day he received his license in 1946, his need for speed drove him to various victories at various competition venues in the 1950s. His 1929 Ford Hi-boy, the "Chopsticks Special," scored a class record at Bonneville. He also set records on National Hot Rod Association drag strips.

Shinoda was a familiar face around Indianapolis as well. He was a pit crewman for the Indy 500 winner four times. And he also designed the paint scheme for Pat Flaherty's 1956 Indy champ.

His competitive—make that rebellious—spirit also helped explain why he didn't eventually climb the corporate ladder in Detroit. "He's brilliant, but he's also an outspoken maverick," wrote *Automobile's* David E. Davis Jr., 20 years ago while running the show at *Car and Driver.* "Anytime the emperor walked into Shinoda's studio without any clothes on, Shinoda made sure he knew he was naked. This sort of honesty does not augur well for long-term success in Detroit, where the proper team spirit in committee work will get you a lot further than charismatic candor. Whatever else history may say about Lawrence K. Shinoda in years hence, it'll never call him a great committee man."

After leaving the Art Center College of Design in Pasadena early—for being "a malcontent," in his words—Shinoda went to work first for Ford in 1955, Packard in 1956, GM from late 1956 to 1968, then Ford again for another short stint. He designed trucks briefly for White and International Harvester in the 1970s, then opened his own studio.

Along with the 1963 Sting Ray, Shinoda's long design resumé included everything from motorcycles, to custom wheels, to the Goodyear blimp. As he told *Motor Trend* in 1973, he didn't want to be remembered "just as the designer who could design show cars.

"The way I look at it is that a designer should be able to design a tractor, a motor home, or anything on wheels, not just wild-looking sports cars," continued Shinoda. "That's basically what a good industrial designer is. He can do any job that comes."

Maybe so, but he is still remembered best for the dream machines he drew up while at Chevrolet. Among the more prominent were Bill Mitchell's Stingray race car, the CERV I and II experimentals, Jim Hall's Chaparral 2C and 2D racers, Mako Sharks I and II, and the Corvair Super Spyder, Monza GT, and Monza SS showcars.

Shinoda's eye-catching automotive drawings were most often easily recognized by their contour line "grids." This is an early rendition of the CERV I race car, built in 1959.

After following fellow GM defector Bunkie Knudsen to Ford in 1968, Shinoda also found himself working on the rival to a potent Chevy product he had helped promote earlier. He supplied the images for both the original Z/28 Camaro and its main Trans-Am competitor, Ford's Boss 302 Mustang. Henry Ford II then rewarded Larry for the latter by firing him, along with Knudsen, late in 1969. When asked later what he thought of corporate life in Dearborn, he said, "you could call it conservative, or you could call it some other things too. They had a strange way of doing things."

Shinoda's way of doing things was always the aggressive way. Taking no for an answer was never his style. After futilely waiting four days in GM offices for an initial interview in 1956, he finally managed to attract the attention of the fin man himself, Harley Earl. Impressed with the young designer's portfolio, Earl asked Shinoda about salary requirements. As he later said in Don Sherman's 1989 *Corvette Fever* interview, "I quickly tacked $200 per month on to what I earned at Packard. Earl rounded the amount of $200 per month higher still and asked when I could report to work."

He did so on September 15, 1956, the same day another Packard refugee, John DeLorean, came onboard at GM. Shinoda then became Mitchell's favored son of sorts after going to work on big Bill's "private racer," the Stingray, in the winter of 1958. From there followed the first Shark, the production Sting Ray, and the Mako Shark II.

Larry Shinoda was awaiting a kidney transplant when he died at age 67. Perhaps now his name will become the stuff of legends.

The Mako Shark II was restyled into the Manta Ray showcar in 1969. A chin spoiler up front and a lengthened, tapered tail were among modifications made that year. *Courtesy* Automobile Quarterly

for New York's International Auto Show, scheduled for April 1965.

No problem.

A nonrunning full-size mockup was rolled out for press release photography in March—rolled out because even though the hood said "Mark IV 396," there was no such thing residing beneath. Originally labeled Mako Shark, as mentioned, its badging had become Mako Shark II after it was decided to convince the public that this was the second in a series of showcars that meant business. Like the XP-755 Shark, which was now the Mako Shark I, the Mako Shark II was very much a prototype. As Pete Estes explained early in 1965, "the reaction of people who view this car during the next few months could very well influence future design decisions." Added *Hot Rod*'s Eric Dahlqist, "let's hope Chevrolet's Special Engineering boys land this one by 1967." At the same time a *Car Life* headline asked, is this the "next Corvette?"

The car in question was a second, fully functional Mako Shark II. This one actually was fitted with Chevrolet's newly introduced Mk IV big-block V-8, only the displacement was 427 cubic inches, not 396. Swapping engines (or in this case, putting an engine where there wasn't one before) represented just one of many adjustments made during the Mako Shark II's crowd-pleasing run on the auto show stage.

Show-goers in April 1965 couldn't have cared less that the original Mako mockup didn't have an engine. It looked fast enough while standing still. "As an overall design it kind of fills the mental outlines of the car Cato always had ready in that seemingly abandoned warehouse for the Green Hornet to rocket off into the night," wrote *Hot Rod*'s Eric Dahlquist in 1965.

A sharply pointed prow led the way, followed by a domed hood that signified power. Bulging wheelhouses at all four corners looked ready to explode, their flared openings barely able to contain the fat Firestones (8.80x15 up front, 9.15x15 in back) found within. The aluminum wheels were similar to the 1967 Sting Ray's optional "knockoffs," but, at 7.5 inches, were much wider.

Adding to the "zoomy" image were cast-aluminum side exhausts that exited the empty engine room halfway up the front fenders. These finned side pipes were painted in crackle black with the edges of the fins remaining polished bright. The paint was later removed after the New York showing and the pipes were fully polished. Side exhausts were then deleted altogether on the second Mako Shark II once its 427 big-block went in place.

Original impressions were both bold and beautiful. Body edges were sharp while contours were seductively soft. Measuring 3 inches lower than the existing Sting Ray's profile, the Mako's definitely integrated roofline rolled back into a tapered exclamation point made even more boldfaced by six window louvers that could be opened or closed electrically. The top itself was hinged at the rear, allowing it to flip open to improve access to the clearly cramped quarters below. A pronounced ducktail brought up the rear. And of course the whole package was painted dark down to light (Firefrost Midnight Blue, to lighter blue, to light gray) to match Mitchell's stuffed shark. Or vice versa.

Inside, the Mako Shark II's seats were fixed. As was the case at the feet of XP-819 drivers, the Mako's footpedals adjusted electrically to and fro. Equally unconventional was the aircraft-style steering wheel, which looked like a rectangle squeezed in slightly on the bottom. Incorporated into the wheel's top horizontal bar were two thumb-rotated controls; turn signals on the left, the automatic transmission shifter to the right. An adjustable knob for a proposed "variable ratio steering" control was found in the wheel's hub.

Like those impractical side exhausts, that futuristic steering wheel was also left off of the Mako Shark's functional alter-ego, which was already in the works while the mockup was wowing New Yorkers in April 1965. When the 427-powered Mako was shown to the press on October 5, it had a typically round steering wheel. Cylindrical-shaped controls for the turn signals and the Turbo Hydra-Matic transmission were now found in familiar locations on either side of the steering column. In place of the side pipes was a conventional full-length exhaust system exiting through two highly stylized rectangular tips at the car's tail.

Gizmos and gimmicks, most of them electrical, abounded throughout the car. The six round taillights (three to a side) in back blinked in sequence, inner light to outer, in Thunderbird fashion, when the turn signals were activated. Working in concert with the front signals were cornering lights hidden behind four "gills" just ahead of each wheel. If the headlights were on when the turn signal was flicked, these gills opened up to let those lights show the way around corners. The driver was alerted to any power failure by a series of console-mounted indicators connected to each driving light by fiber-optic strands.

Headlights consisted of three quartz-iodide beams on a side hidden by long, thin "eyelids" that opened electrically. Though these lights were too low and too bright to be legal in the United States, no one ever stopped the show to make a citizen's arrest during the Mako Shark tour.

Electrical wonderment inside included a digital clock and two other digital readouts for both the fuel gauge and speedometer. Digital instruments are taken for granted today, but represented cutting-edge (and difficultly performed) techno-wizardry in 1965. Rocker switches abounded on the console and door panels as all conventional conveniences were electrically controlled: locks, side glass, and wiper/washers. Washer fluid was "piped" up the wiper arms to flood the Vee'ed windshield where it needed flooding the most—directly in front of the wiper blades. When not in use, those wiper arms hid themselves away beneath hinged cowl sections at the base of the windshield. Additional switches controlled the definitely unconventional rear window louvers, adjustable top-mounted headrests, and flip-up roof.

The electric motors that controlled those last three features were among 17 remote power units required to make all the Mako's toys work. These included a flush-mounted bumper bar in back that extended outward at the flick of one of those console switches. Another switch next to this one flipped the rear license plate around to hide it from view. Although it was claimed that this trick was added to allow the car's tail to appear less cluttered ("for unbroken styling lines," in press release words) on the auto show stage, another value became instantly apparent to street racers who understood the importance of anonymity while leaving the local constabulary in the dust. And wouldn't you know it, Bill Mitchell was one of Woodward Avenue's more famous drag kings.

One more electrical trick attracted a chuckle or two 35 years ago. But it was Mitchell who again got the last laugh. A switch next to the turn signal activator could raise a pair of spoilers as high as 4 inches above that duck-tailed lip in back. According to Chevrolet press releases, these aircraft-like "stability" flaps "increase the down-force or loading by the car's airstream." Skeptics weren't so sure.

"Their effectiveness must be open to debate," wrote *Car Life*'s Dennis Shattuck. "However, the 'stabilizers' make good conversation pieces." They have since made more than that. Many designers later followed Mitchell's lead and put automatically adjustable rear spoilers to work on some of the world's best sports cars. Look who's conversing now.

Shattuck was one of the Mako Shark II's most outspoken critics. Most magazines raved about the car, but not *Car Life*. According to Shattuck's January 1966 review, the Mako Shark II "amply illustrates the 'surface entertainment' idiom. [This] consists of a particular talent to take something that is basically good and clean and pure, then embellish upon it with emblems or textures or patterns which have no relationship with function, but appear to."

Road & Track's critics were much harsher. "The design of the body and the 'styling' of it are, as so often with GM cars, two separate concepts," began an August 1965 *R&T* review of the Mako Shark II mockup. "The basic lines are pleasing and exciting—squint your eyes and see. But styling gimmicks and details have been heaped upon it in such abundance that it's really difficult to see the lines. We suppose that this treatment is some kind of entertainment for the masses. Entertainment it is, in the same vein as comic books or pornography."

On a much more positive note, Shattuck did point out that turning heads was the Mako Shark's top priority. "Its coloration is attention-getting and the car no doubt will stir plenty of discussion, which is just what GM wants," he wrote. On the flipside, he still felt that less should have been more. "The overall shape and proportion is interesting and exciting—it's just that there are too many extraneous convolutions."

So much for form. As far as function was concerned, however, Shattuck was a bit more complimentary. "The car is nonetheless noteworthy," he wrote, "as it contains a variety of potentially available gadgets. In that regard, the Mako Shark II must be regarded as a rolling showcase for future options." Like any successful executive, Mitchell had already covered his ass, offering a disclaimer of sorts concerning that showcase. "Most of these features require further refinement and evaluation before being adopted on production models," he said. To that, Shattuck couldn't resist one last jab. "The Mako Shark II will continue to serve as a styling idea model, updated from time to time with various portions and contours and systems being plucked off it and manufactured on [other] production cars," he concluded. "Boy, just wait until they put those stabilizer flaps onto the Impala!"

Larry Shinoda later tried to put such slings and arrows into perspective. "There was certainly no shortage of reaction in the automobile media to some of the [Mako Shark's] 'added' features that Bill had requested even when some of it might have been just a little short-sighted," he told *Shark Quarterly* in 1997. "But that's the purpose of some of these cars. The public reaction has to be interpreted; you don't just take it at face value. People, by and large, tend to think 'right now' while we are supposed to think in the future. As I look back on the articles which have been written about the car 20 years later, I see a lot of retrospection. The authors now recognize the fact that some of the original criticisms were off-base; the core ideas have been realized."

Most of that criticism was lost beneath the praises heaped on the Mako Shark II during its world tour in 1966. After its press introduction, it was flown to France for an appearance at the Paris Automobile Salon on October 7, 1965. From there it went to London, Turin, Brussels, and Geneva before returning to America for the New York Auto Show in April 1966.

"It was an exceptionally beautiful car that had nothing to do with European nor, what is

In place of the Mako Shark II's rear louvers, the Manta Ray was fitted with a miniscule "sugar scoop" rear window layout. Side exhausts also returned. *Courtesy* Automobile Quarterly

more, with American style, but just with simple, pure style: neat, aerodynamic, and perfect," claimed *Styled Auto*'s staff. "It was a demonstration on how, in a field dominated by chromed, oversprung dinosaurs, an absolutely new and functional car can be made with great ingenuity and simplicity."

"It hasn't the functional beauty and purity of Pininfarina's Ferrari 275 Berlinetta, which anyone would be glad to be seen in," reported *Autocar*. "But let's give it full marks for showmanship and a taste of what is to come."

Once off the showcar circuit, the Mako Shark II paced a few races and also, like other Corvette showcars, served time as Bill Mitchell's personal driver. Then in 1969 it took on a new identity after it was restyled into the Manta Ray. Already measuring some 9 inches longer than a standard Sting Ray, the Mako Shark length grew even more after the Manta Ray conversion. Extra inches came by way of a restyled, stretched tail that took on a tapered look from a profile perspective. The point of that tail was protected by a body-colored Endura bumper. And the louvered rear glass was replaced by a less practical (if that was possible) "sugar scoop" design that featured a radically scaled-down version of the tunneled rear window idea used on the XP-819. The Manta Ray's roofline too came together to a point like the Mako Shark.

Among other updates was a chin spoiler up front and a repaint that played down the shark shading. Side pipes were later added, as were small mirrors mounted up high on the windshield pillars. The biggest news, though, was the Manta Ray's new power source. In place of the iron-block 427 used by the Mako Shark came Chevrolet's all-aluminum ZL-1 427, an exotic, mean-and-nasty mill more befitting of an exotic, one-of-a-kind showcar.

Estimates put the price tag for the original 427-powered Mako Shark II at as much as $2.5 million. Reportedly that price may have even hit $3 million by the time the ZL-1 Manta Ray

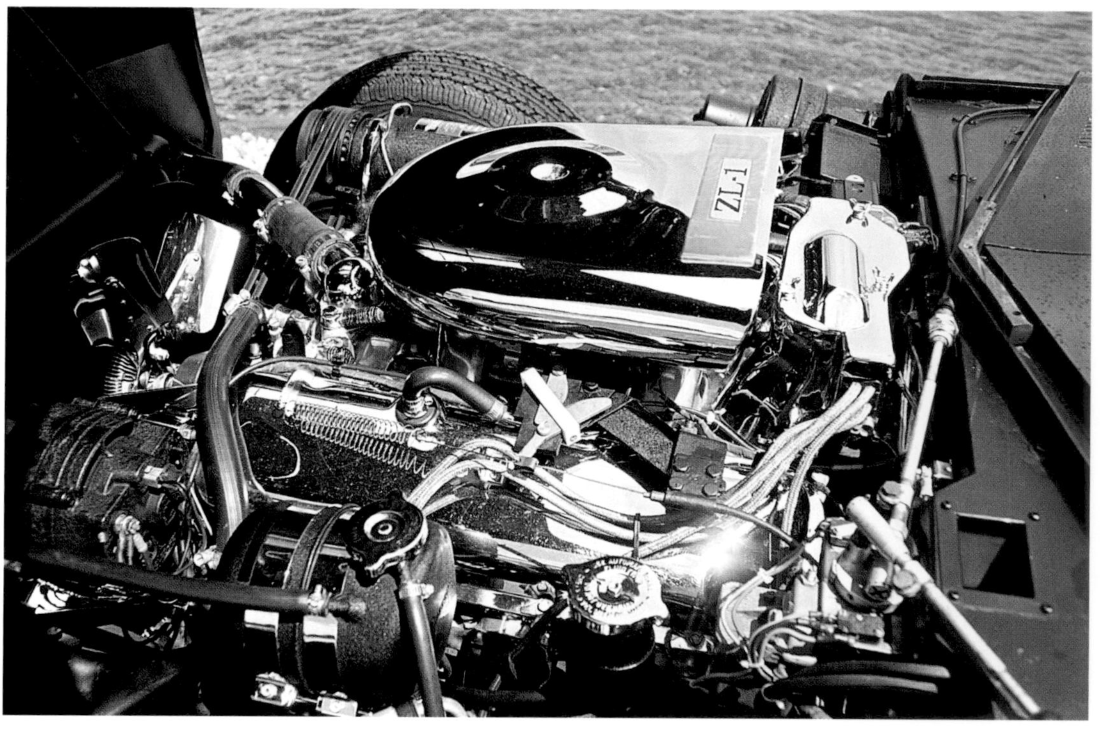

Power for the Manta Ray was updated with the addition of an aluminum ZL-1 427. *Courtesy* Automobile Quarterly

transformation was complete. Was it worth it? What do you think? Publicity may have never come GM's way at a better price per pound. And so much of what made the Mako Shark a show-stopper did find its way into the production Corvette in 1968. Whether that was good or bad can be debated, and was. But one plain fact can't be denied: Corvette popularity reached record heights nearly every year during the third-generation run.

Much work still remained ahead in 1966 if Chevrolet was to make the jump from Mako Shark II to a regular-production Corvette in time for the originally planned 1967 introduction. Design teams were still eating up valuable work weeks toying with Duntov's midengined ideal. Yet another such proposal, mocked up by Mitchell's stylists, appeared in March 1966. This one wore a body with fully enclosed rear wheels and no rear window—rear-view vision was provided by a telescope of all things.

Other more practical midengine experimental models soon followed, but the idea of the perfectly balanced, lightweight Corvette remained a dream. In 1957, planners had run up against retooling costs for the Q-Corvette's original rear-transmission design. That inhibiting reality remained plainly clear 10 years later. The steep price for an all-new transmission/transaxle layout alone was enough to keep the midengine Corvette on the shelf. Despite continued wishful thinking in the press, the next best Vette yet would remain of conventional, front-engined design.

That design was mocked up late in 1964 in Shinoda's secret studio. Compared to the Mako Shark II, this second theme was fashioned more conservatively with practical production in mind. But it still mirrored the basic Mako profile to come. It had a similar tapered roofline and a one-piece top that, in this case, could be completely removed from the car. That Targa-top idea was "borrowed" from the European sports car scene, a move Mitchell wasn't ashamed of in the least. As he told *Collectible Automobile* in 1984, "I wasn't above stealing things from European cars. Not American cars—there was nothing over here to steal."

While Shinoda was busy finishing his model, Henry Haga's team was completing a competing mockup in the regular production studio. Both were then viewed by Mitchell. Haga's car featured soft, rounded lines. "It had a little bit of a flying saucer look to it," said Shinoda later in a *Collectible Automobile* interview. "And Mitchell hated it. He said, 'have you ever seen such a fat pig?' Then he kicked it, and almost the whole back end fell off!"

Mitchell chose Shinoda's theme and passed it on to Haga's studio for its transformation into reality. One of the first changes made was to trade that "boat-tail" roof for a more practical, more pleasing design also borrowed from Europe—in this case, from the Porsche 904. Vertical rear glass was sandwiched between two parallel "flying buttress" C-pillars, a layout that recreated the "tunneled" window style used on XP-819.

The Targa-top idea, also used on XP-819, initially carried over into Haga's studio. And it remained in place atop prototypes until the last minute. With no fixed roof structure in place to help stiffen the platform, the Targa-top machines flexed too much, allowing their windshield frames to twist in relation to the rear roofline "arch." This unwanted torsional movement made the top creak, and it also compromised the car's weather-sealing capabilities. Duntov's crew couldn't solve this problem within established parameters so they had no choice but to add a central reinforcing strut to join the windshield header to that arch. This in turn meant the one-piece roof had to be separated into two sections.

Fixing the roof, however, was the least of Duntov's worries. By then, he had already asked Pete Estes for a deadline extension and gotten his extra year. As mentioned, this time was needed to address various gremlins hiding within that oversexed body. Shinoda's shape was too curvaceous, too bulging. Outward visibility was severely hindered by those tall fender tops; that low, flying-buttress roof; and the big ducktail in back. The slinky shell was also too close to the ground in front where that sharp-edged beak limited the amount of cooling air able to reach the engine. And let's not forget aerodynamics.

An engineering test vehicle was touring GM's Milford Proving Grounds as early as the fall of 1965. A new 1965 Corvette was also run around the track to serve as a measuring stick. Duntov's "bad airplane" tended to lift at both ends at high speeds. At 120 miles per hour, the 1965 Sting Ray's nose rose 2.25 inches, the rear 1/2 inch. In comparison, Engineering's test car hunkered down in back at speed thanks to that large rear spoiler. At 120 miles per hour, its tail dropped 1/4 inch. This depression in turn helped raise the nose, a task the car could already handle well enough on its own. Lift at 120 miles per hour measured 3.75 inches. That first test car might have easily handled regular nonstop service from Dayton to Chicago with scheduled takeoffs every hour on the hour.

All that lift not only made high-speed travel an unstable, turbulent, if not frightening experience, it also typically increased drag. And as all aeronautical engineers know, more drag means more propulsion is needed to reach high speeds. For the record, the 1965 Corvette had to deliver 155 horsepower to the road to attain 120 miles per hour. Engineering's test machine initially required 210 horses to hit the same speed.

Bringing things back down to earth was first achieved by venting the front fenders, a trick first tried on Jim Hall's Chaparral race cars. These vents allowed trapped airflow up front a quicker exit, thus reducing nose lift at the top end. Opening up the fenders brought the prototype's lift down close to stock 1965 Sting Ray levels. At the same time, the modification meant only 175 horsepower was needed to move the car up to 120 miles per hour. Adding a chin spoiler up front—again ala the Chaparral—reduced that power requirement even further to a mere 105 horses. That spoiler also sliced lift to a measly 5/8 of an inch.

Slicing and dicing didn't end there, and it was all the additionally required bodywork that finally convinced everyone involved to push the planned delivery date back from 1967 to 1968. Haga's stylists, joined by Larry Shinoda, took the body back into the studio to address Duntov's other complaints. They cut down those front fender tops to allow the driver a safer look ahead. The rear quarters and roofline were also modified to improve rearward visibility. Downsizing the rear spoiler into a molded-in lip further enhanced the view.

Engine cooling was aided by a reshaped nose that allowed the radiator a more prominent location up front. An "air-dam" lip that ran beneath the car and up around the front wheel openings was also added to better direct cool air toward that radiator. Finally, those fender vents were enlarged to help let hot air escape more easily from beneath the hood. The last two modifications also helped decrease high-speed lift too.

When everything was said and done, the next great Corvette was finally ready for customer deliveries in the fall of 1967. Or was it?

Chapter 2

SEE THREE

Introducing the Latest, Greatest Corvette

Zora Duntov already had enough to deal with in 1967. He became seriously ill that spring and was hospitalized for most of May and June. On top of that, he also was forced to face the reality that the Corvette was no longer his baby. Chevrolet's supposedly wise decision-makers had placed the teenaged two-seater into a foster home late in the C3's birthing process. Even though no one else at GM understood the Corvette as well as Zora, management restructuring at Chevrolet still took America's only sports car out of his capable hands and placed it under the care of the same engineers responsible for the division's full-sized passenger automobiles.

So much for autonomy—for both man and machine. When Duntov emerged from the hospital he found he was now a consultant to the chief engineer's office and the Corvette was just another face in the crowd at Chevrolet Engineering. His authority was all but gone. But the third-generation Corvette's teething problems weren't. Normally all major pains are eased by this late stage in a new-model development process. Not so with the 1968 Corvette.

Before he entered the hospital, Duntov requested that Chevrolet chief engineer Jim Premo personally address one particular hot spot. Sizzling, sexy looks weren't the Shark body's only claim to fame. Excessive heat beneath the hood remained an inherent irritation throughout the third-generation Corvette's long roll into production. Premo undoubtedly recognized the need to soothe this flare-up, but he was reassigned by GM's front office before he could address the problem. His replacement at Chevy Engineering, Alex Mair, apparently concerned himself more with the entire waiting room full of patients instead of one seemingly minor (from his perspective) toothache. Remember, Mair's job was to oversee all of Chevrolet's passenger-car engineering, and the Corvette was now simply one of many Chevrolet products in need of attention. Not special attention, mind you, just attention. Nothing more, nothing less.

So it was that Chevrolet Engineering's restructured pecking order allowed the 1968 Corvette's inherent hot temper to simmer almost unchecked until Duntov returned to work early in July 1967. His first assignment as consultant was to prep the 1968 prototype for its long-awaited press preview, then less than a month away. But all he needed was one tour in the blue big-block coupe then being readied for journalists' scrutiny to recognize that the car would never keep its cool under the magnifying glass. Big-block Corvettes had always run hot, and this particular prototype was no exception. In truth, it was even more so due to that fact that all that cast iron was stuffed into stuffier confines. Not enough outside air could find its way into the radiator to help the coolant flowing within do its job.

Duntov's quick-fix saved the day. He opened up two oblong vents beneath the car's low-slung nose just ahead of the chin spoiler, then enlarged that spoiler to help increase the pressure forcing the airflow up into those openings. From there, the rush of air could only flow

Although it's wearing "Stingray" badges on its flanks, this LeMans Blue coupe is a 1968 model—no Corvettes that year were identified with the familiar script. Perhaps the car's late sales date—midway in August 1968—helps explain the addition. This Corvette perhaps was the last L-89 version built for 1968.

The L-89 option added lightweight aluminum heads to the 435-horsepower, L-71 427 big-block. Only 624 L-89 Corvettes were built for 1968.

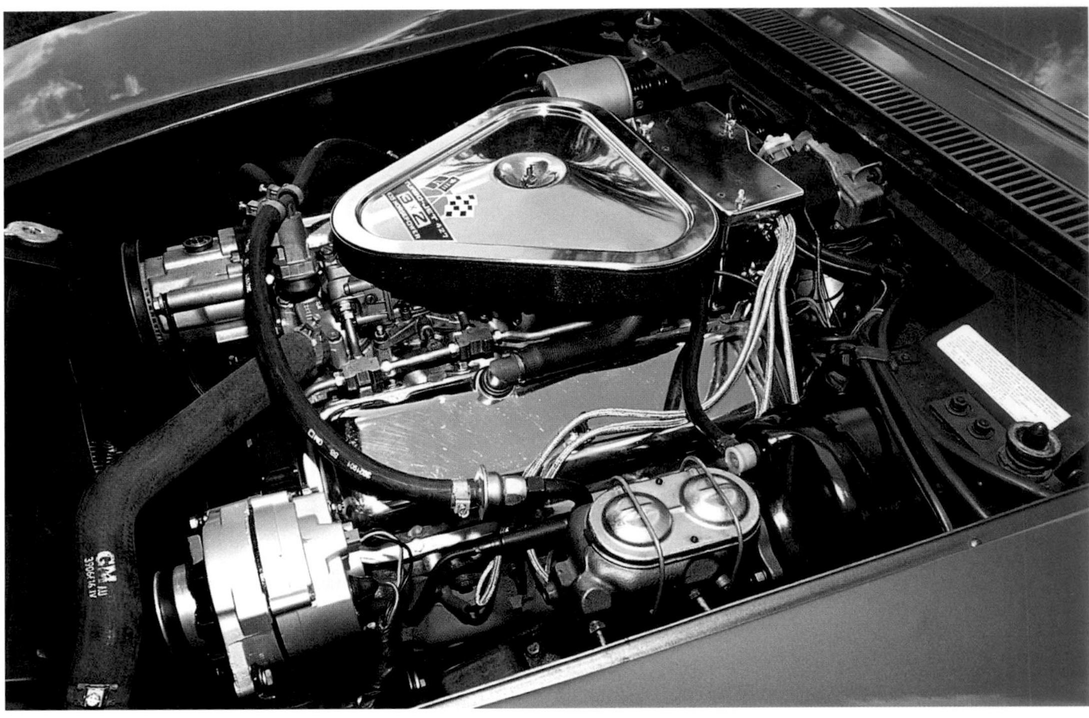

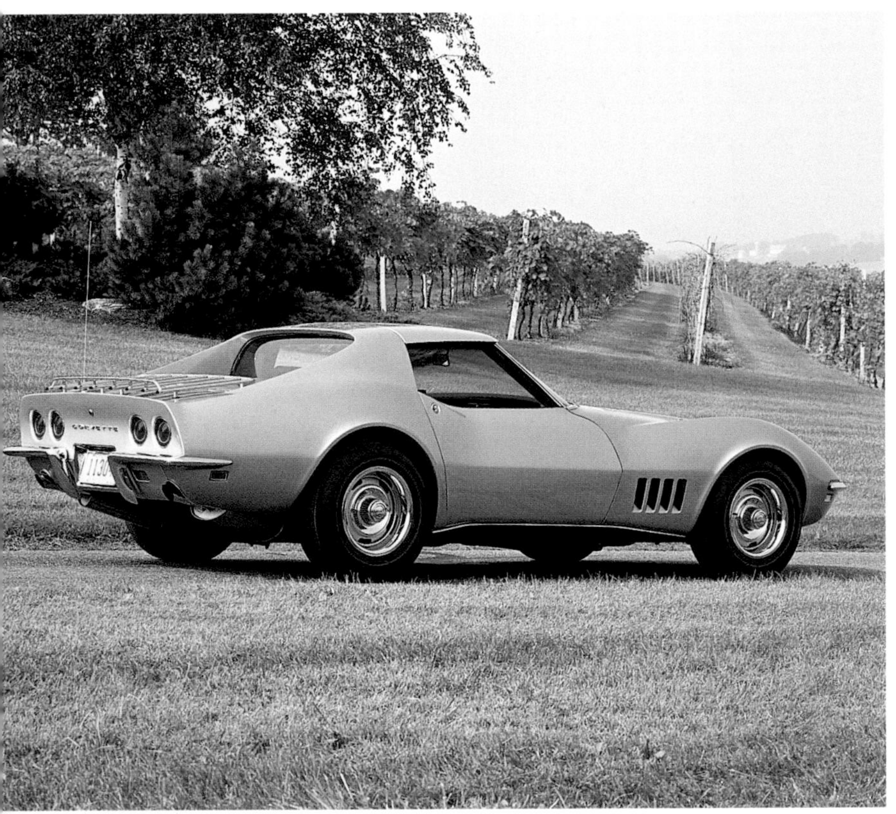

The bare fenders on this Silverstone Silver coupe quickly give away its identity as a 1968 Corvette. Stingray badging appeared in 1969. Red-stripe F70x15 tires, RPO PT6, were a $31.30 option in 1968.

through the radiator as all gaps to either side were closed up. Presto. The big-block prototype ran all day long in 85-degree heat at the Milford Proving Ground during the press introduction, and the temperature gauge stayed within established parameters.

The last major pain relieved? Not exactly.

Immediately ahead for Duntov and his stepchild was one more serious headache. Chevrolet's reorganized plan to build the third-generation Corvette "by committee" created more problems than it supposedly cured. Conventional mass-production tactics worked for passenger cars like Chevelles and Novas, but not for the somewhat-finicky, fiberglass-bodied performance machine that Zora had always hoped would someday challenge the world's best sports cars. It didn't take long for nearly everyone with eyes outside GM to quickly notice how poorly the next great Corvette was being raised in its new home.

After introducing the 1968 prototype to the American press in Michigan, Duntov's next "special consultant" task involved taking another big-block coupe overseas to test European waters in the fall of 1967. Zora's good friend, Belgian journalist Paul Frere, gave the car's performance high marks in his *Motor* review. On the other hand, he also mentioned the body's various rattles and

Four 427 big-blocks were offered in 1968, counting the race-only L-88. Two engines, the 400-horsepower L-68 and 435-horsepower L-71, featured triple carburetors. The L-36 427, shown here, was fed by one four-barrel and produced 390 horsepower. L-36 Corvette production in 1968 was 7,717.

noises. It seemed that anyone with ears also took note.

Back in America, *Car and Driver* editor Steve Smith had both ears and eyes. He also had a sharp pen. In his December 1967 editorial Smith declared the 1968 Corvette he drove was "unfit for a road test." "With less than 2,000 miles on it, the Corvette was falling apart," he wrote. Hot performance couldn't turn his head. Instead he was far more concerned with "the car's shocking lack of quality control."

"Sometimes the pieces chafed against each other, sometimes they left wide gaps, sometimes they were just plain crooked," continued Smith about mismatched body panels. "In the rain, water leaked through a gap in the bolt-on hardtop and dripped on our left shoulders like the Chinese water torture. The surface of the fiberglass was as wavy as a home-built layup. The car rattled and shook on mildly bumpy roads."

We can only wonder what Steve really thought.

As for Corvette customers, they were no strangers to imperfections in the molded shell. Body finish quality had fluctuated considerably during the original Sting Ray's five-year run. But it had never been this bad. And overall fit, as Smith explained, was now downright terrible. *Car and Driver*'s complaints would be echoed again and again by countless buyers who had the misfortune of helping Chevrolet iron out the C3's bugs. To this day, the 1968 model still stands, in many opinions, as the most poorly constructed Corvette of all time. And those fit and finish maladies didn't go away overnight.

Chevrolet's immediate response to this quality-control problem was to right the wrong made midway in 1967. While customer complaints might have eventually inspired the same result, it was Steve Smith's caustic *C/D* column that probably did the most to help reunite the main man and his baby. In 1968, the Corvette program was restored to its rightful place as an exclusive engineering entity. And Zora Arkus-Duntov was finally promoted to the official position he had so long deserved—Corvette chief engineer. From then on, Duntov had the final say concerning essentially every facet of Corvette development and production.

One of the few cases (as well as the most significant) where Zora found himself shouted down in the chief engineer's seat involved the ongoing myth of the mid-engine Corvette. As early as 1965, witnesses were beginning to wonder if the next new two-seater would indeed appear with its engine mounted amidships, this after various scale models featuring this layout were constructed for developmental consideration.

Two years later, Frank Winchell put Larry Nies to work on the attractive XP-880. This

Save for some reworked suspension geometry in back, which in turn required some additional crimping of the exhaust pipes (notice the flattened tube just below the driveshaft), the Shark's chassis carried over from 1967. The triangle-shaped air cleaner on this big-block signifies the presence of the tri-carb 427. *Chevrolet Motor Division*

model looked a lot like their failed XP-819 Corvette with its rear-mounted small-block but actually relied on a Mk IV big-block V-8 bolted in between the driver and rear wheels. Not to be outdone, in 1968 Duntov's engineers began creating their own midengine prototype, the sensational XP-882. These experimental Corvettes were then followed in 1971 by the equally sensational XP-895. Two other more radical midengine machines, fitted with Wankel rotary engines instead of V-8s, appeared in 1973, leading more than one major magazine to announce the arrival of the next new Corvette.

Both *Road & Track* and *Car and Driver* had already made a habit of printing such wishful predictions, and little wonder. Staff opinions from both sources in the 1960s continually favored the exotic European sports car ideal, regardless of price. In their minds not only was the Corvette too conventional and way too heavy to compete with its much more expensive foreign rivals, it was also too blatantly American. "For those who like their cars big, flashy and full of blinking lights and trap doors, it's a winner," claimed an *R&T* review of the 1968 Corvette. On the other hand, "the connoisseur who values finesse, efficiency and the latest chassis design will have to look, unfortunately, to Europe."

By the time *Car and Driver*'s curbside critics did finally get around to road-testing a better-built third-generation Corvette (in their May 1968 issue), they called it "a brilliant car with all of the virtues and all of the vices of American technology. On balance, it's an almost irresistible temptation to buy American." That backhanded compliment, however, was followed a year later by a far less flattering line: "The Corvette's excellent engineering tends to be obscured by some rather garish styling gimmicks that make the uninitiated wonder if the car is a fake—a lurid, bulging, silicone-filled, automotive Playboy Bunny."

"This confusing identity is the result of a confrontation on the part of Zora Arkus-Duntov, who is well and truly the patron saint of all Corvettes, and the Chevrolet styling department," continued that September 1969 *C/D* report. "Duntov's primary aim in his professional life is to make the Corvette the finest sports car in the world. The styling department views his car as a unique opportunity to fool around with the swoopy shapes and flashing lights that somehow to them mean 'sport.' It is within this minor tempest that the Corvette encounters trouble: Duntov on the one hand viewing his automobile as a purposeful, well-balanced sports car, while his rivals see it as a Flash Gordon Thunderbird for the Hugh Hefner school of mass-cult glamour."

Road & Track's staffers were also disappointed in Chevrolet's apparent decision to emphasize flash over innovation. "Rumors came and went about an exciting, advanced new Corvette that would package the engine in the 'midship' position now almost universal in racing machinery and feature new, more efficient body-chassis construction," read *R&T*'s January 1968 road test. "But, alas, all the available money was spent on new styling."

A year later, *Car and Driver* went one step further concerning the prospects of an advanced new Corvette. "The present Corvette will doubtlessly be the last front-engine model," predicted *C/D*. "It remains uncertain if the new rear-engine [sic] version will be introduced in 1971 or 1972. Although a number of prototypes have been tested, a certain amount of turmoil exists within Chevrolet as to exactly what form the new car will take. The present general manager, John DeLorean, is as much an automotive purist as ever reached the top ranks at General Motors, and it is known that he is unhappy with the present Corvette. Rumors from deep inside the company indicate that DeLorean has pronounced that the mid-engine version must be a functional sports/GT car weighing in the neighborhood of 2,600 lbs. and containing an engine of about 400 ci. This places a giant challenge before Duntov and his engineers. [Whether] this can be accomplished with a fiberglass or steel body remains to be seen, but it can be assumed that DeLorean, an engineer himself, will drive hard to make the new Corvette lean and tough. If he succeeds, it could mean goodbye to the [existing] jet-plane gimmickry. And for that we'd all be thankful."

Even more predictions followed, most prominently from *Road & Track*. In 1970, an *R&T* report claimed a midengine Corvette definitely was on the way for 1972; in 1971 yet another feature gave us the "first look" at the "1973 mid-engine Corvette." As late as 1977, *Road & Track*'s ever-optimistic editors were still predicting the arrival of an all-new midmotored Corvette, this time for 1980.

Duntov's dreams for the perfectly balanced, lighweight Corvette, however, had already been dashed well before that last *Road & Track* prophecy hit the stands. Fantasies would be more like it. Zora, Shinoda, Winchell—they all could've built midengine prototypes until the cows made it home and they still wouldn't have affected reality. GM's executive opinion of the plan was plain and simple: Why fix something that wasn't broken? Corvette sales set new records in 1968 and 1969, then started over in 1970 on a steady rise that didn't peak until 1977. Chevrolet held a captive audience for its fiberglass two-seater (with its front-mounted engine) during the 1970s and everyone from DeLorean on up knew it. Even so, corporate execs still allowed Duntov to dream on almost right up to his retirement in early 1975.

When GM squelched the midengine Corvette proposal it resulted in one of the greatest disappointments Zora encountered during his 21 years working with America's only sports car. "Until 1970, 90 percent of what I intended to do, I accomplished," said the Corvette's first chief engineer in a 1980 *AutoWeek* interview. "In 1972, a mid-ship car was touch and go. It was all designed." But it still wasn't to be.

That downer still lay well ahead for Duntov while he was working overtime to rid the new third-generation Corvette of those unwelcomed gremlins. Yet even with its obvious

Body drop time for a 1968 coupe at the St. Louis assembly plant. The powertrain is the base 300-horsepower 327 backed by the optional Turbo Hydra-Matic automatic transmission.

Restyled fender louvers were added in 1970, as were flared wheel openings to help resist rock chip damage to the body.

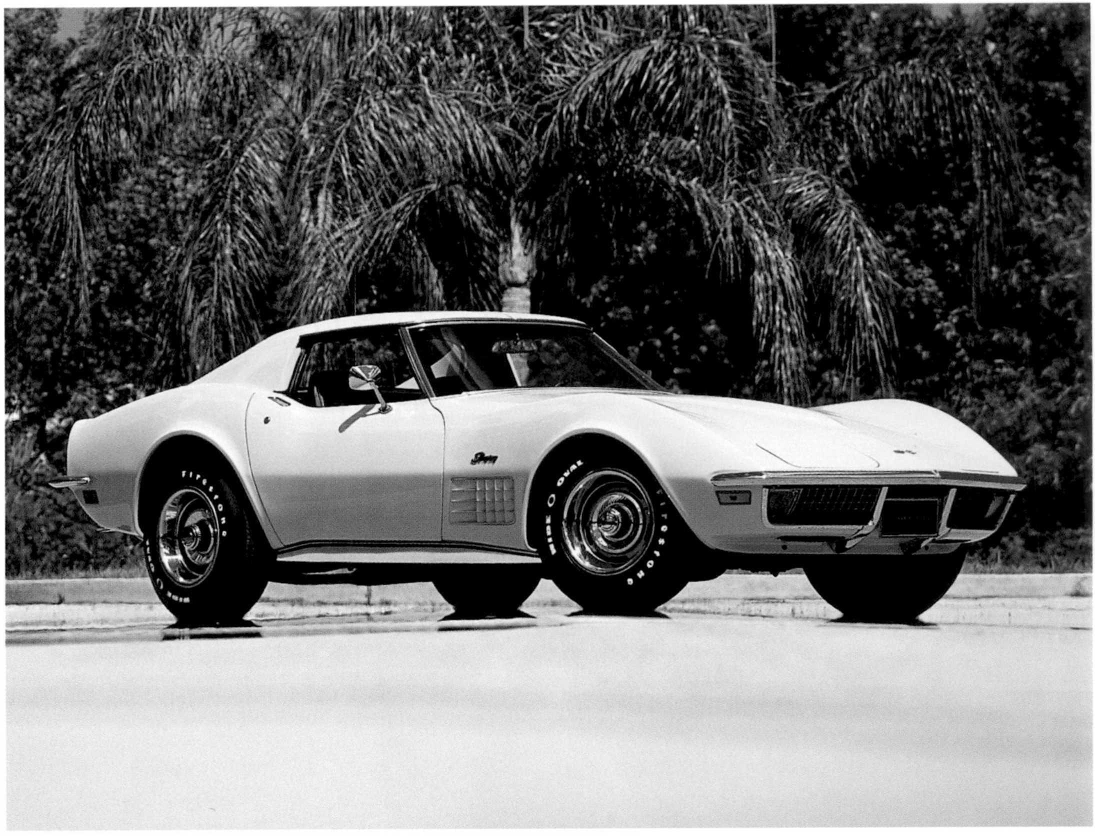

quality-control problems and conventionally located engine, the 1968 Corvette by no means disappointed red-white-and-blue-blooded buyers. By the time the dust cleared, 28,566 of them had stormed Chevrolet dealerships for their own private piece of the ongoing Corvette legacy.

Not all among the automotive press were inclined to sling arrows, either. Far more chauvinistic than *R&T* or *C/D*, *Car Life* couldn't brag enough about the hot, new, built-in-the-U.S.A performance car it described as "the excitement generator." "This 1968 sport coupe is endowed with smooth ferocity," continued *Car Life*'s first review of the latest Corvette. "Longer, lower, wider and sleeker, the new fiberglass envelope should cause a stampede among American sports car purchasers."

Most buyers with a need for speed in this country in 1968 couldn't have cared less about foregoing any possible Continental considerations. These love-it-or-leave-it performance car partisans also didn't need some Euro-phile magazine editor telling them what they should or shouldn't like. They adored big American cars with big American horsepower. Many of them also had nothing against Playboy Bunnies or Flash Gordon, either. And they certainly had no complaints about the Corvette's new look, which titillated them like no Corvette before with its seething, American-style sensuality.

From its low, pointed nose to its flared tail, the 1968 Corvette quickened pulses every bit as easily as the Mako Shark II had done three years before. Those sleek looks also did a decent job of cheating the wind, although most critics still pointed out that much of the car's aerodynamic performance remained a mirage. Less so, however, than in 1967. Test figures for drag and high-speed lift were, according to *Sports Car Graphic*'s Paul Van Valkenburgh in 1970, "very respectable considering that the shape was dictated by GM Styling, and Chevrolet engineers had to sweat acid trying to keep the nose on the ground at speeds over 150."

Although the C3 Corvette gained some high-speed abilities compared to its midyear forerunners, it lost a little ground on the scales, where it weighed in at nearly 3,300 pounds, roughly 150 more than the Sting Ray. It was also 7 inches longer overall at 182.5 clicks. At 69 inches, width was two-tenths less than in 1967, while height dropped from 49.6 inches to 47.8.

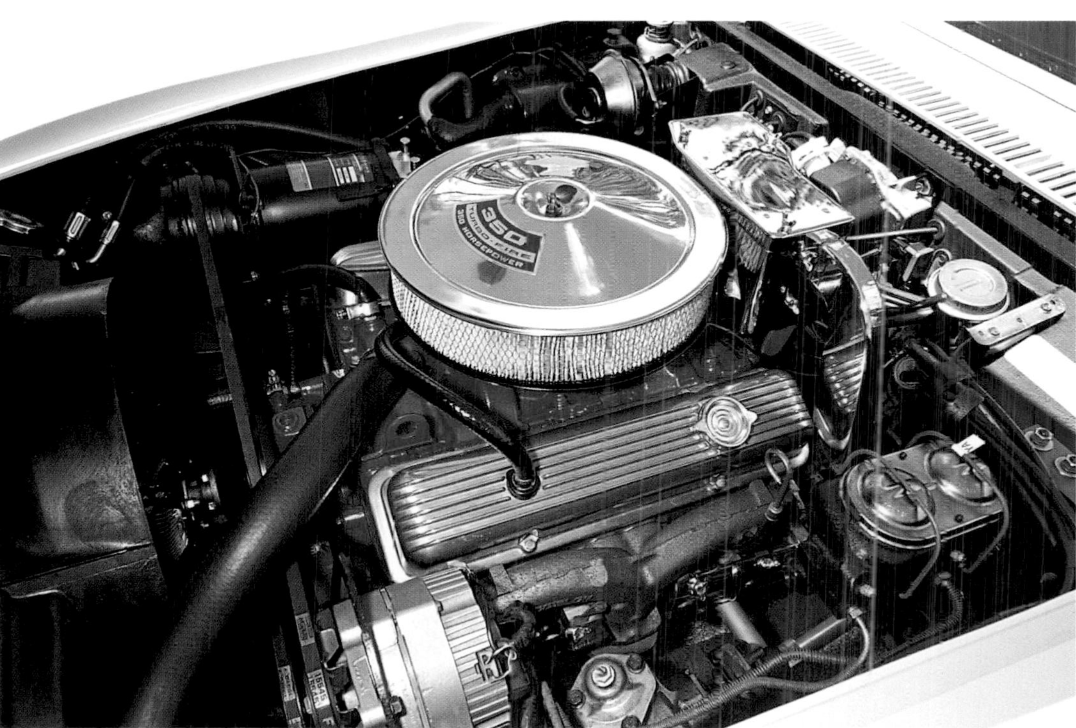

The L-46 small-block, a 350-ci derivative of the 327-ci L-79 V-8, was last offered in 1970. A slightly tamed version of the LT-1 350 with hydraulic lifters instead of mechanical tappets, the L-46, like the L-79, was rated at 350 horsepower. L-46 Corvette production in 1970 was 4,910.

Those last two measurements, working in concert with the radically increased "tumble-home" of the rounded Shark bodysides, translated into a considerable reduction in interior space, demonstrating once more just how much Mitchell's styling dictators controlled the car's functions.

That sexy, claustrophobic form wasn't the only thing to carry over from the auto show stage into production. While the T-top roof superceded the Mako Shark II's one-piece targa top, the production Corvette did share various other design features with its showcar forerunner, not the least of which was its fiber-optic warning light system and its hidden windshield wipers. The latter rested below a vacuum-operated panel that popped open on demand whenever the forecast called for rain. Sleet or snow sometimes represented another situation entirely, although Chevrolet designers claimed that the wipers' lid, as well as the car's vacuum-activated pop-up headlights, could crack their way through 3/8-inch-thick ice. But who would dare subject their 'glass-bodied baby to such climatic calamity, right?

Like the Mako Shark, the 1968 Corvette also arrived without vent windows. Letting the good air in, bad air out was now the job of Chevrolet's new "Astro" ventilation system, which routed fresh breezes in through the cowl,

The ever-popular tilt-telescopic steering column, RPO N37, cost $84 in 1970. N37 sales that year totaled 5,803. This particular L-46 coupe is also equipped with air conditioning, something LT-1 drivers couldn't enjoy until late in 1972.

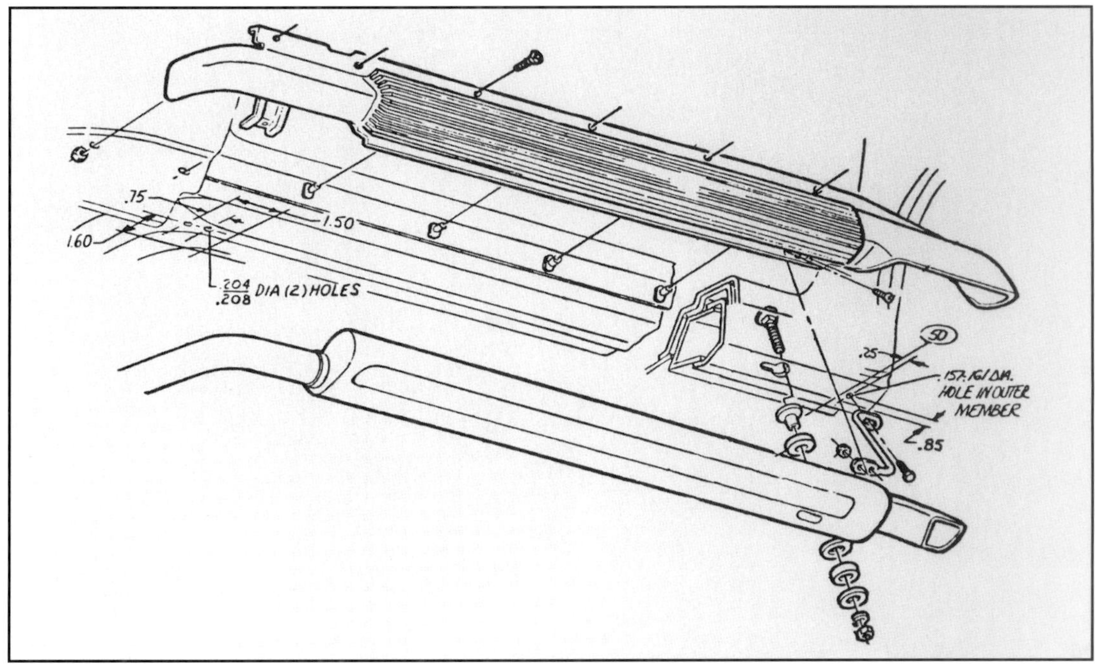

Eye-catching side exhausts were a Shark option only in 1969. The price for the N14 pipes was $147. Sales totaled 4,355.

around interior airspace, and out through grilles located in the rear deck right behind the back window. Convertibles used this ductwork too. Coupe owners in need of a little more wind, along with some extra tanning time, of course could've removed their T-tops. That rear glass detached as well for maximum mussing of the hair, however many follicles remained.

Like the midyear Sting Rays it replaced, the C3 Corvette's first bodystyle rolled on in essentially identical fashion through five model runs. The basic profile, the T-tops, the coupe's removable window—all these readily identifiable features continued unchanged up through 1972. Same for the wheels. Although they were widened from 7 inches to 8 beginning in 1969, those standard 15-inch Rally rims retained an identical style each year, as did the optional full wheelcovers.

While the annual list of minor revamps, inside and out, is a long one, most casual witnesses at a glance still find it difficult to differentiate the Corvettes built from 1968 to 1972. Quick, easy, one-guess giveaways included the optional side-mount exhausts, which were only offered in 1969, and the separate rectangular backup lights, which were of 1968 only. Another less noticeable option, RPO TJ2, added bright trim to the Corvette's fender louvers in 1969 only. The 1968 door handles and dash-mounted ignition switch were also unique. In 1969, the ignition went to the steering column, the pushbutton door releases were deleted, and the backup lights were moved up into the center of the inner pair of taillights. The taillight lenses themselves were later revised slightly in late 1971.

Probably the most obvious clue concerning the 1968 Corvette's true identity involved badging. The Sting Ray name was nowhere to be found on that swoopy shape. Perhaps Chevrolet officials finally opened a dictionary and chose to erase their error. Most spelling compilations describe yet another of Bill Mitchell's favorite sea creatures using one word, as Mitchell himself had done in 1959 for his Shinoda-bodied racer. Whatever the case, when the second edition C3 appeared in 1969 a correctly spelled "Stingray" script was placed on each flank directly above those fender "gills."

Less specific were the round exhaust tips and bezels used in both 1968 and 1969. These units became rectangles on 1970–72 Corvettes. Corvettes in 1968 and 1969 also featured their own style of vertical fender vent; the 1970–72 group received a revised vent that was topped by a bright crosshatch grille. Along with that, 1970–72 Corvettes were fitted with larger side marker lights and rectangular turn signals up front. The 1968–69 models used round turn signal lamps and smaller side markers. The Shark shell in 1970 was also mildly modified with flares around the wheel openings.

Standard on all Corvette coupes built from 1968 to 1973 was a removable rear window, which with a little fuss and muss could be stored behind the seats.

Among the various far less obvious changes made during the 1968–72 run was the deletion of the transistorized ignition and optic-fiber warning light system after 1971. In exchange for the latter, Corvette drivers in 1972 received a horn-honking burglar alarm system as standard equipment. The alarm system was previously an option, RPO UA6, for 1968–71 Corvettes.

Nearly all engineering features beneath the Shark's skin were familiar to any Sting Ray owner who had crawled under a midyear model for a peek. Indeed, all the money had been spent on new styling. Holding up the 1968 Corvette's dirty side was basically the same chassis introduced in 1963, it with the 98-inch wheelbase and independent rear suspension. That's not to say that Duntov didn't have a trick or two up his sleeve.

Yet another inherent problem he addressed in 1968 was the Sting Ray's habit of pitching its nose up whenever the go-pedal was mashed to the floor. Once the nose raised, front wheel geometry went wildly out of whack, meaning the car tended to wander at a time when precise control was preferred more than ever. To help correct this malady, spring rates were stiffened and the rear roll center was dropped from 7.56 inches above the ground to 4.71 inches by lowering the inner pivot points of the lateral suspension arms. Then, to compensate for the increased understeer "dialed in" by these changes, those widened 7-inch Rally wheels were added to allow the use of fatter F70x15 tires. More rubber on the ground meant more resistance to lateral g-forces. Maximum lateral acceleration measured 0.84g for the 1968 Corvette, compared to 0.74 for the Sting Ray. Those wider wheels and tires also meant an increase in track: from 56.8 inches to 58.7 in front and from 57.6 to 59.4 in back.

Did these modifications do the trick? Even *Road & Track*'s ever-critical critics were impressed. "No question about it, the Corvette is one of the best-handling front-engine production cars in the world," claimed a 1969 *R&T* road test.

Initially the C3's standard drivetrain was a complete midyear carryover. Included in the 1968 Corvette's base price ($4,663 for a coupe, $4,320 for a convertible) was the same tried-and-true 300-horse 327 small-block and three-speed manual gearbox installed as standard equipment since 1966. The 327/300 V-8 actually first appeared as an option four years earlier.

Base engine specs then began to grow along with those prices in 1969. A standard 1969 coupe cost $4,781; a convertible, $4,438. Included in both of those deals was a bigger small-block V-8, the 350. Chevrolet engineers had created the 350 in 1967 by stretching the 327's 3.25-inch stroke to 3.48 inches. Bore remained

A removable hardtop, RPO C07, was a $273 option for a Corvette convertible in 1970. Adding vinyl covering (RPO C08) to that roof cost another $63. C07 sales totaled 2,556 that year. Only 832 vinyl roofs were sold.

at 4.00 inches. In the 1969 Corvette's case, almost all other numbers also carried over from the 327 to the 350. Compression remained at 10.25:1 and maximum output was still 300 horsepower at 5,000 rpm. Maximum torque, however, went from 360 ft-lb at 3,400 rpm up to 380 at the same revolutions.

Advertised power levels for the base 350 repeated themselves in 1970 (at slightly lower rpm peaks), then began to drop for the first time in Corvette history in 1971. The reason for the decrease was a compression cut (to 8.5:1) made as part of GM's response to a federal government crackdown on engine emissions. While an even tighter environmentally conscious stranglehold on horsepower lay ahead, advertised outputs for all of GM's engines plummeted further in 1972 when gross ratings were traded for SAE net figures. The 1972 Corvette's standard 350 was listed at a paltry 200 net horsepower.

As for optional engines, the 1968 list was identical to 1967's right down to the prices. At the bottom was the L-79 327, rated at 350 horses. While the L-79's hydraulic lifters helped keep it on the tame side, its 11:1 compression promised wilder times. The price for RPO L-79 was $105.35.

Next came the 427 big-blocks, or "rat motors" as Chevy freaks like to call the division's big-cube Mk IV V-8s. The 390-horsepower L-36 cost $200.15; the 400-horsepower L-68, $305.50; and the thunderous 435-horsepower L-71, $437.10. Topping everything off was the race-ready L-88 427 and the L-89 aluminum head package for the L-71. Prices were $805.75 for the L-89/L-71 and $947.90 for the legendary L-88 with its token 430-horse rating. Production was 7,717 for the L-36, 1,932 for the L-68, 2,898 for the L-71, 624 for the L-89, and 80 for the L-88.

All these 427s—save for the L-88—were fitted with new "low-rise" intake manifolds designed to allow the carburetor (or carburetors) ample clearance beneath the third-generation Corvette's low, low hood. Efficient intake flow (and thus power) was preserved by "sinking" the manifold's underside into the big-block's lifter valley. L-88's didn't require this modification because the scoop on their cool-air hoods supplied the needed carb clearance.

The L-36 and L-68 427s were essentially identical, save for one major adjustment. Both produced their maximum 460 ft-lb of torque at 3,600 rpm. Both also compressed their fuel/air mixture at a 10.25:1 ratio. But while the L-36 relied on a single Rochester Quadrajet four-barrel to shoot the juice, the L-68 sucked down the high-test through the trick triple-carb induction setup introduced for the 1967 Sting Ray. "Three 2-bbl Holley carburetors are used," explained *Car and Driver*'s May 1968 L-68 test, "with the one in the middle providing for normal operation while the end ones, with their vacuum operated throttles, are useful for setting land speed records and snaffling traffic tickets."

Like the L-68, the L-71 too was fed by three Holleys. But it was an entirely different beast. Head-cracking compression was 11.0:1. Four-bolt main bearing caps held the bottom end together. A lumpier cam hammered away at mechanical tappets instead of hydraulic lifters. The K66 transistorized ignition was a required option, as was the M21 close-ratio four-speed transmission.

Those solid lifters allowed the big, hairy L-71 to wind out longer than the L-68 before the muscle fell off. The L-71's 460 pounds of torque arrived at 4,000 rpm. Its 435 hell-bent-for-leather horses showed up at 5,800 revs. As in 1967, the L-71 Corvette in 1968 remained one of America's quickest street machines—road tests produced quarter-mile times in the low (make that very low) 13-second bracket. For more on the even stronger L-88s of 1968 and 1969, see chapter 3.

Changes to the extra-cost engine lineup in 1969 included two new codes. RPO L-46 was added to the small-block ranks to mark the popular 350-horse V-8's graduation from 327 ci to 350. Actually, L-46 replaced L-79. The other code, RPO ZL-1, represented an entirely new breed of 427 V-8, this one with an aluminum block to go along with the L-88's aluminum heads. Again, check out chapter 3 for the tale of the two known factory-installed ZL-1 Corvettes.

All the other optional 427s—they with their cast-iron blocks—rolled over from 1968. Production in 1969 was 10,531 for the L-36, 2,072 for the L-68, 2,772 for the L-71, 390 for the L-89, and 116 for the L-88.

Additional optional upgrades included the introduction of the Corvette's biggest big-block, the 454, in 1970. This monster mill, like the 350 small-block, represented another "stroke of genius" by Chevy engineers. Knowing full well that there was then no substitute for cubic inches, they simply stroked the 427 (from 3.76 inches to 4.00) to add another 27 cubes. The 4.25-inch bore remained constant, as did compression and horsepower. Like the L-36 427 of 1969, the LS-5 454 of 1970 squeezed fuel/air molecules at a 10.25:1 ratio to help churn out 390 maximum horses at 5,400 rpm. Torque output, on the other hand, was a whopping 500 ft-lb, 40 more than the L-36.

While it could melt a Wide Oval with the best of 'em and gulp a gallon of ethyl quicker than you could pump her in, the high-compression 454 in 1970 still could've been considered quite user friendly, thanks in part to its hydraulic cam. "It is by far the most tractable big-engine Corvette unit we've tried," claimed a *Road & Track* road test of the 1970 LS-5 Corvette. At $289.65, RPO LS-5 also wasn't all that hard on the wallet, especially compared to its new little brother, the LT-1 small-block, which cost that plus another $150 or so in spare change in 1970.

Whether or not 440 bucks (or the $480 charged in 1971) was too much to pay for a small-block V-8 depended upon how much a Corvette driver liked playing David to a big-block musclecar owner's Goliath. Rated at 370 horsepower, the first LT-1 solid-lifter 350 could easily slug it out with engines that displaced 100 more cubes, and did so with a vengeance up through 1972. In Corvette terms, the much lighter LT-1 offered customers better handling and similar acceleration in comparison to the nose-heavy big-block models. "As you would expect, the personalities of the LS-5 and the LT-1 are worlds apart," explained a *Car and Driver* review of the Corvette's many different moods. "In performance however, they are neck and neck." To read all about the LT-1, see chapter 4.

The LS-5 gentle giant became even easier to get along with in 1971 after compression was cut to 8.5:1. Advertised output, in turn, dropped to 365 horsepower. Maximum torque slipped to 465 ft-lb at 3,200 rpm. Yet performance still remained high. Rest to 60 miles per hour required only 5.7 seconds according to a *Car and Driver* test, which also reported that the quarter-mile rolled by in 14.1 clicks.

If that wasn't hot enough for you, there was yet another big-block option. The LS-6 454, which first appeared with its 450 horses beneath Chevelle SS hoods in 1970, made its way onto the Corvette options list in 1971 in place of the stillborn 460-horsepower LS-7 promised the year before. Even with compression sliced down from 11.25:1 (in Chevelle trim) to 9:1, the Corvette's LS-6 still produced 425 horsepower, more than enough muscle to propel a fiberglass body into the 13-second quarter-mile bracket. Once more run, don't walk, to chapter 3 to catch up with the rare, rarin'-to-go LS-6 Corvette and the mysterious LS-7 454.

Unfortunately the LS-6 was a one-hit wonder, and understandably so considering how

Coupes outnumbered convertibles by nearly a 2-to-1 margin in 1971, signaling a downward slide that would lead to the topless Corvette's demise four years later.

The fiber-optic light monitoring system, introduced in 1968, was used for the last time in 1971. Those monitor lights appear just below the AM/FM radio on this 1971 convertible.

quickly gas-guzzling, air-fouling big-block V-8s lost face with both the public and GM execs in the early 1970s. Even if Washington in the late-1960s hadn't targeted the internal combustion engine as the main culprit behind this country's air pollution problem, those heavy, high-priced eight-cylinder indulgences would've still run afoul of changing trends and attitudes once gasoline began turning into gold around 1973.

By then the changing trend at Chevrolet involved numbers crunching. Not pricing or production, mind you, those figures continued to rise. But with Corvette demand higher than ever, GM decision-makers began to question the reasons to stock the shelves with so many costly engines. Cylinder heads then started to roll. Counting the L-89 option and the exotic ZL-1, there were seven engine options offered along with the standard 350 in 1969. The Corvette's engine lineup shrank to five early in 1970, then four after the uncivilized LS-7 was cancelled before it could escape into the wild. Gone were all those extra carburetors and aluminum heads that had helped make the 427 the stuff of Corvette owners' dreams.

It was four again in 1971 as a new aluminum-head big-block, the LS-6, debuted while a veteran small-block, the 350-horse 350, retired. Born in 1965 as the L-79 327, the 350-horsepower small-block quickly formed a healthy following. L-79 production that first year was 4,716, followed by 7,591 in 1966 and 6,375 in 1967. Sales jumped to 9,440 in 1968, then reached 12,846 for the 350-cube L-46 rendition in 1969. "Only" 4,910 L-46 Corvettes were sold during 1970's shortened production run.

What was so great about the L-79/L-46? Why did Chevrolet officials drop it like a hot potato after 1970? Why did chief engineer Duntov let them? Last thing first. Zora basically didn't have a choice. Or did he? GM penny-pinchers in 1971 demanded that an engine be dropped from the Corvette lineup, and it was either the LT-1 or the L-46. Duntov campaigned for the former to help keep his baby ahead of the performance pack, though he wasn't happy at all about seeing the popular 350-horse 350 ride away into the sunset.

"He has harsh words for the 'bean counters' who occasionally eliminate a worthwhile option or feature," explained a June 1971 *Car and Driver* report. "The L-46 for example. Until this year you could buy a 350-ci. 350-horsepower engine with a hydraulic camshaft that had very nearly the performance of the LT-1

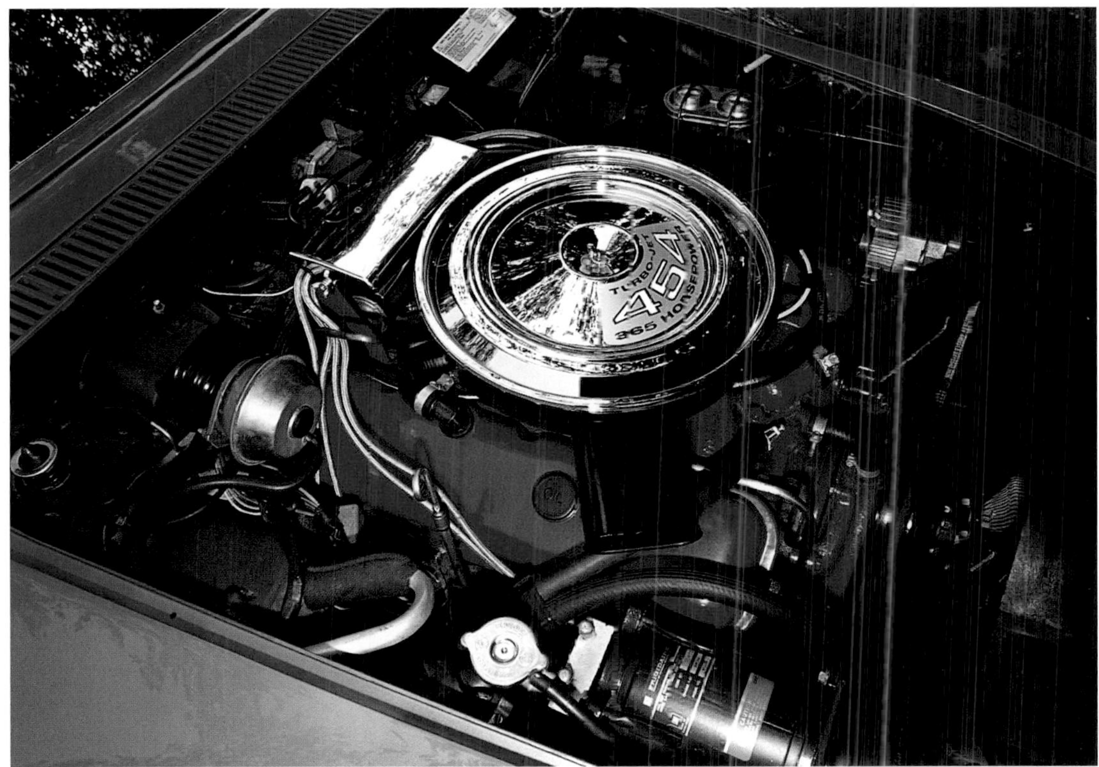

Big news for 1970 was the replacement of the 427 big-block by an even bigger Mk IV V-8, the 454. In 1971 Corvette buyers had two big-block choices: the LS-6 and this LS-5, rated at 365 horsepower. Price for the LS-5 454 was $295. Production in 1971 was 5,097.

but was also compatible with air conditioning. And you could buy it for about $150 compared to $483 for the LT-1. 'Redundant,' decided the bean counters and axed it off the list. Duntov thinks otherwise."

GM decision-makers, though, couldn't have cared less about what Zora thought in this case. At the time, *performance* had become a dirty word at GM, and an anti-Corvette groundswell among corporate killjoys who questioned the money spent on a narrow-niche product like the fiberglass two-seater was just developing. Not even record sales could convince this faction that the return was worth the investment. The LS-7 big-block never saw the light of day in 1970 due to GM's overnight change in attitude concerning the sale of unbridled horsepower. And when execs raised the axe again in 1971, not even the L-46's successful record could save its neck.

Like its L-79 predecessor, the L-46 thrived in its day simply because it was such a great deal. It represented a Corvette customer's best buy as far as horsepower-per-dollar was concerned. It was also far easier to live with than the solid-lifter LT-1, and not just because its driver could stay cooler behind the wheel. That hydraulic cam meant no maintenance hassles and less underhood noise. The LT-1 package also included a stiffer suspension that further compromised the third-generation Corvette's already shaky ride comfort. Ask most drivers who opted for the L-46 in 1970 instead of the LT-1, and they'll tell you the 20-horse trade-off was offset by improved seat-of-the-pants responses and the absence of those pesky solid lifters.

A year after the L-46 was cut, the LS-6 big-block too went as quickly as it had come, leaving Corvette buyers with only three net-rated engines to choose from in 1972. That list included the standard ZQ-3 350, the LT-1 and the LS-5 454. Advertised output for the latter was now down to 270 horsepower, although you would have never known it by looking beneath the hood. For the first time a Corvette big-block carried no horsepower label on its air cleaner lid. Customers in California in 1972 were none the wiser since they didn't even get a look at that lid. Chevrolet officials that year didn't feel it necessary to take the time to put the LS-5 through that state's stringent emissions testing, meaning it failed to meet certification for sale there in 1972. It wouldn't be the first time that a Corvette engine would be "banned" on the West Coast.

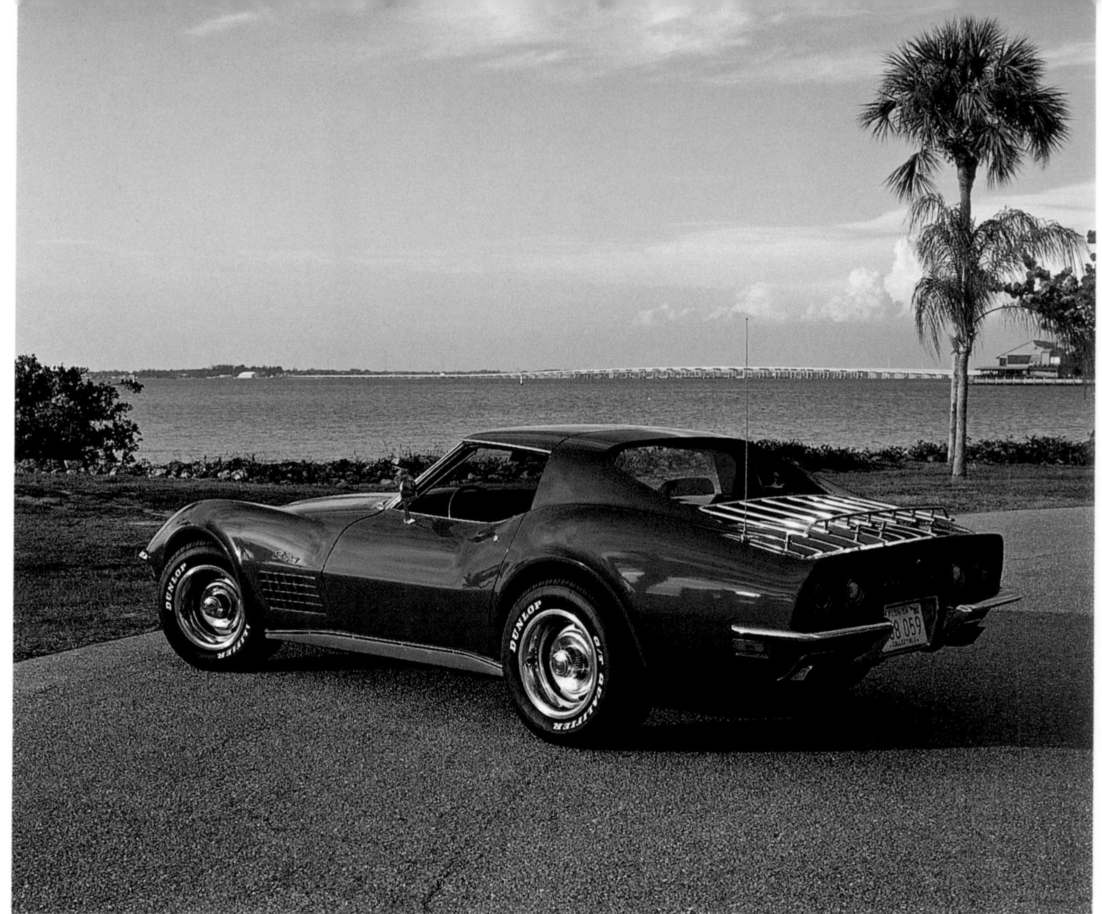

Corvettes built from 1970 to 1973 featured rectangular exhaust outlets, as opposed to the rounded units used in 1968–69. This 1972 coupe represents the last of the breed with chrome front bumpers. The luggage rack was a popular dealer-installed option. Standard power comes from the 200-horsepower 350 small-block.

As for the rest of the 1968–72 drivetrain, the plot wasn't nearly as thick. Optional transmissions for 1968 rolled over from 1967 with one exception. The obsolete two-speed Powerglide automatic, RPO M35, was finally superseded by Chevrolet's excellent three-speed Turbo Hydra-Matic, which had first appeared in 1965. The M40 Turbo Hydra-Matic was made available behind the 1968 Corvette's base 327 as well as the two hydraulic-lifter 427s, the L-36 and L-68. The M35 option in 1967 was priced at $194.35. The M40 in 1968 cost $226.45.

As in 1967, the L-79 small-block was only offered with a four-speed stick, as were the mechanically cammed L-71 and L-88 brutes. Three Muncie four-speeds were again listed: along with the M21 close-ratio (with its 2.20:1 low gear), there was the M20 wide-ratio (2.52:1 low) box and the bullet-proof M22 "Rock Crusher." Both the M20 and M21 were priced at $184.35 in 1968, and either could've been bolted up to the L-79 327, L-36 427, or L-68 427. As mentioned, L-71 installations were limited to the M21, while the M22 was mated only to the L-88, and vice-versa.

Those last two arrangements changed in 1969 when Chevrolet made the tough Turbo Hydra-Matic available behind the two solid-lifter 427s, and not a moment too soon in some minds. "The Turbo Hydro is the best thing that's happened to big-engined Corvettes since high-octane gas," wrote *Hot Rod*'s Steve Kelly. "Those who can overcome the four-speed mystique are in for a surprise" claimed *Car Life*'s Corvette fans. "The Turbo Hydra-Matic fitted to the high-performance 427s is magnificent. It slips from gear to gear in traffic without so much as a nudge. Power tightens the shifts into a series of iron hands, strong enough to light the tires at every change."

When ordered with the base 350 that year, the M40 option was priced at $221.80. It cost $290.40 when mated to the L-71 or L-88. "In the mild engine, the M40 was set to shift up quickly," continued *Car Life*'s July 1969 L-88/automatic review. "In the wild engines, the transmission stays in the lower gear until the driver lifts his foot, right up to redline." Availability of the T.H. automatic continued for the 454 big-blocks, both the LS-5 and LS-6. But it never made it into the LT-1 small-block's realm.

Bringing up the rear in 1968 was the G81 Positraction differential in most cases. Priced at $46.35, the G81 axle was a mandatory extra-cost choice behind all engine/trans combos save for the manual-shifted 327s. Positraction truly was optional for those latter combinations, which came standard with an open differential. The same situation carried over into 1969 before the obvious conclusion was finally reached: Positraction represented the only way to take off. Mandated or not, RPO G81 installations had been on the rise throughout the 1960s. In 1963 the Positraction percentage was 81.6. It was 88.5 in 1967, 94.5 in 1968, and 95.4 in 1969. That figure became 100 percent in 1970 when "posi" gears were made standard equipment on all Corvettes regardless of engine or trannie.

A similar situation occurred involving the third-generation Corvette's standard transmission. Three-speed sticks were for wimps. Real men (or women) demanded four on the floor, and had done so in ever-increasing numbers every year since Chevrolet first offered an optional four-speed to Corvette buyers in 1957. Three-speed Corvettes that year made up 67.5 percent of the mix, automatics 22, four-gears only 10.5. In 1958 the breakdown was 43.1 percent three-speeds, 34.5 fours. Four-speeds then gained the majority the following year, 43.2 percent to 37.4. By 1961, three-speeds were making up only 22.6 percent of the production run. That figure fell to 4.3 in 1963. A mere 1.9 percent of the market stuck with the standard gearbox in 1967, followed by 1.1 percent in 1968.

By this point many Chevrolet dealers were shying away from the rarely made requests for a base three-speed model in fear of being stuck themselves should the buyer back out of the deal. Such requests were answered only 0.6 percent of the time in 1969. Of the record 38,762 Corvettes built that year, a mere 252 hit the streets with three-speeds. Not enough was enough.

In 1970 the M20 wide-ratio four-speed transmission joined the Positraction rear axle on the Corvette's standard equipment list as the three-speed was finally shelved next to the old Powerglide automatic. Both the close-ratio M21 manual box and the Turbo Hydra-Matic automatic could've been ordered in place of the M20 at no extra cost. Yet another former option, tinted glass all around, also was tossed in as part of the standard deal in 1970.

Of course anyone who thought this new deal was a deal had another thing coming. Before 1970, Corvette buyers got what they paid for. After 1970, they paid for what they got. Adding equipment that previously cost extra into the standard package meant simply that Chevrolet had to ask more for that package. After increasing only 2.5 percent from 1968 to 1969, the Corvette coupe's base price jumped 8.6 percent in 1970. And with that jump, the 1970 coupe became the first Corvette to wear a $5,000 standard sticker. The actual figure was $5,192. After coming in at $4,849 in 1970, the Corvette convertible too reached the five-grand plateau in 1971. Its base price that year was $5,259.

John DeLorean and crew at Chevrolet couldn't be blamed for these price hikes. There was nothing personal involved, it was simply good business. Corvette demand was as high as ever as the 1970s dawned. Why not keep charging customers more and more until someone said stop? Buyers proved each year that they wanted more out of their Corvette and they were willing to pay whatever "more" cost. Thus the reasoning behind the addition of more and more standard features. Although many among the sport-conscious press cringed at the direction the third-generation Corvette was taking, it was clear to Chevy execs that adding toys was the best way to go. And who cared if those toys raised the bottom line by leaps and bounds?

Demand for comfort and convenience items like air conditioning, power brakes and steering, and automatic transmission skyrocketed in the early 1970s. This in turn meant that fewer and fewer Corvettes sold were going for anywhere close to those five-grand base stickers. The 454 coupe *Road & Track* tested in 1970 carried a $6,773 price tag. And with a full load of extras, it also carried 3,740 pounds, 47 percent of which rested lightly on the rear wheels. Little wonder that this 390-horsepower Turbo Hydra-Matic Corvette needed 15 seconds to reach the far end of the quarter-mile. And its nose-heavy, luxury-liner nature left few doubts as to what conclusions *R&T*'s critics would make. "The 7.4-liter automatic Corvette was one of the better Corvettes we've driven lately," they began, "but its great weight and incompetence on any but the smoothest roads keep it from being an outstanding GT or sports car."

Maybe so. But by then America's only sports car was well on its way to becoming every bit as much a luxury GT as it was a performance machine. And as horsepower waned further after 1972, the Corvette's softer side grew even more apparent.

PUTTING THE *BIG* IN BIG-BLOCK

Legends Labeled L-88, ZL-1 and LS-6

Not until the arrival of the technologically advanced ZR-1 in 1990 would Corvette drivers find themselves flexing their muscles as strongly as they did during the Shark years. Yet even with dual overhead cams, four valves per cylinder and microprocessor-controlled fuel injection, the 375-horsepower LT5 V-8 could still "only" motivate the first ZR-1s through the quarter-mile in 13 seconds plus a few tenths. Mind you, that much awesome speed was certainly nothing to sneeze at. Nor were the 405 horses unleashed by some extra headwork performed on the high-tech LT5 in 1993. Nonetheless, neither the 375- nor 405-horsepower ZR-1 could claim the crown of the quickest Vette yet.

That honor still belongs to the big-block Corvettes of yore, those fire-breathing, gas-gulping, tire-torturing monster rats that only could have roamed the earth in the days before catalytic converters, 5-mile-per-hour bumpers, and corporate-average-fuel-economy ratings. These beastly rodents only survived for 10 years, which is actually stretching it when you consider that the "smog motor" examples in 1972, 1973, and 1974 were mere shadows of their former selves. The pre-1972 persona was another story entirely. In those days, rat-motored Corvettes ran at the head of the pack with Detroit's most powerful performance machines. This was a direct result of Zora Duntov's willingness to push the outside of Chevrolet's existing performance envelope as far as it would go, even if that meant leading the Corvette away from the world-class sports car ideal he reportedly preferred.

"It is known that Duntov is a great exponent of small-displacement, high-revving engines, and it would seem logical that he would be pushing for the manufacture of smaller, lighter Corvettes powered by the zappy, exciting 302 ci Z/28 engine," explained a 1969 *Car and Driver* report. "But here Duntov faces a difficult personal choice. Because he rightfully believes that his Corvette should represent the pinnacle of Chevrolet engineering, he cannot bring himself to accept producing his car with anything less than the biggest, most powerful engine in the Chevrolet lineup. He feels, with some justification, that it would be absurd to market a 305- or 350-ci Corvette as the top performance car in the division when a customer could buy a Chevelle or Chevy II with a much larger and more powerful engine. Therefore he consents to his once-nimble machine being made bulkier and bulkier by the year."

Compared to the compact, lightweight, all-aluminum LT5, the bulky, cranky, iron-block Mk IV V-8s of the 1960s and 1970s were decidedly low-tech, what with their all-or-nothing carburetors and those conventional pushrods typically operating 16 valves. But relatively speaking, all things are not always equal. Sure, you can call the Mk IV a yeoman powerplant from today's perspective. However, we hope you did so with a smile, mister, 30 years ago if you were driving a big-block musclecar from Ford or Chrysler. Be it 426 Hemi or Boss 429, you still would've been left behind wearing a sheepish grin if you dared take on the hottest of the Mk IV Corvettes.

Zora Duntov rolled out the first race-ready L-88 Corvette in 1967. This L-88, one of 20 built that year, is possibly the first of that run. Notice the unique "L-88" decal on the scoop—no other L-88 was known to have special exterior identification. Racing exhausts are also included here.

Special identification is also found beneath the hood of this particular 1967 L-88 Corvette. Notice the road draft tube (black fitting exiting valve cover just behind "L/88" decal)—smog controls didn't "come into vogue" nationally until 1968. L-88s built for 1967 were totally devoid of emissions hardware.

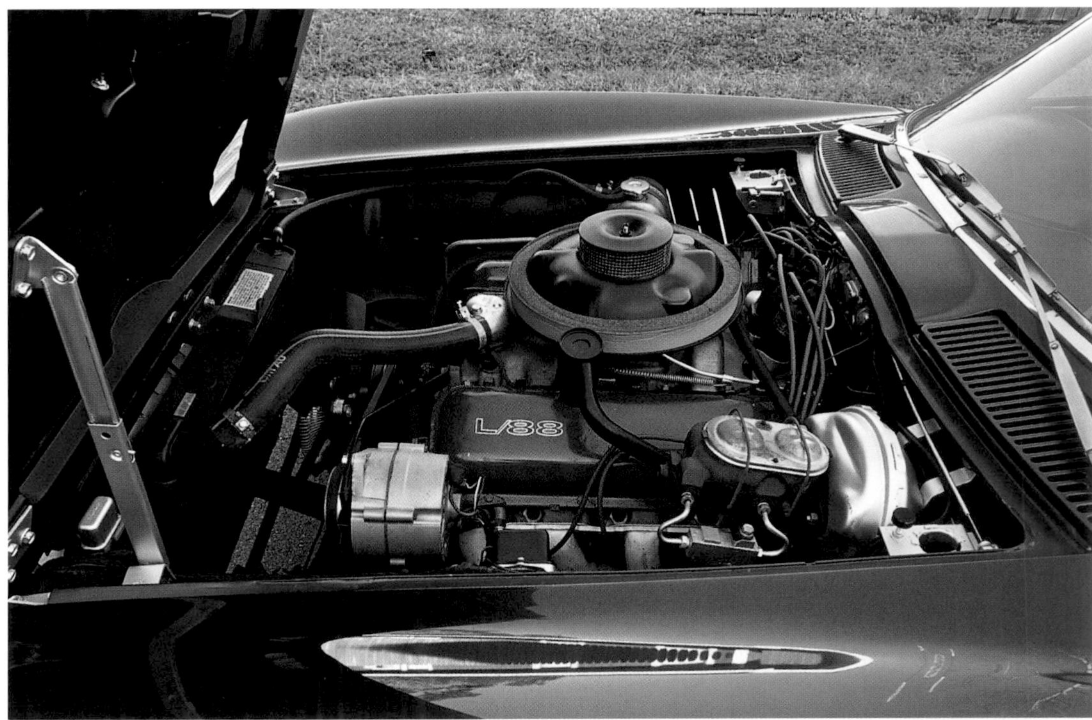

In 1966 a *Car and Driver* road test posted an incredible 12.8-second E.T. for the first 427 Vette. Any faster than that in a street car and you would be . . . well, you probably would be fibbing because street cars simply do not run that fast. Not with full exhausts, standard tires, and 3,500 pounds of body, engine, frame, heater, radio, and so on.

The key term here is *street car*. When Zora was stretching the envelope 30 years ago he had no qualms about putting what were basically racing machines on the street. "Basically" racing machines? No ifs, ands, or buts about it, the legendary L-88 and ZL-1 Corvettes were never intended to simply relocate drivers or passengers from point A to B. Don't let those compliant air pumps used in 1968 and 1969 fool you. The aluminum-head L-88 427 and its all-aluminum ZL-1 brother were built only to run fast. Fast at the track.

That's undoubtedly where all of the first L-88s built in 1967 ended up. Nowhere were these cars promoted to the general public for general use. Nor were they legal for such use due to the fact that they were totally devoid of even the simplest of emission-control devices. And considering that only 20 were sold, it's a fair bet that they were claimed by "insiders" who were well aware of the L-88's intentions, as well as Duntov's. He was counting on the L-88s to promote the Corvette image in sanctioned competition, and he wanted serious racers—customers able to make the right modifications needed to maximize this exotic big-block's full potential—to be the ones doing the taking.

Efforts to guarantee the latter included downplaying the L-88's image, both on paper and in actual physical presence. Outwardly, the first L-88 Corvette looked like any other big-block Sting Ray built in 1967. Save for the distinctive hood (that no one could miss) added the following year, much the same could be said for the 1968 and 1969 L-88s. No specific exterior identification was ever added, this of course to help keep Duntov's not-so-little secret a secret.

"One of the factory's ways to discourage casual buying of L-88s is not to supply a little badge on the fender for the unfortunate many to see and envy," explained *Car Life*'s snitches later in 1969. "The L-88 is the only performance car on the American market we can think of without one."

Another factory ploy involved advertised output. According to Chevrolet paperwork, the L-88 produced 430 horsepower at 5,200 rpm. This claim wasn't necessarily a lie, it just didn't tell the whole story. L-88 427s were delivered from the factory with standard Mk IV exhaust manifolds dumping into a standard dual exhaust system. Duntov and crew knew full well that the first thing a racer would do was deep-six the whole works in favor of wide-open headers. Most in the know agreed that this typical modification alone instantly freed up at least 100 horses. As Chevrolet engineer Fred Frincke later told it, early dyno tests of an L-88 fitted with free-breathing tube headers in place of those stock cast-iron manifolds resulted in a much more realistic figure, as much as 550 horsepower.

Clearly Chevy's promotional pencil-pushers could've never advertised that many horses and not drawn the ire of watchdogs both inside and out of GM. Look what happened when Chevrolet tried to print 450-horsepower decals for the L-72 427 in 1966. That number was erased and 425 was written in before the L-72 was released, apparently because that original label would have offended sensibilities. Or safety crusaders.

Nor did Duntov want such big, bold numbers attracting the attention of Walter Mitty types, they with too many dollars and too few brains. The hope was that Walter and friends would overlook the L-88—it with its "mere" 430 horses—and go for the L-71 with its lineup-leading 435-horsepower decal.

So what was the truth? Chevrolet continued publishing that 430-horsepower figure in 1968 and 1969 even after various upgrades were made. Along with beefier connecting rods, changes in 1968 included a new standard cam (various other over-the-counter bumpsticks were listed in 1968 and 1969) and the midyear addition of Chevy's famed open-chamber heads. Revised cam specs were 347 degrees duration on the intake side, 364 on the exhaust, with 136 degrees of overlap. Lift was 0.5586-inch intake, 0.580 exhaust. L-88 torque output in 1968 was listed as 485 ft-lb at 4,000 rpm. In 1969 it was 450 ft-lb at 4,400 rpm.

Twenty-three years later, *Corvette Fever* published dynamometer test results for a correctly restored/rebuilt L-88. At 4,400 rpm, it was churning out 502 ft-lb of torque. Maximum torque was actually 513 ft-lb at 4,200 turns. As for horsepower, at 5,200 revs the score actually read 489. But that wasn't all. What Chevrolet's little white lies also failed to mention was that 5,200 wasn't the power peak. According to *Corvette Fever*'s 1992 test, the L-88's true maximum output of 514 horses arrived at 6,200 revolutions.

Zora Duntov and Denny Davis keep a watchful eye on an early L-88 427 during dyno testing in May 1966. *Chevrolet Motor Division*

Even a blind man could see that these numbers ran well beyond the realm of anything considered a "street car." Yet that still didn't stop some armchair racers dead set on taking an L-88 to the streets. Sales of Chevrolet's wildest Corvette jumped considerably once word got out. Production of L-88s—both coupes and convertibles—reached 80 in 1968. Another 116 arrived in 1969, including 17 equipped with Turbo Hydra-Matic automatics instead of four-speeds

How many of these actually went from the delivery truck directly to the track? Certainly not all. Unlike the emissions-illegal 1967 L-88, the 1968 and 1969 renditions were fitted with full smog controls, including a PCV valve and Chevrolet's Air Injection Reaction system. Adding the AIR air pump simply made it too easy for Mr. Mitty to try street racing an L-88. Some undoubtedly even tried driving one down to the store. How many of these actually made it to point B? Certainly not all.

Car Life explained the situation in 1969. "Duntov asked that somebody try to get his message across: The L-88 is being bought by

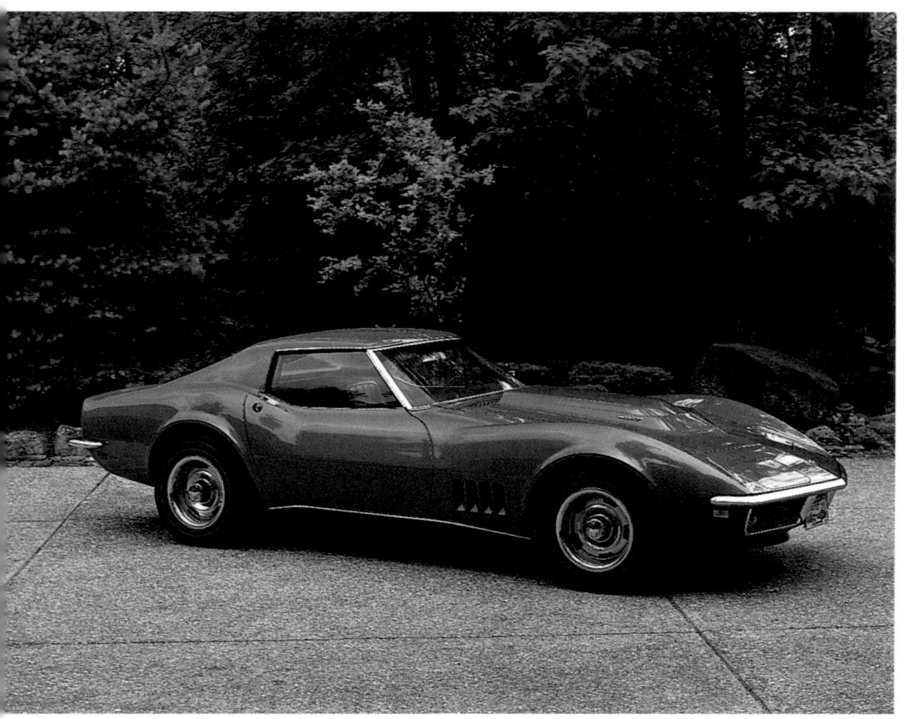

While there was no special exterior badging, L-88 Corvettes built in 1968 and 1969 couldn't be missed with their functional air-induction hoods. Only 80 L-88s were built in 1968, including this coupe. Another 116 followed in 1969. *Tom Glatch*

people who don't know what it is and don't know or care to use it properly. They hear it's the hot thing to have, and that the factory doesn't put L-88 on the order blank, so they order one." They also ordered more than their fair share of headaches. An L-88 Corvette truly was "the hot thing to have," in more ways than one.

If a speed freak wanted to drive one of these unforgiving big-blocks in everyday traffic, it was his prerogative. After all, it was once a free country, right? Free, too, for the foolish. "The L-88, even in showroom form, is closer to being a racer than a cruiser," wrote *Hot Rod*'s Steve Kelly, "and it would seem almost sacrilegious to see an L-88 'Vette serving duty as a transportation machine only." It also would seem almost stupid considering that, as Chevrolet paperwork officially explained, the L-88 was clearly "not intended for street use." As if Chevy had to tell us.

From top to bottom, this purpose-built, off-road powerplant was good to go, and go like no Corvette V-8 ever had before. L-88 roots traced back to 1965 when engineers Frincke, Cal Wade, and Denny Davis began putting together a collection of race-ready big-block parts. These parts then went together to form the foundation for a competition-legal production Corvette that Duntov hoped would pick up where his ill-fated Grand Sports left off. Although Chevrolet wasn't supposed to be in racing—the GM upper office edict that had squelched the Grand Sport project early in 1963 had reportedly decided all that—Zora wasn't about to give up without a fight. He had an L-88 427 running on a dyno as early as October 1965, and he hoped to release it as a Corvette option in 1966.

By then rumors among the press were already doing their own running, rampant-style. *Sports Car Graphic*'s Jerry Titus—one of Duntov's favorite journalists—was among the first to report news of the L-88's impending arrival in *SCG*'s March 1965 issue. "Among the options that will make the [Corvette] competitive is a new four-speed gearbox designed to handle a 'prodified' [read: homologated] version of the [Mk IV] engine," wrote Titus. "An estimated 470 horsepower is expected [for this engine] with application of allowable SCCA modifications." The transmission Titus referred to was the M22 Rock Crusher, which got its nickname from the noises emitted by its big, burly, nearly straight-cut gears. This bulletproof box made it into production as an extra-heavy-duty option in 1966, and would remain the only real racer's choice behind the Corvette's most brutal V-8s up through 1972.

Duntov did file L-88 homologation papers with the Sports Car Club of America and the Federation International de L'Automobile (FIA, the governing body of international racing) in late 1965. And various L-88 components did make it into Roger Penske's hands in 1966. However, RPO L-88 wasn't officially released until early 1967. Originally priced at $947.90, the L-88 427 was complemented by an impressive array of mandatory "options" that ran the bill up even higher. Along with the M22 four-speed, L-88 accompaniment included the K66 transistorized ignition, J56 power-assisted metallic brakes, F41 heavy-duty suspension, and G81 Positraction axle.

Most impressive, though, was the L-88 itself. Beginning with the already stout Mk IV cylinder block with its four-bolt main bearing caps, this competition-bred 427 was fitted with a special crankshaft forged out of 5140 alloy steel, cross-drilled for ample lubrication and tuftrided for hardness. Shot-peened, magnafluxed connecting rods were attached to that crank. At the business ends of those rods were

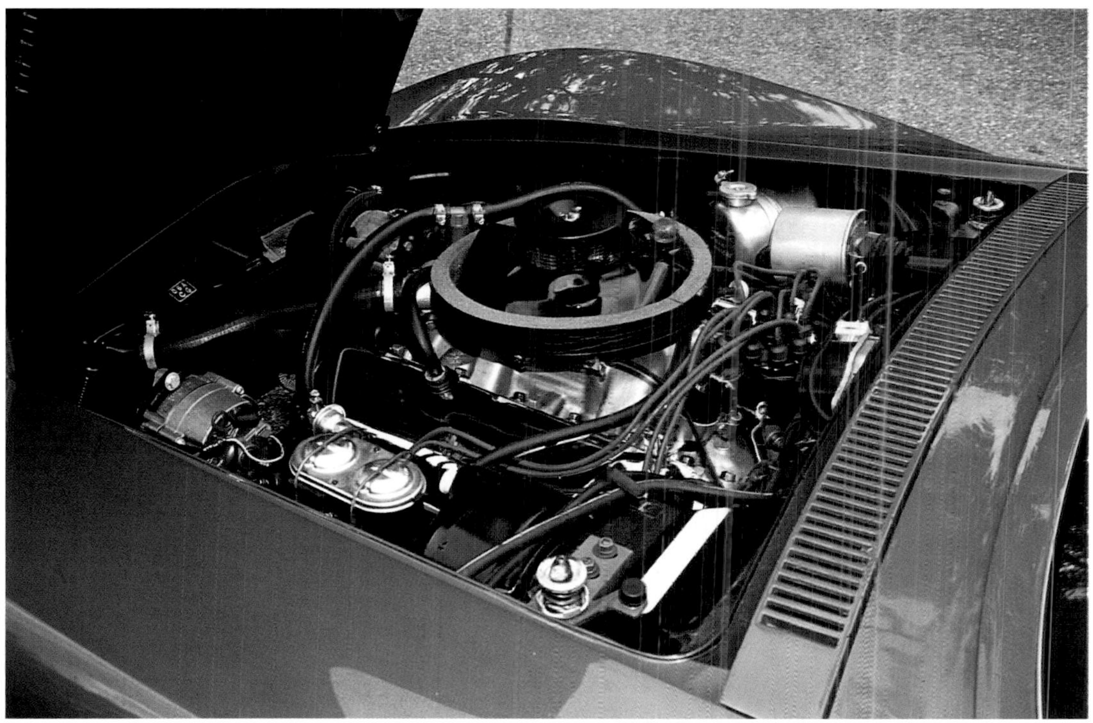

Compare this L-88 view to the 1967 example. Aluminum-head L-88 427s in 1968 and 1969 were fitted with typical emissions controls, which included the air pump hiding here just behind the upper radiator hose. Emissions choked or not, L-88 output remained grossly underrated at 430 horsepower for all three years. *Tom Glatch*

eight forged-aluminum pop-up pistons that could almost split atoms at the resulting 12.5:1 compression ratio. Topping off the L-88's iron block was a pair of weight-saving aluminum heads fitted with large valves: 2.19-inches on the intake side, 1.84 on the exhaust.

Supplying fuel/air to this righteous rat was a huge 850-cubic-feet-per-minute Holley four-barrel. The special high-rise aluminum intake below that carb had its internal partition machined down to create an open plenum for maximum high-rpm performance. Initial specs for Denny Davis' radical solid-lifter cam listed lift at 0.5365 inch for the intake valve, 0.5560 for the exhaust. Duration was 337 degrees intake, 340 exhaust. Thickened 7/16-inch pushrods with hardened ends delivered that lift to those big valves through "long-slot" stamped steel rocker arms rocking on heat-treated, hardened ball-studs. Heavy-duty valve springs were held in place by reinforced retainers and locks.

On the L-88's breathing end, a unique "air cleaner" (using the term very loosely) fit into ductwork in the hood's underside. That duct ran back to the hood's trailing edge where it drew in cooler, denser air from the high-pressure area at the base of the windshield. The L-88s of 1967–69 (along with the 1969 ZL-1) were the only Corvettes fitted with a functional air-induction hood prior to the 1973 introduction of a similar standard-equipment design. And thanks to the extra clearance supplied by that big, bulging rear-facing hood scoop, the L-88 and ZL-1 were the only big-block Corvettes built after 1967 that weren't required to switch over to the low-rise intake manifold necessitated by the Shark body's low hoodline.

Between the L-88 and M22 was an appropriate heavy-duty clutch mated to a small 12.75-inch-diameter flywheel, the latter added in the best interests of increasing rpm potential by reducing reciprocating mass. Cooling came by way of a Harrison heavy-duty cross-flow radiator. Cooling actually came barely by way of this aluminum radiator due to the fact that it wasn't fitted with a fan shroud to help maximize efficiency whenever the tach needle was low to the left. On its own, that missing shroud represented warning enough from the factory against putting the L-88 to use on the street.

At a glance, the aluminum-head 427's off-road status was especially evident during its first year in production. Even if you weren't aware of the L-88's sky-high compression or didn't understand that a big-block Corvette really, really needed that shroud to keep things cool at low rpm, you couldn't miss the "chicken-wire" screen atop the carburetor or that road-draft

The most exotic Corvette ever unleashed "on the street" was the 1969 ZL-1. The all-aluminum 427 V-8 lurking beneath that big ZL-2 hood was also jokingly rated at 430 horsepower.

tube exiting the driver-side valve cover in place of the environmentally correct positive crankcase ventilation system. As you might guess, most race cars avoid inhibiting airflow into the engine with a conventional filter. And they don't need a fan, let alone a shroud, since they rarely get stuck in traffic. Nor are they required to meet federally mandated emissions standards, thus the explanation for the 1967 L-88's inconsiderate venting of crankcase vapors directly into the atmosphere via that draft tube.

Also inconsiderate was the 1967 L-88's interior accommodations. RPO C48, the heater-defroster delete credit offered to Sting Ray buyers from 1963 to 1967, was included as part of the original L-88 deal. Radios were unavailable as well. Same for all other extra-cost creature comforts. The only addition made inside was a label stuck onto the console. It read, "Warning: vehicle must operate on a fuel having a minimum of 103 research octane and 95 motor octane or engine damage may result." "Under no circumstances should regular gasoline be used," reiterated an L-88's delivery paperwork.

Fouling the air, battling that inherent hot temper, paying extra for jet fuel, and cruising without tunes weren't the only hurdles put before those brave souls who dared try to domesticate the wild and wooly L-88. Their task proved daunting enough immediately after turning the key. A lot of fancy footwork followed during cold starts due to the absence of a choke. And even when Chevrolet's retrofit choke kit was added to that enormous four-barrel, the L-88 427 still didn't like to cooperate as its cavernous intake and lumpy, loping cam totally sacrificed low-rpm operation for all-out high-rev usage. Idle speed was a teeth-chattering 1,000 rpm. Automatic L-88s in 1969 were commonly set to idle at two-grand, making shifts out of park a surprising experience unless both feet weren't firmly squashing the brake pedal.

Duntov brought a collection of wild Corvettes to 1969 press leads, including this white ZL-1 convertible. Fitted with fender flares and extra-wide wheels, this road rocket gave *Motor Trend*'s Eric Dalhquist (driving here) the ride of his life. Quarter-mile times were about 11-seconds flat. *Used with permission of EMAP/Petersen Publishing,* Motor Trend *magazine*

The sum of these parts added up to the wildest V-8 ever put on the street—the ZL-1 427. Notice the big Holley double-pumper, the open-plenum intake, and those open-chamber heads with their huge, round exhaust ports. *Chevrolet Motor Division*

All this and some jet-setters still didn't get the picture.

"The L-88 is supposed to be a competition car," explained *Car Life*'s 1969 review of five of the six (the L-89/L-71 was tested, the ZL-1 wasn't) 427 Corvettes offered that year. "Racers remove everything they don't need. Duntov saves them as much trouble as he can by not putting on anything that competition or the government don't require. There's no radiator shroud, because it isn't needed at high speed."

Of course Duntov's engineers easily could have bolted up a typical shroud to the L-88's Harrison radiator—if, that is, they gave a spit about enhancing low-speed operation. As you already know, they didn't. And even when street-wise owners turned the wrench themselves, the L-88's high-compression furnaces still kept things too hot to handle. "The owner of a rental fleet in St. Louis has a shop full of L-88s, which overheat constantly in traffic," continued *Car Life*. "He wishes Duntov would do something. Duntov wishes people wouldn't buy racing cars for use in cities."

The ZL-1's aluminum block was cast with extra material on the bottom end to help hold up like its cast-iron brethren. Those are iron liners in the cylinder bores. Notice the extra "ears" atop each cylinder bank deck. They were added specially to the aluminum casting and drilled for an extra pair of cylinder head bolts to tighten the grip between block and head. *Chevrolet Motor Division*

Although many similarities did exist, simply calling the ZL-1 427 an L-88 with a block made of aluminum instead of iron is not correct. The block itself was an entirely different animal as it had to be specially beefed-up to make up for its less-durable aluminum construction. Behind the 1969 ZL-1 here is a 1967 L-88.

Zora himself was the first to admit that street performance was by no means the L-88 Corvette's forte, especially so in pure-stock form with those spoil-sport cast-iron exhausts. "The horsepower ratings tell the story," added *Car Life*. "Camshafts in the higher rated L-71 and L-89 are designed to give maximum power through the stock exhaust manifolds and mufflers. The L-88 cam is designed to give maximum power, period. It won't give all it has got unless, and until, it has tuned exhaust headers blasting unmuffled into the air."

With socially acceptable mufflers and its optional removable top in place, the auto-trans L-88 convertible *Car Life* tested in 1969 tripped the lights in 14.10 seconds at 106.9 miles per hour, this with a less-than-desirable 3.36:1 rear axle. But while those economy-minded gears sacrificed the car's off-the-line abilities, they naturally assisted things on the top end. At a rod-knocking 6,800 rpm, the L-88's maximum velocity registered at 151 miles per hour.

Hot Rod's Steve Kelly reported better dragstrip results with the same L-88 convertible. He also noted even more potential. "The tall gear in back made 13.56 seconds at 111 miles per hour seem respectable," wrote Kelly in *HRM*'s April 1969 issue. "But we know it's two seconds from where it should be."

The 1969 L-88 was right at the top in another performance category. The weight reduction up front—created by adding those aluminum heads—working in concert with the mandatory heavy-duty F41 suspension, made the L-88 Corvette, in Kelly's words, "the best-handling car built in this country." This was "one U.S. car that'll compete with any $10,000 European, and do it with less money involved," he concluded.

Of course what he failed to mention was that much the same could be said about the L-89 Corvette, as it also featured lightweight aluminum heads and the heavyweight F41 underpinnings. And at $832.15, the L-89 option meant even less money was involved. The tag for RPO L-88 in 1969 was $1,032.15. Furthermore, the 435-horse L-89 Corvette was a street car, it could make it down to the store. And back. In fast enough fashion to suit any card-carrying Walter Mitty club member to a T. The choice was yours. The "L-88 had more potential, but the buyer must extract it for himself," began *Car Life*'s conclusion. "The L-89 was designed to be the hottest Corvette in street trim."

There are those words again. In *street trim* the hottest Corvette of all time was the aforementioned 12.8-second L-72 427 of 1966. The hottest third-generation Corvette? The bodacious tri-carb L-71 and its low-weight, high-priced L-89 derivative of 1968 and 1969 commonly won magazine road test derbies with elapsed times running well into the 13-second range. Yikes.

Take away that "street" qualification and the numbers became even more scary. The L-88, of course, would have beaten everything in sight had Chevrolet public relations people been more willing to show it off. Not only did they not make a test vehicle available to the press until 1969, they also went out of their way to limit results—remember the automatic trans and 3.36:1 gears? Even with its restrictive exhausts, a four-speed L-88 (Turbo Hydra-Matic cars were limited to 2.73:1, 3.08:1, or 3.36:1 differentials only) undoubtedly would have eclipsed the 1966 L-72's record with only a switch to the 4.11:1 optional axle. The stump-pulling 4.56:1 cogs would have salted away the deal without question.

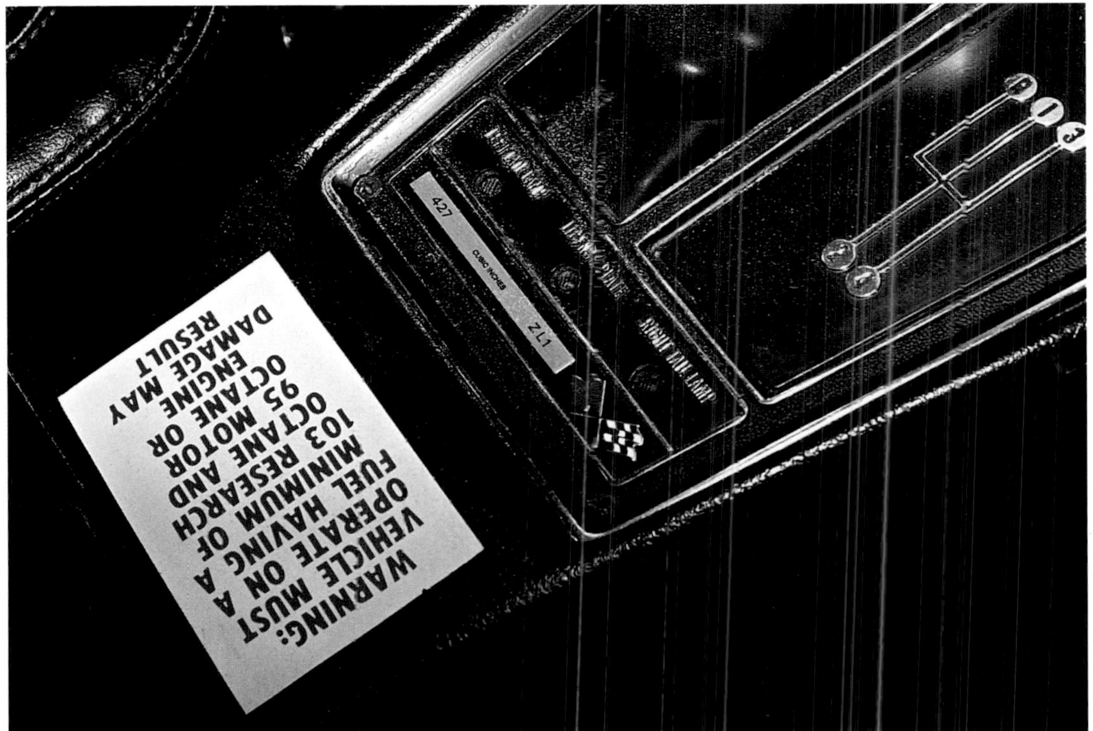

A driver was given fair warning if he dared take a ZL-1 to the streets in 1969. Even if you missed the small console tag, you couldn't help but read the red letters, upside-down or otherwise.

And to think the L-88 still didn't represent the tip of the thermometer in 1969. The hottest Corvette that year—the hottest Corvette to ever make an RPO list, period—was the incredible ZL-1. Why stop there? Never before or since has an American automaker dared deliver so much raw power to the people. Yes, John Q. Public could have walked into his neighborhood Chevy dealership in 1969 and rolled out in a street-legal, emissions-controlled 427 Corvette able to break not simply into the 13-second bracket. Nor the 12. Breaking the sound barrier was more like it.

In July 1968, Zora Duntov and his merry band of speed merchants showed up at the 1969 new model press introduction with two sinister-looking Corvettes; both wearing the familiar ZL-2 air-induction hood already made famous by the L-88. Journalists on hand even figured they were looking at "just" another aluminum-head 427 beneath those bulging hoods because, unlike "regular-production" all-aluminum ZL-1 big-blocks, these test mule engines featured painted cylinder blocks. "All those guys at the 1969 Chevy preview thought it was an L-88," explained a December 1968 *Hot Rod* introduction of Chevrolet's "Better Mousetrap." "Forgot your pocket magnets, right guys?"

What they didn't forget was a big right foot.

Neither one of these mules could've been mistaken for street cars. One was a white convertible with huge, wide-open sidepipes below each door and imposing fender flares at all four corners housing super-fat Firestone treads. Set up by Zora himself, this car was equipped for road-racing duty. Behind its aluminum big-block was a Rock Crusher four-speed that delivered torque to relatively tall 3.70:1 gears out back. Even with those "road gears," this ZL-1 mule was rarin' to run from rest to however fast you wanted to go in a major hurry.

"The ZL-1 doesn't just accelerate, because the word 'accelerate' is inadequate for this car," wrote *Motor Trend*'s Eric Dahlquist after a ride in that great, white whale of a Corvette. "It tears its way through the air and across the black pavement like all the modern big-inch racing machines you have ever seen, the engine climbing the rev band in that leaping gait as the tires hunt for traction, find it, lose it again for a millisecond, then find it until they are locked in."

Once locked in, those racing Firestones propelled Duntov's white ZL-1 through the quarter in 12.1 seconds at 116 miles per hour. Dahlquist also mentioned roaring from 30 miles per hour to 145 (at 6,500 rpm) in what he estimated to be about 1,700 feet. "If the car had a higher gear, one of the engineers casually mentions, it

Tom Langdon and Gib Hufstader built this orange 1969 coupe to especially impress journalists at the 1969 new car introductions. It returned in slightly different form in 1970. The first year, it showcased a ZL-1 V-8. In 1970, it was powered by the LT-2, the 454-ci all-aluminum derivative of the ZL-1. With wide-open headers, slicks, and a high-stall Turbo Hydra-Matic, the car could bolt through the quarter-mile in nearly 10.5 seconds. *Gib Hufstader*

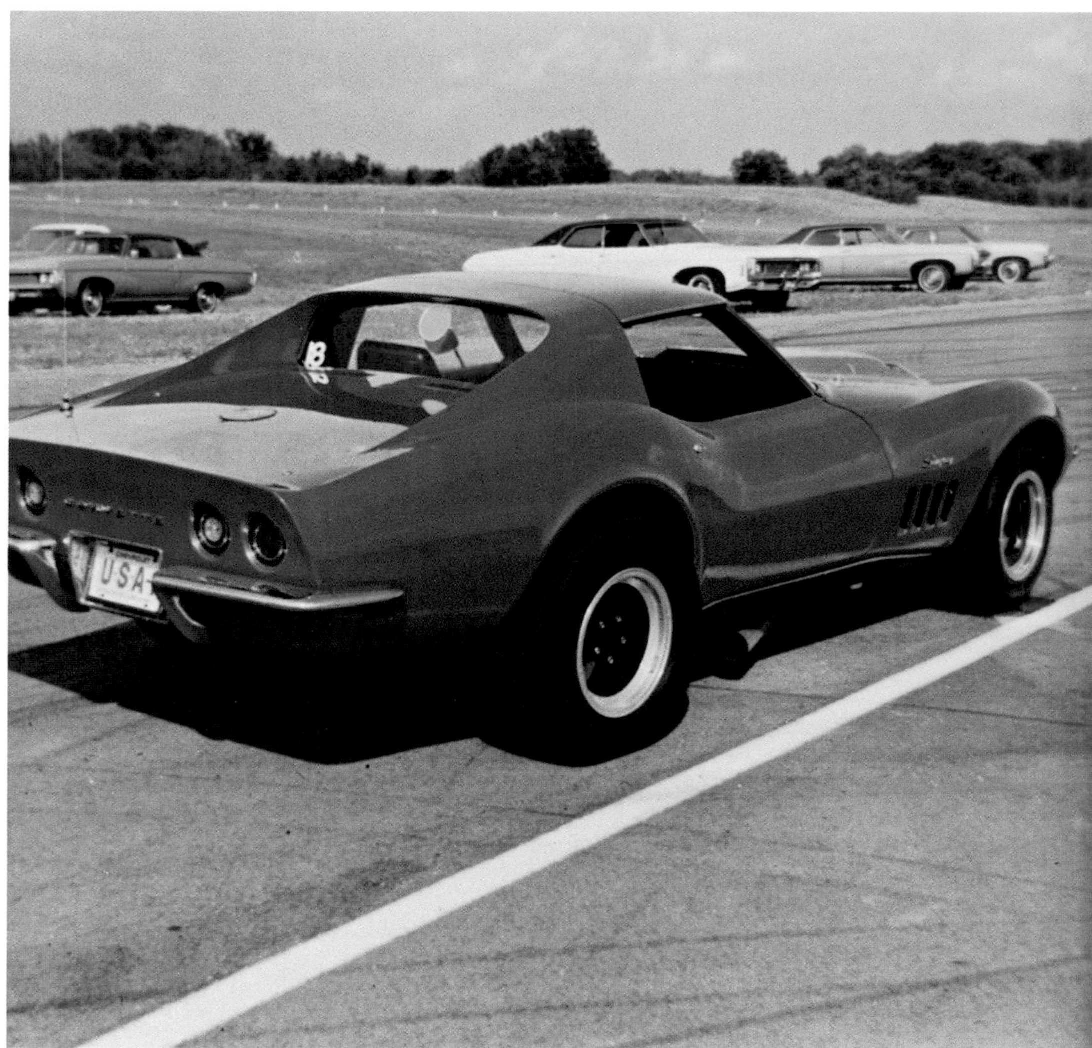

will bust 195, possibly 200," he added. A lower gear (higher numerically) would have easily translated into 11 seconds in the quarter mile. If not less.

Journalists themselves were invited to take the other mule's reins—and hang on for dear life. Created by developmental engineers Gib Hufstader and Tom Langdon, this flaming orange (contemporary magazine reports called it red) coupe was an entirely different animal. "Tom built the engine, I built the car," remembered Hufstader in 1999. "He got about 710 horsepower out of it. I took out all the steel body reinforcement and made the bumper out of fiberglass and chrome plated it, anything to help get the weight down."

Hufstader and Langdon's lightweight ZL-1 coupe featured headers, sidepipes, a special beefed-up, high-stall Turbo Hydra-Matic automatic, 4.88:1 dragstrip gears, and 9-inch racing slicks. Once in the hands of the press, the car's autobox allowed even the meekest, mild-mannered member of the fourth estate to run faster than a speeding bullet without even breaking a sweat. Or at least it felt that way.

"Twenty or 30 people were given the chance to drive this really high-performance car," said Hufstader. "They all had a great time." "It was a terrific machine," added Proving Grounds public relations man Bob Clift. "We all enjoyed driving it. That was back in the good ol' days. Zora used to keep us all excited back then."

Anyone strapped into that orange Corvette on that summer day in July 1968 came away from the experience ecstatic. Running 11-flat through the quarter-mile at about 127 miles per hour was as easy as stomping the go-pedal and

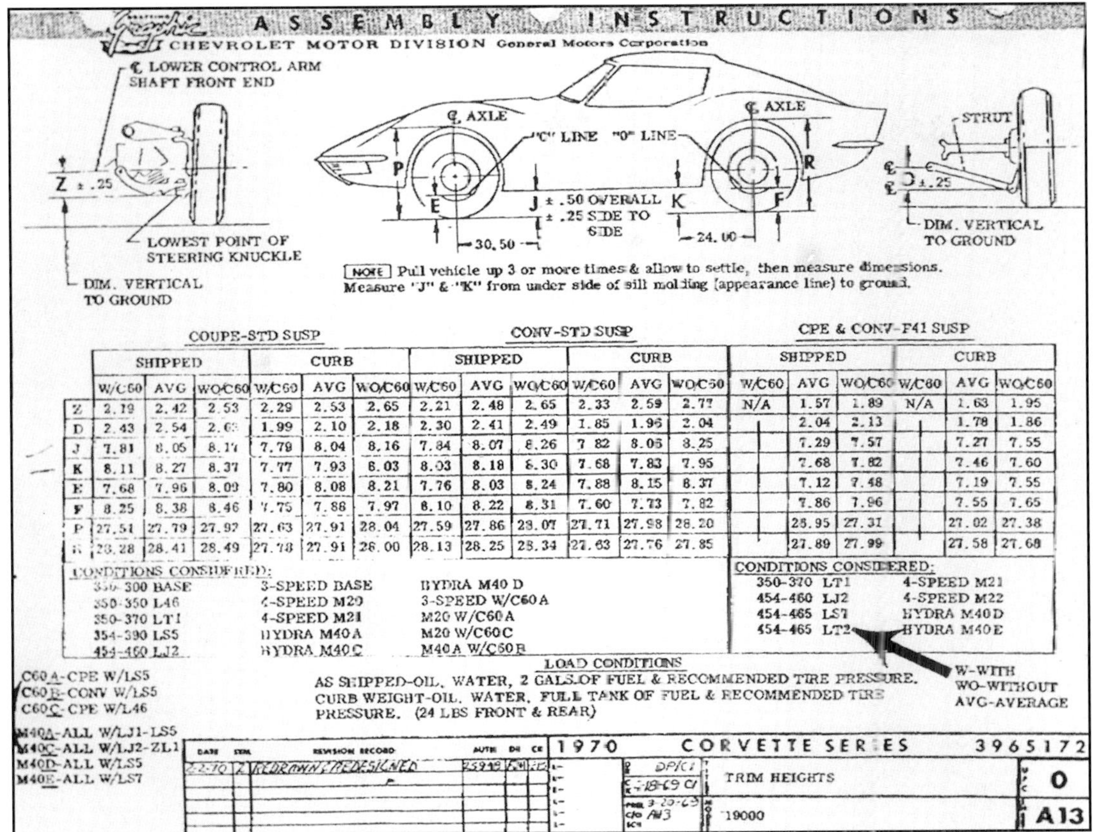

ASSEMBLY INSTRUCTIONS

CHEVROLET MOTOR DIVISION General Motors Corporation

NOTE Pull vehicle up 3 or more times & allow to settle, then measure dimensions. Measure "J" & "K" from under side of sill molding (appearance line) to ground.

	COUPE-STD SUSP						CONV-STD SUSP						CPE & CONV-F41 SUSP					
	SHIPPED			CURB			SHIPPED			CURB			SHIPPED			CURB		
	W/C60	AVG	WO/C60	W/C60	AVG	WO/C60	W/C60	AVG	WO/C60	W/C60	AVG	WO/C60	W/C60	AVG	WO/C60	W/C60	AVG	WO/C60
Z	2.19	2.42	2.53	2.29	2.53	2.65	2.21	2.48	2.65	2.33	2.59	2.77	N/A	1.57	1.89	N/A	1.63	1.95
D	2.43	2.54	2.6[illegible]	1.99	2.10	2.18	2.30	2.41	2.49	1.85	1.96	2.04		2.04	2.13		1.78	1.86
J	7.81	8.05	8.17	7.79	8.04	8.16	7.84	8.07	8.26	7.82	8.05	8.25		7.29	7.57		7.27	7.55
K	8.11	8.27	8.37	7.77	7.93	8.03	8.03	8.18	8.30	7.68	7.83	7.95		7.68	7.82		7.46	7.60
E	7.68	7.96	8.09	7.80	8.08	8.21	7.76	8.03	8.24	7.88	8.15	8.37		7.12	7.48		7.19	7.55
F	8.25	8.38	8.46	7.75	7.88	7.97	8.10	8.22	8.31	7.60	7.73	7.82		7.86	7.96		7.55	7.65
P	27.51	27.79	27.97	27.63	27.91	28.04	27.59	27.86	28.07	27.71	27.98	28.20		26.95	27.31		27.02	27.38
R	28.28	28.41	28.49	27.78	27.91	26.00	28.13	28.25	28.34	27.63	27.76	27.85		27.89	27.99		27.58	27.68

CONDITIONS CONSIDERED:
350-300 BASE, 350-350 L46, 350-370 LT1, 354-390 LS5, 454-460 LJ2
3-SPEED BASE, 4-SPEED M20, 4-SPEED M21, HYDRA M40A, HYDRA M40C
HYDRA M40 D, 3-SPEED W/C60A, M20 W/C60A, M20 W/C60C, M40A W/C60B

CONDITIONS CONSIDERED:
350-370 LT1, 454-460 LJ2, 454-465 LS7, 454-465 LT2
4-SPEED M21, 4-SPEED M22, HYDRA M40D, HYDRA M40E

C60A-CPE W/LS5
C60B-CONV W/LS5
C60C-CPE W/L46
M40A-ALL W/LJ1-LS5
M40C-ALL W/LJ2-ZL1
M40D-ALL W/LS5
M40E-ALL W/LS7

LOAD CONDITIONS
AS SHIPPED-OIL, WATER, 2 GALS.OF FUEL & RECOMMENDED TIRE PRESSURE.
CURB WEIGHT-OIL, WATER, FULL TANK OF FUEL & RECOMMENDED TIRE PRESSURE. (24 LBS FRONT & REAR)

W-WITH
WO-WITHOUT
AVG-AVERAGE

DATE | SYM. | REVISION RECORD | AUTH | DR | CK
2-2-70 | Z | REDRAWN & REDESIGNED | 25949

1970 CORVETTE SERIES 3965172
DP/C1
-18-69
3-20-69
AW3
TRIM HEIGHTS
19000
0
A13

This page from the 1970 Corvette assembly manual lists the LT-2, LS-7, and LJ-2 454s. The LT-2 was supposed to follow in the ZL-1's tracks, the LS-7 in the L-88's. The LJ-2 was intended to replace the triple-carb 427. An LJ-1 is also listed. Could this have been the 3x2 L-68's second coming? Or did the LJ-2 plan include aluminum heads, meaning it was meant to replace the L-89/ L-71? If so, then the LJ-1 may have been the iron-head tri-carb 454 version of the L-71 427.

pointing the high-rising hood in the right direction. Even quicker runs were posted by applying a little street-racer know-how. "We were revving it up to 6,000 [rpm] then dumping it into gear," recalled Clift with a chuckle. "It took off like a striped-ass ape." The best time slip of the day read 10.89 seconds at 130 miles per hour. But all that excitement almost ended up in a downer.

"They got the car back to the shop after [press day] and found many stress cracks where the flywheel attached to the crank," added Clift. "It probably would've come apart after a few more runs. As it was, we did 20 or 30 passes like that, banging the shifts into drive. If it had blown up, that wouldn't have been so great for a press introduction."

Though they nearly tortured it to death, that ZL-1 coupe showed most of those journalists the hottest time they'd ever had behind the wheel of an American automobile. Ten-eighty-nine wasn't just fast, it was ridiculous. Ridiculously easy. "The fact that almost anybody who knows how to drive could jump in and duplicate this run after run may be the most shattering aspect of all," concluded a *Motor Trend* report entitled "The 10-second Trip."

Altered by hallucinogens or not, why anyone in his right mind would want to tear across the pavement that quickly also begged the question of what type of maniac in 1969 would fall in line to buy a ZL-1 Corvette? "First, he will have a lot of money," answered Duntov 30 years ago. A potential customer would've probably needed to have a spare Cadillac lying around because, like its L-88 cousin, the ZL-1 was best (make that only) suited for off-road use. Beyond that, RPO ZL-1 alone cost $4,718.35. For another 70 bucks or so, John Q. could have ordered a standard 300-horsepower 350 small-block that year—and it would have arrived on Mr. Public's doorstep wrapped in a 1969 Corvette coupe. A ballpark bottom-line for the complete ZL-1 Corvette package neared $10,000.

While nine- or ten-grand is still not exactly chump-change today, it was some seriously mean green in 1969, especially for a car as narrow-focused as the ZL-1. Was it worth it? Eric Dahlquist thought so. Calling the car "the first

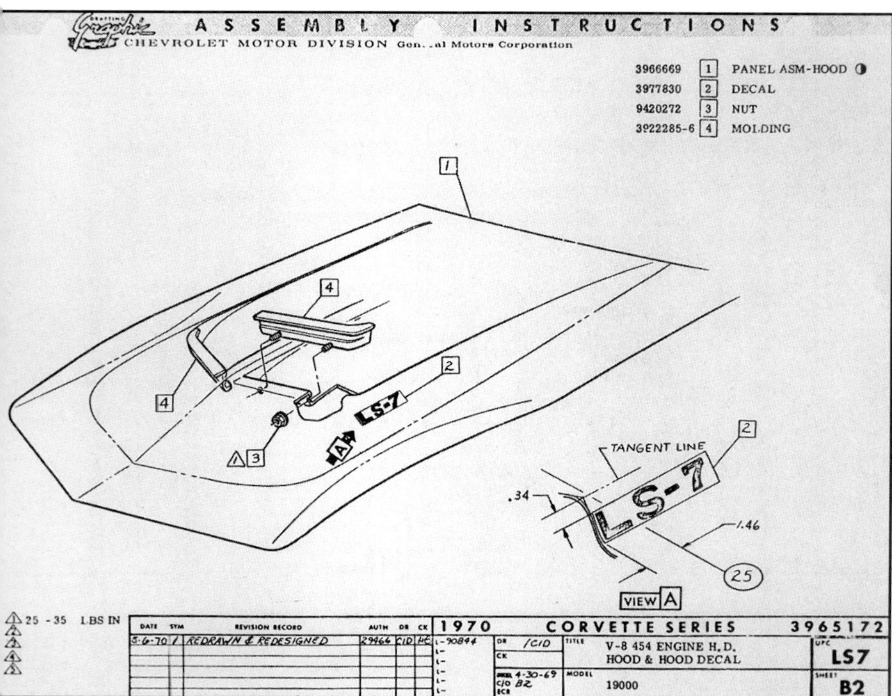

An assembly manual page was devoted to the LS-7 hood's special identification. While small-block fans were treated to a decal denoting the LT-1's presence, no production Corvette big-block (save for perhaps the 1967 L-88 shown on these pages) was ever labeled with anything other than a displacement badge.

American Ferrari," he explained that "you must pay a price for the ZL-1 excellence and it is quite high. [But] considering that an L-88 Corvette goes for $6,000, a $9,000 ZL-1 tab is a reasonable figure. You're going to sell every [ZL-1] you make anyway and your nearest competition is twice as much so why not show the gang in Modena they're not alone anymore?"

In Dahlquist's learned opinion, Duntov indeed had finally done it; he had fathered a world-class Corvette capable of running with Europe's finest sports cars. "They said Detroit could never build anything like a Ferrari because some product planning committee or cost accounting group would pinpoint the economic folly of such low-volume madness, compromise it and send it on to the world just another gimmicked-up cop out," he wrote in *Motor Trend*'s May 1969 issue. "But Duntov, the man, is Man in his old, pure, adventuresome, non-vinyl person, and that's why he was able to create an American Ferrari that is not even partially contemporary Woolworth."

Eric Dahlquist knew American performance cars, and he was convinced that the ZL-1 Corvette represented the ultimate rendition of such. Not only could it run away from anything on wheels (and perhaps a few things with wings), it could do so in the curves as well as down the straightaway. "It is the best handling Corvette ever built," he concluded—which in turn meant it was the best handling American car ever built. "With a 43/57 front to rear weight distribution, the 2,808-pound car is almost neutral with just a shade of understeer that you can overpower at will with the throttle."

Lowered weight, both in total and up front, was, of course, the key to the ZL-1's incredibly well-balanced performance. This was indeed a Corvette that offered the best of both worlds—big-block brute force and small-block nimbleness. In fact, the big, brawny ZL-1 even did its 350-powered brethren one better. Weight-saving aluminum heads on the L-88 and L-89 427s helped those two big-blocks carry only about 60 pounds more than a typical 350 small-block. With an aluminum cylinder block to go with those feather-light heads, the ZL-1 V-8 amazingly tipped the scales at roughly 25 pounds less than a 350.

Duntov may have been, in *Car and Driver*'s words, "a great exponent of small-displacement, high-revving engines." But he also loved his horsepower. "Zora was always anxious for more of everything," explained Gib Hufstader when asked how the ZL-1 fit in with Duntov's ideal for the supreme American sports car. "But the real sin was that people never did buy them." Clearly Dahlquist's justifications couldn't sway wealthy jet-setters who apparently felt the $9,000 ZL-1 tab was an unreasonable figure. "It was a different economy back then," added Hufstader. "People weren't throwing money at cars like they do today. No one wanted to spend that much for just an engine."

Almost no one. Reportedly RPO ZL-1 was checked off twice in 1969.

Explaining how other ZL-1 Corvettes have been spotted over the years is easy enough. Legend has it that as many as 5 test mules or executive toys were built. Some claims say 10 to 12. It then follows that 1 or more of these may have survived, with or without their original engines—probably the latter. And being race-ready powerplants, both the L-88 and ZL-1 427s were also offered individually "in a crate" to racers, professionally or otherwise. It logically follows further that the possibility existed for any number of these crate-motor ZL-1s to have found their way into a street-going 1969 Corvette. Mind you, this is pure speculation; no proof presently exists for any of these possibilities. According to Fred Frincke,

Press release artwork was actually produced for at least one of the "engines that never was for 1970." Shown here is the 460-horsepower LJ-2, the planned triple-carburetor 454. *Chevrolet Motor Division*

Chevrolet's Mk IV engine facility in Tonawanda, New York, built 154 ZL-1 427s, along with 549 L-88s. Tonawanda plant man and diehard big-block researcher Fran Preve claims a different score. His search through Chevrolet's official "Summary of Engines Shipped" papers uncovered 94 ZL-1s manufactured for Y-body Corvette applications: 80 for four-speeds, 14 for M40 automatics. Add to that another 90 all-aluminum 427s built for F-body ponycars by way of performance products manager Vince Piggins famed Central Office Production Order pipeline.

Along with the two recorded factory installations, one other ZL-1 big-block went into the Mako Shark II when it was restyled into the Manta Ray showcar in 1969. As for the remaining Corvette-coded crate engines . . . you tell us.

Sixty-nine ZL-1 Camaros rolled out of Chevrolet's backdoor in 1969 thanks to Piggins' clever use of GM's COPO loophole. Remember, before 1970 GM limited its intermediate and smaller lineups to no more than 400 ci of engine. Chevelles and Camaros could've been ordered with the 396 big-block but not the 427. Normally used for special fleet orders and such, the COPO request line proved to be a quick, easy way around corporate red tape. Piggins' end run resulted in the production of two different 427-powered Camaros in 1969. COPO number 9561 planted the Corvette's L-72 427 between ponycar flanks. COPO number 9560 referred to the ZL-1 Camaro. A third COPO code, number 9562, applied to the L-72 427 Chevelle.

According to longtime Chevrolet test engineer Bill Howell, Vince Piggins was the driving force behind the ZL-1 427's creation. It was Piggins who lobbied his bosses to fund an all-aluminum, big-block racing engine project in 1968, with the intention being to support, among others, Bruce McLaren's successful Canadian-American Challenge Cup team. Small-block Chevy-powered McLaren racing machines had begun their domination of the Can-Am series in 1967. Then Jim Hall had to go and "scratch-build" an aluminum big-block for his Chaparral race team—which was, of course, Chevy's unofficial research and development program. McLaren then threatened to look to Ford for a comparable lightweight big-block to power his 1968 Can-Am cars. Piggins

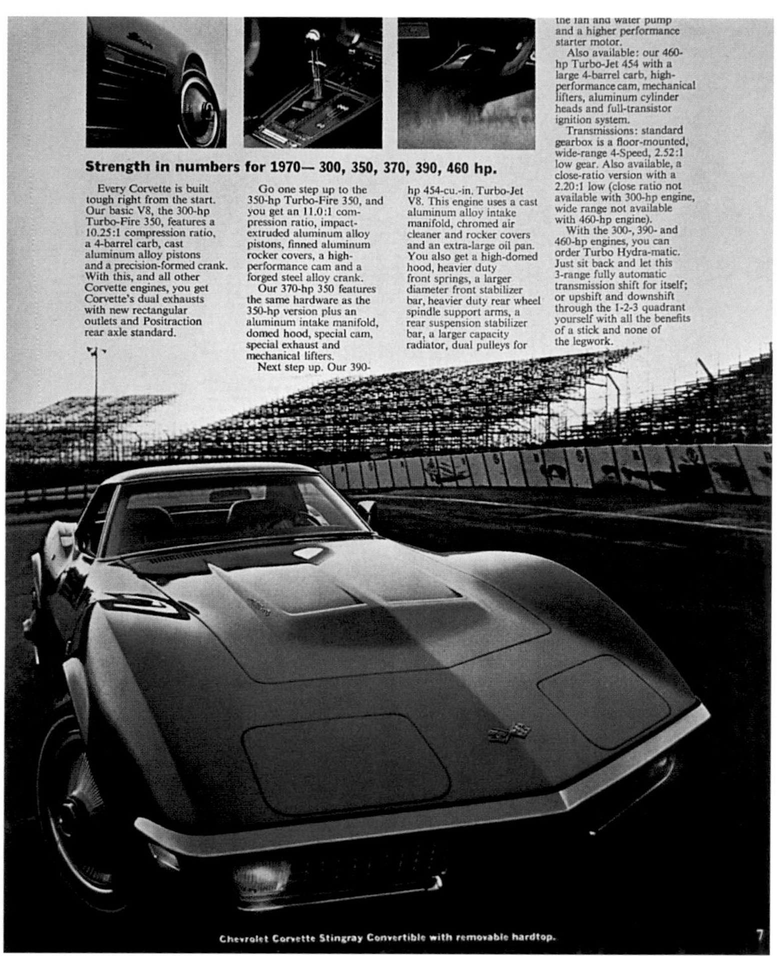

Strength in numbers for 1970— 300, 350, 370, 390, 460 hp.

Every Corvette is built tough right from the start. Our basic V8, the 300-hp Turbo-Fire 350, features a 10.25:1 compression ratio, a 4-barrel carb, cast aluminum alloy pistons and a precision-formed crank. With this, and all other Corvette engines, you get Corvette's dual exhausts with new rectangular outlets and Positraction rear axle standard.

Go one step up to the 350-hp Turbo-Fire 350, and you get an 11.0:1 compression ratio, impact-extruded aluminum alloy pistons, finned aluminum rocker covers, a high-performance cam and a forged steel alloy crank.

Our 370-hp 350 features the same hardware as the 350-hp version plus an aluminum intake manifold, domed hood, special cam, special exhaust and mechanical lifters.

Next step up. Our 390-hp 454-cu.-in. Turbo-Jet V8. This engine uses a cast aluminum alloy intake manifold, chromed air cleaner and rocker covers and an extra-large oil pan. You also get a high-domed hood, heavier duty front springs, a larger diameter front stabilizer bar, heavier duty rear wheel spindle support arms, a rear suspension stabilizer bar, a larger capacity radiator, dual pulleys for the fan and water pump and a higher performance starter motor.

Also available: our 460-hp Turbo-Jet 454 with a large 4-barrel carb, high-performance cam, mechanical lifters, aluminum cylinder heads and full-transistor ignition system.

Transmissions: standard gearbox is a floor-mounted, wide-range 4-Speed, 2.52:1 low gear. Also available, a close-ratio version with a 2.20:1 low (close ratio not available with 300-hp engine, wide range not available with 460-hp engine).

With the 300-, 390- and 460-hp engines, you can order Turbo Hydra-matic. Just sit back and let this 3-range fully automatic transmission shift for itself; or upshift and downshift through the 1-2-3 quadrant yourself with all the benefits of a stick and none of the legwork.

Chevrolet Corvette Stingray Convertible with removable hardtop.

7

The original plan in 1970 was to pick up where the 427 left off with the 454 big-block. The L-88 427 would simply reappear as the LS-7 454. The fabled aluminum-head LS-7 almost made it into production—witness this page from the 1970 Corvette brochure. Other sources listed LS-7 output differently.

stepped in, promised Bruce his aluminum big-blocks, and the rest is racing history. Armed with the ZL-1, McLaren racers destroyed all Can-Am comers from 1968 to 1971, winning 32 of 37 events.

Once thoroughly baptized by fire on the 1968 Can-Am circuit, the ZL-1 427 then made its way in 1969 onto the Corvette's RPO list, as well as into Piggins' COPO delivery system. Although some references identified the ZL-1 V-8 as a "special L-88," creating the king of the 427s was by no means a simple matter of trading cast-iron for aluminum to make the cylinder block match those lightweight heads. While the ZL-1 and L-88 wore similar heads in 1969, the block was a truly unique piece of engineering.

Duntov turned to Fred Frincke for the expertise needed to fashion a high-performance engine completely out of aluminum. Casting was Frincke's forte; he knew his way around a foundry. Winters Foundry was responsible for casting the ZL-1's block, heads and intake. Machining work and assembly was then completed at Tonawanda under a "100-percent parts inspection" policy in production areas that Duntov described as being "surgically clean." Ultimate precision was job one.

Frincke chose heat-treated 356 T-6 alloy for the block, which was cast with thickened walls and beefed-up main webs to compensate for the aluminum's weaker nature. Extra fortification also went into the block's deck to allow for the use of two extra cylinder head hold-down bolts. Head bolts were lengthened or screwed into steel Heli-Coil inserts to help further increase the grip between block and head. Trapped in the aluminum block's bores by the heads were eight cast-iron cylinder sleeves. Provisions for dry-sump oiling was also included in the block's design.

At the bottom end was a fully nitrided crank forged out of SAE 5140 steel and held in place, of course, by four-bolt main bearing caps. The same magnafluxed connecting rods introduced midyear in 1968 for the L-88 were used, they with their beefed 7/16-inch bolts, full-floating wrist pins, and Spiralock pin retainers.

ZL-1's heads—cast from 356 T-6 aluminum too—were based on the open-chamber units also introduced midway through 1968 for the L-88. Combustion chambers in those heads were opened up (thus the name) around the spark plug. Results of this change included a drop in compression (from 12.5:1 to 12:1) for the "Second-Design" L-88 because chamber volume increased from 106.8 cc to 118. Breathing, on the other hand, increased by a reported 30 percent thanks to the revised open chamber's closer relation to the exhaust port. Yet another benefit was lower emissions, which was really the goal of the open-chamber design. This achievement resulted from a 50 percent reduction in the quench or "squish" area, that is the space left over between the piston top and combustion chamber at top dead center.

Revised ports also contributed greatly to the open-chamber head's superior breathing. Although the large rectangular intake passages remained the same size as the first-generation L-88's, they were recontoured internally to help speed the air/fuel mixture into those open chambers. Exhaust ports were radically reshaped from rectangles into round passages to match up to the tube headers that would be quickly bolted up by the Speed Racer set in place of the mis-

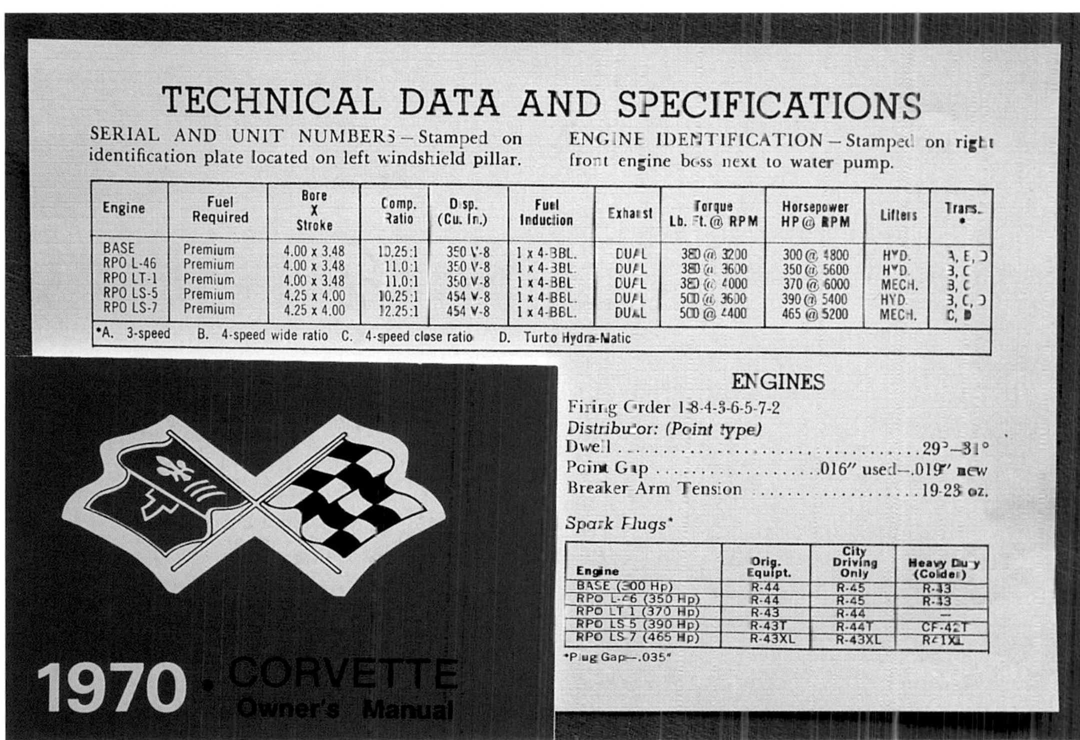

TECHNICAL DATA AND SPECIFICATIONS

SERIAL AND UNIT NUMBERS—Stamped on identification plate located on left windshield pillar.

ENGINE IDENTIFICATION—Stamped on right front engine boss next to water pump.

Engine	Fuel Required	Bore X Stroke	Comp. Ratio	Disp. (Cu. In.)	Fuel Induction	Exhaust	Torque Lb. Ft. @ RPM	Horsepower HP @ RPM	Lifters	Trans.*
BASE	Premium	4.00 x 3.48	10.25:1	350 V-8	1 x 4-BBL.	DUAL	380 @ 3200	300 @ 4800	HYD.	A, B, D
RPO L-46	Premium	4.00 x 3.48	11.0:1	350 V-8	1 x 4-BBL.	DUAL	380 @ 3600	350 @ 5600	HYD.	B, C
RPO LT-1	Premium	4.00 x 3.48	11.0:1	350 V-8	1 x 4-BBL	DUAL	380 @ 4000	370 @ 6000	MECH.	B, C
RPO LS-5	Premium	4.25 x 4.00	10.25:1	454 V-8	1 x 4-BBL.	DUAL	500 @ 3600	390 @ 5400	HYD.	B, C, D
RPO LS-7	Premium	4.25 x 4.00	12.25:1	454 V-8	1 x 4-BBL.	DUAL	500 @ 4400	465 @ 5200	MECH.	C, D

*A. 3-speed B. 4-speed wide ratio C. 4-speed close ratio D. Turbo Hydra-Matic

ENGINES

Firing Order 1-8-4-3-6-5-7-2

Distributor: (Point type)

Dwell .... 29°–31°

Point Gap .... .016" used—.019" new

Breaker Arm Tension .... 19-23 oz.

*Spark Plugs**

Engine	Orig. Equipt.	City Driving Only	Heavy Duty (Colder)
BASE (300 Hp)	R-44	R-45	R-43
RPO L-46 (350 Hp)	R-44	R-45	R-43
RPO LT 1 (370 Hp)	R-43	R-44	—
RPO LS 5 (390 Hp)	R-43T	R-44T	CF-42T
RPO LS 7 (465 Hp)	R-43XL	R-43XL	R-41XL

*Plug Gap—.035"

Another source to prematurely announce the LS-7 454's arrival in 1970 was the Corvette owner's manual. Notice the output figure listed—not even Chevrolet people knew exactly what was going on.

matched, rectangular-passage iron manifolds found on the factory-delivered ZL-1 Corvettes and Camaros.

Like the open-chamber L-88 head, the ZL-1 unit featured 2.19-inch intake valves and enlarged 1.88-inch exhausts. The ZL-1, however, was fitted with new TRW forged aluminum pistons with extra thick tops and strengthened pin bosses. These beefier slugs not only proved more durable than the L-88 units, they also reinstated the aluminum-head 427's original 12.5:1 compression by way of their increased dome area.

The ZL-1 427's solid-lifter cam was even more radical than the L-88's, at least as far as lift was concerned. Intake valve lift was 0.560-inch; exhaust was 0.600. Tom Langdon's tests, however, demonstrated that decreased durations cooperated better with those free-flowing, sewer-sized ports. The resulting shorter-duration cam, working in concert with the various reinforced internals, helped the ZL-1 wind out like no big-block on this planet. Seven-grand on the tach was no problem, and Chevrolet engineers claimed short bursts to 7,600 were within reason. Keeping the juices flowing during those high-rpm trips was the familiar 850-cfm Holley four-barrel.

All that carb, all that rev capability, all that cam, and Chevrolet once again insulted our intelligence with a bogus output rating. Maximum ZL-1 power was listed at 430 horses at 5,200 rpm. And once again everyone knew better. According to Tom Langdon, 525 horsepower was no problem for a ZL-1 right out of the crate. With "some attention to detail to the cylinder heads, etc.," producing up to 600 horsepower was within reason.

Perhaps Corvette buyers finally would have been treated to a larger dose of the truth had the L-88 and ZL-1 returned for 1970. They almost did. Duntov and crew fully intended on tweaking the enlarged 454-ci Mk IV big-block just as they had done with the 427. Early 1970 Corvette assembly manuals even announced this in print. The tri-carb LJ-2 454 would carry on in the best tradition of the L-71. The L-88 would be reborn as the LS-7 454. And the big-cube equivalent of the ZL-1 would be the LT-2. These 454s were all rated more realistically: The LJ-2 was listed at 460 horsepower; the LS-7 and LT-2 shared a 465-horse label

Apparently the LJ-2 never made it much past the drawing board. Not so for the LT-2 454. "We built enough engines to test," explained Tom Langdon in 1999. "The aluminum-block LT-2 went into a showcar for a press review in 1970."

That review was actually held in the summer of 1969 to introduce 1970 models. But that

The LS-6 Chevelle Upstages the Corvette

The LS-7 Corvette's failure to appear in 1970 left the Chevelle SS 454 the temporary king of the Chevy performance hill. Although it cost about $1,300 more, the LS-6 Chevelle outsold its weaker LS-5 SS 454 brother, 4,475 to 4,298.

The Corvette nearly always has been the favored son as far as Chevrolet Engineering was concerned. By the mid-1960s it was reigning supreme. When the fabulous Mk IV big-block was introduced in 1965, it was showcased in its most muscular form beneath a fiberglass hood. Those 396 cubic inches delivered 425 horsepower to a 1965 Corvette's overwhelmed rear rubber. In comparison, the new Malibu SS 396 introduced that year was fitted with a 375-horse version of the Mk IV V-8. Chevelles also were initially limited to no more than 400 cubes. The next year, Corvettes received an even bigger, badder Mk IV, the 427. And even after a GM upper office decree banned the use of multiple carburetor setups for its passenger-car lines, the 1967 Corvette rolled out with yet another even stronger big-block, the 435-horse L-71 427, fed by three Holley two-barrels. The tri-carb 427 remained the Corvette's most formidable street engine up through 1969.

Then came 1970, the year all hell broke loose in Detroit. As the new decade dawned, an escalating horsepower race reached its pinnacle. Runaway competition among the mighty musclecars then roaming the earth even inspired GM's sticks-in-the-mud to drop their 400-cid maximum displacement limit for their intermediate lineups. This then allowed Chevrolet to inadvertently upstage its performance flagship.

For the first time since the legendary 409s were running wild in the early 1960s, a car other than the Corvette stood as the most powerful Chevy on the street. Beyond that, the LS-6 SS 454 Chevelle emerged in 1970 wearing the highest advertised output rating of the entire musclecar era. Such numbers were often misleading back then, either overrated or underrated depending on which way the wind was blowing. But the 450-horsepower label assigned to the Chevelle's LS-6 454 V-8 was no paper tiger. That this rating then soared above all others advertised in 1970 was no coincidence. In many minds, the LS-6 Chevelle deserves the crown of king of the musclecars hands down.

Interestingly, Chevrolet engineers had almost labeled the hottest Corvette 427 in 1966 with a 450-horsepower decal. Cooler heads prevailed, however, and the actual label that did go to press read 425 horsepower. At that time all manufacturers had determined that a 425-horse rating represented the upper limit as far as tolerance was concerned—tolerance by government watchdogs who were already convinced that Detroit's horsepower race was running way out of control. But one year later Chevy engineers inched the Corvette's maximum-performance Corvette 427 to 435 horses. They then threw caution to the wind completely in 1970.

In truth the LS-6's record-setting output rating was undoubtedly a bit on the conservative side, but who was counting? Four-hundred-fifty ponies at 5,600 rpm represented more than enough giddyup power for even the heaviest leadfoot in 1970. Throw in a heaping helping of torque—a massive 500 ft-lb at 3,600 rpm—and melting the rubber to the rims was a foregone conclusion. On street tires with full exhausts the 1970 LS-6 Chevelles could scorch the quarter-mile in a tad more than 13 seconds. A few tweaks, open exhausts, and stickier treads dropped the car well into the 12-second class, a place not too many street cars have ever visited. Ever.

Arguments as to which machine actually won the musclecar era drag race will always persist, especially from the Hemi Mopar, Stage 1 Buick, and W-30 Olds camps. However, whenever the votes are counted it is always the LS-6 Chevelle that comes out on top. In 1970, critics knew even then that Chevrolet had made history. In the words of *Car Life's* road testers, the LS-6 454 was

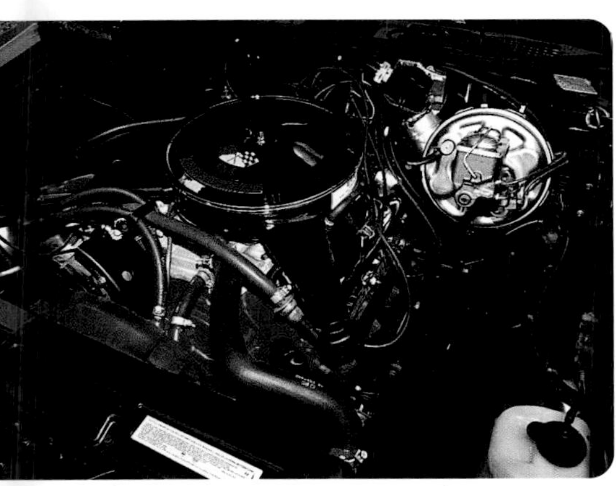

Wearing iron cylinder heads (instead of aluminum) and squeezing fuel/air to a 11.25:1 ratio, the Chevelle's LS-6 454 produced 450 real horsepower. Notice the rare dual-snorkel air cleaner. Most LS-6 Chevelles probably featured the Cowl Induction hood and its rubber-sealed air cleaner. When a standard hood was chosen, the second favorite option was the open-element air cleaner.

"the best supercar engine ever released by General Motors." On the street, the 450-horse SS 454 demonstrated to many rivals that the LS-6 big-block was perhaps the best supercar engine ever released, period. "That's LS as in Land Speed Record," concluded *Motor Trend's* A.B. Sherman after watching an LS-6 Chevelle run from rest to 60 miles per hour in 6 seconds without even breaking a sweat.

Super Stock's staff went even further, comparing the LS-6 to the most powerful man-made force ever unleashed. "Driving a 450-horsepower Chevelle is like being the guy who's in charge of triggering atom bomb tests. You have the power, you know you have the power, and if you use the power bad things may happen. Things like arrest, prosecution, loss of license, broke to pieces, shredded tires, etc."

Like the atom bomb, the LS-6 Chevelle ended up being a doomsday weapon of sorts. It exploded on the scene in 1970 then quickly faded away into history. Even though magazine testers did get their hands on a 1971 LS-6 SS 454, actual production was cancelled as GM officials began closing the book on its musclecar legacy. Fortunately they saved the best for last.

And with the Chevelle SS lineup again relegated to mere mortal status, the Corvette resumed its rightful place atop Chevrolet's performance pecking order in 1971, this time with its own version of the LS-6 454 big-block.

showcar Langdon spoke of was the same 1969 Corvette that journalists had flogged the summer before. "That orange coupe was used in back-to-back press long-leads in 1968 and 1969," added Gib Hufstader. "In 1968 it was a ZL-1; in 1969 it was the LT-2." Again the coupe was equipped with a specially prepared Turbo Hydra-Matic, 4.88:1 gears, and drag slicks. And again most journalists didn't realize exactly what they were looking at beneath that lumpy ZL-2 hood.

"We learned that no one at the press day had bothered, or dared, ask what was actually in the car," explained a *Motor Trend* review of the mystery machine. Fortunately Langdon laid it all out for *MT's* staff. "The engine is a prototype for 1970," he said. "Let's just say [it's] very similar to a current ZL-1 all-aluminum unit. The aluminum cylinder heads are the same as currently released in the ZL-1, as is the camshaft, but this particular car has a special induction and exhaust system."

On top was a truly enormous Holley four-barrel that flowed somewhere between 1,200 to 1,400 cubic feet per minute. At the other end of the process was a set of custom-built 180-degree headers. Looking like something right off a race track, these exhausts matched two pairs of cylinders from opposite banks together into huge collectors to take advantage of the engine's natural firing order pulses. According to Hufstader, these tangled-up tubes freed up about a dozen more horsepower compared to conventional headers. There was also another more noticeable result. "Those 180-degree headers gave the LT-2 a ripping sound," said Hufstader.

Like its ZL-1 427 forerunner, the LT-2 454 eclipsed the quarter-mile in 11 seconds flat with ease. And with anyone at the wheel. According to *Motor Trend*, the best pass was 10.60 seconds at 132 miles pr hour. But the best was also the last.

The all-aluminum 454 was never seen again after its press showing in 1969. According to Hufstader, the LT-2 engine was homologated for competition but was axed well before it got anywhere near the Corvette's official options list for 1970. Times were changing and so were attitudes at GM involving performance—or in the Corvette's case, excessive performance. Corporate killjoys no longer wanted to waste good money on pure flights of fancy. The days of selling race cars on the street were all but over anyway thanks to growing

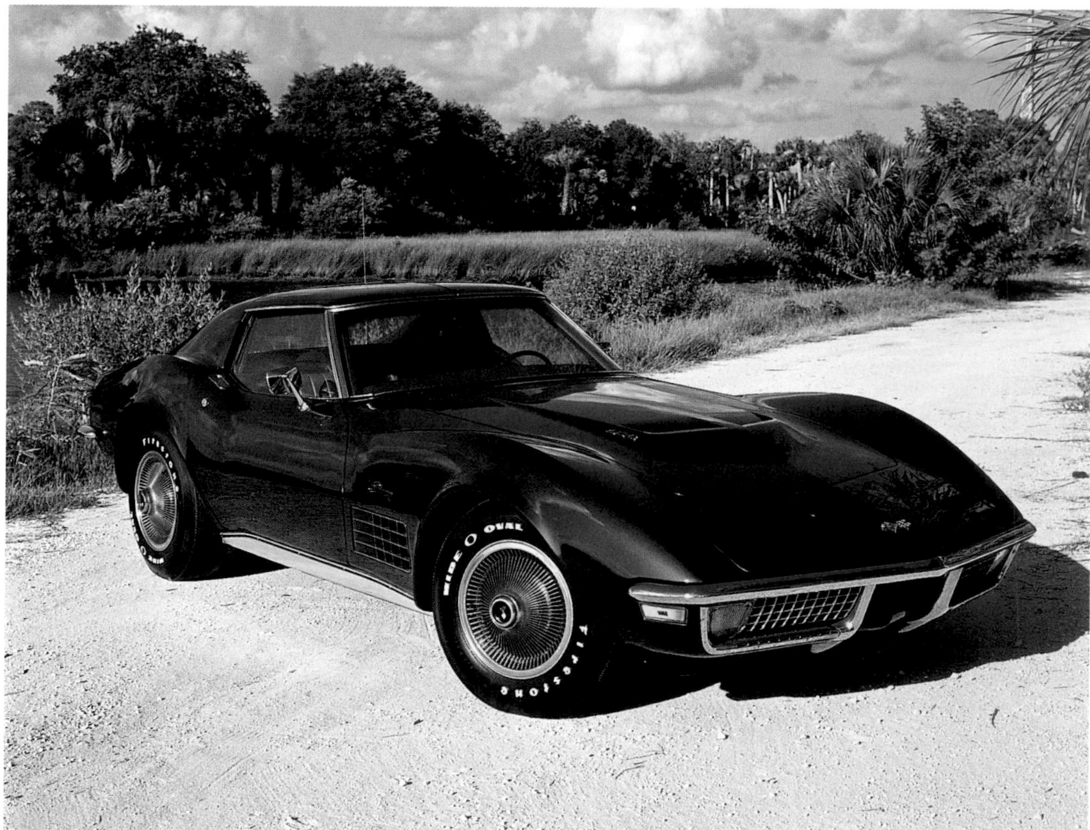

One year after Corvette buyers were teased with the LS-7, the LS-6 454 emerged to revive their faith in Zora Duntov's engineering team. Though tamed by lowered compression, the 1971 Corvette's LS-6 V-8 still rated at 425 horsepower. LS-6 Corvette production was only 188.

safety concerns, ever-tightening emissions standards and wallet-wilting insurance costs.

Of the exotic 454 big-blocks initially mentioned in early plans for 1970 production, the aluminum-head LS-7 came closest to reality. It was not only listed in assembly manuals and AMA spec sheets, it also made it into 1970 factory brochures and owner's manuals, although some confusion existed as to what reality really was. Mundane black-and-white engineering papers and the pretty color brochures listed compression at 11.25:1 and output at 460 horsepower. Like the early assembly manuals, the 1970 owner's manual claimed 465 horsepower, as well as 12.25:1 compression. Solid lifters were a given.

An LS-7 Corvette also made it into the magazine road test arena in 1970, where again a 465-horsepower rating was quoted. Duntov and Hufstader unveiled the aluminum-head 454 at southern California's Riverside Raceway in December 1969. Eric Dahlquist drove the car that day but didn't report any performance times in his March 1970 *Motor Trend* review.

What he did mention was the LS-7's new dual-disc clutch, yet another trick piece transferred from the racetrack to the street. Hufstader today is still proud of this unit, which could handle every pound of big-block torque yet required far less pedal effort than Chevrolet's typical heavy-duty clamper. Doubling the friction area by using two 10-inch clutch discs meant a lower-tension pressure plate could be incorporated. "No one, or nearly no one at the preview missed a shift," claimed Dahlquist. "The harder and faster you went, the better it seemed to work—all day long."

After the day's work was done, it was Paul Van Valkenburgh's turn to drive. And drive. And drive. He picked up the LS-7 coupe at Riverside and returned it to Detroit, recounting his wild 2,500-mile ride in *Sports Car Graphic*'s March 1970 issue. "What's it like to drive a loaded 454-ci Stingray?" he asked. "It's like taxiing a DC3 at full throttle up and down a freshly plowed runway. At least that's what it rides and sounds like." From there, Van Valkenburgh's recount apparently contradicted reality a time or two. According to him, the LS-7 featured a hydraulic cam and 11:1 compression. Go figure.

At least he did crunch some speed numbers. "We easily turned a quarter-mile in 13.8

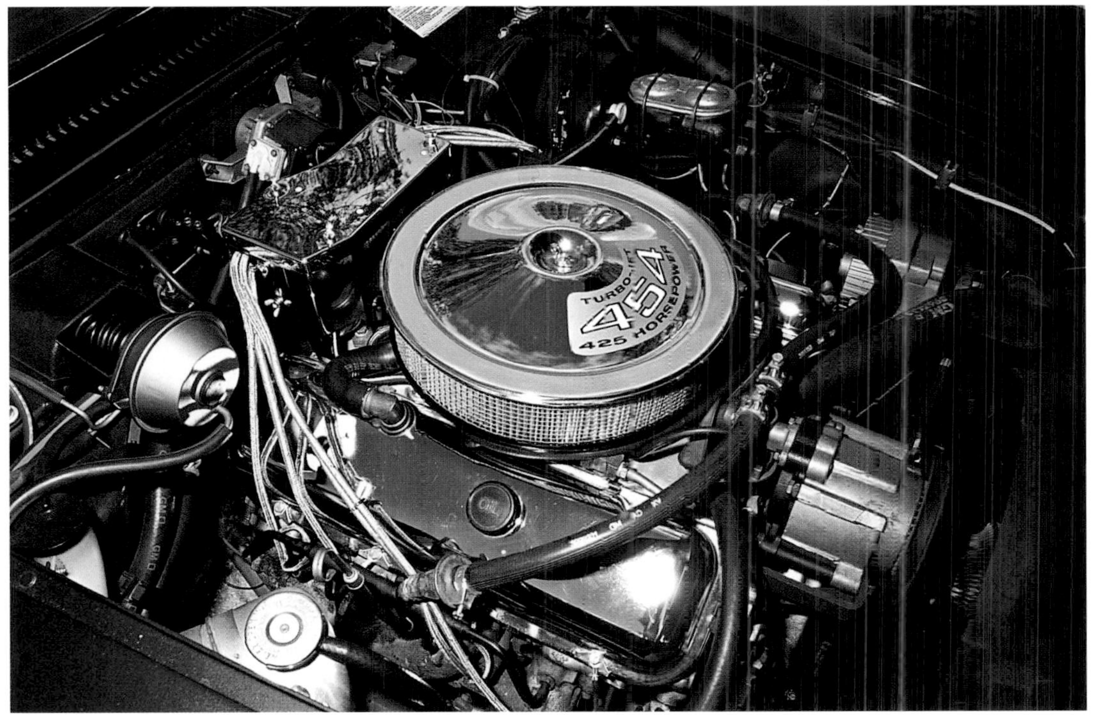

The aluminum-head LS-6 454 received full emissions controls and a timid compression ratio of 9:1, yet it still could burn up the quarter-mile in the 13-second range. It was offered in the Corvette for 1971 only.

seconds and 108 miles per hour—with full fuel, passenger, and luggage for two." And full exhausts, standard Firestone Wide Ovals, smog pump, radio, heater, and so on. And a fan shroud. Unlike the L-88, the LS-7 was set up for street duty. The car itself also featured a conventional, nonfunctional big-block hood, which meant the aluminum-head 454 was fitted with a low-rise intake manifold instead of the high-riser used by the L-88, ZL-1, and LT-2.

Like Dahlquist, Van Valkenburgh loved that clutch. "The roughness of double-disc clutches has been disproven by Chevrolet, as their version is so light and smooth that it precipitates speed shifts—because you can get the clutch pedal down and up before you can get the accelerator up and down." On the other hand (foot?) he wasn't particularly fond of feeding this beast. "A desirable accessory with the 454 LS-7 engine would be a reliable co-pilot to watch the fuel gauge sink and keep feeding cruising range data to the driver between gas stations."

Single-digit fuel "economy" aside, Van Valkenburgh claimed the LS-7 Corvette represented one of the world's best sports car buys as far as "performance-per-dollar" was concerned. He felt all that "awesome power" was definitely worth the price, which he quoted at "well over seven grand." "We close with the old Texas proverb," he concluded. "If you care who's quickest, don't get caught shoveling manure behind someone else's 465 horses.'"

Whether or not the LS-7 could have put the Corvette up on a higher plateau became a moot point once Chevrolet cancelled the advertised option before it could go from paper to plastic. Coupled with GM efforts to tone down its "hot car" image in 1970 were Chevy officials' moves to cut back on costly options that complicated assembly lines. "De-pro" was the company jargon for this de-proliferation program. One de-pro victim was the 350-horsepower L-46 small-block, deleted after 1970. Another was the LS-7. Both losses disappointed Duntov, but at least one other engineer didn't exactly feel the same way concerning the latter cancellation.

"I was opposed to the LS-7, but I was so low down the totem pole it had no effect," said Tom Langdon. "The L-88 already had demonstrated substantial durability problems. A longer stroke inherently creates more problems through increased friction. Increasing the stroke to go from 427 ci to 454 only aggravated the [L-88's] problems. We hadn't even solved the 427's problems yet and we were making [them] worse."

Langdon also didn't agree with another old Texas proverb, the one that claimed that there was no substitute for cubic inches. He felt that in this case there was no need to jump from 427 ci to 454. "Increasing the stroke without enlarging the bore doesn't necessarily translate into a real increase in power," he said. "Some of that extra power is eaten up by increased friction. A good 427 [L-88] would put out about 600 horsepower. The 454 pulled more torque, but power was just about the same as the L-88." Yet another moot point.

By all accounts the 1970 LS-7 Corvette that Dahlquist and Van Valkenburgh drove was the only one built—at least for public exposure. According to research through Tonawanda paperwork, the New York plant shipped seven LS-7 454s to St. Louis, and five of those were returned. Terry McManmon, the National Corvette Restorers Society 1970–72 technical advisor, claims differently. He says Tonawanda officials told him that maybe two to four LS-7 engines were built and all were sent to Chevrolet Engineering in Warren, Michigan, for testing and prototype installations. Another LS-7 mule or two was probably created, but all were dismantled by order. Or were they?

"I asked Zora a few years back about the possibility of an LS-7 Corvette surviving," said McManmon in March 1999. "He told me with a wry smile that he personally signed the order to destroy the LS-7 test cars. But the way he smiled, I wondered if he was giving me the real story."

As for the one known LS-7 Corvette, it was dismantled. Then, according to Gib Hufstader, its aluminum-head 454 was stolen a few years later out of Chevy Engineering's back lot. "I never lost the stuff I tried to hide," said Hufstader, "but this one got away. It was about 1973 or 1975. A couple guys apparently jumped the fence one night and we never saw it again."

With the LS-7 now a soon-to-be-forgotten footnote in the Corvette history books, Duntov's engineers were left with little to show in 1970 for all their fast thinking. The exciting, new LT-1 small-block did debut in 1970. But in the big-block ranks the lukewarm 390-horse LS-5 454 was as hot as it got—beneath Corvette hoods, that is. The LS-7's early demise also left America's only sports car in a unique position: second fiddle. Not only was the 1970 big-block Corvette no longer this country's most powerful performance machine, it wasn't even the most powerful Chevy.

That title was claimed by the LS-6 SS 454 Chevelle, arguably the king of the musclecar era. "The LS-6 was our big success," claimed Hufstader. Wearing cast-iron closed-chamber heads, the original LS-6 454 was rated at 450 industry-leading horses beneath A-body hoods in 1970. Compression was 11.25:1. Although early 1970 paperwork listed RPO LS-6 as an option for both the Chevelle and Camaro Super Sports, that latter combo never arrived—yet another de-pro perhaps?

Oddly, an LS-6 Corvette never showed up in 1970 either. Some, including Tom Langdon, have since claimed that the 450-horsepower 454 didn't become a Corvette option that first year because Chevrolet didn't have a suitable low-rise intake manifold available for the LS-6/Y-body application. Yet it did for the LS-7? Okay, so perhaps flow characteristic differences between the aluminum open-chamber heads and the iron closed-chamber units may have precluded a simple technology swap-out. Maybe, maybe not. There was no problem fitting the LS-5 454 with a hood-clearing intake in 1970.

A better explanation for the situation probably involved Chevrolet's planned pecking order. Even though early paperwork also had the 1970 Chevelle SS getting its own LS-7, the 465-horsepower Corvette would've still claimed no less than a tie for Chevrolet's top power spot in 1970. Planners apparently never even considered an LS-6 option for the 1970 Corvette with the LS-7 deal all but inked. Mention of an LS-7 Chevelle option then quickly evaporated, leaving the promised LS-7 Corvette to roll on toward Chevrolet's late-starting 1970 production run with intentions of once again standing alone atop the division's performance pyramid. According to Gib Hufstader, once the LS-7 454 was cancelled, it was far too late to call up the LS-6 as a stand-in. The waters were muddied even further the following year when Corvette buyers were offered RPO LS-6, but Chevelle customers weren't—this after magazines road tested a 1971 LS-6 SS 454. De-pro again?

"De-comp" might also have been an appropriate catch-phrase for the Corvette's LS-6. Like all GM engines in 1971, it experienced a compression cut, in this case to 9:1. This, in turn, resulted in a corresponding drop in horsepower, from 450 to 425. On the positive side were the aluminum open-chamber cylinder heads bolted on in place of the Chevelle's iron heads. Much of the rest of the 1971 LS-6's makeup also mimicked the L-88. Valve sizes were 2.19 inches intake, 1.88 exhaust. The iron block featured four-bolt mains. Rods were forged steel with big 7/16-inch bolts. Although their dome heights were much shorter than those found in L-88s, the low-compression LS-6 pistons were again TRW forged aluminum pieces.

On top, a 780-cubic-feet-per-minute Holley four-barrel sat on a low-rise, dual-plane intake cast of aluminum. The solid-lifter cam bumped up both valves by 0.519 inch through 1.7:1 stamped steel rockers. Duration was 316 degrees on the intake side, 302 on the exhaust. Ignition was transistorized. Available transmissions were listed as the M21 close-ratio four-speed, M22 Rock Crusher, and M40 Turbo Hydra-Matic. The clutch was the excellent dual-disc unit demonstrated behind the LS-7 in 1970.

Price for RPO LS-6 in 1971 also continued in the best tradition of the L-88. At $1,220, it was little wonder only 188 customers checked off the aluminum-head 454 option that year, leaving the main man disappointed yet again. "It's Duntov's favorite engine and he's tortured because few customers can afford it," claimed a *Car and Driver* report. But this time Zora's letdown may have been self-inflicted. "Maybe for street engine I make mistake," he admitted to *Car and Driver*. "Aluminum heads are expensive and that weight doesn't matter on the street."

Even more expensive was RPO ZR-2, the Special Purpose Turbo-Jet 454 option. Originally mentioned for the stillborn LS-7 in 1970, the ZR-2 equipment group mirrored the ZR-1 racing package offered for the LT-1 small-block from 1970 to 1972 (see chapter 4). Along with the LS-6 454, RPO ZR-2 included F41 heavy-duty suspension, J50/J56 power-assisted heavy-duty brakes, and the L-88's Harrison radiator—without a fan shroud, of course. All comforts and conveniences, including radio and air conditioning, were not available. No way, no how. The only transmission choice was the brutal Rock Crusher.

Equally brutal was that suspension. The seven-leaf spring in back was nearly twice as stout as the standard unit. Front coils were 75 percent stronger. Obviously the ZR-2 was not for soft-tailed drivers. Nor was it for the weak of wallet. The bottom line for RPO ZR-2 was $1,747. A mere 12 were sold in 1971, hopefully to racers only.

On the street, the "standard" LS-6 Corvette did not disappoint those with memories of the L-89 427 still fresh in their minds. *Car and Driver*'s road test of a 1971 LS-6 backed up by that dreaded 3.36:1 economy axle still resulted in a 13.8/104.65 time slip. Zero to 60 equaled 5.3 seconds. As usual, more speed was just an option check-off and turn of the wrench away.

"The LS-6 will definitely produce better times with a higher numerical axle ratio and with a freer exhaust system," read *Car and Driver*'s conclusions. "According to Duntov, 50 horsepower is lost in the mufflers. That, however, is life. You have to have mufflers on the street. California laws say they have to be quiet ones and the LS-6's are—stifled even. The pulses are still distinct but they're muted. Giants in padded cells."

Car Craft's editors made every effort to free those giants. They added headers, sidepipes, 4.56:1 gears, and slicks. Although they expected better, their best test run still produced an E.T. of 12.64 seconds at 114.21 miles per hour. Not long after this sizzling pass, one of *Car Craft*'s less experienced leadfoots put a couple of the LS-6's rods through its oil pan—somewhat of a fitting exclamation point for a story entitled "Goodbye Forever LS-6." *Car Craft*'s crew knew even as they were flogging one of the strongest Corvettes ever built that they would probably never see such speed again from America's only sports car. They were well aware of the fact that the LS-6 was the 'last of the fast Corvettes." Chevrolet had already made it clear that the option wouldn't return for 1972.

De-proliferation took on an entirely new meaning after 1971. Certain extra-high-performance Corvette options were de-pro victims before that year. Afterward, it was horsepower in general that felt the axe. At least before that happened Chevrolet was able to let loose the hot-to-trot legends labeled L-88, ZL-1, and LS-6. They didn't call these production engines big-blocks for nothing. These rats apologized to no one for their rude, raucous, high-revving natures. Sure, Mk IV rat motors would remain a Corvette option up through 1974. But the story just wasn't the same after the LS-6 was cancelled. It truly was, as *Car Craft* announced, the "end of an era."

Never again would the Corvette faithful live so large.

The Mouse That Roared

LT-1 Corvettes, 1970–72

Purists have long scoffed at the notion that the Corvette is a sports car. A true sports car. *Car and Driver*'s ever-caustic Brock Yates may have put it best, from a naysayer's perspective, in 1974 when he claimed that "the Corvette is the Frank Sinatra of sports cars—a hoofer with a gooey frosting of 'stardom' concealing rather limited artistry." He didn't stop there, calling Chevrolet's two-seater "a manifestation of a brand of mass-class, chrome-and-plastic elegance embodied elsewhere in Playboy Clubs, Las Vegas, double-knit suits, diamond pinkie rings, Master Charge cards, Ramada Inns and speedboats with curved windshields." Corvette lovers who still mourn Old Blue Eyes, are lifetime *Playboy* subscribers, jet off to Vegas regularly, and so on, can still find Yates at *Car and Driver*, 2002 Hogback Road, Ann Arbor, Michigan 48105.

More to the point, or at least more to the point being pushed here, were Yates' 1974 comments concerning the Corvette's competition record, which he considered "a compendium of the inconsequential." He pooh-poohed "those endless SCCA amateur championships, where the only time they didn't beat each other, Corvettes were trounced by [Carroll Shelby's] Cobras." And he dismissed "the class structures of international racing [that] make it impossible for Corvettes to compete for overall wins against the lighter European prototypes" as a poor excuse. According to him, "it [still] does dampen national chauvinism to witness those big, red-white-and-blue 454-ci thumpers getting gobbled up by various little rockets from Europe race after race after race." Concluded Yates, "the marque has been on the automotive scene for over 20 years, solidly entrenched as one of the fastest automobiles in the world, yet it has not won a single major motor race! Aside from a couple of victories by John Greenwood in the badly weakened 1973 Trans-Am series and some class wins in endurance competition, Corvettes have been smoked off by everything from Porsches and Ferraris to its factory sister—the Camaro—so often that I view the machine as a bad joke when dressed up in racing numbers."

Again, send your cards or letters to *Car and Driver*, not this author.

Although Yates' opinions may have hit a bit hard, or a lot hard depending on where you sit, they did arrive quite close to home. Being an American car born of American sensibilities helped make the Corvette its own worst enemy—as far as its sports car status was concerned—for many years. From the beginning, it has always been too big, too heavy, too powerful, even too comfortable and convenient. Sports cars, at least from a world view, were meant to be much more nimble, if not spritely. So what if a Corvette can beat a Porsche or Jag from point A to B in the shortest distance? Straight lines are harder to find across the Atlantic where the sports car was born and refined. Germans, Italians, and the British have long built true sport cars: lightweight, surefooted machines able to jaunt about through twists and turns with nary a care. Americans, on the other hand, have rarely built anything other than land yachts: big cars with big engines that spit out, among other things, horsepower by the barrel.

That hood may not have been functional, but that didn't stop the LT-1 small-block from pumping out power like a big-block. Rivals in 1970 who didn't know what that little decal meant had another thing coming.

LT-1 Corvette production, coupes and convertibles, was 1,287 in 1970. Another 1,949 followed in 1971. It cost $447 to drop Chevy's hottest small-block 350 into a Corvette engine bay in 1970.

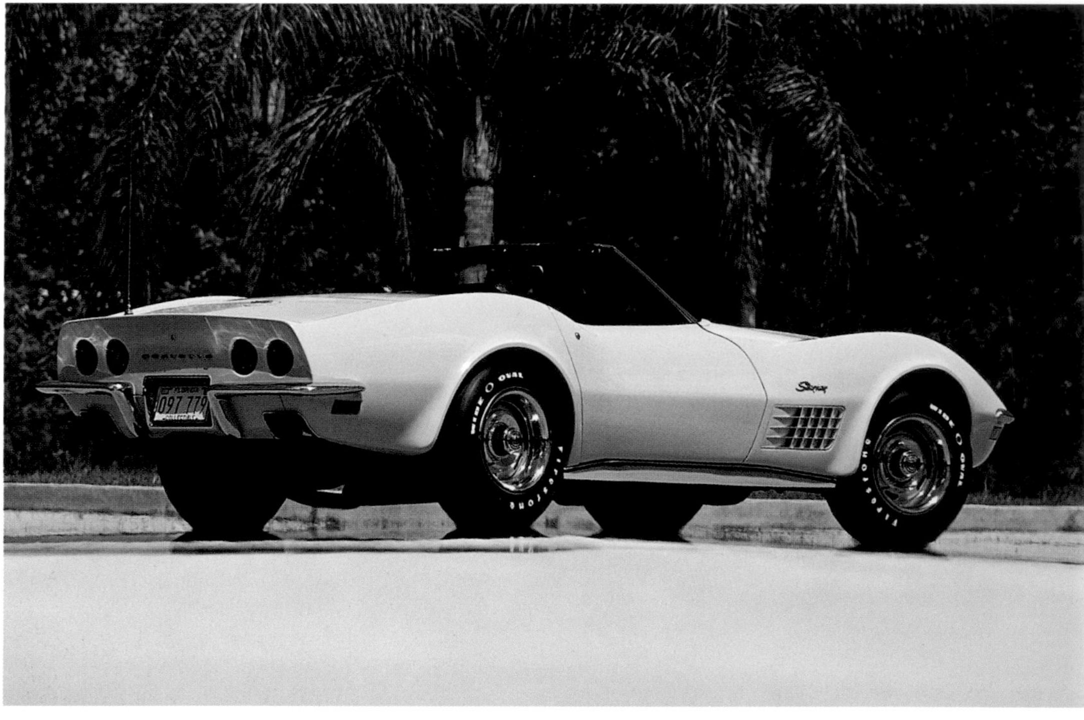

Big-valve heads, a solid-lifter cam and 11:1 compression helped the LT-1 350 produced 370 horsepower in 1970. Air conditioning was not available with the LT-1 in 1970 and 1971.

A wimp in the minds of the typical American horsepower hound, the first Corvette's Blue Flame Six was still a major hunk of macho iron in comparison to nearly all European sports car powerplants of the day, many of which relied on two less cylinders. Then Ed Cole and the gang dropped a V-8 beneath that forward-hinged hood in 1955. Again small by U.S. standards, Chevrolet's ground-breaking 265 small-block nonetheless appeared more like a

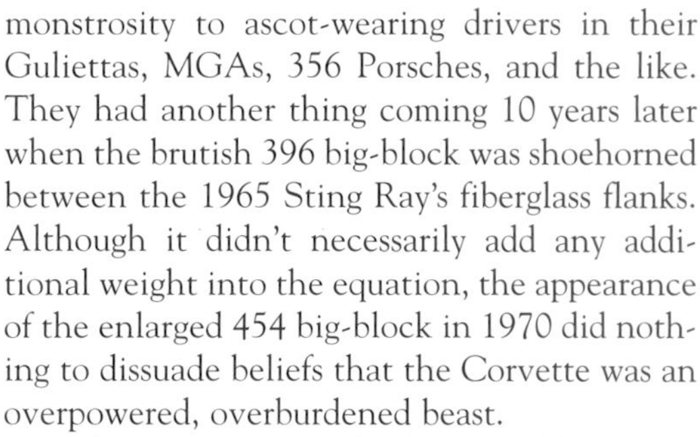

monstrosity to ascot-wearing drivers in their Guliettas, MGAs, 356 Porsches, and the like. They had another thing coming 10 years later when the brutish 396 big-block was shoehorned between the 1965 Sting Ray's fiberglass flanks. Although it didn't necessarily add any additional weight into the equation, the appearance of the enlarged 454 big-block in 1970 did nothing to dissuade beliefs that the Corvette was an overpowered, overburdened beast.

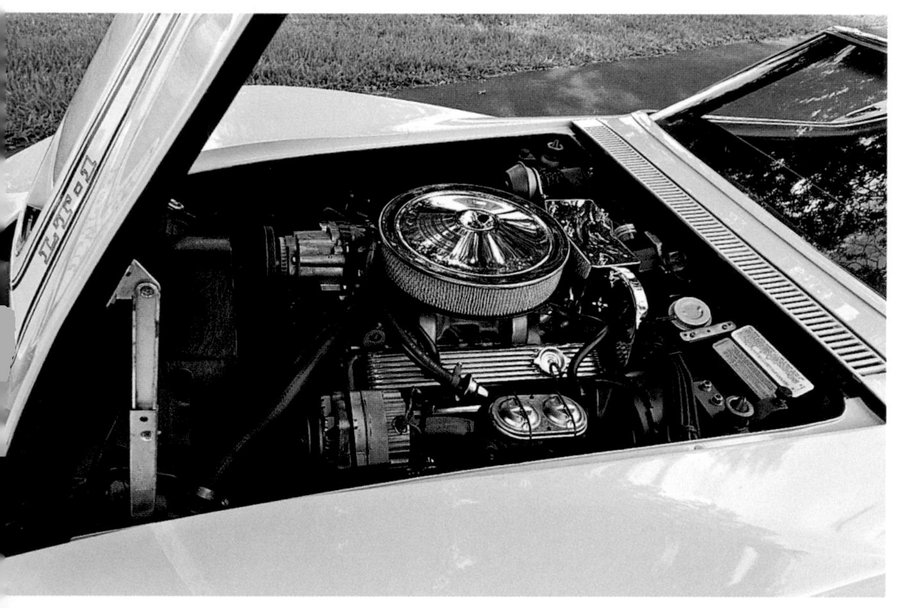

Thus was created the Catch-22 that taunted Zora Duntov throughout his two decades at GM. More horsepower was the key to keeping the Corvette alive beyond 1955, but more power meant more cubic inches, and more cubes meant more engine. More engine, of course, meant more weight; not only more total pounds on the scales, but more unwanted pounds up front over the front wheels.

Don't be fooled, though. Duntov may have tried his darndest to build a better-balanced Corvette with a lighter, yet still strong engine mounted amidships. But that didn't mean he was morally opposed to big-block brute force. On the contrary—he loved the 427. And while his greatest disappointment came when GM finally squelched his midengine idea, he later also expressed dismay that Chevrolet failed to release the all-aluminum LS-7 454 in 1970.

Zora could be both a dreamer and a realist. He was no fool; he fully recognized the budgetary realities at GM, as well as the need to keep the Corvette out in front as America's top-performing automobile. As a 1969 *Car Life* report explained, "We asked Duntov if he had considered a 2,000-lb., 300-bhp Corvette." His reply? "He has, and the closest he's been able to come is a 3,500-lb., 435-bhp Corvette."

Again, class, repeat after me: All that weight required all that power, all that power required all that engine, and all that engine precluded cutting down all that weight.

Being bigger and heavier overall compared to overseas rivals was only the beginning as far as the Corvette's handicap on the international sports car stage was concerned. Superior handling, not supreme horsepower, long has been the top priority among the world-class sporting crowd. Corvette handling, while superior by American perspectives, fell even further behind world-class standards as the car grew heavier by the nose. Until recent years, Corvette owners attempting foreign relations on long and winding roads were more often than not embarrassed by drivers spurring on far fewer horses let loose by much less engine displacement.

Suitable solutions to the problem never did fit within the high-volume, profit-intensive production parameters that were, are, and always will be among the facts of life in Detroit. Although the Corvette has continually stretched the limits at General Motors, job one has always been to keep costs in line at all costs. Duntov's midengine dream machine never made it much beyond the drawing board in the 1970s because such a design would have raised the Corvette's price who knows how far beyond what the market would bear. But while relocating the engine never happened, moving the transmission to the rear did, albeit a quarter century later. Today's C5 is, accordingly, the best balanced Corvette ever, as well as the Corvette best suited to do battle with foreign invaders.

The Corvette most able to represent this country on the world sports car stage 30 years ago wasn't the outrageous L-88 or its more streetable 435-horse cousin. Not even close. Granted, big-block Sharks were among some of the quickest machines ever built. Off the line. But once faced with vectoring left or right again and again they could've easily ended up off the road. The so-called "rat-motored" Vettes, the 427s and 454s, were best suited for stoplight-to-stoplight competition here at home with red-white-and-blue-blooded musclecars like Hemi Mopars and Cobra Jet Mustangs.

The Corvette Duntov undoubtedly would have been more willing to drive in Europe then was the legendary LT-1, introduced in 1970. Built in small numbers up through 1972, the LT-1 probably represented the closest the C3 Corvette came to garnering true respect as a world-class sports car. *Car Life*'s editors in August 1970 called it "the best of all possible Corvettes." "Forget the LS-7," they continued. "Don't wait for the mid-engine prototype. The LT-1 is here, and it's ready." Earlier that summer, *Motor Trend*'s Chuck Koch concluded that the LT-1 was "much closer to its German competitor than most Porsche owners care to admit." According to *Sports Car Graphics* Paul Van Valkenburgh, the 1970 LT-1 was "better in most ways than every Italian/British/German two-seat street GT available at thrice the price."

In 1971 *Motor Trend*'s Eric Dahlquist was also quick to point out how well the LT-1 stacked up dollar for dollar against its much more expensive European rivals. "We were almost embarrassed to find that despite Detroit's

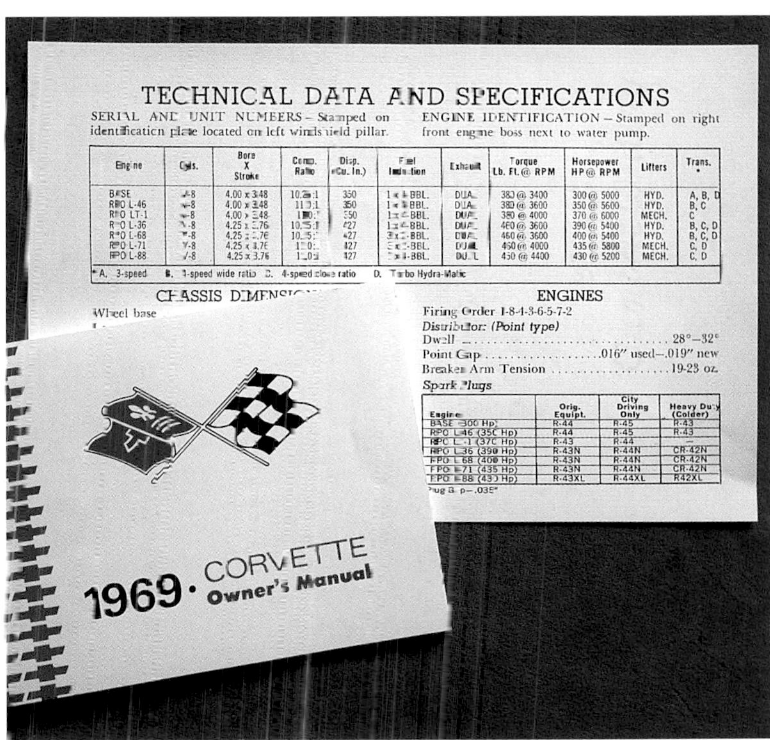

One year before Chevrolet officially announced the LS-7 option then never coughed it up, the paperwork guys were again leaping before they looked. Plans to introduce the LT-1 350 in 1969 fell through, but not before the 1969 Corvette owner's manuals were printed.

The Poorman's Corvette

Comparisons between the Corvette and purported rivals—even dating back to the fiberglass two-seater's earliest days—have never really panned out. Ford's original Thunderbird was a bird of another feather entirely. Studebaker's supercharged Avanti was close but no cigar. Carroll Shelby's Cobras could run, but they couldn't hide their totally uncivilized nature. Shelby's Mustangs, GT 350 or GT 500, had their own niche. American Motors' two-seat AMX was here and gone before anyone really noticed. Pantera? DeLorean? Bricklin? Not a chance. No matter how fast, no matter how sexy, no other car has ever been able to capture the imagination, to stir the souls of both men and women like Chevrolet's 'glass-bodied baby.

But if there was one machine that did a damned good Corvette impersonation it was another Chevy. The Camaro, introduced in 1967 to do battle with Ford's wildly popular Mustang, offered its fair share of performance potential. It was relatively lightweight and could become quite nimble with the right options. It could get downright fast too, with a 396-ci big-block beneath that long hood.

Big-block power, however, compromised handling. The supreme Camaro as far as fully balanced, sports car-type performance was concerned was the famed Z/28, also introduced in 1967. The Z/28's hot, high-winding 302 small-block V-8, coupled with a race-ready chassis, helped turn more than one Corvette crazy's head, especially so if that particular crazy was a few grand short of his dream of living life in the fiberglass fast lane.

Today's horsepower hounds know the concept as "the biggest bang for the buck." There was no doubt that the baddest big-block Corvettes of the late-1960s offered the best bang, but at what cost? Just as there has always been no substitute for cubic inches, there is also nothing stronger than the power of cold, hard cash. How fast you want to go always has and always will depend on how much you have to spend.

Beneath a Camaro's hood, the LT-1 350 was rated at 360 horsepower, 10 less than its Corvette cousin. No matter how you sliced it, though, this ponycar was hot to trot.

By 1970, the Corvette's base price had surpassed the $5,000 plateau for the first time, and for this amount a buyer only received the standard 300-horse 350 small-block. Installing the 454 big-block added another $289 to the bottom line, opting for the 370-horsepower LT-1 small-block upped the ante by nearly 450 bucks.

The original Z/28 package in the late 1960s cost a few dollars more than the Corvette's LT-1 engine option did in 1970. But for about $460, Camaro buyers not only got their own exclusive V-8—the 290-horsepower 302—they also went home with a trick suspension, 15x7 wheels, a nice dose of exterior imagery, and a heavy-duty cooling system. Although other mandatory heavy-duty options (four-speed manual, front disc brakes) did raise the Z/28's price further, a Camaro coupe's base sticker in 1969 was still only a tad more than $2,700.

You get the picture, no? Fifty-five hundred dollars was a lot of dough 30 years ago. Thirty-five hundred was a pile then too, but it wasn't $5,500. All things being relative, the first-generation Z/28 Camaro indeed qualified as a "poorman's Corvette." While the prestige obviously wasn't quite the same, much of the performance was, and it came at a price many considered affordable.

Then along came the second-generation Z/28. You would have to search far and wide to find a car that compared as favorably, as closely, with the Corvette as the 1970 1/2 Z/28 Camaro. Again, its well-balanced performance was a given. But this time around its image took a major turn toward the Corvette's stratosphere thanks to a sexy restyle that most critics couldn't resist. GM's all new F-body shell, introduced in February 1970 (thus the 1970 1/2 designation), created newfound excitement for both Camaro and Firebird buyers. From nose to tail, from top to bottom, this curvaceous, thoroughly modern body represented the biggest styling hit of the new decade. "It's quiet, quick, beautiful and all the parts look and act as though they belong together," claimed *Sports Car Graphic's* Paul Van Valkenburgh in reference to the 1970 1/2 Z/28.

Beauty beneath that bodacious skin included a new powerplant too. The standard small-block for the next-generation Z/28 was the LT-1 350, the same LT-1 as the Corvette's with one exception: The Z/28's LT-1 was advertised at 10 fewer horsepower. Ten horses on paper mattered little, though. More than 1 horsepower per cubic inch was still more than 1 horsepower per cubic inch, and 360 horses were more than enough to move the Z/28 into a higher class of performance. With a much wider, more useful power band compared to the 302, the 350 LT-1 offered an instantaneous brand of throttle response that earlier Z/28 drivers could only imagine.

According to *Car Life's* testers, "the [new] Z/28 is as close to a mild-mannered racing car as the industry has come.

As it has in recent years, talk in the early 1970s had Chevrolet combining the Camaro and Corvette into a more affordable, yet still sporty package. Camaro owners in 1970 almost didn't have to wait for that rumor to become reality. The sexy 1970 1/2 Z28 offered every bit as much performance as the hottest small-block Corvette did that year. Both shared the LT-1 350 V-8—the Corvette as an option, the Camaro as standard power.

Despite the added weight and tougher emissions controls, it's faster than ever, and in a way that makes the car driveable by anybody." That included drivers familiar with Corvette-style performance.

Van Valkenburgh's *SCG* test of the 1970 1/2 Z/28 was a comparison report that pitted the new Camaro against a 1970 LT-1 Corvette. His conclusion came right off the bat in his headline: "They really are all the same in the dark!" In all tests—acceleration, braking, lateral g, and so on—the two ran neck and neck, with the Z/28 actually slightly outscoring the Corvette a time or two. Zero to 60 times were 6.7 seconds for the Corvette, 6.5 for the Camaro.

The only area where the Corvette showed off a noticeable advantage was aerodynamics, but that was expected. On the flipside, the Z/28's advantage was even more noticeable, as well as more meaningful to Average Joe. The as-tested price tags for the two heavily optioned Chevrolets in *SCG's* comparo read $6,357 for the Corvette, $4,690 for the Z/28. Had the Camaro in question not included the RS equipment and a few other optional diddies, the price differential between the two machismo mills would have been every bit of $2,000. Concerning this figure, Van Valkenburgh could only restate the obvious. "Think of the non-automotive things you can spend $2,000 on," he wrote. "If you choose the Vette, you're spending it on something that doesn't even exist—your image."

Haughty Corvette owners in 1970 could look down from above and snicker all they wanted. But it was the Z/28 guys that got the last laugh—and this one lasted all the way to the bank.

myopia and failures they can still build one of the best cars anywhere, not for nine or ten grand, but six," he wrote in praise of the biggest, baddest small-block Corvette to date. The expensive European that Dahlquist used for a measuring stick against the LT-1 was Britain's V-12 E-type Jag. "The Corvette is a better car," he boldly, if not bravely, concluded

The LT-1 earned such accolades by combining rat-like muscle with the nimbleness inherent in Corvettes fitted with the venerable V-8 affectionately known by Chevy-heads as the "mouse motor." With midengined possibilities representing more fantasy than fact, the best a bias-conscious buyer could do in the early 1970s was stick with the 350-cid small-block, which weighed about 150 pounds less than the Mk IV big-block. This, in turn, meant a 350-powered 1970 Stingray achieved a more preferable 50/50 front/rear weight balance, making it more of a treat to drive through the twisties compared to the nose-heavy 454 Corvette. This and the LT-1 brand of 350 V-8 injected 370 horses into the mix.

It had been five years since Corvette buyers had seen a small-block as powerful as the LT-1 350, and its debut instantly invited comparisons to earlier milestones. According to *Car and Driver*, any other power source was "of little interest to the Corvette purist, the man who remembers the soul and vitality of the high-winding fuel-injected 283 when it was the only street engine in the country that put out one horsepower per cubic inch. Today's equivalent is the LT-1."

Like so many other publications over the last 40-something years, *Car and Driver* didn't exactly get the facts right. The Chrysler 300B's optional 354-cid Hemi V-8 was advertising 355 horsepower in 1956, but who was counting, right? As it was, the 283-horse 283 "fuelie" introduced one year later was only the beginning. Top fuel-injected output grew to 290 horses in 1958, 315 in 1961. It hit 360 horsepower when small-block displacement expanded to 327 ci in 1962. By 1964, the injected L-84 327 was producing 375 horsepower. Then along came those big-block bullies the following year, which was the last for the L-84.

Prior to 1970, the hottest noninjected small-block ever cooked up was the L-76 327 of 1964–65. Essentially an L-84 with a four-barrel in place of the Rochester F.I. unit, the solid-lifter L-76 was rated at 365 horsepower. It too

Chevrolet's vaunted small-block legacy began in 1955 with this 265-ci V-8. A short stroke and lightweight valve gear featuring stamped steel ball-stud rocker arms made this all-new, thoroughly modern overhead-valve V-8 rev like nobody's business. *Chevrolet Public Relations*

was discontinued after 1965. The LT-1's debut in 1970 represented both the arrival of a new king of the carbureted mouse motor hill and a return of mechanical tappets to the small-block Corvette lineup.

The 370-horse LT-1 350 also was essentially an enlarged variation of yet another hot solid-lifter Chevy small-block, although saying that begged the question of which came first, chicken or egg? As a June 1971 *Car and Driver* report explained it, the LT-1 "is probably even better known as the Z28, which is what it is called when ordered in the Camaro. Corvette engineers originated the idea so Duntov winces when you say the two engines are the same, but they are."

A second LT-1, this one rated at 360 horsepower, served as the heart and soul for the new Z/28 Camaro introduced early in 1970. Previous Z/28s used the hotter-than-hell 302 small-block hybrid, and it was this engine that the LT-1 was based on. The 290-horsepower 302 was created exclusively for the original Trans-Am Camaro in 1967 by stuffing a 283 crank into a 327 block. A huge 800-cubic feet per minute Holley four-barrel, a loping solid-lifter cam, and big-valve heads helped make the Z/28 302 "a happy and extremely potent screamer," according to *Sports Car Graphic*'s Jerry Titus.

Creating the LT-1 V-8 was simply logical. Knowing that there usually is no substitute for cubic inches, Chevy engineers couldn't help but recognize the obvious. All things being equal, more displacement almost always means more power potential. And by most counts 350 amounted to more than 302. If the Z/28's happy little small-block was such a potent screamer, imagine what 48 more cubes might do for this mighty mouse. So many pieces in Chevy's small-block parts bins mixed and matched so easily, working that Z/28 magic on the 350 V-8 was simply a matter of turning a wrench.

Too bad those bins weren't bottomless.

After serving two years beneath Camaro hoods, the 350-cid small-block finally replaced the venerable 327 V-8 as the Corvette's standard power source in 1969. Initially spec'ed out that year was the base 300-horsepower 350, the 350-horse L-46 350, and the LT-1. That's right, the LT-1. In 1969. Early factory paperwork listed the engine that year, and more than one press source applauded its arrival. "If you're hung up on a Stingray and you want one that handles as well as it hauls, check out the new 370-horsepower LT-1 350-cuber; it's the only way to go," announced a headline in the May

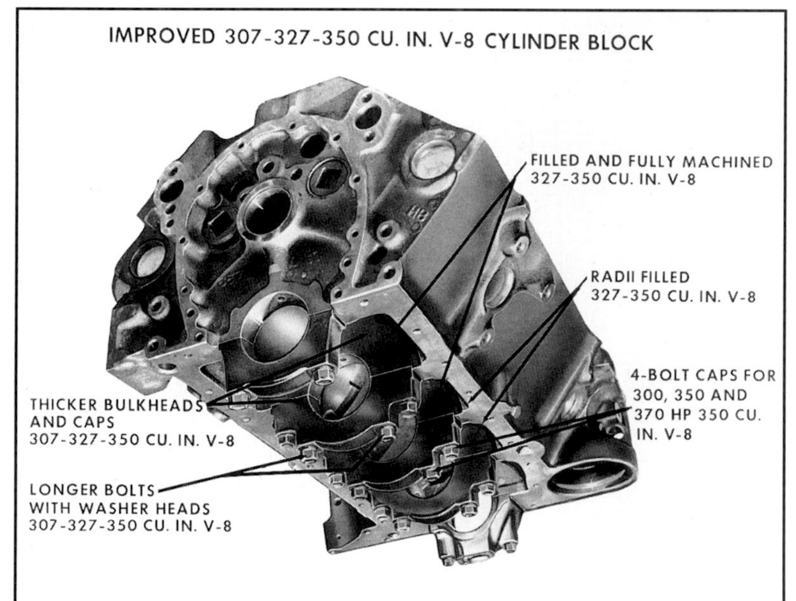

The performance mouse-motor's cylinder block was already one beefy piece even before engineers began building the LT-1 350. *Chevrolet Motor Division*

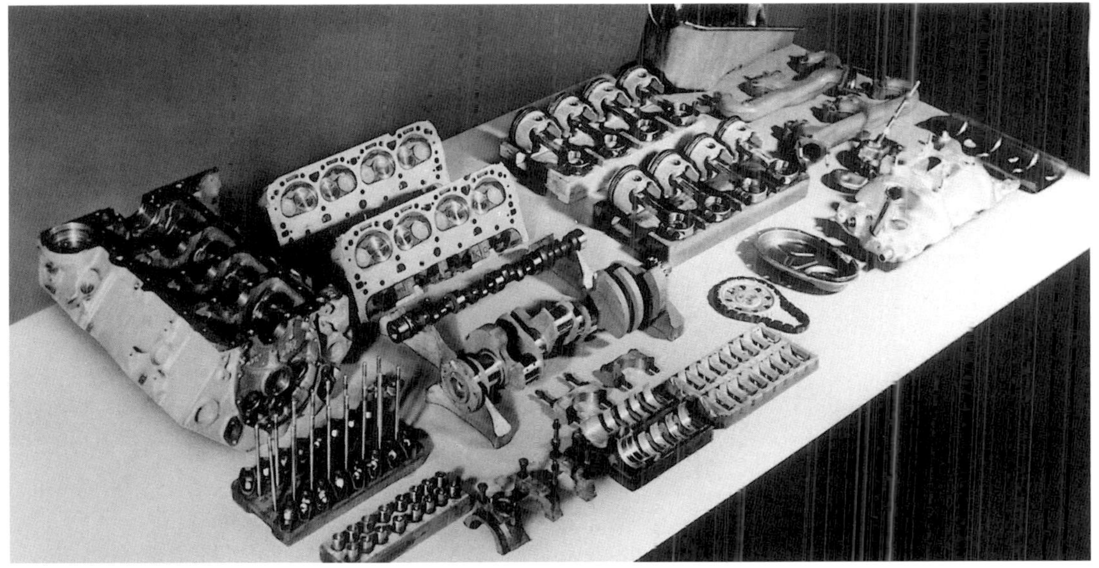

The LT-1's forefather was the first Z/28 Camaro's exclusive powerplant, the 290-horsepower 302. This engine was created specially to legalize the Z/28 Camaro for SCCA Trans-Am racing. It was destroked down within the SCCA's 305-ci limit by inserting a 283 crank into a 327 block. *Chevrolet Motor Division*

1969 issue of *Cars* magazine. "Besides being a super-duty engine with high-rpm potential, it's also relatively light," continued the review a few lines below. "This factor plus its high torque rating makes for a dynamite handling and accelerating package."

Such announcements, however, proved premature as the LT-1 never became a production Corvette in 1969, although one such car apparently was sold. As a July 1969 *Car Life* report explained, "The factory listed the 370-bhp/350-cid engine early in the model year, found they couldn't get all the pieces without depriving the Z/28 market, and cancelled. But before they did the factory shop manuals came out. All the engine specifications were listed."

It wasn't the first time a desirable Corvette option was listed early on then erased. And it wouldn't be the last time that fiberglass fans would be teased with a hot new engine only to see it yanked back out of their reach. But unlike the big-block boys, who even then were licking their lips in anticipation of the promised LS-7 454, mouse motor club members in 1970 got a second chance at their carrot on a string. Better late than never.

The LT-1 engine option was priced at $447.60 in 1970. Included in that deal were the big-valve cylinder heads that had been staples around the Corvette's top-performance small-block parts bin dating back to the fuelie's days. Intake valves were 2.02-inchers; exhausts measured 1.60 inches in diameter. These hot heads were also machined for screw-in rocker studs and used hardened-steel pushrod guideplates. Pushing those rods was an aggressive mechanical cam that dialed in at 317 degrees duration on the intake side, 346 for the exhaust, with 96 degrees of overlap. Valve lift was 0.459 inches intake, 0.485 exhaust.

Four-bolt main bearing caps held a forged crank in place at the block's bottom end. Connecting rods were also forged, as were the aluminum TRW pistons. Compression was a molecule-mashing 11:1. An aluminum high-rise dual-plane intake went on top, itself crowned by a massive model 4150 Holley four-barrel rated at 800 cubic feet per minute. LT-1 Corvettes delivered in California used a slightly different 4150 Holley (the front fuel bowl was vented) to work with the Evaporative Emission Control (EEC) equipment required by that state's clean air cops. At the other end of the process were the big-block's 2.5-inch exhaust pipes in place of the 2-inch tubes normally found behind other 350 small-blocks. Ignition was transistorized by Delco.

Those 370 ponies arrived at 6,000 rpm. Maximum torque of 380 ft-lb came on at 4,000 revs. According to Van Valkenburgh's *Sports Car Graphic* test, this power translated into a 6.7-second ride from rest to 60 miles per hour. *Car Life*'s leadfoots managed 14.17 clicks in the quarter-mile, topping out at 102.2 miles per hour. Of course both the L-88 427 before and the LS-6 454 to come could break into the 13-second bracket with ease. But remember, there was more to the LT-1's appeal than brute

LT-1 Evolution

Corvette performance turned a historic corner in 1992 when Chevrolet engineers introduced yet another milestone small-block V-8 for America's only sports car. And to mark this milestone, the division's image-conscious labelmakers reached back in time for a name familiar to anyone who has followed the rich 45-year history of the popular Chevy small-block.

In the 1960s, the supreme small-block was the L-84 327, the fabled "fuelie" V-8, rated at 375 horsepower. During the power-outage years of the late-1970s, the only name that mattered was L-82. In between came the legendary LT-1 350, the small-block that left many big-block owners believing that size indeed doesn't matter.

Recycling famous Corvette options codes was nothing new when the time came to christen Chevrolet's redesigned 5.7-liter V-8 in 1992. The ZR-1 label, first used in small numbers in 1970, was dusted off in 1990 for the "King of the Hill" Corvette with its sensational dual-overhead-cam, 32-valve LT5 V-8. Two years later Chevrolet officials opted to bring back the LT-1 tag for its latest, greatest small-block. Only this time they dropped the hyphen.

It didn't take long for Corvette buyers in 1992 to recognize that the "dehyphenated" LT1 was more than worthy of the name. According to Dave McLellan, the new-generation small-block earned its revered recognition because of its strength—it was easily more powerful than the original LT-1, which, at 370 horses, ranked right up with the mightiest mouse motors ever built. Consider the name choice a matter of passing the crown along to the latest ruler.

Maximum output for the 1992 LT1 was 300 horsepower at 5,000 rpm; maximum torque was 330 ft-lb at 4,000 rpm. Okay, 300 obviously isn't greater than 370. But remember, advertised outputs before 1972 were gross numbers; along with often being a little on the inaccurate side, they also were dynoed out at the flywheel with no accessory drive drag or external friction losses taken into account. Today's much more honest figures are net ratings; that is, they represent real power delivered right to the road.

As it was, comparing the LT1 with its LT-1 predecessor mattered not at all to drivers who were only familiar with the L98 small-block in their 1991 Corvettes. This time basic arithmetic did apply. Three-hundred horses did dwarf the 245 produced by the L98 350. And if you didn't believe the stats, you could certainly trust the seat of your pants. The LT1 punch literally represented a rebirth for the Corvette in 1992.

The engine itself was surely a rebirth. Next to nothing interchanged between LT1 and L98. Block height, bore spacing, and displacement carried over in the best tradition of the Chevy small-block. Essentially everything else, however, was drawn up on a clean sheet of paper.

Chevrolet's small-block V-8 engineering team was inspired by the ZR-1 Corvette's LT5 V-8. The 5.7-liter LT5 initially produced 375 horses and was later boosted up to 405 horsepower in 1993. While the standard 5.7-liter Corvette small-block was

Chevrolet did away with the hyphen when it dusted off the LT-1 moniker for the Corvette's new standard small-block V-8 in 1992. Helping the wonderfully efficient LT1 350 pump out 300 real horses was the first standard dual exhaust system seen since the Corvette switched to catalytic converters in 1975.

LT1 performance quickly filtered down Chevrolet's performance pecking order after its 1992 introduction. In 1993, a 275-horsepower LT1 became the Z28 Camaro's meat and potatoes. Then in 1994, the new Impala SS (right) debuted with Corvette power beneath its sinister black hood. The Impala SS LT1 was rated at 260 horsepower.

a much more conventional pushrod, two-valve motor, McLellan's engineers recognized that they could squeeze considerably more out of it. Goals for updating the L98 V-8 included at least 50 more horsepower and a higher, flatter, longer torque curve from an engine that at the same time offered increased fuel economy and improved reliability. Tighter external dimensions and quieter running were also among priorities.

India-born Anil Kulkarni was the man given the task of reaching these goals. His engineering team did so and then some. The LT1 became an instant overnight sensation, and not just as the Corvette's heart and soul. In 1993, a 275-horse version of the LT1 helped the redesigned Camaro unseat the 5.0-liter HO Mustang as the performance market's "best bang for the buck." That was followed by a still-hot 260-horsepower LT1 for the Impala SS sport sedan in 1994.

Keys to the LT1's success were improved-flow aluminum heads, 10.2:1 compression, and a much more aggressive roller-lifter cam compared to the L98. Other improvements included a lowered overall height (the better to fit beneath the Corvette's low hoodline) and an unconventional reverse-flow cooling system that delivered coolant from the radiator to the heads first, then the block. This reverse-flow cooling improved combustion efficiency and precision, which in turn benefited both performance and fuel economy.

The LT1 5.7-liter V-8 was joined by an even hotter 330-horsepower LT4 variant in 1996, the last year for Chevrolet's latest legendary small-block. With the arrival of the redesigned C5 Corvette in 1997 came yet another redesigned powerplant, the LS1, leaving the LT1 to retire for a second time. Like its forerunner, its place in automotive Valhalla is guaranteed.

strength. Much more.

Ordering the LT-1 option meant a stiffer suspension was also thrown in as part of the deal, which only further enhanced the small-block Corvette's already nimble nature. "Corvette handling is superior, with any engine," claimed *Car Life*'s test, "and the LT-1 is the best of the bunch. The weight balance is a perfect 50/50 with the small-block engine. The 454 Corvette uses a rear anti-roll bar, to compensate for the weight balance. The 350 Corvette doesn't need it, because there is no problem for which to compensate."

Other comparing critics weren't so kind to the 454 Corvette, which in LS-6 trim in 1971 weighed in at about 300 pounds more than the LT-1. Stiffer springs and an extra sway bar simply couldn't correct the big-block's forward weight bias. "Despite these changes to compensate for the larger engine, the 454 proved to be quite unpredictable and unsettling on the track," concluded Koch in a 1972 *Motor Trend* base-350/LT-1/big-block run-off. Veteran Corvette racer Tony DeLorenzo, who did all the hotshoe work for that triple-car test, found this out firsthand. "The 454 really got it on in the power department," he told Koch. "However, of the three cars it is the poorest handling. It is a wildly oversteering car, particularly in the fast corners, where it had the tendency to want to get away from you." Physical laws are never broken, at least in most states.

Perhaps the bravest, boldest claim concerning LT-1 handling came from Koch after comparing the 370-horse Corvette to a Porsche 911E for *Motor Trend*'s May 1970 issue. "Off the strip and onto the road course, this is where the Porsche should reign supreme," began Koch. "For years now the words Porsche and handling have been synonymous." Okay, tell us something we didn't know, Chuck. He did. "Here is where we experienced the biggest surprise of the test. The Corvette was just as fast, if not faster through the corners as the Porsche."

Most Americans probably also felt the 1970 LT-1 Corvette was every bit as cool, if not cooler than the Porsche. They were wrong in one respect. Air conditioning could not be installed when the 370-horse 350 was ordered. Nor could the Turbo Hydra-Matic. "Chevrolet is telling you something," explained *Car Life*'s LT-1 review. "You cannot get an automatic transmission, air conditioning or power-assisted

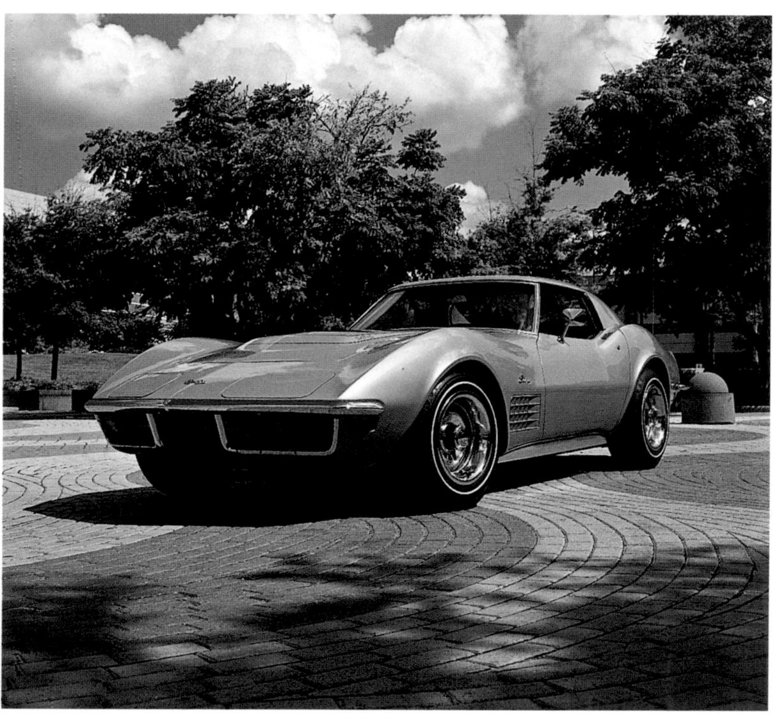

Chevrolet was able to let loose one more LT-1 Corvette in 1972 before the handwriting on the wall let everyone in on the story—the days of truly hot, high-winding V-8s, small- or big-block, would soon be over.

steering. It's hard to find mechanical reason for all of these exclusions. The same engine comes with an automatic in the Z/28, and the bigger Corvettes turn 6,500 rpm and come with the Corvette-only power steering. Our suspicion is that the keen types at Chevrolet just don't want to waste all their engine and chassis work on somebody who drives with his fingerprints."

Maybe so, but leaving off the air conditioning compressor was the only thing to do considering all the cooling problems that had been inherent in the C3 design from the beginning. Compounding that natural fact was the LT-1's own hot-blooded temperament, something any high-compression engine lives with. Keeping that blood from boiling was tough enough without a compressor pulley to crank. Why push its luck?

As for the automatic exclusion, who cared? A stick was the only choice for any sports car, and in the LT-1's case that choice was limited to two four-speeds: the wide-ratio M20, or the close-ratio M21 box. Standard rear gear ratios behind the transmissions were 3.55:1 for former, 3.70:1 for the latter. The 3.55:1 "economy" ratio was an optional choice for the close-ratio trannie, as were stump-yanking 4.11:1 cogs. Optional rear-axle accompaniment for the wide-ratio four-speed came in 3.36:1 and 3.70:1 ratios.

A third four-speed, the gnarly M22 "Rock Crusher," was also available to LT-1 buyers in 1970, but only by way of the race-ready ZR-1 package. That Chevrolet later applied this now-famous label to its King of the Hill Corvette for the 1990s was no coincidence. The first-edition ZR-1 was no pretender to the throne. In its day, it surely stood as the supreme small-block Corvette, and that may have been selling it a tad short.

Some even consider the LT-1/ZR-1 to be a "small-block L-88" of sorts. No, it didn't have aluminum heads or upwards of 500 horsepower. But it also didn't have that cranky, cantankerous nature and all those extra big-block pounds up front, either. Like the L-88, the ZR-1 was a complete, ready-for-the-track package with a mean and nasty chassis that could both take punishment and dish it out with the best of 'em. Although big-blocks could still out-accelerate

Air conditioning ducts were not things many LT-1 buyers could brag of nearly 40 years ago. No 1970–1971 LT-1 Corvettes were fitted with the cool option. And it wasn't until well into the 1972 run that engineers were finally able to make the combo work. Some estimates put cool-running 1972 LT-1 Corvette production at 240. Others claim 286 were built.

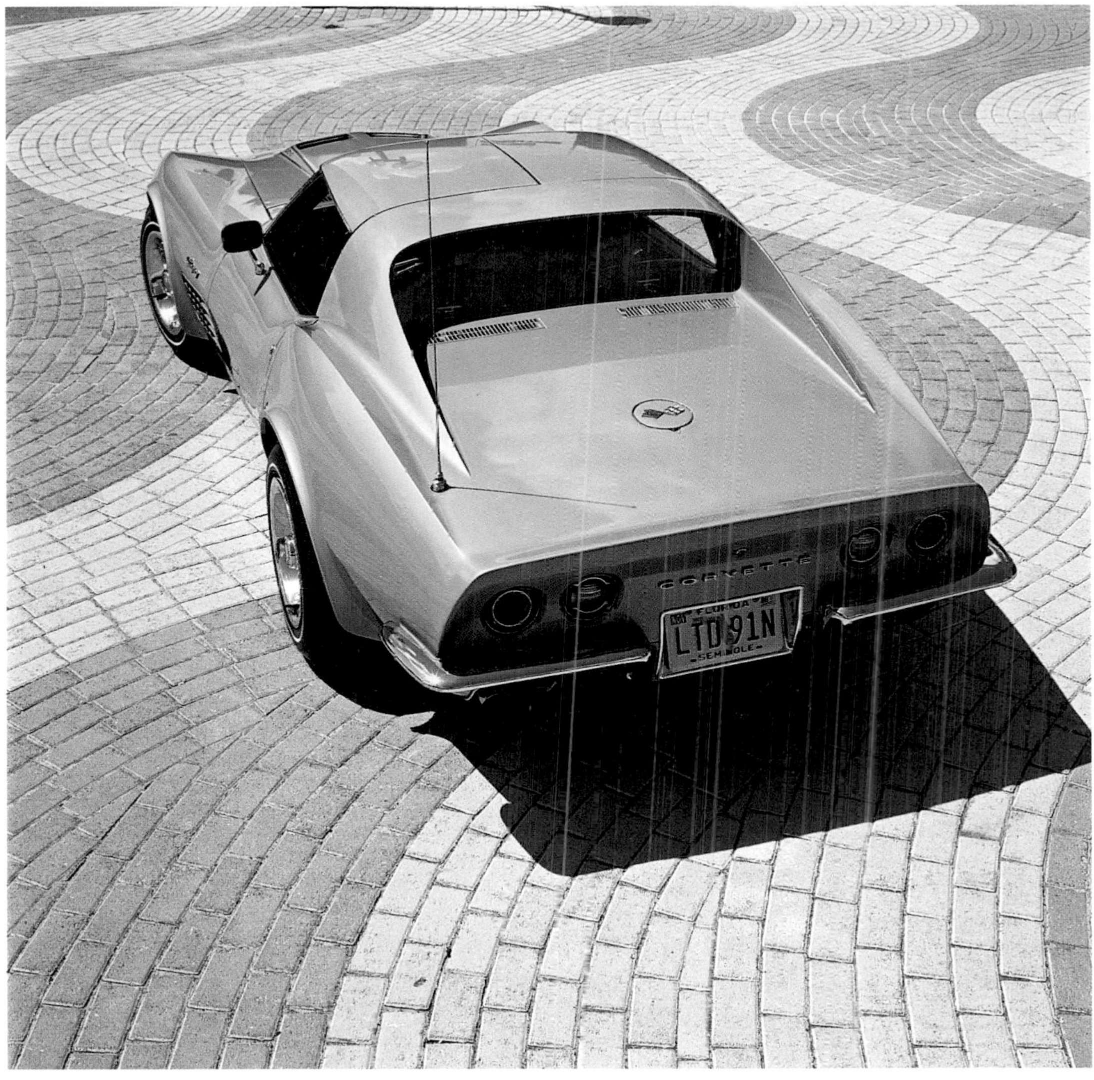

The LT-1 option's price hit $483 in 1972. Still, 1,741 buyers with a need for small-block speed anted up for the last "mouse that roared." This particular 1972 LT-1 played a cameo role in the movie *Apollo 13*, this even though the actual Apollo 13 drama unfolded in 1970.

this macho mouse-motored machine, they had another thing coming in the curves. If the "standard" LT-1 was indeed the "best of all possible Corvettes," then the ZR-1 truly was as good as it gets.

Unlike its modern counterpart, the first ZR-1 attracted very little attention in 1970. Few noticed in part because the option wasn't included in brochures—by most accounts, it wasn't officially mentioned in company paperwork until it appeared in a Chevrolet Motor Vehicle Price Schedule dated April 1, 1970. Even fewer chose the option once they did find it; this was perhaps due to its $965.95 asking price. Apparently the first LT-1/ZR-1 wasn't built until February 1970. Only 24 more rolled out of St. Louis that year.

Footnoted in that price schedule as an "indicated change" for the 1970 options list, the "ZR-1 Special Purpose Engine" was "not recommended for normal traffic situations." The equipment list went like this: "Not available when power windows, power steering, air conditioning, audio alarm system, rear window defroster, wheel covers, or radio is ordered. Includes 370-horsepower 350-ci engine, special four-speed close-ratio transmission, HD power brakes, full transistor ignition system, aluminum radiator, special springs with matching shock absorbers, special front and rear stabilizer bars." Since no radio was present, no shielding was needed for the distributor and spark plug wires.

Three items on that list were exclusive to the ZR-1 Corvette and all three were carryovers from the L-88s of 1967–69. The F41

With compression lowered to 9:1 and output now listed as a net figure, the LT-1 was rated at 255 horsepower in 1972. Also note the absence of an engine decal—no Corvette V-8s in 1972 had them, probably because Chevy engineers were not at all proud of the new decompressed, net-rated numbers. Barely discernible in this shot is Zora Duntov's autograph on the air cleaner lid. Duntov had actually specified this car to be the test mule for the LT-1/air conditioning combination. It was the first sweat-free LT-1 Corvette built.

special suspension and J56 heavy-duty brakes, like the aforementioned M22 four-speed, were not offered for any other model in 1970.

Standard Sharks were not known for their ride right out of the box, and the beefed-up LT-1 was even less respectful of seat-of-the-pants responses. Imagine, then, how rough and ready the ZR-1 was. Shorter, stiffer coils up front and a seven-leaf rear spring made up the F41 additions. Spring rates were nearly doubled. Although both front and rear heavy-duty sway bars were mentioned, no ZR-1s have ever been spotted wearing a bar in back.

The J56 brakes included the J50 power booster, heavy-duty Delco-Morraine four-piston calipers and fade-resistant metallic linings. Front pads were fixed more firmly in place by two mounting pins each, compared to the rear pads, which typically only used one pin. Cast-iron caliper mount braces were added up front to restrict vibration during hard stops. This brake system was all but identical to the L-88's save for the fact that its dual-circuit master cylinder didn't incorporate a proportioning valve.

The brakes, suspension, and gearbox weren't the ZR-1's only ties to the L-88. The two also shared a heavy-duty nodular-iron flywheel and leg-cramping 10.5-inch clutch. Measuring only 12.75 inches across, compared to the stock LT-1's 14-inch unit, the ZR-1's smaller flywheel helped the high-winding 350 wind up even easier by reducing the rotating mass it had to sling around. Installing this flywheel, in turn, required a smaller bellhousing and the L-88's high-torque starter motor. Another L-88 piece, the ZR-1's large-capacity Harrison aluminum radiator, dated back to the first Mk IV motor Corvette, the 425-horse 396 in 1966. It was fitted with a fan shroud to further aid cooling.

The ZR-1 package itself was fitted to both coupes and convertibles, and it was offered each year the LT-1 was. News in 1971 included a price increase to $1,010 and the introduction of a big-block running mate, the ZR-2. For this year only, the ZR-1 shared its Rocker Crusher four-speed with another Corvette, the LS-6 model. The 12 LS-6/ZR-2 Corvettes built were joined by only 8 LT-1/ZR-1s in 1971.

Corvette brochures finally acknowledged the ZR-1 in 1972, and production for that final year "soared" to 20. These cars all came without fan shrouds with the intention being to once and for all re-emphasize the obvious fact that ZR-1 Corvettes were "not recommended for normal traffic situations." Extra cooling capability via that shroud wasn't needed as long as a ZR-1 stayed in the fast lane, preferably on a racetrack. Transistorized ignition, initially mentioned in 1972 paperwork, was also deleted that year.

Chevrolet's first ZR-1 Corvette retired along with the LT-1 after 1972. Tightening emissions controls, soaring insurance costs, and rising fuel prices all helped ring the death knell for the big, bad small-block. First, its sky-high 11:1 compression was brought back down to earth in 1971, dropping to 9:1. Advertised horses, in turn, fell to 330 (at a slightly lower 5,600 rpm), while the LT-1 option price jumped to $483. When gross horsepower numbers were replaced by net figures in 1972, the LT-1's advertised maximum output shrank even further to 255 horsepower. Maximum torque was 360 ft-lb in 1971, 280 in 1972, both again arriving at 4,000 rpm.

LT-1 buyers were treated to one last surprise just before the car's demise. In July 1971, a build order was issued for an "air conditioning and engine cooling development vehicle" to test whether or not an A/C compressor could peacefully coexist with the solid-lifter small-block. This car was built in September and delivered to the Engineering Center in Warren, Michigan, "to be used for experimental purposes and/or industrial processing." From there it went to GM's Mesa Proving Grounds in Arizona for some serious testing under the sun.

With its wimpy 9:1 compression, the LT-1 was not nearly the same hothead it had been in 1970. Basically all engineers did was add deep-groove pulleys to resist throwing the accessory drive belt at high rpm. The typical LT-1 tach with its 6,500-rpm redline was also deep-sixed in favor of a rev-counter redlined at 5,600 rpm, this to remind drivers that they needed to keep cool on the throttle to stay cool behind the wheel. Once this War Bonnett Yellow coupe—shown, by the way, on these pages—passed its trial by fire in the desert, Chevrolet officials finally decided to add civilized comfort into the "who-cares-about-the-heat-index?" LT-1 mix.

"So many have asked for it we just had to include the C60 air conditioning as an option," announced *Corvette News* editor Joe Pike in 1972. "If you purchase your Corvette with an LT-1 engine, wide-range transmission and 3.55 ratio rear axle, you now have the option of adding air along with the rest of the goodies. This option, however, is not available with other optional transmissions or axle ratios." The $447.65 C60 option was installed on as many as 240 LT-1 Corvettes during the last four months of 1972 production.

Production of all LT-1s, cool-running or not, was limited, though relatively consistent throughout the three-year run. The numbers read 1,287 in 1970, 1,949 in 1971, and 1,741 in 1972. Although some magazines, in typical fashion, spoke too soon concerning the arrival of a fourth LT-1 Corvette in 1973, anyone with eyes could've recognized that the days of solid lifters and huge Holley four-barrels were over. The mouse that roared would roar no more.

Chevrolet wasn't about to unveil one of the greatest small-block V-8s (if not the greatest) ever built without it being dressed for the occasion. Special valve covers and the expected chrome-topped open-element air cleaner were part of the LT-1 deal. *Chevrolet Motor Division*

GOODYEAR
EAGLE ST
GOODYEAR

Chapter 5

Soft Touches

The "Bumperless" Years Begin in 1973

Despite press predictions to the contrary, no radical changes were ever made beneath the C3 Corvette's skin. While a new nose was added in 1973, followed by a revised tail in 1974, the basic platform remained all but identical to its 1963 forerunner.

We said it before and we'll say it again—"If it ain't broke, don't fix it." Actually, a GM board member had said it best in June 1972 after viewing one of Duntov's midengine prototypes at the Milford Proving Grounds. "What do you want a new car for?" he blurted out. "You're selling all you can make right now."

Indeed, the 1973 Corvette did a hotcake impersonation like no Corvette ever before on the way to becoming the first of the breed to break the 30,000-unit sales barrier. In a standard 12-month model run, that is. Remember, John DeLorean had "cheated" in 1969. Two months after the former Pontiac chief took over as Chevrolet general manager on February 1, the St. Louis assembly line was shut down by a strike, one of eight UAW work stoppages experienced by GM plants nationwide at the time. The St. Louis strike lasted from April 10 to June 9. Once the Corvette line restarted, DeLorean decided to make up for lost ground. Normally, 1970 production would have begun in September 1969. But Chevy's new general manager put 1970's startup on hold and let the 1969 run continue until December, resulting in that asterisk-marked 38,762-unit sales record.

On the flipside, 1970's late start in January coupled with yet another plant shutdown from April 6 to May 6—this one brought on by a parts shortage caused by a Teamsters strike—resulted in a drastic drop in production following 1969's sky-high output. The final score for 1970 read only 17,316 Corvettes, the lowest total since 1962. But from then on yearly sales didn't stop increasing until 1978.

As mentioned earlier, the downside to the record-setting production runs in 1968 and 1969 was a startling lack of quality control. DeLorean's predecessor, Pete Estes, temporarily added a third shift at the St. Louis plant in 1968 to speed things along, with the result being a new calendar-year (both 1968 and 1969 models) production record of 32,473 Corvettes—the first 30,000+ January-to-December run in the car's 15-year history. Around-the-clock production also resulted in some of the most shoddily-built Corvettes of all time. A 1970 *Road & Track* survey discovered that 'the worst thing about Corvettes, according to the owners, is the workmanship—or the lack of it." *R&T*'s pollsters talked to 177 owners and found that 18 percent of those who drove 1963–67 models felt workmanship was the worst feature. Forty percent of 1968–69 owners picked production quality as the worst feature of their cars.

Although workmanship would improve considerably after 1970, keeping ahead of growing demand would still occasionally compromise production standards—which simply had to remain high for a car the likes of the Corvette. F. James McDonald helped make quality control an even tougher task. A manufacturing

Dwindling demand helped convince Chevrolet to give up on the convertible Corvette after 1975. This Bright Yellow droptop was one of only 4,629 topless models built that year, compared to 33,836 coupes. An open-air Corvette wouldn't return until 1986.

The first major change since 1968 came in 1973 when the Corvette received a new plastic front end. Beneath that monochromatic nose was a structure guaranteed to let the car bounce back from 5-mile-per-hour collisions. The 1973 Corvette's tail remained identical to the 1972's.

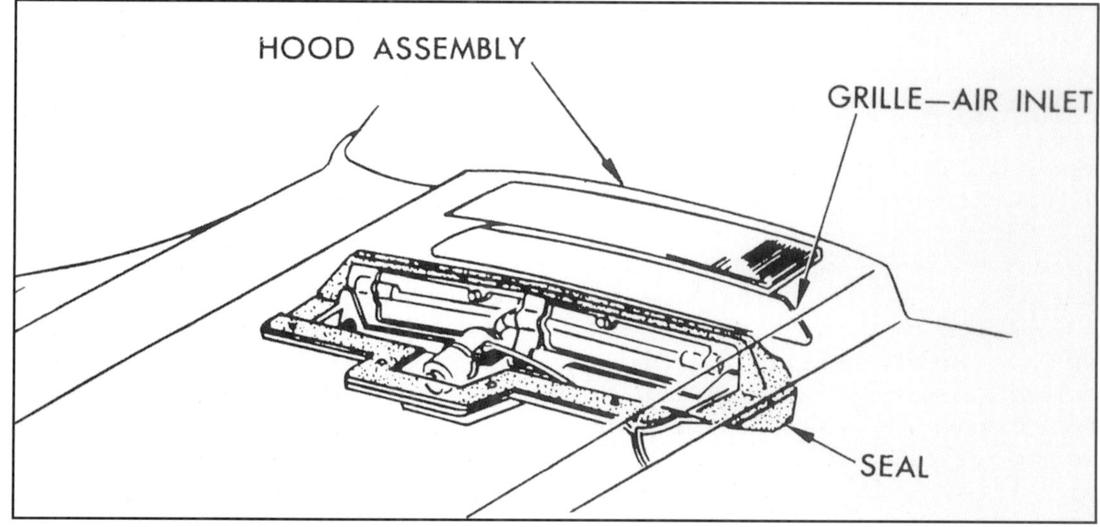

Before 1973, the only Corvettes with functional induction systems were the "Airbox" models of the 1950s and the L-88s and ZL-1s of 1967–69. New for 1973 was a functional hood that allowed air pressure that formed at the base of the windshield to force its way through a duct to the carburetor.

specialist and former head at Pontiac. McDonald took over as Chevrolet general manager on October 1, 1972. In 1974, McDonald gave the go-ahead to pick up St. Louis' production pace from eight Corvettes an hour to nine. Fortunately this move did not lead the Corvette down to the roughshod depths of 1968 and 1969. Just as it had done in 1973, the 1974 Corvette copped honors as the "Best All-Around Car" in *Car and Driver*'s annual readers pole. As it was, McDonald wasn't around to witness the results of his decision either way—former Cadillac exec Robert Lund moved over to Chevrolet to take F. James' place in December 1974.

Actually McDonald had little choice but to step up the production pace in 1974. Growing customer demand warranted the increase. Even with its four-month advantage, the 1969 sales standard probably would have been topped in 1973 had St. Louis been able to build Corvettes fast enough. The 1973 calendar-year run—32,616 cars—was a new record. The final 1973 model-year tally—30,464 Corvettes—represented only what the assembly line could bear. Another 8,200 orders were returned to dealers unfilled.

Supply continued to soar each year thereafter. Chevrolet sold 37,502 1974 Corvettes, followed by another 38,465 1975 models. The 40,000 plateau went by the boards the following year as a new all-time high was established at 46.558 units. Yet another record came in 1977 as 49,213 Corvettes rolled off the St. Louis line. Interestingly it had taken 15 years for Chevrolet to build its first quarter-million Corvettes. Hitting the half-million mark required only eight more years. The 250,000th example, a Riverside Gold convertible, was built on November 7. 1969. Had things been normal, this milestone machine would have been a 1970 Corvette. But due to DeLorean's extended run, it remained a '69 model. The 500,000th Corvette, a white coupe, was later driven off the line by Robert Lund on March 15, 1977.

"The St. Louis plant is operating two nine-hour shifts daily and working overtime two Saturdays a month just to meet sales demand," said Lund that day. "Current demand is running more

Only three engines were offered for the 1973 Corvette: the base 190-horsepower L-48 350, the 250-horsepower L-82 350, and the 275-horsepower LS-4 454. All three, even the L-48 shown here, were topped by an air cleaner that sealed to the hood's underside, this because standard equipment beginning in 1973 included an air-induction hood.

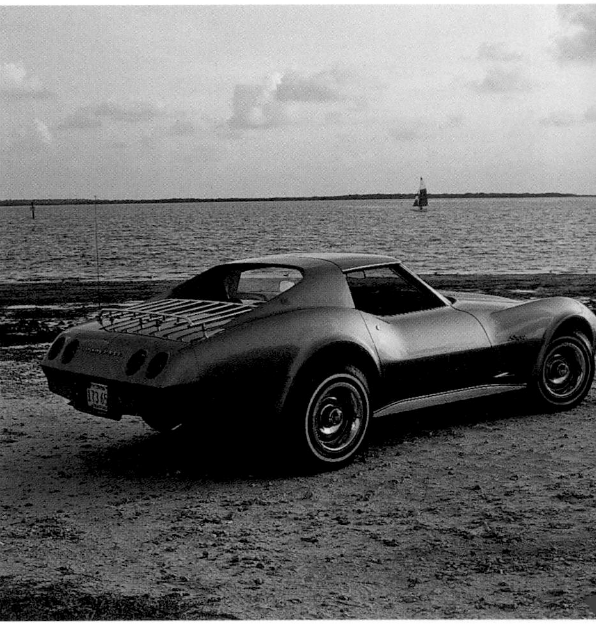

Difficulties forming the body-colored tail cap left Chevrolet with no choice but to create the thing in two pieces. The luggage rack on this 1974 454 Corvette was a dealer-installed option. The bright exhaust tips are owner-installed preferences.

Things came and went for the 1974 Corvette. This year was the first for a rubber bumper in back and the last for the 454 V-8. Chevrolet cancelled the big-block option after selling 3,494 454 Corvettes, including this coupe, in 1974.

than 29 percent ahead of last year." Predicting yet another Corvette sales record was even easier than shooting fish in a barrel in 1977.

Although it paled in comparison to its 1968–72 forerunners from a power perspective, the second of the C3 Corvette's three "five-year plans" clearly ended with a bang unlike anything heard before. On top of showing production increases for each year from 1973 to 1977, those last two record runs still rank third (1977) and fifth (1976) on the Corvette's all-time sales success scoreboard.

Recognizing those three groups is easy enough. The first, spanning 1968–72, had traditional chrome bumpers at both ends. The 1973–77 Corvettes introduced body-colored, crash-proof bumper systems. Corvettes built from 1978 to 1982 featured a new fastback glass rear roof section. All groups were based on the same platform introduced in 1968, and all still showed off Bill Mitchell's "Coke-bottle" body, at least in the middle.

Trading that classic chrome bumper for a urethane-covered, energy-absorbent front end was the result of new federal automotive safety standards that specified that all 1973 cars be able to bounce back from 5-mile-per-hour impacts. Beneath that monochromatic plastic nosepiece was a steel bumper beam attached to the frame by two ductile steel "Omark" draw bolts. If everything worked right, light collision energy was absorbed by the permanent deformation of the steel beam, coupled with the Omark bolts extrusion through two corresponding dies incorporated into the mounting points on the frame. Both the squished bolts and bent bar required replacement after a 5-mile-per-hour bump, but the plastic nose simply rebounded back into shape, hopefully none the worse for wear. Further safety enhancement was found inside the 1973 Corvette's doors where steel guard beams were added to protect occupants from side impacts.

Even more protection was added in 1974 when the 1973 energy-absorbing nose design was repeated in back. In place of that familiar ducktail rear and twin chrome bumpers was another resilient plastic cap, this one molded in two pieces. In 1975 the Corvette's body-colored end cap was redone in one piece without that telltale seam down the middle. Beneath that solid cap, a new aluminum bumper bar was attached to the frame with twin hydraulic cylinders. At the same time, the 1975 Corvette was also fitted with a new plastic honeycomb framework beneath its nose to help supply additional low-speed cushioning.

Amazingly all this extra reinforcement, steel or otherwise, didn't add on nearly as many pounds as most detractors feared early on. Reportedly that plastic-covered bumper system up front—which stretched total length by 3 inches—only increased overall weight by 35 pounds in 1973. All told, the typical 1973–77 Corvette curb weight went up about 250 pounds compared to its 1968–72 predecessor.

The 1973 nose job also included a new hood. Like the L-88 hood of 1967–69, this fiberglass lid incorporated ductwork that drew in cooler, denser air from the high-pressure area at the base of the windshield—but only at times when that pressure was truly high. Once a heavy foot depressed the throttle linkage beyond a certain point, a switch activated a solenoid, which in turn opened a flap hidden beneath a grille at the hood's trailing edge.

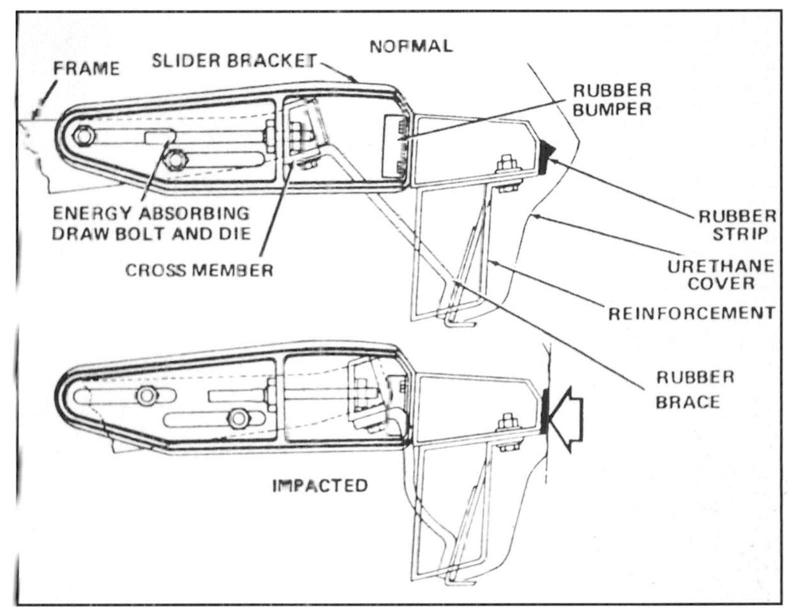

In the beginning, both the front and rear bumper systems worked the same beneath those plastic covers—a long bolt and die destroyed each other to help absorb the punishment. This system was refined a few times along the way.

Stripped of compression and hounded by everyone from insurance agents to safety crusaders to fuel conservationists, the Corvette's Mk IV big-block finally took its last ride in 1974 after leading the way since 1965. Output for the LS-4 454 in 1974 was 270 horsepower. Notice that this 1974 454 Corvette is missing its standard-issue plug wires and ever-present ignition shielding.

The Corvette's soft nose was refined in 1975 to include a special "honeycomb" cushion to help better resist minor bumps and collisions.

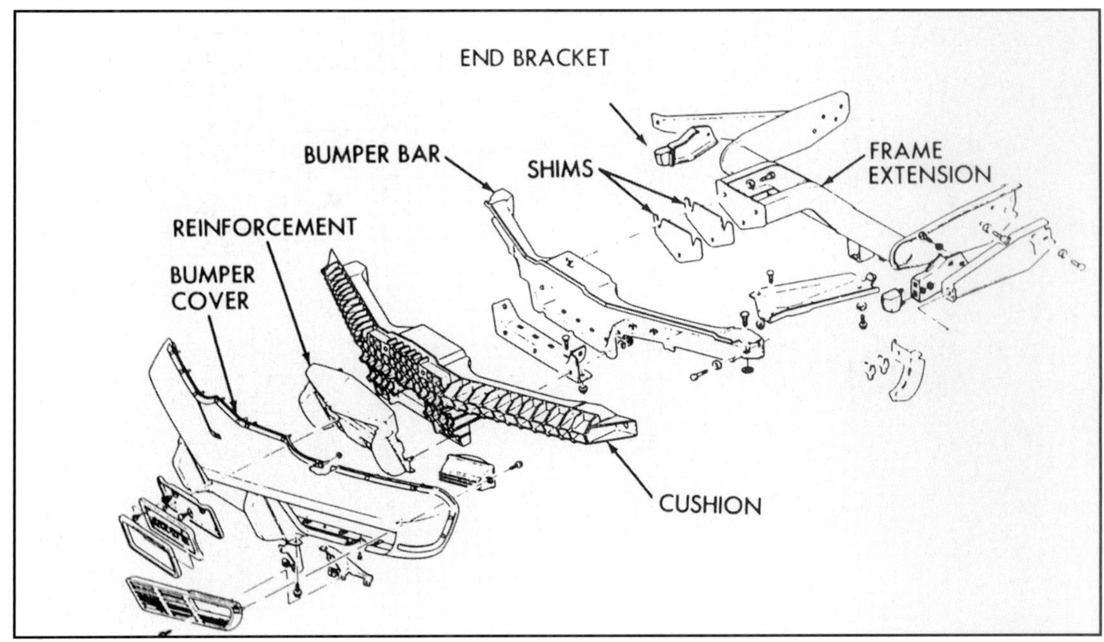

Opening this flap allowed that denser air to whistle directly to the air cleaner, which was sealed to the hood's underside by a rubber doughnut.

Along with allowing Corvette engines to breathe easier at top end, the new standard hood also did away with a Shark feature that had had many witnesses shaking their heads from its inception in 1968. The 1973 Corvette hood ran all the way back to the windshield uninterrupted, thus doing away with the pop-up panel that had formerly hidden the hideaway wipers on 1968–72 models. Called "GM Futurama styling at its worse" by *Car and Driver*, that panel was too slow and clunky and didn't always cooperate as designed. It was also a waste of weight-adding machinery considering that the wipers could simply hide beneath an extended hood's rear lip and operate without additional moving parts, as demonstrated effectively enough in 1973.

Modifications in 1976 did away with the C3 hood's cowl flap, which apparently whistled too loudly for most drivers. In place of the solenoid-activated induction setup was a simpler system that rammed in airflow through a duct that ran forward over the radiator support to pick up some of the radiator's cooling breezes. Even though the 1976 Corvette's hood no longer used the cowl-induction equipment it still kept the intake grille. That opening wasn't deleted until 1977.

Okay, so the cowl-induction hood did make some unwanted noise. But the rest of the revamped 1973 Corvette was easier on the ears overall compared to its 1968–72 predecessors. Larger mufflers were installed to tone down the exhaust note and extra sound deadener was added both under the hood and in the interior cabin's floor and side panels. The exhausts were tamed even further in 1974 with the addition of two small resonators.

The 1973 Corvette was also easier on the seat of the pants. New rubber cushioned body mounts were added to reduce the amount of vibrations transferred from the road to the driver through the frame. Also helping reduce ride harshness were the standard steel-belted radial tires introduced for 1973. Both Firestone and Goodyear supplied these GR70-15 treads, which ran more smoothly at highway speeds and improved wet-weather braking performance. On the other hand, magazine road tests showed that the radials reduced maximum cornering ability, as well as maximum stopping power on dry surfaces.

Initial plans in 1973 included offering optional aluminum wheels, RPO YJ8, to complement those radials and to help offset some of that extra federally mandated fat. Each YJ8 rim would have cut off 8 pounds of unsprung weight—had they been installed. Manufacturing gremlins, however, forced a recall of these wheels after about a couple of hundred sets were

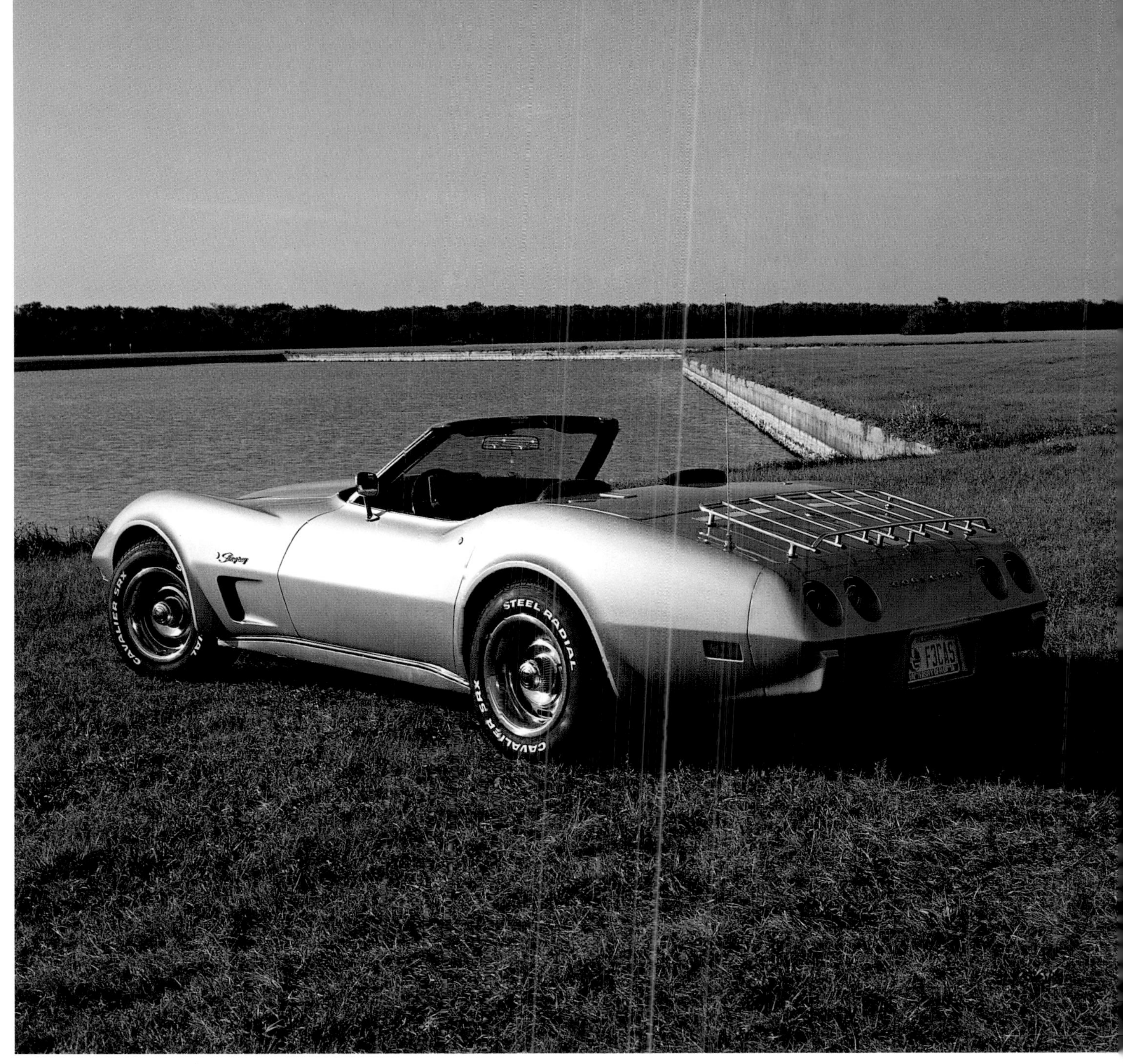

cast because quality wasn't up to snuff. Sound familiar? A similar situation occurred in 1963 when Chevrolet first tried to introduce cast-aluminum knock-off wheels for the Sting Ray. Just as some of those knock-offs surely made it into the wild 10 years before, Chevy paperwork in 1973 showed that as many as four Corvettes apparently were delivered with YJ8 wheels. Additional sets may have "slipped out the backdoor" as well.

RPO YJ8 didn't become an official (read successfully produced) option until 1976. The package included four aluminum wheels with a standard steel spare to keep the cost down. The price in 1976 was $299. It was $321 in 1977. Production was 6,253 for the former, 12,646 for the latter.

Third-generation Corvette owners who understood the value of reducing unsprung weight and cared little about harsh rides were treated to yet another new option, RPO Z07. Offered from 1973 to 1975, the Z07 package included considerably stiffer springs and shocks at both ends, a thicker front sway bar (a rear sway bar was also listed), and heavy-duty power brakes with dual-pin-mounted pads up front and fade-resistant

In 1975 the Corvette received a one-piece rear body section.

Heir to the Throne

Another era in Corvette history came to an end in 1975. Sixty-five-year-old Zora Arkus-Duntov officially retired on January 1, after 21 years and 7 months with General Motors. Two decades before he had boldly written Chevrolet chief engineer Ed Cole about a job after seeing the Corvette prototype on stage at GM's Motorama auto show in New York. "Now there's potential," he remembered thinking in a 1967 *Hot Rod* interview. "I thought it wasn't a good car yet, but if you're going to do something, this looks good." Duntov's letter led to a job as an assistant staff engineer at Chevrolet beginning May 1, 1953. "Not for [the] Corvette or anything of that sort," he told *Hot Rod*'s Jim McFarland, "but for research and development and future stuff."

"Considering his present stature, it is surprising to find that Duntov was not a part of the original Corvette project," began a December 1972 *Car and Driver* account of Zora's latest achievements. "However, he was soon drawn into it and he is certainly the architect of its performance image that began to emerge with the 1956 models. Since then his influence has grown to the point where he is known worldwide as the Father of the Corvette, a position all the more remarkable in Detroit, the land of the committee car. So it follows, then, that if you are to understand the Corvette you must not only drive it with an open mind but also hear of it from Duntov."

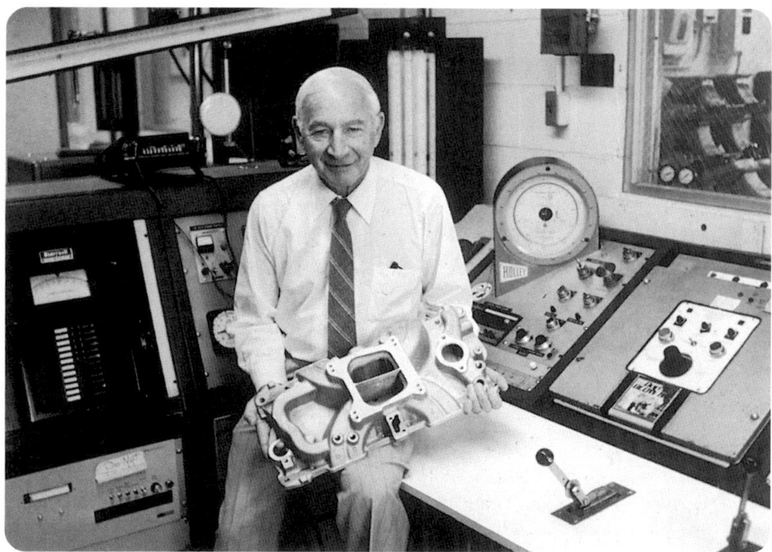

Zora Arkus-Duntov joined General Motors in 1953 and retired in 1975.

"That was the first Corvette that reflected my thinking," he told *Road & Track*'s Allan Girdler in 1989, in reference to the revamped, restyled 1956 model. After "fiddling on the side" (his words) in 1953 and 1954, Duntov was officially named Chevrolet's director of high-performance vehicle design and development in 1956, with his main focus of course being the division's highest-performance vehicle. His legendary, long-running "Duntov cam" appeared the following year, as did another major milestone—Ramjet fuel injection. Zora worked alongside engineer John Dolza to create the fabled "fuelie" small-block, which then led the way as the Corvette's top performance option up through 1964.

After only a few years on the job, Duntov was widely recognized as the man with his thumb firmly planted on the Corvette's pulse. Yet he wasn't officially named Corvette chief engineer until 1968, this after some bureaucratic bumbling had temporarily cut him out of the loop late in the C3 development process. From 1968 to 1974, he reigned supreme.

For those who've always wondered, but were afraid to ask, the Father of the Corvette got his name as a result of himself having two dads. The son of Russian parents, Zora Arkus was born in Belgium on Christmas day, 1909. Later, after returning to her hometown, by then known as Leningrad, Zora's mother divorced and remarried Josef Duntov. Both Zora and his brother, Yura, then took on the hyphenated last name out of respect to Misters Arkus and Duntov.

Those two monikers were merged even tighter together after the brothers fled Europe just ahead of Hitler's blitz in December 1940. In 1942 Zora teamed up with Yura to open a machine shop in New York. This endeavor quickly grew into the Ardun Mechanical Corporation—Ardun, of course, being short for Arkus-Duntov.

The company's main claim to fame was the legendary overhead-valve Ardun head conversion for Ford's flathead V-8. The plan was to produce these exceptional cylinder heads for Ford, but the deal fell through. No worry. British sports car builder Sydney Allard began offering the Ardun-head Ford V-8 in his J2 sports racers in 1949. Zora himself went to work for Allard in England soon afterward. He also drove an Allard racer at Le Mans in 1952.

Zora then returned to the States in time to get his first look at a Corvette in January 1953. An avid speed freak dating back to his youngest days, Duntov continued racing even after going to work for Chevrolet. He drove again at Le Mans in 1953, despite Ed Cole's insistence that he stay home and attend to his new position. His job was still there, of course, after the 24-hour race. It also remained intact following the class victories he scored while piloting a Porsche Spyder at Le Mans in

1954 and 1955. From then on, however, driving fast Corvettes remained his prime passion.

A bold race driver. A dashing, unforgettably handsome man who knew how to show off with style. An engineering genius with few equals. A fair-minded gentleman leader. If there was anything bad to say about the man, no one was talking following his death in April 1996.

"I was impressed with his continental poise, sophistication and his honesty and dedication to performance and to his work as an engineer," began Gib Hufstader's respectful homage. "He appreciated people who were very dedicated to doing a good job, to getting the job done. For some of us, it was a dream come true to work with him."

How did a mere mortal pick up where Zora left off in 1975?

The man handed the task of keeping the dream alive was David Ramsay McLellan. McLellan had begun his engineering career in 1959 after graduating from Wayne State University. His first job was in the noise-and-vibration laboratory at GM's Milford Proving Grounds where he demonstrated a knack for developmental design work. Dave moved on to Chevrolet early in 1969 to apply his talents to the new second-generation Camaro. A brief assignment in 1971 had him at GM's Technical Center working on John DeLorean's proposed "K-car" program. To Duntov's distinct dismay, the K-car was intended as a platform combining the Nova, Camaro, and Corvette. After this ill-fated proposal was rightly shot down, McLellan remained at the Tech Center as a full-time chassis engineer for the Camaro/Nova group.

Dave McLellan spent most of 1973 and 1974 at the Massachusetts Institute of Technology's Sloan School of Management. Not only did his GM bosses encourage this move, they also paid for it. Clearly he was being groomed for something big. With his MIT master's degree in hand, he returned to Chevrolet in the summer of 1974 as one of Duntov's staff engineers. Six months later, Zora stepped down and McLellan rose to the post that he already knew was his for the taking.

What wasn't so apparent was how Dave McLellan was going to make his mark on America's only sports car. The 1975 Corvette was, of course, well into its sales run by the time he took the reins. The following year's final product then too was already cast in stone, meaning the 1976 Corvette would follow closely in the tracks of every Shark born since 1968. The same went for the 1977 model. The new regime didn't make a noticeable impact until the Corvette was fitted with "fastback" rear glass in 1978. This minor makeover, however, represented nothing more than make-work, something to pass the time until McLellan's creative juices could boil over into the marketplace. That wouldn't happen for another five years.

The names *Duntov* and *Corvette* had become all but synonymous within three or four years after Zora's arrival at Chevrolet. It took about eight years for the moniker McLellan to edge its way near the household category. Dave first made his presence known in a really big way on March 24, 1983, when he introduced the long-awaited 1984 Corvette to Californians. The rest of America got its first look at his redesigned C4 on April 21.

Dave McLellan started his career at GM's Milford Proving Grounds in 1959 and became one of Duntov's staff engineers in the summer of 1974. When Duntov retired in 1975, he assumed control of the Corvette program.

C4 development dated back to 1978—a time when Duntov's midengine proposals remained fresh in everyone's minds. Including Zora's first and foremost. Though retired, he still dropped by McLellan's offices in Warren, Michigan, about once a month. The Father not only couldn't just walk away from his baby, he also couldn't quite forget the one dream that was never fulfilled, this even though GM execs had already all but dashed it to pieces.

Michael Lamm explained the situation in his 1983 book, *The Newest Corvette*. "In a 1978 conversation, Zora acknowledged to McLellan that Chevrolet wasn't committed to the midengine concept," he wrote, "although when I questioned Duntov in late 1982, he expressed some disappointment that the new [1984] car had abandoned the midship layout."

McLellan did dabble with a mid-engine mule early on, whether out of respect for the old man or as a product of at least a partial belief that Zora was right. "Partial" because Dave was undoubtedly much more of a realist than Duntov. He knew his bosses would never fund any really radical innovation. "The Stingray kept selling very robustly even into the early 1980s," said McLellan to Lamm in 1983. "And this trend made it harder to sell management on any new Corvette program, front- or rear-engined. Given our limited manufacturing capacity at St. Louis, given that you couldn't market any more cars of the more expensive mid-engine configurations—at the time management wasn't interested in these other sides of the game."

Dave McLellan stepped down in 1992. David Hill then became the Corvette's third chief engineer.

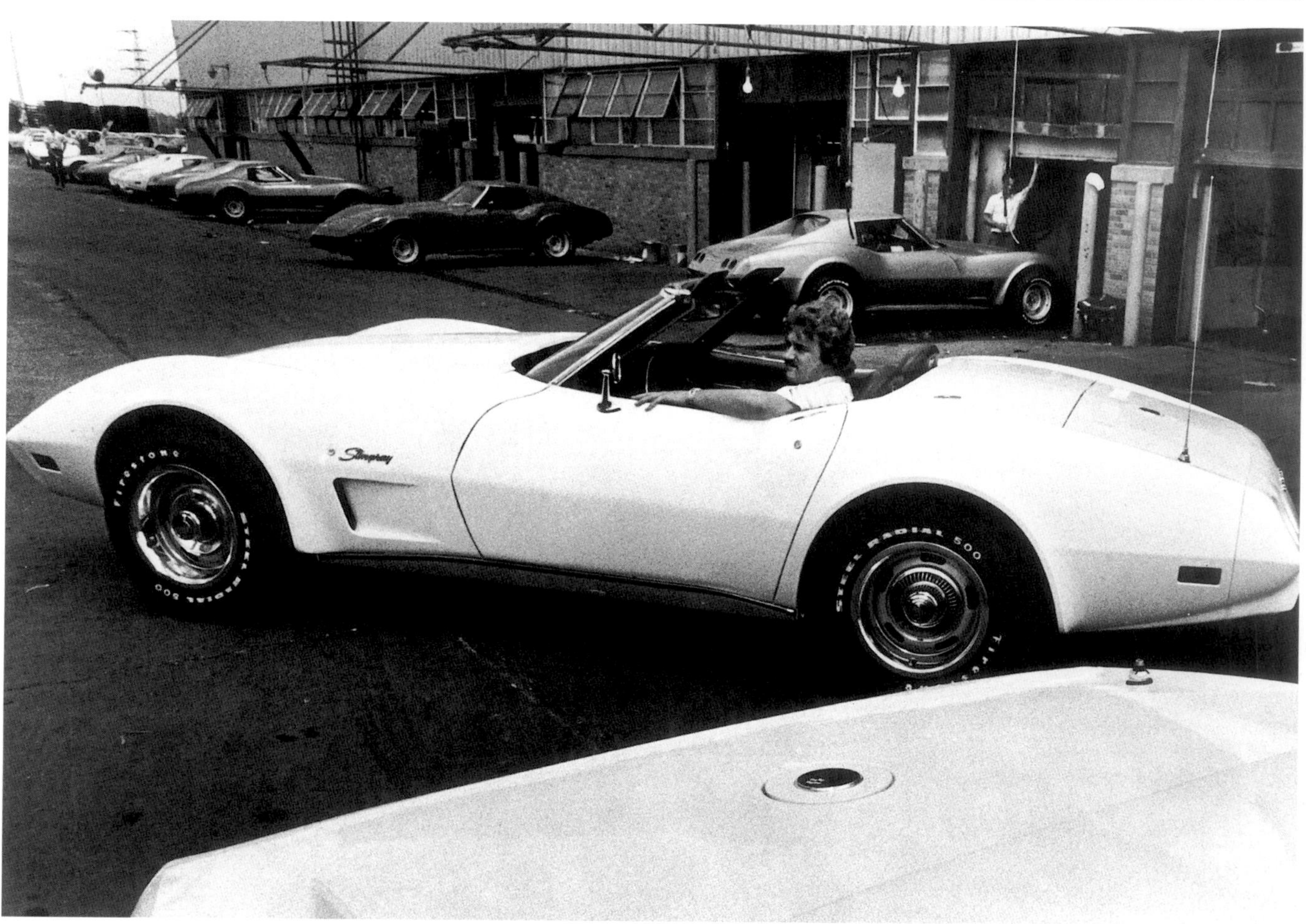

Bob Shell, inspection general foreman at the St. Louis plant, drives the last Corvette convertible off the line on July 31, 1975. *St. Louis Mercantile Library*

metallic linings all around. Like similar competition-oriented options before it, RPO Z07 was clearly intended for the track, not the street. Thus it could not be ordered with the mundane base 350 small-block or air conditioning. The M21 close-ratio four-speed was also mandatory.

RPO Z07's price was $369 in 1973, $400 in 1974 and 1975. Production figures reflected the option's not-ready-for-prime-time nature. Only 45 Z07 Corvettes were built in 1973, 47 in 1974 and 144 in 1975.

RPO FE7, the Gymkhana suspension package, was far more plentiful, because it was both easier on the wallet and the pants where that wallet resided. Introduced in 1974, it simply included a thickened front sway bar and higher-rate springs—no stiffened shocks or brawny brakes were included. Nor were there any ordering restrictions or additional mandatory options. Standard 350, automatic transmission, air conditioning—it didn't matter, the FE7 option could be added with no questions asked. Its price? A measly $7 in 1974 and 1975. That figure went up to $35 in 1976, then to $38 in 1977.

In this case, production figures reflected the FE7 package's softer sell, at least from a pricing perspective. While the less-gnarly FE7 group wasn't labeled an off-road option and Z07 was, the former still was not recommended for "casual use." An FE7-equipped Corvette could rattle a tooth or two, yet that apparently didn't hinder buyers who didn't mind trading comfortable kidneys for improved road-hugging capabilities. Chevrolet sold 1,905 FE7 packages in 1974, 3,194 in 1975, 5,368 in 1976, and 7,269 in 1977.

In other 1973–77 news, the removable rear window formerly included on all 1968–72 Corvettes was dropped in favor of fixed glass. Duntov did this to eliminate an unwanted backdraft that would occur at high speeds with windows up and roof panels removed. The breaker-less High Energy Ignition—with its

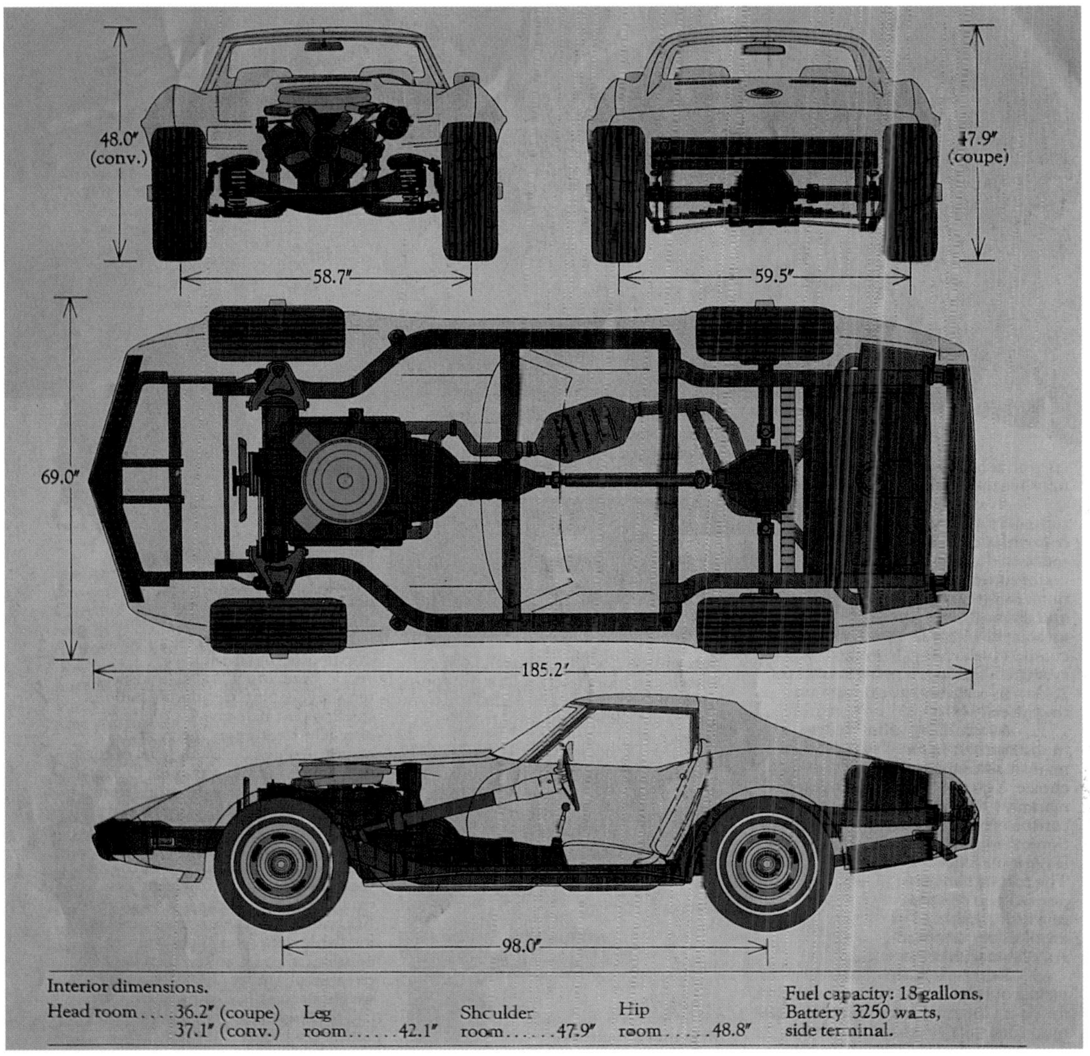

Also new for 1975 was a catalytic converter exhaust system. And since only one "cat" was used beneath the car's floorboard, a system of two Y-pipes routed exhaust into a single flow then back into dual mufflers. True dual exhausts wouldn't be seen again beneath a Corvette until the ZR-1 debuted for 1990. Standard duals reappeared for all models behind the LT1 350 in 1992.

hotter, more reliable spark—was made standard in 1975. A steel underpan was added in 1976 to increase rigidity and improve heat insulation. And a lighter (13 pounds or so) Delco Freedom battery joined the standard equipment list that year as well. Finally, the familiar Stingray script was deleted once and for all from Corvette fenders in 1977.

Clearly Corvettes built after 1973 were better cars as far as noise, vibration, and harshness were concerned. That was the idea. Duntov chose to improve his pride and joy as best he could within the rules imposed upon him. In one hand were safety czars' mandates that forced him to add weight to the car. In the other were stringent smog standards that limited how much horsepower he could use to try compensating for those extra pounds. Performance initially was the loser in the deal.

That the sporting crowd continued flocking into the fiberglass fraternity in ever-greater numbers from 1973 to 1977 wasn't exactly indicative of an ever-growing ability to stir the soul during those years. On the contrary, standard V-8 muscle sank to an all-time low: 190 horsepower in 1973, 165 in 1975. Mind you, these were net ratings, but they still represented an unprecedented downturn compared to 1972's 200 SAE net standard horses.

Along with horsepower, the engines themselves began disappearing after 1972. The LT-1's failure to return for 1973 in turn meant the end of the road for solid lifters, those noisy, rev-sensitive mechanical tappets that for more than 15 years had reminded Corvette drivers that the engine beneath that fiberglass hood did indeed mean business. "At first it seems unthinkable," began *Car and Driver*'s December 1972 obit.

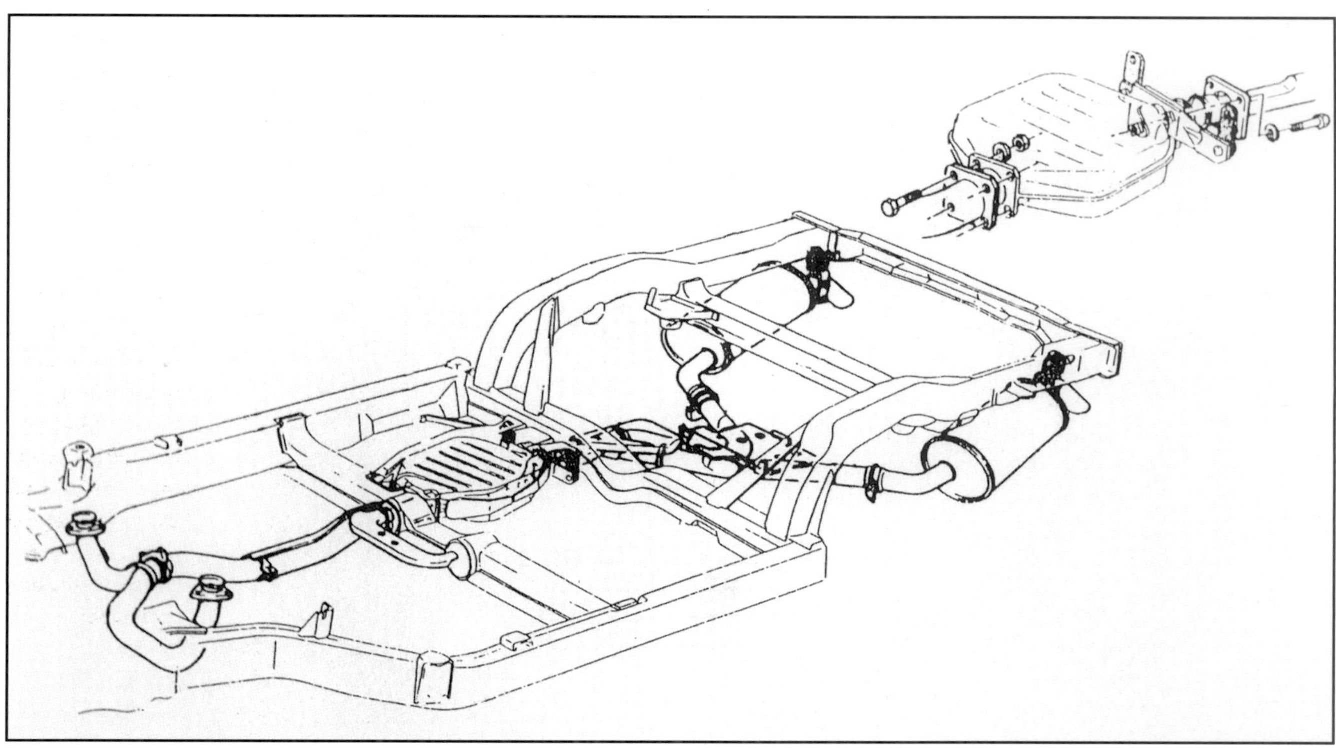

A more detailed look at the exhaust system used beginning in 1975 shows how Chevrolet allowed us all to think that Corvettes still had dual exhausts. Twin catalytic converters were considered, but in the end this single-unit layout won out.

"High winding engines and valve train clatter have been Corvette trademarks since 1956. To the enthusiast, it was those solid lifters that separated the Corvette engines from their weaker passenger car siblings. And now, with the passing of the LT-1, it is reasonable to say that The Corvette Engine no longer exists."

Even after the LT-1's demise, Corvette buyers in 1973 still had three V-8s to chose from, same as in 1972. Joining the base 350 small-block and the optional LS-4 454 big-block was a new RPO code—L-82. Though it filled in the space left behind by the LT-1, the L-82 small-block was actually a descendant of the hydraulic-lifter L-46 350, discontinued after 1970. Featuring 9:1 compression, big-valve heads and a relatively aggressive hydraulic cam, the L-82 350 produced 250 horses, which still stood tall despite *Car and Driver*'s claim that Corvette-style power had blacked out. L-82 compression never slipped during the 1973–77 run, and in fact topped all Corvette engines built in those years. L-82 output in 1974 was again 250 horsepower. But it dropped to 205 in 1975, then leveled out at 210 net horses in 1976 and 1977.

The explanation for the L-82's power outage? Those industrywide (Chevrolet wasn't alone) compression cuts made in 1971 had represented Detroit's first step toward the mandated use of lower-octane unleaded gasoline, which reportedly ran cleaner than the tetraethyl lead-laced jet fuels previously used to keep high-compression Corvette engines alive and well. While the cleaner-running aspects of unleaded gas could've been debated then, and were, the real reason behind the introduction of low-lead fuels in 1971 was to prepare the market for the next wave of federally ordered clean air requirements, scheduled to be met by 1975. To comply with these more stringent emission-control standards, Detroit engineers concocted the contaminant-burning catalytic converter, which didn't mix at all with leaded gasoline.

So it was that the limited availability of low-lead gas in 1971 set the stage for ethyl's swan song. By July 1, 1974, every retail outlet in America "at which 200,000 or more gallons of gasoline was sold during any calendar year beginning with 1971" was required by law to offer unleaded fuel of at least 91 octane.

This requirement, in turn, allowed Chevrolet engineers to introduce a catalytic converter exhaust system for the 1975 Corvette. A single large-capacity converter was installed after a design featuring two smaller units failed durability tests. Two Y-pipes were used to at least preserve the appearance of a sporty dual exhaust system. The first one funneled exhaust flow

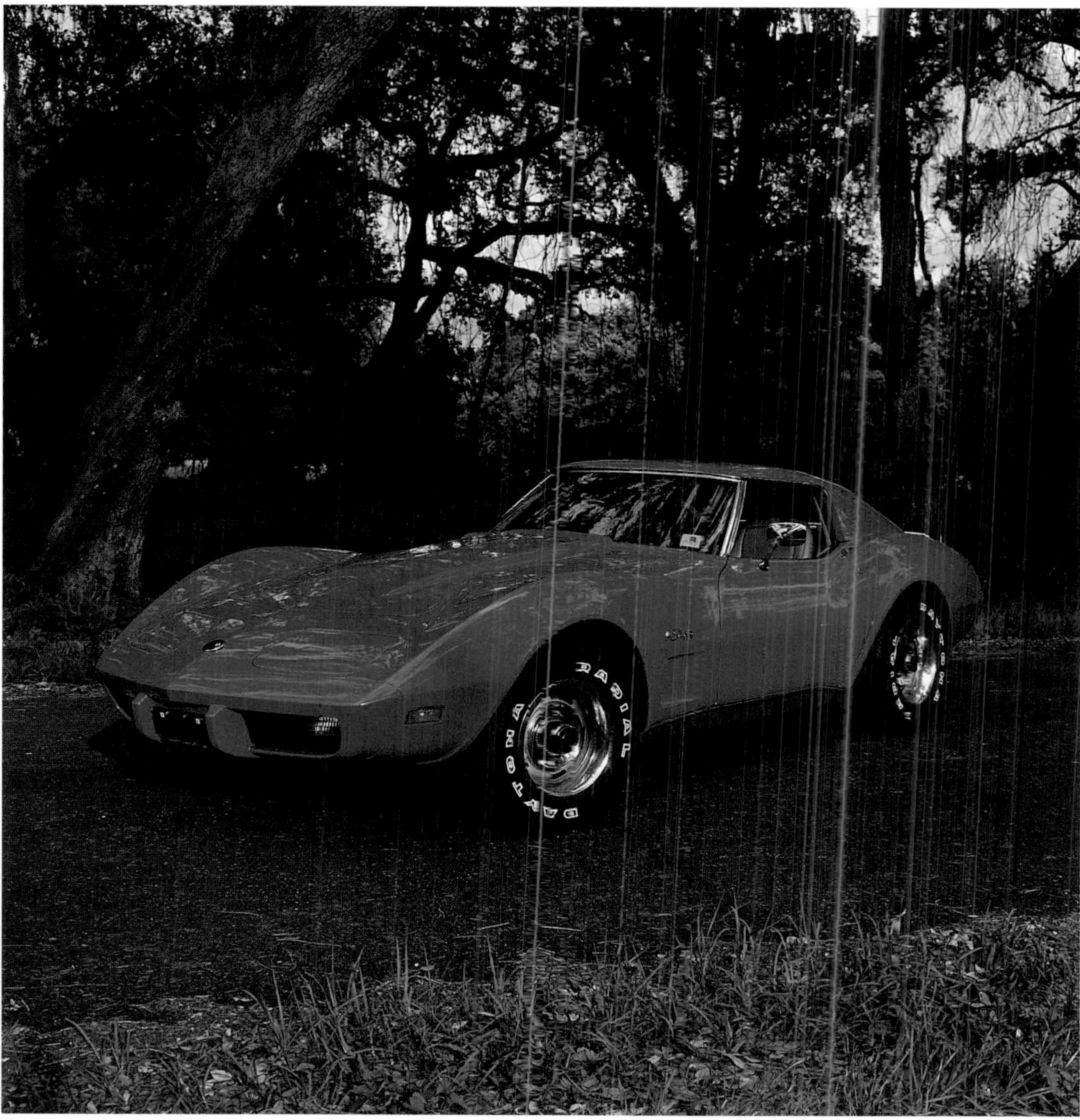

Corvettes for 1976 received a steel floorboard section to increase rigidity and improve insulation. The cowl flap induction setup was also traded for a forward-inlet system to reduce noise. Though the hood no longer drew fresh air in from the base of the windshield, the ornamental vent remained for one more year.

from both sides of the engine together into one tube to enter the converter. From there a reversed Y-pipe did the opposite in back to deliver the cleansed spent gases to typical twin mufflers at the tail. Corvette buyers after 1974 could then pretend their cars still had dual exhausts. True duals wouldn't make a comeback until the LT5-powered ZR-1 debuted for 1990. Standard Corvettes were finally refitted with a real dual exhaust system as part of the second-generation LT1 upgrade made for 1992.

The restrictive single-exhaust setup put a severe crimp on things in 1975. Thus the base 350's abysmal 165-horsepower rating and the L-82's corresponding output drop. Fortunately some extra tinkering brought both these ratings back up—180 horsepower for the former, the aforementioned 210 for the latter—for 1976 and 1977. However, no amount of hocus-pocus could've restored the once-mighty Corvette engine that failed to make the 1975 lineup. The Mk IV big-block V-8, the Corvette's toughest engine option since its introduction in 1965, was dropped from the RPO list after 1974.

Even with its low 8.25:1 compression, the LS-5 454's successor, the LS-4, still remained atop of the Corvette's performance pecking order in 1973 with its 275 horsepower. And it stayed there with its 270 horses the following year. Big numbers, however, weren't enough to keep the 454 big-block alive. Diminishing demand for the expensive-to-own, relatively inefficient LS-4 was the common excuse given for its demise.

The Mid-Engine Program

Zora Arkus-Duntov always understood the logic behind the midengine layout. The design offers various advantages, not the least of which involves getting all that weight off the nose. Reducing the pounds pounding the front wheels lightens up steering effort. This, in turn, means faster manual steering ratios can be used without overtaxing the driver's arms. And moving the engine to the middle not only better balances the load, it can also translate into a preferred lower center of gravity, this because all that motive mass can be mounted closer to the road with no steering or suspension components barring the way. The cockpit can be lowered, too, primarily because the pilot doesn't have to look over a big V-8 perched directly in his line of sight.

Additional advantages were even more obvious to Duntov. "The mass distribution of, say, about 40 [percent] front/60 rear will offer much better traction and handling," he told *Car Life's* Gene Booth in 1968. "You can utilize your power much more accurately."

Or so he thought when GM hired him in May 1953. "Duntov recalls that he was proposing a rear- or midship-mounted engine Corvette to Chevrolet management back in 1954," wrote Booth in his June 1968 account of Zora's hopes and dreams. "The original 6-cylinder car had hardly gotten out of the mold, and Duntov had barely settled in his then-new job in Research and Development, but already different configurations were being considered."

"I came up with a report shortly after," added Zora. "I convinced myself that a car of 40/60 weight distribution doesn't need much to make it well behaved. I remember the wording. I said, 'If you inflate the tires corresponding to their respective load, the car is in the ballpark.' Then you have to do a few things; but the car will turn, it will not spin out, and if you make it break away, it will do it slowly and correctably."

So why didn't Chevrolet begin building a superbly handling midengine Corvette then? "My boss felt that it wasn't as simple as that," answered Duntov. Zora's relocated-engine ideal wasn't considered again until 1959. But no one on the street really paid all that much attention when the mid-engine CERV I racer appeared in 1960. After all, this obviously was an engineering experiment. Much the same could be said when the all-wheel-drive CERV II followed in 1964.

Then Duntov proposed yet another mid-engine racer, the GS 3, in April 1964. Also included in that proposal were two lightweight production Corvettes; one with its engine mounted

Built in 1959, the CERV I racer/engineering testbed helped lay the groundwork for development of the 1963 Sting Ray's independent rear suspension. It also helped put midengine thinking on the fast track around Chevrolet Engineering. *Chevrolet Motor Division*

up front, the other with a powerplant located amidships. These ideas never made it off the drawing board, but they did lay the groundwork for more innovative thinking to come.

Duntov's dreams remained just that in 1964. But R&D engineer Frank Winchell's came true, albeit briefly. Created later that year, Winchell's XP-819 Corvette attempted to prove that moving the engine to the tail, Corvair-style, was the way of the future. Track tests proved otherwise.

Winchell then returned to the drawing board in 1967, resulting in the sleek XP-880. This midengine experimental was running by February 1968, then was officially named "Astro II" in preparation for a public introduction at the New York Auto Show in April. Although it looked stunning, the Astro II's wimpy two-speed automatic transaxle—borrowed from a 1963 Pontiac Tempest—ruled out any chances for additional development.

Picking up where Winchell's XP-880 left off was the XP-882, which Duntov began putting together early in 1968. Unlike previous prototypes, the XP-882 featured a transverse-mounted engine. This unique design was nearing testing stages early in 1969 when new Chevrolet general manager John DeLorean cancelled the project. He directed designers instead to try a less expensive course using a more conventional platform based on the Camaro chassis then being readied for 1970.

Fortunately this "Cormaro" idea was itself quickly cancelled after it was learned that both Ford and American Motors would be showing up at the 52nd annual New York Auto Show in April 1970 with their own midengine proposals, the Pantera and AMX/3, respectively. In response, Chevrolet revived the XP-882 project and put together its own 1970 exhibit labeled simply "Corvette prototype."

"We'll stake our reputation on this being the Corvette of the future," announced a July 1970 *Road & Track* report, "but don't expect it until 1972 at the earliest." Six months later, *R&T's* Ron Wakefield explored the midengine proposal further.

The Reynolds Metals people helped the XP-895 midengine experimental lose some weight with a body made entirely of aluminum. This idea would have never meshed with production realities. *Reynolds Metals Company*

The Italian-styled "2-Rotor" Corvette kicked off the shortlived Wankel development era. Two rotors weren't enough, so Duntov and Gib Hufstader just had to add two more.

Safety nazis be damned, the design team added gullwing doors to the sensational "4-Rotor" Corvette. Duntov and company did manage to extract ample power from the four-rotor setup, but GM gave up on the rotary experiment and opted instead to leave well enough alone. Corvettes to this day remain powered by V-8 engines mounted over the front wheels.

"We have now established beyond a doubt that the car was indeed a prototype for future production—1973, to be exact—and can report full details on the 1973 Corvette," he wrote in the January 1971 issue.

Further toying with the XP-882 platform in 1971 resulted in the more pleasing XP-895. But as much as this prototype looked like the next step into the future, the XP-895 still weighed every bit as much as a regular-production Corvette. To breach this hurdle, DeLorean turned to the Reynolds Metals Company in 1972. Reynolds redid the XP-895 body in aluminum and delivered it to Chevrolet Engineering. A year or so later, Chevy engineers used that lightweight shell to create an XP-895 variant that weighed about 500 pounds less than the original. Costly production processes, however, killed the Reynolds Corvette idea before it ever got rolling.

As for the basic midengine Corvette idea, it was KO'ed more than once. By DeLorean in 1969. By GM's executive board in 1972. But the XP-882 platform just wouldn't die.

Yet another resurrection followed after GM bought out the patent rights to the Wankel rotary engine in November 1970. In June 1971, GM president Ed Cole gave the go-ahead to the XP-897GT project. Wearing a Pininfarina body atop that same transverse-engine chassis, this car, the so-called "2-Rotor Corvette," debuted in September 1973. Duntov never did like the rotary Corvette idea, but he had no choice in the matter.

"Ed Cole was enamored with the Wankel engine," said Zora in a 1980 *AutoWeek* interview. "And he kept twisting my arm. 'What about a rotary Corvette?' Originally, the rotary engine was intended for the Vega. But the idea of sharing the Vega powerplant with the Corvette was nonsense. Still Cole asked me to produce a rotary Corvette and I was in a dilemma. Then DeLorean comes to styling and looks at the midengine Corvette. He knows already that the decision has been made to produce this Corvette, but with the Wankel engine. I told him it was not powerful enough and he lost his composure. 'You're some genius!' he shouted. 'Invent something!'

Duntov turned to Gib Hufstader, who then did the 2-Rotor job two better. Hufstader's much more powerful "4-Rotor" Corvette debuted one month after the XP-897GT. Using two Wankel engines coupled together, this truly fast gull-winged beauty was, according to *Car and Driver*, "the betting-man's choice to replace the Stingray." Whether or not that was a good bet was rendered a moot point after Cole announced in September 1974 that GM was postponing the use of the Wankel rotary engine after running into problems getting it emissions certified.

Two years later, the 4-Rotor Corvette's Wankel was replaced by a conventional small-block V-8 as the name was changed to "Aerovette." The body remained the same, as did those tired, old rumors. According to a February 1977 *Road & Track* prediction, the Aerovette would become the 1980 Corvette. Too bad Chevrolet was still selling conventional Corvettes like there was no tomorrow.

By 1978, Dave McLellan was busy working full-time on the new fourth-generation Corvette—it with its engine mounted up front. Zora had retired three years earlier and his hopes for a world-class midengine Corvette had all but retired with him. As work on the Shark's replacement finally began, Chevrolet officials once and for all decided to put the dream to rest.

Indeed, the painful realities of 50-cent gallons of low-lead and insurance premiums as heavy as car payments did dissuade jet-setters from choosing the LS-4 option in 1973 and 1974. Throw in the fact that the L-82 was both cheaper to insure, better on fuel, and only 25 horses short, and the big picture became obvious. Even though it cost more, the $299 L-82 350 outnumbered the $250 LS-4 454 5,710 to 4,412 in 1973, and 6,690 to 3,494 in 1974. In 1969 Chevrolet had rolled out nearly 16,000 big-block Corvettes. Five years later, bigger apparently was no longer better.

With the 454 in the archives, the Corvette engine lineup was left with only the standard 350 and the optional L-82 in 1975—the first time in 20 years that only two power sources were available. And with the L-82 being the only choice left for buyers wanting the most Chevy engineers had to offer, Chevy's bean-counters couldn't resist upping the RPO ante to $336. The L-82's price jumped (make that soared) again to $481 in 1976, then to $495 in 1977. But apparently the sticker shock wore off quickly. After L-82 sales dropped to 2,372 in 1975, they rebounded to 5,720 in 1976 and 6,148 in 1977.

For some Americans, there was only one drivetrain choice available during those last two years. The L-82 was not offered on 1976 and 1977 Corvettes sold in California because the optional performance V-8 did not meet that state's tougher emissions standards. Four-speed transmissions were also "banned" out West for those years, meaning the only combo a Californian could buy was the 180-horsepower 350 backed by the Turbo Hydra-Matic automatic.

And that auto box wasn't the TH 400 previously used behind all engines. Corvettes fitted with the standard 350 in 1976 and 1977 received the mundane TH 350 as product planners opted not to "waste" the more expensive, heavy-duty Turbo Hydra-Matic on engines that didn't put out enough punishment to merit its use. The TH 400 remained the weapon of choice whenever an L-82 buyer forked over the extra cash for the M40 automatic transmission option in 1976 and 1977. "Heavy" M40 prices were $134 for former, $146 for the latter. The lighter TH 350 M40 package was a no-cost option behind the base 350.

Engines and transmissions weren't the only things to fade from a Corvette buyer's sight in the 1970s. One year after the last big-block Corvette rolled into the sunset, the same thing happened to the convertible model. GM's explanation this time involved both safety concerns and, again, nose-diving demand. From 1953 to 1962, all Corvettes had been convertibles, and not even the stunning Sting Ray coupe could change the way Americans looked at Chevrolet's two-seater. After nearly matching droptop production its first time out in 1963, the Corvette coupe then lost favor as the wind-in-the-hair crowd temporarily regrouped. The coupe's cut of yearly production was 37.3 percent in 1964, 34.7 in 1965,

Decision-makers drew sharp criticism in 1976 after adding this sport steering to the Corvette's interior. Save for the cross-flag medallion, it was the same four-spoke wheel used in Chevy Vegas.

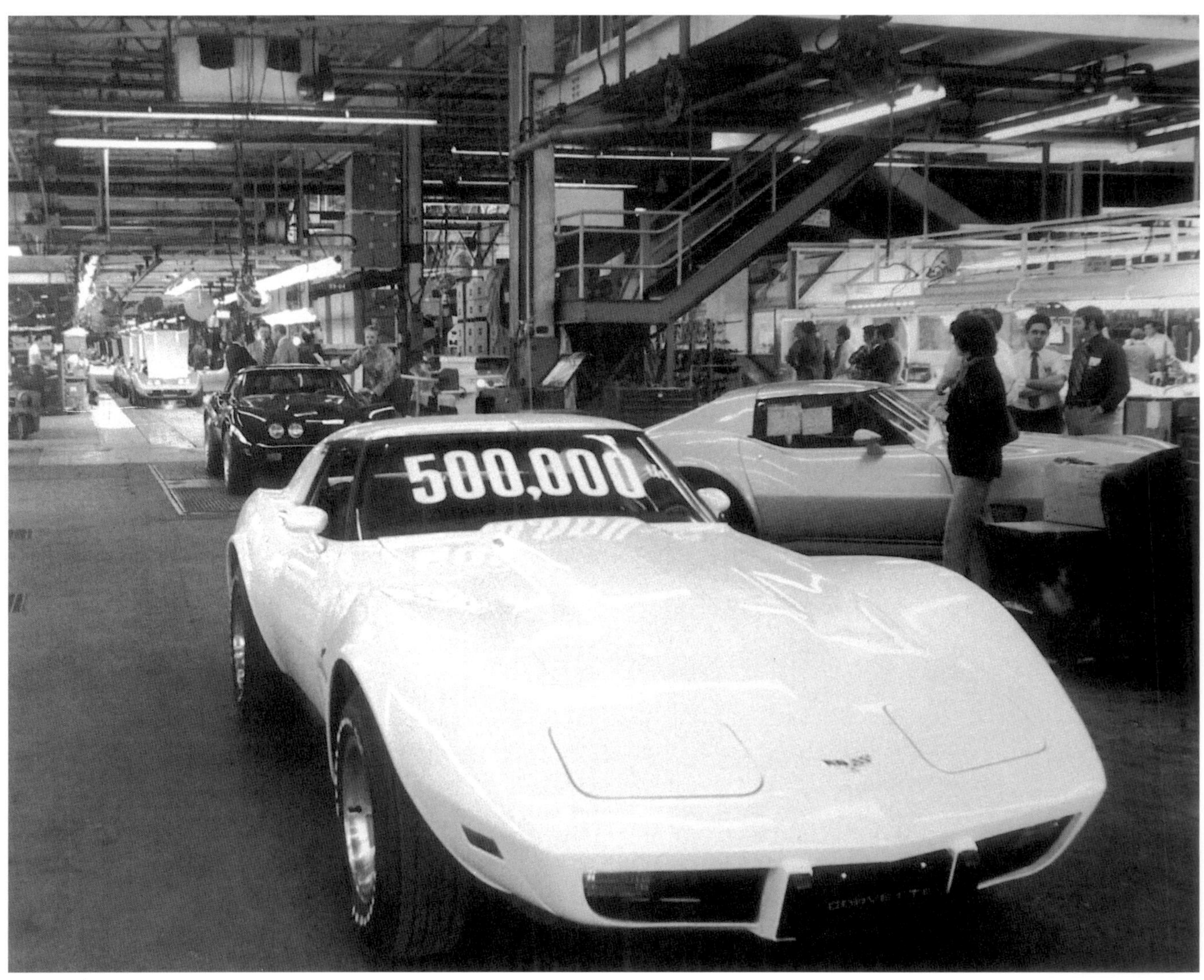

The 500,000th Corvette rolled off the St. Louis line on March 15, 1977. *Chevrolet Motor Division*

35.9 in 1966, and 37.1 in 1967. The coupe percentage remained in that same ballpark in 1968 when the Shark body debuted with its removable roof panels.

Stingray sport coupe sales then more than doubled in 1969 as the percentage hit 57.2 percent. It then became the convertible's turn to hold the short end of the stick. Droptop sales went from 18,630 in 1968, to 6,648 in 1970, and to 4,943 in 1973. The convertible's piece of the pie sank from 38.4 percent in 1970, to 32.7 in 1971, 24.1 in 1972, and 16.2 in 1973. Those last 4,629 ragtops built in 1975 represented a mere 12 percent of the total production run that year. Another end of an era? So we all thought. Then. Fortunately topless Corvettes returned to center stage in 1986.

Declining Corvette convertible demand was the result of various factors, not the least of which was a general trend of disinterest felt across the board in Detroit. By 1976, all factory-built American convertibles were history, apparently because comfort-conscious American drivers were growing more spoiled by the day. During the 1960s, staying cool had taken precedence over being cool. High-profilin' open-air touring lost favor while sales of expensive air conditioning options began heating up considerably at decade's end at any dealership near you, be it allied to GM, Ford, or Chrysler.

America's only sports car was no exception. RPO C60, optional air conditioning, was introduced to Corvette customers along with the all-new Sting Ray in 1963. Its price was $421.80. Only 278 buyers (equal to 1.3 percent of the total

1963 Corvette market) were willing to spend that much then. Again, the key word was "then." By 1968 C60 installations were making up 19.8 percent of the production run. In 1969 the figure was 30.6. It was 52.7 in 1971, 70.8 in 1973, and 82.8 in 1975. Once more, as demand picked up, so too did the price. Six years after it first appeared, the Corvette's air conditioning option had only risen $6.90 in cost. The C60 tag then went up to $447.65 in 1970, $452.00 in 1973, $490 in 1975, and $553 in 1977.

Air conditioning's soaring popularity in the 1970s represented just one facet in what many purists felt was the "sissification" of the once-macho fiberglass two-seater. Whatever the case, buyers still kept snapping up more and more Corvettes loaded down with more and more comfort and convenience options. Who could blame them? Horsepower was becoming harder to come by, why not leave that ongoing debate concerning the Corvette's sports car status completely behind and build yourself a sexy luxury GT?

Various other "kinder, gentler" options accordingly experienced their own newfound sales success in the 1970s. Power steering, power brakes and leather appointments, all introduced along with air conditioning in 1963, also jumped up the Corvette pop charts with a bullet. Power windows, added to the options list in 1956, did, too. The percentage of 1963 Sting Rays equipped with RPOs J50 (power brakes) and N40 (power steering) was 15.5 and 14.2, respectively. By 1970 those figures had soared to 53.6 and 68.8, and they didn't stop there. Ninety-seven-point-seven percent of the Corvettes built in 1975 were fitted with optional power steering; 93.1 percent had power brakes.

Power windows were rarely seen during the 1950s. And in 1967 RPO A31 still only found its way into 17.6 percent of the Sting Rays built that year. By 1973 the percentage of A31 power window installations was at 46. It reached 63.8 the following year, 83.1 in 1976, and 90.1 in 1977.

The situation in 1976 became as obvious as it had been in 1970, the year when Chevrolet product planners made Positraction and a four-speed standard equipment. Late in 1976, power steering, power brakes, and the custom interior trim group (with its leather seats) became part of the base Corvette package. All Corvettes built for 1976 featured power brakes, while only 173 hit the streets without power steering. Power steering and brakes were fitted to every 1977 Corvette as standard equipment, and the same would've been said about the custom interior group's leather seats had not Chevrolet also offered leather-trimmed cloth seats at no extra cost that year.

Of course all these additions to the standard package meant a corresponding rise in the base price. While horsepower was on the wane in the 1970s, pricing was riding an increasing curve upward. A Corvette's base sticker edged beyond $6,000 (by $1.50) for the first time in 1974. It jumped to $6,810.10 in 1975, then hit $7 604.85 the following year. In 1977 it was a whopping $8.647.65, this due to the inclusion of that extra dose of standard comfort, convenience, and class. Yet even with such intimidating price hikes customers continued buying their favorite fiberglass dream machine.

Clearly the Corvette thrived in a seller's market from 1973 to 1977. Chevrolet sold so many Corvettes primarily because performance fans had next to nothing else to choose from coming out of Detroit. Basically the only thing on four wheels remotely comparable to the Corvette in those days was Pontiac's Trans Am and, to a lesser degree, Chevy's own Z28 Camaro.

Car and Driver's April 1976 issue even went so far as to compare the Corvette and Trans Am with Ford's little Mustang II Cobra II, Dodge's Dart Sport, and, gulp, Chevy's C-10 Silverado pickup truck in an article titled "Finding the Fastest American Car." At 15.3 seconds, the L-82 Corvette's ET won out, followed closely by the 455 Trans Am's 15.6 time slip. The Trans Am went fastest 0–60, nosing out the Corvette by a tenth with a 7-flat clip. The Corvette took actual Fastest American Car honors at 124.5 miles per hour followed curiously by the 360-powered Dodge Dart with its 121.6-mile-per-hour top end.

A Corvette fan could've looked at it two ways a quarter century ago. Even with all those power cutbacks, America's only sports car remained America's fastest, best-handling automobile in the 1970s, a time when true speed was truly hard to come by. Yet in a few short years the Corvette was transformed from an intimidating animal into an image-conscious status machine targeted more toward the wannabe crowd than real rally runners.

Perhaps those plastic bumpers said it all. By the late-1970s, Corvettes could have been considered soft touches in more ways than one.

OFFICIAL PACE CAR
GOODYEAR

Chapter 6

Life In the Fastback Lane

A New Profile Debuts in 1978

Witnesses who felt things had gotten a touch soft in the Corvette camp in the mid-1970s had another coming at the turn of the next decade. Although engineers in the late 1970s and early 1980s did manage to keep their fingers in the horsepower dyke—no small achievement considering those stifling emissions standards—they had no choice but to give Corvette customers what they wanted. And what they wanted wasn't exactly what Zora Duntov originally had in mind when he began envisioning a future for the fantastic plastic showcar he first stumbled across in December 1953. Then again, Zora was no longer the boss by the time his baby was celebrating its 25th birthday.

"Keeping [customers] content is Dave McLellan's job as the Corvette's chief engineer," explained a December 1978 *Car and Driver* report on the latest status of America's only sports car. "While he does his best to keep the Corvette's power-to-weight ratio respectable, McLellan's primary mission is satisfying the current Corvette buyer hooked on comfort and convenience. Yes, this is a drastic turnabout from the Zora Arkus-Duntov era of Corvette development. Chevrolet's one and only engineering demigod did his best to keep the Corvette a half-civilized racer—not too convenient, but plenty satisfying, with a big-block prime mover stuffed under the hood. Zora made sure the right things happened when you stepped on the gas."

The right things were still happening when a driver stepped on the Corvette's gas in 1978, just not to the same degree as they had during the third-generation's early days. A lot had changed in 10 years. No-lead had turned to gold. "Internal" and "combustion" had become dirty words, although less so after all those smog controls went to work. Horsepower, too, had become taboo due to its perceived threat to innocent highway travelers. And what little was left in the high-horsepower range after 1970 had become almost impossible to insure, at least for mere mortals taking home mild-mannered paychecks.

But two things didn't change: the Corvette's basic platform and American's lust for that sexy body. "Big-blocks and Zora Arkus-Duntov have gone away together," continued *Car and Driver*, "leaving Dave McLellan with an 11-year-old design and at least 50,000 customers who want to buy it every year." Indeed, demand continued to overwhelm supply through the end of the decade, this even though the car essentially remained old news. Chevrolet killjoys could nail down the lid on the convertible. They could deep-six the 454. They just couldn't stop the madness, no matter how hard they tried. They kept rolling out basically the same Shark year in, year out, and fiberglass fans still kept cheering. They let power dwindle down to the nubbins and drivers still kept driving. They raised prices through the roof and buyers still kept buying.

After selling 49,213 Corvettes in 1977, Chevrolet rolled out 46,774 more in 1978, all identified with special "25th Anniversary" badging and fitted with the first major body modification to appear since 1968. McLellan's

In 1978 Chevrolet celebrated two milestones: 25 years of Corvettes and the fiberglass two-seater's first selection as Indianapolis 500 Pace Car. All 46,776 Corvettes built in 1978 wore 25th anniversary badges and 6,502 of those cars were Limited Edition Indy Pace Car replicas like the one shown here.

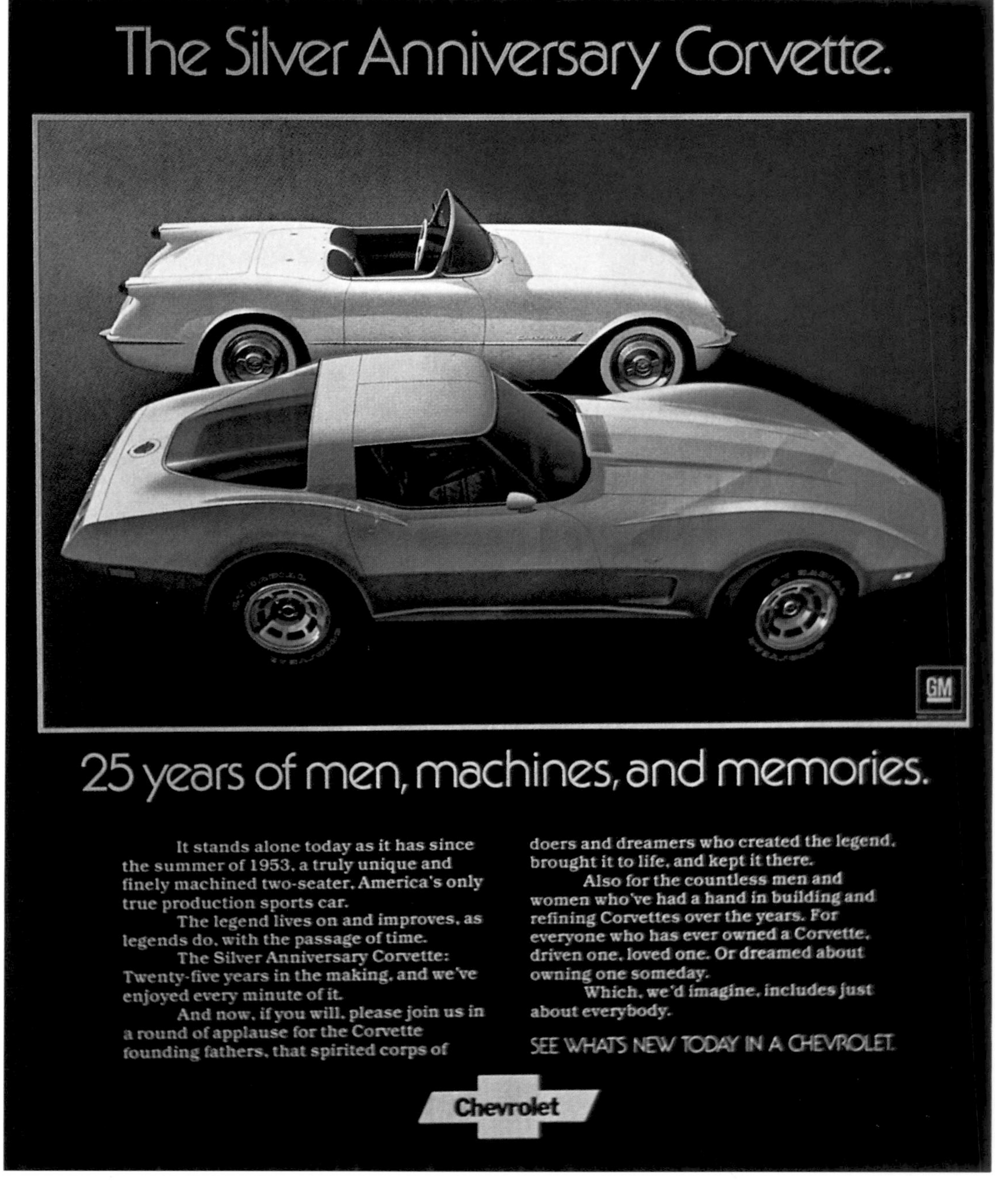

The Silver Anniversary Corvette.
25 years of men, machines, and memories.
It stands alone today as it has since the summer of 1953, a truly unique and finely machined two-seater. America's only true production sports car.
The legend lives on and improves, as legends do, with the passage of time.
The Silver Anniversary Corvette: Twenty-five years in the making, and we've enjoyed every minute of it.
And now, if you will, please join us in a round of applause for the Corvette founding fathers, that spirited corps of doers and dreamers who created the legend, brought it to life, and kept it there.
Also for the countless men and women who've had a hand in building and refining Corvettes over the years. For everyone who has ever owned a Corvette, driven one, loved one. Or dreamed about owning one someday.
Which, we'd imagine, includes just about everybody.
SEE WHATS NEW TODAY IN A CHEVROLET.
Chevrolet
GM

Chevrolet also commemorated the Corvette's 25th birthday with a Silver Anniversary paint scheme in 1978. Priced at $399, the Silver Anniversary option added exclusive two-tone paint. Sport mirrors and aluminum wheels were also required.

design team finally made its own mark on the Corvette by adding that "fastback" rear glass, "a universally appreciated Good Move," in *Car and Driver*'s words. "The large rear window freshened up the Corvette's profile, and it also added space and light to help relieve the claustrophobia inside this, the most tightly coupled car known to man."

While that sloping rear window did increase storage area behind the seats, it didn't allow access to that space. Making that glass roof a lift-up hatchback would have been the logical move. McLellan, however, opted not to complicate matters. Reaching over the Corvette's high, wide rear quarters to gain such access would not have been an easy task. At least that was the opinion around Warren. Then. Apparently Corvette customers themselves didn't give those missing hinges a second thought. They couldn't get enough of that sleek, new shell in 1978.

The production run to end all production runs then came the next year. Sales for 1979

Exclusive seats and upholstery were included in the Indy Pace Car replica deal. Notice also the Citizens Band radio mike on the console. CB radios were Corvette options from 1978 to 1985. The AM/FM stereo with CB, RPO UP6, was amazingly popular in 1978, even at $638 a pop, good buddy. UP6 installations totaled 7,138 that year.

totaled 53,807, a new all-time high that still stands today and probably will forever. Only one other model year tally has come close: the extended run for the first C4 in 1984. That year's (make that year-and-half's) final count was 51,547.

Never before had so many Corvette buyers been so willing to spend so much for so little performance. "GM's assembly plant in St. Louis cranked out more than 46,000 Corvettes last year," added *Car and Driver*, "and to the best of our knowledge, not a soul bought one for less than full sticker. The more the buyers spend, the less they seem interested in buying real sports cars. Corvette customers opt for automatic transmissions, cruise controls, and power windows in droves."

In 1969, the Corvette's long, long RPO list was dominated by dominating performance options like aluminum cylinder heads, side-mount exhausts, metallic brakes and super-duty four-speeds. By 1976 the list had shortened considerably and among its most popular RPO codes were A31 (power windows), C60 (air conditioning), J50 (power brakes), N41 (power steering), and N37 (tilt-telescopic steering column).

The options lineup was long again in 1978, only this time it was stuffed full of the likes of the U75 power antenna, the D35 sport mirrors, the UP6 AM/FM stereo with Citizens Band radio, and the CC1 removable glass roof panels. It was all the added fluff like this that had *Road & Track*'s ever-critical critics up in arms in 1980 concerning the Corvette's latest tack, which in their minds was heading even further away from Zora's original ideal. "Someone is evidently missing the point, but is it 50,000 proud Vette buyers each year or us?"

Good question. That buyers were flocking into Chevy dealerships in record numbers to snap up a supposed performance machine that was more luxury showboat than sports car was one thing. That they continued doing so while

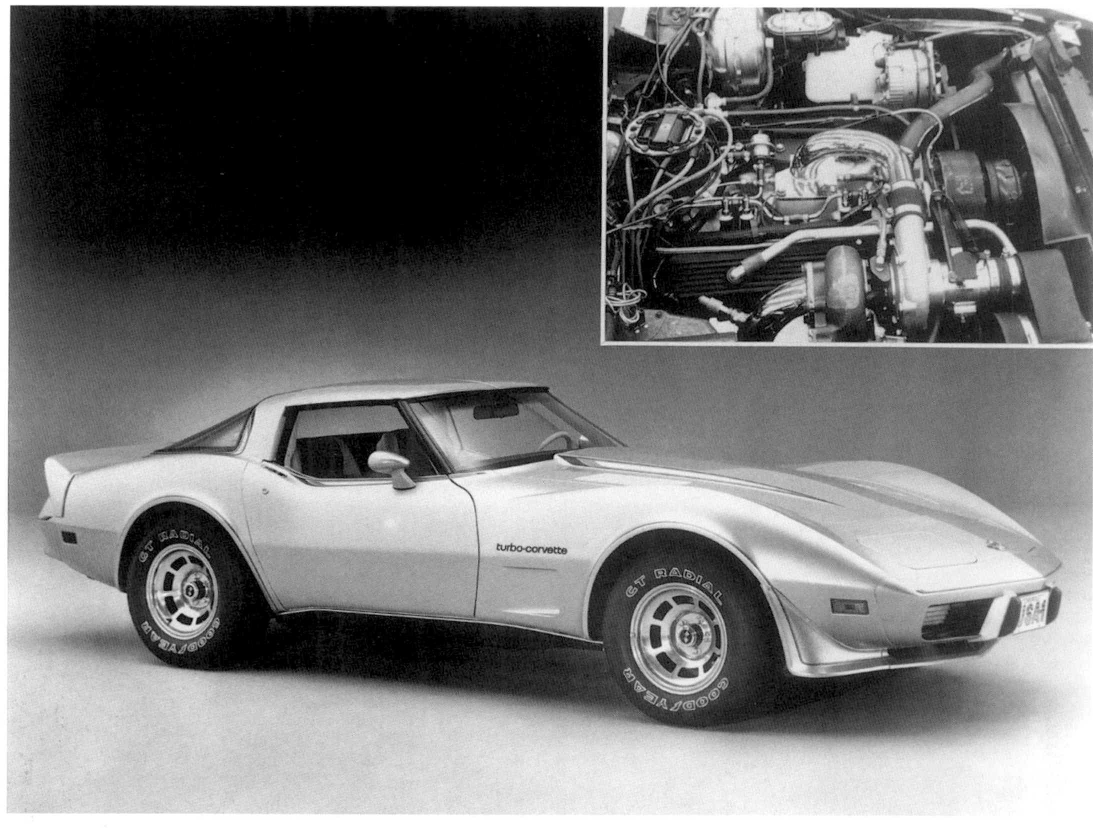

McLellan's engineers in 1979 put together this showcar to experiment with an alternative power source never tried by Duntov—turbocharging. An AIResearch TO3 turbo was combined with fuel injection to up the L-48 350's 195 horsepower to about 280 or 290, according to development engineer John Pearce. According to *Car and Driver's* Don Sherman, performance for the 1979 Turbo Corvette was only slightly better than the naturally aspirated L-82 model. Zero to 60 was 6.3 seconds for the Turbo, 6.6 clicks for the L-82. Quarter-mile time was 15-flat for the former, 15.3 for the latter. *Chevrolet Public Relations*

prices were also rising at record clips was another. It surely appeared to be a violation of the laws of economics.

A standard Corvette in 1958 cost $3,591. Ten years later the base price (for a 1968 coupe) had only risen to $4,663, an increase of 23 percent. The base sticker then skyrocketed by 100 percent over the next 10 years. A 1978 Corvette's bottom line began at $9,351.89. From there that line would shoot up by 96 percent in only five years. The 10-grand barrier was shattered in 1979 as the standard sticker reached $10,220.23. It was $13,140.24 in 1980, $16,258.52 in 1981, and a whopping $18,290.07 in 1982.

Of course not every customer was entirely willing to ride the Corvette's steep ascent up that pricing curve. Sales "dropped" to 40,614 in 1980 and 40,606 in 1981. Sure, those two figures paled a bit in comparison to 1979's lofty record. But they undoubtedly didn't disappoint Chevrolet officials, who would have been happy with anything above 25,000. As it is, 1980 and 1981's totals still stand as the sixth- and seventh-best Corvette counts ever. And those numbers looked awfully good when sales finally did come back down to earth in 1982. "Only" 25,407 Corvettes were sold that year as buyers were distracted by rumors of an all-new fourth-generation model to come for 1983.

Helping increase the 1978–82 pricing curve's rate of climb was yet another expansion of the Corvette's standard equipment package. Once again, Chevy's decision-makers took note of customer preferences and responded accordingly. Of the 46,774 Corvettes sold in 1978, 37,858 had tilt-telescopic steering columns, 37,638 were fitted with air conditioning, and 36,931 featured power windows. All told, these three options cost $910 in 1978, $966 the following year. Then, effective May 7, 1979, this comfort/convenience trio was made a part of the standard Corvette deal, raising the base price by $706. Various other additions also eventually helped hike the 1979 standard price to $12,313.23.

As heavy as base bottom lines were during the last five years of the C3 run, most window stickers seen in 1978–82 were even heavier thanks to the droves of extra-cost equipment added on. The K30 cruise control option, introduced in 1977, was ordered 31,608 times in 1978

Marvin Lloyd, then an 18-year veteran at Chevrolet's St. Louis assembly plant, performs the body drop on the last Corvette built in Missouri. The date was July 31, 1981. Corvette production had commenced at the new Bowling Green plant about two months before. *St. Louis Mercantile Library*

and was included on 96 percent of the Corvettes sold in 1982. RPO K30 cost $99 in 1978. The renamed K35 cruise control option in 1982 was priced at $165. A rear window defogger, RPO C49, appeared on 66 percent of the 1978 Corvettes built and 91 percent of the 1981s. The C49 price ranged from $95 in 1978 to $129 in 1982. Those highly coveted aluminum wheels tacked on another $340 in 1978, $458 in 1982. The installation percentage was 26 in 1978, 63 in 1979, 84 in 1980, 90 in 1981, and 66 in 1982. Easily the heaviest hit on the RPO list was the AM/FM stereo with CB radio. In 1978 it cost $638, good buddy. Five years later, Corvette drivers who wanted to always know Smokey's "20" needed to hand over $755. Only 1,987 did, compared to the 7,138 who gave a big 10-4 to the UP6 radio offering in 1978.

Performance options, meanwhile, were few and far between. The FE7 Gymkhana suspension package was the only sport-minded chassis upgrade available from 1978 to 1982. Metallic brakes and off-road underpinnings were things of the past. New for 1978 were fatter 60-series steel-belted radials, but it took a few years for these wide white-letter treads to catch on. Pricing didn't help matters. In 1978, the P225/70R15 tire option cost $51. The P225/60R15 tires, which required fender trimming at the factory, wore a $216.32 tag. Two years later, the price had nearly doubled to $426.16. Optional 70-series rubber, accordingly, easily outsold those P225/60 tires each year until 1982, when the latter outnumbered the former 3 to 1 despite a price differential of $542.52 to $80.00.

Fortunately the relatively hot L-82 350 was still around as the 25th Anniversary Corvette's only optional V-8. Its output in 1978 actually increased from 210 horsepower to 220 thanks to the addition of a less restrictive exhaust system

Corvettes at the Brickyard

Chevrolet is no stranger to The Brickyard, the fabled Indiana home to the Indianapolis 500. The Bow-Tie boys can brag of leading the pace lap at Indy more times than any other manufacturer. When a Monte Carlo did the honors on May 30, 1999, it marked the 12th occasion a Chevy product has performed as the prestigious Indy 500 pace car.

A Fleetmaster convertible was the first in 1948, followed by the sensational, all-new 1955 Bel Air seven years later. The equally sensational Camaro emerged in 1967, just in time to take its rightful place at the head of the pack at Indy that year. Camaros repeated as pace cars in 1969, 1982, and 1993. In between, a Beretta convertible toured Indy in 1990.

Curiously, Chevrolet's fiberglass two-seater was on the scene for a quarter century before it made its debut as an Indy 500 pacer in 1978. Seemingly making up for lost time, America's sports car then returned to The Brickyard for three additional encores over the next 20 years.

A convertible model rejoined the Corvette lineup after an 11-year hiatus in 1986 and was immediately chosen as the pace car for the 70th running of the greatest spectacle in motorsports. Chevrolet officials that year were more than proud of the fact that their latest Corvette needed no special engineering modifications to help bring Rick Mears, Danny Sullivan, Michael Andretti, and the rest up to speed. Save for the safety-conscious strobe lights, five-point harness and onboard fire system, the yellow, 230-horsepower ragtop that lead the pace lap on May 31, 1986, was basically identical to all the other 1986 Corvette convertibles sold to the public. The Corvette's second pace lap appearance also represented the second time that a street-legal, stone-stock machine hit the bricks at Indy. The first? Chevrolet's 1978 Corvette.

Retired U.S. Air Force Brigadier General Chuck Yeager, a man who certainly knows a little something about setting the pace, was the celebrity driver in 1986. Yeager, of course, was the first man to fly faster than the speed of sound on October 14, 1947. Flying much lower and slower, Bobby Rahal won the 1986 Indy 500.

The Corvette's first appearance as the prestigious pace car for the Indianapolis 500 came in 1978. A street-going pace car replica (on left) of course followed. Corvettes have since paced Indy three more times, with replicas also being produced in 1986 (top), 1995 (right), and 1998. *Chevrolet Public Relations*

After the race, Walter Mitty types were typically offered pace car replicas. Only this time Chevrolet considered every Corvette convertible built in 1986, 7,315 in all, to be street-going Indy pacers, regardless of color. No special adornments or limited-edition options packages were offered. It simply was left up to the buyer to add a dealer-offered commemorative decal to the doors of his or her 1986 droptop. Most didn't.

Chevrolet image-makers did things a bit differently nine years later after division general manager Jim Perkins drove the third Corvette to pace the Indy 500 around the legendary track on May 28, 1995. This time a truly limited limited-edition pace car replica package was offered. Not even a blind man could miss this one. Only 527 Indy 500 Pace Car Replica convertibles were sold, all wearing a Dark Purple and Arctic White finish with perhaps the splashiest graphics yet seen on a commemorative pacer. Completing the deal, listed as RPO Z4Z, were special leather seats embroidered with Indianapolis 500 logos. Price for the Z4Z option was an eye-popping $2,816.

Even more eye-popping, in terms of both visual impact and the bottom line, was the fourth Indy pace car Corvette, this one based on the totally redesigned C5 platform. When introduced in 1997, the C5 came only in targa-top form. Convertible lovers had to wait a year. By the time a topless C5 did appear in 1998 it was already a foregone conclusion that this sexy, speedy soft-top would be chosen to set the pace at Indianapolis.

Once again the Corvette needed no additional wrench-turning to do the job. With the 345-horse LS1 up front, the 1998 C5 easily ranked as the most capable Indy pace car Corvette yet. And if you thought the 1995 pace car stood out in a crowd . . .

The second-edition Z4Z Indy Pace Car Replica package included even higher doses of high-profile imagery. Glowing Radar Blue paint was accented by glaring yellow graphics that ran down each side and culminated in a checkered flag flowing up over the rear wheels onto the rear deck. Screaming yellow wheels, yellow stripes on the hood, and yellow inserts for the black leather seats added further exclamation.

Additional Z4Z equipment included electronic dual-zone heating and air conditioning, a Delco AM/FM radio/CD player with Bose speakers, memory package, Theft Lock, a digital clock, and floor mats. The JL4 Active Handling system, a new option priced at $500 for 1998 C5s, was also included in the Z4Z options group. The 4L60-E four-speed automatic transmission was "standard" at no extra cost. Adding the six-speed manual required another $815 on top of the $5,039 Z4Z asking price. Total production for the wallet-wilting 1998 Indy Pace Car Replica was 1,163.

The Corvette will, without a doubt, be back on track at Indianapolis soon enough—as part of the 50th anniversary celebration in 2003 perhaps?

The first Corvette rolled off the Bowling Green assembly line in Kentucky on June 1, 1981. Eleven years later, the 1 millionth Corvette (shown here) was built there on July 2, 1992. *Chevrolet Public Relations*

and a dual-snorkel air induction setup that improved breathing on the top end. Engineers were just then figuring out how to reverse the downward performance spiral created by ever-tightening emissions standards and demands for better fuel economy. Results of this roller-coaster ride up a new learning curve even included a power boost for the standard L-48 350, which went from 180 horsepower in 1977 to 185 in 1978. L-48s sold in California and high altitudes that year were rated at 175 horses.

Either way, L-48 or L-82, the quarter-century-old Corvette remained this country's top performance automobile. Or so said *Car and Driver* in a turnabout of opinion late in 1977. "After a number of recent Corvette editions that prompted us to mourn the steady decline of both performance and quality in this

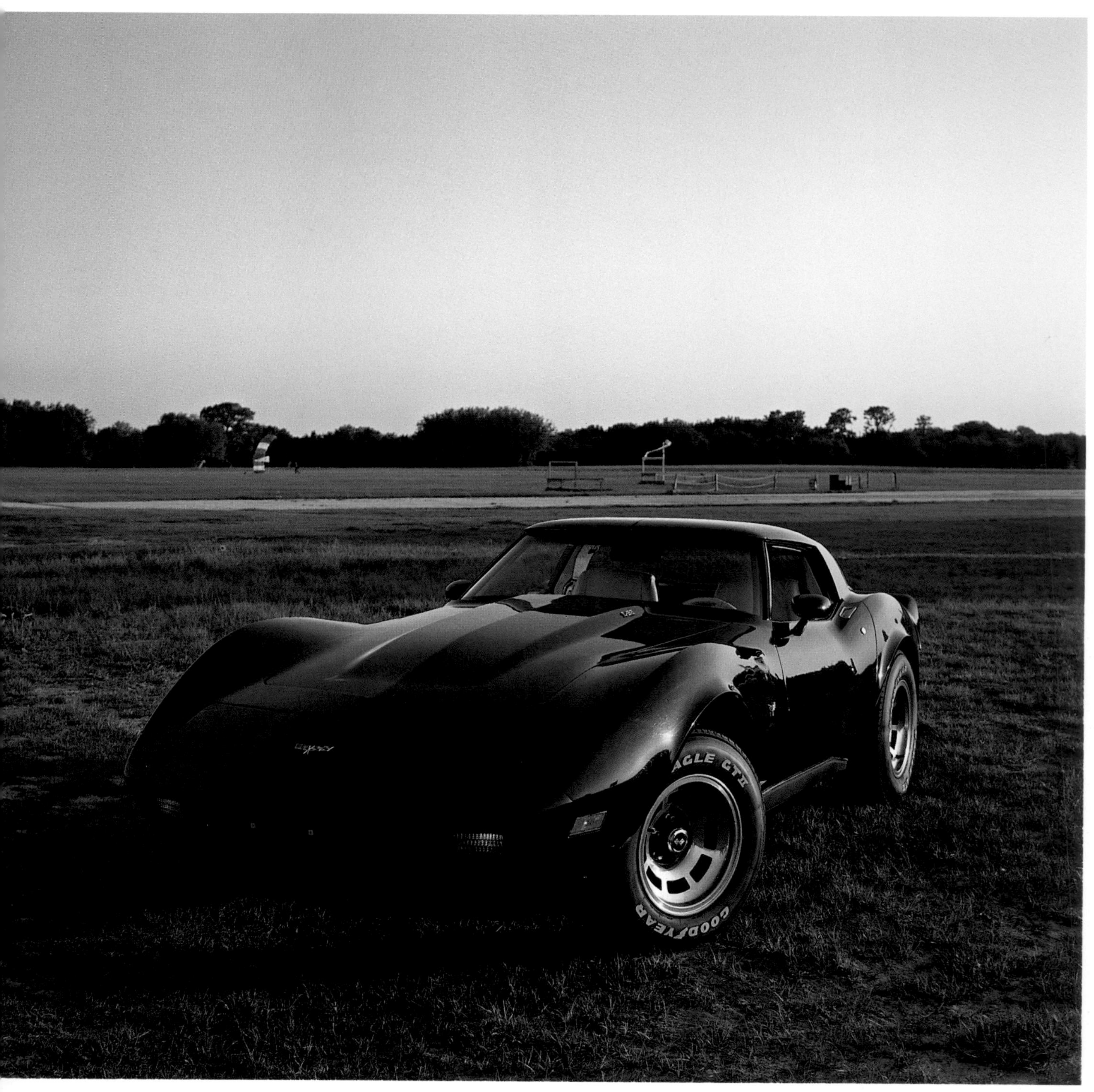

Chevrolet stopped offering Tuxedo Black paint as a Corvette option in 1969. Black returned in 1977. Some black Corvettes were sold in 1975 and 1976, but not necessarily by Chevrolet. A special paint option in those years allowed buyers to take delivery of their car in primer. They could then have it painted in any color they preferred. This L-82 Corvette is one of 10,465 ordered through regular channels in black in 1979. Black was by far the most popular Corvette color that year, outnumbering the second-favorite, white, by nearly 2,000 sprayings.

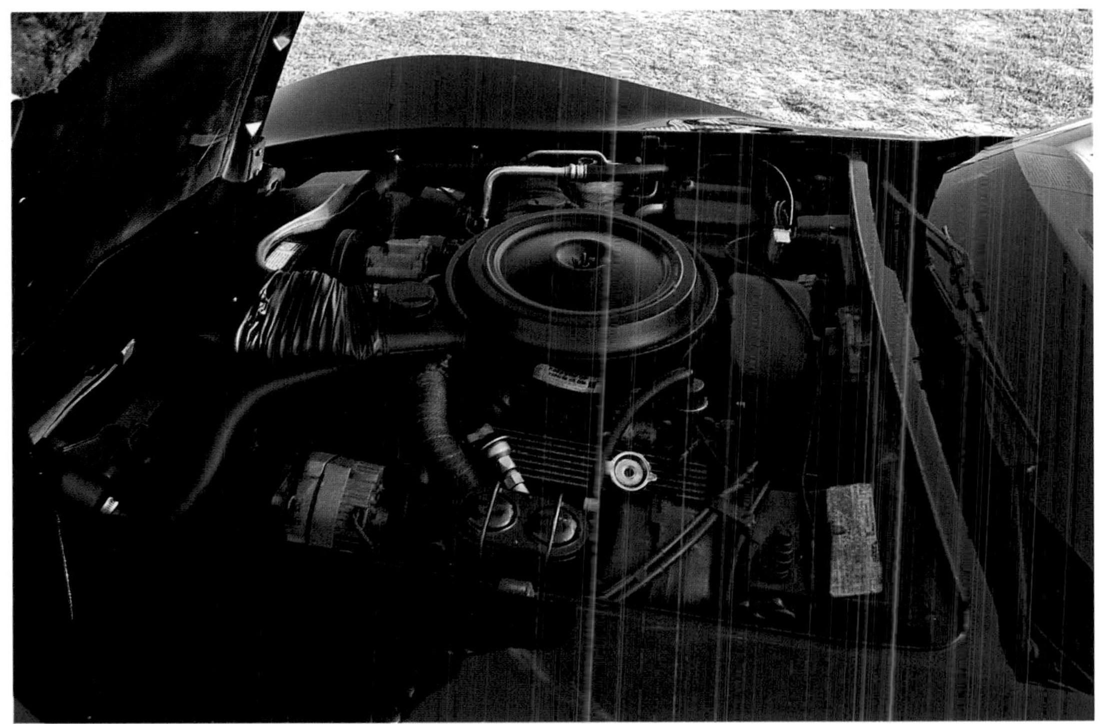

From 1975 to 1980, the only engine option available to Corvette customers was the L-82 350. The 1979 L-82, shown here, was rated at 225 horsepower. The asking price was $565. L-82 Corvette production that year was 14,516.

once-proud marque, we can happily report the 25th example of the Corvette is much improved across the board. Not only will it run faster now—the L-82 version with four-speed is certainly the fastest American production car, while the base L-48 automatic is no slouch—but the general drivability and road manners are of a high order as well." L-48 performance was quoted at 7.8 seconds for the time-honored 0-60 run, 123 miles per hour on the top end. The L-82 reportedly could reach 133 miles per hour.

Additional tweaking increased L-82 output to 225 horsepower in 1979. The L-48 that year also received the L-82's dual-snorkel induction equipment and "open flow" mufflers, which helped up its output ante to 195 horsepower. Although the L-82 350 received another power boost to 230 horses in 1980, it was the end of the line for the Corvette's last optional "hi-perf" V-8. Engineers were never able to certify the "high-compression" (9:1) L-82 for sale in California during the years 1978 to 1980. Chevrolet then cancelled the L-82 option outright, leaving a 190-horsepower 350 as the only power choice in 1981.

Corvette buyers in California were limited to one engine only, the base 350, since 1976. Then that state's extra-strict emissions standards were tightened even further in 1980.

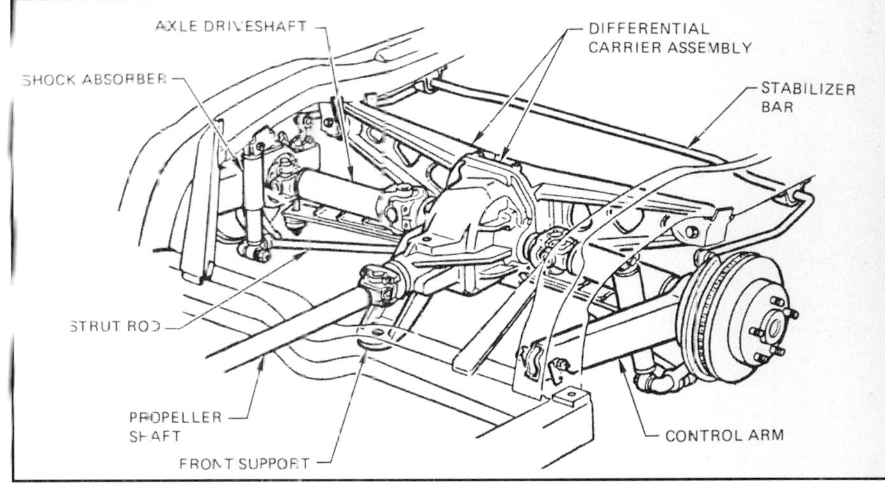

Dave McLellan's main goal during the C3 years was to shave off as many pounds as possible from the platform to try to improve performance through the back door. Various lightened components—including aluminum wheels, tubular steel headers (instead of cast-iron exhaust manifolds), and magnesium valve covers—were introduced during his tenure. In 1980 a new differential housing and corresponding frame cross-member, both done in aluminum, were installed.

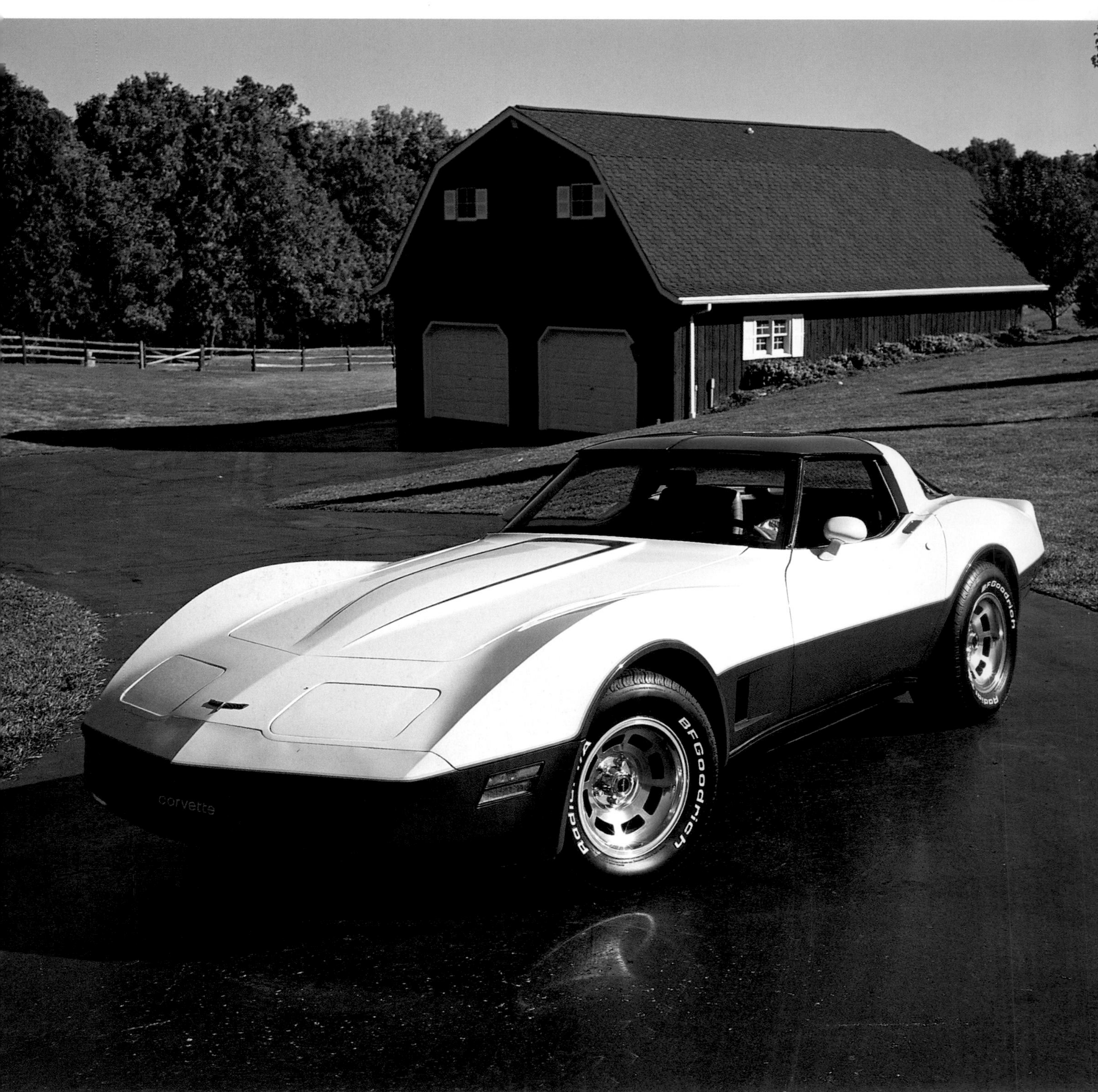

Chevrolet began offering contrasting paint schemes for the Corvette in 1956. The "440" code exterior finish added a second color to the bodyside "cove" panels. This option was dropped after 1961. Two-tone paint schemes returned in 1978 for the Indy Pace Car replica and Silver Anniversary models. Then came RPO D84 in 1981. All D84 two-tone Corvettes that year were created in Bowling Green to help show off the new assembly plant's superior paint facilities. This beige/dark bronze Corvette is one of 5,352 two-tone cars sold in 1981. Another 4,871 D84 cars were finished out in 1982.

Chevrolet failed to certify either of its 350-ci V-8s for sale there that year. So in place of the 190-horsepower L-48 (and in exchange for a $50 credit) came the LG4 305-ci V-8. Although it was taken right from the mundane passenger-car parts shelf, the West Coast-legal LG4 still produced only 10 fewer horses than the L-48 thanks to the use of stainless-steel tubular headers and a "Computer Command Control" system that automatically adjusted carburetor mixture and ignition timing on demand. LG4 sales in 1980 totaled 3,221.

The LG4's lightweight headers (with oxygen-sensor smog controls) and computer "brain box" were transferred to a new 350 small-block, the L-81, in 1981. Not only was this 190-horsepower V-8 certified for sale in all 50 states, it was also available in California with either a four-speed or an automatic transmission. This meant a bushy, bushy blonde beach boy could specify a bitchin' manual-trans Corvette for the first time since 1975. But he could only do so for one brief year. Chevrolet didn't offer a four-speed stick at all for the 1982 Corvette in any state. Not since 1954 had a complete model-year run been limited only to automatic transmission installations. Luckily a four-speed option returned for the new C4 Corvette in 1984.

Various other features on the new next-generation Corvette were also "returning." McLellan's engineers had been working on the C4 since 1978, and more than once over the following years they let some of that developing technology slip out into the latest C3 model. Easily the biggest slip came in 1982 when an intriguing new powerplant appeared for the final third-generation Corvette.

"It's a harbinger of things to come," said McLellan about that car that preceded his sport coupe de grace. "For the 1982 model is more than just the last of a generation; it's stage one of a two-stage production. We're doing the power team this year. Next year, we add complete new styling and other innovations."

While Corvette fans would have to wait more than half a year to finally see the redesigned C4 in the spring of 1983, they got to try out the new car's engine and transmission some 18 months before. Designated L-83, the 1982 Corvette's 350 V-8 used refined versions of the tubular-header exhaust system and Computer Command Control equipment that first appeared along with the LG4 California V-8 in 1980. And like the L-81 350 of 1981, the L-83 also used weight-saving magnesium valve covers. The real news, however, came atop the engine.

McLellan's men called it "Cross Fire Injection." To many witnesses, the setup looked very much like the rare, twin-carb option used on some Z/28 Camaros in 1969. But those weren't carburetors beneath that cool-looking air cleaner. They were two computer-controlled Rochester throttle-body fuel-injection units mounted diagonally on an aluminum cross-ram intake manifold. Making this TBI (throttle body injection) system work was an ECM—Electronic Control Module—that was capable of dealing with up to 80 variables (ignition

A federal law required all 1980 automobiles, including America's only sports car, to be fitted with speedometers reading no higher than 85 miles per hour. Performance by then was down, but not that low. Shown here is the emasculated speedo in an 1981 Corvette.

THE
Heartbeat
OF AMERICA

The third-generation Corvette run ended with an exclamation point in the form of the 1982 Collectors Edition. Special paint and wheels were part of the package, as were extra-wide white-letter tires. Replacement rubber has long since replaced those P225/60R-15 treads on this Collectors Edition Corvette.

Exclusive leather upholstery, luxury carpeting, multitoned door panel treatment, and a leather-wrapped steering wheel were standard inside the 1982 Collectors Edition. A new four-speed automatic transmission with a lock-up torque converter and automatic overdrive was also standard. Chevrolet didn't bother certifying a four-speed in 1982, making this the first time since late in 1955 (a few three-speed manuals were installed near the end of the 1955 run) that all Corvettes built in a given year were automatics.

timing, fuel/air mixture, idle speed, and so on) adjustments per second to maximize performance and efficiency. Although this TBI setup wasn't exactly a fuel-injection system in the truest sense of the term—not like the Rochester-supplied unit used by Corvettes from 1957 to 1965—it did produce something former fuelie drivers were familiar with: instant throttle response.

Enhancing overall response even further was the new 700-R4 four-speed automatic transmission, which was also electronically linked to the ECM. Shifts and the torque converter's lockup clutch feature were all precisely controlled by the ECM depending on varying speed and load data inputs. This power team combo clearly was as high as high tech had ever been beneath a fiberglass hood to that point. Yet even with all that techno-wizardy, the 1982 small-block still only produced 200 horsepower. "A far cry from the 400 bhp-plus days of the L88 and L68," began *Road & Track*'s verdict on the last C3, "but not exactly a shrinking violet by today's wheezing standards."

McLellan's plans to put those 200 humble horses to work most effectively involved putting the Corvette on a diet. Accordingly, the new C4 in 1984 was lousy with weight-saving aluminum components, including a lightweight differential housing and corresponding frame mount first introduced in 1980. The 1984 Corvette also relied on a fiberglass mono-leaf spring in place of the steel multileaf unit used by most third-generation Corvettes. This idea first appeared in 1981 for automatic cars with standard suspensions. The plastic mono-leaf weighed only 8 pounds. The steel leaf spring setup it replaced tipped the scales at 44 pounds.

To both showcase all this new technology and mark the end of the Shark era, Chevrolet in 1982 put together a special model the likes of which Corvette buyers had never seen before. The 1982 Collector Edition was, in Dave McLellan's words, "a unique combination of color, equipment, and innovation [resulting in] one of the most comprehensive packages ever offered to the Corvette buyer." Actually Corvette customers had cast their eyes on something similar just five years before as the 1978–82 group featured special-edition offerings at its bookends. The Collector Edition helped close things out in 1982. Kicking off the fastback years in 1978 was the Limited Edition Corvette.

Casual witnesses and disappointed investors alike best remember that 1978 model as

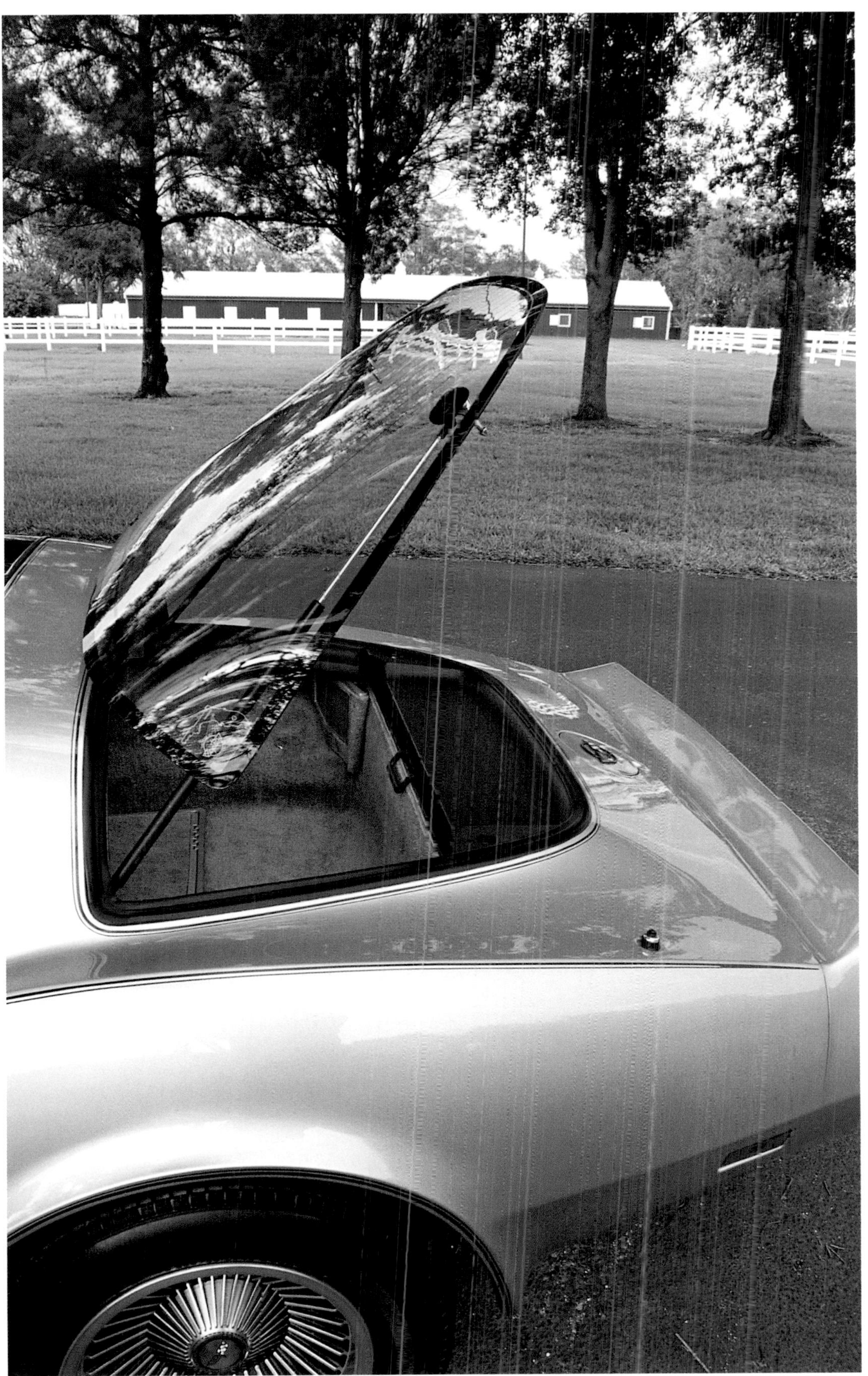

Removable glass roof panels topped off the Collectors Edition, while a welcomed hatchback window brought up the rear. The optional power antenna was also included in the $22,537 deal.

Many thought the 1982 Corvette's 200-horsepower 350 small-block was fitted with dual four-barrel carburetors. But beneath that air cleaner were twin throttle-body injectors. Used by both the Corvette and Camaro, this TBI setup was called "Cross-Fire Injection", even though it wasn't fuel injection in the true sense of the term. Tuned-port injection (TPI) design debuted in 1985, and this actually represented the "fuelie" Corvette's return after a 20-year hiatus. *Chevrolet Motor Division*

the Indy Pace Car replica. For the first time, America's only sports car was chosen that year as the Indianapolis 500's prestigious pacer. And just as they had done with Camaro Indy pacers in 1967 and 1969, Chevrolet officials opted to put special pace car replicas on the street in 1978 to help mark the moment.

As the name implied, the original plan was to make this package a limited-edition collector's piece. The *Wall Street Journal* even went so far as to print a cover story in March 1978 touting the Indy Pace Car Corvette as a sure-fire ride to riches. Those lucky enough to get their hands on one of these rare machines reportedly would be able to turn it around for many times its original sales price after only a matter of months. Initially the window sticker read $13,653.21, $4,300 more than a base 25th anniversary Corvette coupe. Once word got around, however, the going price soared as high as $30,000. Those unlucky enough to buy at that price soon found out that some old adages never lie: If it sounds to good to be true, it probably is.

Perhaps that adage would not have rang so honestly had Chevrolet only built 300 Indy Pace Car Corvettes as originally planned. But all speculation ran right down the drain after Chevy's litigation-shy decisionmakers decided to build at least one Pace Car replica for every dealer in America. Apparently the idea was to avoid any lawsuits from potential buyers or dealers (translated: opportunistic exploiters) left in the lurch with nothing save for complaints of unfair, monopolistic sales practices. Whatever the case, the final "limited-edition" count for the 1978 Indy Pace Car's production run reached 6,502. Most (if not all) of those who originally jumped on the Limited Edition Corvette bandwagon 20 years ago are still waiting to make hay today.

Included in the Limited Edition's original price, however astronomical, was a long list of options combined with a heavy dose of special treatments. On the outside was an exclusive black-over-silver two-tone paint scheme accented by red pinstriping. Official Indy 500 decals were expected. A front air dam, rear spoiler, aluminum wheels (also with red pinstripes), and glass T-tops were part of the deal as well. Inside was an exclusive leather interior

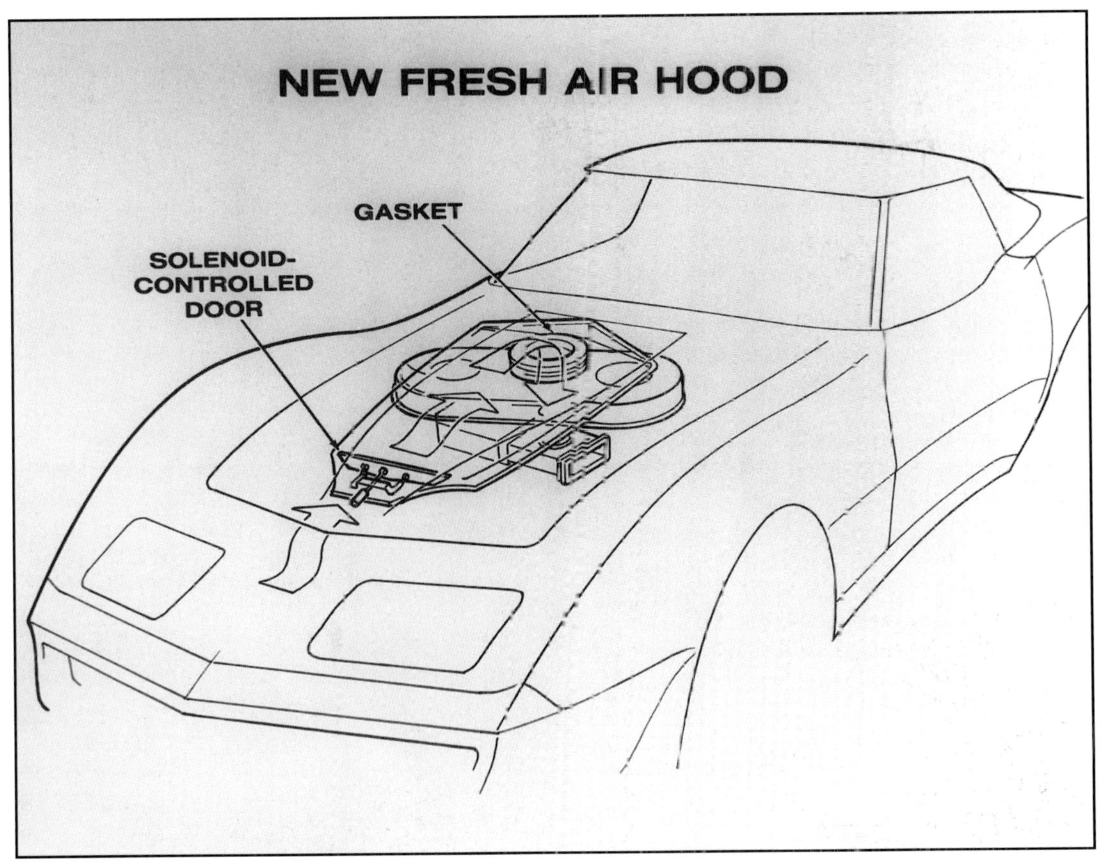

The 1982 Corvette was also fitted with a new air-induction hood that directed some of the radiator's cooling flows into a special duct formed into the hood's underside. At the front of the duct was a solenoid-controlled flap that opened on demand. Cooler, denser air then rushed to the duct's rear where it flowed through an opening in the air cleaner's top, which was sealed to the hood. *Chevrolet Motor Division*

done in silver-gray—called "smoke" by Chevrolet. Lightweight buckets were also exclusive to the Limited Edition's interior. Optional extras included in the Indy Pace Car package were power windows, door locks and antenna; a rear window defogger; air conditioning; sport mirrors; tilt-telescopic steering column; white-letter P225/60R15 tires; heavy-duty battery; AM/FM 8-track stereo with dual rear speakers; and the Convenience Group. Included in that last collection, RPO ZX2, were a dome light delay, headlight warning buzzer, underhood light, low-fuel warning light, interior courtesy light, floor mats, intermittent wipers, and passenger-side vanity mirror on the visor.

For those who wanted to bridge the gap between the standard 1978 Corvette with its 25th anniversary badges and the heavily loaded high-priced Indy Pace Car replica, there was the Silver Anniversary option, RPO B2Z. Priced at $399, the B2Z package added another exclusive two-tone paint scheme, this one done in light silver over dark silver. Dual sport mirrors and aluminum wheels were required options along with that commemorative paint. Silver Anniversary Corvette production in 1978 was 15,283.

Optional two-tone paint would return to the Corvette's RPO list in 1981, again wearing a $399 price tag. Four D84 combinations—Silver/Dark Blue, Silver/Charcoal, Beige/Dark Bronze, and Autumn Red/Dark Claret—were offered, with sales of those combinations totaling 5,352. The D84 price rose to $428 in 1982 and included three new combos—White/Silver, Silver/Dark Claret, and Silver Blue/Dark Blue—along with 1981's Silver/Charcoal. Total two-tone paint sales in 1982 hit 4,871.

Like the Silver Anniversary Corvette, the Indy Pace Car of 1978 also didn't just roll off into the sunset without passing something on to later models. The Limited Edition Corvette's high-back bucket seats became standard equipment in 1979. But not everyone thought this was an improvement. *Car and Driver* called the far-from-form-fitting bucket "an abysmal failure." "The new seats were sold to management on their weight-savings merit, and their molded-plastic design is in fact 22 pounds lighter," continued the *C/D* complaint.

What Came After C3

Dave McLellan's claim to fame as Corvette chief engineer came in March 1983 when the redesigned 1984 Corvette was introduced. Shown here is serial number 00001, the "first 1984 Corvette." This car originally was raffled away as part of a charity promotion.

It's doubtful any future Corvette generation will break the longevity record of the C3. Fifteen years is a long time, especially in today's automotive market where the "what have you done for me lately" attitude prevails like never before.

The fourth generation came close, although not by plan. Talk of an all-new, totally redesigned fifth-generation Corvette began as early as 1988. The hope then was to introduce it in time for the car's 40th anniversary in 1993. That would have cut the C4 run off at 9 years, leaving the 10-year history of the original solid-axle Corvette as the second longest span among the five generations. But C5 development was delayed again and again as GM went awash in red ink. In its place, the C4 continued rolling on for 13 years before the book was finally closed at the end of 1996.

How soon they forget. In the mad rush to laud the C5 as the best Vette yet, few onlookers in early 1997 seemed to recall a similar sensation seen nearly a decade and a half before. Like the C5, the first C4 was honored by *Motor Trend* as its prestigious "Car of the Year," and rightly so. Okay, the C5's award didn't come until the convertible version was introduced in 1998, but that's only because the targa-topped sport coupe initially unveiled in January 1997 appeared too late to make *Motor Trend's* 1997 balloting.

The first C4 showed up tardy for its coming-out party too. Dealer introductions for the Shark's long-awaited replacement didn't begin until March 1983. By then Chevrolet officials had already decided to simply forego an official 1983 model year entirely. The last C3 was the 1982 model. The first C4 was the 1984. No 1983 Corvettes were sold to the public.

Chevrolet's extended 1984 run for its newest two-seat sensation then resulted in a near-record production total. The 51,547 1984 Corvettes built stands second only to the 53,807 produced for 1979. Forget Joe Dimaggio's 56-game hit streak; that 1979 Corvette standard without a doubt will stand forever. Will the market ever again bear such excess? Will demand ever again inspire such a supply? Will Chevrolet ever again sell 50,000 Corvettes in a year? Ask these questions again in 2003.

Such sales success like that of 1979 represented one of the main reasons why the C3 was allowed to run for so long. C4 roots originally took hold in 1978 with the plan then being to introduce the car as a 1982 model. Yet, despite a national recession, the Corvette entered the 1980s selling stronger than ever. Yearly production for both 1980 and 1981 surpassed 40,000. Why fix something that wasn't broken?

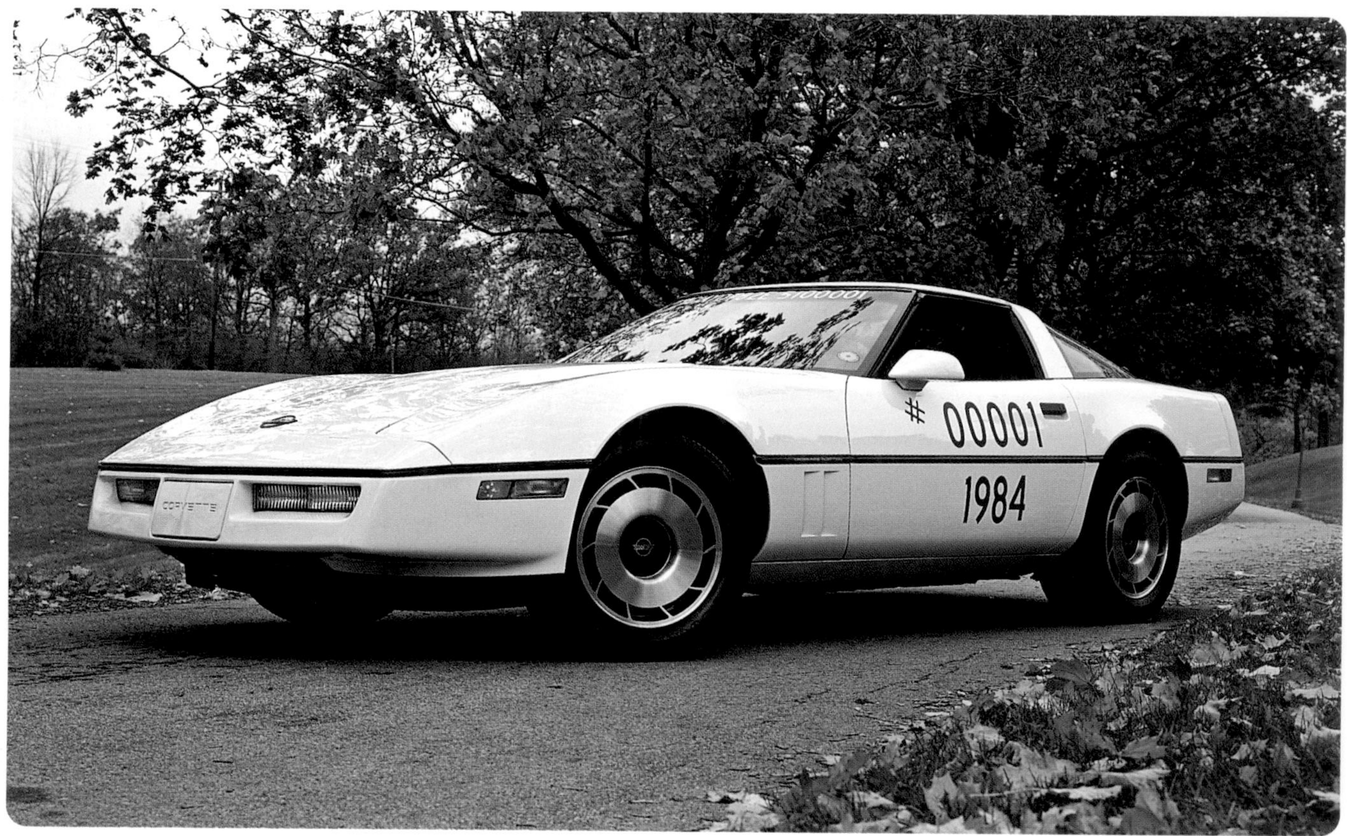

On top of that, Chevrolet officials also didn't want to tackle start-up tasks for both a new assembly line and a new model at the same time. Corvette production at the Bowling Green facility began in June 1981 with the venerable C3 remaining the focus. Various development gremlins then surfaced, like they do so often, to help delay the C4's introduction further. Most agreed, however, that the end result was worth the wait.

In their February 1984 Car of the Year issue, *Motor Trend's* editors concluded that the C4 had risen to a new plateau. "The [1984] Corvette has the highest EQ [Excitement Quotient] of anything to come out of an American factory. Ever. Its handling goes beyond mere competence; call it superb, call it leading edge, call it World Class. *We* certainly do."

Indeed it was the C4's new chassis that set it apart from what came before. Highlights included transverse, mono-leaf fiberglass springs front and rear; Girling four-wheel disc brakes; revised suspension locations at both ends; and the liberal use of aluminum components throughout to save weight. Independent suspension continued in back, but it was improved markedly with a five-link design in place of the old three-link setup. On the clean side of the car, a totally fresh restyle incorporated improved function into its form by way of a large "clamshell" hood that allowed easier engine access.

Later C4 upgrades included the introduction of the fuel-injected L98 in 1985, a convertible Corvette's return in 1986, the ZR-1's emergence in 1990, the rise of the LT1 in 1992, and the LT4 and Grand Sport debuts in 1996. Fans of the fourth-generation Corvette certainly have a lot to remember.

That so much history was overshadowed with seemingly no regrets in 1997 simply helped demonstrate the C5's own historic nature. This truly was the first all-new Corvette. All other next-generation models before brought along something from their past—the first C4 still relied on the C3's Cross-Fire 350 V-8 used in 1982. Hell, even the original Corvette in 1953 borrowed many of its components from Chevrolet's mundane passenger-car parts bins. Everything about the C5 was engineered exclusively to help make this the best Corvette yet. Chief Engineer David Hill's goal was to create the most comfortable, most convenient, easiest to handle, hardest charging Corvette of all time. He didn't disappoint.

Listing the C5's impressive roll call is not something easily done in a few hundred words. Or a few thousand. The incredibly durable, wonderfully efficient, wildly powerful LS1 V-8 could fill a book all on its own. Then there's the world-class chassis with its rear-mounted transmission for better balance, the incredibly rigid frame with its central tunnel and hydroformed side rails, and that beautiful body that cuts through the wind like no other Corvette shape before.

So much of what makes the C5 the best generation yet involves that new frame. Its super strength means that nearly all of the creaks, rattles, and rolls inherent to the C4 design are gone. Its rigidity allowed engineers to dial in much more precise suspension settings—with next to no frame flex, suspension location geometry basically remains constant and true. All this adds up to a more sure-footed, more comfortable ride. The C5 not only handles at extremes better than any previous Corvette, it also leaves passengers with more positive seat-of-the-pants impressions in everyday driving. And dress-wearing drivers will appreciate the lower doorsills—made possible by those hydroformed frame rails—that make getting in and out less of a reach for the feet.

All this sure-footed comfort is especially apparent to convertible drivers. Even though the droptop model was introduced later in 1998, the C5 platform was essentially designed first as a convertible. Unlike a C4 convertible, which required extra bracing to compensate for its missing roof, the C5 convertible needs no major additions to keep itself in shape. This also means no extra unwanted weight is added into the convertible equation, an inherent physical law common to ragtop construction since the beginning of time.

C5 convertible owners can also take their car to the club with little muss or fuss thanks to that trunk in back, a Corvette feature last seen in 1962. Chevrolet promotional people in 1998 were more than willing to point out that the new Corvette trunk was capable of carrying not one, but two golf bags. In 1999, a third C5 variation—the lighter, lesser-priced fixed-roof coupe, or hardtop as Chevy calls it—was also fitted with a trunk. This introduction meant that, for the first time ever, Corvette buyers were faced with three different models to choose from.

More than 30,000 customers chose the C5 in 1998. Continued sales success in such quantities will certainly guarantee a long, happy life for the fifth-generation Corvette. But the C5 still has a long way to go to reach the C3's record. Indeed, 15 years is a long time.

A convertible Corvette was again reborn one year after the sensational C5 debuted in 1997. Droptop C5s were not built that first year. They appeared in 1998 just in time for *Motor Trend* to name the latest, greatest Corvette its "Car of the Year."

Everything beneath the 1982 Corvette's skin worked in unison to maximize both performance and efficiency. Chevy promotional people also bragged of the car's new low-restriction "dual exhaust system"—it was, of course, still the same design used beneath Corvettes since 1975. Exhaust flow, however, was improved by a freer-flowing catalytic converter. Also improved was the Cross-Fire Injection V-8's new computer, which could adjust fuel flow as much as 80 times a second. The 1981 computer-controlled carburetor's best variable adjustment rate was 10 times per second.

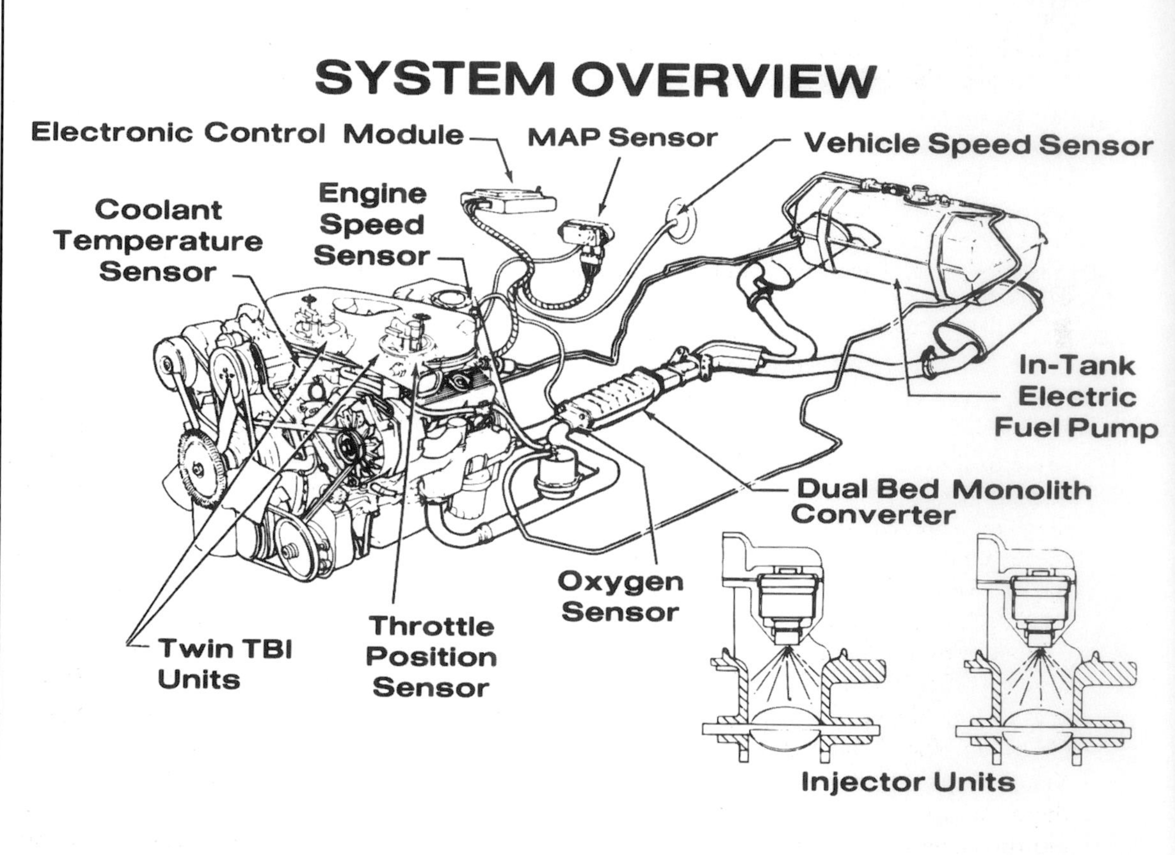

"The problem with parts engineered down to the last ounce is that aesthetic appeal is oftentimes the first pound to go. The Corvette's seat shells have the throwaway feel of parts molded by Rubbermaid."

While critics could be picky about their seats, they couldn't complain about another Indy Pace Car feature carried over into 1979. Those front and rear spoilers added on in 1978 became an option, RPO D80, the following year. Priced at $265, the D80 spoilers found their way onto 6,853 Corvettes in 1979 and went a long way toward reducing unwanted drag. In 1980, new front and rear caps with integral spoilers were added.

Yet another exterior modification appeared two years later. Available only for the Collector Edition, frameless hatchback glass was hinged on in 1982 to technically expand Corvette bodystyle choices to two for the first time since the convertible departed after 1975. Apparently McLellan and crew decided that anyone able to pay the extra asking price for the 1982 Collector Edition probably would have some hired help on hand to do all that long-reach loading into and out of the rear storage area.

At 18 grand, a base Corvette in 1982 was already expensive enough. Fully loaded with options and extras like the 1978 Indy Pace Car, the Collector Edition became the first Corvette to enter the $20,000 zone. The exact suggested price was $22,537.59, $4,250 more than that standard sport coupe. Helping hike that price up were exclusive "turbine" alloy wheels wearing white-letter P255/60R15 Goodyear Eagle GT rubber, glass roof panels done in unique bronze tinting, a rear window defogger, a power antenna, and special identification inside and out.

Like the Limited Edition and Silver Anniversary Corvettes of 1978, the 1982 Collector Edition featured unique paint, this time a silver-beige finish accented by graduated gray decals and accent striping. That exclusive color carried over inside, where silver-beige leather was found on the seats and door panels. Leather wrapping also went onto the steering wheel and luxurious, extra-deep pile carpeting covered the floor.

Unlike the 1978 Limited Edition model, the 1982 Collector Edition did not tease potential collectors into a frenzy. "The Collector Edition is sure to become a hot item, much like the Indy Pace Car in 1978," wrote *Road & Track*'s Joe Rusz. "You may recall that because of their scarcity, Pace Cars sold for as much as $28,000, about double the sticker price. McLellan tells me this won't happen with the Collector Edition because the new Bowling Green plant will turn out as many cars as the market will bear." Indeed, the new Kentucky home to the Corvette built Collector Edition models as fast as demand demanded. It was that simple: no leading on, no lawsuits. When the demand finally stopped, the final count for the year was 6,759.

While the Collector Edition did honor the Corvette's third-generation on its way into the history books, it also helped mark the opening of a new age, the Bowling Green era, if you will. Chevrolet officials wanted to show off the new Kentucky plant's advanced paint facility, and the attractive Collector Edition proved to be just the ticket to do just that.

Actually it was those two-tone Corvettes that debuted in 1981 that first demonstrated the new assembly facility's merits. The book finally closed on the St. Louis story on August 1, 1981, as the finishing touches were put on the last Missouri-built Corvette. The first Kentucky-built model had rolled off the new Bowling Green line on June 1, meaning the Corvette's past briefly overlapped its future. Solid-colored Corvettes built in St. Louis that year were done in lacquer as always. Meanwhile, Bowling Green rolled out two-tone after two-tone using a new enamel-based paint enhanced with clearcoats. Of the 40,606 Corvettes built for 1981, 8,955 began life in Kentucky.

Rumors of a move to a larger, more modern plant began surfacing along the Mississippi as early as 1973. Built in 1920, the Chevrolet plant in St. Louis was not only archaic, it was also severely limited in size and scope. That the Corvette team had managed to build nearly 50,000 cars a year there during those hot-to-trot years in the late 1970s was more a testament to their dedication than it was proof that the Fisher Mill Building, located on Natural Bridge Avenue, was capable of carrying on into the 1980s.

Corvette production had moved into the Fisher Mill Building just before Christmas 1953. "We selected St. Louis as the exclusive source of Corvette manufacture because the city has a central location and excellent shipping facilities and we have always found here an ample supply of competent labor," explained Edward Kelly, Chevrolet Motor Division's general manufacturing manager. The first Corvettes began forming in St. Louis on December 28, 1953. Some 25 years and three generations later it had become painfully obvious that the legacy had run as far it could. Environmental Protection Agency cops were hounding officials at the aging plant about its paint facility, which wasn't anywhere near up to snuff as far as federal air quality standards were concerned. And Dave McLellan knew full well that his baby, the planned C4, could never be born in St. Louis. Cutting-edge innovation and obsolete production facilities just didn't mix.

The solution to the problem was a 550,000-square-foot complex formerly used by the Air Temp Division of Chrysler Corporation and the Fedders Corporation in Bowling Green. GM bought this building, expanded it to 1 million square feet and modernized it with the latest in state-of-the-art assembly technology. Most important, this new assembly plant wouldn't be home to anything but fiberglass two-seaters. "The Bowling Green facility, which will build Corvettes exclusively, is an investment in Corvette's future," explained a 1981 Corvette brochure. "It represents the experience and knowledge learned over all those years [in St. Louis]."

So it was that a new, thoroughly modern production facility was up and running in time to build a new, thoroughly exciting fiberglass two-seater for 1984. After 15 years, the Shark's tale finally came to a close in 1982. As for the old St. Louis plant, it was boarded up in the fall of 1987 after building 13 million Chevrolet cars and trucks. About a half million of those were third-generation renditions of America's only sports car. Call them rough, call them soft, it didn't matter. They were all Corvettes.

Enough said.

Index

Models

CORVETTE
4-4-63